ANTHROPOLOGICAL PAPERS

MUSEUM OF ANTHROPOLOGY, UNIVERSITY OF MICHIGAN

NO. 74

THE ARCHAEOLOGY OF THE SIERRA BLANCA REGION OF SOUTHEASTERN NEW MEXICO

by
JANE HOLDEN KELLEY

ANN ARBOR, MICHIGAN
1984

Dedicated to
Don Lehmer and Mark Wimberly

Printed in the
United States of America

ISBN 0-932206-96-4

CONTENTS

TABLES

CHARTS

FIGURES

PLATES

MAPS

FOREWORD TO THE 1984 EDITION

The amount of archaeological excavation that has been carried out in the Southwest over the past century is staggering. Thousands of sites have been tested or excavated and tens of thousands more have been recorded. Almost nothing has escaped the archaeologist's attention, from scattered artifacts on deflated dune surfaces to huge, multi-storied pueblos. Libraries have been filled with survey and excavation reports, and museums are packed to the bursting point with artifacts. Given this intensity of interest and research, it is almost incomprehensible that a major portion of the Southwest—all of southeastern New Mexico—should remain virtually unknown archaeologically. Most of the area has never been surveyed and only a handful of professional research projects have been conducted in the region since the turn of the century.

The most obvious reason for the lack of interest in such a large part of the Southwest is the absence of picturesque cliff-dwellings or mesa-top villages which attract so much attention on the Colorado Plateau. Equally critical in diverting interest away from southeastern New Mexico is the mistaken view held by many Southwestern archaeologists that the area was "marginal" to puebloan horticultural adaptations, and that consequently its archaeological record holds little if any potential for contributing toward an understanding of puebloan developments. This is a curious position given the current popularity among Southwestern archaeologists of "marginality" in explanations of culture change. Marginal areas are of particular interest precisely because of their marginality. Such areas often are the ones most sensitive to changes that affect a cultural system. Not only do marginal areas often provide the earliest signs of system stress, but the more ephemeral nature of communities on the adaptive margins of a system makes their stratigraphy less complex and easier to decipher archaeologically.

But attributing the scarcity of large puebloan communities in southeastern New Mexico to the area's "marginality" reflects mistaken notions about its physical environment. The environmental diversity of southeastern New Mexico is easily as great as that of most areas within the puebloan heartland. Moreover, the region's horticultural potential prehistorically probably was much greater than most Southwestern archaeologists would suspect. Today's rainfall is comparable to, or higher than elsewhere in the Southwest. The timing and predictability of precipitation are also comparable. Vast areas of arable soil are available along the Pecos and its many upland tributaries, as well as around the margins of the hundreds of shallow basins and playas that dot the lowlying areas. The growing season in the uplands is no different than at similar elevations on the Colorado Plateau, and at lower elevations, such as in the Pecos Valley, it is substantially longer. Most important, surface water was unusually abundant until quite recently, even in what today appear to be some of the most inhospitable portions of southeastern New Mexico. Several rivers, fed by one of the largest artesian systems in North America, poured into the Pecos between Roswell and Carlsbad. All of these rivers, including the Berrendo, North and South Spring, Hondo, Peñasco, and Felix, are essentially dead today in their lower reaches. However, as late as the 1870s and 1880s several of these rivers supported a fishing industry that supplied catfish and other fish to Fort Stanton and Las Vegas, New Mexico. Late nineteenth-century farmers near the mouth of the Hondo in the Roswell area irrigated their fields with water diverted from beaver dams. In addition, numerous springs headed at the base of the Caprock or Llano Estacado and emptied into the shallow basins that dot the landscape east of the Pecos. Until the nineteenth century, many of these also held water, perhaps year-round, providing both cultivable land and habitat for thousands of ducks that migrated up the Pecos flyway. These springs and basins also dried up in the last century, as overgrazing altered the landscape and deep well drilling and diversion lowered the watertable.

Thus, it is extremely unlikely that we can attribute the absence of large puebloan communities in southeastern New Mexico to the area's environmental "marginality." Social, political, and economic factors probably played an extremely important role in shaping the culture history of southeastern New Mexico and in fact may have been as important in defining the nature and limits of puebloan adaptations as rainfall, soils, or temperature. Southeastern New Mexico was peripheral to the puebloan area, not marginal.

If these assertions are in any way correct, the archaeological record of southeastern New Mexico becomes exceedingly important as a resource for understanding the factors, beyond the physical constraints of land and climate, that shaped the course of cultural developments in the Southwest. What, for example, underlies the interaction, both cooperative and competitive, between horticulturalists living at the periphery of the puebloan world and nomadic hunters and gatherers living at the periphery of theirs? What determines the geographic location of this interface, and how has it shifted over time?

How did populations along the periphery respond to changes in the economic or political structure of major communities such as Casas Grandes within the puebloan heartland? That the eastern periphery was linked by exchange to the Casas Grandes system, as well as to other systems in the Southwest, is amply attested by the presence of marine shells, copper bells, macaws, northern Mexican ceramics, Rio Grande glazes, St. Johns Polychrome, turquoise, and obsidian in several southeast New Mexican prehistoric communities.

Equally important, what were the effects of sociopolitical or economic changes in communities along the eastern periphery on Casas Grandes and other Southwestern cultural systems? Although the commodities that entered the exchange networks from the east are less well known, bison robes, meat, and tallow were certainly among the more important ones. Other commodities undoubtedly were also important but remain to be documented.

The culture history of southeastern New Mexico is obviously of interest in its own right, but an understanding of the nature and dynamics of culture change in communities occupying the puebloan periphery holds the promise of providing important clues to processes operating within the Southwestern heartland. This potential of the southeastern New Mexican archaeological record is only now coming to be recognized, and the pace of research is steadily increasing. Regrettably, however, urban expansion, landleveling for irrigation, timbering, potash mining, gravel quarrying, oil and gas exploration, and dam construction have been proceeding at an unprecedented rate and have already obliterated an unknown but substantial part of the region's fragile archaeological record. Pothunting has also taken its toll, destroying many of the larger and more deeply stratified sites.

The sites in southeastern New Mexico that remain reasonably intact have become precious and irreplaceable resources. These will have to be carefully managed and judiciously but creatively "squeezed" with all the insight archaeologists can muster, in order to make the fullest possible use of their research potential.

Materials recovered from previous excavations in the region also take on tremendous importance. A great deal can yet be learned from reanalyses of existing collections. Analyses of the isotope chemistry of human and animal bones, studies of ceramic design elements and clay composition, trace-element determinations in obsidian and turquoise, and systematic reevaluation of faunal and botanical materials are but a few of the highly productive avenues of research that can be pursued using existing museum collections.

Finally, publication and wide dissemination of existing data are also crucial if we are to understand the cultural development of southeastern New Mexico. It is in this vein that the University of Michigan Museum of Anthropology became interested in publishing Jane Holden Kelley's 1966 doctoral dissertation. Obviously, a dissertation which was completed nearly twenty years ago, and which reports on excavations carried out ten years earlier still, will be out of date in many respects. The theoretical interests and methodological approaches of the field have changed since the 1950s and 1960s, and the Southwestern data base to which Kelley compared her materials has since grown enormously. Nevertheless, the thesis contains a wealth of valuable information, available nowhere else in the literature, documenting many important sites in southeastern New Mexico, most of which no longer exist. For example, Kelley's dissertation contains the only detailed report on the enigmatic ten-room pueblo, Bloom Mound, located just outside of Roswell. This little pueblo produced at least seven copper bells and a variety of other materials almost certainly derived from Casa Grandes. The site was leveled by pothunters in the 1940s, and most of the small number of artifacts that made their way into the Roswell Museum were subsequently destroyed in a flood. Many other sites of comparable importance and interest, such as the Bonnell Site in the Hondo Valley and the Smokey Bear Ruin on the north side of the Capitan Mountains, are reported in the dissertation. Bonnell is now a gravel quarry and Smokey Bear resembles a lunar landscape. Moreover, Kelley develops a basic chronological framework for the upland portion of southeastern New Mexico which remains as valid today as it was when it first appeared. Unfortunately, the dissertation has been virtually inaccessible to the profession since its appearance. It is over 600 pages long and filled with photographs of artifacts and features which do not reproduce well. As a consequence, only a small number of specialists have ever even seen a copy.

After considerable discussion with the author, we decided to publish the dissertation without revision. Revision would have required major rewriting which would have substantially delayed publication. Moreover, while most of the basic site data were presented in appendices at the end of the dissertation, a great deal of data, not repeated in the appendices, had been incorporated directly into the text. Revising the text without losing these data or totally redoing the appendices proved to be so complex and time-consuming a task that we decided to publish the document as is. Only minor editing has been done. The reader should bear in mind, therefore, that parts of the discussion will be very dated, particularly some of the theoretical sections and the inter-regional comparisons. But as a basic record of major excavations carried out on a shoestring budget in the early 1950s, the quality and detail of reporting are outstanding. Kelley's study is one of the most important existing documents on the archaeology of southeastern New Mexico. We feel that its publication will bring a valuable resource out of obscurity and will be a major contribution to the archaeology of the region. We also believe that the information in Kelley's dissertation will help to illuminate the fascinating cultural developments that were taking place along one of the Southwest's most interesting peripheries. Without Kelley's meticulous reporting of the sites she excavated, a major record of the archaeology of this region would be lost forever. We are delighted to make it available for the first time to professional and enlightened avocational archaeologists.

John D. Speth
Ann Arbor, Michigan
May 1984

PREFACE — 1984

As is the case in so many parts of the world, archaeological resources in the Sierra Blanca Region of southeastern New Mexico are being damaged at an alarming rate. A primary reason for publishing a modified version of a dissertation presented in 1966, which was in turn based on fieldwork carried out in the 1950s, is that it represents a source of information about now damaged or destroyed archaeological resources. To give a few examples, the Bonnell Site has been completely destroyed in favor of a sand and gravel pit; Block Lookout or Smokey The Bear Site now resembles a World War I battlefield, and it is doubtful if much more can be salvaged from Bloom Mound. Since the particular localities in which we worked in the 1950s have received little archaeological attention in the intervening years, our work has not become obsolete as rapidly as would otherwise have been the case. Today other archaeologists are finding the region a useful testing ground for problems of contemporary interest. The basic data contained in the dissertation may prove useful to this new crop of researchers and it may also help to call attention more generally to a neglected region of the Southwest.

Both the fieldwork and the dissertation are products of their time. Consequently, they are in many respects quite dated by today's standards. The problem orientation was historical in nature. The approach was inductive — often narrowly — and descriptive. Induction, however, is not simply a monolithic entity, and we employed a variety of forms of reasoning, the comparative method, pattern recognition, analogy, and other logical procedures.

Southeastern New Mexico was by no means an archaeological blank in 1950 when we began our work, but it was close enough to one to foster a pioneering, exploratory attitude which was reinforced by the expeditionary conditions under which we lived and worked and by our relative isolation from other archaeological workers in the Southwest. The open-ended goals of the 1950s fieldwork reflected this attitude as we attempted to establish a first level informational plateau about prehistoric horticulturalists in a large area reaching from the Pecos Valley to the upper slopes of Sierra Blanca and, in the other direction, from the Peñasco Valley to the Gallo Drainage.

Sociological and pragmatic factors played a substantial role in shaping the field research. Among these may be mentioned the expeditionary atmosphere, recruitment of personnel and availability of resources. The organizational framework of the research was a field school which, by and large, recruited students with little prior background in archaeology. Continuity of personnel from one season to the next was slight. Resources were on the scanty side, even for the 1950s; by today's standards, they were slender indeed.

During the fieldwork, the main emphasis was on data collection. Scarcity of facilities and resources did not encourage extensive analysis in the field. Rather, this step was left to the few individuals with a deeper interest in archaeology who volunteered their services after the conclusion of the field seasons. Rightly or wrongly, we felt that our responsibility to the data and to the archaeological profession would be discharged through the presentation of brief, descriptive reports.

It was only after conclusion of this sequence of fieldwork that my involvement with the assembled data and collections took on a new dimension. I had been involved in all field seasons, and, as much as anyone, I understood what we had done. I had tended to see the Sierra Blanca work as useful training for my projected Mesoamerican dissertation research. As it turned out, I did not go to Mesoamerica as planned; rather suddenly I needed an alternative dissertation topic. The obvious choice was the Sierra Blanca research in which I had already invested so much time.

In this new context, a whole series of new demands were made on the data. The most immediate task was to make a fuller and more systematic analysis of the collections than had previously been done. Resources were no more plentiful for this phase of the research than for earlier ones. After I was allowed to use the hayloft of the old Texas Tech dairy barn as a laboratory, the one resource I had in abundance was space. My father built row upon row of trestle tables in this space so that I was able to lay out the more than 3 tons of collections with ease. Thereafter I proceeded in near solitary splendor. The one-person-show character of the analysis resulted in further limitations. I was not then and am not now, a qualified physical anthropologist, faunal expert, geologist or mineralogist. Nor were there resources to acquire the services of such experts, except on a catch-as-catch-can and volunteer basis.

Eventually the collections had to be packed up, and we moved to Nebraska where the next stage of the dissertation took shape. Not unexpectedly, questions arose which could have been better dealt with had the collections and sites been more accessible.

A dissertation in the modern world of the 1960s had to be "problem oriented," as I was firmly told by my committee. I conceived the problem orientation primarily in terms of historical relationships between regions and localities, relying heavily on distributional evidence and trait diffusion. The

Sierra Blanca Region horticulturalists appeared to be conservative in the sense of maintaining a wide range of traits that had passed out of usage in more central parts of the Southwest. This, I suggested, was attributable to the cultural and geographical marginality of the region — a kind of cultural lag.

The Sierra Blanca data and collections, then, were first used as the basis for individual site reports. Later they were reassembled in the dissertation for a cultural historical treatise. Later still, I undertook a Restudy Project (Kelley 1979) which was designed with a full appreciation of limitations inherent in the data and collections. One of the purposes of the Restudy Project was to overcome some of the limitations resulting from the character of the previous stage. More significant, however, was that portion of the project aimed at better understanding relationships between localities in terms of specialized manufacture and movement of artifacts bewteen sites and localities. Ceramic petrographic analysis and X-ray diffraction studies tend to support a view of extensive movement of pottery between sites and localities rather than site-specific manufacture and use. Although we can claim support for our arguments, the evidence is not yet strong enough to claim confirmation. Nevertheless, we were able to use older collections to address questions of craft specialization and exchange networks — and these are among the topics being studied by archaeologists today.

Although awareness of and action for conservation, preservation and salvage of archaeological resources is now widespread in the profession, other potential steps for extending archaeological resources remain underexploited. One such step is fuller utilization of existing data and collections. Older collections accumulated for other purposes clearly have built-in limitations and cannot serve all contemporary research needs. But if research designs take full account of the constraints, older collections can still be useful. As archaeological resources diminish, we will be forced to maximize resources in a number of ways. If recourse to older collections is to be a part of our future, it would seem reasonable to prepare now by encouraging the retention and curation of total collections and their documentation.

That our Restudy Project was feasible at all was due, first of all, to the scope of the artifact recovery during fieldwork. With the exception of manos and metates, which were mostly left in the field, we saved virtually everything that was portable and perceived to have informational value. The retrieval of lithic remains, for example, was unusually complete for Southwestern projects of the 1950s. There were, of course, many things now perceived to have scientific value which we did not collect.

Equally important to the Restudy Project was the continuing completeness of the collections. Although the collections and documentation suffered some attrition over the years, they were sufficiently intact to serve as the basis of a study with very different goals from earlier uses of the data. Stratified sampling procedures could be applied in selecting sherds for technical analysis; stylistic analysis of selected ceramic types could be based on the entire range. If only exhibitable and "typical" sherds had been saved and curated, our recent research would have had less value and would, perhaps, have been impossible.

What is published here, however, is the dissertation. The editors and I discussed the advisability of updating this now outdated document. For various reasons, we decided against this option. For one thing, the most valuable portion of the dissertation is the compilation of basic descriptive data on sites which since have been largely or totally destroyed. As of the present time, this still represents the most extensive archaeological documentation for the particular localities concerned. For another, a thorough revision of the theoretical framework of even those problems considered in the dissertation and an updating of the comparative material from other regions would, quite simply, result in such a different document that it would become pointless to publish it as having anything to do with the dissertation. We finally decided that it is the dissertation and not a replacement document which has a certain value. In any event, there are now others better qualified to write the sequel which will inevitably address a very different range of archaeological problems.

Although we have opted to publish the original document virtually unchanged, it is not inappropriate for me to comment on certain aspects of the dissertation.

Chapter 1 must be seen as a somewhat naive drag-net attempt to garner any and all information I could find on natural resources relevant to economic, craft, and subsistence activities. Were I undertaking this research today, such data would be systematically collected during fieldwork and integrated into considerations of adaptive processes. As it was, much of this information was collected after fieldwork terminated, or its collection was incidental to the archaeological work. It simply did not occur to us to collect zoological specimens in the field, for example, and even if it had, we lacked resources and expertise to perform well in such areas. I made an attempt to match regional botanical data with ethnobotanical information from other parts of the Southwest in a not very explicitly used form of analogical reasoning aimed at better understanding potential resources and how they might have been used.

Chapter 2, entitled "Regional Review of the Ecology and Archaeology," deals primarily with archaeological sequences in surrounding regions: Chupadero Mesa, south-central New Mexico from the Tularosa Basin to the Rio Grande, the Pecos Valley, and The Llano Estacado. Later research in these areas has so changed the archaeological data base and problem orientation as to render this chapter badly out of date. It does provide, however, a reasonable state-of-the-art picture for the time the dissertation was being written and therefore has contextual value for this document.

In Chapter 3, the focus is more directly on the Sierra Blanca research. The setting, the sites we investigated, and three proposed phases are summarized.

Chapter 4 is characterized by an exhaustive use of the comparative method for examining cultural traits and their distribution. The data base is partitioned in ways that crosscut the partitioning presented in the previous chapter based on sites, localities, and phases.

The comparative method and the related phenomenon of pattern recognition have long been among the more powerful and routinely-used anthropological and archaeological tools, yet they have tended to be ignored in recent methodological debates which have focused on other logical matters. They are essentially inductive in nature, and induction generally seems to be in a state of ill repute. While archaeologists are tightening up their methodology, some attention should be spared for these and other members of our methodological repertoire. Like any other matter of scientific method, there are questions of what should count as evidence for what purposes and what are the most appropriate criteria for judging results as supportive or non-supportive of an argument.

Chapter 5, "Origins and Development of Sedentary Life in Southeastern New Mexico," is the most outdated section of the dissertation in terms of contemporary theory and data. It must be emphasized that alternative hypotheses need to be considered and assessed for all the topics discussed. With regard to "abandonment" of the Sierra Blanca Region (or perhaps it is better to say with regard to the apparent cessation of sedentary village life partially based on horticulture), for example, I still feel that *if* the northern horticulturalists of the Sierra Blanca Region passed into the ethnographic record in any identifiable form, the most likely place to look is among the Piros, Tompiros, and Jumanos. This is a big "if" and remains highly speculative. Even if true, it is not of overwhelming interest in and of itself. But if confirmed, we would have more directly linked ethnographic information to serve as the basis of one kind of analogical reasoning. Certainly presumed historical continuity has served as the basis of analogy often enough in Southwestern archaeology.

On the basis of available evidence, it still appears that a sedentary, horticulturally-based way of life ceased to exist in the Sierra Blanca Region at the end of what I call the Glencoe and Lincoln phases. If, as we suspect, this is related to stress on the cultural systems, it would be interesting to know what forms of stress operated, and if the people acted to perpetuate their accustomed life style, presumably by moving on or by choosing to maintain their geographical position, to mention only two alternatives. If it could be convincingly argued that some people moved and joined the Piro, Tompiro, and Jumano villages, we would be in a stronger position to say that one alternative selected was maintenance of life style. Alternatively, if we could show that some people modified their adaptive strategies by expanding their non-horticultural activities, we could say that part of the population opted to maintain its geographical position. These are not mutually exclusive propositions, and it seems more likely that there were multiple responses to multiple variables.

During the 1950s and 1960s, the constructs of major cultural and areal divisions of the Southwest such as Anasazi and Mogollon took on, for me at least, a corporate reality. It seemed terribly important that I establish the historical derivation of cultures in the Sierra Blanca Region. The northern part of the region was best interpreted as having Anasazi roots, while the southern part seemed Mogollon-derived, and the middle was a mixture. Indeed, no part of the Sierra Blanca Region was neatly and cleanly anything except itself. These concerns haunted me and therefore haunt the dissertation. Such areal constructs are of great value as organizational devices for certain purposes, but they must be continually reevaluated with regard to content and with a view to their usefulness in any particular context. To say that the Corona and Lincoln phases have their primary historical roots in Anasazi is perfectly defensible, but this is considerably less enlightening than looking at what happened beyond the root stage.

Cultural lag is a topic that one heard more about in anthropology a decade or so ago. In historical perspective, prehistoric horticulturalists in the Sierra Blanca Region do seem to exhibit this phenomenon. The picture has not been substantially revised by contradictory evidence insofar as I am aware. The region must still be viewed as falling near major areal boundaries, whether these are defined in cultural or geographical terms; almost by definition it is marginal with regard to large, areally defined constructs. I regarded the edge position of the region relative to the Southwestern culture area as a major factor contributing to the apparent cultural lag. The boundary position at the edge of the Southwest fronting on the South Plains was invoked in an interpretation of the unusual range of trade goods found at Bloom Mound. These arguments are probably no less sound now than they were in 1966. Archaeologists, however, are far less interested in such topics at the present time and place a higher priority on addressing a different range of problems.

What we now regard as the portion of the dissertation having the greatest value for contemporary and future research is, curiously enough, the basic descriptive data presented in lengthy appendices. Allocation of so much expensive publication space to descriptive data is quite unusual today. I would suggest then, as we attempt to extend archaeological resources, one of the problems facing the profession is access to basic data. Not only are archaeological resources in the ground diminishing, but the realities of publication costs, combined with a professional emphasis on the results of research as opposed to fuller presentation of the research steps and the data on which findings were based, have acted to further limit access to the data against which archaeological inferences must ultimately be tested.

Needless to say, if I were undertaking fieldwork in this region today, I would approach it quite differently. Should I live long enough to undertake research in the year 2000, it would be different again. Not only would the problem orientation be different, but methods, techniques and pragmatic factors would also change. I hope today, as I did in 1956 and 1966, that good archaeologists will exploit the very useful potential of the Sierra Blanca Region. As new plateaus of knowledge and understanding emerge, this document can follow normal disciplinary growth patterns and recede into obscurity.

Jane Holden Kelley
Calgary, Alberta

ACKNOWLEDGMENTS — 1966

This project has gone on intermittently for 16 years. It is a natural consequence that many individuals have contributed their time and knowledge. It is with great pleasure that I am able to partially acknowledge the assistance I have received. I am deeply indebted to the officials of Texas Technological College, the institution that sponsored the fieldwork in southeastern New Mexico from 1950 to 1956 upon which this study is based. Within the College, the work was carried out under the auspices of the Museum and the Department of History and Anthropology. They have allowed me to use this information for a thesis and supported the project materially with equipment, funds, and personnel. I was ably assisted in the field by F. Earl Green, Rex Gerald, Virginia Gerald, and Herbert R. Harvey, who served as field assistants, and by the 64 students who did the actual excavations. Joe Stewart and Carl Darwin worked in the project laboratory doing pottery analysis in 1962 and 1963.

Our hosts in the field granted permission to excavate, furnished camping facilities, and extended Southwestern hospitality. Our longest sojourn was at the Bonnell Site with Ralph Bonnell and his family. George Turner, now deceased, owned the old Phillips Ranch which was managed by his brother Bill Turner in 1955. Sid Goodloe assumed ownership of this property in 1956. The Briton family managed the Block Ranch for Mrs. Tobe Foster. Our work in the Gallo Valley was carried out on the Clint Sultemeier, Frank Sultemeier, Carl Hiner, Ivor Ryberg and Clark ranches. In the Peñasco Valley, we worked on the Wolf ranch.

During our work at Bloom Mound, Colonel Sayre of the New Mexico Military Institute, David Gebhard of the Roswell Museum, Howard Brawn, and Don Brenner made old excavation records and artifacts from the site available for study. Jack Harkey of Carrizozo, New Mexico, and Clark Pfingsten of Lincoln, New Mexico, allowed us to study their private collections. John Boyland of the Lincoln County Museum put the museum's archaeological collections at our disposal.

Peter Hurd of San Patricio, New Mexico, and Ernest McDaniel of Glencoe, New Mexico, are sensitive observers of wildlife and ecological conditions, and both shared their knowledge of the region with us. Bob Stewart of the New Mexico Fish and Game Department at Ruidoso, New Mexico, M. E. Guck, Forest Ranger at Capitan, New Mexico, and Clemens F. Weindorf of the Soil Conservation Service at Capitan, New Mexico, provided useful lists, charts, and bibliographic leads on ecological matters. Since this project was going on throughout the time I was training to become an archaeologist, a great many teachers, fellow students, and other professional anthropologists and geologists have influenced me. Archaeologists who helped this project in a direct fashion include Fred Wendorf, Stanley Stubbs, Stewart Peckham, Arthur Jelinek, Elizabeth King, H. P. Mera, Erik Reed, and T. N. Campbell.

My father, W. C. Holden, gave me my first taste of archaeology when I was 4 years old, and put me in charge of these field sessions. His insistence that I write up these materials as a thesis is at last bearing fruit. Joyce Wike assisted by arguing for brevity and stylistic improvements in the thesis, and John Champe gave expert organizational advice. Technical assistance in the preparation of the final manuscript was given by Robert Eisele, drafting; Wayne Nelson, photography; Valerie Nammour, proofing; Wade Cox, ink drawings; Pat Allgood, drafting; Linda Murphy, typing; and Jean Le Riche, typing. Jimmy Le Riche and Anna Middleton helped to assemble the thesis. My thesis committee offered helpful leads, and my thanks go to J. O. Brew, Stephen Williams, and William Bullard. My husband, David H. Kelley, has assisted this long-term project on all fronts, which I deeply appreciate.

ACKNOWLEDGMENTS — 1984

Preparation of the dissertation for publication was aided by Barry MacDonnel, Ornella Cavaliere, Eric Poplin and Lesley Nicholls, of the University of Calgary. The University of Calgary graciously provided a publication grant. John Speth masterminded things at Michigan, where Kay Clahassey prepared the cover design and Mary Hodge coordinated production and editing.

INTRODUCTION

The archaeology of southeastern New Mexico has not kept pace with other regions in the Southwest, although initial investigations showed great promise. The Cosgroves, W. S. Stallings Jr., H. P. Mera, and Stanley Stubbs worked there, and they communicated frequently with key amateurs and with each other. Several important excavations and surveys were carried out by them, and most of the major pottery types were defined during the 1930s. H. P. Mera published the first general review of southeastern New Mexico in 1943, and Donald Lehmer published his *Jornada Branch of the Mogollon* in 1948; these two summaries furnish a point of departure for anyone working in southeastern New Mexico today.

The Texas Technological College field archaeological program from 1950 to 1956 was conducted in a region that lies east of the crests of the Sacramento, Sierra Blanca, and Gallina mountain chain, in the vicinity of the modern New Mexican towns of Roswell, Mayhill, Ruidoso, Capitan, and Corona. This region was chosen for fieldwork because of its geographical location on the eastern frontier of the Southwest, bordering the Plains. The archaeological program of Texas Technological College had, in the past, dealt with other regions of the eastern Pueblo frontier and western Plains. The initial hope that evidence of cultural contacts between the two culture areas would be found was not realized. We therefore turned our attention to the problems of defining the cultural units that we encountered and to tracing their relationships and development.

This study interprets the prehistory of the Sierra Blanca Region, and relates it to the prehistory of southeastern New Mexico, of which it is a part, and to adjacent regions of the Southwest.

Chapter 1 summarizes the general ecological characteristics of the whole of southeastern New Mexico and analyzes the potential resources afforded by the area's natural environment. Chapter 2 reviews the specific ecological setting and archaeological data from several regions of New Mexico. The archaeological sequence of the Chupadero Region is based on Toulouse and Stephenson (1960), that of south-central New Mexico is based on Lehmer (1948), and that of the Pecos Valley from Fort Sumner to Roswell is based on Jelinek (1960). Archaeological information from the Guadalupe Mountains and the Pecos Valley from Carlsbad to the Texas border came from the Lea County Archaeological Society, the Laboratory of Anthropology survey, and publications by Ferdon (1946) and Howard (1935).

Chapter 3 presents a summary of the Sierra Blanca Region, including environmental data and a brief review of the excavations conducted by Texas Technological College. Three new phases have been defined on the basis of this fieldwork; the characteristics of the Glencoe, Corona, and Lincoln Phases are also presented in Chapter 3.

A descriptive survey and detailed analysis of individual culture traits using the comparative method follows, in Chapter 4. Traits found in the Sierra Blanca Region serve as a baseline for systematic comparisons within the archaeological sequences of the other regions in southeastern New Mexico and other parts of the Southwest.

From the archaeological picture resulting from this analysis, a discussion of the origin and development of sedentary life in the Sierra Blanca Region and in southeastern New Mexico becomes feasible. Chapter 5 puts forth some suggestions about the ethnic identity of the Glencoe and Lincoln Phase peoples and their fate. Geographical marginalism affected crucial cultural processes that were instrumental in producing the culture of the Glencoe, Corona, and Lincoln Phases.

The final and most voluminous parts of this report are the Appendices, where the site reports have been placed. In the course of preparing this study, the most convenient unit for analysis was a locality of small geographical extent, usually part of a drainage system. Thus, each appendix describes one locality. Each appendix summarizes local ecological conditions and presents all available archaeological information. The latter category includes the survey results, the site reports of the Texas Technological College expeditions, and any other data that have been published or to which I had access. Within each locality, sites are organized by the phases set up in Chapter 3.

While this study presents a comprehensive coverage of our field activities and represents a final report on the work at certain sites as of 1966, the overall picture is far from complete, and this must be regarded as a preliminary study. Many details need to be filled in. It is entirely possible and indeed probable that the conclusions reached here will be reconsidered in years to come. The very nature of the archaeology is such that each new site reported will add appreciably to our concepts of the prehistory. Suggestions for future research are tendered to indicate some major problem areas that urgently need attention.

Chapter 1

A SURVEY OF NATURAL POTENTIAL RESOURCES OF SOUTHEASTERN NEW MEXICO

INTRODUCTION

Southeastern New Mexico is a land of topographical and ecological contrasts. Much of this part of the State of New Mexico belongs to the Basin and Range physiographic province, characterized by a dramatic juxtaposition of abrupt mountains and flat basins. The eastern fringe of New Mexico belongs to the Great Plains Province. Ecological conditions are closely related to topography. Arid Lower Sonoran Zones are to be found in the Pecos Valley, Tularosa Basin, Jornada del Muerto, and Rio Grande Valley. Upper Sonoran Zones are formed on the Llano Estacado or Southern High Plains and on the flanks of the two mountain chains. Higher life zones occur along the mountain ridges.

From the Pecos Valley westward, a variety of ecological zones are compacted into a small geographical area. For hunters and gatherers, subsistence would depend upon the exploitation of a number of zones, as nowhere is there an abundant food supply. Agriculturalists could settle in places that furnished the necessary environmental conditions for their crops. As we shall see, these conditions were found within rather narrow ecological limits in the Sierra Blanca Region.

To project the total environmental picture into the past, one needs climatic reconstruction based on pollen analysis, Late Pleistocene and post-Pleistocene geology, and so forth. Since no such data have been published for southeastern New Mexico, this treatment will of necessity be brief, general, and limited to modern conditions that can be projected back in time for only a few centuries.

INORGANIC RESOURCES

Stone

San Andres limestone forms the uppermost geologic bed over the entire eastern slopes of the eastern ranges and is to be found in more limited quantities in every region. Much of the exposed limestone is weathered and soft, but harder limestones outcrop. Limestone cobbles are common in streams and in terraces. Rectangular blocks of harder limestone were used in house construction, and limestone cobbles and pebbles were used for both ground and chipped stone tools.

Sandstones are outcropped frequently at higher elevations where older beds have been exposed; elsewhere sandstone is scarce. Shale and siltstone are likewise most abundant in the higher mountains where older beds are outcropped, and in the cut valleys. Jelinek (1960:56) reports a siltstone workshop in the Pecos Valley.

Siliceous rocks such as quartz, quartzite, chert, and flint may be found as pebbles in Glorietta sandstone, Santa Rosa conglomerate, and the Chinle Formation which are present in the higher mountains and cut valleys. Some silicified shale beds were mined, and one such locality is described in Appendix 2. While this black shale was only a medium grade, it was the best siliceous material available in quantity over a large area. Good cherts, chalcedonies, and similar siliceous materials in nodular form were probably difficult to locate. No major chert sources have been recognized. Siliceous materials become much more scarce in the Pecos Valley. The relatively high proportion of chipped stone tools made of siltstone and compact limestone reflects this shortage.

Igneous rocks are most abundant in the higher elevations. Rhyolite is common in dikes. The source of igneous rocks in the lower elevations is primarily pebbles. This raw material is apparently too hard to be easily worked, but some ground stone tools are made of it, and there are a few chipped stone implements of basalt, again stressing the scarcity of siliceous rocks.

Clay

Clay exposures yielding material suitable for covering houses and making pottery seem to be widespread. Old terraces are rich in this resource and there are clay lenses and beds in the San Andres and Yeso Formations. Much of the clay from which pottery could have been made has inclusions of sand.

Ornamental Stones and Pigments

Turquoise was mined at Oro Grande by Pueblo IV times; the beginning of this operation is not known. Sites in the lower Tularosa Basin yielded some turquoise ornaments, but in general this was a scarce commodity. Individual finds of quartz crystals, amethyst, and micaceous schist suggest that a variety of stones valued for ornamental purposes were difficult to obtain. A number of pigments were used archaeologically; iron oxide and chalk were available as pebbles derived from higher elevations. Malachite probably had a more localized source in copper-bearing deposits.

Metal and Coal

Metal deposits of iron, gold, copper, magnesium, tungsten, and others are of little commercial value today and apparently were not utilized prehistorically. Large reserves of bituminous coal exist just west of the town of Capitan. While the main reserves are subsurface, some low grade coal outcrops. There is no evidence that this resource was exploited aboriginally.

RESOURCES PERTINENT TO AGRICULTURE

Water

The amount of rainfall and snow moisture corresponds closely to elevation (see Fig. 1). Not only the annual average but also the extremes of precipitation are of interest to people living in a region. Figure 2 shows the variation in precipitation at selected stations, with 1954 the last year recorded. Roswell and Carrizozo stations show 2 and 3 years respectively when less than 5 inches of rain fell. All stations except Ruidoso and Cloudcroft recorded a number of years with less than 10 inches of moisture. Again making an exception of Cloudcroft, years with more than 30 inches of precipitation are rare. Dryland farming is uncertain in an area that has less than 15 inches of precipitation a year; it becomes hazardous with less than 10 inches. Much of this region is so marginal for dryland agriculture today that flood-water irrigation is strongly suggested for prehistoric farming in the valleys, if climatic conditions were comparable.

Winter moisture may be dissipated from the point of view of growing plants, unless that precipitation is stored as snow. See Figure 3 for monthly distribution of moisture at three stations and Figure 4 for length of the growing season.

The mineral content of the stream water is generally high. Mourant (1963:Pl. 4) maps the results of chemical analysis of spring water, springs, and wells from the Hondo Drainage. Only at highest elevations, close to the the headwaters of the streams, is the water low in mineral content. As the Pecos River is approached, the chloride content jumps from 500 to 2500 parts

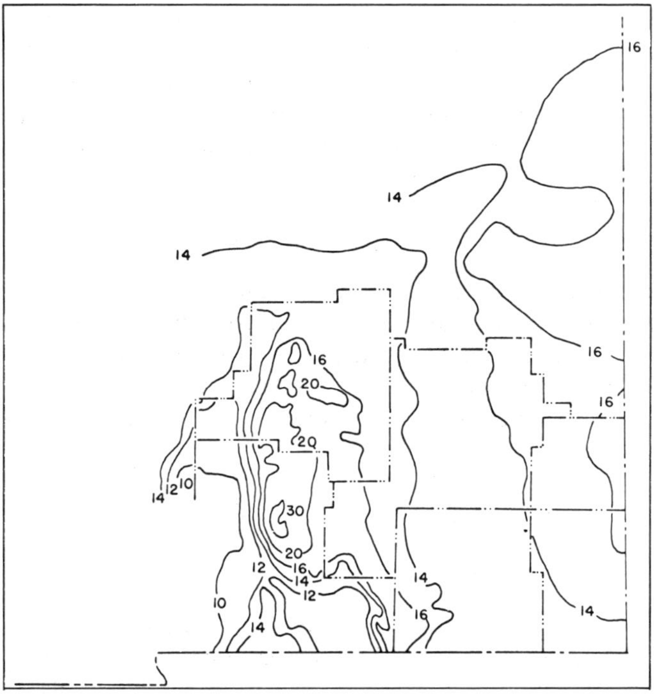

Figure 1. Relief and average annual precipitation in southeastern New Mexico (based on Reynolds 1956: Exhibit 2).

per million. It is quite likely that this situation has existed throughout the period of human habitation because of the nature of the uppermost geologic beds.

Springs, located throughout the mountains, would have been useful sources of potable water. Many have a high mineral content due to the absorption of minerals from limestone. A few springs originating in sandstone deposits are today famous for the sweet water they produce.

Soil

Alluvium in the U-shaped valleys that originate along the eastern slopes of the eastern ranges seldom exceeds 20 feet in depth. These long, narrow bands of rich soil were important for agriculture prehistorically. Around Capitan Mountain, there is an almost continuous band of outwash fans due to the steep gradient that has encouraged erosion of the upper slopes. The precipitous slopes of the western side of the Sacramento-Sierra Blanca ranges has not allowed U-shaped valleys to develop. The Organ-San Andres-Oscura Moun-

Selected Stations	Years of Weather Records		Precipitation Extremes		No. of Years Over or Under Average				
					Over			Under	
			High	Low	30″	20-30″	10-20″	10″	5″
Elk–Lower Peñasco Elev. 5350′	1895–1954	(59 yrs.)	39.10″ (1905)	8.63″ (1924)	2	6	47	4	0
Roswell Weather Station Elev. 3602′	1878–1954	(76 yrs.)	32.93″ (1941)	4.87″ (1910)	1	6	49	18	2
Arabela Elev. 5700′	1916–1922 1931–1945	(6 yrs.) (14 yrs.)	43.74″ (1941)	9.97″ (1933)	1	5	14	1	0
Capitan Elev. 6348′	1911–1954	(43 yrs.)	30.74″ (1941)	8.40″ (1922)	1	9	29	4	0
Fort Stanton Elev. 6231′	1856–1861 1868–1872 1881–1896 1900–1954 (Total =	(5 yrs.) (4 yrs.) (15 yrs.) (54 yrs.) 78 yrs.)	28.70″ (1857)	6.06″ (1945)	0	6	63	9	0
Ruidoso Elev. 6855′	1942–1954	(12 yrs.)	27.95″ (1942)	14.50″ (1947)	–	–	–	–	–
Cloudcroft Elev. 8650′	1902–1954	(52 yrs.)	48.10″ (1941)	15.01″ (1917)	9	25	18	0	0
Mayhill Elev. 6400′	1917–1954	(37 yrs.)	42.96″ (1941)	8.60″ (1951)	?	16	?	2	0
Alamogordo Elev. 4250′	1890–94, 1898, 1901–43 (48 yrs.)		29.37″ (1941)	5.20″ (1917)	0	1	31	16	0
Carrizozo Elev. 5438′	1909–1954	(45 yrs.)	35.60″ (1931)	3.25″ (1917)	1	4	23	13	3
Corona Elev. 6664′	1910–1954	(44 yrs.)	36.11″ (1941)	6.58″ (1917)	1	4	23	6	0

Fig. 2. Variation in recorded precipitation at selected stations.

tains have such precipitous slopes that U-shaped valleys with alluvial bottomlands are poorly developed. Soils throughout these mountains tend to be spotty and shallow.

Soils derived from limestone decomposition and eolian action blanket the eastern Sacramento-Sierra Blanca slopes, the Pecos plains, and the Llano Estacado. These soils are shallow, with occasional pockets up to 20 inches deep. In many places the underlying limestone is exposed. Unconsolidated materials are deep in the Tularosa Basin but dunes, salt marshes, and extreme aridity have prohibited the exploitation of soil resources for agriculture, except at the basin margin. The Jornada del Muerto and the Rio Grande Valley, like the Tularosa Basin, have deep unconsolidated materials that have been ex-

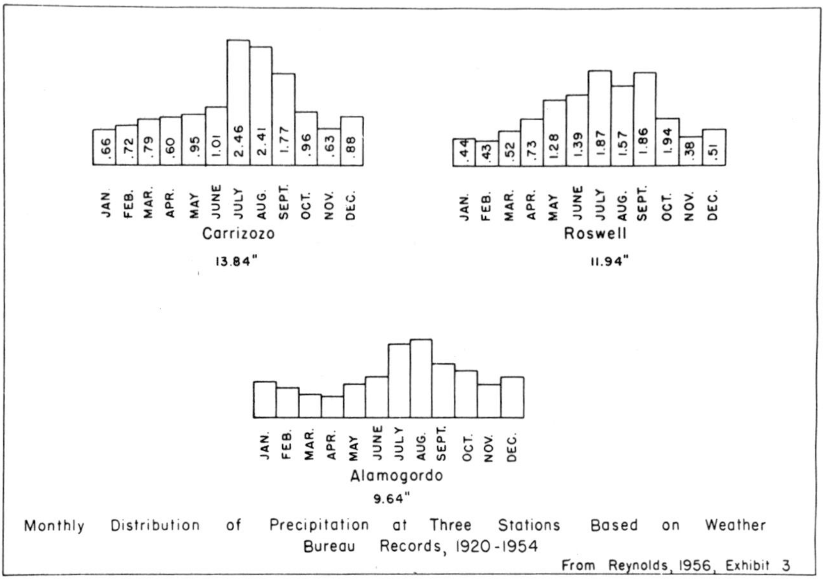

Figure 3. Monthly distribution of precipitation at three stations.

ploited agriculturally only where water was available.

Temperature

Annual mean temperature varies from 63° F in the extreme southeast corner of the state to 50° F in the high Sierra Blanca and Sacramento Mountains (Fig. 5).

Agricultural Resources and Limitations

In discussing agricultural potentials, it is convenient to divide southeastern New Mexico into two parts, using an imaginary east-west line drawn through Carrizozo to distinguish between the different ecological conditions of the northern and southern parts of the subarea.

The land available for agriculture in the southern part of southeastern New Mexico was limited, discontinuous, and widely separated. Land suitable for farming with the techniques and crops at their disposal had been effectively occupied by Pueblo III times. Even with large-scale irrigation and deep plowing, the amount of land now under cultivation is not much greater than that utilized prehistorically, except in the Roswell and Artesia Basins. Much of the southern part of the subarea such as the Organ Mountains, the Guadalupe

Selected Stations	Average Frost Date Spring	Fall	Average Frost Free Period	Extreme Frost Dates Late	Early
Chaves County– Elk Elev. 5350′	Apr. 27	Oct. 18	174 days	May 24, 1946	Sept. 22, 1924
Roswell Elev. 3602′	Apr. 6	Oct. 31	208 days	May 7, 1917	Oct. 10, 1909
Lincoln County– Carrizozo Elev. 5438′	Apr. 15	Oct. 27	195 days	May 26, 1944	Oct. 16, 1908
Corona Elev. 6664′	May 3	Oct. 19	169 days	June 3, 1947	Sept. 16, 1951
Fort Stanton Elev. 6231′	May 5	Oct. 9	157 days	June 4, 1947	Sept. 13, 1913
Ruidoso Elev. 6855′	June 10	Sept. 20	102 days	June 25, 1951	Aug. 19, 1950
Otero County– Alamogordo Elev. 4250′	Apr. 5	Nov. 7	217 days	May 7, 1917	Oct. 14, 1900
Cloudcroft Elev. 8650′	May 15	Oct. 2	140 days	June 18, 1912	Sept. 9, 1953
Mayhill Elev. 6400′	May 9	Oct. 7	151 days	May 24, 1946	Sept. 23, 1946

Fig. 4. Frost data (from Reynolds 1956).

Mountains, and the Tularosa Basin and Jornada del Muerto interiors, was hostile to farming in prehistoric times and remains so today.

In those limited places with favorable farming conditions, the land actually available was often limited to a narrow valley, with the result that the human population was scattered in small villages. Small farming groups were separated from other farming groups by the distance between valleys, by mountain ranges, or by the arid basin interiors. These were not total barriers to face to face contact, but they contributed to the isolation of certain localities.

ORGANIC RESOURCES

Plants as Potential Resources

All modern Indian groups in the Southwest have an extensive knowledge of native plants and they utilize the native flora to varying degrees. Some of the plants used widely in modern times have a long history of utilization, as excavations in dry caves have shown (Chart 1).

We conducted no original botanical or ethnobotanical research. However, in an effort to understand the potential botanical resources and their possible uses, I undertook a survey of plant lists from the area and of Southwestern ethnobotanical literature and arranged the plants native to southeastern New Mexico into potential use-categories (see Charts 1 and 2).

Food Plants

Not all Southwestern groups share identical ethnobotanical information, and the degree of dependence on wild products has varied in response to complex cultural preferences, success of agricultural pursuits, and the geographical limits of the wild plants. There are, nevertheless, a number of plant use-categories that are shared by all or most groups. All modern Southwestern groups for which there is published ethnobotanical data use some wild products for: (1) seeds that may be reduced to flour; (2) fruits; (3) greens and/or vegetables; and (4) condiments and accessories. A fifth category of heart and stalk plants is applicable for many groups even though these products had to be obtained by trade.

Certain plants that were widely prized and sought regularly were piñon nuts, *Yucca baccata* fruits, mesquite beans, cactus 'tuna', lambsquarter, and wild strawberries. Some wild plants of limited distribution were popular beyond their homeland; an extensive commerce in mescal was formerly carried out between the Apache and various pueblo groups (Castetter 1935:11).

Other wild foods were regarded as starvation fare. Utilization of such foods would be heavier in years of crop failure. The grass *Eriocoma cuspidata* was so regarded by the Zuni, who became knowledgable foragers of these seeds in lean years (Stevenson 1915:67).

Fiber Plants

Major fiber producing plants, in order of their importance in the Southwest, are yucca, beargrass (*Nolina microcarpa*), agave, and sotol. All are available in the area under consideration, although the latter two are limited to the southern, more arid sections. Minor fiber sources are mesquite bark, cattails (*Typha*), willow wands, and various grasses.

Wood Sources

Wood for making tools and weapons was more limited in its geographical distribution because of the ecological requirements of trees. Regional differences exist in the types of wood used for implements. In the Lower Sonoran sections of the Guadalupe Mountains, southern Pecos Valley, Tularosa Basin, and Jornada del Muerto, mesquite, screwbean, and occasional cottonwoods were the best woods available. Because of this scarcity, stalks of sotol and

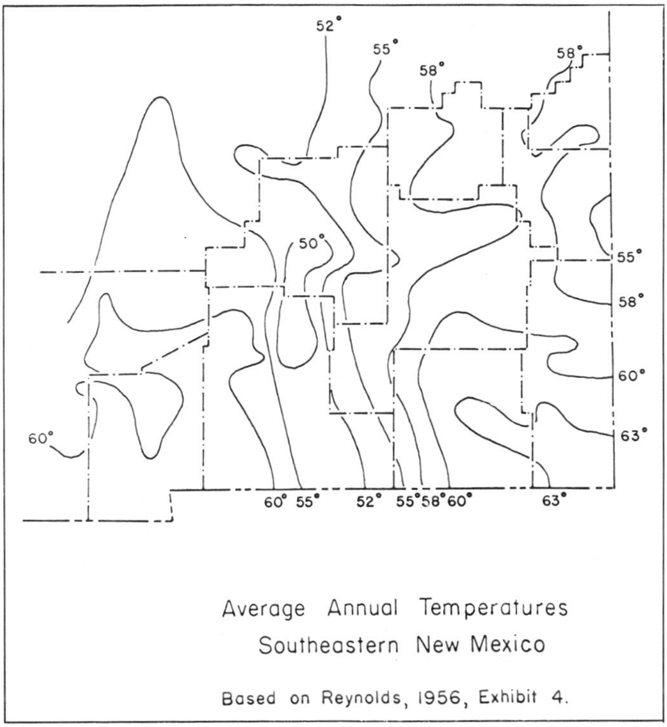

Figure 5. Average annual temperatures, southeastern New Mexico.

agave were important sources of woody material (Cosgrove 1947:50, 56). For the Upper Sonoran Zone, where most of the village sites were located, piñon and juniper grew on the slopes, and cottonwood, walnut, and willows were found in the adjacent valleys. Oak, pine, spruce, and other trees of the higher life zones were available in the mountains.

Stone or adobe housing would exploit mainly inorganic resources for construction materials and would use plant products mainly for roofing materials, support posts, and furnishings. Pithouse construction placed a greater emphasis on the exploitation of plant resources, with timber a major component of pole-walled houses covered with brush and reeds and plastered with clay or soil.

Medicinal Plants

The extent to which native plants were used for medicinal and ceremonial purposes was tied to systems of belief for which we have no pertinent data. Of the many plants used by the Navajo for this purpose, at least 71 of those listed by Vestal (1952:67–71) are native to southeastern New Mexico and could have served in this capacity.

Animals as Potential Resources

The Upper Sonoran Life Zone had the most abundant and varied fauna, although each of the life zones supported animals that could have been exploited for food, by-products, or both. We have archaeological evidence that a number of large mammals were hunted.

Bison were killed in the Pecos Valley prior to 1840 (Bailey 1931:14), and well-defined bison trails leading from the High Plains into the Pecos Valley were visible as late as 1902. The frequency of bison bones in excavated sites indicates that their range included the Pecos Valley and plains but not the mountain valleys.

Three species of deer are found today, each fitting into a different ecological niche. Mule deer range in the higher elevations. Arizona white-tailed deer prefer brushy country and are plentiful at medium elevations from the Sierra Blanca Mountains south into Texas. The Virginia or Texas white-tailed deer are found on lower mountain slopes and into the valleys and basins (M. E. Guck, Forest Ranger at Capitan, personal communication). Skeletal resemblances between the various deer species and antelope make positive identification of body bones difficult.

Antelope were abundant throughout the historical period. They are herd animals which range through the open to semi-open country of the Upper Sonoran and Lower Sonoran Life Zones; horn cores found in sites of the Sierra Blanca Region prove that these were taken aboriginally.

We have no evidence that bighorn sheep were used for food, but their frequent portrayal in petroglyphs and on artifacts shows that they had special significance. Their range was in the rougher mountains, such as the Guadalupes and the Organs.

Merriam's elk was exterminated by 1900, but it had been common at higher elevations prior to this. There is no archaeological evidence that elk were hunted, and I know of no petroglyphs or pictographs that portray this distinctive animal.

Small black-cinnamon bears may still be found, and Bailey (1931:362–63) postulates an extension of the Texas grizzly bear into southeastern New Mexico until recent years. A few bear teeth have been found archaeologically, and bear effigies are known, suggesting religious importance. There is no evidence that bears were exploited for food or fur.

Large cats whose range was mainly in the mountains include the jaguar (*Felis onca hernandesii*) and two species of panther or cougar (*Felis concolor hippolestes* and *aztecus*). The smaller bobcat (*Lynx rufus uinta*) extended down into the Upper Sonoran Life Zone.

Members of the *Canis* family include the lobo wolf, the red and the gray fox, and the coyote. Peccary also occurred. We have no evidence that any of the cats, members of the Canis family, or peccary were exploited extensively, although a wolf limb bone has been tentatively identified from the Bonnell Site.

Cottontails and jackrabbits were numerous and frequently hunted, as indicated by the substantial numbers of their bones in refuse. Other small animals that could have been exploited (but for which we have little information) are squirrels, prairie dogs, rats and mice, muskrats, beavers, porcupines, badgers, skunks, shrews, and bats.

At least 127 species of birds are present with some regularity in southeastern New Mexico, and many other migratory species pass through (based on Bailey 1928). Of potential importance as a food resource are the prairie chickens, doves, Merriam turkeys, and three species of quail. Prairie chickens inhabit Upper and Lower Sonoran environments; some of the doves are to be found on the mountain slopes, others are confined to the mountains. The only eggshells found archaeologically have been attributed to turkey. Nine species of ducks which migrate through this area in the fall would have furnished a potential seasonal food. While any bird could supply feathers, the more brightly-colored species include Treganza's Blue Heron, the Long-crested Jay, the Piñon Jay, and the Painted Bunting. Birds of prey are often valued for their feathers. Both Bald Eagles and Golden Eagles occur, as do eight species of hawks and one species of falcon. Six species of owls include the large horned owl and the tiny pygmy owl. The roadrunner or chaparral, famous as a rattlesnake killer, occurs in a Lower Sonoran environment.

Fish seem to have been ignored as a food source prehistorically, although they are frequently depicted on petroglyphs and on shell pendants. Some fish were available in every type of water. In the cool or cold mountain streams there was the cut-throat trout. At lower elevations in these streams were minnows and two species of chub. Larger rivers at lower elevations (the Pecos and Rio Grande) supported a varied fish population in the deeper, permanent holes; when the rivers were flowing, a wide variety of fish would be generally available. American eels penetrated far upriver. Larger species, now recognized as a good source of food, include four species of catfish, spotted and rock bass, and five members of the sucker family (Koster 1957). Among the water invertebrates, freshwater mussels were exploited prehistorically as a source of ornamental shell but, apparently, not as a food.

Amphibians and reptiles are most common in Upper and Lower Sonoran Zones (Bailey 1913:19, 34–35). Both life forms are frequently found in petroglyphs. Soft-shelled turtles of the sort that live in soft-bottomed rivers and streams were found archaeologically in Pecos Valley sites (Jelinek 1960:59).

The degree of utilization of animal soft parts, especially the hide, seems to have been minimal in the Hueco Phase if one can judge from the dry cave materials reported by Cosgrove (1947:136) from the Hueco region, by Ferdon (1946:17) from Hermit's Cave, and by Roosa (1952:133–45) from a cave in Capitan Mountain. Fiber was far more important as a raw material. In the former region, the only leather objects were pouches; fur cloth was made of rabbit skin wrapped around yucca cords, and sinew was used for atlatls, darts, fending sticks, and arrows. Recognizable leather sources included deer, rabbit, antelope, rodent (prairie dog and squirrel), coyote or wolf, and porcupine (Cosgrove 1947:136). This is in strong contrast to the conditions reported by the Espejo Expedition of 1582–83 for regions along the Rio Grande ("Journal of Diego Perez de Luxan," in Hammond and Rey 1929:57–73), where deerskin bodices or scapularies and skirts, buffalo skin cloaks, buffalo skin shoes and deerskin boots were worn, and skins were valued enough to serve as gifts. It would seem that hunting increased in importance after the introduction of agriculture. The sixteenth-century emphasis on leather for wearing apparel, especially footwear, may reflect Athapascan influences.

Summary Statement on Organic Resources

Southeastern New Mexico, with several life zones compressed into a relatively small space, offered a variety of plants and animals as potential resources, but nowhere was there a constant, abundant, natural food supply. In order to utilize these resources at a hunting-gathering level, limited nomadism seems mandatory. The modern Mescalero Apache probably typify an old pattern, although undoubtedly on a larger geographic scale than their pedestrian predecessors, with their seasonal exploitation of mescal, mesquite, piñon nuts, acorns, and so forth (Castetter and Opler 1936:10–14).

After agriculture was introduced, dependence on native plants undoubtedly decreased; on the other hand it seems clear that hunting increased in importance. The sedentary people of the Lower Tularosa Basin apparently utilized mesquite beans as an important adjunct to agricultural products, judging from the quantity of mortars and pestles in Mesilla and El Paso Phase sites. Piñon nuts were probably a minor staple food in the Chupadero Region and for the people of the Glencoe Phase; *Opuntia* fruit and walnuts were widely gathered. One problem for future research is to determine the extent to which the different cultural groups utilized wild products, and to specify the range of wild products that were important to the agricultural villagers.

CHART 1
SELECTED LIST OF NATIVE PLANTS USED FOR FOOD
(Based Primarily on Castetter 1935)

Technical Name	Common Name	Mescalero Apache	Navajo	Pima	Papago	Zuni	Acoma Laguna	Rio Grande Pueblos	Hopi	Ventana Cave	Gila Caves	Hueco Caves
Acacia greggii	Cat claw			x								
Agave parryi	Mescal or century plant	x		x	x			trade	trade	x	x	x
Allium spp.	Wild onion	x	x	x			x		x			
Amaranthus spp.	Amaranth or pigweed		x									
	tumbleweed	x	x			x	x	x	x			
Amelanchier prunifolis	Serviceberry		x					x				
Anogra albicaulis	Evening primrose	x										
Asclepias spp. *(galioides)*	Milkweed					x	x	x	x			
Astragalus spp.						x	x	x	x			
Atriplex canescens	Saltbush											
confertifolia	Saltbush											
nuttallii	Saltbush											
argentea	Saltbush											
cornuta	Saltbush											
elegans	Saltbush			x			x	x	x			
coronata	Saltbush											
philonitra	Saltbush											
powellii	Saltbush											
sabulosa	Saltbush											
Berberis haematocarpa	Algerita	x						x				
repens												
Chenopodium spp.	Lambsquarter	x	x	x	x	x		x	x			
Cleome serrulata	Rocky Mt. bee plant		x			x		x	x			
Dasylirion wheeleri	Sotol	x										
Echinocactus spp.	Hedgehog cactus	x	x	x			x	x				
Eriocoma cuspidata	Indian millet											
(Oryzopsis hymenoides)	Sand bunch grass		x			x			x			
Euphorbia spp.												
(serpyllifolia)	Spurge					x						

CHART 1, continued
SELECTED LIST OF NATIVE PLANTS USED FOR FOOD
(Based Primarily on Castetter 1935)

Technical Name	Common Name	Mescalero Apache	Navajo	Pima	Papago	Zuni	Acoma Laguna	Rio Grande Pueblos	Hopi	Ventana Cave	Gila Caves	Hueco Caves
Fragaria bracteata	Wild strawberry	x	x					x				
Frasera speciosa	Deer's ears	x										
Helianthus spp.	Sunflower	x	x					x				
Juglans major	Walnut, nogal											
minor		x	x				x	x	x		x	x
nigra												
Juniperus monosperma	One-seeded juniper											
scopulorum	Rocky Mt. juniper							x				
pachyphloea	Alligator juniper											
Lycium pallidum	Squawthorn		x			x	x	x	x			
Monarda menthaefolia	Horsemint or oregano	x						x	x	x		
Reomammillaris spp.	Various cactus	x										
Rolina microcarpa	Bent grass											
Opuntia spp.	Cholla, or prickly pear	x	x	x	x	x	x	x	x	x	x	
Panicum obtusum	Panic grass	x								x		
Phoradendron juniperinum	Juniper mistletoe			x				x				
Physalis fendleri longifolia	Ground-cherry					x	x	x	x	x		
Pinus edulis	Piñon	x	x			x	x	x	x		x	x
Pinus flexilis brachyptera	Pine		x			x						
scopulorum												
Poa fendleriana	Grass											
Portulaca oleracea	Purslane-verolaga		x			x	x	x	x			
Prosopis glandulosa	Mesquite	x	x	x	x	x	x	x		x		x
Prosopis pubescens (syn. of *Strombocarpa pubescens)*	Tornillo or screwbean	x		x				x				x
Prunus americana	Wild plum		x					x				
Prunus melanocarpa	Chokeberry (capulin)		x				x	x				

Quercus spp. esp. *utahensis gambelii*	Oak	x	x	x	x		x	x			x	x
Rhus trilobata	Skunk bush											
	3-leaved sumac	x	x			x	x	x	x			
Ribes inebrians	Currant		x			x		x	x			
inerms	Gooseberry	x						x				
Rosa fendleri	Rose	x	x									
Rubus arizonicus	Red raspberry		x									
Sambucus microbotrys	Elderberry	x										
Solanum fendleri	Wild potato	x				x	x	x				
Solanum jamesii triflorum	Wild potato berries					x	x	x	x			
Sporobolus spp.	Dropseed grass	x	x									
Tradescantia spp. *(occidentalis)*	Spiderwort						x		x			
Vitis arizonica	Wild grape	x	x				x	x				
Yucca baccata	Soapweed	x	x	x		x	x	x		x	?	?
glauca			x	x			x	x				
elata	Soapweed or palmilla	x										

CHART 2
POTENTIAL PLANT RESOURCES OF SOUTHEASTERN NEW MEXICO, ARRANGED BY ARBITRARY USE-CATEGORIES

1. Seeds that could be ground into flour

A. Grass seeds

a. Major species

Muhlenbergia spp.	Muhly grass
Oryzopsis hymenoides (syn. *Eriocoma cuspidata*)	Indian millet or sand bunch grass
Panicum spp.	Panic grass
Sporobolus spp.	Dropseed grass

b. Minor species

Bouteloua spp.	Grama grass
Eragrostis diffusa	Lovegrass
Koeleria cristata	Junegrass
Nolina microcarpa	Beargrass
Poa spp. (esp. *fendleriana*)	Poa grass
Sorghastrum nutans	Indian grass

B. Other small seeds

Amaranthus graecizans	Tumbleweed
Amaranthus palmeri	Pigweed
Atriplex spp.	Saltbush
Camelina microcarpa	False flax
Capsella bursa pastoris	Shepherd's purse
Chenopodium spp.	Lambsquarter
Dysodia papposa	Fetid marigold
Mentzelia pumila	Stickleaf
Sophia incisa	Tansy mustard

C. Larger seeds

Helianthus spp.	Sunflower
Juglans spp.	Walnuts
Pinus edulis	Piñon nuts
Prosopis glandulosa	Mesquite beans
Prosopis pubescens	Screwbean or tornillo
Quercus spp.	Oak acorns

D. Cactus seeds

Opuntia spp.	Cholla
Opuntia spp.	Prickly pear

CHART 2, continued

2. Fruits

A. Small fleshy fruits

Berberis haematocarpa	Algerita berry
Fragaria bracteata	Wild strawberry
Lycium pallidum	Squawthorn
Physalis spp.	Ground-cherry
Prunus americana	Wild plum
Prunus melanocarpa	Chokecherry
Rhus trilobata	Skunk bush
Rubus arizonicus	Red raspberry
Sambucus microbotrys	Elderberry
Vitis arizonica	Wild grape

B. Cactus fruits

Echinocerus spp.	Hedgehog cactus
Opuntia spp.	Cholla
Opuntia spp.	Prickly pear
Yucca baccata	Yucca
Yucca elata	Yucca

3. Greens and vegetables

A. Cactus

Echinocereus spp.	Hedgehog cactus
Neomammillaria	Fishhook cactus
Opuntia spp.	Cholla
Opuntia spp.	Prickly pear

B. Other species

Acanthochiton wrightii	?
Amaranthus graecizans	Tumbleweed
Amaranthus retroflexus	Pigweed
Asclepias spp.	Milkweed
Astragalus diphysus	Milk vetch
Capsella bursa pastoris	Shepherd's purse
Chenopodium spp.	Lambsquarter
Cleome serrulata	Rocky Mt. bee plant
Cymopterus spp.	Wild celery
Cyperus fendlerianus	Sedge
Dysodia papposa	Fetid marigold
Juniperus monosperma	One-seeded juniper
Lathyrus lencanthus	Wild pea
Ligusticum porteri	Chuchupate
Portulaca oleracea	Purslane
Rumex occidentalis	?
Tradescantia occidentalis	Spiderwort
Typha latifolia	Cattail
Vicia americana	Vetch

CHART 2, continued

C. Root and tuber vegetables

Hoffmanseggia densiflora	Camote de raton or Indian potato
Pseudocymopterus montanus	?
Solanum fendleri	Wild potato
Solanum jamesii	Wild potato

4. Hearts and stalks

Agave parryi	Agave, mescal, or century plant
Dasylirion wheeleri	Sotol
Yucca baccata	Yucca
Yucca elata	Yucca
Yucca glauca	Yucca

5. Condiments and food accessories

A. Condiments

Allium spp.	Wild onion
Artemisia ludoviciana	Sage
Atriplex spp.	Saltbush
Cleome serrulata	Rocky Mt. bee plant
Cymopterus fendleri	Wild celery
Dracocephalum parviflorum	Dragon head
Hedeoma nana	Pennyroyal
Humulus lupulus neomexicanus	Hop
Juniperus monosperma	One-seeded juniper
Monarda menthaefolia	Horsemint or oregano

B. Food accessories

a. Sugar or "sweetening"

Amaranthus blitoides	Amaranth
Amaranthus palmeri	Amaranth
Acer negundo	Box elder maple
Acer neomexicana	New Mex. maple (sap)
Castilleja lineata	Indian paint brush
Chenopodium fremontii	?
Euphorbia serpyllifolia	Spurge
Pinus scapulorum	Pine (inner bark)
Populus tremuloides	Aspen (inner bark)
Rhus cismontana	Sumac (bark)

b. "Butter"

Pinus edulis	Piñon nuts

CHART 2, continued

c. "Chewing gum"

Asclepias spp.	Milkweed
Pinus edulis	Piñon (resin)
Populus wislizeni	Cottonwood (buds)

6. Beverages

Agave parryi	Agave
Mirabilis multiflora	Wild Four-O'Clock

Chapter 2

REGIONAL REVIEW OF THE ECOLOGY AND ARCHAEOLOGY

A brief review of the status of archaeological knowledge in the southeastern quarter of New Mexico sets the stage for the detailed trait comparisons which must be made. At the same time this review serves to place the Sierra Blanca Region into a wider archaeological context.

Publications concerned with all or a large part of southeastern New Mexico are those of Mera (1943), Lehmer (1948), and Wheat (1955b:29–33). Lehmer drew a pear-shaped region that extended from Carrizozo on the north to Villa Ahumada, Chihuahua, on the south. Mera defined an eastern brown-ware area that had its western limits at the San Mateo, Magdalena, and Black Mountains (Mera 1943:1). As Wheat pointed out, the latter division meets the Mimbres Branch and includes what has become known as the San Marcial Phase, which Lehmer specifically excluded from the Jornada Branch (Wheat 1955:30).

DATING PROBLEMS

As of 1966, relatively few tree-ring dates have been obtained within southeastern New Mexico, and as a result, absolute dating in terms of the Christian calendar is not feasible for most sites or phases reported here. Dating of the sites described here thus relies heavily on trade pottery types that originated in other regions of the Southwest, where they have been dated with some precision. However, the element of time lag, or of sloping time horizons, has not been sufficiently well worked out to warrant using the dates assigned to these trade types in their homeland. Using tree-ring dates as an absolute time scale, Breternitz (1962) has convincingly demonstrated that a substantial time lag existed between the point of origin of a pottery type and its occurrence as a trade type some distance away in eastern Arizona.

Much of the chronologically significant trade pottery in southeastern New Mexico originated in Anasazi regions where the types have been pegged to a period or periods in the Pecos Classification. Thus, the Lino series may be assigned to Basketmaker III - Pueblo I, Red Mesa Black-on-White to Pueblo II, St. Johns Polychrome and Heshotauthla Polychrome to Pueblo III, and the Rio Grande Glaze series to Pueblo IV. As techniques become available for refining the chronology in southeastern New Mexico, the gross scheme effected in this report can be more finely redrawn. The terms Pueblo I, II, and so forth, are used herein as a *relative* chronological yardstick based primarily on trade pottery. The cultural implications of these terms, as originally set forth in the Pecos Classification or as subsequently modified, are largely ignored here.

CHUPADERO REGION

The Setting

Chupadero Mesa, the Salinas-Medano locality, and mesa slopes of the northern Jornada del Muerto are encompassed within the Upper Sonoran Zone which is contiguous with that part of the Upper Sonoran Zone covering so much of central New Mexico, a factor that facilitated the diffusion of agriculture into the region. East of the mesa, there is grassland with isolated stands of piñon and juniper. Here, and on the mesa proper, water is an eternal problem as there are no streams (Howard 1959). A few shallow lakes tend to become quite saline. Chupadero Mesa is somewhat higher than the Salinas-Medano locality, and accordingly has more precipitation and tree cover. On the south and west, the mesa slopes are timbered with piñon and juniper, and intermittent streams flow toward the Rio Grande.

Archaeological Sequence

The six foci set up by Toulouse and Stephenson (1960:40–41) provide a skeletal framework of cultural development from early Pueblo III to historic times. These authors use the *focus* as their basic archaeological unit; I have taken the liberty of equating their foci with *phases*, the working archaeological unit employed in this report.

Archaeological research has emphasized late prehistoric and mission sites, and the earlier phases are in need of more thorough documentation. A Pueblo I site was found and partially excavated as a result of a pipeline survey. The Laboratory of Anthropology survey cards give some indication of temporal placement of unexcavated sites and furnish a clue to site frequencies in the different pueblo periods.

A Preceramic Site

Hearths and hammerstones were found at LA 2539 (Fenega and Cummings 1956:220).

Gran Quivira Pithouse Village (LA 2579)

The site probably contained six to eight pithouses scattered over a flat area which is now Upper Sonoran grassland. Two circular pithouses, an exterior hearth, and five extramural hearths have been reported (Fenenga 1956:226–29; Green 1955:182–85). Jornada Brown and Lino pottery types were found on the floor of both houses. Fenenga suggested a Basketmaker III date; a Pueblo I date seems equally plausible.

Claunch Focus

No excavated sites (Toulouse and Stephenson 1960:40–41). Type site: G. Q. #19 (Site 19, Gran Quivira Monument survey). Date: early Pueblo III (?). Toulouse and Stephenson listed Jornada Brown, Los Lunas Smudged, San Francisco Red, Chupadero Black-on-White, and indented Corrugated Utility as associated pottery types. It is probable that their San Francisco Red was of local manufacture and not imported, as the type designation implies. Widely scattered house units of one, two, and three rooms were noted, but no structural information was given.

The Laboratory of Anthropology survey located 20 sites in this region with similar pottery complexes, sometimes with the addition of Red Mesa, Socorro, Mimbres, Chaco 2, and San Marcial Black-on-Whites as well as Wingate Black-on-Red.

Toulouse and Stephenson (1960:41) feel that the Claunch Focus coexisted with the Arroyo Seco Focus, and that the former was the last of the local brown-ware tradition while the latter heralded the beginning of the Puebloan "foci." It is more likely that the two were sequential and that there was more continuity than they imply.

Arroyo Seco Focus

No excavated sites (Toulouse and Stephenson 1960). Date: Late Pueblo III (?). Type site: Arroyo Seco Ruin (G. Q. #3). Square, masonry pueblos with a central plaza were said to characterize the focus. The type site was described as a pure Chupadero Black-on-White site (Toulouse and Stephenson 1960:41), but Corrugated Utility and St. Johns Polychrome were typical of the focus (ibid.:40). It is probable that the total pottery complex will be found to include Jornada Brown, Chupadero Black-on-White, Tularosa Black-on-White, Mimbres Black-on-White, and Galisteo Black-on-White. Twelve sites in the Laboratory of Anthropology survey have these and earlier pottery types.

Gran Quivira Focus

Type site: early Gran Quivira (G. Q. #6), a small ruin a few hundred feet south of the main ruins at Gran Quivira (Toulouse and Stephenson 1960:40–41). Date: early Pueblo IV. The pottery includes Corrugated, Chupadero Black-on-White, and a variety of Rio Grande Glaze I types. At least eight large sites in the Laboratory of Anthropology survey belong here; a number of sites that apparently began in this phase continued to be occupied in later phases.

Pueblo Pardo and Pueblo Colorado Foci

Type sites are Pueblo Pardo (G. Q. #7) and Pueblo Colorado (G. Q. #12); excavations have been conducted at the former site. Date: Pueblo IV (Toulouse and Stephenson 1960:40–41).

Pueblo Pardo was first settled in the Gran Quivira Phase, and it was not abandoned until about 1630 (Toulouse and Stephenson 1960:3). An E-shaped house block was flanked on the east by additional units. Three circular kivas were located, one of which was excavated. Locally-made brown pottery survived into the historic period; 4.6% of the total sample was of this type. The most common utility pottery was a plain gray, which almost completely replaced Corrugated; only 16 sherds of the latter type were found. Chupadero White ware, which made up 15% of the total sample, included Chupadero Black-on-White, Casa Colorado Black-on-White, Tabira Black-on-White, Tabira Plain, Miscellaneous Chupadero, and Unnamed Miscellaneous Tabira (ibid.:21). Rio Grande glazes and other painted and glazed types accounted for about 43% of the total.

Salinas Focus

Date: Historic. Type site: Abo. Gran Quivira Mission also belongs to this phase (Toulouse and Stephenson 1960:40–41).

Abo was a settlement of the Tompiro Indians, mountain-dwelling relatives of the Rio Grande Piros (Toulouse 1949:1). Missionary efforts began as early as 1626; the mission settlement was abandoned between 1672 and 1675. The mission was one of the wealthier in New Mexico due to exploitation of two natural resources: piñon nuts and salt from the saline lakes (ibid.:3–4).

A kiva in the west court was constructed, apparently during the building of the church, "as there was no other sign of Indian occupation underlying the church in this neighborhood, except refuse under the main altar" (Toulouse 1949:11). One would expect an older kiva to be under the altar, as was the one at Awatovi (Montgomery, Smith, and Brew 1949:65), and one would not expect a kiva to be built at all in the mission period. Montgomery felt that this case was not as aberrant as it first appeared, but that it represented a unique form of the doctrine of superposition in which the use of the kiva for kitchen refuse was substituted for the more usual form of ritual superposition of a Catholic sacred altar over a pagan sacred structure (Montgomery, Smith, and Brew 1949:137).

Locally made pottery represented the final expression of the Chupadero Region pottery series. A smoothed utility type that made up from 25% to 65% of the ceramic samples ws similar to Kidder's late culinary ware at Pecos (ibid.:14). Salinas Redware was the second most numerous type. In the Chupadero wares, a few sherds of Chupadero Black-on-White gave evidence that the type persisted to this date. More common were Tabira Black-on-White, Tabira Polychrome, and Tabira Plain. Toulouse (1949:18) commented on the similarity between the disc base of earlier Chupadero ware and annular bases from western Mexico.

Summary

Sites known from the Laboratory of Anthropology and Gran Quivira Monument surveys indicate a continuous occupation of the region from Basketmaker III or Pueblo I times to the better known pueblos of the late prehistoric and historic periods. Villages of pithouses were associated with exterior storage pits in Pueblo I. It may be postulated that these were followed by small, shallow pithouse or surface house units scattered in an open village pattern. Pueblo structures were typical of the region from Pueblo III to historic times.

SOUTH-CENTRAL NEW MEXICO FROM THE TULAROSA BASIN TO THE RIO GRANDE

The Basin and Range topography of this territory is best described in four parts: the Tularosa Basin, the San Andres-Organ mountain ranges, the Jornada del Muerto, and Rio Grande Valley. Two archaeological sequences have been set up for this territory: the southern sequence extends into all of the regions mentioned above; the northern sequence is limited to the northern Tularosa Basin.

The Setting

Tularosa Basin

The floor of this basin is nearly flat, sloping gradually toward the south. A large alkali marsh in the interior is banded on the east by gypsum dunes, the White Sands, 6 to 12 miles wide. Escarpments and shorelines of a Pleistocene lake have been noted (Meinzer 1922:541–52). Arid components of the Lower Sonoran Life Zone characterize the flora and fauna (Bailey 1913:14; Meinzer and Hare 1915:196–206). Known archaeological sites are along the basin fringes where a narrow Upper Sonoran Life Zone is present.

Jornada del Muerto

This is actually a series of basins, some of which retain occasional drainage in shallow lakes. The basin floor slopes from 4700 feet in elevation at San Marcial to 4200 feet at Las Cruces. The entire basin lies within the Lower Sonoran Life Zone. Insofar as we know now, the interior has attracted only transients; the permanent sites that are reported are in ecologically more favorable localities on the edges of the basin.

Rio Grande Valley

Forming the natural western limit of southeastern New Mexico, the river is bordered by an arid Lower Sonoran landscape from Socorro south to the Texas border. The water available in the river does not compensate for the generally unfavorable environment, and prehistoric sedentary occupation was spotty and sporadic.

The Organ, San Andres, and Oscura Mountains

These form part of a chain which includes the Franklin Mountains of Texas and the Montoso-Manzano-Sandia ranges to the north. The highest elevations run close to the longitudinal median of the mountains giving approximately equal slopes on both the east and west sides. Long, gradual slopes, such as the east flank of the Sacramento-Sierra Blanca ranges, are nonexistent; this means that more limited sections were available for agriculturally-based people in these ranges. The Tularosa Basin on the east and the Jornada del Muerto on the west support arid Lower Sonoran life forms. There is an abrupt change from the Lower Sonoran of the flanking basins to the Upper Sonoran of the ranges. These desert mountains have large expanses of exposed rock between the sparse vegetation on the slopes. Small patches of timber crown the highest elevations and represent the Transitional Life Zone. As one proceeds north, the ranges become less arid and the Upper Sonoran Zone increases in width. Very little is known of this region archaeologically.

Archaeological Sequence of the Southern Regions

The more arid, Lower Sonoran environment was used little by aboriginal inhabitants. Known sedentary sites are located on the basin fringes in a grasslands belt of the Upper Sonoran Zone.

Archaeological site reports deal with Pueblo II and late Pueblo III - Pueblo IV sites. The intervening period is less well known. The archaeological sequence used here was set up by Lehmer (1948).

Mesilla Phase

Type Site: Los Tules (Lehmer 1948:75–78). Date: Pueblo II. Both the pithouse village of Los Tules on the Rio Grande and the lower level of La Cueva in the Organ Mountains were assigned to this phase by Lehmer. La Cueva was explored in the hope that perishable materials of this phase would be preserved. This did not prove to be the case. The ceramic stratigraphy in the cave gave clear evidence that El Paso Brown preceded El Paso Polychrome in time. At Los Tules, considerable variation occurred in pithouse form. Eleven houses formed a scattered village. Pottery was predominantly El Paso Brown, with minor amounts of decorated El Paso Brown, Mimbres Black-on-White, Mimbres Corrugated, San Francisco Brown, and Alma Plain. Maize agriculture was basic to the economy, although some wild product or products were processed in mortars.

Doña Ana Phase

No excavated sites were reported by Lehmer (1948:78–80). Date: Pueblo III (?), or A.D. 1100–1200 as given by Lehmer (ibid.:89). Lehmer's survey data suggested that both adobe surface structures and pithouses were in use. His major criterion for defining the phase was the pottery complex which consisted of all the types listed above for the Mesilla Phase and El Paso Polychrome, Chupadero Black-on-White, Three Rivers Red-on-Terracotta, and St. Johns Polychrome. Roger Green (1956:15) placed his Site 1, located in the Sacramento Mountains, in this phase on the basis of the time and space dimensions set up by Lehmer. It is possible that the site is earlier, if St. Johns Polychrome is considered as a diagnostic type of the Doña Ana Phase. Green's site is reassigned to the newly formulated Glencoe Phase in this report.

El Paso Phase

Of all the phases of southeastern New Mexico, this is the best documented (Lehmer 1948:80–84), and our ideas about its time, space, and content dimensions will be least affected by new excavations. Site reports dealing with the Bradfield Site (Lehmer 1948:38–54), Alamogordo Sites 1 and 2 (Bradfield 1929; Stubbs 1930; and Lehmer 1948:54–57), and Twelve Room House Ruin (Moore 1947:94–114) furnish concrete evidence about this phase which began in mid-Pueblo III and lasted until early Pueblo IV, when the lower Tularosa Basin was apparently abandoned. Adobe pueblo villages, often with large internal plazas, were located toward the margins of the Tularosa Basin. The pottery complex was distinctive for this time period in the Southwest in that El Paso Polychrome seems to be the only native pottery type. A large number of trade pottery types are significant for dating and for determining directions of trade relations.

Summary

Current evidence favors limiting the Mesilla, Doña Ana, and El Paso

Phases to the lowland localities of the Tularosa and Jornada del Muerto Basins and adjacent Rio Grande Valley. The Mesilla Phase was contemporary with and has its closest relationships to the Three Circle Phase. Pueblo architecture, which began to diffuse into the region during the Doña Ana Phase, was the only building form of the El Paso Phase. Aside from this architectural innovation, other aspects of culture show remarkable continuity from one phase to the next. In the Organ and San Andres Mountains, the culture is best classified as a late manifestation of the Hueco Phase, although some agriculture was practiced and contemporary pottery was acquired.

Archaeological Sequence of the Northern Tularosa Basin

Taylor Draw Site

Pueblo II. The site report has not been published, but it is briefly mentioned (Peckham 1957b:70). The whole village was dug. A number of circular pithouses with ramp entries and ventilator shafts were placed along a ridge overlooking Taylor Draw at the northern edge of the basin. Each pithouse was associated with contiguous slab-lined granaries. A kiva with a ventilator and a banquette lacked a *sipapu*. The bulk of the pottery was a brown type that has not been formally named; it is what Mera has called "coarsened Alma" (Peckham, personal communication). The diagnostic trade ware was Red Mesa Black-on-White.

Capitan Phase

This is thought to be contemporary with the Mesilla Phase (Lehmer 1948:84–85). Jornada Brown was the main pottery type; it was associated with a broad lined red-on-terracotta which may be the type subsequently named San Andres Red-on-Terracotta by McCluney (1962:49–55). Some sites were reported to have large quantities of Mimbres Black-on-White, especially Bold Faced (Lehmer 1948:85). The only site definitely attributed to this phase, in print, is Site 2000 in the Peñasco Valley, which in this study is placed in the Glencoe Phase (see Appendix 7).

Three Rivers Phase

Surface pueblos were built (Lehmer 1948:85). In addition to the pottery types of the Capitan Phase, El Paso Polychrome, Chupadero Black-on-White, and rare sherds of St. Johns Polychrome were associated. Lehmer did not discuss the Three Rivers or Falls Ranch sites (LA 1231 and 2455) where the Cosgroves excavated, but these sites presumably belong in part to this phase. Twenty-five percent of the sherds from that site were reported to be Three Rivers Red-on-Terracotta by the Cosgroves in 1932 (Cosgrove and Cosgrove 1932:99), but their notes on this site published since then indicate that the percentage was 25% of the Black-on-White instead of 25% of the total (Cosgrove and Cosgrove 1965:11). The Laboratory of Anthropology sherd list from these sites suggests that these sites began in the Three Rivers Phase and terminated in the San Andres Phase.

San Andres Phase

Adobe walled house blocks grouped around plazas were typical. Pottery types were the same as those listed for El Paso Phase sites in the southern part of the basin (Lehmer 1948:86). The two phases are thought to be contemporary.

Summary

It is probable that village sites will be limited to the basin fringes where there is an Upper Sonoran environment. Excavation and surveys are badly needed to understand how the Pueblo II Anasazi developments at Taylor Draw are related to the Jornada Branch phases that Lehmer defines. The latter need to be validated by excavation and survey and their relationships to adjacent regions clarified.

GUADALUPE MOUNTAIN REGION

Low precipitation, high evaporation, and high annual temperatures impart a rugged desert character to the terrain. The most arid components of the Upper Sonoran Life Zone are present on the slopes. Agave, sotol, and yucca were utilized extensively by prehistoric hunters and gatherers. Higher elevations are in the Transitional Life Zone.

The reports on Burnet Cave (Howard 1935) and Hermit's Cave (Ferdon 1946) constitute the entire archaeological literature of the region. Of 14 sites listed in the Laboratory of Anthropology survey, 5 are caves and the others are camps or midden sites. The latter are prominent collections of fire-cracked rocks. All 14 sites yielded pottery, most of which was probably imported, although some of the brown types may be of local manufacture. In particular, the type called Carlsbad Red in the Laboratory of Anthropology survey may be local. El Paso Polychrome was acquired in small amounts from the lower Tularosa Basin; certain textured sherds originated in Chihuahua; Lincoln Black-on-Red and Corrugated types came from the Sierra Blanca Region. One Rio Grande Glaze V sherd reported in the Laboratory of Anthropology survey suggests that this region maintained its hunting/gathering population after the villages of horticulturalists to the west and north were presumably abandoned.

It is not known whether agriculture was practiced. Cosgrove found corn in the Hueco Mountains to the south, and I have seen corn from caves in the Sacramento Mountains. Ferdon, however, found no evidence of corn in Hermit's Cave, and the only "metate" he found was a basin milling stone which presumably was used for wild products. Corn was also absent from the upper levels of Burnet Cave (Howard 1935). Closest cultural affinities of the Guadalupe cave dwellers are to the Hueco Phase in the Hueco Mountains of Texas, and until there is evidence to the contrary, it is convenient to assign them to the same phase.

THE PECOS VALLEY

The Setting

Originating in the Edwards Plateau of Texas as a tiny tributary of the Rio Grande, the Pecos River cut northward through soft Mesozoic rocks just east of the mountains. These events probably occurred in the early Pleistocene (King 1948:152–53). As it progressed northward, it beheaded the drainages that in Pliocene times had reached east from the Rocky Mountains across the plains.

In modern times the Pecos receives water from the Sangre de Cristo Mountains in northern New Mexico and from feeder streams entering from the west. Very little water enters the Pecos River from the east because of its proximity to the Llano Estacado.

Differences in the ecological character of the valley above and below Carlsbad require that the two sections be considered separately, although both belong to the Lower Sonoran Life Zone (Bailey 1913:12–13).

The Valley South of Carlsbad

From Carlsbad south to the Texas border, the valley belongs to the Chihuahuan Biotic Province as set up by Dice (1943:58–61). More arid components of the Lower Sonoran Life Zone such as creosote, ocotillo, and lechuguilla dominate the flora. Grass is sparse. High annual mean temperature is coupled with low precipitation.

The Valley from Carlsbad to Fort Sumner and the Adjacent Pecos Plains

North of Carlsbad, the precipitation rises and the mean annual temperature decreases (Fig. 5). This section of the valley is described by Bailey as the least arid part of the Lower Sonoran Zone in New Mexico (1913:13). Cottonwoods, willows, and other Upper Sonoran forms grow along the river, although adjacent slopes are covered with mesquite, creosote, and lechuguilla. Grass is more abundant than in the southern sector. Today the Artesia and Roswell Basins are intensively farmed as a result of deep alluvium and artesian water, but these resources would have been of little value to prehistoric farmers.

Surface water is limited. There are a few shallow saline lakes. The Pecos River is intermittent with a few standing pools, and the side streams run only during the infrequent rains. Sand dunes have developed in both the valley and the rolling plains found to either side. This region is one of low relief and no abrupt ecological changes.

North of Capitan Mountain and west of the Pecos River, the undulating Pecos Plains extend as far north as Vaughn, New Mexico. The same Permian, Triassic, and Cretaceous rocks that make up the geological structure of Sierra Blanca Mountains to the southwest and the Llano Estacado to the east underlie the surface. The modern rolling plains were formed as the uppermost limestone beds eroded after the early Pleistocene development of the Pecos River. Sand dunes are well developed in places, and the underlying limestone is frequently exposed by blowout action. Soil is typically shallow except along the valleys. Few drainage systems are well developed and most streams lose their momentum and dissipate due to the low relief and general porosity of the surface, coupled with low rainfall. The Pecos plains are contained within the Upper Sonoran Life Zone. Dice's description of the arid grasslands belt of the Navajonian Biotic Province is apropos here (1943:39–42). Only a few campsites are known from this region, but it has not been extensively surveyed.

Archaeological Sequence

From Carlsbad to the Texas Border

A survey carried out by members of the Lea County Archaeological Society is of great interest. Corley and Leslie (n.d.) report that 150 sites have been located by Society members. Of these, 146 are campsites and 4 have some type of architecture. One of the latter sites, located about 40 miles southwest of Hobbs and 30 miles east of the Pecos River, contained a pithouse and about six separate surface rooms (Mr. Corley, personal communication, 1959). This promising site was destroyed by looters in a single afternoon. The major projectile point type from this site was what the Lea County Archaeological Society calls Type No. 23, described by Mr. Corley as "deeply serrated with little tang or base." Some were 2 inches long, but most were smaller. Almost 100 of these points were collected in the vicinity of the site; one came from a burial ca. 100 yards from the site. The only pottery mentioned by Mr. Corley was Ochoa Corrugated.

This site, and any others like it, represented the southernmost outpost of sedentary life in the New Mexico portion of the Pecos Valley; in addition, they are the only known example of villages east of the Pecos River in this section of New Mexico.

The Laboratory of Anthropology survey records seven campsites from this region, each of which had pottery similar to that found in the Guadalupe Mountains.

Roswell to Fort Sumner

Jelinek has proposed four phases for the Fort Sumner locality and two phases for the Roswell locality (1960:157ff.). With the exception of Jelinek's Site P4 (Pueblo II) and Bloom Mound (late Pueblo III - early Pueblo IV), all are campsites. Many of the latter are in "blow-outs."

The Fort Sumner Locality

18 Mile Bend Phase: The type site of P4 is located on the Pecos River close to Fort Sumner. The site has four spatial divisions, and Jelinek feels that three phases are represented. The only structure completely excavated prior to 1960 was a pithouse in the part of the site designated P4ab. An encircling bench 10 inches above the floor had upright stone slabs placed at the outer periphery. Red Mesa Black-on-White was found on the floor with locally made brown types, indicating a Pueblo II date.

A second structure was partially excavated in another part of the site, P4c. A central clay-lined hearth was surrounded by four post holes. A short entrance passage on the east was flanked by two large posts. Secondary posts suggested a circular structure, "however, . . . several vertical sandstone slabs in alignment argues for a rectangular adobe walled surface structure" (Jelinek 1960:83).

Trade sherds from P4c included 4 Red Mesa Black-on-White, 3 Santa Fe Black-on-White, 24 Kwahe'e Black-on-White, and 21 unspecified Pueblo II types. Chupadero Black-on-White and Corrugated were also present. Presence of the latter two types caused Jelinek to postulate a Pueblo III date for this house, although he noted that there may have been two occupations of the structure.

Jelinek has subsequently located a pithouse village with a kiva (personal communication, May 1963). The results of his latest work will greatly expand our knowledge of the Pueblo II period in this region.

Mesita Negra Phase: No sites have been excavated: a Pueblo III date was suggested. Jelinek reported that shallow, slab-lined pithouses were typical, and that the population peak for the Fort Sumner locality was reached during this phase.

McKenzie Phase: Site P4c (?) and various camp sites. Date: Pueblo III (?). The house described above from P4c may belong here. Aside from that structure, all other evidence strongly suggests that agriculture was permanently abandoned in the locality. Grass pollen increased markedly and a bison hunting economy was indicated (Jelinek, personal communication, 1963).

Roswell Locality

The Crosby Phase is thought to be contemporary with the Mesita Negra Phase. The high ratio of sherds to stone artifacts is interpreted by Jelinek as evidence of an agricultural economy. The Roswell phase is equated with the McKenzie Phase. The high ratio of stone artifacts to sherds is interpreted as evidence of a bison-hunting economy. Jelinek classifies all post-A.D. 1300 archaeological developments in both the Fort Sumner and Roswell localities as "Late Hunters." This designation is inappropriate for Bloom Mound (Appendix 6), which belongs to the latter time period. We visited three sites in this locality, and they are entered in the archaeological record in Appendix 8.

Summary

In the Fort Sumner locality, a pithouse site (P4) was built during the Pueblo II period. It is not clear whether Site P4 supported an agriculturally-based village into Pueblo III times, but by mid-Pueblo III times, the locality was abandoned by farmers. On the basis of a pollen study, Jelinek has suggested that increasing aridity was the main reason for this (personal communication, 1963).

The Roswell locality apparently did not support sedentary agriculturalists until Bloom Mound was built, probably in mid- or late Pueblo III. In this study, Bloom Mound is considered as an outpost of the Lincoln Phase. The locality was permanently abandoned by farmers at the end of the Glaze I period.

THE LLANO ESTACADO

Permian, Triassic, and Cretaceous rocks form a low relief base for Tertiary and Quaternary continental deposits. Dominant topographic features today are the playas or shallow basins and surface deposits resulting from eolian activity. Ecologically, the region belongs to the grasslands belt of the Upper Sonoran Life Zone, or to what Dice calls the Kansan Biotic Province (1943:26–27). Known archaeological sites are temporary camps, mostly exposed by blowout action. Surface collections from these camps are often mixed chronologically.

SUMMARY

Certain regions in southeastern New Mexico are archaeological blanks. We have little or no information for the Los Pinos Mountains, the Sierra Oscura or the San Andres Mountains. The main localities where agricultural village life developed were: (1) the Sierra Blanca Region, described in Chapter 3, (2) the Chupadero Region, (3) south-central New Mexico, and (4) the Pecos Valley.

The Chupadero Region had villages by Pueblo I, and the sequence was probably continuous until the historical period. Its closest relationships were with the Middle Rio Grande. This region was undoubtedly a donor of people and cultural traits to the northern Sierra Blanca Region.

Sites in south-central New Mexico showed a different orientation. Earliest primary affiliations of the Mesilla Phase were to the Three Circle Phase of the Mimbres. Future work in Chihuahua should extend these phases farther south. The local pottery series showed remarkable continuity and conservatism. El Paso Brown and El Paso Polychrome were apparently the only two types ever manufactured in this region. While many types were acquired by trade, the total percentage of non-local pottery remained small. Adobe surface pueblos of the El Paso Phase shared many traits with late pueblos over the Southwest. The absence of separate and obvious ceremonial structures is typical of much of southeastern New Mexico.

Sites in the northern Tularosa Basin belong to both the northern and southern cultural traditions, and more work is needed to unravel these relationships.

Settled life was not continuous in the Pecos Valley, but a few villages were widely scattered in time and space. During Pueblo II times, one or more of the villages built in the Fort Sumner locality were basically marginal Anasazi with a typical southeastern New Mexican pottery complex. Bloom Mound at Roswell has been interpreted as an extension of Lincoln Phase culture into the Pecos Valley in late Pueblo III/Pueblo IV times.

Chapter 3

ARCHAEOLOGICAL SITES OF THE SIERRA BLANCA REGION

Willey and Phillips (1958:19) remark that the geographical boundaries of archaeological regions are frequently determined by the vagaries of archaeological investigation. The Sierra Blanca Region is a case in point, as its boundaries coincide with the territory in which our fieldwork took place. It is a simplified reference term by which this particular sector of southeastern New Mexico can be specified (Fig. 6). The upper reaches of the Gallo, Macho, Hondo, and Peñasco Valleys are roughly between 5400 and 6200 feet in elevation. All of these valleys rise in the Sacramento-Sierra Blanca-Gallina Mountains and flow east to the Pecos Valley. One site that is tentatively assigned to a Sierra Blanca Region Phase is located in the Pecos Valley some miles to the east of the Sierra Blanca Region proper and at a lower elevation.

THE SETTING

The Sacramento and Sierra Blanca Mountains are mainly monoclinal, with long slopes to the east and steep, faulted escarpments on the west (Fig. 7). San Andres limestone of Permian age covers the eastern slopes. Older, harder rocks are exposed in the higher elevations and on the steep west face. Quaternary deposits are alluvial and eolian. The latter do not form a continuous cover, and the San Andres limestone is frequently exposed. Volcanic activity contributed to the final shape and height of a number of peaks such as Sierra Blanca and Nogal. Capitan Mountain had a different geologic origin from the rest of the range. Jutting out to the east of the main chain, it is a laccolith formed by magma spreading out under the San Andres limestone, which was arched and lifted (Allen and Kottlowski 1958:9–10). Most of the limestone has eroded off of the crest exposing the igneous core. The extreme gradient of the upper elevations of Capitan Mountain, over 50%, has created a veritable network of arroyos which deposit eroded materials in overlapping outwash

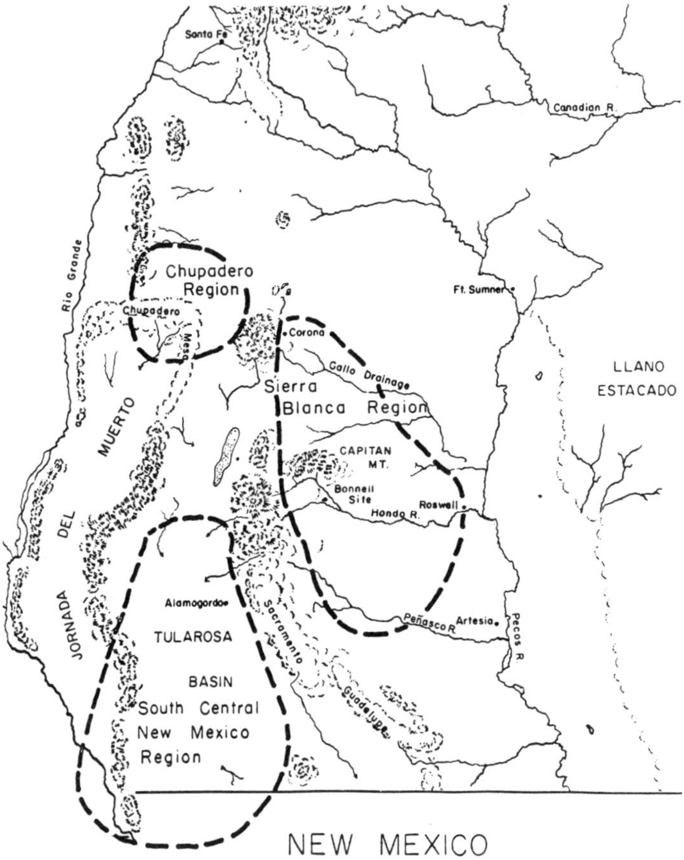

Figure 6. Regions of southeastern New Mexico. The approximate limits of the three main regions of southeastern New Mexico where agricultural villages are known archaeologically—the Chupadero Region, the Sierra Blanca Region, and the Tularosa Basin or south-central New Mexico Region — are shown above.

fans, resulting in a wide band of alluvial soil that was significant to prehistoric farmers.

The Tucson, Jicarilla, and Gallina Mountains, created by the same geologic forces that produced the Sacramento-Sierra Blanca ranges, may be considered foothills of the more massive Sierra Blanca. Carrizo Peak reached 9656 feet, due to secondary volcanic activity. A number of small peaks are isolated laccoliths. A well-developed drainage system, the Macho, rises in the Tucson-Patos Mountains and flows east to the Pecos. North of this there is rarely sufficient water to maintain long drainage systems, and the streams now flow east toward the Pecos until they are dissipated.

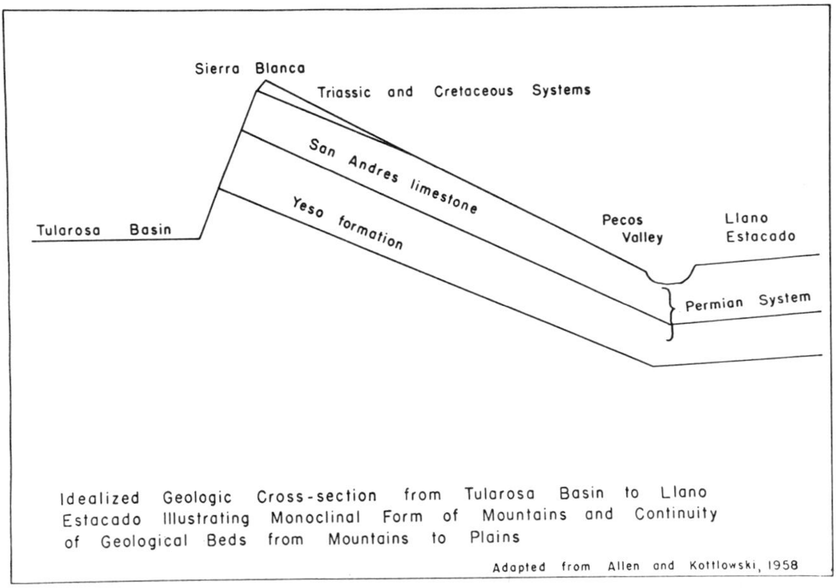

Figure 7. Idealized geological cross-section, Tularosa Basin to Llano Estacado.

The Upper Sonoran Life Zone of the long east slopes of these mountains constitutes the largest ecological zone. Junipers and piñon grow in scrubby orchardlike forests. Some oaks appear at the upper edge of the zone. Yuccas, prickly pear, and milkweed are common. Grasses grow, often in clumps, and bare spaces are common on the lower slopes. Above this, the highest mountain ranges have a well-developed Transitional Zone where yellow pine is dominant and where elk, deer, wolves, and big cats were prominent prehistorically. The Canadian Zone is fully developed on Sierra Blanca Mountain, where open parks and spruce-lined gulches occur. Larger animals include deer, elk, and bear. The Hudsonian Zone is present only on the northeast slope of Sierra Blanca Peak. The treeless peak of Sierra Blanca probably can be called true Arctic-Alpine (see Fig. 8).

Prehistoric farmers settled in the locations most favorable for primitive agriculture. Village sites tend to be located within the narrow ecological limits of the piñon-juniper belt of the Upper Sonoran Zone, close to the border of the Transitional Zone, where there is water and alluvium for farming. These conditions are often found in the alluvial valleys of the Sacramento and Sierra Blanca Mountains at elevations of 5400 to 6200 feet. Similar conditions are

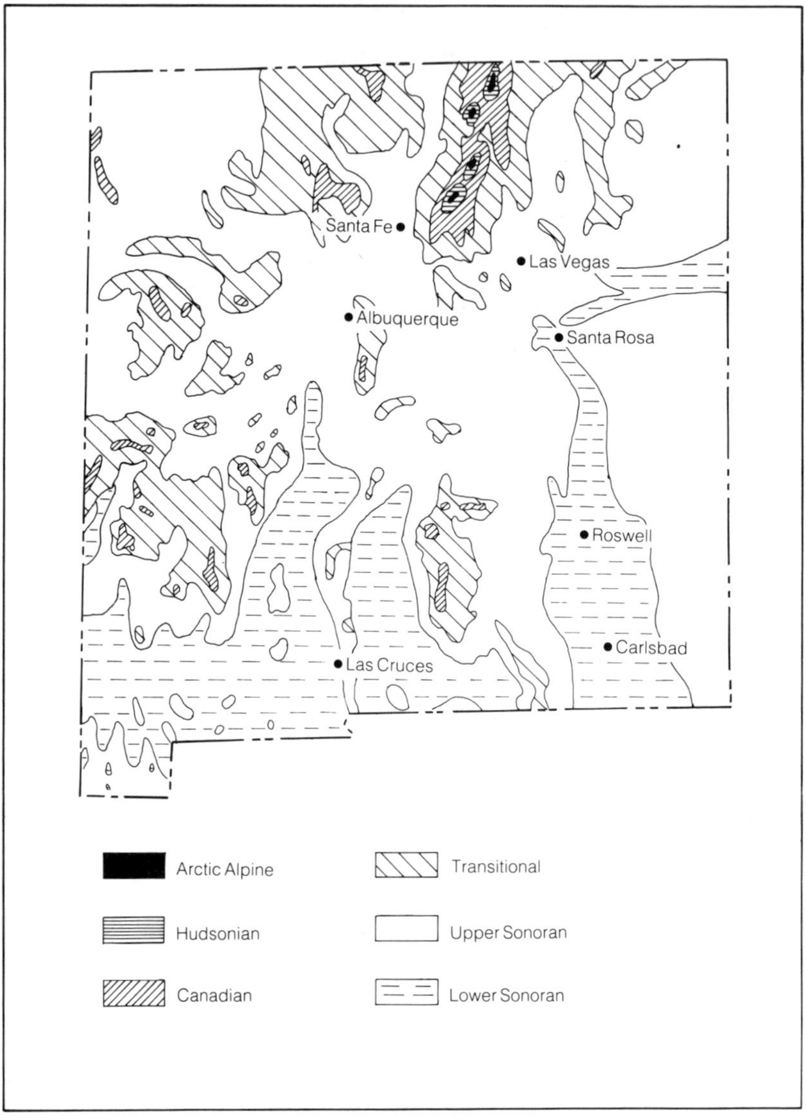

Figure 8. Life zones of New Mexico (after Bailey 1913).

found at these elevations around Capitan Mountain where the overlapping outwash fans supply alluvium and springs supply water. A few sites occur within the Transitional Zone. Environmental limitations of the long east mountain slopes between valleys and in the higher life zones are such that habitation sites are rare and of a temporary nature. These sectors were probably exploited by the agriculturalists as places to hunt or collect various natural products.

HISTORY OF THE FIELDWORK

For six weeks each summer from 1950 through 1956, archaeological parties from Texas Technological College were, in part, under my direction in the field. The initial problem with which we were concerned was the question of Plains-Southwestern contacts in this particular region. The base from which we conducted operations was the Bonnell Ranch, 14 miles east of Ruidoso. In the first season, we set about becoming familiar with the local terrain and ecology; we visited a number of archaeological sites in the immediate vicinity, and excavations were begun at the Bonnell Site. Preliminary results of excavation and the general archaeological picture we were acquiring through contacts with amateur archaeologists and from limited surveys convinced us that there was little evidence of Plains-Southwestern contacts. Our program was reoriented toward a fuller definition of the time, space, and cultural context of the Bonnell Site. Most of the actual man-hours of fieldwork were centered on this site from 1950 through 1954.

After two seasons of work, a fairly comprehensive picture of the cultural content of the Bonnell Site had emerged. The problem then became one of fitting this site into a wider, regional context. Comparative data were available from south-central New Mexico (Lehmer 1948), but the localities immediately to the north and south were virtually unknown archaeologically. In 1952, therefore, small crews on temporary assignments began a series of small-scale excavations in adjacent localities, and some reconnaissance was undertaken. Preliminary investigations were started in the Gallo Valley in 1952. A site in the Peñasco Valley was explored in 1953 in an effort to establish the southern boundary of sedentary village life in the Sierra Blanca Region. During the 1954 season, excavations were undertaken in a number of widely separated locations. This was in part due to requests from Fred Wendorf that we salvage sites in highway or pipeline right-of-ways. Two sites in the Peñasco Valley were "salvaged"; we dug a house at Gran Quivira Pithouse village, previously discovered in a pipeline survey, and we assisted Wendorf in clearing LA 2945 near Corona. That same year, we maintained a small crew at the Bonnell Site, carried out a project at Bloom Mound in cooperation with the Roswell Archaeological Society, and investigated additional sites in the Gallo Valley.

In 1955, Rex Gerald conducted a brief training session at the Bonnell Site. Thereafter, part of the staff joined Dr. C. Bertrand Schultz of the University of

Nebraska in excavating Hermit's Cave, while the rest of the crew moved to the Phillips Site on Carrizo Creek, a tributary of the Upper Macho Drainage. The latter site was selected because it showed a blend of architectural styles isolated during our excavations and survey of the Gallo Valley the previous year.

We returned to the Phillips Site in 1956. The planned excavations at this site were not concluded because the new owner was facing both a drought and a heavy mortgage, and he felt that the excavations destroyed grass unnecessarily as well as attracting a steady stream of visitors who trampled down still more grass. For this reason, we transferred our operations to the Block Lookout Site north of Capitan Mountain. Fieldwork was terminated at the close of the 1956 season.

THE SITES

Key sites are briefly described below and shown on Map 1. Full excavation and survey reports are appended at the end of this study. (Note: The work at Hermit's Cave, Gran Quivira Pithouse Village, and Gerald's excavations at the Bonnell Site are not included in this report.)

Mayhill Sites 1 and 2

We undertook the salvage of pithouses at two sites in the vicinity of Mayhill, New Mexico, at the request of Fred Wendorf in 1954. Both had been partially destroyed by previous highway construction, and both were in the right-of-way of proposed highway improvements. Our excavations were confined to the house remnants visible in the highway cuts. At Mayhill Site 1, the remaining section (perhaps one-fourth) of a square or rectangular pithouse was cleared. Only one large support post remained; several small post holes were placed against the intact pit walls at floor level. No pottery or artifacts were recovered. The house remnant at Mayhill Site 2 was roughly circular, with a fully encircling bench and a sloping lateral entry that opened to the east. The pottery was mostly Jornada Brown, some of which had red line or red slip decorations. The presence of Chupadero Black-on-White in limited quantities and the absence of other trade types suggested an early Pueblo III date.

Site 2000

Site 2000 was tested by a Texas Technological College crew during the 1953 field season when we were interested in establishing the southern boundary of

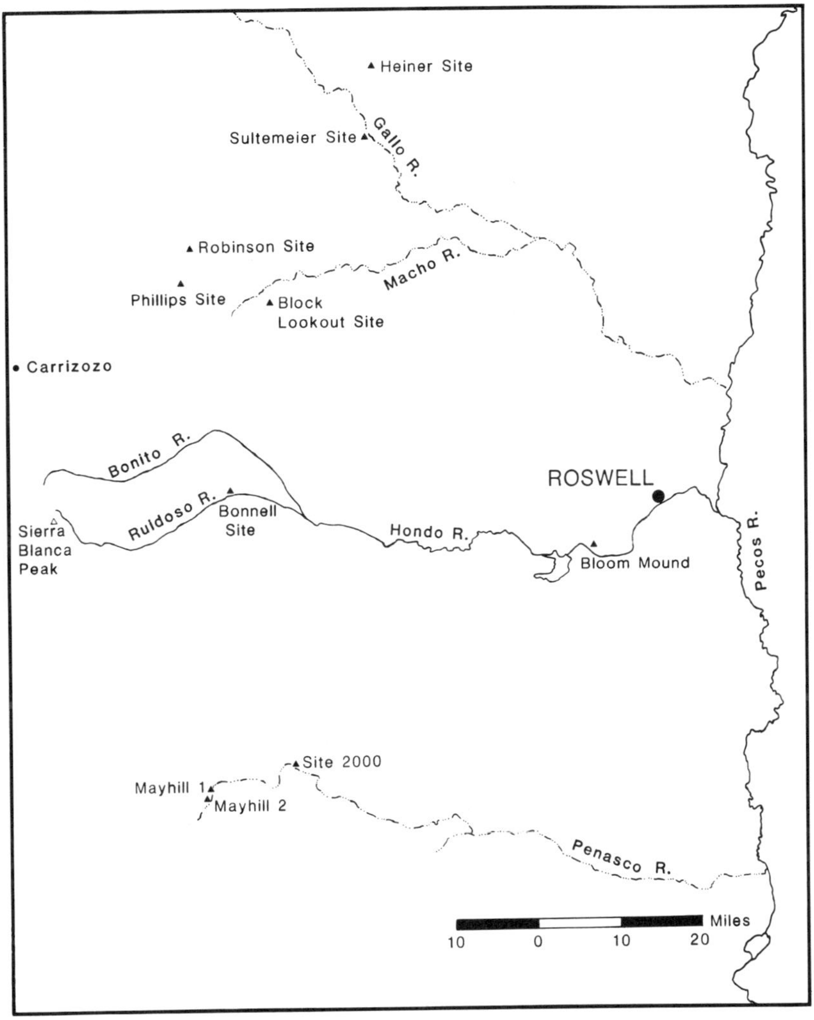

Map 1. Excavated sites in the Sierra Blanca Region.

sedentary village life along the eastern slopes of the Sacramento Mountains. This site had been investigated some years earlier (Jennings 1940).

A shallow pithouse and part of an overlapping pithouse were cleared in the part of the site that Jennings designated 2000 B. The former structure was nearly square; it had a central firepit and a variation of the four central post support pattern. The pottery collected by Jennings and in our excavations suggested that the site was occupied from early Pueblo III until middle or late Pueblo III times.

The Bonnell Site

From 1950 to 1954, approximately 805 man-days were spent in excavating the largest occupational "mound" at this site on the Ruidoso River. Full constructional details were not available for many of the 33 structures because of the extensive destruction that the site had previously undergone. Medium depth to shallow square or rectangular pithouses and surface *jacal* structures were built in a compact or nucleated plan. Rebuilding in the same space was a normal procedure for Bonnell builders. Four building periods are described in Appendix 5. Individual pithouses were built during the first and third building periods. The second building period was characterized by pit rooms placed so closely together that they must have created multi-room buildings, a practice that apparently reflects the experimental use of the pueblo concept of multi-room structures, executed in traditional, familiar building media. Surface *jacal* structures were constructed in the fourth building period. The pottery complex dates the site in the late Pueblo III - early Pueblo IV time period. Jornada Brown formed a substantial percentage of the total pottery sample. Three Rivers Red-on-Terracotta, Lincoln Black-on-Red, Chupadero Black-on-White, and Corrugated pottery types were either made locally or acquired by intraregional trade. El Paso Polychrome presumably came from El Paso Phase sites in the lower Tularosa Basin. More distant trade types included Mimbres Black-on-White, Chihuahuan types, Gila Polychrome, St. Johns, and Heshotauthla Polychromes, and Rio Grande Glaze I. The latter type furnished the most useful chronological marker. A small, primitive species of corn was grown. Deer, antelope, and rabbits supplied an important secondary food source as well as the raw materials for making objects. Some artifact types found at this site had passed out of common usage in more centrally located sectors of the Southwest. Trough metates with a mano rest at the closed end and bone gaming sticks may be mentioned.

Clint Sultemeier Site

Surface indications of a type of architecture with which we were not familiar led us to investigate a site on the sandy banks of the Gallo River during 1952. Upright stone slabs outlined shallow rooms. A house unit consisting of a living room and two storage rooms was excavated, as were two isolated rooms. Artifacts were scarce; there was little trash. The pottery from this and from other sites with this type of architecture suggested an early Pueblo III date. Jornada Brown and Chupadero Black-on-White were the most important pottery types.

Hiner Site 1

This large pueblo site on one of the tributaries of the Gallo River appeared, from surface indications, to consist of three separate structures; two of these were square buildings with a central plaza, while the third was a linear room block. In 1954, we excavated five adobe-walled rooms in the northeast part of the largest pueblo structure and a room outlined with upright stone slabs, appended to the south wall of the same pueblo building. Corrugated and Chupadero Black-on-White pottery were major components of the pottery complex; Jornada Brown was third in importance. El Paso Polychrome, Glaze I, Heshotauthla and St. Johns Polychromes, and Gila Polychrome were present in small quantities. A late Pueblo III - early Pueblo IV date is indicated.

Phillips Site

Small house units outlined with upright stone slabs were scattered over several acres of the valley bottom and adjacent terraces of Carrizo Stream near Carrizo Mountain. This remote village was apparently founded early in Pueblo III times, judging from surface pottery collections. The earliest type of construction at the site was the slab-outlined house unit, of which we excavated two examples belonging to the early and middle Pueblo III period. A larger house unit of this same construction was built late in Pueblo III times, showing that this style of building probably survived until the site was abandoned. In the latest house unit identified at the site, juxtaposition of architectural forms included shallow rooms outlined with stone slabs, masonry walls used in conjunction with a small, medium-depth, slab-lined pithouse, surface masonry walls, surface adobe walls, and a square pithouse with four central post supports. This eclectic conjunction of architectural forms reflects a stage of acculturation in which new pueblo building concepts were being integrated with the older way of building.

Block Lookout Site

A site on the highest part of a prominent hill on the north flank of Capitan Mountain was partially excavated in 1956 by one of our field parties under the direction of Herbert R. Harvey. Rooms outlined with upright slab stones on the east slopes of the Lookout hill were not investigated; they probably belong to an earlier occupation of the site. Our excavations emphasized the latest occupation at the site. A linear, adobe pueblo of perhaps 20 rooms arranged in a double row fronted east on a square, subterranean chamber which was equipped with an eastern ventilator, a firepit, and a cupped stone plastered into the floor that may represent a *sipapu*. The pottery complex was similar to that described for Hiner Site 1, and a similar date is indicated.

Bloom Mound

By using the results of Texas Technological College fieldwork in 1954 and the results of previous excavations carried out by the Roswell Archaeological Society, a partial picture of the architectural features, the pottery complex, and the artifact assemblage of Bloom Mound has been established, from which we can infer something of the character of this important site. A linear pueblo composed of a double row of adobe-walled rooms fronted east on a large, square, subterranean chamber. The site was modest in size, containing perhaps 12 surface rooms. The entire pueblo and adjacent chamber had burned, trapping some of the inhabitants along with their worldly possessions; as a result, the artifact yield for amateur and professional archaeologists has been unusually high for a site in this region. Even when one makes allowance for this fact, the recovered material culture is exceptionally abundant and luxury items such as copper bells, *Oliva* shell tinklers, disc beads, and an inlaid stone pipe are more common at this site than at any other site in the region. One possible explanation for this affluence could be that this was a small trading center. Its location within the Pecos Valley would have allowed economic exchange with agricultural peoples to the west and with Plains hunters to the east. Strong contacts were maintained with El Paso Phase peoples, as evidenced by the large amounts of El Paso Polychrome and by close similarities in certain ornamental and ceremonial categories of artifacts. Except for the high percentage of El Paso Polychrome, the pottery complex was similar to the late Pueblo III - early Pueblo IV period sites described above. Close similarities between Bloom Mound and Block Lookout in pueblo construction, the shape, size, and placement of the subterranean chamber, the pottery complex, and various categories of artifacts place the two sites in the same phase.

PHASES

The phase is the working unit employed in this report, in keeping with current trends in Southwestern archaeology. Three new phases have been formulated on the basis of our field data.

The Glencoe Phase

Geographical Extent

The Peñasco Valley forms the known southern boundary for this phase which extends northward to the Ruidoso and Bonito valleys of the Hondo Drainage, to Nogal Mesa, and to Nogal Canyon (Fig. 9). The Glencoe Phase had its beginnings early in Pueblo III, and all of the above mentioned localities were occupied during most of this period. The Peñasco Valley was the first locality to be abandoned, late in Pueblo III. In the Nogal Mesa locality and in the Bonito Valley, the Glencoe Phase gave way to the Lincoln Phase during the latter part of Pueblo III. The last stronghold of the Glencoe Phase was the Ruidoso Valley, where the culture was undergoing profound changes due to the acceptance of a number of traits from the Lincoln Phase on the north when that valley was abandoned at the end of the Glaze I period in Pueblo IV.

Throughout most of the background work for this report, two separate phase names were applied to materials now grouped into this one phase. In the final analysis, we decided that the culture continuity was such that two phases were not warranted. Instead, early and late divisions of the phase are made.

The Archaeological Sample

Data from the following sites have contributed to the formulation of this phase:

Site	*Location*	*Reference*
Site 2000	Peñasco Valley	(Appendix 8)
Mayhill Site 1	Peñasco Valley	(Appendix 8)
Mayhill Site 2	Peñasco Valley	(Appendix 8)
Green's Pithouse	Peñasco Valley	(Green 1956 and Appendix 8)
Bonnell Site	Ruidoso Valley	(Holden 1952 and Appendix 5)

In addition, information from surveys or from other sources is available for eight sites in the Ruidoso Valley, two sites on Nogal Mesa, one site in Nogal Canyon, and two sites in the Bonito Valley (Appendix 4). The fullest site report deals with the Bonnell Site, which must be considered as atypical of the phase because of the acculturation process mentioned above.

Conflicting Phase Designations

Site 2000 was assigned to the Capitan Phase by Lehmer (1948:85). Green placed his site in the Doña Ana Phase, as defined by Lehmer (Green 1956:15), with the result that these two sites, which are close together geographically and which are culturally similar, were assigned to different phases which actually reversed their chronological position. Further complications were created by having members of the northern and southern Jornada phase sequences present in the Peñasco Valley only a few miles apart.

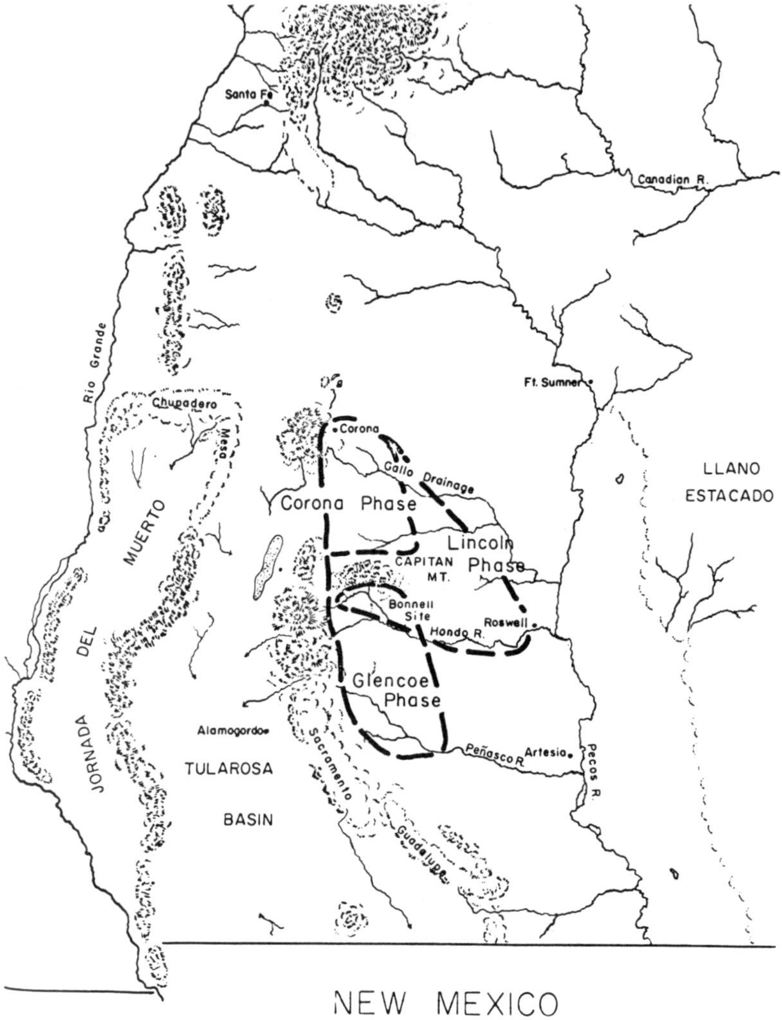

Figure 9. Areal extent of phases in the Sierra Blanca Region.

The Bonnell Site was said to be a member of the San Andres Phase of the northern Jornada Branch of the Mogollon, following Lehmer's scheme (Holden 1952:127). Jennings' and Holden's phase assignments were reiterated by Wheat (1955b:32–33). In the light of our excavations, it has become evident that the cultural content of these three sites and of other sites in this vicinity is sufficiently distinct to warrant the establishment of a separate phase.

Ecological and Topographical Distribution

Most sites were concentrated in the piñon-juniper belt of the Upper Sonoran Zone; fewer sites occurred in the grasslands belt of that life zone as well as in the lower reaches of the Transitional Zone. The topographical location of the sites varied somewhat, but all were close to streams. Some sites were on the valley floor, others were on terraces adjacent to streams, while still others were on ridges trending towards the streams. Main valleys were favored.

Village Plan

Typically, the village layout was an open, scattered arrangement of pithouses. At the Bonnell Site, however, pithouses were closely bunched together. It is estimated that five to ten houses would have been occupied contemporaneously in a village, so that village size was small. Trash was deposited in abandoned houses and in sheet fashion throughout the village.

Pithouse shapes were not standardized early in the Glencoe Phase. Nearly square pithouses, rounded pithouses with lateral entries, and rectangular pithouses with rounded sides were built within a few miles of each other in the Peñasco Valley. There is some evidence that there was a trend toward a fairly standardized form: the nearly square pithouse with straight sides, four centrally located posts, and a central firepit. This is the type of house found at Site 2000 and in Nogal Canyon, for example. Later, when the Glencoe Phase survived only in the Ruidoso Valley, pithouse architecture was subjected to building principles that stemmed from pueblo building practices of the Lincoln Phase. At the Bonnell Site, contiguous pithouses formed multi-room units which were structurally weak and poorly designed.

Ceremonial structures have not been recognized. If they existed early in the phase, either they have not been excavated or else they are not easily distinguished from domestic structures. Dwellings probably served as the scene of ceremonial activities. The size, shape, and location of Houses 1 and 15 at the Bonnell Site suggested that they served a specialized function; however, the cultural content of each house was domestic.

The Pottery Complex

Jornada Brown pottery is a major component of the ceramic complex at all Peñasco Valley sites belonging to the early part of the phase. Late in the phase at the Bonnell Site, this type made up from 22% to 72% of the sherd lots from house floors, with an overall average in excess of 50% for the sherds collected at the site.

Categorical statements about other pottery types would be misleading, as these reflect the geographical proximity of individual localities to nearby sources of trade pottery, such as the Peñasco Valley to the lower Tularosa Basin, and the Ruidoso Valley to more northern pottery centers. Furthermore, the time difference between early phase sites in the Peñasco Valley and late phase sites in the Ruidoso Valley introduces another bias.

In the early Glencoe Phase sites in the Peñasco Valley, 90% of the pottery was Jornada Brown. Some red slipped sherds probably represent local variants of Jornada Brown. Chupadero Black-on-White, Mimbres Bold Face Black-on-White, and Three Rivers Red-on-Terracotta were acquired in small amounts.

The situation in the upper level at Site 2000, where Jennings reported that 89% of the pottery was El Paso Polychrome, may represent an unusual concentration of that type in a single dwelling, as our subsequent excavations in houses of comparable age failed to yield such a high percentage of that type. The importance of El Paso Polychrome as a trade ware in the Peñasco Valley points up the geographic proximity to the source in the lower Tularosa Basin.

In the late Glencoe Phase pottery complex at the Bonnell Site, Chupadero Black-on-White, El Paso Polychrome, Lincoln Black-on-Red, and Three Rivers Red-on-Terracotta were acquired regularly from adjacent localities, or in some instances may have been manufactured at the site. Gila Polychrome, Ramos Polychrome, St. Johns Polychrome, Heshotauthla Polychrome, Playas Red Incised, Babicora Polychrome, and Rio Grande Glaze I had their origins farther afield and were present in smaller numbers.

Subsistence

Corn, mesquite beans, and game were part of the diet of the early Glencoe Phase culture in the Peñasco Valley. The relative importance of agriculture, gathering, and hunting cannot be accurately assessed, but it is my impression that gathering played a larger role here than it did elsewhere in the Sierra Blanca Region and that hunting was somewhat less important. The number of arrow points and the quantity of bone scrap at the Bonnell Site suggests that hunting became more important in the late Glencoe Phase.

Artifacts

The various artifact categories will not be itemized here, as the reader may easily refer to the site reports in the Appendices for those details. Some general similarities and differences between early and late Glencoe Phase artifacts are noted. Full-grooved axes, stone "palettes" with small depressions, and a preference for the metapodial bones of deer or antelope in bone tool manufacture are some of the traits common to both early and late sites. In general, tools of the late Glencoe Phase show a greater similarity to contemporary Lincoln Phase tools than they do to earlier Glencoe Phase tools. Metates from early Glencoe Phase sites in the Peñasco Valley are of the open-ended trough type with a concave grinding face. Most metates from the late

Glencoe Phase Bonnell Site have mano rests at the closed end of the trough, although some flat slab metates were found. The latter type are typical of the Lincoln Phase, and their presence at the Bonnell Site may be due to diffusion from the Lincoln Phase. Throughout the Glencoe Phase, metates were used free standing, and mealing bins were unknown.

Most points from Site 2000 were corner-notched, whereas side-notched arrow points were the most numerous form at the Bonnell Site. Side-notched points were probably introduced into the Sierra Blanca Region shortly before the Peñasco Valley was abandoned, and there was not enough time for this type to become popular in the latter locality.

Personal ornaments were scarce in early Glencoe Phase sites; a single mussel shell pendant fragment has been reported. Jennings (1940:9) mentioned that mussel shell fragments occurred, but it is not clear whether the bivalves were used as food or as a source of shell. Various types of ornaments were made from freshwater mussel shell at the Bonnell Site, and the working of this type of shell is a culture trait of the Glencoe Phase. *Olivella, Glycymeris, Oliva,* and *Strombus* shell ornaments were found in limited numbers at the Bonnell Site. While bone and various types of stone were used to fashion ornaments at this site, shell was the preferred or most available raw material. Bone gaming pieces, not yet reported from early Glencoe Phase sites, were numerous at the Bonnell Site.

Burial Practices

The way in which the dead were interred remained much the same throughout the Glencoe Phase. Individuals were flexed, placed on their backs or sides, and buried in house fill, under house floors, or in the sheet trash between houses. Personal ornaments were occasionally placed on the body and, in a few instances, "killed" bowls were laid over the face.

Summary

The Glencoe Phase is known to have occupied two valleys and adjacent territory along the eastern slopes of the Sacramento-Sierra Blanca Mountains. The mixed subsistence pattern was primarily adapted to an Upper Sonoran environment. Contiguous ecological zones were exploited to a lesser extent. Sedentary life was late to develop here, in comparison with other parts of the Southwest. The sedentary population seems to have been small and thinly spread. The culture that these people possessed was not overladen with luxury items. Some of their major cultural traits were long out of fashion in more central regions of the Southwest. This basic conservatism seen in architecture, pottery, and artifact types is thought to be due to the remote and marginal position.

The Corona Phase

Geographical Extent

Known sites of this phase are located in the upper Gallo Drainage, in the upper Macho Drainage, and along the north and southeast slopes of Capitan Mountain (Fig. 9). It is probable that similar sites will be found to the west of these localities.

The Archaeological Sample

No single site has received intensive investigation, and the traits that can be best described come from surface indications and limited excavations. As a result, we have a fair idea of village layout, domestic architecture, and pottery types, but virtually no data about the ceremonial aspects of culture or about many artifact categories.

Sites assigned to this phase are:

Clint Sultemeier Site 1	(Appendix 1)
Hiner Site 2	(Appendix 1)
Clark Site 2	(Appendix 1)
Black Stump Canyon Site	(Appendix 1)
House Units 1 to 39, and 43, Phillips Site	(Appendix 2)
Las Tablas Site	(Appendix 3)
Blue Water Sites	(Appendix 4)

Ecological and Topographic Distribution

Sites are rather consistently located in the piñon-juniper belt of the Upper Sonoran Zone. Villages were placed in broad valley bottoms, or on flat areas close to a water source.

Village Plan

The village layout was an open, scattered arrangement of small house units. No plaza or other type of formal spatial design has been recognized. Village size varied from a few to 50 or more house units which covered perhaps 10 acres. Trash deposition was in a thin sheet over the village. One of the most noticable things about these sites is the paucity of trash. It appears that the sites were not occupied intensively or for extended periods of time.

Architecture

House units of one to nine rooms were outlined with upright stone slabs which were easily visible when we visited the sites. These were shallow pithouses which must have had a *jacal* superstructure. Our efforts to locate wall posts were seldom successful. Internal posts were sometimes present. Some rooms were equipped with firepits; it is assumed that these were domiciles. Rooms that lacked firepits or rooms with flagstone floors were probably used for storage. Two of the sites had circular or hemispherical arrangements of upright stone slabs which may be found upon excavation to be ceremonial structures.

The Pottery Complex

The two major pottery types were Jornada Brown and Chupadero Black-on-White. A number of other types have been found on Corona Phase sites, but we need more detailed excavations effectively to identify associated minor types. A post-Pueblo II date is indicated by the absence of Red Mesa Black-on-White which might reasonably be expected in a Pueblo II site in this region. It is known that the succeeding Lincoln Phase began in mid- to late Pueblo III, and the Corona Phase is therefore assigned to an early Pueblo III date.

Summary

Although the traits that can be definitely attributed to the Corona Phase are limited, the distinct house type, village layout, and pottery complex are quite different from the more fully documented Lincoln Phase which later occupied much the same territory. It is desirable to formulate a separate phase name. Like the Glencoe Phase, the Corona Phase has some major cultural traits that were out of date elsewhere in the Southwest.

The Lincoln Phase

Geographical Extent

Sites of this phase have been found in the upper Gallo Drainage, in the upper Macho Drainage, along the north and southeast flanks of Capitan Mountain, in the Bonito Valley of the Hondo Drainage, and in the lower Hondo Valley close to the Pecos River (Fig. 9). This territory includes the whole of that occupied by the Corona Phase, plus a major southern extention into the Hondo Drainage. The lower Hondo Valley site, Bloom Mound, is separated from the core region by some 40 miles, but the cultural relationships between it and other Lincoln Phase sites are so close that it has been tentatively assigned to the same phase.

The Archaeological Sample

Eight sites have received archaeological attention:

Hiner Site 1	(Appendix 1)
Frank Sultemeier Site	(Appendix 1)
LA 2945	(Wendorf 1956:87–105)
Ryberg Site 3	(Appendix 1 and Wendorf, 1956:89)

Phillips Site	(Appendix 2)
Block Lookout Site	(Appendix 3)
Block Headquarters Site	(Appendix 3)
Bloom Mound	(Appendix 6)

The Laboratory of Anthropology survey, our own survey, brief published site or pottery descriptions, and information acquired through local museums and local amateur archaeologists are summarized in Appendices 1, 2, 3, 4 and 6. These have amplified our knowledge of site distribution, allowed more precise definition of the geographical boundaries of the phase, and added some details about the cultural content of the phase.

Dating

This phase began in mid-Pueblo III, as indicated by the common occurrence of St. Johns Polychrome on many sites. The only tree-ring dates so far available for the Sierra Blanca Region came from the Armstrong Ruin (LA 1225) in the Gallo Valley. Stallings tested one room for tree-ring material which gave these dates: 1342, 1348C, 1362, 1364, and 1366C (Smiley, Stubbs, and Bannister 1953:37).

A fairly large and stable population existed until the Glaze I period in Pueblo IV, when most of the region was abandoned. A few Glaze II and Glaze III sherds collected in some sites in the upper Gallo Drainage show that a greatly reduced population lingered in that valley a little longer.

Ecological and Topographical Distribution

The favored ecological niche of the Lincoln Phase farmers was the piñon-juniper belt of the Upper Sonoran Zone, where most known sites are located. A few sites are found at a higher elevation in the Transitional Zone, and Bloom Mound is at a much lower elevation in the Pecos Valley, which is normally classified in the Lower Sonoran Zone. Bailey (1913:13) makes it clear that this particular stretch of the Pecos River supports Upper Sonoran Life forms.

Sites were placed in various topographic situations. Some, such as Block Headquarters Site, Frank Sultemeier Site, and Hiner Site 1, were on broad, flat areas well removed from the major streams. In both the Gallo and Bonito (Hondo) Valleys, some sites were in the main valley bottom, and others were on ridges or terraces adjacent to, but some distance from, streams. Block Lookout was on the top of a high hill that can be described as defensive in that the location afforded excellent visibility in all directions.

Architecture

Stone masonry and coursed adobe were used to build multi-room pueblos. Two basic ground plans have been recognized so far: (1) a linear houseblock fronting east on a plaza and subterranean chamber, and (2) an enclosed square built around a small plaza. More pueblo patterns will be identified when more comprehensive work is done. Pueblo size ranged from an estimated 10 or 12 surface rooms at Bloom Mound to an estimated 120 rooms in one of three visible pueblo buildings at Hiner Site 1. The linear pueblos were much smaller than the pueblos built around a plaza.

At the Phillips site, true pueblo architecture never became established. Individual rooms made of adobe or coursed stone masonry were used in conjunction with pithouses and slab-outlined rooms to create multi-room house units.

Ceremonial structures excavated at Bloom Mound and at Block Lookout were roughly square, deep, subterranean structures with central fire pits; these were located just east of the linear house blocks. The Bloom Mound structure had no specialized features, beyond an ash pit located east of the fire pit. The Block Lookout chamber was equipped with a bench, eastern ventilator, possible deflector, and a "substitute *sipapu.*" The latter feature is discussed more fully in Chapter 4. To date, no ceremonial chambers have been fully excavated in the enclosed pueblos, but a plaza test at Block Headquarters Site exposed part of a subterranean structure which had two large support posts located some distance in from the walls. If these are square ceremonial chambers similar to the one at Block Lookout Site, they will take up all or most of the available space in the small central plazas of the square pueblos.

Several of the pueblos are known to be built on deep cultural fill. Since testing has not revealed older buildings underneath, further testing should be done. Trash was disposed of in rooms and in sheet fashion around the pueblo. No specialized trash mounds have been recognized, but a search should be made for this feature.

The Pottery Complex

In contrast to the preceding Corona Phase, Corrugated became the major utility type and Jornada Brown decreased in importance. Chupadero Black-on-White continued its popularity. Innovations in bowl form and design mark a style which has been named the Capitan variant of Chupadero Black-on-White. Lincoln Black-on-Red was made locally. Three Rivers Red-on-Terracotta and El Paso Polychrome were imported in small quantities from the Tularosa Basin. St. Johns Polychrome, Heshotauthla Polychrome, and an assortment of types on the Glaze I horizon from the Rio Grande were imported regularly. Gila Polychrome and Chihuahuan types were acquired in lesser numbers.

The pottery complex shows considerable overlap with that of the late Glencoe Phase. Trade pottery from the Little Colorado and Rio Grande regions was much more common in Lincoln Phase sites than in contemporary Glencoe Phase sites, while Gila Polychrome and types originating in the Tularosa Basin and in Chihuahua were generally more numerous in the latter phase. Bloom Mound, assigned to the Lincoln Phase, seems to be unique in its overall proportion of trade pottery, and especially southern trade pottery such as El Paso Polychrome, Chihuahua types, and Gila Polychrome.

Subsistence

Corn agriculture was supplemented by the gathering of wild vegetable products and hunting. The unusually small and primitive corn from Block Lookout Site was analyzed by Gallinat and Harvey (Appendix 3). Since larger corn was grown in the region (See Appendix 4, Feather Cave) the retention of such a small-eared variety of maize must have been due to its drought resistant adaptation to local ecological conditions. The corn from the Bonnell Site, Glencoe Phase, is very similar. Corn from Bloom Mound, however, is a much larger variety. One of the many details to be cleared up in future research is the distribution of different varieties of corn throughout the Sierra Blanca Region and an interpretation of their significance biologically, ecologically, historically, and culturally. More information is needed about the total agricultural complex.

Various wild products were gathered. "Thorn apples" (*Crataegus*), sunflower seeds (*Helianthus annuus*), cholla buds (*Opuntia arborescens*?), and walnuts were found at Block Lookout. Game may have been a substantial element in the diet, for deer or antelope bones were numerous, as were smaller animal bones.

Artifacts

Portable artifacts of the Lincoln Phase are itemized in the site reports. Only the more diagnostic categories of artifacts will now be summarized.

Slab metates and shallow metates of the one-end-closed trough type with a mano rest were mobile; they could be propped up with rocks to a good grinding angle and stood against the wall when not in use. Mealing bins, typical of this period elsewhere in the Southwest, were only beginning to be used here. One mealing bin at LA 2945 was made of slab metate fragments set in a mud matrix to form a troughed, one-end-closed grinding area (Wendorf 1956:91). Subrectangular to oval manos were biconvex to rectangular in cross-section. One grinding face was most typical, although multiple grinding faces were used. One-handed grinding stones were found at most sites, but the reciprocal containers have not been recognized.

Only full-grooved axes have been formally reported; one three-quarter grooved axe was said to have been found by an amateur archaeologist. Arrow shaft straighteners with transverse grooves occurred.

Corner-notched arrow points were the most common form, but side-notched points like the Harrell type of Texas were introduced early in the Lincoln Phase, and these were well represented in all sites. By and large, other chipped stone tools were made on random interior flakes, and the forms of scrapers, gravers, drills, and knives were not standardized.

Bone awls were often made of deer or antelope ribs; at least this bone was preferred in the Gallo Valley. This contrasts with the choice of metapodials in the late Glencoe Phase just to the south. Scapula scrapers, bone tubes, punches or flakers were made and used.

Tubular pipes were made of stone and pottery; the latter was sometimes decorated with simple punctation and incision.

Differences exist in the number and variety of ornaments found at Bloom Mound and at other Lincoln Phase sites. In the former site, disc beads, *Oliva* tinklers, and copper bells were numerous. Elsewhere, *Olivella* beads and freshwater mussel shell pendants were more common and individual specimens of *Strombus* and *Glycymeris* were reported.

Burial Practices

Burials were made beneath room floors, in room fill, and between houses. When several graves were placed in the same room, earlier burials were frequently disturbed by subsequent interments. Bodies were flexed and laid on their backs or sides. No consistent grave orientation was observed. The inclusion of grave offerings or personal property was rare. When items were interred with an individual, ornaments and decorated pottery bowls were chosen. Children were more likely to have grave furniture than adults.

Local Economic Specialization

It is comparatively easy to recognize trade items originating beyond the region. It is, however, far more difficult to unravel the amount of intraregional economic specialization. This can be demonstrated in a few instances for the Lincoln Phase. Siliceous shale mines on Carrizo Mountain were apparently controlled by the inhabitants of the Phillips Site. Siliceous stone with desirable fracturing properties was hard to find in the region, and the mined black shale represented a scarce commodity. Lincoln Black-on-Red pottery, manufactured in some abundance at the same site, undoubtedly furnished the Phillips villagers with another negotiable commodity.

The relative abundance of luxury goods which differentiates Bloom Mound from other Lincoln Phase sites may in part be a consequence of destruction by fire. If this was a small trading center, as has been postulated, we may have an example of local economic specialization that was not based on control of a scarce commodity insofar as we can tell. Rather, by virtue of its geographical position, it may have served as the scene of economic exchanges between various groups. The inhabitants may well have been middlemen or merchants who occasionally supplied products to interested parties.

SUMMARY

The Sierra Blanca Region was earlier described as a convenient term by which one could refer to the territory where the Texas Technological College archaeological program centered from 1950 through 1956. Data obtained from the excavation of several sites scattered throughout this region contributed to the formulation of three phases (see Table 1). It is believed that each of these phases comprises a distinguishable archaeological unit within the limits discussed by Willey and Phillips (1958:22).

The Glencoe Phase is the only archaeological unit now recognized for the southern part of the region. As such, it has an unusually long duration, lasting from early Pueblo III until the Glaze I horizon of Pueblo IV. As pointed out elsewhere in this chapter, I was inclined for some years to create two phases that would be comparable in their temporal dimensions to the Corona and Lincoln Phases in the northern part of the region, and that would be more on the order of phases in the south-central New Mexican sequence, the Middle Pecos Valley, or the Chupadero Region.

One deals with time, space, and cultural content in archaeological units. Which of these factors receives precedence in the establishment of archaeological units is an old problelm. In the case under consideration, cultural content was deemed to have more weight. It might be noted that a similar division of the southern sequence of the Jornada Branch would result in the elimination of the Doña Ana Phase; the break between the Mesilla and El Paso Phases would be drawn at the point in time when pueblo architecture was accepted. In the Chupadero Region, the Pueblo Pardo and Pueblo Colorado Foci could easily be combined. Archaeological units which punctuate fairly gross cultural changes would serve a useful purpose while the framework of southeastern New Mexican prehistory is being constructed.

Horticulturalists in the northern and southern parts of the Sierra Blanca Region derived their basic culture from separate sources. These relationships will be traced in the next chapter.

TABLE 1
CORRELATION OF PHASES AND SITES NOT YET ASSIGNED TO PHASES, OF AGRICULTURAL VILLAGERS, SOUTHEASTERN NEW MEXICO

Pecos Classification	Sierra Blanca Region		Chupadero Region	South-central New Mexico		Pecos Valley	
	Southern Localities	Northern Localities		Southern Tularosa Basin to Rio Grande	Northern Tularosa Basin	Fort Sumner Locality	Roswell Locality
Fully Historic			Salinas Phase				
Pueblo V			Pueblo Colorado Phase Pueblo Pardo Phase				
Glaze I							
Pueblo IV	Late Glencoe Phase	Lincoln Phase	Gran Quivira Phase	El Paso Phase	San Andres Phase		Bloom Mound (Lincoln Phase)
Pueblo III	Early Glencoe Phase	Corona Phase	Arroyo Seco Phase Claunch Phase	Doña Ana Phase	Three Rivers Phase		
Pueblo II				Mesilla Phase	Capitan Phase and Taylor Draw Site	18 Mile Bend	
Pueblo I			Gran Quivira Pithouse Village				

Chapter 4

INTRA- AND INTERREGIONAL COMPARISONS OF INDIVIDUAL CULTURE TRAITS

PLACEMENT AND INTERNAL ORGANIZATION OF SITES IN THE SIERRA BLANCA REGION

Ecological Distribution of Sites

The close relationship between ecological conditions and village location was more than fortuitous, as a wide range of ecological choices was available. The selection of a village site was influenced by a number of factors, foremost among which would have been the requirements of crops relative to farming techniques. The geographical distribution of alluvium and water resources within the piñon-juniper belt of the Upper Sonoran Zone along the eastern mountain slopes more or less predetermined the geographical limits of farming. Suitable agricultural conditions were found in the valleys and around Capitan Mountain between roughly 5400 and 6200 feet in elevation. Only a few sites are located outside of these ecological limits. Site 2000, in the grasslands belt of the Upper Sonoran Zone, is in the most arid situation of all sites investigated outside the Pecos Valley.

Bloom Mound is nominally within the Lower Sonoran Zone of the Pecos Valley; the Upper Sonoran character of local vegetation has already been stressed. The ecological constraints that appear to characterize other horticulturally-based village sites in the Sierra Blanca Region do not apply to the Pecos Valley sites, and, for the moment, we do not have an adequate understanding of how their differing ecological situation fits with observed cultural relationships.

Somewhat more use was made of the lower limits of the Transitional Zone by horticulturalists. Four sites in the Peñasco Valley and a number in the Ruidoso-Bonito Valleys fall within this zone.

Topographical Location of Sites

Villages were placed with a regard to farmland and water. They were therefore normally confined to the vicinity of streams. The topography of Capitan Mountain with its encircling alluvial band created by outwash fans presented a somewhat different set of alternatives from the river valleys.

Corona Phase sites were frequently placed on tributaries of the larger streams. Those Corona Phase sites around Capitan Mountain were closer to the mountain than were later sites. The valley bottoms were preferred locations.

Lincoln Phase sites tended to cluster in the main valleys, where they were sometimes placed in the valley bottom. More frequently a location on a ridge, terrace, or hill was selected. Lincoln Phase sites were often placed farther away from water than Corona Phase sites.

Known Glencoe Phase sites are located on elevations immediately adjacent to streams. Broad terraces were chosen, where they existed. At higher elevations where terraces were narrow or nonexistent, ridges trending toward streams were selected.

The Factor of Defense in Site Locations

Visibility of surrounding terrain, topographical inaccessibility, the availability of water, and the physical defensive potential of the site are separate factors that could operate in the selection of a location for defensive purposes. By and large, sites in the Sierra Blanca Region are not well situated with regard to defense, nor have defensive building measures been recognized. Lincoln Phase pueblo architecture with its compact organization and thick walls was inherently more defensible than isolated pithouses of the Glencoe Phase or the scattered house units of the Corona Phase; however, there is no reason to think that defense was a major function of this architectural style.

Corona Phase sites were open, scattered villages, vulnerably placed on valley floors immediately adjacent to streams. Defense was not a concern of these people.

Most Lincoln Phase villages likewise show a disregard for defensive measures. Block Lookout, however, is so far removed from the convenience of water and is so obviously situated for maximum visibility, that some consideration for defense is inferred.

Glencoe Phase sites are frequently placed where visibility is excellent, and yet they do not seem to be defensive in character.

The "fortification" described in Appendix 4 is the only site that is unquestionably defensive, and we have no clue as to when it was built or where it would fit in the archaeological sequence.

Village Organization

Corona Phase house units were arranged in an open, scattered village pattern. Smallest sites with only two or three visible house units may have been field houses. Larger villages containing up to fifty units spread over as much as ten acres would be better described as *rancherias*. It is not clear how many units were occupied at the same time nor is the total life span of a village known. House units were not extensively reused or remodeled. When new structures were needed, they were built a short distance away. Sheet trash deposits were typically thin. No courts, plazas, or other focal points have been recognized. Several sites have circular depressions, suggesting a specialized community structure, but none have been excavated. At the Robinson and Clark sites, these were placed at one edge of the village. At the former site, the slab-outlined circular depression was on the north; at the latter site it was on the west. Each house unit probably contained living quarters and storage rooms; at least some rooms contained firepits and others did not. There was no consistent orientation of the units, except that they were roughly placed with the cardinal directions. Some house units with one living room containing about 130 to 160 square feet of floor space may have been occupied by a nuclear family. An extended family may have been the resident social unit in larger house units.

Lincoln Phase sites were self-contained compact pueblos that occupied a minimum of ground space. The actual composition of villages varied. An enclosed square with a central plaza was sometimes associated with additional linear units, as at Hiner Site 1. Some linear house blocks fronted on an eastern subterranean structure, as at Block Lookout.

Probably all Lincoln Phase villages had a court or plaza and associated subterranean structure. The subterranean structure at Block Lookout was sufficiently excavated to show its major characteristics. Testing at Block Headquarters Site proved that there was a subterranean chamber in the plaza, and such a possibility was strongly suggested by the plaza test at Hiner Site 1.

At the Phillips Site, the older type of slab-outlined house units was mixed with a hodgepodge of adobe and masonry structures in an open village pattern during the Lincoln Phase.

Pueblo structures were usually built on a deep accumulation of trash; the same space was utilized for a long period of time. Rebuilding and remodeling were common.

Lincoln Phase sites varied in size from an estimated 20 rooms at Block Lookout to an estimated 200 rooms at Hiner Site 1. Most of the buildings were only one story high, but some, such as Ryberg Site 3, may have been multistoried structures. The increase in number of rooms per site and in the total number of sites suggests that the peak of population expansion in this region occurred during the Lincoln Phase.

The Glencoe Phase village layout was quite different from that of the Corona and Lincoln Phases. Pithouses were typically scattered.

Mound A at the Bonnell Site, which has the most completely known village plan of the Glencoe Phase sites, cannot be considered as typical of the phase. Closely grouped, individual pithouses were built in two of the four building periods. It is unlikely that more than five or seven structures were occupied simultaneously throughout most of the history of the site. Perhaps as many as nine or ten structures were occupied during the second building period, when an unusual village pattern emerged. If the reconstruction favored here is correct, a tiny plaza some 20 by 40 feet was bounded on the east and west by house units composed of contiguous pithouses or pit rooms. A two-room building was placed across the south end of the plaza. The large pithouse on the north of the postulated plaza burned, and the pit depression was used for trash.

The most striking feature of the Bonnell village layout was the congested arrangement of pithouses and the frequent rebuilding in the same limited space, an arrangement that was in no way dictated by the topography since the village occupied only a fraction of a long, flat terrace. Wheat (1955b:33) pointed out that this nucleated village layout was similar to that of the Galaz Site.

Insofar as can be determined, most structures of the Glencoe Phase were used as living quarters. Two of the houses at the Bonnell Site were unusually large and may have had a dual function. Absence of storage pits or definite storage rooms leaves unanswered the question of how they handled their agricultural produce.

PITHOUSES AND OTHER SUBTERRANEAN STRUCTURES

These observations are based on information from the following sites.

Glencoe Phase sites:	
Site 2000	(Appendix 7; Jennings 1940)
Mayhill Sites 1 and 2	(Appendix 7)
Green's Mayhill Site	(Green 1956)
Bonnell Site	(Appendix 5)
Nogal Canyon Site	(Appendix 4)
Corona Phase sites:	
Escondida Site	(Appendix 4)
Clint Sultemeier Site	(Appendix 1)
Black Stump Canyon Site	(Appendix 1)
Hiner Site 2	(Appendix 1)
Phillips Site	(Appendix 2)
Las Tablas Site	(Appendix 3)

Lincoln Phase sites:

Block Lookout Site	(Appendix 3)
Bloom Mound	(Appendix 6)
Phillips Site	(Appendix 2)
Robinson Site	(Appendix 2)

Raw Materials and Their Utilization in Pithouses

Wood and clay or soil were the major building materials used in pithouses. A great deal of timber was felled in the course of building any pithouse village. Several hundred posts or post holes as well as collapsed wall or roof timbers were found at the Bonnell Site. With this great reliance on wood, it is likely that it was worked into many perishable objects; only some charred wooden beads have been preserved.

Pine was used for the larger supports and roof timbers. Piñon and juniper were used for the smaller poles and posts. Cottonwood, used occasionally for braces and for split planks, was too soft for major load-bearing. Walnut and other available hardwoods were not exploited.

Clay or soil were used for covering roofs and probably walls. This material has good insulating properties which are especially useful during the winter when insulation is needed and few rains occur. Torrential summer rains must sometimes have resulted in a melting house.

Glencoe Phase pithouse builders could not handle stone or adobe effectively, whereas the Lincoln Phase builders constructed adequate structures of both stone and adobe. The latter reserved subterranean construction for their ceremonial chambers. The slab-lined shallow pithouses of the Corona Phase were more akin to Glencoe pithouses in the raw materials utilized and the way in which these were handled.

Pithouse Shape

Sierra Blanca Region

Early in the Glencoe Phase, house shapes were not standardized. A roughly circular house and a squarish house with straight sides were excavated at Mayhill Site 2. The house remnant reported by Green (1956:13) had slightly outcurving sides. A trend toward a more standardized form may be seen during the Glencoe Phase: the houses at Site 2000 and many of the houses at the Bonnell Site were square with straight sides.

The shallow slab-lined dwelling and storage rooms of the Corona Phase were rectangular. Circular depressions reported from several sites have not been excavated.

The only subterranean structures in the Lincoln Phase were the ceremonial chambers. Their shape was identical to the larger straight-sided, square pithouses of the Glencoe Phase, from which they were probably derived.

Comparisons

Circular pithouses were most typical of the western pueblo area (Bullard 1962:117), although circular houses occurred elsewhere at one end of the rectangular-with-rounded-sides range. Within southeastern New Mexico, both houses at Gran Quivira Pithouse Village were circular, as were some of the houses at Taylor Draw. The shape of the houses at P4ab and P4c is not clear. At Los Tules, there were four rectangular, one square, one oval, and four circular pithouses. These circular pithouses and the one at Mayhill Site 2 may or may not be historically related to the circular houses at Taylor Draw and Gran Quivira Pithouse Village.

Rectangular to square pithouses with rounded sides were typical of the eastern Anasazi (Bullard 1962:117). Both circular and rectangular-with-rounded-sides houses of pre-Pueblo II age have been excavated near Albuquerque (Peckham 1957b:39–70). The closest parallel in the Sierra Blanca Region is Green's house (1956:13).

Unless the houses at Site P4ab or P4c were square to rectangular, the only pre-Pueblo III examples in southeastern New Mexico were those at Los Tules, and these would seem to be the most immediate source of the common Glencoe Phase house shape.

Rectangular houses, often with equilateral sides, were known in Mogollon regions by the San Francisco Phase and survived into the Three Circle Phase or even later (Bullard 1962:115). Houses of the La Junta Focus at the confluence of the Conchos and Rio Grande Rivers were similar in basic shape to Glencoe Phase houses and Lincoln Phase ceremonial structures.

Summary

During Pueblo I and II, circular, "rectangular with rounded corners," and straight-walled rectangular-shaped houses were made in southeastern New Mexico. The more northern examples belonged to the first two categories and have general Anasazi affinities. The more varied southern Pueblo II lot included the rectangular shape that was to become common in the Glencoe Phase and in Lincoln Phase ceremonial chambers.

Depth of House Pits

Sierra Blanca Region

The deepest structures were the early Glencoe Phase house near Mayhill (Green 1956:18) and the Lincoln Phase subterranean chamber at Bloom Mound, both 7 feet deep. The Lincoln Phase subterranean chamber at Block

Lookout had a maximum depth of 4 feet 10 inches. All other regional examples ranged from medium depth to very shallow.

Comparisons

The original pit depth of House 1 at Gran Quivira Pithouse Village was approximately 5 feet 6 inches (Fenenga 1956:229). Taylor Draw pithouses were of medium depth and those at Sites P4c and P4ab were shallow. The Los Tules houses were from 0.5 to 1.0 m deep, judging from drawn plans (Lehmer 1948:18–23).

Summary

Deep houses were unusual throughout southeastern New Mexico. The majority of houses were of shallow to medium depth. At the shallow end of the scale, the houses merge into a surface *jacal* building tradition.

Treatment of Pit Walls

Sierra Blanca Region

Slab-lined walls will be discussed separately. Pit walls were occasionally plastered, as in House 1 of the Bonnell Site and in the subterranean chambers at Bloom Mound and Block Lookout. More commonly walls were left untreated and their texture depended on the type of deposit into which they were cut. When dug through gravel, as were House 4 of the Bonnell Site and Green's deep Mayhill house, the walls were rough with protruding cobbles. When dug through top soil, as at Peñasco Site 2000 B and in many houses at the Bonnell Site, the walls were fairly smooth.

Comparisons

Wall plaster was rarely used in other pithouses reported from southeastern New Mexico. Only House 11 was plastered at Los Tules (Lehmer 1948:24). Both of the houses at Gran Quivira Pithouse Village had unplastered walls.

Floor Treatment

Sierra Blanca Region

A common regional practice was to surface the central portion of the floor around the firepit with clay plaster. This was probably the case in the pithouse reported by Jennings (1940:3). No evidence of surfacing was noted in House 4, Bonnell Site. A number of the Bonnell Site houses had packed-earth floors. When houses were cut into a deposit that produced a level surface, this formed all or part of the floor. In House 1, Bonnell Site, the house was cut into gravel on the south side and into a clay deposit on the north side. The clay deposit was left unaltered while heavy clay plaster was applied over the gravel. The subterranean structure at Bloom Mound was cut into a gypsum deposit which created a hard, sparkling floor. Green's house near Mayhill had 1 to 2 inches of clay plaster (Green 1956:12).

Comparisons

Lehmer reports that floors in Los Tules houses were "simply the sandy pit bottom" (Lehmer 1948:24). The two houses at Gran Quivira Pithouse Village had unplastered floors (Green 1955; Fenenga 1956); comparable data are not available for Taylor Draw or Site P4ab.

Lateral Entrances and Ventilators

Lateral Entries in the Sierra Blanca Region

Lateral entrances were not a regular architectural feature. The early Glencoe Phase house at Mayhill Site 2 had a sloped entryway on the east which opened at the bench level. One post was placed where the entry joined the house; the companion post had undoubtedly eroded away.

No entryways were recognized at the Bonnell Site during excavation. A photograph of House 19 suggested strongly that an eastern lateral entry was present. Two post holes at the middle of the east wall of House 1 were first thought to be entry supports, but an intensive search failed to detect an entry.

Entrances were absent in the Peñasco Valley houses of the Glencoe Phase, in the two Lincoln Phase subterranean chambers at Block Lookout and Bloom Mound, and in House 13, House Unit 46 at the Phillips Site. In the shallower houses, there would have been little need for an entry. We did not recognize any well-worn or well-packed floor areas such as would develop at doorways. Deeper houses and subterranean chambers probably had roof openings.

Comparisons

Elsewhere in southeastern New Mexico lateral entrances were more common, although by no means universal. At Los Tules, the four rectangular houses had sloping entrance passages. The small square house (number 9) and the oval and circular houses did not have lateral entries (Lehmer 1948:16–23). Lateral entries occurred in two of the four houses at Taylor Draw (Peckham, personal communication, 1966). No entry was found in the two houses at Gran Quivira Pithouse Village. Jelinek believes that a lateral entry was present in the house at Site P4c, but it was not traced (1960). The few lateral entries found in the Sierra Blanca Region faced east. Those at Los Tules were oriented to the east and southeast.

A Ventilator in the Sierra Blanca Region

The only known ventilator from the Sierra Blanca Region was in the middle of the east wall of the subterranean chamber at Block Lookout. A deflector stone was tentatively identified.

Comparisons

The trait was absent at Los Tules, but it occurred in the kiva at Taylor Draw, and in one house at Gran Quivira Pithouse Village (Fenenga 1956:229). A ventilator was found in Kiva A at Pueblo Pardo of Pueblo IV age (Toulouse and Stephenson 1960:16).

The absence of ventilators at Los Tules points up the eastern Mogollon affinities of that site, as ventilators were rare in that region. The presence of ventilators in the Gran Quivira Pithouse Village and at Taylor Draw emphasizes their eastern Anasazi heritage.

Most pithouses in the Sierra Blanca Region and elsewhere in southeastern New Mexico lacked both ventilators and deflectors. Antechambers were unknown anywhere in the subarea. Bullard points out that these three structural adjuncts supply fresh air to subterranean houses (1962:137). It might be argued from the absence of these features that these pithouses were not tightly made and that air could circulate more freely through the structure, making techniques of introducing fresh air unnecessary.

While pithouses in most Anasazi and Mogollon regions typically have one or more of the three features, occasional structures are found in some sites that lack all three traits. In the Mimbres Region, for example, these traits were absent in House 23, Harris Site, which belongs to the Three Circle Phase (Haury 1936:Pl. XXVII, Fig. 24), in Houses 128, 133, 113A, 140, 141, and 142 at Cameron Creek Village that cannot be assigned to phases (Bradfield 1931:Map opposite p. 62), and Houses AB, M, E, and perhaps others at the Swartz Ruin that cannot be assigned to phases (Cosgrove and Cosgrove 1932:Pl. 238).

Of the pre-Pueblo II pithouses in the Middle Rio Grande, only Room 2 at LA 3290 lacks all three fresh air features (Peckham 1957b:48). La Junta Focus houses are shallow, rectangular, and lack ventilators, antechambers, or passages.

Benches

Sierra Blanca Region

Two early Glencoe Phase house remnants (Mayhill Site 2 and Green's pithouse—cf. Appendix 8) had unplastered benches encircling the remaining portions of the houses. The Lincoln Phase subterranean chamber at Block Lookout had a well-made bench 27 inches wide that extended around all excavated portions of the house, 27 inches above the floor. Plaster was continuous with the floor and back wall. In the excavation of House 15, Bonnell Site, a "bench" was left on the west side of the house. In retrospect, it seems that this feature should be considered an "archaeological artifact."

Comparisons

Benches are known from three Pueblo II sites. At Los Tules, the circular structure (number 5) had an encircling bench. Since this was the only structure having this feature, Lehmer suggested that it may have been a ceremonial chamber (1948:23). A bench was present in the Taylor Draw kiva (Peckham 1957b:70) and in the house at Site P4ab (Jelinek 1960:65). Benches were absent in the Pueblo I Gran Quivira Pithouse Village and in the Pueblo IV kiva at Pueblo Pardo. A questionable bench or shelf was found in Room 5 at the latter site (Toulouse and Stephenson 1960:15). El Paso Phase sites, such as Twelve Room House, Bradfield Site, and Alamogordo Sites 1 and 2, lack this trait completely.

Bullard concludes that benches are primarily an Anasazi trait with the only major exception occurring in the Forestdale region, adjacent to western Anasazi regions. Full benches are typical of western Anasazi and three-quarter benches occur in the eastern Anasazi area in the periods prior to A.D. 900 (Bullard 1962:146–49). None of the Pueblo I or II pithouses reported so far from the Middle Rio Grande have benches, but the number of excavated structures is small and Bullard (1962:148) points out that only 30% to 40% of the Anasazi houses in his sample have this trait.

Insofar as our limited information may be stretched, all examples from southeastern New Mexico appear to be of the fully encircling type, except for the small bench or shelf in a pueblo room at Pueblo Pardo. It is premature to conclude that this is evidence of western Anasazi or Forestdale region contacts or influences, but this geographical exception to Bullard's findings should be noted.

Interior Pits and Depressions

Sierra Blanca Region

These are not a regular feature of houses in the Sierra Blanca Region. The Glencoe Phase house at Mayhill Site 2 had a small, unplastered pit dug through the bench. The house that Peckham excavated in the same site had two deep pits in the eastern part of the floor.

A small, unplastered pit was found in the house at Site 2000. An earlier bell-shaped pit within the same structure had been filled and the house floor extended over it. At the Bonnell Site, small unplastered pits 15 to 18 inches deep were associated with Houses 6 and 12. The niche or wall recess in House 15 may be included here. Similar shallow, unplastered pits were found in the slab-lined pithouses of the Corona Phase and in Lincoln Phase pueblo rooms.

Shallow, basin-shaped depressions about 6 inches deep were present in Houses 1 and 8 at the Bonnell Site and in the house at Site 2000 B. These also occur in Corona Phase slab-lined houses and in Lincoln Phase pueblo rooms.

Comparisons

Outside of the Sierra Blanca Region in southeastern New Mexico, two of the houses at Los Tules had single interior pits that were small, judging from the published plans (Lehmer 1948:18–19). Interior pits were rare at Taylor Draw (Peckham, personal communication, 1966). None were reported from Site P4c (Jelinek 1960:83); they were definitely absent from the two structures at Gran Quivira Pithouse Village (Fenenga 1956:229; Green 1955:182–85).

Firepits and Fire Areas

Basin-shaped Firepits

These are known from the Bonnell Site, where House 1 had a well-made, plastered firepit with a low rim created by an extension of the interior plaster about an inch above the floor. Three other fire basins or depressions at the same site were shallower and more crudely made. The firepits that Jennings (1940:4) described for the upper level houses at Site 2000 A might be classed as basin shaped with sloping walls and a rim or coping.

Cylindrical Firepits

This more common and more standardized type can be divided into deep forms, in which the depth is greater than the diameter, and shallow forms 3 to 6 inches deep. Both typically have straight sides; a few firepits with in-sloping sides seem to be a minor variation on the cylindrical shape. The bottoms are usually flat in the shallow type and may be slightly concave in deeper firepits. The pits usually open flush with the floor. In a few cases clay rims or copings were added above the floor level.

The deeper type of cylindrical firepit was more characteristic of earlier sites, while the shallower type increased in popularity late in Pueblo III. Direct superposition of the two types occurred in three houses at the Bonnell Site, where the other ten examples of the shallow type were in later houses. Jennings (1940:4) noted a similar shift from the deeper cylindrical firepit of his lower level to the shallower versions in the upper level. A Corona Phase firepit at the Clint Sultemeier Site was of the deep cylindrical type. Shallow cylindrical firepits were found in some houses at Lincoln Phase sites, although there was a tendency to retain the deeper firepits for ceremonial chambers.

Internal Fire Areas

Known examples of areas on house floors where fire was built are limited to the Bonnell Site. This occurred in two rooms that lacked firepits. In the third room, fire was built on the floor adjacent to a firepit. In one case a clay coping delineated the fire area.

Slab-lined Fire Box: The only known regional example was at Black Stump Canyon, Corona Phase (Appendix 1).

Cooking Stand or Drying Rack: A number of small post holes, inclined inward around a firepit in House 13 at the Bonnell Site, suggest that some sort of an apparatus stood about 3 feet high.

Location within Structures: Central placement of the firepit seems to have been a standardized construction principle in all pithouses and ceremonial structures in the Sierra Blanca Region.

Functional Implications

The presence of firepits is usually thought to mean that the structures were used for domiciliary or ceremonial purposes, and their absence implies a storage function or perhaps seasonal occupation in warm weather. All of the early Glencoe Phase houses in which the middle of the room was intact possessed firepits; only two houses at the late Glencoe Phase Bonnell Site lacked this feature. We can postulate that all or most structures of this phase were principally used as residences. Specialized storage rooms are assumed for Corona and Lincoln Phases because a number of rooms lacked firepits or fire areas.

Comparisons

Firepits and fire areas were placed on one side of the Los Tules houses. Four of the Los Tules houses lacked fire areas, an unusually high percentage in a pithouse village. Two houses had basin-shaped, clay-lined firepits. A circular, straight-sided, unlined firepit 0.75 m deep in House 1 was the only example from southeastern New Mexico of a cylindrical firepit of Pueblo II age or earlier which was analogous in shape to the type that became fairly standard in Pueblo III - early Pueblo IV times in the Sierra Blanca Region. It is, however, unusually deep.

Firepits from the Pueblo I and II sites of Gran Quivira Pithouse Village and Site P4ab and P4c were basin shaped, usually with clay copings. The central position of these firepits in the houses was more like that in the Sierra Blanca Region. At Taylor Draw, the fire area was a roughened, burned spot located off center toward the ventilator (Peckham, personal communication, 1966).

Firepits, usually clay lined, were typically of the shallow, cylindrical type in the El Paso Phase. These were also the most typical form at the Three Rivers Site (Cosgrove and Cosgrove 1965:2-5), where one rectangular slab-lined fire box was found in Room 4.

Bullard (1962:158) points out that rectangular fire places gained in popularity in both Anasazi and Mogollon areas after A.D. 900. Rectangular firepits were present in the pithouses underlying the pueblo at Swartz Ruin, and they became the dominant form in the Mimbres Phase pueblo; however, some of the shallow cylindrical-shaped firepits were still made in the Mimbres Phase (Cosgrove and Cosgrove 1932:9, 19).

Rectangular to oval slab-lined fire boxes were typical in the Chupadero Region by the Pueblo Pardo Phase (Toulouse and Stephenson 1960:15) and the historic kiva at Abo Mission had a fire box of this type (Toulouse 1949:11).

Summary

Circular firepits, usually of cylindrical form, were typical of all phases in south-central New Mexico and in the Sierra Blanca Region. There was a shift from deeper to shallower forms in late Pueblo III times. Central placement of firepits was common in Glencoe and Corona Phases.

Slab-lined fireplaces were normal by late Pueblo III in the Mimbres, Chupadero, and Middle Rio Grande regions, but only two instances of this trait are known from south-central New Mexico and the Sierra Blanca Region. Retention of circular firepits in the Sierra Blanca Region during Pueblo III and IV is one further example of the marginalism and cultural lag that characterized this region.

Ash Receptacles

Sierra Blanca Region

Ash shelves were an integral part of the cylindrical firepits in two separate floors of House 13, Bonnell Site. At the same site, a rectangular slab-lined box contained ashes in House 15, while a similar feature in House 10 contained no ashes at all.

The subterranean chamber at Bloom Mound had a sub-floor ash pit covered with a perforated metate that afforded an opening 5 inches in diameter. This feature was just east of the cylindrical firepit.

Comparisons

Ash receptacles are absent in the Pueblo I and II sites in southeastern New Mexico, as well as in the El Paso Phase sites in the lower Tularosa Basin. They were present at Pueblo Pardo.

Summary

Ash receptacles were absent in south-central New Mexico and rare in the Sierra Blanca Region where they belonged to the late Glencoe and Lincoln Phases. The closest region in which this is a common trait is the Chupadero Region, which probably served as the source of this and related traits.

Houses Outlined with Upright Stone Slabs

Distribution in the Sierra Blanca Region

This type of construction is one of the distinguishing characteristics of the Corona Phase. Surveys of Hiner Site 2, Black Stump Canyon, and Las Tablas gave useful information. Five structures were fully or partially excavated at Clint Sultemeier Site 1, and a single room in House Unit 43 was excavated at the Phillips Ranch Site.

This type of house continued to be made in the Lincoln Phase, when it was customarily associated with other types of structures. Examples are Room 2 at Hiner Site 1, the Robinson Site, and the Lincoln Phase house units at the Phillips Site. At the latter site, three rooms in House Unit 48, the two rooms of House Unit 45, and part of Room 12 of House Unit 46, were excavated.

Isolated examples of this construction technique are known from the Glencoe Phase. Upright stone slabs were placed around parts of two rooms at Site 2000 C in the Peñasco Valley. The two rooms partially outlined with stone cobbles at the Bonnell Site may represent a variant of this type of construction.

Description

Living rooms and storage rooms in the Corona Phase were rectangular. Some circular structures have been observed but none excavated. Room dimensions ranged from 5 feet to perhaps 12 feet. The houses were constructed by digging shallow pits 3 to 12 inches below the ground surface; these pits were partially lined with upright stone slabs. Modern surface erosion in the valleys may have reduced pit depths. There are usually large gaps between slabs, which may be the original pattern, or, since these slabs are exposed on the modern surface, stones may have been removed. The structures were often placed in the soil or sand of valley floors and the slabs may have served to stabilize loose pit walls; however, the pits were so shallow that this seems unnecessary. This cultural trait crystallized into a major architectural form in the Corona Phase, where whole villages were built of slab-lined structures.

A few interior supports were located, and in some cases posts 5 to 6 inches in diameter were set on the floor and mud built up around them. Posts never exceeded 6 inches in diameter. No standard interior support system has been recognized, and the number of posts found in excavated structures seems insufficient to account for walls and roof. It is assumed that pole or *jacal* walls were made. Surface erosion may have removed post holes set outside of the slab-lined pit. Burned clay with wattle and daub impressions was found.

Cylindrical firepits that opened flush with the floor are known, and a house in Black Stump Canyon had a rectangular slab-lined firepit. Small, crude subfloor pits were found, and a shallow clay-lined pit was adjacent to the firepit in

Clint Sultemeier Site 1, Room 1. Rooms with firepits are thought to be living quarters, and rooms lacking this feature probably functioned as storage rooms. One of the latter had a flag-stone paved floor. Other floors were packed earth.

Comparisons

The idea of using upright stone slabs around pit walls is an Anasazi trait that can be traced to Basketmaker III. Bullard found only two occurrences of this trait outside of the Anasazi area prior to A.D. 900, and he ascribed both cases to Anasazi influence (1962:150). Slab lining was used in connection with storage pits, house pit walls, bench facings in kivas, and in surface storage rooms associated with pithouses during Basketmaker III and Pueblo I (Bullard 1962:149–50, 173). The surface indications of house units outlined with upright stone slabs described by W. H. Jackson and W.H. Holmes for the Mesa Verde Region (Brew 1946:219–20) sound almost identical to the Corona Phase sites in southeastern New Mexico, although the two are widely separated in time and space.

During Pueblo II in southeastern New Mexico, slab-lined surface granaries were associated with pithouses at the Taylor Draw Site. In the Fort Sumner locality, slabs were set deeply into the periphery of the bench of the house at P4ab. Upright slabs were noted for the partially excavated structure at P4c, which may be of the same date or somewhat later. Shallow slab-lined pithouses were cited as the characteristic architectural form of the Mesita Negra Phase of Pueblo III age (Jelinek 1960:163). The superficial appearance of the Corona Phase slab-outlined houses is more like the surface granaries at Taylor Draw than the pithouse at P4ab.

The widely scattered house units of 1, 2, and 3 rooms that Toulouse and Stephenson (1960:40–41) note for the Claunch Phase of the Chupadero Region (early Pueblo III) may be related to the slab-lined houses of the Corona Phase, but upright slabs are not mentioned.

There are suggestions that contiguous slab-lined rooms may occur in the Galisteo Basin and the northeastern pueblo frontier in the vicinity of Cimarron. Historic period kivas at Paa-ko were slab lined (Lambert 1954:32). An excavation at North Ponil Site 1 near Cimarron has been partially reported by Baker (1964) and Lutes (1959) and mentioned by Wendorf (1960:59ff.). A foundation of crudely-shaped sandstone blocks enclosed within a line of post holes spaced at 8- to 12-inch intervals was in the lowest level. The floor was uneven and there was a slab-lined firepit (Lutes 1959:59). At a higher level in the same site, they found three contiguous semi-subterranean slab-lined structures (Wendorf 1960:59ff.). The same pottery types were associated with both levels (Baker 1964). The painted pottery is Kwahe'e Black-on-White and/or Taos Black-on-White. Wendorf (1960:59) feels that the Ponil pottery resembles Taos types of A.D. 1000 to 1200, but that it is probably locally made. Lutes (1959:59–68) dates the painted pottery at ca. A.D. 900 while Baker (1964) places the dates at A.D. 1150-1250. Some sherds have been tentatively identified as Upper Republican.

Wendorf (1960:55–65) says that the slab-lined structures resemble contemporary structures found at Taos, but notes that the latter are associated with deep pithouses. Ellis (1964:316–27) suggests that the sites east of the Sangre de Cristo may represent seasonal occupations by groups from Taos. Baker (1964) says that Bertha Dutton told him that slab-lined houses similar to those of the Ponil Phase had been found in the Galisteo Basin.

In his survey of Chihuahua, Sayles mentions that "enclosures were outlined by boulders laid on edge or flat stones placed vertically. These were either single rooms, or parts of a larger group where the majority of the walls were composed of other materials" (Sayles 1936:31).

The slab wall construction of the Antelope Creek Focus is quite different. Double upright slabs were rubble filled and other upright slabs were set inside this base (Holden 1930:27), or slab bases were used for crude horizontal masonry (Krieger 1946:43). The latter construction is found in Room 11, House Unit 46, Phillips Ranch Site, and will be discussed separately in this chapter. Antelope Creek structures differ from those under consideration here in many other details such as the long tunnels, the flanking storage or antechambers, and in their consolidated building arrangement.

Summary

It would appear that slab-lined semi-subterranean houses were a minor architectural component of several eastern New Mexico regions, and that these spread out of the Middle and Upper Rio Grande. Slab-lined pithouses and slab-lined granaries were present in southeastern New Mexico during Pueblo II (Site P4 and Taylor Draw). This eastern slab-lined architectural tradition is undoubtedly related to and derived from the Basketmaker III - Pueblo I forms from the Anasazi area (See Bullard 1962:150). The Corona Phase is the only instance now known where this type of construction crystallized into a dominant architectural pattern associated with fairly large villages. It spread south into Glencoe Phase sites as a minor architectural form that coexisted with pithouses.

Cobbles Used in Structures

Description

The use of rounded cobbles in connection with pithouse structures may be a variant of slab lining, as cobbles were used to line pits in the same way that upright slabs were. The only structure in the Sierra Blanca Region that used cobbles was the south house unit at the Bonnell Site, composed of Rooms 7 and 8, where cobbles partially lined the shallow pit walls and were used to create a two-course masonry partition wall.

Comparisons

In North Ponil Canyon, northeastern New Mexico, a "foundation of crudely shaped sandstone blocks was enclosed within a line of post holes spaced at 8 inch intervals" (Lutes 1957a:59). At the Switchback Ruin in the Reserve Region, Houses 2 and 3, which lacked lateral entries, had a one-course row of basalt boulders that probably served as a partition wall between the two structures (Peckham 1957a:10–38).

A Slab-lined Pithouse with Masonry Walls

Description

Vertical slabs lined the pit wall of House 11, House Unit 46 at the Phillips Site (Appendix 2). A double-faced wall of horizontal masonry began at ground level. Internal dimensions of the room were small, about 7 feet square. It may have been used as a storage room as it lacked a firepit. Its exterior appearance must have been rather vault-like.

Comparisons

Comparable construction practices have been reported as a minor architectural element from widely separated places in the Southwest and the adjacent Canadian River, but nowhere is this a major architectural form. In the Antelope Creek Focus, some use was made of vertical slabs to line shallow pit walls, topped with horizontal masonry (Krieger 1946:43). The same basic construction occurred at Reeve Ruin, (Di Peso 1958:35) and at Point of Pines (Wendorf 1950:23). All known examples are associated with other Anasazi traits. This may be an independent response to the introduction of pueblo architecture.

Although the various masonry-walled pit rooms described for western New Mexico (Peckham 1958:81-94; Cosgrove and Cosgrove 1932:9; Haury 1936:84; Peckham, Wendorf, and Ferdon 1956:37; Schroeder and Wendorf 1954:92–95) did not have a base course of vertical slabs, this may have represented an alternate response to the introduction of masonry structures to pithouse dwellers. The practice probably goes back to Basketmaker III, when slab-lined pits had above-ground walls of adobe turtlebacks (Kidder and Guernsey 1919:43; Bullard 1962:150).

House Units Composed of Contiguous Pit Rooms

Distribution in the Sierra Blanca Region

Corona Phase slab-outlined rooms fit into the category of house units composed of contiguous pit rooms. These have been described and their cultural relations traced in a preceding section, and they will not be reviewed here.

Contiguous pit rooms that created multi-room structures characterize the second building period at the Bonnell Site of the late Glencoe Phase. Three house units were built (Appendix 5).

Description of the Bonnell Site House Units

The west house unit consisted of four contiguous pit rooms arranged in linear fashion. The east house unit had three pit rooms aligned, and there may have been a second row of rooms attached. The south unit had only two rooms.

To a certain extent, each room was a separate structural unit that contained its own major supports of roof and walls. Two, four, six, and irregular post support patterns were represented in the house blocks. The superstructure construction suggested by each support pattern must be reconsidered for the unit as a whole, as proximity and alignment of these rooms strongly suggests that they could not maintain an independent existence.

The center houses in both east and west house blocks probably had slightly pitched gable roofs. Roofs on the flanking buildings could have been slanted shed fashion against that of the center house, or they could have been flat. The two-post support of Room 9 suggests a gable roof, but two gable roofs in juxtaposition would result in an intervening trough which would present drainage problems.

Bonnell Site builders had a model of multi-room structures in the Lincoln Phase adobe and masonry pueblos being built only 10 miles or so to the north and in the larger pueblos of the El Paso Phase just to the west in the Tularosa Basin. The idea of multi-roomed structures diffused without the accompanying constructional skills.

Comparisons

Analogous situations may be represented at certain sites where the ideas of using masonry or creating multi-room structures preceded the actual arrival of surface pueblos by a short period of time. At the Galaz Site, for example, three contiguous masonry-lined pithouses are transitional between Three Circle and Mimbres Phases (Haury 1936:84). A masonry-lined pithouse in the Reserve Region was the prelude to Tularosa Phase surface pueblos (Peckham 1958:81–94). Peckham's statement in regard to a similar situation in Rooms 2 and 3 and the Switchback Site is pertinent here: "The common masonry wall and shallow depth of these two rooms gave them the appearance of a small surface pueblo although the rooms possessed features commonly associated with pithouses. Apparently the architectural innovation of contiguous masonry surface rooms was not accepted by the Mogollons without a period of trial and transition. The joining together of two or more dwellings, particularly subterranean ones, was an unfamiliar situation for a group whose previous village plan was one of scattered pithouses" (Peckham 1957a:36).

The above examples were followed by the appearance of fully surface pueblos. Such a development did not occur in the Glencoe Phase because the Sierra Blanca Region was abandoned at the end of that phase. Had abandonment been postponed, the Glencoe Phase peoples would surely have made the transition to surface pueblos during Pueblo IV times. House Unit 46 at the Phillips Site provides a slightly different example of a transitional step in the acceptance of pueblo architectural concepts (Appendix 2).

Superstructure Construction

The position of major support posts is the key to reconstruction of the house form above the pit.

Four Central Posts, Sierra Blanca Region

The four central post pattern was usually used in the larger, deeper structures. Examples are Houses 1, 3, 4, and 15 at the Bonnell Site, the house at Site 2000 A 2, probably the two superimposed structures at Site 2000 A 1, the house Peckham excavated at Mayhill Site 2, House 13 in House Unit 46 at the Phillips Site, and the subterranean chamber at Bloom Mound. Although the subterranean chambers at the Block Lookout and Block Headquarters sites were not fully cleared, they too probably had four central posts. Variations on this pattern are seen in House 7, Bonnell Site, where a fifth post was set in the center, and in the house at Site 2000 B, where a filled storage pit in one corner caused the fourth post to be set south of the firepit.

In these houses, the distance from supporting posts to outside wall is roughly one-half that between supporting posts. By using the sustained span principle, the major weight of the superstructure would have been carried on the main supports and little or no weight carried on the walls.

The four central post system is usually reconstructed as having a flat central section between the main supports; small poles leaned from the cross beams of the central roof section to the ground surface around the pit (Bullard 1962:128–29). This was probably the type of construction used in most of the houses listed above.

The subterranean chamber at Bloom Mound and the pithouse remnant excavated by Green in the Peñasco Valley were both 7 feet deep. Two main supports located close to the corners in the latter structure caused Green to infer a four post system (1956:15). These supports were much closer to the pit walls than in other houses in the region. These two structures were so deep that they could have been roofed at ground level or slightly above. It is probable that the central section was slightly raised to afford better drainage and that the side roof construction was like that described by Bullard (1962:128). Depth of pit walls gave full head-room over the entire floor area of the deep houses.

A reconstruction of pithouses at the Bonnell Site (Holden 1952:82) was based primarily on architectural features of House 1. After this was published, vertical post holes and post fragments were found behind the plastered pit wall of that house, suggesting an alternative reconstruction with vertical walls. These posts, from 3 to 6 inches in diameter, were embedded deeply below floor level, and they extended above the ground level of the pit wall. Wall plaster was not removed from other sections of the house, and more of these posts may have been present on west, north or east walls. Plaster had eroded from the south wall, and no posts were embedded in that wall. These posts could have served as retaining agents in the pit, or could be part of a vertical wall.

Comparisons

Buildings with four post supports were present by Pueblo I times in southeastern New Mexico, as both structures at Gran Quivira Pithouse Village had this pattern. It is also found at Taylor Draw and Site P4ab and P4c. Patterns at Los Tules are quite varied; the four post support is present.

Most of the Basketmaker III and Pueblo I pithouses reported for the Middle Rio Grande show this pattern (Peckham 1957b:41; Vytlacil and Brody 1958:161–68).

The four post system, among others, was known in the Mimbres Region by the Three Circle Phase. In most published plans of houses with four post supports, the posts are set fairly close to the walls, and a sloping side roof would not greatly affect the amount of floor space where head-room was available. The house that Green (1956:13) dug near Mayhill conforms to the usal placement of posts near walls, as do most of the Los Tules examples. Most houses in the Sierra Blanca Region have the major posts located farther into the room, and if a sloping side roof was used, the amount of usable floor space would be materially diminished.

Six Support Posts, Sierra Blanca Region

Houses 3 and 13, Bonnell Site, had four centrally located posts and two additional supports against the west wall. In House 13, the two west posts were aligned with the other four posts. In House 3, double posts were set in the northwest and southwest corners. Each of these structures formed the middle room of a house block of contiguous pit rooms. The larger number of posts may be related to their structural position in the house block. Roofs could have been flat or gabled. Walls were undoubtedly vertical.

Comparisons

If gable roofs were used on these houses, there were probably nearby antecedents to serve as models. Lehmer (1948:24) and Bullard (1962:130) agree that this type of roof was probably used on some houses at Los Tules. The latter author notes that the gable roof was the major or only roof form in the Mimbres Region during the San Francisco Stage and that it was probably retained into the Three Circle Phase (Bullard 1962:131).

Two Support Posts

Only House 9, part of the east house block at the Bonnell Site, had two major posts. A gable roof is possible, but its structural interdependence with House 13 on the north suggests a shed-type roof. This house was in such a shallow pit that it must have functioned as a surface structure. An adobe wall remnant or wall base formed the south limit of the house. Two upright posts 3 to 4 inches in diameter were set on the outside of this feature.

Irregularly Placed Posts

Smaller, shallower houses of the late Glencoe Phase constructed more like surface pole or *jacal* structures share the irregular post placement with the slab-outlined structures of the Corona Phase. Support posts had a maximum diameter of 6 inches, and many were smaller. At the Bonnell Site, Houses 2, 8, and 14 definitely show this pattern, and Houses 5, 6, 10, 11, and 12 seem to have had this type of support system.

Roof Construction

Wherever collapsed roofing was found, the same sequence of construction was observed. Large cross beams supported small poles overlaid with brush, tied grass or reeds, topped with a heavy clay layer. Split planks were used as cross beams in House 1, Bonnell Site. Split planks were also reported from Site 2000 A (Jennings 1940:9).

Secondary Interior Posts

Most fully excavated houses have a number of posts that could have been structural braces or part of the interior furnishings of the house. The scarcity of recognizable storage facilities in Glencoe Phase sites suggests that some of the interior posts, and perhaps some exterior ones as well, supported storage racks or shelves. At the Bonnell Site, only House 4 lacked secondary posts. The pattern of small interior posts was different at each of the six floor levels of House 13 at the same site indicating that interior room furnishings were subject to change fairly often.

Minor Construction Elements Involving Posts

Posts were sometimes placed on stone footings when the post hole was dug in loose fill (Houses 3 and 8, Bonnell Site). Posts frequently had rounded bottoms which were charred. This probably did not result from felling the trees by burning, but rather it is interpreted as a means whereby the butt ends were given a smooth surface by burning and sanding for even weight distribution.

ADOBE AND/OR MASONRY SURFACE STRUCTURES

Within the Sierra Blanca Region, surface structures with solid walls were limited to the Lincoln Phase. The fully or partially excavated rooms that form the basis of the following discussion include:

5 rooms:	Hiner Site 1	(Appendix 1)
1 room:	Frank Sultemeier Site	(Appendix 1)
12 rooms:	LA 2945	(Wendorf 1956:87–105)
1 room:	Ryberg Site 3	(Appendix 1; and Wendorf 1956:89)
3 rooms:	House Unit 46. Phillips Ranch Site	(Appendix 2)
1 room:	Block Headquarters Site	(Appendix 3)
7 rooms:	Block Lookout Site	(Appendix 3)
1 room:	Bloom Mound	(Appendix 6; Holden 1952)

Shape of the Pueblo Structures

Surface observations and limited excavation have revealed two basic plans, and other shapes will undoubtedly be recognized in the future. Linear structures at Block Lookout and at Bloom Mound were comprised of 10 to 30 rooms in a double row that faced eastward on a subterranean chamber that was probably located in a plaza. LA 2945 was a linear house unit; however, it is doubtful if the entire complex was excavated.

Square enclosed pueblo units with a small central plaza were built at Hiner Site 1, Frank Sultemeier Site, and Ryberg Site 3. Surface indications at some Lincoln Phase sites in the Bonito Valley indicate that this pueblo shape was present there. If ceremonial chambers were located within these plazas, they must have taken up all or most of the plaza space. One of the striking characteristics of this shape pueblo is its compactness.

Enclosed pueblos were consistently larger than the linear pueblos. Whereas 10 to 30 rooms were estimated for the former, the latter commonly had 100 to

200 rooms. In at least one case, a village consisted of two enclosed square pueblos and a linear house unit (Hiner Site 1).

Lincoln Phase pueblos often give the impression of having been designed as a unit. Alterations of the basic shape were minimal.

Comparisons

El Paso Phase pueblos are much more sprawling and spread out than those of the Lincoln Phase. The plazas are much larger, subterranean chambers are absent, and room size shows much more variation.

Pueblo shapes of the Arroyo Seco and Gran Quivira Phases are more analogous to those of the Lincoln Phase. The later, more irregular pueblo shapes of the Pueblo Pardo and Pueblo Colorado Phases do not have known counterparts in the Lincoln Phase.

Wall Construction and Building Materials

The builders of Lincoln Phase pueblos used a range of raw materials, mechanical skills, and engineering knowledge that contrasted strongly with those used by Corona and Glencoe Phase peoples.

Adobe Construction

Entire pueblo structures at Hiner Site 1, LA 2945, Block Lookout, and Bloom Mound were made of adobe. At the Phillips Site, adobe walls abutted a masonry room. Interior walls varied from 8 to 12 inches in thickness. At Hiner Site 1, the outside wall of the pueblo was 12 inches thick; the outside wall at Block Lookout was 2 feet thick. Adobe at Block Lookout had a high rock content, while that at Hiner Site 1 had only a few small pebble inclusions.

Wendorf recognized coursed adobe at LA 2945, and this was probably the usual construction technique. Adobe walls at LA 2945 were set in a trench (Wendorf 1956:94).

Comparisons

Coursed adobe walls seated in foundation trenches were used contemporaneously in a number of widely separated sites in eastern New Mexico, such as at Forked Lightning Ruin in the upper Pecos Valley (Kidder 1958:15), at Pindi in the Rio Grande (Stubbs and Stallings 1953:25–28), and in El Paso Phase sites (Lehmer 1948:44, 55, 56). Exterior walls at Alamogordo Sites 1 and 2 were about 1 m thick in places; such massive construction had no parallel in Lincoln Phase buildings. Adobe walls were usually smoothed but unplastered. At Block Lookout, however, heavy plaster covered the rather rocky adobe surface.

Masonry Walls

Shaped sandstone blocks (Wendorf 1956:89) or sandstone slabs selected for their elongated flat shape were used. Four types of above-surface masonry have been distinguished:

(1) Coursed masonry without core, laid in mortar, was found at Ryberg Site 3 and at the Frank Sultemeier Site.

(2) Coursed masonry without core, with no visible mortar, was used at Block Headquarters Site and in two walls of House 15, House Unit 46, Phillips Ranch Site.

(3) Double rows of coursed stones without core, but with occasional stones turned perpendicular to the wall to "tie" the two sides of the wall together, were used in two walls of Room 15, House Unit 46, Phillips Ranch Site.

(4) Rubble-filled walls faced on each side with large horizontal stone slabs set in small amounts of mortar had occasional stones placed perpendicular to the wall to "tie" the wall together. This type was limited to House 11, House Unit 46, Phillips Ranch Site, where the masonry was placed at ground level above a slab-lined pithouse. Wall plaster on masonry walls was noted at the Frank Sultemeier Site; most walls apparently were unplastered.

Comparisons

Wall construction of Pueblo Pardo is described as follows: ". . . masonry walls constructed of uncut, limestone slabs set in adobe mortar. . . . The masonry was irregularly coursed, and both inner and outer wall surfaces were smooth and even, but not faced. The walls were uniformly 1.0 foot thick. . . . All room walls, except the north and east walls of Room 5, were plastered on the interior. . . ." (Toulouse and Stephenson 1960:6). This corresponds to the first type of masonry listed above for the Sierra Blanca Region.

Roof Construction

The method of roofing pueblo rooms was basically the same as that described for pithouses. Cross beams were covered by poles, brush or grass, and clay or earth.

Interior Posts

Size, number, and placement of posts in most pueblo sites suggested that they functioned as house furnishings or braces rather than as primary supports. At Hiner Site 1, for example, three rooms lacked interior posts, one room had a single central post, and two posts were located close to the walls of two other rooms.

An important exception was Block Lookout. Three to seven medium-sized posts were found close to the wall in all of the fully excavated rooms. Further excavation at this site is needed to determine whether the trend toward four supports located close to the corners was a regular construction feature.

Firepits

In our small sample, each site was internally consistent in the type of firepits represented; other sites of this phase had different shapes of firepits. Three adobe-walled rooms and the slab-lined Room 2 on the south edge of Hiner Site 1 had shallow, straight-sided, circular firepits. The same type of firepits were found at LA 2945. Basin-shaped firepits were present in two surface rooms at Block Lookout. The only firepit from surface rooms at Bloom Mound, described in the Roswell Archaeological Society scrapbook, was 10 inches in diameter, 16 inches deep, and tapered inward toward the bottom. In the subterranean chamber at this site, a similar deep, cylindrical firepit was found. No firepits were found in excavated structures at the Phillips Site.

The same types of firepits were present in Lincoln Phase surface pueblo rooms as were found in the Corona and Glencoe Phases, and comparative data given there are apropos here.

Fireplace features present in Corona and Glencoe Phases that were absent in the Lincoln Phase were rectangular slab-lined fire boxes and clay copings or rims built on the floor around the firepits.

Ash Box

This trait was rare in Corona and Glencoe Phases, and we had only one example in the Lincoln Phase sites. A rectangular slab-lined box that did not contain ashes was located east of the firepit in Room 2, Block Lookout.

Sub-floor Pits

Small, unplastered sub-floor pits and depressions were present in the surface pueblo rooms occasionally. Two were found at Hiner Site 1 and one at Block Lookout. They were similar in shape, size, and placement to the few examples known from Corona and Glencoe Phases.

Use of Upright Stone Slabs

The hallmark of the preceding Corona Phase was the generous use of upright stone slabs. This trait survived in greatly curtailed form into the Lincoln Phase. In the Gallo Drainage, a number of rooms along the south side of the Hiner Site 1 pueblo were outlined with upright stone slabs; a firepit in the only excavated slab-outlined rooms there suggested that some or all of these rooms were living quarters. Upright stone slabs were placed within adobe surface rooms at the same site. Wendorf (1956:94) noted the use of vertical stone slabs to reinforce the bases of adobe walls at LA 2945. Slab outlined houses coexisted with masonry and adobe structures at the Phillips Site in the Lincoln Phase where the architecture was quite aberrant.

Doorways

Lincoln Phase

None have been reported for this phase. The walls at LA 2945 were so low that doors with a high sill would have been eroded away. Sufficient wall height remained at most other sites to demonstrate that doorways were absent.

Comparisons

Doors were found at Pueblo Pardo (Toulouse and Stephenson 1960:14). Doors were present at the El Paso Phase Bradfield Site but were absent at Alamogordo Sites 1 and 2 (Lehmer 1948:45, 56, 58). Doors were found at the Three Rivers Site (Cosgrove and Cosgrove 1965:5). Stubbs and Stallings (1953:29, 31) commented on the few doors at Pindi, as did Kidder (1958:24) for Forked Lightning.

Jacal Construction

Distribution

Jacal construction associated with shallow pits is clearly demonstrated for Houses 7 and 8 of the south house unit at the Bonnell Site. Houses 18 and 26, Bonnell Site, are surface *jacal* houses. It is assumed that the shallower pithouses at this site and the slab-lined pithouses of the Corona Phase had lightweight superstructures of similar construction.

Comparisons

Jacal or pole-walled structures placed either in shallow pits or at ground level represent one architectural variant in the Anasazi area from Basketmaker III to Pueblo II. An even older example could be the "houses" found at LA 2605 in La Plata, Colorado, by Fenenga and Wendorf (1956:207–14). Brew (1946:220–21) reviews the evidence for structures of this type and notes some structural differences between *jacals* in different localities.

At Pindi, a *jacal* structure with pole and posts set in an adobe base was found below the surface pueblo, as was a pithouse; these belong to the Pueblo II period (Stubbs and Stallings 1953:24–25). At the Cerros Mojinos Site on the Rio Puerco of the east, Group A was composed of four *jacal* rooms. *Jacal* construction was also present in other house units. This site is dated as late

Pueblo II - early Pueblo III (Fenenga and Cummings 1956b:242–55).

The history of *jacal* structures in the Anasazi area needs further attention. They apparently make their first appearance in the northern part of the Anasazi area, where they were an important architectural component from Basketmaker III to at least Pueblo II times. By Pueblo II times this house type was present near the Rio Grande, and it survived into Pueblo III and early Pueblo IV times in southeastern New Mexico and into Pueblo III times in northeastern New Mexico.

CEREMONIAL ARCHITECTURE IN SOUTHEASTERN NEW MEXICO

Kivas can rarely be identified with certainty in southeastern New Mexico. In the often quoted words of Watson Smith, "there are many cases in which the relationships of a given room within its architectural complex, its difference in shape or size from other associated rooms, and its positional relation to them, will be of greater significance than any or all of its internal features as such" (1952:161–62). In the various excavated sites in southeastern New Mexico, certain rooms or structures differ from associated rooms or structures in size, shape, or internal appointments, and most archaeologists working here have suggested that these distinctive rooms functioned partially or wholly as ceremonial chambers.

Review of Archaeological Evidence

The earliest known village site is Gran Quivira Pithouse Village (Pueblo I). Two dissimilar structures were excavated; one was a round pithouse which lacked auxiliary features such as a lateral entrance or a ventilator (Green 1955:183). The other, smaller and irregular in shape, was equipped with a ventilator and a small cupped stone or "mortar" plastered into the floor northeast of the firepit (Fenenga 1956:229). The cupped stone plastered into the floor might have had a specialized function, in view of the other known occurrences of this trait.

No problems of interpretation arose in identifying the Pueblo II kiva at Taylor Draw. It was circular, equipped with a ventilator and a banquette, and it lacked a *sipapu*.

At Los Tules, Lehmer felt that "the unusual depth, the bench, and the unusual posthole arrangement of House 5 all serve to set it apart, and it seems possible that it was some sort of a special chamber, possibly analogous to the Anasazi kiva" (1948:24).

Evidence from the early Pueblo III period is not extensive. No possible ceremonial chambers can be cited for the early Glencoe Phase. Circular depressions outlined with upright stone slabs in Corona Phase sites may have had a specialized function; none of these have been excavated.

More evidence is available for the late Pueblo III - early Pueblo IV period. Pueblo Pardo had at least three kivas. Kiva A was a circular subterranean structure with a ventilator, firepit-ash pit complex, loom holes, and a "small rectangular stone with a rectangular depression cut in the top, located near the center of the kiva and set into the floor, which probably served as a *sipapu*" (Toulouse and Stephenson 1960:19). These authors were the first to suggest that this floor feature could represent a *sipapu*. The later, rather curious kiva at the Mission of Abo had a ventilator but lacked a *sipapu* (Toulouse 1949:11).

Subterranean rooms were absent in El Paso Phase sites in the lower Tularosa Valley. Suggested ceremonial chambers were rooms contained within a house block that were unusually large, that tended to have symmetrical floor features, or that had some unusual features. Twelve Room House Ruin was a small, isolated, linear pueblo house of the early El Paso Phase. Room 3 could have had a specialized function because of its unusual size (Moore 1947:Pl. 8). Lehmer (1948:39) limited the Bradfield Site to a single, linear pueblo house and its adjacent midden which formed only a part of a larger village. "There was nothing about any of the rooms to suggest definitely the kiva features of the north, but it seems possible that Room M may have served as some sort of communal chamber. It was unusually large, and its floor features were placed with unusual regularity" (Lehmer 1948:46).

More of the village plan of Alamogordo Sites 1 and 2 was delineated; in each case, a large plaza was flanked on three or four sides by an adobe pueblo structure. Subterranean structures were absent. Room 5 in House 1, Site 1, was much larger than the others, "again raising the possibility that it was used as some sort of communal chamber" (Lehmer 1948:55). Room 41, House 2, Site 1, contained a number of unusual features, including "a semicircular adobe bin (?) 60 cm. long, 45 cm. across, and 25 cm. deep, built against the west wall . . . , a circular firepit in the center of the room . . . and a smooth stone measuring 30 by 45 cm. laid in flush with the floor" (Lehmer 1948:57). This is the earliest reference to a stone plastered into the floor of a room whose suggested function was ceremonial. Rooms 41 and 21 were unusually large, and either or both may have had specialized functions. House 1 in Alamogordo Site 2 was "remarkable for its size. . . . The posthole arrangement is very similar to that in the supposed communal chamber at the Bradfield Site" (Lehmer 1948:58).

In Lincoln Phase sites, subterranean chambers were associated with surface pueblos at Block Headquarters, Block Lookout, and Bloom Mound. The incompletely excavated chamber at Block Headquarters must have taken up most of the space in the interior "plaza." The square subterranean chamber at Block Lookout had an eastern ventilator, the only post-Pueblo II occurrence of this feature in southeastern New Mexico, a fully encircling bench, and a small cupped stone or "mortar" plastered near the center of the floor just west of the firepit. The subterranean chamber at Bloom Mound was also situated east of a linear pueblo unit. Comparable in size and depth to the Block Lookout structure, it lacked a bench, a ventilator, and a stone set into the floor.

At the late Glencoe Phase Bonnell Site, the size, depth, and location of Houses 1 and 15, which were occupied sequentially, set them apart from other structures at the site. There is no internal evidence that they served as other than domestic dwellings.

Sipapus

No true *sipapus* have been reported from southeastern New Mexico for any period. It has been suggested that cupped stones plastered into the floor of ceremonial chambers functioned as a substitute. Four instances of this trait were reviewed above.

Some supportive evidence for this theory may be gleaned from the upper Pecos River Region. No *sipapus* were found at Forked Lightning, at Dick's Ruin, or, with two possible exceptions, at Pecos Pueblo (Kidder 1958:29–42, 47, 251). The two non-conventional *sipapus* in Kivas 7 and 16 at Pecos were larger than usual and held ceremonial objects (Kidder 1958:198–203). The *sipapu* in the kiva at Arrowhead Ruin (Holden 1955a:105–06) was so large that its identification as a *sipapu* may have been an error in the light of the general absence of this feature in the upper Pecos Valley.

Flat or slightly cupped stones were plastered into the floor south of the firepit of the kiva at Dick's Ruin, into one of six kivas at Forked Lightning, and into five of the Pecos kivas (Kidder 1958:159, 174, 182, 200, 208, 261). These stones were larger than the postulated substitute *sipapus* of southeastern New Mexico, and their uniform location was at variance with the irregular placement of the stones in the latter area. The absence of true *sipapus* combined with this particular feature raises the possibility that substitute *sipapus* plastered into the floor were typical of much of the eastern pueblo periphery.

There is no mention of slabs plastered into the floor of Pueblo I and II sites in the Middle Rio Grande (Wendorf 1954b:13–28; Peckham 1954:41–52; Peckham 1957b:39–70). This trait may have been present in Pueblo III, as Kiva E at Pindi had four smooth, flat stones set into the floor on the west side of the firepit (Stubbs and Stallings 1953:39). These authors suggested that the approach to the firepit was from this side and that the slabs represented a late provision to prevent wear (ibid.:44). Since the other kivas had worn spots in similar places, this seems reasonable; it may be significant that this kiva also lacked a conventional *sipapu*.

Should further research show that these stones were indeed substitute *sipapus,* we would have a concrete, easily identifiable trait related to the religion of the aboriginal inhabitants of southeastern New Mexico. Once ceremonial structures can be recognized, our knowledge about other aspects of religion can be enlarged.

Summary

During Pueblo I in the Southwest, pithouses were "becoming less specifically a domicile and more specifically a communal chamber or kiva. . . . some domestic activities were probably always carried on in kivas, as they are today, and this would have been especially true in this period of transition. Nor can identifying differences in structural details between pit houses and kivas be determined at this period" (Bullard 1962:103). The evidence from Gran Quivira Pithouse Village suggests that this statement is also true of southeastern New Mexico.

The Pueblo II kiva at Taylor Draw was similar to kivas in the Middle Rio Grande at this period, except that it lacked a *sipapu* (Peckham 1957b:39–70). Circular kivas showing a number of specialized kiva features were in use in the Chupadero Region during the Pueblo Pardo Phase and at the historic Abo Mission. A fully documented sequence from the Chupadero Region should show that circular subterranean kivas had a continuous history from Pueblo II times to historic times in that region.

In the Mesilla and Glencoe Phases, pithouses that differ in shape or size from other pithouses at the same site are most likely to have had ceremonial functions. Absence of specialized features and the domestic nature of the artifacts recovered from such houses make it possible that these structures also served as dwellings.

Rooms within El Paso Phase pueblo buildings may have been used for ceremonial purposes. Unusually large rooms sometimes have specialized features that reinforce such an interpretation.

Corona Phase ceremonial architecture is not known. Excavation of circular depressions outlined with upright stone slabs may reveal a variant of circular kivas.

Several Lincoln Phase sites have square subterranean chambers adjacent to a pueblo building or inside an enclosed plaza. True kiva features are often absent, although one structure had an eastern ventilator and a "substitute *sipapu*." I have recently heard of another square kiva, located at a pueblo site on upper Bonito stream of the Hondo Drainage which had an alignment of hearth, ladder holes, and ash pit, with a row of loom holes off to one side

(Peckham, personal communication, 1966). It is postulated that these square chambers developed out of the square domestic house of the Glencoe Phase rather than being derived from the rectangular kivas of the western pueblos.

Flat or cupped stones plastered into the floor are interpreted as "substitute *sipapus*." They have been reported from El Paso, Pueblo Pardo, and Lincoln Phase sites. It is further suggested that the "substitute *sipapu*" may prove to be a characteristic of much of the eastern pueblo frontier.

FOOD PROCESSING TOOLS

Metates and Basin Milling Stones

None were found in Corona Phase sites. The following types occured in Glencoe and Lincoln Phase contexts.

Trough Metate with One End Closed

With the exception of the early Glencoe Phase sites in the Peñasco Valley, this was the most common type. It may be considered one of the diagnostic artifacts of the late Glencoe and Lincoln Phases. Considerable variation in depth of the trough and corresponding height of the sides was primarily related to depth of the original stone and degree of usage. Some of the metates with deeper troughs may have had a fairly deep trough pecked into the stone at the time of manufacture. In others the trough seems to have developed through usage.

The flat closed end, usually deliberately ground smooth, was 4 to 6 inches wide. This is hereafter called a "mano-rest"; it differs from the "Utah" type of metate in that the mano rest was flat and not depressed. Identical flat places were developed on some basin milling stones and on flat or slab metates.

Provenience

Sites	*Excavated Specimens*		*Surface*
	Whole	Frag.	
LA 2945	2		
Hiner 1	1	2	
Phillips	1		
Bloom Mound	4	4	
Block Lookout	10		Present
Block Headquarters			Present
Hulbert			Present
Pryor Farm, Blue Water			Present
Bonnell	8	9	

Flat or Slab Metates with "Mano Rests"

One well-made specimen from the Bonnell Site had been little used. The stone had a uniform thickness of about 1 inch over the grinding surface; the flat "mano rest" was slightly raised above the grinding surface.

Flat or Slab Metates

At the Bonnell Site, three specimens, which had flat to slightly concave grinding surfaces, were excavated. One of these had an incipient "mano rest." A few of these were observed on the surface, and three were excavated from rooms at Block Lookout. The common occurrence of nearly flat-surfaced manos in Lincoln Phase sites in the Gallo, Macho, and North Capitan localities probably means that slab metates were common there.

Concave Faced Trough Metates

The four specimens described by Jennings (1940:8, Pl. VII) from Site 2000 were used with a back-and-forth motion. The grinding surface covered the entire face of the stones; the concave face does not appear to be truly troughed, judging from the photographs.

Basin Milling Stones

These were used with an elliptical motion; the reciprocal tool was undoubtedly a small grinding stone. Wild seed products were presumably processed in these grinding containers. Three were found at the Bonnell Site, one of which had a "mano rest."

Position of Metates and Milling Stones in Sites

Whole metates tended to be located within rooms. Some rested on the floor and a few were leaned against the wall.

Degree of Wear

Broken implements were discarded, of course. Whole implements were usually in excellent shape. It was rare to see a worn out metate, milling stone, or mano. Only one metate of the many I have examined, including many in private collections which are not tabulated, was worn through.

Secondary Uses of Metates

The metate referred to above which was worn completely through was placed over the ash pit in the ceremonial chamber at Bloom Mound. A small depression in the old grinding surface of a metate fragment from the Bonnell Site transformed this specimen into a "palette." Dry pigment was occasionally ground on metate surfaces.

Mealing Bins

The only possible instance of a mealing bin was reported from LA 2945. "Four fragments of at least two metates [were] arranged and plastered in proper position to form a troughed, grinding area with one end closed. Clay was employed to fill the spaces between the fragments, thus permitting use as a complete metate" (Wendorf 1956:91).

Comparisons

The earliest recorded metate came from Gran Quivira Pithouse Village (Pueblo I). It was a "rectangular tablet. . . . The work surface is very slightly concave in the long axis, flat in the transverse plane. . . ." (Fenenga 1956:230).

Eight metates were reported from Los Tules (Lehmer 1948:32–33). Four were described as troughs, open at one end. In the illustration, this type appeared to be similar to the metates that Jennings got at Site 2000 (1940:8). Three basin milling stones and a flat or slab metate were also present at Los Tules.

Shallow trough metates with one end closed were found at Taylor Draw (Peckham, personal communication, 1966). Comparative information is not available for the other northern Pueblo II sites, and Site P4.

Although quantification is lacking for the three El Paso Phase sites in the lower Tularosa Basin, slab metates, one-end-closed troughed metates without mano rests, and basin milling stones occurred there (Lehmer 1948:50 and 64). At the early El Paso Phase site of Twelve Room House Ruin, Mrs. Moore (1947:94–114) reported eight troughed metates with one end closed with concave faces, more like the Site 2000 and Los Tules specimens. Mrs. Moore noted stones that were probably used to prop the metates to a convenient plane.

Slab metates (21) outnumbered troughed metates (9) at Pueblo Pardo. The latter had well-made shelves or mano rests at the closed end. Basin metates (5) probably functioned as milling stones (Toulouse and Stephenson 1960:26). At Abo Mission, slab metates had virtually replaced troughed metates. The only example of the latter form came from fallen wall debris (Toulouse 1949:23).

Trough metates with one end closed are considered to be the most typical Mogollon form (Wheat 1955b:111). They were widespread throughout the Southwest until Pueblo III times when they were gradually replaced by flat types associated with mealing bins. Trough metates survived later in some regions than in others, as for example at Pinedale in the thirteenth century, and both slab and one-end-closed trough metates were in use at Aztec and Pueblo Bonito (Woodbury 1954:59).

Summary

Troughed metates with a flat mano rest at the closed end were the most common type in late Glencoe and Lincoln Phases (late Pueblo III - early Pueblo IV times). This type was less numerous, but nevertheless present during the same time period in the Pueblo Pardo Phase.

Retention of troughed metates in the Sierra Blanca and Chupadero Regions during late Pueblo III and early Pueblo IV times was functionally related to the absence of mealing bins. As Woodbury (1954:59) pointed out, "As long as the metate was moveable, and was propped on the floor each time it was used, the roughed shapes were more convenient. The bordering ridges kept meal from spilling off the grinding surfaces. . . ."

Slab metates were present during Pueblo I at Gran Quivira Pithouse Village and during Pueblo II at Los Tules. This type metate was a minor but persistent element in late Glencoe, Lincoln, and El Paso Phases. It had become the most common metate form in the Chupadero Region by the Pueblo Pardo Phase, and it was perhaps the only form employed during the historic Salinas Phase.

The most common metate type during the early Glencoe, the Mesilla, and the El Paso Phases had rather concave faces and lacked mano rests.

Basin milling stones for processing wild products found in the Mesilla and El Paso Phases are indicative of a regional exploitation of a wild food resource. The only reported milling stone from the Sierra Blanca Region was at the Bonnell Site.

Manos and Grinding Stones

A thorough classification of manos from the Sierra Blanca Region would be desirable; incomplete observations were made in the field and few manos were transported to the laboratory. Specimens have been described as completely as possible for each site.

Manos of the Lincoln Phase tended to be rectangular in cross-section and sub-rectangular to oval in outline. Manos of the Glencoe Phase were oval in cross-section and had near flat to slightly to very convex grinding surfaces that tapered upward toward the ends. Multiple grinding surfaces were rare in all localities. One-handed grinding stones, usually with battered ends, were found in all phases.

Mortars and Pestles

Portable, well-developed stone mortars were rarely found in the Sierra Blanca Region, but mortar holes in rock outcroppings occurred. Perhaps piñon nuts were hulled or ground into flour in the many mortar holes developed in Grindstone Mesa (Appendix 4).

Provenience of Mortars

Site	*No. of Mortars*	*No. of Pestles*
LA 2945	1	0
2000 A	1	1
Bonnell	2	3
Block Lookout	1(?)	0

Small mortars from the first three sites were 4 to 6 inches in diameter. The "mortar" from Block Lookout was plastered into the floor of the subterranean chamber, and its function as a substitute *sipapu* has been discussed.

Small pestles were found at two sites. The one from Site 2000 A was only 2⅝ inch long and 1⅜ inch in diameter (Jennings 1940:9). Those from the Bonnell Site were about 4 inches long and with slightly convex battered ends.

Comparisons

Chupadero Region: The "mortar" from Gran Quivira Pithouse Village was, like the Block Lookout specimen, plastered into the floor and it is believed that it was a *sipapu*. "Mortars" described for Pueblo Pardo had such shallow depressions that they will be considered with "palettes." A pestle 6 inches long came from the pueblo Mission at Abo (Toulouse 1949:23).

South-central New Mexico: Mortars and pestles were a regular component of material culture from Mesilla to El Paso Phases. Earliest pestles were elongated, and Lehmer (1948:32) points out that their considerable weight and smooth working surfaces were used for crushing, not pounding. Reciprocal mortars were not present at Los Tules, but mortar holes in rock outcrops were common around Mesilla Phase sites, and portable mortars were noted at other Mesilla Phase sites (ibid.). Elongated pestles continued into the El Paso Phase, when a short form appeared for the first time. The latter is similar to pestles found at the Bonnell Site. At Alamogordo Sites 1 and 2, boulder mortars occurred, sometimes set into room floors (Lehmer 1948:64). Lehmer (1948:50) felt that mortars and pestles decreased in importance from Mesilla to El Paso Phases.

Summary

South-central New Mexico is the only region in southeastern New Mexico in which these food processing tools played a major role. Exploitation of a wild product, such as the mesquite bean which was limited to the Lower Sonoran Life Zone, formed a substantial food resource throughout the periods of established village life.

Most of the reported portable "mortars" from the Sierra Blanca and Chupadero Regions are classified in this report as substitute *sipapus* and palettes. A number of bedrock mortars at Grindstone Mesa in Ruidoso may have been where piñon nuts were processed, perhaps by Glencoe Phase peoples.

Summary

Slab metates were a minor type throughout southeastern New Mexico at all periods. Trough metates with a smoothed mano rest at the closed end were the most typical form of the late Glencoe and Lincoln Phases and they occurred in the Chupadero Region where they were gradually replaced by the flat form. The trough metates of the early Glencoe Phase and of the Mesilla and El Paso Phases had a concave face and lacked mano rests. Mortars and pestles for processing a wild food product, probably mesquite beans, were common in the latter two phases.

OTHER GRINDING IMPLEMENTS

"Palettes"

Description

The term as used here refers to shallow, cupped, depressions placed in a larger stone background. Similar objects are variously referred to as grinding slabs (Woodbury 1954:Fig. 23g–j), paint grinding stones (Kidder 1932:72 and Figs. 48, 49) and mortars (Toulouse and Stephenson 1960:27, Fig. 29b). The depth and size of the depressions are within the range of small shallow "mortars," including the substitute *sipapu* stones, but the stone background of "mortars" is not as large.

The depressions were seldom over ½ inch deep; the diameter of the depression could range from about 1 to 4 inches. Square depressions were made rarely. Some stones had depressions of two sizes in opposite faces; in no case were two depressions placed on the same face. The surrounding stone was sometimes unaltered and sometimes ground smooth. Flat pebbles or cobbles, broken metates, and manos were used as a background for these depressions.

Their function is open to question. Few had pigment in the depressions, although if liquids were used and the depression washed, traces might not remain. Dry pigment was frequently ground on the flat surfaces of these objects and as well as on a variety of other surfaces.

Provenience

Site	*No.*
Bonnell	8
Site 2000	2

All recorded Sierra Blanca Region examples are from Glencoe Phase sites.

Comparisons

The only comparable specimens from southeastern New Mexico are the mortars from Pueblo Pardo (Toulouse and Stephenson 1960:27) that fall within the specifications of "palettes" as used here.

Summary

The term "palette" may not fully reflect the function of this class of artifacts, as little pigment was found in the depressions. Known examples are Pueblo III and IV in age. To date, this type of artifact is known only from the Glencoe and Pueblo Pardo Phases in southeastern New Mexico.

Grinding Slabs

Description

Flat or slightly concave stone slabs could have been used for a variety of purposes, one of which was grinding dry pigments. None of the Sierra Blanca Region examples were square or rectangular. Some ovoid grinding slabs had been roughly shaped; others were unaltered slabs. Sandstone and limestone were favored raw materials. An upper size limit of 10 inches was found to separate these implements from metates.

Provenience

Site	*No.*
Bonnell	7
Hiner 1	7
Bloom Mound	3

Comparisons

South-central New Mexico: The three tabular or rectangular "palettes" from the Bradfield Site, El Paso Phase, with flat to slightly concave grinding surfaces may be analogous. One had a coating of gritty clay (Lehmer 1948:52). They were more deliberately shaped and had better ground surfaces than the Sierra Blanca Region specimens.

Chupadero Region: At Pueblo Pardo, thin slabs of limestone and sandstone were rectangular to oval in outline; all retained traces of red pigment (Toulouse and Stephenson 1960:27).

Summary

Well-shaped grinding slabs were present in El Paso and Pueblo Pardo Phase sites, being most numerous in the latter phase. Those of the Sierra Blanca Region were less well shaped, never rectangular, and unshaped slabs were often used. All known specimens from southeastern New Mexico belong to the late Pueblo III - early Pueblo IV period, but it seems likely that they were used in earlier times. These grinding slabs were often used to grind pigments, a function they shared with the "pallettes" with depressions, large sherds, and other flat stone surfaces.

STONE ABRADING TOOLS

Grooved Abraders

Within the Sierra Blanca Region, the only known sandstone abrader was in the Roswell Museum collections from Bloom Mound. This artifact type was not reported from south-central New Mexico. In the Chupadero Region, one of the arrowshaft tools described by Toulouse and Stephenson (1960:28) may have been an abrader, as it was crudely made of coarse sandstone and it had a single groove.

Grooved abraders were apparently rare in southeastern New Mexico; the only two examples are from late Pueblo III or early Pueblo IV contexts.

Striated Abrader

A small limestone pebble with a number of deep striations such as would result from pointing bone awls was found at one of the Alamogordo sites (Lehmer 1948:69). No comparable items have been described from the Sierra Blanca or Chupadero Regions; it seems curious that they should be absent.

Flat Abraders

Woodbury used the term *flat abraders* for non-grooved, abrasive stones which could be held in the hand to shape and smooth objects (1954:98). These were apparently absent from southeastern New Mexico, as they were at Pecos.

HAFTED TOOLS

Axes

Provenience

Within the Sierra Blanca Region, the following axes have been recovered:

Excavated at Site	*Full-grooved*	*Three-quarter Grooved*	*Chipped Axes with Notches*
Phillips	1	1 (?)	1
LA 2945	2		1
Bloom Mound	4		1
Bonnell	14		
Total	21	1 (?)	3

Surface Finds or Specimens in Lincoln County Museum	
2000 A	1
Upper Stanton	1
Double Crossing	1
Nogal Canyon	1
Pryor Farm (Blue Water)	Present

Types

No axes have yet been found in early Glencoe or Corona Phase sites. Full-grooved, ground-stone axes were typical of late Glencoe and Lincoln Phases. The largest number of axes was found at the Bonnell Site (Appendix 5).

The finest specimen at the Bonnell Site showed no signs of wear and could have been new or "ceremonial." The limestone specimen in the Lincoln County Museum from the Double Crossing Site was so thin that it would seem that a functional application to a tree trunk would have shattered it. Notched, chipped stone axes found at three sites showed evidence of hard usage. The single three-quarter grooved specimen reported from the Phillips Site was in Jack Harkey's private collection.

Comparisons

Chupadero Region: No axes were found at Pueblo Pardo. A chipped fibrolite axe with a pecked groove was found outside the cemetery wall at Abo Mission.

South-central New Mexico: No axes were found at the Bradfield Site, although full-grooved axes were well represented in private collections. A few had a secondary groove which passed over the poll at right angles to the primary groove (Lehmer 1948:52). Axes were not tabulated from Alamogordo Sites 1 and 2, but they were ". . . fairly numerous and usually well made. Full- and three-quarter grooved varieties occurred in about equal numbers" (Lehmer 1948:66). Some notched, ground-stone axes were also present.

Summary

Surprisingly few axes have been reported from most regions of southeastern New Mexico, considering the importance of wood as a building material. Full-grooved and three-quarter grooved forms were in use in the El Paso Phase. Within the Sierra Blanca Region, the full-grooved form was a heavy favorite. None of the spiraled-grooved type described by Kidder (1932:50–51) and Stubbs and Stallings (1953:105) have been reported from southeastern New Mexico. Fibrolite was imported only in historic times.

Grooved Hammers, Mauls, and Other Hafted Tools

Sierra Blanca Region

Hafted tools for pecking or pounding were rare; however, a few specimens were found in every phase. A spherical hammerstone from the Bonnell Site was full grooved at the midsection. Full-grooved mauls from the Bonnell Site (late Glencoe Phase) and from Hiner Site 2 (Corona Phase) resembled each other in shape, weight, and placement of the groove toward the poll. Three mauls were reported from Bloom Mound (Lincoln Phase). The remaining Lincoln Phase example from Block Lookout was made from a mano that had the full groove placed at the midsection.

Comparisons

Chupadero Region: Grooved hammerstones and a grooved maul were present at Pueblo Pardo.

South-central New Mexico: The spherical-to-ovoid mauls reported from the Alamogordo Sites 1 and 2 (Lehmer 1948:66) fit Woodbury's description (1954:45) of spherical full-grooved hammers, except for the off-center groove on the Alamogordo Site specimen (Lehmer 1948:Pl. XXXIVa).

Summary

Woodbury commented that in general the full-grooved hammers are to be found where full-grooved axes were in use, and this is true for southeastern New Mexico. Grooved tools were never numerous, however.

Hafted stone hoes and picks were a diagnostic tool type of the El Paso Phase, and one was reported from the site at Three Rivers (Cosgrove and Cosgrove 1965:5), showing that the trait had spread into the northern Tularosa Basin. None have yet been reported from the Sierra Blanca or Chupadero Regions.

HAMMERSTONES

Hammer or pecking stones were used in all regions and phases of southeastern New Mexico. Pebbles of chert, quartzite, and even heavy igneous rocks were selected. Gradations from barely battered to spherical have been found, although the well-used, spherical forms were rare. It was more common to use a pebble and then discard it. Cylindrical and discoidal forms were absent.

Provenience of Specimens Transported to the Lab for Study

Block Lookout	4
LA 2945	4
Phillips	3
Bloom Mound	3
2000 A	1
Bonnell	14
Hiner 1	1

These do not represent the total number, as some specimens were left in the field. A number of other tool categories functioned in part as pecking or hammerstones. For example, most small grinding stones were battered on the ends.

COOKING ACCESSORIES

Comales

Sierra Blanca Region

A flat stone with a black, soot-like coating found at the Bonnell Site may have been a *comal* or griddle. No others were reported from the Sierra Blanca Region.

Comparison

Comales were common in the Pueblo I Gran Quivira Pithouse Village (Fenenga 1956:231) and they occurred at Pueblo Pardo (Toulouse and Stephenson 1960:28) and at Abo Mission (Toulouse 1949:23). We may conclude that they were typical of the northern Anasazi phases in southeastern New Mexico and that they were not in use in south-central New Mexico.

Pot Lids

Sierra Blanca Region

The only objects identified as possible pot lids were some disc bases of Chupadero Black-on-White pottery that had been slightly smoothed around the edges from the Bonnell Site.

Comparisons

South-central New Mexico: A thin, roughly circular limestone slab ground to a convex surface on one side was found at Los Tules, and Lehmer (1948:33) suggests its use as a pot lid. A similar specimen came from one of the Alamogordo sites (ibid.:69).

Chupadero Region: The 36 stone discs at Pueblo Pardo (Toulouse and Stephenson 1960:30) may or may not have served this function.

Fire Dogs

Sierra Blanca Region

A cylindrical stone of the floor of Room 13, House Unit 46, Phillips Site, may have been a "fire dog" or an anvil. No other possible examples were encountered in the Sierra Blanca Region.

Comparisons

South-central New Mexico: This trait was apparently absent from Mesilla and El Paso Phases and from the site at Three Rivers as well.

Chupadero Region: Slab-lined firepits equipped with both stationary and movable fire dogs were associated with the latest houses excavated.

Cooking Racks

Sierra Blanca Region

The post holes encircling a firepit in House 13, Bonnell Site, have already been discussed with architectural features. They are mentioned here for the sake of functional interpretation.

Summary

The cooking accessories considered above reveal some differences in food preparation habits. *Comales* or griddles were probably used for making thin corn bread like *piki*, much as Stephen (1936) described for the Hopi. Griddles were found in every phase in the Chupadero Region for which data are available, and when the intervening phases are explored, griddles will probably be found. Equipment for making *piki* is lacking from all phases in south-central New Mexico, and only one possible example of a griddle was found in the Sierra Blanca Region. "Fire dogs" have the same geographical distribution, as might be expected if griddles and "fire dogs" were functionally related.

"Fire dogs" could also support cooking pots. The technique of supporting cooking pots above the fire is not evident for either south-central New Mexico or the Sierra Blanca Region. The postulated cooking stand or rack could represent an alternative solution. It is possible that pots rested in the ashes or coals; however, if the small interior firepits were used, air flow to the fire would seem to present a problem. Outdoor hearths may have been used for most of the cooking, in which case hearth stones could have supported the cooking pots.

CEREMONIAL, ORNAMENTAL, OR RECREATIONAL ARTIFACTS

Stone and Pottery Animal Figures

No stone and clay animal figures have been recovered from controlled excavations in the Sierra Blanca Region, but specimens have been collected by amateurs from Lincoln Phase sites. These will be considered with other examples from southeastern New Mexico. All of these are zoomorphic; insofar as we know, no anthropomorphic representations have been found in these media, although human figures were executed in petroglyphs and pictographs.

Provenience

Sites	*Number of Figures*	*References*
Phillips Site	3	Appendix 2
Nogal Mesa Site	1	Appendix 4
Las Cruces District	3	Lehmer 1948:53
Alamogordo Sites	4	Lehmer 1948:66
Pueblo Pardo Site	1	Toulouse and Stephenson 1960:30
Abo	3	Toulouse 1949:23
Total	15	

All were from the late Pueblo III - early Pueblo IV periods. Both stone and clay figures were fashioned. The largest of the above specimens was from Abo (14 inches long). The smallest were perhaps 2 inches long.

Most common were the block-like figures depicting bears and mountain sheep; one of the figures from the Las Cruces district looked suspiciously like a buffalo (Lehmer 1948:Pl. XXXVb). This general category of blocky figures most closely resembles certain Chihuahuan specimens (Sayles 1936:Pl. XVIII), a small quartz figure from Paa-ko (Lambert 1954:PL. XXXII), and a Zuni fetish (Chapman 1947).

Incense Burners (?)

Two specimens, one from Bloom Mound (Appendix 6) and one from one of the Alamogordo sites (Lehmer 1948:70), were similar in shape. Both were cylindrical; a terraced or stepped "altar" motif rose from the base. The Bloom Mound specimen was made of clay, and it had a slight depression on the upper surface. It was in Room C, which yielded a number of decorative and possibly ceremonial objects. The Alamogordo specimen was carved from a single piece of white stone on which faint traces of green, brown, black and blue decorations were visible; it was buried under a room floor. Lehmer mentions that the latter was almost identical to one in the Morrow collection at Las Cruces.

Pipes

Provenience in the Sierra Blanca Region

Pipes were a regular feature of Lincoln and late Glencoe Phase sites. Their absence from Corona and early Glencoe Phase sites may reflect the small available artifact sample.

Sites	*Stone Elbow*	*Stone Tubular*	*Pottery Tubular*
Bonnell	1	2	5
Bloom Mound		2	
Double Crossing			1
Block Lookout			3
Phillips			2
Total	1	4	11

Tubular Pipes in the Sierra Blanca Region, Southeastern New Mexico

Undecorated, tubular pottery pipes were the most common form of the late Glencoe and Lincoln Phases. In side view they were slightly convex. Two pipes from Block Lookout had punctation-incised decorations; one of these had a flange that delineated mouth and body sections. Stone tubular pipes were found at two sites. A simple tubular pipe fragment and a pipe fragment with a raised lip came from the Bonnell Site. From Bloom Mound, an unusually long stone pipe had one stone inlaid and a socket for a second inlay. The fourth stone specimen, from Bloom Mound, had a raised lip like the Bonnell specimen.

Tubular Pipes in South-central New Mexico

Mesilla Phase: Conical clay pipes found at Los Tules (Lehmer 1948:29) were similar to clay pipes from Swarts Ruin (Cosgrove and Cosgrove 1932:Pl. 103). This type did not survive into subsequent phases nor did it spread into the Sierra Blanca Region.

El Paso Phase: Tubular stone and clay pipes were common (Lehmer 1948:48, and 61). These differ from Glencoe and Lincoln Phase specimens in having straight to slightly concave lines in side view, and the bowl opening is larger (Lehmer 1948:Pl. XXXVIb).

Three Rivers or San Andres Phase: An incised tubular pipe was found at the Three Rivers Site (Cosgrove and Cosgrove 1965:3).

Tubular Pipes in the Chupadero Region

Pueblo Pardo Phase: None reported.

Salinas Phase: One incised clay tubular pipe was found in a refuse deposit at Abo Mission.

Elbow Pipes in Eastern New Mexico

A few pipes of probable Plains origin were widely scattered over eastern New Mexico. A stone elbow pipe was found at the Bonnell Site in an early Pueblo IV temporal context. It was not certain that elbow pipes were prehistoric at Pecos (Kidder 1932:85). Those at Paa-ko were definitely in the prehistoric levels (Lambert 1954:114–16).

Summary

Simple tubular pipes were the most common form throughout southeastern New Mexico. In south-central New Mexico there was a shift from the conical pipes of the Mesilla Phase to the longer, somewhat flared, tubular pipes of the El Paso Phase. Clay tubular pipes were preferred in the Glencoe Phase. Clay and stone pipes were equally important in the El Paso and Lincoln Phases. An unusually long, inlaid pipe from Bloom Mound was undoubtedly acquired by trade and it would be instructive to trace its place of manufacture. Pipes decorated with incised and punctate designs have a northerly distribution within southeastern New Mexico, suggesting distant affinities to the fancy pipes of Pecos, Forked Lightning, and Loma Lothrop (Kidder 1932:160–78). Elbow pipes occur rarely.

Gaming Pieces

Games of chance for pleasure or for ceremonial purposes must have been popular in the Sierra Blanca Region, as 53 gaming pieces were recovered from the Bonnell Site, and they were present at the Phillips Site (1), Block Lookout (2), and Bloom Mound (8).

Description

Round, rectangular, and lenticular forms occurred, often in sets which were matched in shape, thinness, and general workmanship; pieces of individual sets were surely made by the same artisan. Two sets (from Houses 1 and 3, Bonnell Site) each consisted of 10 matched rectangular or lenticular pieces and 3 matching round pieces with central, drilled pits. A set of 6 lenticular pieces from House 8, Bonnell Site, had red pigment on the cancellous surfaces.

Comparisons

While this type of game was popular with Glencoe and Lincoln Phase peoples, it was not widely practiced elsewhere in eastern New Mexico in the late Pueblo III - early Pueblo IV period. Bone gaming sticks were absent from all phases in south-central New Mexico, as well as from Pueblo Pardo, from Pindi, and from Pecos. One was recovered at Paa-ko (Lambert 1954:156).

Closest relationships are to Pueblo I to III gaming pieces in Anasazi regions. Those illustrated in Morris and Burgh (1954:Fig. 95) were similar in shape to the Sierra Blanca Region series, but the latter group did not have such consistent scoring of one face. By Pueblo III, bone gaming pieces were declining in frequency in the Anasazi regions, as only 16 were recovered from Pueblo Bonito (Judd 1954:279).

Dice or gaming pieces from Tularosa and Cordova caves were never numerous but at least one was found in each phase (Martin et al. 1952:190). A few bone gaming pieces came from Swartz Ruin (Cosgrove and Cosgrove 1932:61). One gaming piece came from the Tularosa Phase site of Apache Creek (Martin et al. 1957:81).

Wooden sticks or counters were in use in the Hueco Mountains (Cosgrove 1947:152–53), but bone pieces were not reported.

Summary

Bone gaming pieces continued in common use in the Glencoe and Lincoln Phases until early Pueblo IV times, whereas they had passed their peak of popularity in most other parts of the Southwest by Pueblo III times.

Bone Whistles

Provenience

The following specimens have been found in the Sierra Blanca Region:

Site	*No. of One-stop Tubular Whistles*	*Bitsitsi Whistle*
Bonnell	2	
Block Lookout	1	
Bloom Mound	7	1

Description

One-stop whistles were made from slender long bones. All reported examples were less than 4 inches in length. Two matched bone pieces found together at Bloom Mound are interpreted as a *Bitsitsi* whistle.

Comparisons

A single one-stop flageolet from Pueblo Pardo was made from a turkey bone (Toulouse and Stephenson 1960:31). The *Bitsitsi* whistle from Bloom Mound is similar to Pindi specimens (Stubbs and Stallings 1953:Pl. 35c). Wheat (1955b:144) notes that whistles occur only in the Forestdale Branch of the Mogollon, where they were probably an intrusive northern trait.

Summary

Distributional evidence gives a clue to their historic derivation, as whistles and related artifacts are absent in south-central New Mexico and in most of the Mogollon area while they are present in the Chupadero Region, Middle Rio Grande, and upper Pecos Valley. Lincoln and Glencoe Phase whistles therefore are assumed to be related to eastern Anasazi whistles.

Bone Tubes

Tubular bone objects may be grouped with bone beads, as Toulouse and Stephenson (1960:Pl. 40) have done. Some of the longer, more slender tubes may have been part of a shaman's paraphernalia or served other functions.

From the Sierra Blanca Region, elongated, unincised bone tubes have been reported from the Glencoe Phase. Bone tubes were missing from the cultural inventory of south-central New Mexico and apparently from all Mogollon regions, as the large bone tubes described by Wheat (1955b:144) are quite different from these. On the other hand, elongated bone tubes are present in the eastern Anasazi, and a relationship between these and the Glencoe Phase specimens is assumed.

Miscellaneous Bone Items Probably Used for Personal Adornment

A large bone tube from the Bonnell Site had two cut slits in one side (Pl. 59d). Encircling marks appear at each end and at the midsection; some of these are incisions and others are worn as if a thong or string had been tied around the item. "Ceremonial," musical, and ornamental functions have been suggested.

A flat, carved bone from the Bonnell Site was similar to a specimen from Bloom Mound (Pl. 74). The latter had two long, parallel prongs like a hair pin. A "pendant" illustrated from one of the Alamogordo sites (Lehmer 1948:Pl. XXV) was fashioned in a related manner. A two-pronged bone object from Pecos had a simple, squared end (Kidder 1932:Fig. 206f). Another specimen that closely resembles these three was found by the author in an unnamed site just north of the Lubbock Lake Site on the Texas South Plains, where it was associated with Scallorn arrow points, other chipped stone tools, and numerous bison bones. The shape of these artifacts would permit their use as hair pins.

TABLE 2
DISTRIBUTION OF ORNAMENTS,
SIERRA BLANCA REGION

Ornament Categories	Bonnell	Bloom Mound	Block Lookout	F. Sulte-meier	Phillips	Hiner	Total
Strombus	1 Bead		1 Breast Plate				2
Olivella beads	226		64				290
Oliva beads or tinklers	2	42					44
Glycymeris bracelets	1					1	2
Disc beads (all materials)	2	1770 to 2182(?)				1	>1773
Ground-stone pendants	3	2					5
Worked turquoise	3						3
"Mussel" shell							
Perforated							
Geometric	12	5					17
Zoomorphic	2						2
Unperforated							
Zoomorphic	1						1
Geometric	16						16
Cut pieces	16				1		17
Bone beads							
Tubular	3	6					9
Flat	1						1
Wooden bead	1						1
Bone "hair ornaments"	1	1					2
Gypsum ornament (?)	1						1
Copper bells		7					7
Shell buttons or pendants, species unidentified	1			1			2
Misc. stone pendant or bead		1					1
Total	293	>1834	65	1	1	2	>2196

Ornaments

Materials

Olivella, Oliva, and *Glycymeris* shells were acquired from the Pacific coast. Two specimens were made of *Strombus* from Atlantic waters. Local freshwater shells have not been identified to species; a thorough analysis of the shell material would probably show that other species were imported.

Stones used to make beads and pendants included siltstone, compact limestone, quartz, amethyst, turquoise, gypsum, and others as yet unidentified.

Bone beads were made in flat, tubular, and small disc forms. Some pronged bone pieces from Bloom Mound and the Bonnell Site were discussed above. Wooden and other perishable materials must have been used for decorative purposes, as attested by the charred wooden bead from the Bonnell Site.

Aside from the disc beads that were so common in El Paso Phase sites, in the Hueco Caves, and at Bloom Mound, the most favored raw material throughout southeastern New Mexico was shell. Turquoise, held in such high esteem elsewhere in the Southwest, was used sparingly and one assumes that it was difficult to obtain.

Distribution

Table 2 lists the distribution of ornaments in sites in the Sierra Blanca Region. The largest sample of material culture came from the Bonnell Site, and it was from this site that we got the most varied ornament inventory. All species of imported shells were represented by at least one specimen, and "mussel" shell ornaments were varied in form. Disc beads were not well represented at the Bonnell Site, and no copper bells were found. In general, the Bonnell ornaments have a home-made look, with only a few choice items obtained by trade.

Bloom Mound also produced a large array of material culture, and the emphasis in their ornamentation was quite different from that at the Bonnell Site. *Oliva* tinklers and copper bells were imported. The number of copper bells recovered from Bloom Mound (7) is an impressive quantity for any site in the Southwest, including Hohokam sites. Disc beads were the most numerous ornament category. "Mussel" shell pendants were present. The absence of *Olivella* beads from Bloom Mound is puzzling, in view of the large sample of goods recovered and of the extensive trade indicated by other factors. Other sites are represented by such small artifact samples that generalizations are not in order.

Place of Manufacture

Freshwater bivalves were locally worked in the Sierra Blanca Region. Cut and unworked shell scrap found at the Bonnell Site indicated that it may have been a local manufacturing center. Cut shell also occurred at Site 2000 in the Peñasco Valley. Imported shell objects apparently arrived in the Sierra Blanca Region as finished products; at least no scrap of imported shell types has been found. Disc beads in El Paso Phase sites and at Bloom Mound may be of local manufacture because many raw materials such as siltstone are to be found locally. No bead abraders such as are illustrated by Judd (1954:86) have been found, but simple sandstone abraders could have been used. Since bone was locally worked at all sites, the decorative bone objects may well have been made locally.

Comparisons

South-central New Mexico: Olivella and *Glycymeris* shell ornaments were found in the Mesilla Phase. These shells were present in considerable numbers in the El Paso Phase, when discoidal beads became popular and *Conus* tinklers were used. In both phases shell pendants were often made in a conventionalized fish form. An illustrated pendant from a cache in the Hueco Basin looks very much like a parrot (Moore and Wheat 1951:Pl. 22w). Stone ornaments and charms were also fairly numerous, and bone rings were made (Lehmer 1948:29, 48, 62). This emphasis on discoidal beads and the common occurrence of tinkler beads had its closest parallels to Bloom Mound in the Sierra Blanca Region. It is probable that the *Glycymeris* specimens at the Bonnell Site and Hiner Site 1 were obtained from or channelled through the lower Tularosa Basin region. Copper bells have been reported from the El Paso Phase, and one copper bell was found at Three Rivers, where it probably dates from the San Andres Phase. Bloom Mound copper bells were probably obtained from El Paso Phase villages.

Mimbres Region: In the Mimbres Phase, the shell inventory was similar to, but more elaborate than, those of El Paso and Lincoln Phases.

Hueco Caves: Materials from the Hueco Caves cannot be accurately dated. Discoidal beads strung on hair and yucca cord, pieces of perforated gypsum strung on yucca fiber cord, *Olivella* beads, turquoise chunks, fish bones, freshwater mussel pendants, bone beads, a reed necklace, and a seed necklace were reported (Cosgrove 1947:151–52, Fig. 144, 146, 147). *Glycymeris* shell was apparently absent; the popularity of disc beads was reminiscent of El Paso Phase sites and of Bloom Mound.

Chupadero Region: The ornamental assemblage from Pueblo Pardo was not large and probably not representative. A perforated, shaped scapula may have been a pendant, and bird bones were made into tubular beads. Two pendants were made of freshwater mussel shell and one small *Olivella* was found (Toulouse and Stephenson 1960:31–32).

Upper Pecos and Middle Rio Grande Region: Turquoise was used for a few pendants, and it was the major material used for disc beads at Pecos. All of the shell species recognized for southeastern New Mexico were present at Pecos in expectably larger numbers. When the total quantity of goods from Pecos is compared with the lesser quantities found in southeastern New Mexican sites, the number of *Oliva* and *Conus* tinklers from Bloom Mound and El Paso Phase sites looms large. The *Strombus* pendant illustrated by Kidder (1932:Fig. 165a) is similar in shape and technique of decoration to the one from Block Lookout (Pl. 34).

Sites such as Arrowhead, Pindi, and Paa-ko seem poor in the general area of ornamentation when compared to Pecos, or even to sites in southeastern

New Mexico. Since so many of the shell types present at Pecos are also found in El Paso Phase sites, it is possible that one route of the shell trade to Pecos led through the lower Tularosa Basin and up the Pecos River, via Bloom Mound.

Summary: It is difficult to unravel the history of the shell trade and of trends in ornamentation with the spotty archaeological record at our disposal. *Glycymeris* and *Olivella* shells were being acquired by Pueblo II times in the Mesilla Phase. No shells or ornaments were found at Gran Quivira Pithouse Village, or in the Pueblo I and II middle Pecos Valley sites. Our few early Pueblo III sites yielded no pertinent information. By late Pueblo III, *Glycymeris* was being traded to the Sierra Blanca Region. *Conus* and *Oliva* tinkler beads were plentiful in El Paso Phase sites and at Bloom Mound. Local, freshwater mussel shell was worked into geometric shapes in Pueblo Pardo, El Paso, Lincoln, and Glencoe Phases. Fish and bird zoomorphic motifs were executed in freshwater bivalve shell in the El Paso and Glencoe Phases.

Copper bells were limited to El Paso and San Andres Phases in the Tularosa Basin and to one site of the Lincoln Phase.

The widely distributed bone beads were perhaps made locally in all regions. Bone rings, limited to the Mesilla and El Paso Phases, did not diffuse eastward or northward.

Turquoise was a scarce commodity in the Sierra Blanca Region. It was more plentiful in south-central New Mexico where the Oro Grande mines were located. It was likewise more abundant at Pecos.

Summary

Bone tubes, bone whistles or flageolets, the *Bitsitsi* whistle, bone gaming pieces, and tubular pipes, especially those decorated with incision, have ties to the eastern Anasazi area.

The *Strombus* pendant, *Strombus* bead, and elbow pipes originated in areas to the east. Since it is probable that trade routes followed the valleys across the Plains, it is unlikely that these items were directly acquired via the South Plains. A more probable route was along the Canadian River, perhaps through Pecos Pueblo where similar goods have been found. A reverse route from Sierra Blanca Region sites to Pecos may have supplied the latter pueblo with *Oliva* and *Conus* tinklers, *Glycymeris* shells, and other western imports.

Bloom Mound, alone among Lincoln Phase sites, shares a number of specific traits with the El Paso Phase: "incense burners," copper bells, *Oliva* tinklers, and a definite preference for disc beads.

"Mussel" shell pendants were an important element in personal adornment for both Glencoe and Lincoln Phase peoples, a trait shared with the El Paso

Phase and late Hueco Phase. *Glycymeris, Oliva,* and *Olivella* shells were common to all these phases.

Blocky animal figures, the stone substitute *sipapu* (discussed with architectural features), *Olivella* shells and bone beads are known from south-central New Mexico, the Chupadero Region, and the Sierra Blanca Region.

WEAPONS COMPLEX

The artifacts described below are those found in open sites. Perishable items such as nets, snares, traps, clubs, and so forth, were preserved only in dry caves.

Arrow Shaft-straighteners

Description

Arrow shaft-straighteners from the Bonnell Site, typical of those found elsewhere in the Sierra Blanca Region, are described in some detail in Appendix 5. The majority of specimens have a single transverse groove. Elaborate shaft-straighteners with well-made ridges or multiple grooves were rare. Few specimens would have been suitable for use in pairs, and it is doubtful if any were so used.

Provenience

Site	*No. of Shaft-straighteners*
LA 2945	1
Bonnell	15
Hiner Site 1	4
Block Lookout	4
Nogal Canyon	1

None were reported from early Glencoe or Corona Phase sites; however, they were common in late Glencoe and Lincoln Phase sites.

Other Regions

Absent in the Mesilla Phase, arrow shaft-straighteners of the transversely grooved type were common in El Paso Phase sites. The seven specimens from the Bradfield Site were rather uniform in shape and workmanship; double transverse grooves occurred. Examples from Alamogordo Sites 1 and 2 were more irregular; in most cases, the original pebble shape was not altered greatly. Some of these specimens had been carved into effigy figures of the human foot and various animal forms (Lehmer 1948:64).

Five shaft-straighteners from Pueblo Pardo had longitudinal grooves, and some had a ridge parallel to the groove (Toulouse and Stephenson 1960:28). Limestone and micaceous schist were used to make these tools.

Use of Shaft-straighteners

The coarse stones used in the Bradfield Site specimens, including vesicular lava, made it likely that these were used as abrading instruments; perhaps wooden arrow shafts were in use in the El Paso Phase (following the suggestions of Woodbury 1954:109). Raw materials were not noted for the other El Paso Phase specimens. On the other hand, the fine-grained materials used in Sierra Blanca Region specimens and in those reported from Pueblo Pardo (Chupadero Region) may well have been used for straightening arrow shafts of cane or reeds (ibid.). The presence of natural and carved ridges on some specimens may be related to the latter technique. The form of specimens illustrated from Alamogordo Sites 1 and 2 (Lehmer 1948:67) suggest that arrow shafts (of cane and reed?) were straightened in El Paso Phase sites, as well as abraded. It seems unlikely that any of the arrow shaft-straighteners reported from southeastern New Mexico were used in pairs.

Summary

Arrow shaft-straighteners with transverse grooves were present in El Paso, Glencoe, and Lincoln Phases; a middle or late Pueblo III date is indicated for the introduction of this artifact type. The Pueblo Pardo Phase specimens had longitudinal grooves and well-developed ridges. We do not know when the tool type entered the Chupadero Region, but it was definitely present in Pueblo IV.

The arrow shaft-straighteners of the subarea are of the type that first appeared in the Southwest during Pueblo II, but which diminished in frequency in central and western New Mexico after Pueblo III (Woodbury 1954:111). They were present at Pecos, but their earliest appearance there is in a Glaze II association (Kidder 1932:80). None of the fancier Pecos types have been reported from southeastern New Mexico. It must be remembered that all of southeastern New Mexico, except the Chupadero Region, was virtually abandoned by horticulturalists by the Glaze II period. Elongated, loaf-shaped, and ridged shaft-smoothers, which were more popular in Pueblo III, IV, and V sites in western New Mexico, were never introduced into southeastern New Mexico.

Projectile Points

Point frequency in the Sierra Blanca Region

Sites	*Number of Points*
Clint Sultemeier 1	3
2000 A	2
Phillips	44
Hiner 1	7
Frank Sultemeier	1
Block Lookout	65
Bloom Mound	65
Bonnell	161

Points were absent from the earliest Glencoe Phase sites, uncommon in Corona Phase sites, and well represented in late Glencoe and Lincoln Phase collections.

Some larger, thicker, heavier specimens from the Bonnell, Phillips, and Bloom Mound sites have been called dart points in this report. This form was never numerous in these sites, and the actual function of these points is open to question. The most common arrow point forms were corner- or diagonal-notched, side-notched, and unnotched triangles.

Dart Points in Southeastern New Mexico

PaleoIndian or Early Lithic points are common surface finds; however, the only reported excavated specimen is the Burnet Cave Folsom point (Howard 1935). Atlatls and darts with pointed wooden or stone tips were found in caves in the Hueco Mountains, where the bow and arrow was absent (Cosgrove 1947:48–54). The illustrated points were small, with a 1⅞-inch maximum length, and all but one had side or diagonal notches (Cosgrove 1947:Fig. 131a–f). These fall within the range of Ellis-Ensor types which survived until A.D. 500 or 1000 in Texas (Suhm and Jelks 1962:187–90). The exception (Cosgrove 1947:Fig. 131d) was similar to the Langtry type, which lasted until approximately A.D. 700 or 800 in adjacent regions of Texas (Suhm and Jelks 1962:205, Pl. 103).

The small size of these dart points reflected a trend toward miniaturization of point types that were larger elsewhere, as, for example, in central Texas. This same tendency was noted in South Plains dart points during a photographic survey of private collections from that region of Texas. Over 2600 points were photographed by the author in a cooperative project with the South Plains Archaeological Society during 1961–63. Some 900 points could be classified as "Archaic" dart points. The South Plains specimens exhibited the same outline as central Texas types but were consistently smaller. In private collections from both the South Plains and southeastern New Mexico, the Ellis-Ensor shape was conspicuous, but earlier, rectangular-stemmed points were virtually absent. It may be that Early Lithic points survived later in the South Plains and in this part of the Southwest.

Diffusion of the Bow and Arrow into Southeastern New Mexico

Available evidence suggests that the bow and arrow diffused into southeastern New Mexico about A.D. 900 or 1000. The bow and arrow was the primary weapon of the sedentary agriculturalists while the atlatl and darts survived to a later date among the gathering peoples of the southern mountains. Darts and arrows were present in the second level at Hermit's Cave, the latter being more numerous (Ferdon 1946:25). This culture level antedates the upper level which contained Chupadero Black-on-White and Lincoln Black-on-Red pottery.

Farther south at the mouth of the Pecos River, Kelley (1950:71–74) and Taylor (1949:73–88) postulated that bows and arrows belonged to the Chisos Focus, beginning about A.D. 900.

In the middle Pecos Valley around Fort Sumner, Jelinek defined the Yeso Phase as the latest preceramic culture. Yeso type points would be called Scallorns if found a few miles to the east, and the knife blades which he illustrated would be called Ellis and Ensor dart points (Jelinek 1960:Pl. IVB).

Certain points from Glencoe and Lincoln Phase sites were called dart points in this report because of their weight, thickness and width. They were almost identical to the Hueco Caves series of dart points. The absence of perishable shafts from these open sites made it impossible to determine if darts were still in use at this time.

Arrow Point Sequence

Points were absent from Gran Quivira Pithouse Village, the only excavated Pueblo I site in southeastern New Mexico. Jelinek's Yeso points may belong in the Pueblo I period, and these were corner or diagonal notched. This form apparently was dominant in Pueblo II sites in the northern part of the subarea, as Jelinek reported them from P4, and they were present at Taylor Draw. A barbed, diagonally-notched arrow form with a small stem (like the specimen in Jelinek 1960:Pl. VIII A1, or like Fig. 61t-x in this report) was especially distinctive and occurs in many Southwestern regions in Pueblo I and II (Haury 1936:Pl. XVII a–b, Morris and Burgh 1954:Fig. 81,1f–i).

By Pueblo II times, and perhaps earlier, rather crude side-notched points, often with convex bases, were being made. These resemble miniature Ensor dart types, and these arrow points probably originated as diminuitives of older dart forms rather than as a diffusion of a new type of arrow point.

In the southern part of southeastern New Mexico during Pueblo II, both corner- or diagonal-notched and side-notched arrow points were made (Lehmer 1948:Pl. VII). A Livermore point from Los Tules was probably acquired through trade from Texas. Slender, triangular points with straight or concave bases (Lehmer 1948:Pl. VIIa–c) were in use from Mesilla to El Paso Phases. This latter type, which seems atypical of the Pueblo II period in the Southwest, may be a regional development; the same point type continued into the El Paso Phase and occurred in the late Glencoe Phase.

Early Pueblo III arrow points were not well represented, and it was not clear whether the triangular forms (notched and unnotched), so common in Pueblo III and later sites over the Southwest, arrived in southeastern New Mexico at the beginning or middle of this period. They were the dominant type of the late Glencoe and Lincoln Phases.

Unnotched triangular points with a width-length ratio of at least 1:2 are called Fresno points in Texas, where the side-notched forms are called Harrell points. The dates of their appearance in southeastern New Mexico and in the Southwest correspond to the sudden and widespread appearance of these closely related types in Texas, on the Great Plains, and elsewhere. It is obvious that in this case we are dealing with the widespread diffusion of a point type, in contrast to the postulated *in situ* development of the earlier side-notched arrow points of Pueblo I and II.

The diffusion of Fresno and Harrell types was not uniform, as the types were absent from the El Paso Phase sites. At the Bradfield Site, all points were of the slender, triangular form that first appeared at Los Tules. These were also typical at the Alamogordo sites, where a minority of corner-notched and crudely side-notched points occurred (Lehmer 1948:48–49, 62). One of four points from Pueblo Pardo was of the Harrell type, showing that while the type had diffused to the Chupadero Region, it had not replaced older forms. Distributional evidence of the Harrell and Fresno types suggests that these diffused into the Sierra Blanca Region from the South Plains rather than from adjacent regions in the Southwest.

Summary

During preceramic times, it is doubtful if hunting was very important in the mountain regions of southeastern New Mexico. All excavated dry caves show a strong emphasis on collected wild products. The bow and arrow apparently arrived about A.D. 900, at about the time that agriculturalists were becoming established. It is possible that the agriculturalists initiated the diffusion of the bow and arrow. Hunting was more important to certain agricultural groups than it had been to the earlier collectors.

SMALL TOOLS USED IN CRAFTS

Most artifact categories included here receive less than their fair share of attention from archaeologists and their typology is far from satisfactory. Data from Sierra Blanca Region sites are detailed as fully as possible in the site reports (Appendices 1 to 8). Comparative data from south-central New Mexico lacks quantification, and these tool categories were not well represented at Pueblo Pardo.

Chipped Stone Tools

Throughout southeastern New Mexico, chipped stone tools other than projectile points did not achieve standardization. The general scarcity of good grades of siliceous materials was noted in Chapter 1. Limestone, basalt, siltstone, and other materials of poor fracturability were pressed into service for piercing, cutting, and scraping. Flakes, usually with a low working angle, were seldom altered extensively and the original flake form can be seen in most specimens. The tool categories and frequencies for Sierra Blanca Region sites are given in Table 3.

TABLE 3
DISTRIBUTION OF EXCAVATED CHIPPED STONE TOOLS, SIERRA BLANCA REGION

Tool Types	Clint Sulte-meier 1	Mayhill 2	Bonnell	Block Lookout	Bloom Mound	Phillips	LA 2945	Total
Knives	1		8	4	5			18
Bifacial ovates			2					2
Drills			9	2	1	2		14
Gravers			11		1			12
Bifacial retouched flakes								
One edge			4	8		9		21
Two edges			2					2
Scrapers								
Side			9	6	5		5	25
End			1					1
Core planers			3	1				4
Unifacial retouched flakes	10	3	87	16	not recorded	18		134
Choppers:								
Bifacial							3	3
Unifacial		1	3			4		8
Miscellaneous			2	1				3
Total	11	4	141	38	12	33	8	247

Few of the chipped stone tool categories lend themselves to comparative treatment because of the lack of standardization in the tools themselves. Unused or barely used flakes were excluded from this analysis. The amount of work carried out with random, unshaped flakes at the Phillips Site, for instance, was far greater than the tabulation of classifiable tools indicates. This particular site was close to a silicified shale mine that was exploited during the Lincoln Phase by individuals from this village, and the quantity of shale flakes is described in Appendix 2.

Drills were apparently absent in Corona and early Glencoe Phases, for which the artifact sample was small. Drills were likewise absent from the Mesilla Phase, where a more representative tool sample was obtained at Los Tules. Drills of the late Glencoe, Lincoln, El Paso, and Pueblo Pardo Phases were mainly of the expanded-stem type, although a few straight-stemmed specimens occurred.

It is my impression that small chipped stone tools were comparatively more numerous in Glencoe and Lincoln Phases than in either the El Paso or Pueblo Pardo Phases. Hunting seems to have been more widely practiced in the Glencoe and Lincoln Phases, possibly resulting in more leather work which would call for more chipped stone tools; perhaps the whole hunting–leatherworking complex was in part due to proximity to the Plains.

Bone Awls

Provenience and gross quantity of bone awls from Sierra Blanca Region sites is given in Table 4. Types of awls are described in the site reports, Appendices 1 to 8. A preference for rib bones was noted in Lincoln Phase sites, whereas metapodial bones were more frequently chosen for awls in Glencoe Phase sites.

TABLE 4
DISTRIBUTION OF EXCAVATED BONE TOOLS, SIERRA BLANCA REGION

Sites	Awls	Weaving Tools (?)	Scraping-polishing Tools	Punches and Flakes	Miscellaneous
2000 A	5				1
2000 B	1				
Bonnell	98	1	28	13	33
Phillips	5				4
LA 2945	1				
Block Lookout	22			6	5
Hiner 1	7		1	1	1
Bloom Mound	29	1	1	3	16
Total	167	2	30	23	60

Awl heads carved into stylized mountain sheep designs found at Site 2000 and the Bonnell Site (Pl. 59e, obverse view in Pl. 60A, f) are almost identical with awls bearing mountain sheep designs from Swarts Ruin (Cosgrove and Cosgrove 1932:Pl. 59).

Only one awl was found at Los Tules, suggesting that crafts requiring awls were not well developed during the Mesilla Phase. Awls increased in frequency during the El Paso Phase, and they were well represented in contemporary Glencoe and Lincoln Phase sites. Awls were not numerous at Pueblo Pardo in comparison to other artifact categories.

Other Small Bone Tools

Other categories of bone tools were not sufficiently well represented to trace their history in the Sierra Blanca Region.

The largest artifact sample is from the Bonnell Site, and it is from there that we have the most diverse selection of bone tools. Twenty-eight bone tools were used for scraping or polishing; many of these were made from deer scapulae. Punches or flakers were made from antler tines or split long bones.

Scapula scrapers were absent from both south-central New Mexico and the Chupadero Region. One scapula scraper was found at Pecos (Kidder 1932:Fig. 196e). The Sierra Blanca specimens and that from Pecos reflect Plains influence along the eastern frontier. Fleshing tools, present at Pecos, did not penetrate into the Sierra Blanca Region.

Detailed comparisons of minor bone tools are not possible at this time. It is my impression that bone tools are more numerous and varied in Glencoe and Lincoln Phases than in the El Paso and Pueblo Pardo Phases. As mentioned in regard to chipped stone tools, this may reflect the importance of hunting and of crafts based on hunting by-products, which in turn may reflect Plains influence or proximity.

Polishing Stones

Proveniences

Sites	*Polishing Pebbles*
Bonnell Site	15
Hiner 1	5
Phillips	2
Block Lookout	26
Bloom Mound	6

Discussion

Small quartz and quartzite pebbles from 1 to 3 inches in diameter were suitable for polishing pottery. Large polishing stones, sometimes referred to as floor polishers, have not been reported.

Comparisons

Small polishing pebbles were absent in the El Paso Phase, presumably because they were not used in the manufacture of El Paso Polychrome which was finished by scraping. The sherd scrapers typical of both the Mesilla and El Paso Phases may have performed this task. Polishers were found at Pueblo Pardo.

DISPOSAL OF THE DEAD

Customarily, interment involved flexing the body and placing it in a shallow grave which was roughly oriented with a cardinal direction. The grave could be located in house fill, below the floor of occupied structures or in the sheet trash between houses (Table 5). Variability in grave locations is most clearly demonstrated at the Bonnell Site, where most of one section of the village was cleared. At other sites, the percentage of sub-floor or room burials is probably unrealistically high because excavation was largely limited to architectural units.

TABLE 5
DISPOSAL OF THE DEAD, SIERRA BLANCA REGION

	Intentionally Buried					Badly Scattered or Un-buried Individuals	Total
Sites	Extra-mural	Within House Limits	In House Fill	Sub-floor	With Offerings		
Mayhill 2			2*				2
2000 A	1	3			2		6
2000 B	1						1
Hiner 1	1*						1
LA 2945	1*	1*		1	1		4
Block Lookout		1	5	2			8
Bonnell	12	3	2	5	2	4(?)	28(?)
Bloom Mound						15 or more	15+
Total	16	8	9	8	5	19+	65+

*Those burials probably made before or after the excavated architectural units were occupied.

Grave offerings were rare. In one of three burials at LA 2945, a mano was placed between the back of the skull and the pit edge (Wendorf 1956:95). Jennings (1940:9) reported that two of four burials at Site 2000 A had bowls inverted over the face, and that one of these bowls had been "killed." At Block Lookout, one infant had a *Strombus* pendant or breast plate, and a second infant had a necklace of *Olivella* beads and a small bowl was next to the body. Only two of the twenty-two individuals at the Bonnell Site definitely had non-perishable goods placed with the body. One infant had a four or five strand *Olivella* necklace and a "killed" bowl had been placed over the face. An adult had a "killed" bowl inverted over the face. The latter burial was unusual in that the bottom of the grave had been burned and a few fire-cracked rocks were in the grave fill. In general, grave offerings were rarely made, and they were more likely to be placed with children than with adults.

Comparisons

Flexed burials, usually extra-mural, in small graves with few or no offerings, were typical of the Mesilla and El Paso Phases. Sub-floor burial was practiced in some El Paso Phase sites. If, as Lehmer (1948:82) suggested, El Paso Phase burials were localized in trash heaps, this would be a major contrast with the Sierra Blanca practices. Grave offerings were apparently rare in both phases.

Cremation, flexed inhumation, and extended inhumation were practiced in both Pueblo Colorado and Pueblo Pardo Phases (Toulouse and Stephenson 1960:34–35). Cremations were placed in small sub-floor pits. Inhumations were placed in cists, some of which were slab lined. This variation in techniques of disposing of the dead contrasts sharply with the more standard burial form of the Glencoe and Lincoln Phases.

Cremations of unknown date were found in Burnet Cave in the Guadalupe Mountains (Howard 1935:67–69), and cremations occurred in the lower Pecos Valley (Cosgrove 1947:162). A few cremations were found at Swarts Ruin (Cosgrove and Cosgrove 1932:25–26), but flexed inhumations were more common. It was a rare Mimbreño who was unaccompanied by grave offerings or personal adornment. The burned grave at the Bonnell Site may be related to the Mimbres practice of placing ashes and burned materials in the grave (Cosgrove and Cosgrove 1932:27).

Flexed inhumations with relatively few accompanying objects were typical of Pueblo III and IV in the Middle Rio Grande and Galisteo Basin. The extended position was rare in the Rio Grande, but occasional examples have been noted from Pueblo I (Peckham 1957b:55, 69) to late prehistoric times (Lambert 1954:165).

WOVEN MATERIALS

In rare instances, charred woven materials have been preserved in Sierra Blanca Region sites. Mats, coiled basketry, and a textile fragment from Bloom Mound are described in Appendix 6.

POTTERY OF THE SIERRA BLANCA REGION

Type names and formal descriptions of all pottery types used in this report are in the literature. Some new variants are recognized in this study and the range of variation of some types is expanded.

In considering the ways and means of presenting the pottery data in this study, an attempt was made to apply the Type-Cluster-System scheme of Wheat, Gifford and Wasley (1958:34–47). Jelinek (1960:App. B) used this framework for pottery from the middle Pecos Valley, thereby establishing a precedent in southeastern New Mexico pottery taxonomy. The conservatism and lag manifest in these regions made it impossible to assign types and ceramic systems to a single period.

The pottery that would belong to a Jornada Brown system or to a Chupadero Black-on-White system spans several periods in the Pecos Classification and was of wide geographical extent. The time span of a Jornada Brown system would be on the order of the "Hopewell Zoned Stamped Ceramic System" that Phillips set up as a trial case (Phillips 1958:124). Furthermore, the limitation of type clusters and ceramic systems to a single class of pottery was contrary to the ceramic relationships assumed by most archaeologists who have worked with this pottery. The application of this scheme resulted, in this case, in separating certain small groups of sherds bearing painted decoration from sherds that appeared to be identical in every other respect. Decorated brown sherds never exceeded 5% of a ceramic lot, and more frequently ran from 0% to 2%. In Jelinek's Jornada Brown system, these decorated vessels were assigned variant status of the undecorated types, contrary to the original intentions of Wheat, Gifford, and Wasley (1958:41). Most archaeologists working in southeastern New Mexico have implicitly or explicitly accepted the close relationship between certain decorated and undecorated sherds, and used descriptive terms attached to type names to show this relationship (Jennings 1940:5–6; Mera 1943:12; Jelinek 1960:App. B; Stubbs, personal communication). Certainly this way of thinking was firmly embedded in my own pottery sorting as reflected in the sherd lists accumulated over 15 years.

Native Types and Variants

Jornada Brown

For the present, this type encompasses most of the brown pottery native to the region, allowing considerable variation in temper, color, thickness, and other attributes.

Jornada Brown was not formally described in print until Jennings (1940) worked a site on the Peñasco River, although the pottery had long been known informally. Jennings called it "Common" or Unnamed Brown, and Mera (1943:12) proposed the name Jornada Brown, Red-on-Brown, or Polychrome, as the case was, for the pottery Jennings described. This term has subsequently been applied to such a variety of sherds that the specifically defined factors of temper and surface polish frequently have been ignored.

Temper may offer the best tool for identifying geographical variants and localized manufacturing centers in a type that otherwise presents such a monotonous face to the world. Jelinek (1960:App. B) felt that crushed rock was the major tempering component for all five of his brown types. Several geologists who examined sherds of each of his types, at my request, unanimously agreed that the well-rounded grains characteristic of four of Jelinek's five types were sand grains reflecting the petrological composition of their source rather than manufacturing traditions. South Pecos Brown had angular feldspar tempering along with smaller rounded grains which may well have been crushed rock, although F. E. Green (personal communication) tells me that certain sands are just as angular as this near their source. The petrological structure of feldspar is such that rounding may not occur even when the particles are rolled over considerable distances. Rex Gerald tested the hypothesis that crushed rock vs. sand temper could be used to separate brown ware pottery; he concluded that rounded sand may be distinguished from angular sand and/or crushed rock by visual means, but that "crushed rock temper cannot be distinguished from sand temper" (Danson 1957:124).

Clays with sand inclusions could have been used, making additional tempering unnecessary. According to one ceramicist, many clay deposits have such inclusions; beds of such clays exist in southeastern New Mexico (F. E. Green, personal communication).

Individual potters could have varied the temper of their vessels according to the function planned for each pot. This has been done by the modern Papago potter, Avalina Ignacio (Fontana et al. 1962:34).

If Alma Plain sherds were subjected to a thorough petrographic analysis, a number of temper types probably could be differentiated. Archaeologists working in those regions have refrained from splitting this fundamental type.

Martin (in Martin and Rinaldo 1960) assigns his plain brown sherds from Table Rock Pueblo, Arizona, to the Alma Plain type, although all of his sample was sherd tempered.

Origin of the Type: Most archaeologists have seen a genetic relationship between Jornada Brown and Alma Plain. Mera (1943:9) pictures the southeastern New Mexico brown pottery as a coarsening of Alma Plain due to regional modification at an undetermined date.

Geographical Distribution: The Sierra Blanca Region was a manufacturing center of Jornada Brown. As the major utility type, it was undoubtedly manufactured by local family units, a factor that may have contributed to the lack of standardization in the type. Jornada Brown extended east to the Pecos Valley and west to the Gran Quivira locality. Peckham (personal communication, 1965) who recently reexamined Fenenga's pottery from Gran Quivira Pithouse Village, felt that those brown sherds were good examples of the Jornada Brown type. Similar brown types centered in the lower Tularosa Basin and adjacent Rio Grande Valley (El Paso Brown as defined by Lehmer [1948:94]) and in the northwest part of southeastern New Mexico (the coarsened Alma discussed by Mera [1943:9–10]). One of many problems facing future archaeologists is the adequate typological and geographical differentiation of the various brown pottery types.

Working from the published literature, it is virtually impossible to chart the distribution of Jornada Brown in regions where other brown types were manufactured. Its diffusion to the east and northeast can be traced with some assurance. It is a common component on the many surface sites on the Llano Estacado, and it has been reported from northwestern New Mexico (Dick 1953:267–84; Renaud 1937).

Temporal Distribution: The following sites and phases, dated primarily by associated pottery types, show the temporal range established for Jornada Brown:

Pueblo I	Gran Quivira Pithouse Village
Pueblo II	Site P4ab
Pueblo III	Corona, early Glencoe and early Lincoln Phases
Pueblo IV	Late Glencoe and late Lincoln Phases

Regional differentiation of southeastern New Mexico brown pottery had taken place by Pueblo II, when El Paso Brown had developed in the lower Tularosa Basin (Lehmer 1948:94) and "Coarsened Alma," for lack of a better name, was in use at Taylor Draw (Peckham, personal communication, 1965).

Undecorated Variants: Roswell Brown, defined as a separate type by Jelinek (1960:App. B), is subsumed under the broader category of Jornada Brown in this report. Gallo Micaceous is set up as a variant of the Jornada Brown type.

Decorated Variants: Jornada Red-on-Brown, Roswell Red-on-Brown, Jornada Black-on-Brown, Jornada Red-slipped, Roswell Red-slipped, and Jornada Polychrome are considered in this category.

Chupadero Black-on-White and Related Types and Variants

Mera (1931:1–4) first named Chupadero Black-on-White and, later, its smoothed or unstriated variant, Casa Colorado Black-on-White. Hawley offered a more restricted definition in which a white slip was specified (1936:67). A technological note on this type was supplied by Shepard (Kidder and Shepard 1936:349). Toulouse (1949:18–19) recognized Tabira Black-on-White as a late outgrowth of Chupadero Black-on-White. Jelinek (1960:App. B) offered a Chupadero Black-on-White ceramic system and listed as constituent types Chupadero Black-on-White, Crosby Black-on-White, and Middle Pecos Black-on-White.

Chupadero Black-on-White existed from at least early Pueblo III until historic times. In such a long-lived, decorated line of pottery, some stylistic changes must have occurred but, to date, only Pueblo IV and later variants have been demonstrated. This type forms a stable part of the ceramic complex in several regions within the northern part of southeastern New Mexico. Mera (1931:1) postulated a geographical center around Chupadero Mesa, hence the name. It occurs in such substantial quantities (20% to 30% of the total pottery complex) in sites from the Chupadero and Sierra Blanca Regions that widespread manufacture is indicated. On the other hand, the type is fairly uniform, suggesting a limited center or centers. At the very least, the degree of standardization argues against family unit production of the type. The idea that one-fifth to one-third of the pottery utilized by virtually every family in the regions mentioned above was traded any great distance implies economic specialization beyond that indicated by other evidence.

Chupadero Black-on-White as a Trade Item: This was perhaps the most exportable of locally made pottery types, as indicated by the following references:

Lesdos Site	Lambert 1956a:67–68
Swarts Ruin	Cosgrove and Cosgrove 1932:95–98
15 miles North of Sabinal, Chihuahua	Cosgrove and Cosgrove 1932:95–98
Ringo Site	Johnson and Thompson 1963:465–81
Cerros Mojinos	Fenenga and Cummings 1956b:254
LA 2554, 2557, 2565, 2572	Fenenga and Cummings 1956a:223–26
Pindi	Stubbs and Stallings 1953:60
Paa-ko	Lambert 1954:48–49
Lynam Site	Gunnerson 1959:145–54, Lister 1948:35–41
25 sites near Watrous	Renaud 1937
Pecos	Kidder and Shepard 1936:346–49
Rowe	Kidder and Shepard 1936:346–49

Near Abilene, Texas	Krieger 1946:144
Confluence of Little Wichita and Red Rivers	Krieger 1946:132
Culberson County, Texas	Krieger 1946:83
Titus Focus, East Texas	Krieger 1946:208
Tobias Site, Kansas	Wedel 1959:245
Mound Lake, Texas	Jennings 1952:307

Dates: Origin of the type has not been firmly fixed. It was absent from Gran Quivira Pithouse Village (Fenenga 1956:232; Green 1955:184), Taylor Draw (Peckham 1957b:70), and Site P4ab in the Pecos Valley (Jelinek 1960:App. B) which were Pueblo I and Pueblo II in age. Jelinek reports Chupadero Black-on-White in association with Red Mesa Black-on-White and Kwahe'e Black-on-White at Site P4c. If this did not represent a mixed collection, the type could have developed in the late Pueblo II period. It was well established in the northern part of southeastern New Mexico during Pueblo III early Pueblo IV. As villagers abandoned the Sierra Blanca Region, manufacture of all pottery types ceased at the end of the Glaze I period. This type and its successor, Tabira Black-on-White, continued as a vigorous member of this pottery complex in the Chupadero Region until about A.D. 1650.

Origin: Chupadero Black-on-White evolved more or less directly from San Marcial and Socorro Black-on-White. The possibility of more remote affiliations was suggested by Krieger (1946:154) and Toulouse and Stephenson (1960:39). Krieger pointed out that the disc bases of Chupadero were similar to Paint Creek and Henrietta Red vessels, and he felt this trait may have diffused into the Southwest form the east. Apparently Toulouse would route the diffusion through western Mexico, as he drew parallels with Isabel Kelly's Jalisco material. He pointed out that the only other disc bases in the Southwest were vases at Pueblo Bonito (see Judd 1954:210). Mesa Verde and Kayenta cups have flat bases, but Toulouse felt they represented a separate tradition.

Capitan Variant of Chupadero Black-on-White: Bowl rims ½ to ¾ inch wide were flared at an angle to the bowl wall; bowls were usually unslipped and black paint was applied directly onto a gray background. Atypical decoration, such as rim ticking and lines curved from the center of the bowl interior to the rim were used. Paint was frequently glazed.

Capitan variant sherds were never numerous and they always were found with larger numbers of more traditional Chupadero Black-on-White in Lincoln Phase sites. In addition to the instances reported in this study, the variant was present in a site in the upper Bonito Valley of the Hondo Drainage excavated by Stewart Peckham (personal communication, September 1965).

Three Rivers and Other Red-on-Terracotta Types

Three Rivers Red-on-Terracotta was the first regional pottery type to appear in the literature. The Cosgroves visited a large site at Three Rivers in 1925 where this was a major component of the pottery complex (Cosgrove and Cosgrove 1965). Since this type occurred as a trade ware in the Mimbres area where the Cosgroves and Paul Nesbitt worked, it was further mentioned in the various Mimbres reports (Cosgrove and Cosgrove 1932; Nesbitt 1931). Mera and Stallings (1931) included a somewhat more formal discussion of the characteristics of this type in their paper on Lincoln Black-on-Red pottery. When McCluney (1962:49–55) named and described San Andres Red-on-Terracotta, he suggested that it was ancestral to Three Rivers Red-on-Terracotta. In this he had been anticipated by Mera and Stallings (1931:2–4), who drew attention to a widespread Red-on-Terracotta which they felt might eventually require a new name.

Origin: Red-on-Brown and red slipped variants of Jornada Brown served as the immediate source. Ultimately the impetus may be traced through Mogollon Red-on-Brown and San Francisco Red traditions into the Post-Classic Red-on-Buff horizon of western Mexico.

Geographical Distribution: Its center seemed to be around Three Rivers at the east edge of the Tularosa Basin. It was present in substantial quantities in Hondo Drainage sites, and it diminishes in frequency as one proceeds north to the Macho and Gallo Drainages, south to the Peñasco Valley and east to the Pecos. Outside of the Sierra Blanca Region, both types were represented in collections from the Llano Estacado such as that from Mound Lake (Jennings 1952:310) and sites reported by Watts (1939:77–91). A recent reexamination of sherds in the museum at Texas Technological College from Blue Mountain Shelter (originally reported in Holden 1938:208–21) showed Three Rivers Red-on-Terracotta to be present. Krieger (1946:83) reported Three Rivers Red-on-Terracotta from Culberson County in Texas. Three Rivers Red-on-Terracotta was found at Pindi (Stubbs 1953:17) and at Swarts Ruin (Cosgrove and Cosgrove 1932:98–99).

Dating: San Andres Red-on-Terracotta was made in Pueblo II, as it was found at Taylor Draw (Peckham, personal communication). It survived into the Glencoe and Lincoln Phases, or until early Pueblo IV. Three Rivers originated early in Pueblo III. It was a common component in Corona and Glencoe Phase sites. Apparently the type was made until the Glaze I horizon of Pueblo IV.

Lincoln Black-on-Red

Lincoln Black-on-Red was described by Mera and Stallings (1931), using Three Rivers Red-on-Terracotta as the starting point for the description. It was assumed that Lincoln Black-on-Red evolved out of Three Rivers Red-on-Terracotta.

Mera and Stallings (1931:7) stated that the temper and paste of Lincoln

Black-on-Red was the same as Three Rivers Red-on-Terracotta. This has not proved to be the case.

Lincoln Black-on-Red was apparently a late Pueblo III innovation in late Glencoe and Lincoln Phases. It had a more limited geographical distribution than its ancestral types. The major manufacturing centers were north of Capitan Mountain. It was certainly made at the Phillips Site, where Jack Harkey reported excavating 40 bowls in varying stages of manufacture from a single room. The type has been found at a number of sites on the Llano Estacado, and Krieger (1946:47) reported it from Alibates Ruin and Antelope Creek.

The most common stylistic variant is the one originally described. Minor variants encountered in the course of the fieldwork described in this study include Lincoln Red-on-Red, Lincoln Black-on-Red with thin-lined decoration, Lincoln Black-on-Red Glaze, and Lincoln Black-on-Red Polychrome.

Corrugated Pottery of Local Manufacture

In mid-Pueblo III times, the practice of making corrugated utility pottery diffused into the northern part of the subarea. Smudged Corrugated was present at the Pueblo II site of Los Tules in the Rio Grande Valley (Lehmer 1948:94); however, distributional evidence indicates that this was not the source of Lincoln Phase Corrugated pottery. The Chupadero Region and the Middle Rio Grande seem to be more likely sources.

This pottery competed with local brown utility types, and gradually replaced them in the Gallo and Macho Drainages during the Lincoln Phase. Corrugated did not compete effectively with Jornada Brown in the Glencoe Phase or with El Paso Polychrome in the El Paso Phase.

Shapes of corrugated were similar to the wide-mouthed ollas of Jornada Brown. Both had slightly everted lips, virtually no neck, and globular bodies. Exterior corrugations and the usual gray to black color were the major differences. A number of sherds which had not received secondary firing through use as cooking pots were brown in color. There is considerable variation in temper and paste consistency, apparently reflecting localized manufacture. It was probable that the same clay and temper sources were used for this type as for Jornada Brown, since, in the Gallo Drainage, Jornada Brown and Corrugated contain comparable amounts of mica. Jelinek noted that, in the Pecos Valley, some Corrugated had the same temper and paste as Roswell Brown.

Intraregional Trade

All of the pottery types discussed in the preceding section, with the possible exception of Jornada Brown and Corrugated, were probably manufactured by specialized potters instead of by family units. These types were undoubtedly involved in short-distance trade transactions, but manufacturing centers have not been pinpointed with enough precision to trace their routes. It has been suggested that sites close to Three Rivers produced Three Rivers Red-on-Terracotta. The long life span of this type and variations observed in temper, hardness, color, and decoration make it likely that other manufacturing centers were involved in making this pottery. Lincoln Black-on-Red was made at the Phillips Site, and it was best represented in Macho Drainage sites of the Lincoln Phase. It was in these localities that several design variants of Lincoln Black-on-Red developed. Chupadero Black-on-White is something of an enigma, as the relative standardization seems incompatible with individual family production. It was used by virtually every family in the Sierra Blanca Region for several centuries. El Paso Polychrome could, in a few instances, have been made in the Sierra Blanca Region, but it was usually traded in from the adjacent Tularosa Basin.

Interregional Trade Pottery

El Paso Polychrome

This pottery was relatively standardized, and the original description by Stallings (1931:1–13) has been quite adequate. The geographical center was in the lower Tularosa Basin where 80% to 95% of the pottery in El Paso Phase sites was of this type. Manufacture within the Sierra Blanca Region was especially suggested by the high percentage of El Paso Polychrome at Bloom Mound, where some sherds lacked the characteristic temper and paste, and at Site 2000 in the Peñasco Valley.

El Paso Polychrome achieved wide popularity as a trade ware. In addition to those sites listed by Lehmer (1948:83), El Paso Polychrome was found at the Lesdos Site (Lambert 1956b:259–83), Reeve Ruin (Di Peso 1958:149), a ceremonial cave in the Winchester Mountains (Fulton 1941:24), Casas Grandes in Chihuahua (Cosgrove and Cosgrove 1932:93–95), and the Ringo Site (Johnson and Thompson 1963:465–81). Eastward, it occurred in surface camps on the Llano Estacado; Krieger (1946:80) noted 30 sherds from a campsite 15 miles from Plainview, Texas. It was fairly common in Pecos, Culberson, Hudspeth, and El Paso Counties in Texas (Krieger 1946:83).

Chihuahuan Types

Ramos Polychrome, Babicora Polychrome, and Playas Red Incised enjoyed some popularity in southeastern New Mexico. As one would expect, these types were most numerous in the regions adjacent to their homeland; El Paso Phase sites invariably contained sherds of Chihuahuan types. Moore and Wheat (1951:147) described a cache found near El Paso in which ten Chihuahuan vessels were associated with Chupadero Black-on-White, El Paso Polychrome, Tucson Polychrome, and numerous ornaments. Ramos Polychrome was the Chihuahuan type most favored by Glencoe and Lincoln Phase peoples, although other types arrived in lesser numbers. Lincoln Phase sites north of Capitan Mountain had negligible quantities of those types.

Mimbres Types

Classic Mimbres Black-on-White and Mimbres Corrugated of the Three Circle Phase occurred at Los Tules (Lehmer 1948:27). Mimbres Bold Face, otherwise known as Mangus Black-on-White, was a minor trade type in southeastern New Mexico until the Glaze I horizon in Pueblo IV. Most authorities have indicated that the Mimbres Region was abandoned about A.D. 1200; Fred Wendorf once casually suggested to me that the Mimbres people might have migrated into southeastern New Mexico as their pottery was consistently found in late Pueblo III - early Pueblo IV contexts there. The small amounts of Mimbres Bold Face in Glencoe and Lincoln Phase sites imply, to me, a more distant but contemporary source. Haury (1936:130) noted that "Some ruins east of the Rio Grande consistently yield an association of Mimbres and Chupadero Black-on-White, and El Paso Polychrome, suggesting a possible overlap, and thus necessitating a later date, say 1250, for the Mimbres Culture in this outlying district." It is not impossible that a reinvestigation of the Mimbres Region would show some late sites that produced Mimbres Bold Face into Pueblo IV times.

Types from Southwestern New Mexico and Southeastern Arizona

The following types were important from Pueblo III until early Pueblo IV times.

St. Johns Polychrome: This type has been considered a fairly reliable horizon marker because of its wide distribution and limited time span, as Kidder pointed out in 1936 (Kidder and Shepard 1936:351–52). It was introduced into southeastern New Mexico late in Pueblo III, and coexisted briefly with Glaze I in the Lincoln and Glencoe Phases. A similar overlapping of St. Johns and early Rio Grande glazes existed in Middle Rio Grande sites (Wendorf 1956:104).

Springerville Polychrome: This glazed version of St. Johns is the latest pottery type reported from the Peñasco Valley. The type has not yet been reported from other localities.

Wingate Black-on-Red: Surface collections from Gallo Valley sites have shown that Wingate Black-on-Red was present. Excavation in late Pueblo III sites should demonstrate its association with St. Johns Polychrome.

Heshotauthla Polychrome: This type occurred in the same context as St. Johns Polychrome within the subarea.

Upper Gila Corrugated: This type, never well represented, was present in Glencoe and Lincoln Phases.

Tularosa Black-on-White: A single sherd from the Bonnell Site, Glencoe

Phase, and a few sherds from Block Lookout, Lincoln Phase, indicated that the type was occasionally acquired. A vessel of unknown provenience in the Roswell Museum belonged to this type. Occasional sherds were noted on Lincoln Phase sites.

Gila or Tonto Polychrome: The wide time range of these types in Arizona has meant that they were not useful for direct dating in the Sierra Blanca Region. At the Bonnell Site, where there was some stratigraphic control, Gila Polychrome arrived slightly after Glaze I. For a short period, this was the most important trade pottery in Glencoe and Lincoln Phase sites.

Anasazi Types

Lino Types: During Pueblo I, these were present at Gran Quivira Pithouse Village. No other sites of this age have been investigated.

Red Mesa Black-on-White: Locally made brown pottery was associated with this type at Taylor Draw and Site P4ab (Peckham 1957b:70; Jelinek 1960).

Miscellaneous Black-on-White: In Gallo and Macho Drainage localities, small numbers of Anasazi Black-on-White in Pueblo III and early Pueblo IV contexts have been reported, mostly from surface collections. Chaco 2 and Mesa Verde Black-on-White were presumably earlier than Santa Fe and Galisteo Black-on-Whites, but excavations are needed to delimit their distribution. Capitan and the adjacent mountains form the apparent southern border of Black-on-White types originating in the Middle Rio Grande - Galisteo Basin regions.

Rio Grande Glazes: The Peñasco Valley was abandoned prior to the introduction of glaze types. In Ruidoso Valley Glencoe Phase sites and throughout the territory of the Lincoln Phase, Glaze I was a common intrusive. Few post-Glaze I sherds have been found in the Sierra Blanca Region, and either Glencoe and Lincoln Phase sites were abandoned during the Glaze I period, or else trade routes were thoroughly disrupted. In the Gallo Drainage, a number of glazes and polychrome glazes were collected by the Laboratory of Anthropology, including Los Padillos Polychrome, San Clemente Glaze, and Arenal Glaze Polychrome. These types were probably channeled into the Gallo locality from Chupadero Region sites, where Middle Rio Grande pottery was prominent; some of the types were undoubtedly manufactured in the latter region.

Los Lunas Smudged: This was a minor member of the Lincoln Phase pottery complex. It was found in Laboratory of Anthropology surveys of the Gallo locality, and a restorable bowl was excavated at Block Lookout.

Summary

The study of trade pottery is a matter of some importance in southeastern New Mexico because dating of sites and phases frequently hinges directly or indirectly on trade pottery and because it affords one of the most important lines of evidence of cultural contacts. Within the Sierra Blanca Region, the chronological positions of the Glencoe, Corona, and Lincoln Phases have been postulated on the basis of their ceramic complexes.

Elements that Cross-cut Pottery Types

Form and Function

Similarity between Jornada Brown and Corrugated wide-mouthed ollas was in part due to function. Both served as the primary storage, water, and cooking utensils. The similarity in form and in paste-temper continuity in some cases suggests that new techniques of surface treatment and firing were applied to an old line of pottery. The shape of Chupadero Black-on-White jugs was, in at least one instance, imitated in Three Rivers Red-on-Terracotta; since the base of the Three Rivers jug was not found, it is not known whether the imitation possessed the disc base. Bowl forms overlapped between Jornada Brown, Chupadero Black-on-White, Three Rivers Red-on-Terracotta, and Lincoln Black-on-Red. At one extreme, Chupadero Black-on-White and Three Rivers Red-on-Terracotta bowls tend to be hemispherical; at the other extreme, Jornada Brown and Lincoln Black-on-Red bowls have straighter sides (however, see Pl. 64b for a straight-sided Chupadero Black-on-White). "Squash jars," small-mouthed, globular vessels without necks may have been limited to Chupadero Black-on-White. Small jars with narrow mouths that could be easily closed with a wooden plug or corn cob were made in Jornada Brown and Chupadero Black-on-White. These probably were used in much the same way as the small ollas or "seed jars" of El Paso Polychrome and Jornada Brown. Miniature Chupadero Black-on-White and Jornada Brown pots have been found, as well as some miniatures that were too nondescript to classify.

Rim Forms

Direct rims, often flattened, were typical of bowl forms in all types. Rims everted at an angle to the vessel wall occurred on Capitan variants of Chupadero Black-on-White bowls and on a single Jornada Brown-Roswell variant bowl. Olla rims were more distinctive. Direct rims were typical of wide-mouthed Jornada Brown ollas. Thickened everted rims occurred on Jornada Polychrome, on Corrugated, and on some Jornada Brown; El Paso Polychrome had the most extreme form of thickened everted lip.

Firing Techniques

Jornada Brown, Three Rivers Red-on-Terracotta, San Andres Red-on-Terracotta, and Lincoln Black-on-Red were fired in an oxidizing atmosphere. Firing clouds were frequently produced. Gray to black Jornada Brown sherds and vessels suggest that a reducing atmosphere was sometimes achieved, although it would be difficult to prove that this was not the result of refiring. Chupadero Black-on-White and Corrugated were customarily fired in a reducing atmosphere. Exceptional sherds and vessels of the latter types were oxidized, again illustrating that variation in firing techniques occurred in actual practice.

Among the group of types customarily fired in an oxidizing atmosphere, it is not clear whether an attempt was made to fire some types at a higher temperature than others. The greater hardness of Three Rivers Red-on-Terracotta, coupled with the results of some kiln tests at Texas Technological College on sherds of this type, showing that a brighter terracotta color was achieved at high temperatures, indicate that this type may have received higher firing temperatures. The amount of iron in the various clays was not measured, and this would have been a vital factor in the final color.

Design Motifs and Styles

The execution of Jornada Red-on-Brown and Jornada Polychrome displayed a similar proficiency as opposed to the slapdash style of El Paso Polychrome. Overlap and duplication occurred in the linear motifs used on Jornada Red-on-Brown and San Andres Red-on-Terracotta, and in Three Rivers Red-on-Terracotta and Lincoln Red-on-Red. Three or four lines, ⅛ to ¼ inch wide, created designs quartering the bowl or just circling the bowl interior under the rim in the latter two types. Red paint applied to the rim or red paint extended over the rim onto the bowl exterior was known for San Andres Red-on-Terracotta, Three Rivers Red-on-Terracotta, and Jornada Brown decorated variants. Red-slipped or red-washed vessels were made in Jornada Brown, Three Rivers Red-on-Terracotta, and Lincoln Black-on-Red. Duplications of design elements occurred, although a whole motif or style was rarely transferred from one type to another. The use of a solid stepped element in a band or panel design, checkerboards, elongated triangles, and pendant triangles were particularly common on Chupadero Black-on-White and Lincoln Black-on-Red, and some were introduced into Three Rivers Red-on-Terracotta. Design exchange was most frequent in late Pueblo III and early Pueblo IV times in Lincoln Phase sites of the Macho Drainage. Some of this was due to exchange of local design ideas and some seemed to reflect an imitation of imported Glaze I vessels. Other elements that seemed to have been inspired by traded wares were the application of white lines to the exterior of Lincoln Black-on-Red, local attempts to glaze Chupadero Black-on-White and Lincoln Black-on-Red, creation of Lincoln Polychrome and Three Rivers Polychrome, and the use of animal figures on Chupadero Black-on-White and Three Rivers Red-on-Terracotta. Many of the elements shared by Chupadero Black-on-White and Lincoln Black-on-Red suggested a transfer from the latter to the former. Chupadero Black-on-White hatching was never applied to other local types.

Jornada Brown decorated bowls, San Andres Red-on-Terracotta, Three Rivers Red-on-Terracotta, and Lincoln Black-on-Red had the same spatial arrangement of decorated zones on bowls. Jornada Brown decorated ollas, Jornada Polychrome, and El Paso Polychrome had paint applied to the neck and upper portion of the body. The use of a wide band of decoration around the widest part of the vessel was limited to Chupadero Black-on-White jugs.

Construction

Coiling was the usual method of manufacture for all types. A minor construction technique involving the use of flattened wide clay "coils" to make bowls seemed to be limited to Lincoln Phase sites in the Macho Drainage and the Glencoe Phase sites in the Ruidoso Valley. These "coils" were eradicated on the interior of the bowls but remained visible on the exterior. This technique was applied to both Chupadero Black-on-White and Lincoln Black-on-Red vessels. Construction techniques that did not diffuse beyond a single type were the disc base of Chupadero Black-on-White and the extreme thinness of El Paso Polychrome.

Surface Treatment

The interior striations of Chupadero Black-on-White jugs were imitated in Jornada Brown ollas and in Three Rivers Red-on-Terracotta jugs. Exterior scoring or roughening was used on Chupadero Black-on-White bowls and on San Andres Red-on-Terracotta. Matte finish by finger smoothing could be seen on most of the types. It was undoubtedly a step in the manufacturing process of all types. Tool polishing on one surface was a final step for some Jornada Brown, Three Rivers Red-on-Terracotta, Lincoln Black-on-Red, Corrugated, and Chupadero Black-on-White. Surface texturing by brushing, incision, and punctation was limited to Jornada Brown, among the native types. Models for the latter practices were available in imported Chihuahuan textured types.

Summary

The pottery types manufactured within the Sierra Blanca and adjacent regions shared a number of individual elements or modes and afford a good example of the "Ceramic School" that Smith discusses (1962:1175). Some of these modes had a minimum of cultural meaning beyond the sharing of a ceramic tradition common to most of the Southwest. Overlap in olla and bowl shapes would be of this order. The spatial arrangement of similar linear designs on Jornada Brown decorated variants, San Andres Red-on-Terracotta, Three Rivers Red-on-Terracotta, and some Lincoln Black-on-Red pointed up the genetic relationships between these types, as well as reflecting an on-going close relationship between the potters making these types. The makers of Lincoln Black-on-Red accepted new design motifs with a greater frequency than did potters making any other type. The exchange of design elements between Lincoln Black-on-Red and Chupadero Black-on-White in a limited geographical region where both types were locally made suggests closer cultural contacts. Both types may have been made in a single village or even by the same potter. The diffusion of design elements from a distance was fostered by local imitations of imported pottery.

DESCRIPTION OF FOUR POTTERY TYPES NATIVE TO THE SIERRA BLANCA REGION

Jornada Brown

Form

Globular ollas or jars were customarily between 10 inches and 14 inches high; occasional specimens were taller. Some ollas were flat bottomed; most or all could have sat without support. The mouths were usually 6 to 7 inches in diameter, and an unthickened, direct rim was typical. Necked vessels were rare but occurred. The relative frequency of ollas to bowls has not been established for any phase; bowls were always in the minority. Bowls tended to have slightly slanting sides. Small "seed jars" and miniatures have been found.

Construction

Coiled construction was used, and the unpolished vessels were smoothed by hand or with the fingertips. Polished vessels bear polishing marks.

Thickness

Most vessels were at least ¼ inch thick, and a few were over ½ inch thick.

Paste

Sherds showed some variation in paste consistency, but most could be described as soft and friable. Central carbon streaks were sometimes present.

Color

The final color of brown pottery depends upon firing temperature and the amount of oxygen present at the end of the firing process. Pots changed color during the firing and refiring would produce a different colored pot. To demonstrate color variation, a number of sherds from the fill of House 1 at the Bonnell Site were matched against the Munsell Soil Color Chart (Table 6).

The color range could have been expanded by enlarging our sample. Light to medium reddish browns and yellow reddish browns were most frequent, with darker browns and black to gray occurring. Firing clouds caused considerable color variation in single vessels. There was an overlap at the lighter end of the color scale in the yellow-brown range between Jornada Brown and Three Rivers Red-on-Terracotta; it was usually possible to distinguish between the two types on the basis of temper, evenness of the vessel wall thickness, hardness, and surface finish.

TABLE 6
COLOR RANGE OF JORNADA BROWN SHERDS FROM HOUSE 1, BONNELL SITE, MATCHED AGAINST THE MUNSELL SOIL COLOR CHART

Color	Hue	Value/Chroma
Body Sherds from Level 6		
Reddish brown	5 YR	5/4
Reddish gray	5 YR	5/2
Reddish brown	5 YR	5/3
Dark reddish gray	5 YR	4/2
Light reddish brown	5 YR	6/4
Light reddish brown	5 YR	6/5
Rim Sherds from Level 7		
Reddish brown	5 YR	5/4
Light brown	7.5 YR	6/4
Pinkish gray	5 YR	6/2
Reddish brown	5 YR	5/3
Dark gray	5 YR	4/1
Reddish gray	5 YR	5/2
Dark reddish brown	5 YR	6/3
Light reddish brown	5 YR	3/6
Dark red	2.5 YR	3/6
Reddish brown	2.5 YR	4/4
Dusky red	2.5 YR	3/2
Body Sherds from Level 1		
Light reddish brown	5 YR	6/3
Brown	7.5 YR	5/4
Yellowish red	5 YR	5/8
Pink	7.5 YR	7/4

Surface Finish and Treatment

Most of the Jornada Brown type was unpolished or matte finished and was probably finger smoothed—at least no tool marks were visible. Polishing occurred on olla exteriors and on bowl interiors, and tool marks were visible on these specimens. Steward Peckham once remarked that he was tempted to sort all the brown sherds into polished and unpolished categories and let it go at that. Polishing occurred with a variety of tempers, color, vessel shapes, wall thickness, and so forth. Textured surfaces were rare but individual sherds in our collection showed brushing, punctation, and incising. Some textured pieces must have been local imitations of Chihuahuan trade pieces; others possibly reflected a potter's experimental mood.

Temper

Sand grains of quartz and feldspar were the most frequent tempering agents. An almost continuous gradation from sherds showing no macroscopic temper through very fine grained to large coarse particles was noted. Most sherds I have examined fall in the medium size range. Certain sherds had a mixture of rounded quartz grains and angular feldspar fragments. Only angular feldspar was visible in others. Pearlite was recognized in some sherds. Mica was present in most sherds, if examined with a hand lens. Both bronzite and muscovite (colorless) mica occurred. Sherds were described as micaceous only when the mica content was clearly visible to the naked eye.

Undecorated Variants of Jornada Brown

Roswell Variant: Defined as a type by Jelinek (1960:App. B). Specialized temper set this apart from other native brown pottery of the Sierra Blanca Region and Pecos Valley. Orthoclase feldspar, which produced distinctive orange flecks in the temper, was accompanied by plagioclase feldspar and quartz, with the latter predominating. This particular temper combination is easily recognized and, in my opinion, means that this pottery was manufactured at a single center or in a single locality, not yet identified. Sherds with this temper were frequently, but not always, polished. Jelinek (1960:App. B) who did not recognize polishing as an essential feature of Roswell Brown, reported this temper type in corrugated sherds. The single reconstructed Roswell Brown olla from the Bonnell Site had a straight direct rim 1½ inches high which expanded to a globular vessel. One bowl fragment had straight walls and a narrow rim that turned at a right angle to the wall. This variant seemed to be limited to the eastern side of the Sierra Blanca-Sacramento mountains. It has been found in the upper Gallo, Macho, Hondo, and Peñasco Valleys and along the Pecos River. It probably was limited in time to Pueblo III and IV. Jelinek (ibid.) suggested dates of A.D. 1000 to A.D. 1250 or 1300; our excavations showed that it lasted into Pueblo IV.

Gallo Micaceous Variant: Visible amounts of clear (muscovite) mica characterize most of the brown pottery from Corona Phase sites in the upper Gallo Drainage and on Carrizo Creek in the upper Macho Drainage. This is interpreted as the result of using local clay deposits with micaceous inclusions. Ollas with direct rims were the only vessel form recognized in our collection, but bowls were probably made. Attributes of color, hardness, thickness of vessel walls, and so forth, were within the range of the Jornada type. This variant has been found in both Corona and Lincoln Phase sites of Pueblo III - early Pueblo IV age.

Decorated Variants of Jornada Brown

Jornada Red-on-Brown: The main geographical center seemed to have been in the Hondo Valley and east to the Pecos Valley. Decorated brown sherds never formed a large percentage of the pottery complex. This category was best represented in certain lots of sherds from the Bonnell Site, where all variants of decorated brown sherds formed only 5% of the total sherd lot. Broad red line decoration (about ¼ inch wide), red bands (about 1 inch wide), and red slips were applied to vessels that otherwise would have been classed as Jornada Brown. Bowls received this treatment more frequently than ollas.

Roswell Red-on-Brown: Jelinek (1960:App. B) specified broad red line decoration extending down from a painted red rim at 45° to 90° angles. Red slipped or red washed interiors were also noted. An unpolished bowl with the temper characteristic of Roswell Brown, in the collection of the Roswell Museum, had a distinctive linear design (Pl. 1).

Jornada Black-on-Brown: Known from a few sherds in the Gallo Drainage, black paint was used to apply decoration like Jornada Red-on-Brown.

Jornada Polychrome: Ollas with thickened direct rims had red and black designs painted on the upper portions of the vessels. A few bowls have been reported; a slightly thickened, flattened rim form and polychrome decoration were the main attributes that set this apart from Jornada Brown.

Chupadero Black-on-White and Related Types and Varieties

Form

The most common was a nearly spherical vessel with a flat disc base, a constricted neck, and a flaring mouth. Called a jug in this study, it has also been called a pitcher or a jar by other archaeologists. A single handle of one, two, or three coils was customarily applied between rim and shoulder. Within the area, this form was limited to the Chupadero Black-on-White type. Bowls were usually shaped like a hemisphere, although straighter sides occur. Bowl rims were direct and unthickened, except in some late variants when the rim was turned at a near right angle to the bowl wall. The disc base was used on bowls as well as jugs, although some partially reconstructed bowls from the Bonnell Site seem to have been made entirely of coiling. Minor forms were "squash jars" (or a neckless globular vessel), miniatures, and animal effigies. A squash jar was found at Paa-ko (Lambert 1954:Pl. XIV, lower left); in our excavations rim sherds of this form were found at Block Lookout and most of a vessel was found at the Bonnell Site. Two animal effigies were in the Lincoln County Museum (Fig. 29) and sherds of animal effigies were found at the

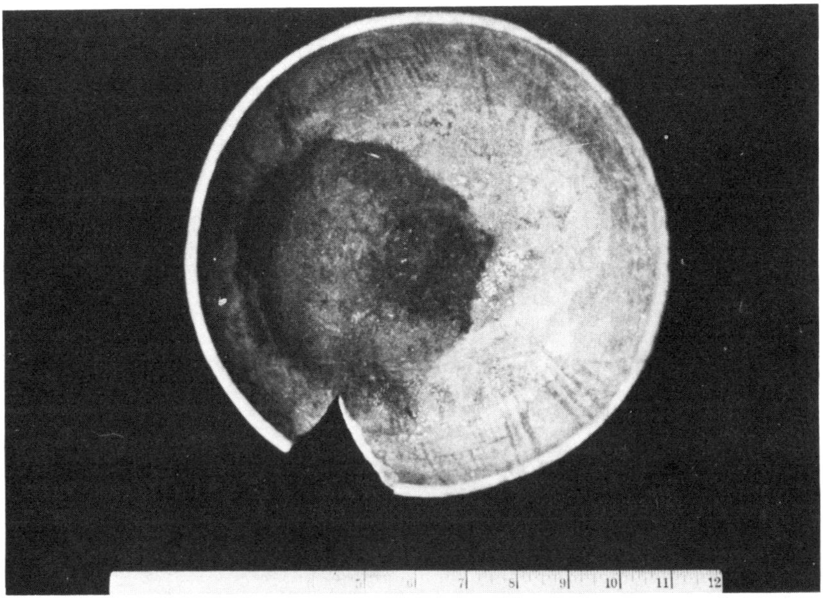

a

b

Plate 1. *a*. Roswell Brown bowl, Roswell Museum Collection; *b*, Chupadero Black-on-White bowl, Jack Harkey Collection.

Bonnell and Phillips Sites. Small "seed jars" with constricted necks were made (Pl. 80a). The use of lugs and small handles attached on the shoulder was rare, but Lincoln Phase examples have been observed (Pl. 2a).

Construction

The disc base is unique in Southwest pottery (see Toulouse and Stephenson 1960:39). Upper parts of jugs and bowls were coiled. Upon occasion, three or four bands or slabs of clay about 1 inch wide were joined to create a bowl. Handles of jars were welded to the exterior surface or inserted through the vessel wall.

Surface Treatment

Interior striations on jugs and the roughened exterior of bowls were a hallmark of the type. Jug exteriors were customarily well smoothed, and sometimes polished; however, barely smoothed specimens were known. Polishing marks were seldom visible. Bowls of slab construction had unsmoothed slab marks on the exterior. A few bowl sherds were basket impressed.

Slip

Contrary to Hawley (1936:67), the presence of a slip was not essential. When present, slips varied from chalky white to cream to gray. In our collections, unslipped sherds were most frequent in early Pueblo IV sites of the Lincoln Phase.

Paint

Black mineral paint was applied with considerable variation in thickness or heaviness. Occasionally this paint fired red or reddish brown. The paint sometimes glazed in early Pueblo IV examples, apparently in imitation of imported glazed vessels.

Design

In a pottery type or pottery sequence of this temporal and geographic magnitude, it would seem reasonable to find geographical and temporal stylistic variations, but remarkably few have been isolated. A number of atypical designs such as feathers and flowers were applied to Tabira Black-on-White (Toulouse and Stephenson 1960:21). In early Pueblo IV, there was considerable experimentation in design motifs; single lines from the center of bowls curved to the edge of outflared rims. Rim "ticking" almost certainly was introduced from Galisteo and Santa Fe Black-on-Whites. These latter designs, combined with the new outflared rim, are designated herein as the Capitan variant.

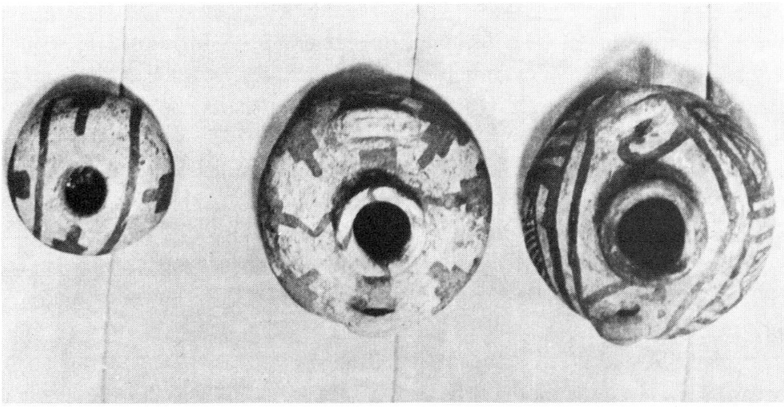

a

b

Plate 2. *a*, Chupadero Black-on-White miniatures, Jack Harkey Collection; *b*, Chupadero Black-on-White jar with zoomorphic design, Ivor Ryberg Collection.

The most common motif of Chupadero Black-on-White consisted of enclosed hatching adjacent to solid black elements (Pl. 3e). Sometimes lines were used in nested squares or rectangles surrounding a small central element, such as a stepped triangle (Pl. 3d). Interlocking scrolls (Pl. 64a), single scrolls, and frets (Pl. 64b) were common elements. By leaving the central element unpainted and blocking in the rest of the panel with black paint, a negative effect was achieved (Pl. 1b; Pl. 3c; Pl. 64a). Animal or naturalistic figures were rare; the only example I have seen is pictured in Plate 2. On jugs, the design was contained in a band around the widest part of the vessel, leaving bottom and shoulder sections undecorated. Lines or other elements were placed around the neck of jugs (Pl. 3e). The central section of bowl interiors was usually left undecorated. Lines just below the rim and at the bottom of the design area often created a band effect, although in some cases the design extended to the rim. On all forms, the design was executed in sections: the basic design was repeated every one or two sections, albeit the repetitions were sometimes roughly executed. At least four sections or panels were normal, and five, six, seven, and eight sections have been noted. Spatial divisions of the sections were not always evenly distributed. Execution of the designs sometimes achieved mathematical precision.

Three Rivers Red-on-Terracotta and Related Types

Paste and Temper

Three Rivers Red-on-Terracotta had a rather distinctive temper in which quartz grains appeared as evenly spaced, rather sparse, white flecks. The paste was harder than any of the Jornada Brown variants or Lincoln Black-on-Red. Three Rivers vessel walls were usually very uniform in thickness (¼ inch was common). San Andres Red-on-Terracotta had temper variation more like the Jornada Brown types, and it was not as hard as Three Rivers Red-on-Terracotta.

Form

Shallow bowls with direct rims were overwhelmingly the most common form (Pl. 63b). Sherds from the Bonnell Site showed that a globular jug with a constricted neck and a thick coiled handle was made. The resemblance of this vessel to Chupadero Black-on-White jugs was heightened by the use of interior straitions. Wide-mouth ollas may have been made occasionally in this type, but I was unable to secure rim sherds of this form.

Surface Treatment

Interiors and exteriors of Three Rivers Red-on-Terracotta bowls were usu-

a b c

Plate 3. Chupadero Black-on-White vessels, Jack Harkey Collection.

ally well smoothed and the interior was often polished. Rims and the upper part of the bowls were usually more highly polished than the bottom of the interior, due to usage which wore away the surface polish. Bowl exteriors varied from highly polished to smoothed to roughened. Roughened or scored bowl exteriors may have been an imitation of Chupadero Black-on-White or Alma Scored. San Andres Red-on-Terracotta bowls had a smoothed but unpolished interior, and exterior roughening was normal. As mentioned above, Three Rivers Red-on-Terracotta jug (and olla?) interiors were sometimes striated and roughened; in this case analogies to Chupadero Black-on-White were clear.

Construction

Coiled construction was used.

Decoration

Historically, the broad red line decoration of San Andres Red-on-Terracotta (some of which was very broad indeed) and Three Rivers Red-on-Terracotta antedated thin-lined designs. The broad red lines were used to form compositions similar to those of some of the Jornada Red-on-Browns. Two, three, or four broad lines would be applied on the interior of the bowl just below the rim. San Andres Red-on-Terracotta often had ½ inch to 1 inch of red paint extending down from the rim on bowl exteriors as did red-slipped Jornada variants. Some designs extended into the central portions, and designs that quartered the bowl were frequent (Pl. 63b).

Thin lines were used in much the same fashion later in time. There was a form of Lincoln Black-on-Red and a Lincoln variant (Red-on-Red) that used thin-lines to produce designs identical to thin-lined Three Rivers Red-on-Terracotta. Three Rivers Red-on-Terracotta and San Andres Red-on-Terracotta rarely had other than line decoration, although one zoomorphic design was present on a sherd from the Bonnell Site. Peckham found "one sherd of what can only be called Three Rivers Polychrome. The usual Red-on-Terracotta, but with the space between the red lines filled in with black. It is probably the result of some influence from El Paso Polychrome, since the black paint appeared to be carbon" (Peckham, personal communication, 9 September 1965).

Slips

These types were customarily unslipped; however, occasionally a red slip was applied to the entire interior of the bowl; it was carried over the rim onto the exterior for ¼ inch to ½ inch. Some of the terracotta-colored interiors appeared to have a thin self slip or wash.

Vessel Color

McCluney (1962) characterizes San Andres Red-on-Terracotta as having a light brown to buff color that does not approach the light orange color of Three Rivers Red-on-Terracotta. A matching of Three Rivers and Jornada Brown sherds against the Munsell Soil Color Chart showed some overlap between them (Table 7). Some Three Rivers Red-on-Terracotta vessels have been fired to an orange color that cannot be confused with any other local pottery type, but many bowls were fired to a less distinctive light brown to buff.

Paint Color

The decoration of San Andres Red-on-Terracotta could vary from red to dark red; it did not approach the bright red-orange of the Three Rivers paint.

Variants of Three Rivers Red-on-Terracotta

Three Rivers Red-on-Terracotta, broad lined, thin lined, red slipped, and polychrome have been discussed above.

TABLE 7
COLOR RANGE OF THREE RIVERS RED-ON-TERRACOTTA SHERDS FROM HOUSE 1, BONNELL SITE, MATCHED AGAINST THE MUNSELL SOIL COLOR CHART

Color	Hue	Value/Chroma
Vessel Color		
Reddish yellow	5 YR	6/8
Reddish yellow	5 YR	6/6
Light reddish yellow	5 YR	6/4
Pink	7.5 YR	7/4
Light Brown	7.5 YR	6/4
Red Paint		
Dark red	2.5 YR	3/6
Red	2.5 YR	4/6
Red	2.5 YR	4/8
Red	10 R	4/6

Lincoln Black-on-Red

Paste and Temper

Sand temper varied in size and frequency. Paste was not as hard as in Three Rivers Red-on-Terracotta. Walls could be from ¼ inch to ½ inch in thickness.

Form

Only bowls with direct rims have been reported.

Surface Treatment

Bowl interiors were smoothed, and sometimes polished. Exteriors were usually smoothed; in one construction technique, bands or slabs were not obliterated on the exterior.

Construction

Coiled construction was most frequent. A number of sherds and vessels from the Phillips Ranch Site show construction by bands or slabs of clay about 1 inch wide (Pl. 14).

Slip

Red polished slips were sometimes applied to bowl interiors. The red color of the unslipped vessel was a result of firing temperature and technique.

Color

Bowls are red to dark reddish brown.

Designs

In the "classic" style, a banded design just below the rim on bowl interiors consisted of solid black step motifs, elongated right angle triangles, and other geometric forms. White lines were occasionally drawn on bowl exteriors, in imitation of St. Johns Polychrome and/or Rio Grande Glaze I.

Variants of Lincoln Black-on-Red

Lincoln Polychrome: A single sherd of true polychrome was found in our excavations. Black and white paints were used to create the interior design.

Lincoln Red-on-Red: Sherds with reddish orange linear designs on Lincoln pottery were found only at sites in the Macho Drainage, where they were fairly numerous. Three and four thin red lines formed designs that extended into the central portions of the bowl, dividing it into quarters.

Lincoln Black-on-Red, Thin-lined: In this style, thin black lines around the interior of the bowl rim were identical to thin red-lined designs on Three Rivers Red-on-Terracotta.

Lincoln Black-on-Red Glaze: The black paint occasionally glazed on late vessels; Stanley Stubbs referred to this as "Lincoln Glaze" (personal communication). Since glazed vessels were being imported at this time, the Lincoln Glaze was probably a deliberate imitation.

REGIONAL SUBSISTENCE PATTERNS IN THE SUBAREA

A rough index of the importance of broad food categories can be gleaned from the relative numbers of projectile points (reflecting hunting), manos and metates (reflecting corn agriculture), and basin milling stones and mortars (reflecting gathered wild products). Quantification of one or all categories is lacking for a number of sites, and in some cases where quantification is available, the sample is too small to be meaningful. Nevertheless, certain trends stand out (Table 8).

Perishable materials from the Hueco Caves, Hermit's Cave, Feather Cave, and other caves explored by amateur collectors show that the pre-pottery economy was based firmly on gathered wild products.

In the Sierra Blanca Region, our artifact samples from Pueblo II and early Pueblo III sites are too small to allow inferences. Lincoln and Glencoe Phase sites usually had a high proportion of projectile points to vegetable food processing tools, and hunting seems to have played a major role. The abundance of animal bones reinforces this interpretation. Plant collecting was carried out, as indicated by the basin milling stones at Bonnell. Gathered products may have been processed close to their source; Grindstone Mesa may have been used to hull or make flour of piñon nuts.

TABLE 8
RELATIVE FREQUENCY OF FOOD PRODUCING ARTIFACT CATEGORIES IN SOUTHEASTERN NEW MEXICO

Phase	Site	No. of Metates	No. of Manos	No. of Points	No. of Mortars and Milling Stones
	Gran Quivira Pithouse Village	Present	Absent	Absent	Absent
Corona	Clint Sultemeier 1			3	
Glencoe	Bonnell	21	121	161	3
	2000 A	4	?	2	1
Lincoln	Hiner 1	3	8	7	
	LA 2945	2	6	0	1
	Phillips	1	8	45	
	Block Lookout	13	23	65	
	Bloom Mound	8	11	65	
Mesilla	Los Tules	8	?	6	
Doña Ana or El Paso	Twelve Room House Ruin	8	15	2	
El Paso	Bradfield	Present	Present	Present	
	Alamogordo	Present	Present	Present	Present
Pueblo Pardo	Pueblo Pardo	35	56	4	

In south-central New Mexico, wild plant products seem to have been a steady and major food source. Lehmer (1948:32, 50) comments about the numbers of bedrock mortar holes in the vicinity of sites of Mesilla and El Paso Phases. It is his impression that mortars and pestles were less important in and around El Paso Phase sites than in preceding phases (Lehmer 1948:50, 81). Mortars were imbedded in room floors of the Alamogordo sites. Points were apparently fairly numerous, as were manos and metates. Subsistence obviously depended heavily on all three categories of food, but relative percentages for the different phases await quantification. Of all the regions of southeastern New Mexico where agricultural village life existed, this region maintained the greatest reliance upon wild vegetable products.

If one can generalize from the excavations at Pueblo Pardo to the entire Chupadero Region during the late prehistoric periods, agriculture played a more central role here than in either the Sierra Blanca or south-central New Mexican Regions. Hunting was of minor importance and no tools suitable for processing wild vegetable products were reported.

Summary

Until about A.D. 900, or perhaps a little earlier in the western regions, the economy of all southeastern New Mexico relied heavily on gathered wild products. Hunting was not a major concern. Corn agriculture probably diffused through ecologically favorable localities before the spread of pottery, but gathered products were still the mainstay of life. Certain regional differences will probably be recognized when the preceramic period is better documented. This way of life apparently continued in isolated regions, such as the Guadalupe Mountains, until the subarea was abandoned.

During Pueblo I, agriculture and village life were established close to the Middle Rio Grande, and the several comales at Gran Quivira Pithouse Village suggested that corn was the staff of life. Northern Pueblo II villages give the impression of relying on corn agriculture. Jelinek has unpublished pollen evidence which shows the Middle Pecos Valley was less arid during Peublo I and II times (personal communication).

In the southern part of the subarea, a mixed economy characterized the Mesilla Phase. This regional reliance on gathered wild products continued into the El Paso Phase.

During late Pueblo III and early Pueblo IV, hunting was important in the Sierra Blanca Region. Hunting was not of comparable importance in contemporary Chupadero Region or Middle Rio Grande sites.

SUMMARY OF CULTURAL RELATIONSHIPS IN THE SIERRA BLANCA REGION

Traits Shared by Early Glencoe and Mesilla Phases

The squarish pithouse with four central posts and a central firepit that became characteristic of the Glencoe Phase was probably derived from square and rectangular pithouses of the Mesilla Phase. Scattered pithouses without apparent arrangement are typical of Mogollon phases until about A.D. 1000, in contrast to the more formal arrangement of Anasazi villages after Pueblo I. Within southeastern New Mexico, known Pueblo II village models were (1) the scattered village plan of Los Tules and (2) the more formally arranged Taylor Draw. Early Glencoe Phase sites probably derived their village plan, as well as their basic house type, from the Mesilla Phase. Metate form was also shared.

Anasazi Traits in the Early Glencoe Phase

Two pithouses in the Peñasco Valley have shapes and features indicative of Anasazi influences, although comparable shapes and features occur in the Mesilla Phase. It is not clear whether we are dealing with Anasazi traits channeled through the Mesilla Phase or with more direct influences. The house types in question are Green's (1956) squarish pithouse with outcurving sides, in which the main posts were set close to the corners, and the circular house at Mayhill Site 2 with an eastern lateral entry and fully encircling bench.

Corona Phase Traits of Anasazi Origin

The use of upright slabs to line shallow house pits is definitely an Anasazi trait. No sites have yet been excavated with this architectural trait in the Chupadero or Middle Rio Grande Regions, but it should be instructive to have sites of the Claunch Phase reported in detail.

Lincoln Phase Traits Shared by Phases in the Chupadero Region

Strong parallels are seen in pueblo construction and plan. There are basic similarities in the pottery complexes, especially during the Claunch and Gran Quivira Phases. Considerable duplication and overlap has been noted for a number of artifact categories, including food processing tools, pipes, bone whistles, slender bone tubes, and so forth.

Differences Between Lincoln and Pueblo Pardo Phases

Certain traits present in the latter phase did not diffuse into the Lincoln Phase, and quantitative differences illustrate cultural lag. Round kivas, doors, room benches, extended burials, cremations, griddles, and slab-lined firepits were unknown in the Lincoln Phase. Mealing bins were perhaps known in the Lincoln Phase; however, they were not in common usage. Slab metates were far more prevalent in the Pueblo Pardo Phase. The pottery complex of the Pueblo Pardo Phase had a much larger percentage of decorated types of Middle Rio Grande origin or inspiration, due to geographical proximity to the source.

Continuity Between Early and Late Glencoe Phase Traits

It should be remembered that the Peñasco Valley, where sites of the early Glencoe Phase have been excavated, was abandoned in late Pueblo III before the Lincoln-derived traits of the late Glencoe Phase had a chance to diffuse. Therefore there are many superficial differences in the pottery complex and in small tools. The basic house type and settlement pattern continued into the late part of the phase.

Traits Shared by the Late Glencoe and Lincoln Phases

By late Pueblo III, there were Lincoln Phase pueblos within 10 miles of the Bonnell Site, which is the main source of information about the late Glencoe Phase. A number of pueblo building concepts were tried out in the building media with which the Glencoe Phase peoples were traditionally familiar. Multi-roomed structures composed of contiguous pit rooms and a nucleated village pattern may be cited. Lincoln Phase kivas are so similar to the typical Glencoe Phase house that an historical connection seems probable. Because of contemporaneity and geographical proximity, the pottery complexes of the two phases were quite similar. The more conservative nature of the Glencoe Phase was reflected in a high proportion of Jornada Brown. Troughed metates with a flat "mano rest" at the closed end were identical in the two phases. Similar mussel shell pendants and ornaments were manufactured. The subsistence pattern of both the Lincoln and late Glencoe Phases emphasized hunting, with similar types of projectile points, more than did earlier phases within the region and more than El Paso and Pueblo Pardo Phases in adjacent regions. A small variety of corn was grown by Lincoln and late Glencoe Phase farmers, although larger varieties have been found in some Lincoln Phase sites.

Relationships Between the El Paso Phase and the Late Glencoe and Lincoln Phases

El Paso Polychrome formed a standard part of the late Glencoe Phase pottery complex, and to a lesser degree, of the Lincoln Phase pottery complex. Slender triangular points with concave or straight bases were common in El Paso Phase sites and they occurred at the Bonnell Site. A disproportionate number of El Paso Phase traits, especially in the ceremonial and ornamental artifact categories, appear at Bloom Mound in the Pecos Valley, a site tentatively assigned to the Lincoln Phase. These include "incense burners," copper bells, and certain types of beads and shell ornaments. It has been postulated that Bloom Mound was a small trading center, perhaps a way station on a Pecos Pueblo - Tularosa Basin route.

Traits Common to the Sierra Blanca Region, the Chupadero Region, and South-central New Mexico

Basic cultural foundations were much the same for all three regions, as they were part of the Southwestern horticultural tradition. Pithouses were replaced by pueblo architecture throughout southeastern New Mexico, with the exception of the Glencoe Phase, as in so many other parts of the Southwest. This widespread trend has not yet been adequately explained in terms of culture process. While basic traits such as pithouses, pueblo buildings, metates, pipes, and so forth occur, few traits have specific parallels in type or form in all three regions. The most detailed similarities are found in the blocky stone or clay animal figures, in the stone *sipapus*, in *Olivella* beads, and in certain widely traded items such as pottery types (although the quantities of particular trade types are not equitably distributed).

Plains Traits and Their Probable Diffusion Routes

Elbow pipes (Bonnell Site) and the *Strombus* pendant (Block Lookout) undoubtedly came from the east. These sorts of trade goods would tend to follow established routes, and as has been noted before, these routes follow the rivers. The nearest and most likely route would be through the Canadian or Arkansas Valleys. Pecos Pueblo is a likely receiving point for such items; from there these could be dispersed through further trade networks. Other Plains traits that could have been obtained more directly from South Plains tribes are hunting equipment, hunting techniques, and tools for processing skins. Scapula scrapers, point types, and the greater number of chipped stone tools in the Glencoe and Lincoln Phases may reflect this type of contact and cultural exchange.

Traits Showing Cultural Lag

A number of traits found in the Sierra Blanca Region were typical of earlier periods in more centrally located regions of the Southwest. Their presence during Pueblo III and early Pueblo IV in this region is interpreted as a function of cultural lag dependent on the remote and marginal position. Individual examples of equally late occurrences elsewhere in the Southwest can be found for all or most traits. It is the large number of out-of-date traits and their quantitative importance in the Sierra Blanca Region that is significant. Glencoe Phase sites consistently show a higher degree of conservatism than do Corona and Lincoln Phase sites. The following traits may be mentioned: pithouses as the major architectural form, slab-lined shallow pithouses, firepits as opposed to fire boxes, the high percentage of undecorated brown pottery, troughed metates, the absence of mealing bins, and bone gaming pieces. Much of the culture seems to lag about one period in the Pecos Classification behind other regions of the Southwest.

Summary

It is clear that the primary cultural influences which contributed to the formation of the early Glencoe Phase came from the Mesilla Phase and perhaps from the little known Doña Ana Phase as well. The Corona Phase and the subsequent Lincoln Phase have their closest ties to phases in the Chupadero Region. The late Glencoe Phase, while retaining some basic traits of the early Glencoe Phase, was in the process of acculturating a large number of Lincoln Phase traits when the region was abandoned.

Chapter 5

ORIGINS AND DEVELOPMENT OF SEDENTARY LIFE IN SOUTHEASTERN NEW MEXICO

RELATIONSHIPS BETWEEN THE HUECO AND MESILLA PHASES

Prior to the advent of sedentary village life about A.D. 900, the mountain regions of southeastern New Mexico were occupied by peoples with a hunting-gathering economy, with a heavy emphasis on gathering. The Hueco Phase, best known from the Guadalupe and Hueco Mountains, is the only cultural entity yet defined for the long period between Early Man hunters and the Mescalero and Lipan Apaches in other regions. Lehmer surveyed the pertinent data in 1948, and little has been done to expand our knowledge of this rather nebulous phase since that date. From Roosa's analysis of the sandals from Feather Cave in the Capitan Mountains (1952:133–46) it is clear that this is or a closely related culture extended into the Sierra Blanca Region.

For purposes of this report, the Hueco or other similar undefined phases are of concern as a possible base from which sedentary village life in south-central New Mexico and the Sierra Blanca Region developed, and as a contemporary, dissimilar culture, located in adjacent mountainous regions, involved in various types of relationships with the sedentary cultures.

Lehmer felt that "The Mesilla Phase was a continuation of the Hueco Phase with the distinguishing traits, architecture and pottery, derived from the Mimbres Branch via the San Marcial Phase" (1948:78). Continuity was seen in stone tools, and Lehmer noted that the Mesilla Phase agricultural complex might have been passed on from the Hueco Phase. Whatever decisions are made about cultural and/or population continuity from Hueco to Mesilla Phases will affect the problem of the origin of the early Glencoe Phase, which was closely related at the time of its inception to the Mesilla Phase.

Wheat (1955b:30–31) argued that the Hueco Cave Dwellers were not an eastern variant of Cochise, and that the basic traits of Mesilla Phase culture were derived rather directly from Mogollon regions to the west. Whether it represents a true Mogollon branch or a Mogollonized branch has not been settled.

One can say with some assurance that the Mesilla Phase did not evolve out of the Hueco Phase in the same manner that early Mogollon culture is said to have evolved out of Cochise. Agriculture in the Hueco Phase was probably diffused as an independent complex from elsewhere in the Southwest; we do not yet have adequate studies of when agriculture appeared in southeastern New Mexico, nor do we know the agricultural complex in any detail. Mesilla agriculture could as well represent a second diffusion of crops and techniques. Certainly the ecological setting of Hueco agriculture in the mountainous regions is different from the lower fringes of the Upper Sonoran Zone and Lower Sonoran Zone exploited by Mesilla Phase farmers in the Rio Grande Valley and in the Tularosa Basin. Other Mesilla Phase elements, such as pottery, house types, and village organization have such strong ties to San Francisco and Three Circle Phases to the west that one must assume strong cultural diffusion or the arrival of some new people.

Pueblo I and II villages in the northern part of the subarea have their closest relationships to eastern Anasazi culture in the Middle Rio Grande. Since earlier cultures have not been described, it is uncertain what type of culture the villages such as Gran Quivira Pithouse Village, Taylor Draw, and Site P4 coexisted with or displaced. If the earlier population had a food gathering economy with a fairly sparse population, the few villages would not necessarily have displaced the older peoples immediately, and a food gathering culture may have occupied the territory around the agricultural villages for some time. In the Sacramento, Guadalupe and Hueco Mountains, the Hueco Phase or at least a non-agricultural, non-village way of life may have continued until late in Pueblo IV times, as indicated by the sherd of Rio Grande Glaze V Polychrome from site LA 546 in the Guadalupe Mountains.

There are very few data which would illuminate the relationships between the sedentary and non-sedentary peoples. Most of the evidence comes from the non-sedentary end of the scale. Sierra Blanca Region pottery reached the late Hueco Phase peoples in the Guadalupe Region, and most non-perishable tools of the Hueco Phase have close counterparts in Sierra Blanca Region or lower Tularosa Basin villages. The perishable goods, so prominent in the dry caves of the Hueco Phase, are poorly represented in village sites. Some of the coiled basketry from Bloom Mound resembles Hueco specimens reported by Cosgrove.

For the present, the relationship of the Hueco and perhaps other undefined but related phases to later sedentary cultures must remain an open question. More work in the Sacramento, Guadalupe, and Hueco Mountains is urgently needed to elucidate the beginnings, cultural context, internal development, and relationship of the non-sedentary cultures of that region to the sedentary cultures.

Did big game hunters occupy some or all of the subarea, as the Folsom point from Burnet Cave suggests, or was the mountainous region always part of the gathering-based Desert Culture? Is the sharp cultural break between the Southwest and the Great Plains in this part of New Mexico one that has great antiquity, or is it only operative for the Pueblo period? Were sedentary, agricultural peoples able to expand into this region because of a hospitable ecology, or did the resident gatherers assimilate agriculture and village life?

PRIMARY SOURCES OF PUEBLO I–II CULTURE IN SOUTHEASTERN NEW MEXICO

Two distinct cultural configurations were present in southeastern New Mexico by Pueblo II. The northern configuration was basically Anasazi while the southern Jornada culture was derived from Mogollon. The sparse sedentary population was cast in the role of pioneers.

The practice of firing pottery in an oxidizing atmosphere diffused into southeastern New Mexico during or before Pueblo I. Virtually every village site in that quarter of the state from Pueblo I to Pueblo IV produced some locally made brown pottery. This technique of pottery firing is thought to be derived from Alma Plain. It may be that brown pottery, like some aspects of agriculture, diffused independently. However and whenever brown pottery arrived, it became a part of the basic culture of the subarea. As part of a common substratum of southeastern New Mexico culture, it has a minimal usefulness in determining the direction from which other cultural traits came. It is more instructive to look at the associated minor pottery types and other cultural traits.

The only Pueblo I site reported to date is Gran Quivira Pithouse Village, which Fenenga (1956:226) designated as Mogollon on the basis of the high percentage of locally manufactured brown pottery. Circular pithouses had a four post support pattern; one of the houses had a ventilator. Pueblo I circular pithouses with this roof support system could be derived either from Anasazi or from what Bullard has called Peripheral Mogollon; the presence of a ventilator argues for the former interpretation. Types of Lino Gray were found on the house floors and in the ventilator. San Marcial Black-on-White was in house fill.

The Pueblo II site of Taylor Draw shows its Anasazi heritage even more clearly. Circular pithouses and slab-lined surface storage rooms were arranged in units that gave a planned village layout quite unlike the contemporary Mesilla Phase site of Los Tules. The kiva has its closest affinities to the eastern

Anasazi. Brown pottery was the most numerous type, although Red Mesa Black-on-White was more diagnostic of cultural relationships.

The Middle Rio Grande is a likely center from which these Pueblo I and II traits could have spread. Brown sherds thought to be of southeastern New Mexican origin have been found in Middle Rio Grande sites (Peckham 1957:70). Other brown sherds from these Rio Grande sites have been classified as Alma Plain, suggesting contacts with the Mogollon heartland. At LA 3290, 22.4% of the sherds were brown (Alma Plain), raising the possibility that some pottery was being fired in a oxidizing atmosphere in the Middle Rio Grande, as this seems like an unusually high percentage to account for by trade alone. Two skeletons from LA 3290 with intermediate occipital deformation (Reed 1957:89) cannot be interpreted as strong evidence of Mogollon influence; neither do they show the more typical Anasazi lambdoid flattening.

The southern Pueblo II Mesilla Phase is known primarily from the site of Los Tules, although it extended over the southern part of the Tularosa Basin. Here again, the basic pottery was brown; associated Mimbres types originated in west-central New Mexico. The pithouses of Los Tules included circular, oval, and rectangular shapes, variously covered with gable, flat, and presumably conical roofs. While individual elements, such as circular houses and four post supports, could be from Anasazi sources, this particular combination is Mogollon in origin. The scattered, unplanned village layout and the absence of kivas are consistent with a Mogollon origin.

SUBSEQUENT DEVELOPMENT OF SEDENTARY VILLAGE LIFE IN SOUTHEASTERN NEW MEXICO

All known Pueblo I and II sites were abandoned by the end of Pueblo II, and the degree of continuity between the Pueblo II and Pueblo III Phases is not clear. In Pueblo III, the Chupadero, south-central New Mexico, and Sierra Blanca Regions had extensive sedentary village occupations. As the sites that Mera (1940a:14–17) briefly mentioned for the territory between the Chupadero and Sierra Blanca Regions are investigated, the apparent geographic break may be eliminated, and it may become desirable to combine phases in the two regions.

In the Tularosa Basin, the Mesilla Phase gave way to the Doña Ana Phase. No excavations have been carried out in sites belonging to the latter phase. Lehmer reported that it was a transitional phase when both pithouse villages and pueblos were built and the older El Paso Brown pottery was being replaced by El Paso Polychrome. Continuity has been demonstrated for various types of tools and ornaments. A dependence on gathered wild products as a secondary food source has been noted for all three phases.

The pueblo architecture that apparently began in the Doña Ana Phase, and which replaced all other house types in the El Paso Phase, could have been introduced from a number of regions. It is possible that it came from the Middle Rio Grande, via the Chupadero Region, from the Mimbres Phase of the Mimbres Region, or from Chihuahua. The linear house blocks and U-shaped or square house blocks built around a large plaza were not duplicated in the Chupadero Region, insofar as we know now. The spaciousness of the plaza in proportion to the room blocks at the Alamogordo Sites imparts a Chihuahuan flavor. Aside from accepting pueblo architecture, the El Paso Phase was remarkably conservative. Pottery obtained through trade was varied as to type and point of origin: Chupadero Black-on-White was the major trade type, indicating strong contacts with the Sierra Blanca or Chupadero Regions. Roughly 80% of the pottery, however, was the locally made El Paso Polychrome.

Developments in the Chupadero Region between Pueblo I and Pueblo IV are not well known. From the number of sites listed in the Laboratory of Anthropology surveys and from the phases briefly outlined by Toulouse and Stephenson (1960:40-41), it is clear that this was a major population center that should be considered as intermediate between southeastern New Mexico and the Rio Grande. One of the greatest needs for further work is in the Pueblo II and III periods in the Chupadero Region.

Sedentary village life may have existed in the Sierra Blanca Region prior to Pueblo III times, as is suggested by a few sites which have only brown pottery. Houses have not been found. For the time being, the story of village life must begin with the early Glencoe and Corona Phases of Pueblo III date.

The Glencoe Phase in the Sacramento and Sierra Blanca Mountains was most closely related to the Mesilla Phase; in some ways, it looks like a marginal Mesilla Phase survival in isolated mountain localities at a time when the Doña Ana Phase had grown out of the Mesilla Phase in the Tularosa Basin. The suggestion has been made that the mountain villages (herein assigned to the Glencoe Phase) might represent seasonal habitations of people living in the Tularosa Basin. The substantial differences in house type, pottery complex, food processing tools, and in other aspects of material culture make this seem unlikely. Furthermore, sites such as the Bonnell Site give evidence of continuous, not seasonal, occupation. A separate phase designation is merited by its different ecological setting, its Pueblo III date, its ceramic complex, and a trend toward standardization of square pithouses with four post supports and flat roofs.

The major architectural style of the Corona Phase was Anasazi in inspiration, although we cannot trace its immediate antecedents. The basic pottery complex was shared to some extent by the early Glencoe Phase to the south and more completely with the Claunch Phase to the west.

Within the Sierra Blanca Region, then, the early Pueblo III phases show the same north-south cultural dichotomy which was evident in Pueblo I and II phases to the northwest and southwest.

The Corona Phase gave way to the Lincoln Phase. Architecture and most of the pottery types of the latter phase were very like those in the Chupadero Region, and close contacts must have been maintained between these two regions. The number of known pueblo sites in the Lincoln Phase implies a population increase over the preceding Corona Phase, and an actual movement of peoples out of the Chupadero Region may have occurred. The Lincoln Phase occupied more territory than the Corona Phase, with an extension south of Capitan Mountain into the Bonito Drainage, and with an isolated colony at Bloom Mound in the Pecos Valley.

Immediately to the south, the late Glencoe Phase continued the conservative way of life established earlier. Pueblo architecture was *not* accepted, and Corrugated pottery did not make much headway in displacing the locally made brown pottery for utility purposes. Many traits were accepted from the Lincoln Phase. If the region had not been abandoned at this juncture, it is probable that these conservatives would have succumbed to diffusing styles in architecture and pottery.

ABANDONMENT — WHEN AND WHY

The Peñasco Valley was the first southeastern New Mexico locality to be abandoned by the sedentary villagers. Since the latest recorded pottery type is Springerville Polychrome, a date of A.D. 1300 ± 25 is suggested for the exodus. Sedentary farmers evacuated almost all of the Sierra Blanca Region before Glaze II pottery reached the region. A few sherds of later glazes have been found in the Gallo Drainage; however, most of the population departed at the end of the Glaze I period. The Tularosa Basin was abandoned at approximately the same time, as Glaze I and Arenal Glaze Polychrome are the latest reported pottery types in El Paso Phase sites. By 1400, or even before, the history of sedentary life in two large regions of southeastern New Mexico came to an end. In the Chupadero Region, Indian settlements survived into Spanish contact times.

It is difficult to say why this territory was abandoned. Many Southwestern archaeologists have dealt with terminal occupations. Climatic change and consequent events such as arroyo cutting, disease, social disintegration, and Enemy Peoples have been used singly or in tandem to explain this widespread phenomenom. Our data allow limited comments about the first and last mentioned possibilities.

At this time we do not have the necessary data from pollen analysis and geology to make an analysis of climatic or of environmental shifts that would have rendered these regions uninhabitable for agriculturalists. Arroyo cutting may have increased about A.D. 1350, as it did in eastern Arizona, where it has been suggested that the total rainfall may not have changed appreciably, although the pattern of annual rainfall shifted to torrential summer rains conducive to arroyo cutting (Schoenwetter, in Martin, et al. 1962). If this were the case, the water table in the Gallo, Macho, Hondo, and Peñasco Drainages might have been lowered, and so the entire Sierra Blanca Region would have been adversely affected. A similar situation would have developed in the Tularosa Basin. On Chupadero Mesa, the water supply came from surface lakes which may have been able to capture and retain the water from torrential summer rains without resultant erosion. If so, this could be the reason why this region alone in southeastern New Mexico was able to maintain sedentary villages. To resolve this problem, ecological interpretations based on pollen analysis, sediment studies, and so forth need to be carried out in southeastern New Mexico.

The Athabascans have been a favored Enemy People. The most recent evidence suggests a late entry of Athabascan groups into the area (Dittert, Hester, and Eddy 1961:346–65; Gunnerson 1956:346–65; Gunnerson 1960:252). The Espejo Expedition of 1582–83 did not encounter indentifiable Apache groups along the Rio Grande. The Apache intrusion into southeastern New Mexico probably occurred after 1600. Certainly Apache, and possibly Comanche, were raiding missions in eastern New Mexico by 1659. It is generally agreed that the final withdrawal of surviving Indians from the Salinas Missions to the vicinity of Socorro in the Rio Grande Valley was occasioned by Apache raids coupled with a series of crop failures (Toulouse 1949:4).

Other candidates for the villanous role of Enemy People include (1) the pre-Apache, non-sedentary groups who inhabited the more remote mountainous sections of southeastern New Mexico; (2) the pre-Apache foot nomads of the Plains, who may have been feeling the pressure from Apaches or other groups pushing down the western Plains; and (3) inter-village hostilities which may have occurred.

Two archaeological cases of hostile activities have been noted. Bloom Mound was burned and some of the inhabitants killed. The undated hilltop fort, now in the Mescalero Reservation, was highly defensive, implying a last ditch stand for a group displaced from their customary dwelling place. Apparently the fort is not remembered in Mescalero Apache folklore, and it may pertain to the prehistoric period under consideration.

In lean years, face-to-face contacts might decrease and be less friendly. In really hard times, hostilities broke out. Bloom Mound, advantageously placed to trade with the Plains buffalo hunters and to act as a way station on the Pecos-Tularosa Basin trade route, was isolated and unprotected when hostilities arose. Deteriorating environmental conditions would be reflected in increased hostile activities. Kidder (1958:309–10) discusses the interrelationship of these two factors for Pecos, basing his comments on J. Charles Kelley's (1952) well-reasoned arguments about the abandonment of the Rio Grande between El Paso and the Conchos River. It is probable that during good times when crops were good, hunting was profitable, and wild food plants were abundant, harmonious relationships must have existed between the several dissimilar groups in the Sierra Blanca Region. Trading and visiting would have been mutually advantageous, and Bloom Mound must have been host to many parties.

The burning of Bloom Mound coincided in time with the abandonment of the rest of the Sierra Blanca and south-central New Mexico regions. No direct evidence of hostile activities at other village sites has been recorded. Some, but not all, of the later villages were located away from water on vantage points that afforded visibility in all directions. An assured water supply would seem to be an essential ingredient for defense; it is possible that enough water could be stored in jars to last through short raids, or there may have been larger water storage facilities within the sites that have not been found archaeologically. Aside from the factor of increased visibility, none of the village sites were extremely defensive.

ETHNIC IDENTITY

The historic inhabitants of the Salinas-Medano Missions were Piro speakers, as has been convincingly demonstrated by Scholes and Mera (1940:265–99). The Spaniards distinguished between the Tompiro and the Jumanos, but the languages may have been related dialects, as indicated in this passage from Fray Freita's writings:

> Fray Garcia de San Francisco is the only religious who knows and preaches in the Piro language, the language of the pueblos of El Socorro, and of the pueblos of Seneca, El Alamillo, and Sevillita; he can also make himself understood by the Indians of the pueblos of Umanos, Abo and Tabira. . . . [Scholes and Mera 1940:283]

In view of the close archaeological connections between phases in the Chupadero Region and the Corona and Lincoln Phases, it is possible that Piro speakers of the Tanoan stock once spread as far south and east as the Bonito Valley of the Hondo Drainage.

Davis (1959:73–84) postulated removal of Tanoan speakers from Cochise culture, because the geographical center of Azteco-Tanoan is to the southwest.

Such a derivation could be responsible for the use of brown, oxidized-fired pottery and occipital flattening of skulls in the Middle Rio Grande and in the Chupadero and northern Sierra Blanca Regions. In the same paper, Davis explored the time depth of various Tanoan languages, using glottochronolgy. Sixty-three Piro words were available of the 100-word basic vocabulary established by Swadesh. The time depth of 1200 years suggested for Piro would differentiate it from the more northern Tanoan languages about A.D. 750, a date that fits fairly well with the earliest Pueblo I and II cultures in the subarea. It is therefore possible that the sedentary peoples in the northern part of southeastern New Mexico were Piro speakers from the earliest sedentary occupation. This gives greater time depth to the Tanoans in the Chupadero and Sierra Blanca Regions than did Mera's suggestion that the Tanoans drifted south with pueblo architecture and Chupadero Black-on-White pottery (Scholes and Mera 1940:293).

The Espejo Expedition of 1582–83 passed through several Piro towns in the Rio Grande Valley. Luxan's diary gives us glimpses of Piro life at that date (Hammond and Rey 1929:72–76). Villages varied in size from 20 to 100 "houses," which must have referred to households, as the rest of his description obviously refers to pueblos, not individual houses. Luxan's estimates of number of "houses" and total village population for six Piro villages indicate that he calculated an average of eight individuals to a household unit. Two-story pueblos had rooms which were used for specialized functions. Mealing bins, in ground floor rooms, were made of four to eight metates placed together. Earthen jar stands (*tinaxeros de barro*) supported water jars. Bows and arrows were few and poorly made; instead the Piro fought with clubs and bludgeons equipped with stone heads. The kivas were located in the plaza, and roof entry was through a trap door and ladder. Stone benches encircled the whitewashed interior of the kiva. Turkeys were grown for their feathers which were used in making feather blankets. Articles of clothing mentioned by Luxan include small cotton blankets worn by both women and men to cover their privy parts, tanned deerskin jackets or tanned deerskins tied to the body, feather cloaks, and shoes or boots of tanned deerskin. Penis decoration was also mentioned. Maize, beans, gourds, and cotton were cultivated.

The ethnic identity of the southerners, archaeologically represented by the Glencoe, Mesilla, Doña Ana, and El Paso Phases, is even more tentative. Within historic times, the aboriginal inhabitants of these regions have been various groups of Apache settled there by the Spaniards, and the groups around El Paso that were known as the Caguate and Tanpachoans in the sixteenth century and the Mansos in the seventeenth century. Only the latter groups can be considered as possible descendants from the people of the Mesilla or El Paso Phases. Lehmer (1948:86) concluded that the cultural inventory of the Mansos was so distinct from that of the El Paso Phase that the

Mansos could not be connected with the Jornada Branch. The brush-covered houses, skin clothing, temporal agriculture, and little pottery described by Bandelier for the Mansos bear little resemblance to the pueblo-dwelling, pottery-making, agriculturalists of the El Paso Phase.

A more roundabout, remote sort of relationship between the La Junta and El Paso Phases has been charted by Newcomb (1961:Ch. 9) and Kelley (1949:89–114). The villages which the Espejo Expedition visited from the mouth of the Conchos to El Paso were inhabited by people who were to some extent the cultural descendants of the Jornada Branch. It is difficult to tell whether there were actual migrations of Jornada peoples down the Rio Grande or an existing population that accepted pottery and pithouses from the Mesilla and Doña Ana Phases, or if both sorts of diffusion were at work.

A house remnant from the earliest site reported for the La Junta Focus, Site 3109–5 (Kelley 1949:89–114), was similar to the square pithouses of the Glencoe Phase. Later La Junta Phase houses sometimes had *jacal* walls placed inside the pit wall, a construction technique present in the Glencoe Phase. Altars or platforms within rooms are typical of the La Junta Phase; Lehmer (1948:80) cites similar altars in southern El Paso Phase sites. Small stone platforms in Mimbres Phase sites were located in plazas. The "altars" in Antelope Creek Focus sites have close parallels to the La Junta Phase examples.

La Junta Focus pottery came, directly or indirectly, from Jornada regions. At Site 3109–5, the nine sherds were classified as five El Paso Brown, one "affinis" Three Rivers, one plain polished Red-on-Brown, one plain brown, and one deep corrugated. Later in the La Junta Focus, El Paso Polychrome became the dominant type, and Chihuahuan types were acquired regularly by trade. Chupadero Black-on-White was found at Site 5702–3. Presumably the local brown pottery types of later times, such as Conchos Plain and Conchos Red-on-Brown, evolved out of brown, red-on-brown, and red-slipped types that were found over southeastern New Mexico and parts of Chihuahua.

Troughed metates were in use in the Bravo Valley Aspect, as they were in the Sierra Blanca Region. A number of tool categories, especially those connected with fishing and gathering, are continuations of older Archaic forms, and as such have no parallels in the Jornada Branch. The high value which the historic inhabitants at the mouth of the Conchos placed on buffalo skins suggests Plains tastes or ties, as the buffalo hides had to be acquired from some distance. The diamond-shaped, four-beveled knives of the La Junta, Concepcion and Conchos foci (Kelley 1954:45–51) are also suggestive of Plains connections.

The economy of the Bravo Valley Aspect and of the sixteenth- and seventeenth-century groups between the Conchos and El Paso was more diversified than in any of the Jornada Phases. Fishing was not practiced in any Jornada Phase.

It would seem that certain traits connected with sedentary living diffused down the Rio Grande from the Jornada regions. These influences, probably from the Doña Ana Phase, merged with local cultures to create an agricultural village-dwelling population. The most pure Jornada ties may be isolated in the early La Junta Focus. Subsequent local development and other external influences caused the culture to become more differentiated from that of the Jornada regions. While El Paso Phase pottery reached the mouth of the Conchos, El Paso Phase pueblo architecture did not. After 1400, the El Paso Phase had ceased to exist. Jornada traits survived in attentuated form in this marginal region.

The Bravo Valley Aspect has certain parallels with the Glencoe Phase in that both received basic elements from the Mesilla and Doña Ana Phases; both retained traits that went out of style in the more central regions; and pottery was the cultural element in which continued cultural contact between the marginal and central regions was best reflected.

The ethnic identity of the Jornada peoples cannot be linked to the historic tribes in the lower Rio Grande Valley. On the basis of distributional evidence, I think it not impossible that the Jornada peoples (or some of them) were Uto-Aztecan speakers. How closely they were related to the Suma, regarded by both Sauer (1934) and Scholes (Scholes and Mera 1940) as Uto-Aztecan speakers, cannot be surmised.

MARGINALISM AND CULTURAL CONSERVATISM

Southeastern New Mexico was geographically marginal to the rest of the Southwest. The northern part received primary cultural influences from the Middle Rio Grande, a region that was itself considered to be culturally marginal to Anasazi culture until about A.D. 1200 (Wendorf 1954c:202). The southern or Jornada part of the subarea was marginal to the Mimbres Region from about A.D. 900 to A.D. 1100.

A number of traits were flourishing in the Sierra Blanca Region at a time when they were long out of fashion in more centrally located parts of the Southwest. The time lag is frequently about one period in the Pecos Classification. The time necessary for traits to reach to this somewhat remote region resulted in a sloping diffusion horizon. The distribution of Sierra Blanca people in small, scattered communites, especially those of the Glencoe Phase, slowed down diffusion. There were only two main directions from which primary cultural influences compatible to village-dwelling farmers could come. The semi-remoteness, the demographic situation, the sloping diffusion horizon and the limited number of contacts with other agricultural peoples resulted in an internal process whereby cultural conservatism was fostered.

Wendorf (1954c:215), in discussing the Upper Rio Grande after A.D. 1200, suggested that a variety of slightly different cultural influences may be responsible for dynamic new cultural growth and development. The Sierra Blanca Region represents a case in which the number of similar cultural influences has been restricted by its geographical position. Viewing the region as a circle, about 180° fronted eastward on non-agricultural, hunting and gathering groups who surely affected the way of life in the Sierra Blanca Region, but whose culture was too dissimilar to serve as a stimulus toward dynamic development in the core areas of a villager's way of life. The remaining half of the circle faced Southwestern agriculturalists. Cultural influences compatible with an agricultural, village-dwelling ethos were limited to the western half of the circle, where there were only two main lines of communication to the ongoing developments in more centrally-located sectors of the Southwest.

Some of the effects of this geographical and cultural marginalism were: (1) sedentary village life began later than in the more central regions; (2) traits that were older in other regions persisted into later times; (3) there was an absence of traits that were contemporary in other regions; (4) the cultural inventory was simple, or less elaborate, than elsewhere; (5) selective diffusion of some cultural complexes resulted in a transformation of certain aspects of culture; (6) there were fewer unique traits; and (7) by limiting the variety of cultural influences through geographical factors, the diversity conducive to dynamic cultural development was minimized.

Sedentary village life began about A.D. 700 in the northern part of southeastern New Mexico, on the Pueblo I time horizon. This was undoubtedly a function of cultural lag, and it may simply represent the length of time necessary for the diffusion of a trait or complex of traits.

Some traits out of vogue elsewhere in the Southwest persisted as part of the cultural complex of the Sierra Blanca Region. Slab-lined surface houses of the Corona Phase, the square pithouses of the Glencoe Phase, troughed metates in Glencoe and Lincoln Phases, the large percentage of undecorated brown pottery in the Glencoe Phase, and bone gaming pieces of the Glencoe Phase serve to illustrate this point.

A number of traits present in adjacent regions failed to penetrate the Sierra Blanca Region. Some that reached the Lincoln Phase did not spread south to the Glencoe Phase. Circular kivas and various construction features of pueblo architecture such as doorways were in use in the Chupadero Region, but as yet are not known for the Lincoln Phase. Pueblo architecture did not penetrate south of the Bonito Valley in the Sierra Blanca Region.

As might be expected, the Chupadero Region occupied an intermediate cultural position between the Sierra Blanca Region and Rio Grande in respect to retention of older traits and absence of traits that were extant in the Middle Rio Grande. As an example, slab metates had been accepted and were the most numerous form, but trough metates continued in use in the Pueblo Pardo - Pueblo Colorado Phases. Such distinctive Rio Grande traits as spiral-grooved axes, rectangular kivas, room kivas, and kiva murals apparently never reached the Chupadero Region.

Single culture traits, such as metate form, diffused without recognizable changes. When a complex of traits connected with a particular aspect of culture were shifted from one region to another region, either by stimulus diffusion or actual migration, the component parts of the complex were reworked. If we had sufficient data, it is probable that every major complex would show this sort of creative reworking or reassembling of component parts, with some features dropping out. The religious complex is a case in point.

In general, the cultural inventory of the Sierra Blanca Region seems meager in comparison to other parts of the Southwest at comparable dates, and there is little that is unique to the region. Most cultural traits and trait complexes can be traced to outside sources, and the total cultural content was somewhat simplified in the diffusion process. This is true of domestic architecture, the religious complex, and the locally made pottery.

The best case of the regional development of a major cultural trait may be the square ceremonial chambers of the Lincoln Phase. I feel that these developed out of the domestic architecture of the Glencoe Phase, and that they did not originate in the western Pueblo area as did the rectangular kivas of the Rio Grande. The pithouses of the Glencoe Phase in turn represent a local standardization of basic architectural techniques and concepts that were derived basically from the Mesilla Phase.

In speculating about the reasons why the Sierra Blanca Region did not achieve a cultural florescence, two reasons come to the forefront. First, the development was cut short by the abandonment of the region. Second, its marginal position was such that diverse cultural influences and populations did not enter the region. A situation comparable to the florescence of Rio Grande Anasazi culture after A.D. 1200 (based on the fusion of slightly diverse elements that entered that region about that time) did not develop in the Sierra Blanca Region.

SUGGESTIONS FOR FUTURE WORK

The scanty nature of published archaeological reports for southeastern New

Mexico has been apparent throughout this study. It is quite clear that future work will cause some basic modifications of interpretations made here. Any site which was dug and reported would significantly increase our knowledge. Some key problem areas could be made less critical through limited, judicious excavations.

We need to know a great deal more about the culture that existed prior to the introduction of sedentary villages into southeastern New Mexico. How far does the Hueco Phase extend geographically? Can other phases be isolated? Can the non-sedentary people of the Sacramento, Guadalupe, and Hueco mountains from A.D. 900 to A.D. 1600 be placed in the Hueco Phase, or should new phases be defined? Open sites in the desert basins and valleys need to be correlated with the cave materials from the mountains. The Organ–San Andres mountains need to be explored. Publication of the Feather Cave report by the University of New Mexico will materially increase our knowledge of this time period. In regions where sedentary village life was never established, we need more careful work to demonstrate how the older Hueco pattern was modified by having sedentary villages nearby, and to ascertain if these regions were abandoned prior to the arrival of historic tribes, or if there is cultural continuity into historic times.

The intensity and extent of the Pueblo I and Pueblo II Anasazi culture needs to be delineated. Where in the Tularosa Basin and the eastern mountains is the dividing line between those Pueblo II sites of Anasazi derivation with associated Red Mesa Black-on-White and those Pueblo II sites of Mogollon derivation associated with Mimbres types? A search should be made for Pueblo I and II sites in the Sierra Blanca Region and in the territory between this region and Chupadero Mesa.

The early phases in the Chupadero Region, briefly set forth by Toulouse and Stephenson (1960:40–41), need to be documented through excavation since this region is of critical importance in any interpretation of southeastern New Mexican prehistory. The territory around Los Pinos Mountain should be surveyed and the cultural affiliations of the local cultural sequence specified. The nature of contacts with the Galisteo Basin needs to be explored.

In the Sierra Blanca Region, the cultural content of all three phases defined in this report, especially the early Glencoe and Corona, needs to be known in greater detail. Some of the circular, slab-lined structures of the Corona Phase need to be excavated to determine if they are, in fact, ceremonial structures. The geographical boundaries of the early Glencoe Phase should be delineated, and more information is needed about the postulated continuity between early and late Glencoe Phase sites. The extent of the Lincoln Phase intrusion into the Pecos Valley, now known only from Bloom Mound, needs to be clarified.

Sites of the Doña Ana Phase have not been excavated. This was a vital transitional period, and as such, it needs clarification.

The agricultural complex is not well known from any region. In the absence of preserved materials, pollen analysis might be of assistance. Corn from all of the localities needs to be compared. The primitive, Bat Cave-like variety from Lincoln and Glencoe Phase sites raises the question of where this variety survived in the Southwest. Pollen analysis could also contribute significantly toward an environmental reconstruction of past ecological conditions and allow us to assess the role of environmental change in the abandonment of various regions.

Chronology needs to be more finely drawn, and when tree-ring dating is feasible, this can be begun. A more thorough pottery analysis than has been attempted here would clarify this problem somewhat.

A detailed collection of petroglyphic and pictographic materials should be made before these are further defaced. Comparative studies of the styles and subject matter are needed.

Finally, study of the physical anthropology of the southeastern New Mexico aborigines, now virtually unknown, could shed light upon some of the archaeological problems.

Appendix 1

ARCHAEOLOGY OF THE UPPER GALLO DRAINAGE

INTRODUCTION

The upper Gallo Drainage includes the upper parts of the Gallo River and its tributary, Bonito Arroyo (Map 2), which head in the higher elevations of the Gallinas Mountains to the west and flow in a general southeasterly direction. All are classed as intermittent streams and are now virtually dry except during summer rains. Maps show that these streams dissipate about halfway to the Pecos River. A few small pools of water survive in the deeper holes for longer periods. Today there is little surface water and modern inhabitants get their water from wells.

Elevation varies from 6600 feet above sea level in the western part of the locality to approximately 5800 feet in the southeastern part. Known archaeological sites are in partially wooded rolling foothills. Vegetation is typical of the Upper Sonoran Zone and includes species of both grassland and piñon-juniper belts. Larger trees occur at higher elevations where there is a precipitation advantage. Soil Conservation Service maps categorize the valley environs as wooded foothills with shallow sandy soil which border on open grassy plains with the same soil type.

Along many low ridges the uppermost limestone beds are exposed, presenting a rough, solution-pitted surface. Underlying the limestone, and exposed where stream erosion has occurred, are medium to massive bedded sandstones that are buff in color that break into fairly uniform slabs 1 to 2 inches thick which were utilized as a building material.

Most prominent of modern surface features are the sand dunes resulting from eolian activity. Massive dunes occur in the broad valley on both sides of the modern stream channel, the dunes east of the river being larger. There is some evidence that much of this eolian activity occurred in recent times. For example, we noted a fence line buried to a depth of 4 feet with windblown sand.

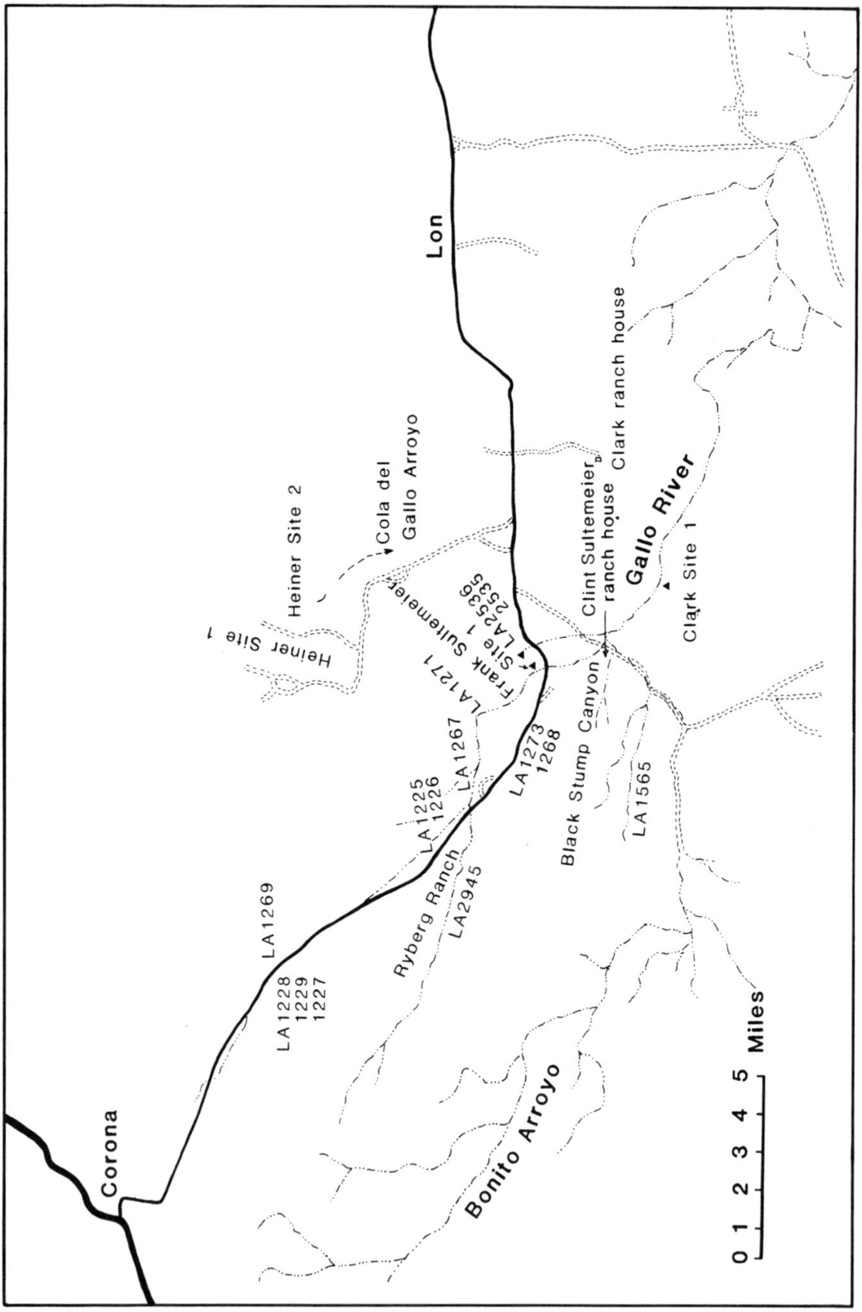

Map 2. Location of known sites, upper Gallo Drainage, New Mexico.

Several factors argue for more surface water existing at the time the prehistoric sites were occupied. The amount of surface water now available would not support the population indicated by the size and number of prehistoric sites in the upper Gallo Drainage. The lower fill in the rooms of some Lincoln Phase sites was of gray silty materials overlain by tan eolian sand. As a result of the modern eolian activity, much of the best farmland in the valley bottoms is now under dunes.

Previous Work

The Laboratory of Anthropology in Santa Fe has recorded sites in this locality for many years. Sites included in their survey, as of 1955, are considered later in this chapter. Smiley, Stubbs, and Bannister (1953:37) published a series of tree-ring dates from LA 1225. Site LA 2945, excavated as part of a highway salvage program, was reported by Wendorf (1956:87-105).

Fieldwork

Eight sites were surveyed and limited excavations conducted at five of these in 1953 and 1954 by Texas Technological College field crews.

EXCAVATED SITES OR FEATURES NOT ASSIGNED TO A PHASE

Clint Sultemeier Site 2

Location

The Clint Sultemeier Site 2 is located approximately NE¼, S2, T3S, R15E. A deep pit was located some 600 feet east of the Clint Sultemeier ranch house. No other surface features were noted in the vicinity.

The Excavated Feature

The pit was 5⅓ feet in diameter and 5 feet 7 inches deep (Pl.4; Pl.7b). A circle of upright stone slabs had been set from 3 to 14 inches back from the edge of the pit mouth. Dug through sand, pit walls were well plastered with clay ⅓ to 1½ inches in thickness. A shallow, curved indentation in the south wall could have served as a foot hole. Flagstones were stacked in the lower 12 inches of the pit, above which it was filled with blown sand. A sherd of Jornada Brown pottery was in the fill at a depth of 3 feet. Below the flagstones were eight Jornada Brown sherds, five of which were the heavily micaceous Gallo Variant of that type.

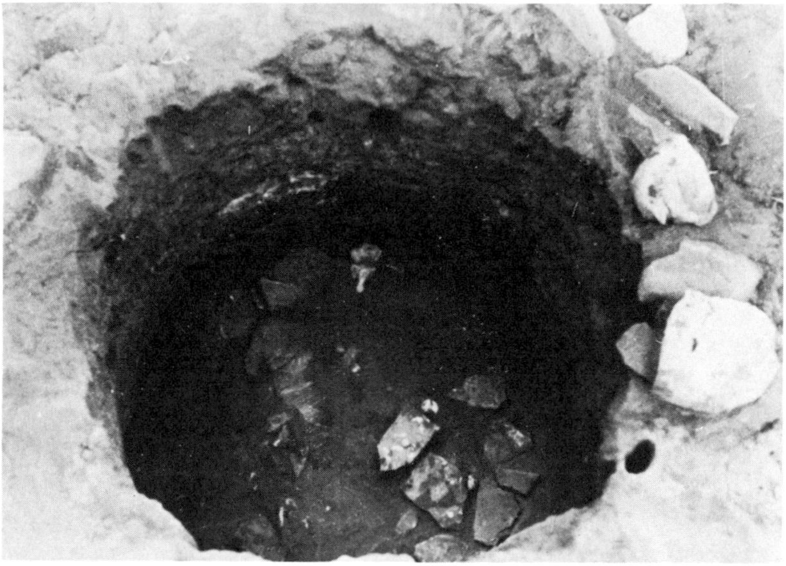

a

b

Plate 4. Pit, Sultemeier Site 2.

Clark Site 1

Location

Clark Site 1 is near the center of S7, T3S, R16E. The isolated feature described below was located on a terrace on the west bank of the Gallo River. Piñon trees grow on the site.

Surface Indications

Upright stone slabs, about 8 feet in diameter, were visible on the surface. They formed almost a complete circle.

The Excavated Feature

Upright slabs ringed the mouth of a large cylindrical pit. An entrance and two toe-holes were shaped on the south side (Fig. 10; Pl. 5). Holes a few inches below the mouth show that a roof was made of cross beams and poles. Two upright posts on either side of the entrance depression indicate that this too had a low cover. This pit was larger than the one at Clint Sultemeier Site 2; it measured 6 feet 4 inches to 6 feet 8 inches in diameter. From the rim of the pit to the floor was 9 feet, from the modern surface to the floor was 10 feet 2 inches. The fill was wind blown sand. A few rocks were in the bottom. Water had stood in the pit several times. A one-end-open trough metate was found about halfway down in the fill, and four sherds of Jornada Brown pottery were in the bottom, all four belong to a single olla with a highly polished exterior.

Isolated Feature at the Frank Sultemeier Site

Location

This feature was found at W½, S26, T2S, R15E.

The Excavated Feature

A test pit 75 feet east of the mound exposed a large storage pit (Fig. 11) that was similar in form to those at Clint Sultemeier Site 2 and Clark Site 1. The mouth of the pit was 18 inches below the modern surface. The trashy fill over the pit consisted of numerous burned sandstone rocks, a metate fragment, charcoal, sherds, poorly preserved bone, and a side-notched point; these remains pertained to the Lincoln Phase occupation of the adjacent pueblo. The pit itself, 7 feet in diameter and approximately 7 feet deep, had a layer of flat rocks covering the bottom of the floor. The straight sides were plastered only for the lower 2 feet. In contrast to the trashy fill over the mouth of the pit, the wind-blown sand within the pit contained only a few scattered Jornada Brown sherds and a corncob 4½ feet above the pit floor.

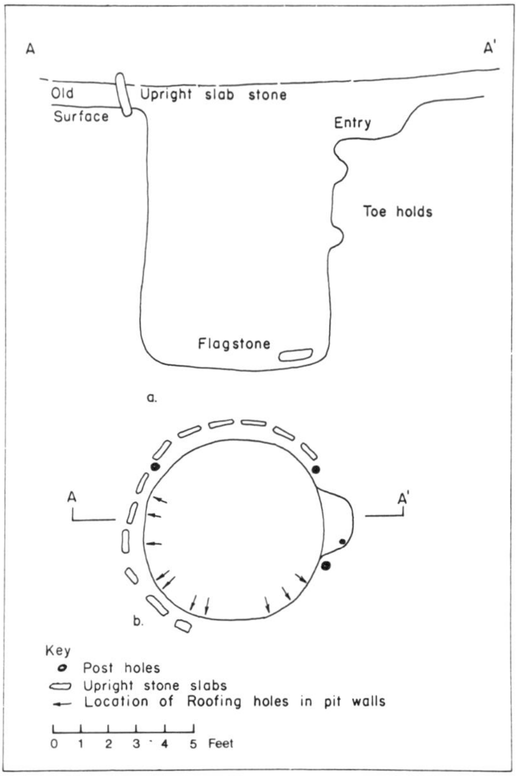

Figure 10. Pit, Clark Site 1: *a,* Cross-section of pit; *b,* Top view, showing upright stone slabs around pit mouth, entry, and posts for roof supports.

Comment on the Three Preceding Features

Since the three pits contained only Jornada Brown sherds, they may antedate the Corona Phase. None had been secondarily used for trash deposition or burial. Evidence from Clark Site 1 shows that some of these cylindrical pits were roofed. To date, accompanying cultural features such as houses have not been recognized. All three pits were located close to streams. In one case, the pit was dug through sand in the valley floor, and in another case it was placed so that it received surface slope drainage. The pit walls testified that water had stood in the pit several times. The topographic placement of these two pits would seem to limit their usefulness for grain storage.

We considered the possibility that these pits served as wells, and the placement of the pit at Clint Sultemeier Site 1 would seem to support such a hypothesis. However, the other two features were not suitably placed to collect or hold water.

Plate 5. Pit, Clark Site 1.

Plate 5. Pit, Clark Site 1.

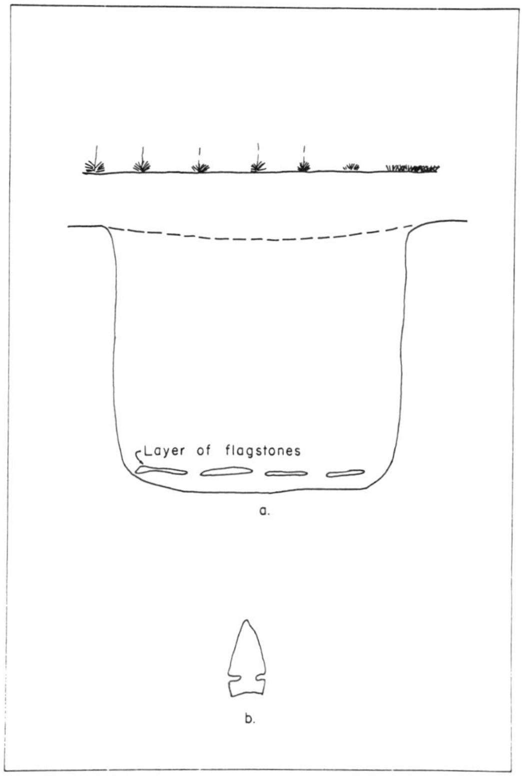

Figure 11. *a*, Cross-section of pit, Frank Sultemeier Site. Pit size: 7 feet in diameter and 7 feet in depth. *b*, Projectile point found in the pit fill. Length: 23 mm.

AN EXCAVATED SITE OF THE CORONA PHASE

Clint Sultemeier Site 1

Location

NE ¼, S2, T3S, R15E. This site is on the flat valley floor of the west bank of the Gallo River a short distance above the junction of this river with Bonito Arroyo.

Surface Indications

Isolated rooms and small house units containing two and three rooms were visibly outlined with upright stone slabs. Slab-outlined structures cover at least an acre on the west side of the river, and drifted sand probably covers additional rooms. On the opposite bank of the river, under the modern ranch house, are other cultural remains that could have formed part of the same village. Sherds were fairly abundant on the surface over several acres on both sides of the river. Chert chips and occasional stone artifacts could be found. The Clint Sultemeier family had an extensive collection from the site. Four slab-outlined rooms were excavated; a fifth was outlined by Dr. Carl Schmidt, a visitor in our camp.

Architecture

Three of the five structures were adjacent but not contiguous. Rooms 1, 2, and 3 lay in a north-south line (Fig. 12).

Room 1: An irregular rectangle in form, Room 1 was the largest of the three adjacent rooms and measured ca. 11½ x 8¾ feet (Pl. 6; Pl. 7a). The rough clay floor was about 9 inches below the present surface. A firepit 8½ inches in diameter and 9 inches deep with straight, plastered sides was floored with a stone slab; a thick layer of ash was present in the bottom. Just west of the firepit was an empty clay-lined pit 8 inches deep. At least four of the nine interior post holes must have furnished wall and roof support. The depth of the main post holes varied from 6 to 14 inches. A cluster of five post holes 3½ to 5 inches deep in the northeast corner may have had a different function. Eight worked fragments of chalcedony and quartzite, a bifacial tool of red jasper, a black chert side-notched arrow point, and some sherds to be described separately were found.

Rooms 2 and 3: Both rooms were floored with flagstones and neither had a fireplace (Pl. 6). These rooms probably served as storerooms for the people who lived in the larger, adjacent Room 1. Room 2 measured about 9 feet by 7½ feet while Room 3 was about 7¼ x 6½ feet (Fig. 12). Interior posts, which were set on the flagstones, had clay built up around their bases. A small subfloor pit in the southwest corner of Room 3 contained a few sherds. No artifacts were found in Room 2; two Chupadero Black-on-White pottery discs came from Room 3.

Room 4: Upright stone slabs outlined this isolated room on three sides (Fig. 13). Erosion had removed the south wall and most of the floor. No artifacts were found.

Room 5: Two walls were traced, and a post hole was located near the northeast corner (Fig. 14). The clay floor was exposed along the north and east wall. No artifacts were found.

Artifacts

The paucity of artifacts was probably due to the shallow fill of the houses and the eroded surface as well as the frequent artifact collecting of local ranchers.

Chipped Stone: Ten flakes of quartzite, chert, chalcedony, limey chert, and flint showed slight unifacial retouch. Nine of these were thin internal flakes;

the longest was 3 inches in length. A quartzite pebble was broken in half, and the edge had been used. Two complete points and a point tip came from the site. The small, symmetrical, side-notched point of black chert and a gray flint point tip were surface finds. An asymmetrical ovate of red mottled jasper from Room 1 was 2⅝ inches long, 2 inches wide, and ½ inch thick; large flakes were removed from both faces, and the ovate had some edge retouch.

Worked Sherds: Two rectangular worked sherds of Chupadero Black-on-White were found in Room 3.

Pottery

Over one-half of the sherds were undecorated Jornada Brown, with small numbers of decorated variants (Table 9). Chupadero Black-on-White comprises 32% of the total count. A questionable Glaze I sherd and an equally questionable Gila Polychrome sherd came from Room 3. A basket-impressed white sherd was examined by Stanley Stubbs, who was not familiar with the type.

SURVEYED SITES OF THE CORONA PHASE

Black Stump Canyon Site

Location

Black Stump Canyon Site is located at about NE ¼, S4, T3S, R14E. The canyon was 3 miles west of the Clint Sultemeier ranch headquarters. At the point where the site is located, the valley is about one-half mile wide, and the valley floor is level. Piñon-juniper grow in an open stand.

Surface Indications

The outlines of slab-lined houses and house units covered some 10 acres. The settlement pattern was similar to Clint Sultemeier Site 1 and Hiner Site 2.

A room 10 x 7 feet, exposed by recent road grading, had a floor of hard-packed earth. Toward the center, a fire box full of ashes was made of three rock slabs set into the floor.

Pottery

Jornada Brown sherds, Gallo Micaceous variant, are assumed to be of local manufacture; the Roswell Brown variant may have been imported. The partially corrugated olla has a thickened everted rim and a smooth neck; slightly smoothed corrugations extend about halfway down the vessel, and the lower portion is smoothed. Temper is large and angular; the paste is friable. Since one vessel and one other sherd are represented, the percentage of corrugated is unrealistically high (Table 10).

TABLE 9
SHERD TABULATION,
CLINT SULTEMEIER SITE 1

Pottery Type	Rooms						Surface	Total	
	2			3		4		No.	%
	Floor	Fill	Fill & Floor	Fill & Floor	Sub-floor Pit	Fill & Floor			
Jornada Brown, undecorated Jornada variant				2	2	1	x	5	
Gallo Micaceous variant	43		25	17		18	x	103	
Roswell Brown variant	2	1	3	8	1	1	x	16	
Total								124	56.6
Jornada Brown, decorated									
Roswell Red-slipped-bowl	1			1				2	
Total								2	0.9
Chupadero Black-on-White Bowls	6	5	3	8		8	x	30	
Jugs	17	4	10	16	1	4	x	52	
Total								82	37.4
Glaze I				1(?)				1	0.5
Jornada Polychrome				1				1	0.5
Gila (?) Polychrome				1(?)				1	0.5
Unclassified									
White	1							1	0.5
Other				7				7	3.2
Total	70	10	41	62	4	32		219	
Floor & Fill	80			66					

x = present

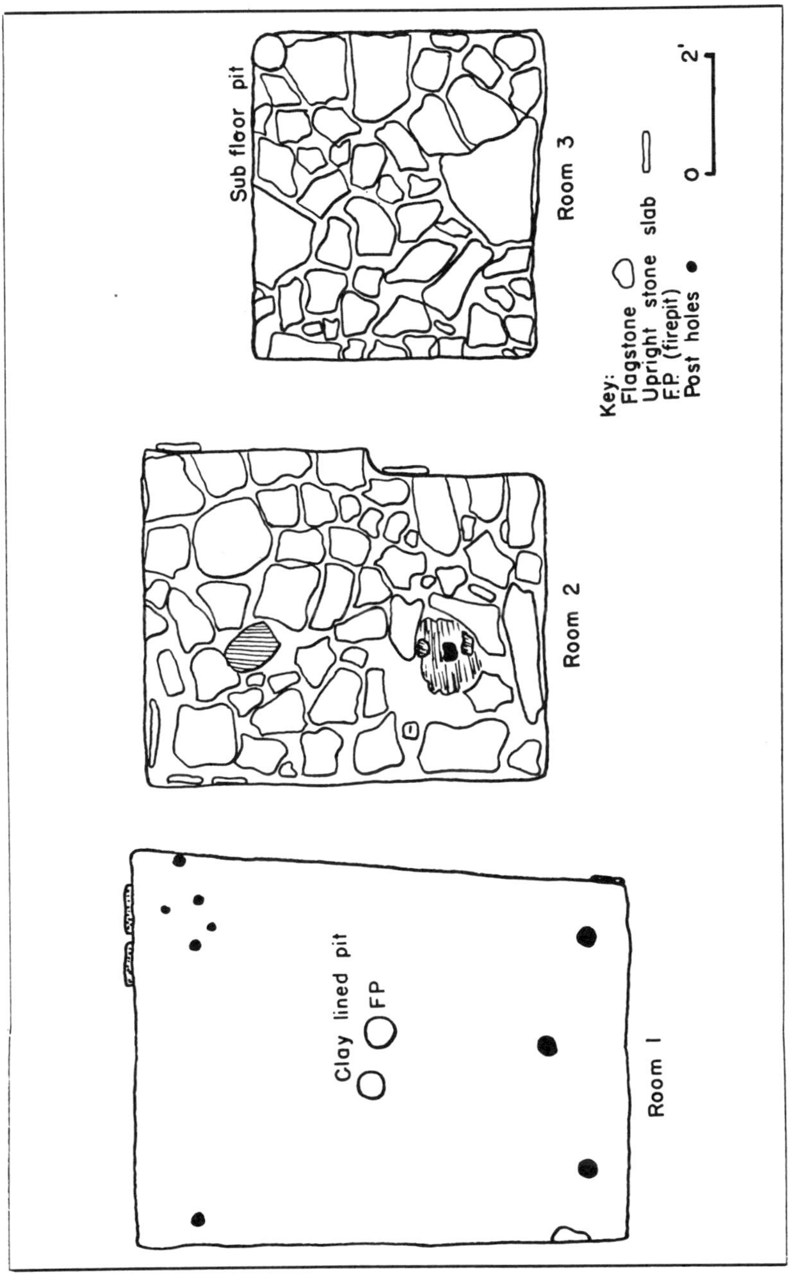

Figure 12. Plan of Rooms 1, 2, and 3, Clint Sultemeier Site 1.

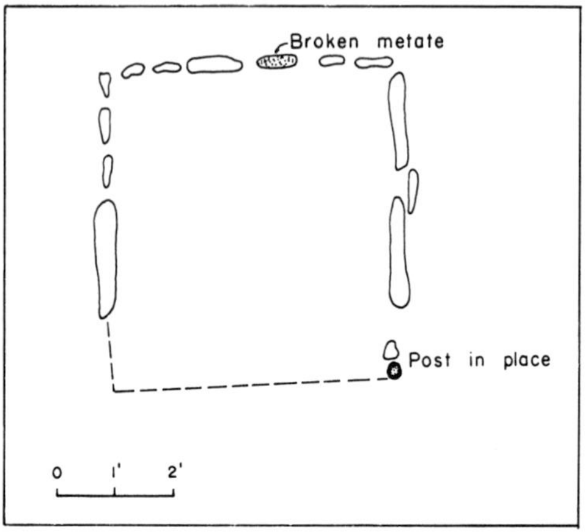

Figure 13. Plan of Room 4, Clint Sultemeier Site 1.

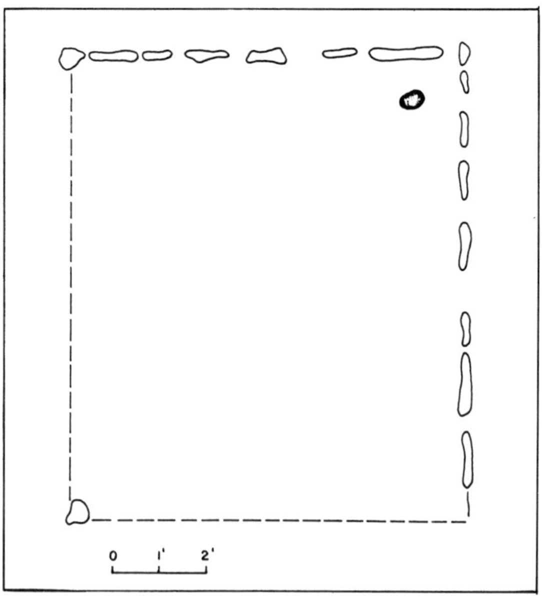

Figure 14. Plan of Room 5, Clint Sultemeier Site 1.

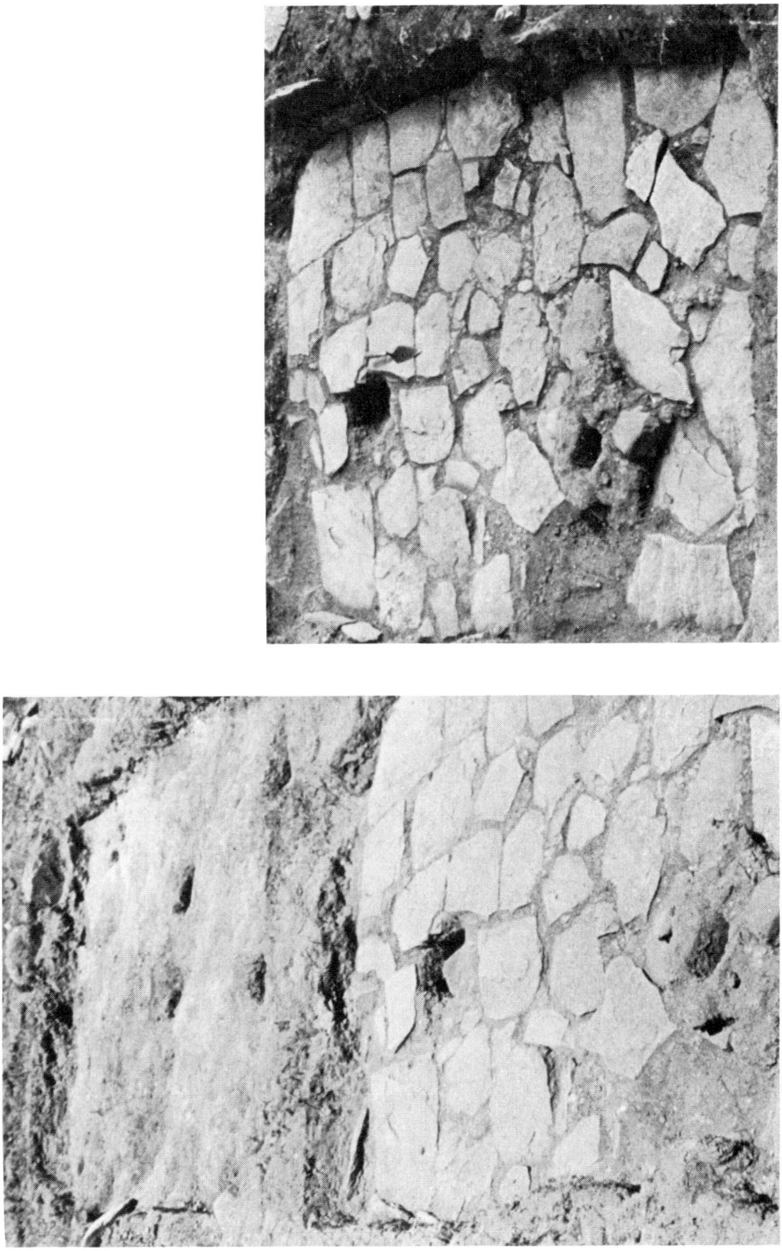

Plate 6. Rooms 1 and 2, Clint Sultemeier Site 1.

Plate 7. *a*, Room 1 detail, Clint Sultemeier Site 1; *b*, Pit, Clint Sultemeier Site 2.

Phase Designation

Assignment of this site to the Corona Phase is based primarily on the slab-outlined architecture arranged in an open settlement pattern. Percentages of Jornada Brown and Chupadero Black-on-White are large enough to make this reasonable. However, other types normally thought to be somewhat later occur on the surface of this site.

Hiner Site 2

Location

Hiner Site 2 is in approximately the SW ¼, S36, T1S, R16E. The site is about 3 miles east of the Hiner ranch house on the south bank of the Cola del Gallo Arroyo, a tributary not shown on available maps. An unused fence line that runs through the site was unstrung as a result of a survey about 1940 that moved Mr. Hiner's boundary farther east. Ecologically, the site is slightly higher in elevation than other sites in the locality, and today supports pine and piñon as well as various yuccas.

Surface Indications

Individual rooms and small house units outlined by upright stone slabs parallel the arroyo for 200 feet.

An unusual number of artifacts were present on the surface, due to the site's isolated location and the fact that Mr. Hiner did not welcome amateur archaeologists.

Artifacts

Chipped stone: Quartz, quartzite, and red flint or jasper were common raw materials. Occurring in smaller quantities were opal, obsidian, chert, other flints, and chalcedonies.

Small corner-notched and crude side-notched points were collected. Worked flakes showed no definite type, and no piece was found with enough retouch to be called a scraper. A flint graver was made on a flake.

Ground stone: Loaf-shaped manos were common. Small pebble grinding stones, 3 to 4 inches in diameter, occurred. A full-grooved maul was found.

Pottery

A high percentage of brown sherds was observed but no count was made. Jornada Brown, Gallo Micaceous variant, was the most common type; non-micaceous Jornada Brown, Roswell Brown, and Jornada Polychrome were present. Chupadero Black-on-White was the second most numerous sherd category. One sherd of Three Rivers Red-on-Terracotta and one sherd of Glaze I were collected.

TABLE 10
BLACK STUMP CANYON SITE, SURFACE SURVEY SHERD COUNT

Pottery Type	No.	%
Chupadero Black-on-White		
Jug	110	
Bowl	24	
Basket-impressed bowl	1	
Total	135	39.24
Jornada Brown, Undecorated		
Gallo Micaceous variant	103	
Roswell variant	15	
Total	118	34.30
Jornada Brown, decorated		
Roswell Red-slipped bowl	2	0.58
Jornada Polychrome	4	1.16
Corrugated		
Type undifferentiated. Partially corrugated. Single vessel.	51	
Los Lunas Smudged (?)	1	
Total	52	15.12
El Paso Polychrome	15	4.36
Three Rivers Red-on-Terracotta		
Undecorated sherds	3	
Broad-lined	2	
Red-slipped bowl sherd	1	
Total	6	1.74
Unclassified Black-on-White	12	3.49
Grand Total	344	

Clark Site 2

Location

Clark Site 2 is located at S ½, S35, T2S, R16E. An extensive site covering several acres lies just east of the Clark ranch house on the north bank of an unmapped tributary of the Gallo River.

Surface Indication

Rooms outlined by stone slabs were visible. Most seemed to be scattered individual rooms. One rectangular, multi-roomed structure had nine clearly outlined rooms, each approximately 9 x 14 feet, and additional rooms were indicated. One circular, slab-outlined structure and a semicircular arrangement of upright slabs were noted. Few sherds were present on the surface. Manos, trough metates with mano rests, and a variety of flakes were seen but were not collected.

Pottery

Only 20 sherds were picked up after a fairly extensive search:

Jornada Brown	9
Three Rivers Red-on-Terracotta, olla	1
Chupadero Black-on-White, jug	5
Chaco Black-on-White II	2
Unidentified Black-on-White	2
Broad-lined Red-on-Terracotta, not typed, with a gray, coarse paste	1
Total	20

EXCAVATED SITES OF THE LINCOLN PHASE

Frank Sultemeier Site

Location

Frank Sultemeier Site is located at W½, S26, T2S, R15E, on the north bank of the Gallo River.

Surface Indications

A rather square mound some 200 feet square with a central depression was interpreted as a square pueblo with a plaza in the center. The tops of a few masonry walls were exposed by erosion and pot hunters had dug out a few rooms. There was an abundance of pottery on the surface, as well as some chipped stone.

Excavated Features

A single room in the southeast corner of the pueblo was excavated; a pit that predated the pueblo has been described earlier in this appendix.

Room 1: Dimensions of the room were 7 feet 10 inches (north-south) x 6 feet 6 inches (east-west). Walls standing to a height of 21 inches were made of sandstone slabs 1 to 3 inches thick separated by heavy layers of mud mortar. The north and south walls had been plastered, but no plaster was found on the east and west walls. Flagstones covered most of the floor. There were no internal posts. The size, the flagstone floor, and the absence of a firepit suggested that this was a storeroom. A corner-notched arrow point was excavated 4 inches above the floor, and a shell pendant lay on the floor.

Hiner Site 1

Location

Approximately S25 of T1S, R15E. The site was about 0.3 miles south of the Carl Hiner ranch house. No trees grew on the site, although piñon grows in the vicinity.

Surface Indications

Two large, roughly circular mounds had central depressions. Two linear mounds were located immediately east of the circular mounds. The southwestern structure, chosen for limited excavation, was about 140 feet in diameter and contained an estimated 120 rooms. Our excavations and visible surface features indicated that adobe-walled rooms stood three rooms deep on four sides of the plaza. Stone slabs outlined small rooms on the outer edges of the structure which may have been lean-to additions to the main building (Map 3).

Excavations

Five adobe-walled rooms in the northeast corner of the structure were excavated (Fig. 15; Pl. 8), as was one of the slab-outlined rooms on the south. After we had cleared the five adobe-walled rooms, sub-floor tests below Rooms 1, 3, and 4 demonstrated that the adobe walls rested on a deep fill, rich in cultural materials. A test pit in the center of the plaza was carried to a depth of 6 feet through almost sterile heavy black soil. A skeleton was found at this depth, and the rest of the time allocated for completing the test pit was consumed in cleaning the skeleton. The floor of the plaza or subterranean chamber, which would have been well below ground level, was never reached.

Architecture

The five adobe-walled rooms on the northeast corner will be described together (Fig. 15). Rooms 1, 3, 4, and 5 had single floors; Room 6 had three superimposed floors. Room 2, a slab-lined room on the south side of the pueblo, will be considered last. None of the excavated rooms had burned.

Room 1: The single interior feature was a centrally-located post some 5 inches in diameter. The north wall, which was the outside wall of the pueblo, was about 12 inches thick. Interior walls were about 8 inches thick.

Artifacts found in Room 1 included two loaf-shaped, rectangular manos which had two opposed grinding faces. A one-handed grinding stone was ground on one face. A shaft-straightener fragment made of an unshaped limestone pebble had a short transverse groove. Chipped stone tools included a scraper-chopper of black shale (3½ inches long, 2¼ inches wide, and 1¼ inches thick), and an unworked chert flake. The single polishing pebble was made of black chert. Three bone awls were made of split and polished ribs.

Room 3: A firepit was located in the southwest quarter of the room and post holes were placed in three corners.

Artifacts found in Room 3 included four sandstone mano fragments of the

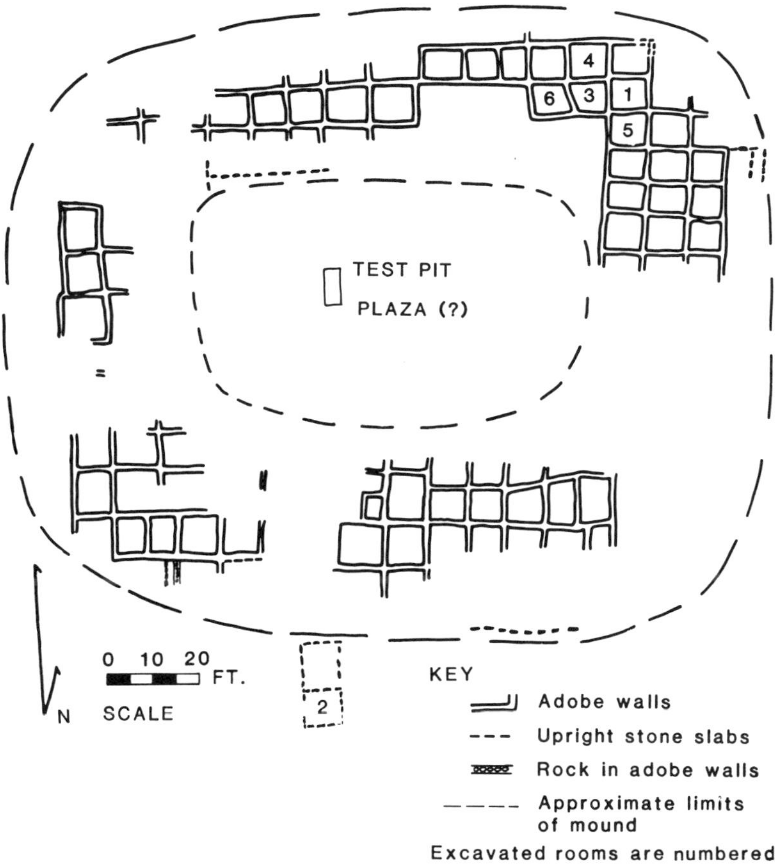

Map 3. Sketch map of visible walls, Hiner Site 1, Mound 1.

loaf type. Each had two opposing, parallel grinding faces. One oval pebble grinding stone 5 inches long was ground on only one face. Five sandstone slabs from 8 to 15 inches in length showed signs of grinding; red pigment adhered to four. Chipped stone artifacts included a snub-nosed scraper of white quartzite and three projectile points; of the latter, two had small side notches and one was corner notched. A stone disc bead (½ inch in diameter, ⅛ inch thick) had a biconical perforation. The single bone tool was a split rib awl.

Room 4: A well-plastered central firepit was 11½ to 12 inches in diameter and 3½ inches deep. An upright slab (15 x 8 x 1 inch) stood in the northwest corner. Two stones were set on edge towards the middle of the room.

Artifacts found in Room 4 included a metate fragment which was turned upside-down over the firepit. A second metate fragment with a mano rest was upside-down on the floor.

Room 5: A shallow depression 15 inches in diameter was in the south side of the room. Several upright stone slabs had been placed around the wall (Pl. 9).

Artifacts found in Room 5 were as follows. A large trough metate with a mano rest at the closed end and a flat grinding slab were on the floor. A loaf-type mano fragment had two opposing grinding surfaces. A small, corner-notched projectile point was found. Three awls, all over 5 inches long, were lying together in a corner.

Room 6: Two to three inches separated each of the three floors. The uppermost floor had a new fireplace; the lower two floors shared a firepit. The firepits were 11½ inches in diameter and 13 inches in diameter, respectively; both were approximately 4 inches deep with straight, plastered walls. Three holes in the floor may have been post holes. A sub-floor pit in the northwest corner, 8 inches deep and 12 inches in diameter, contained a lump of red clay, a worked deer scapula, and several split bones. An infant had been buried from the middle floor level in a small grave (13 inches east-west, 9½ inches north-south, and 8 inches deep); the body was flexed, with the head to the east and the face to the north.

Artifacts found in Room 6 included a sandstone grinding slab (10 x 9 x 2 inches), upside-down on the uppermost floor. A fragment of a loaf-shaped mano had four grinding faces; pecking marks on the unground surfaces showed that the mano had been shaped before use. A small pebble (3 inches in diameter and 2 inches thick) had been ground on two flat faces and on two edges. A hammerstone had been battered until it assumed a spherical shape. Two shaft-straighteners were unusually small. One quartz polishing pebble was found. Two of the nine flakes or small cores were similar in color to Alibates flint, but it is probable that they were derived from other beds. Red chalcedony or jasper, quartz, quartzite, and chert were represented.

Figure 15. Plan of Rooms 1, 2, 3, 4, and 5, Hiner Site 1.

Plate 8. Hiner Site 1: *a,* Rooms 3 and 6, looking west; *b,* looking north across excavated rooms.

Plate 9. Room 5, Hiner Site 1.

A flat section of cut scapula had one edge slightly beveled from use; the other edge had been nicked. A double-pointed punch and a tool with a blunt point on one end and a scraping or smoothing area on the other end were both made of split ribs. A long-bone splinter (bison?) had one end smoothed from use with a scraping or gouging motion.

Room 2: Stone slabs set on edge outlined this room, which was an appendage to the south wall of the pueblo (Map 3). A cylindrical firepit in the northeast quarter of the room was 8 inches in diameter and 5 inches deep. The floor was of packed earth.

Artifacts found in Room 2 included a small shaft-straightener made on a limestone pebble, which had both ends battered. One of two rectangular Chupadero Black-on-White worked sherds had a groove that could have served to suspend it as a pendant. There were three unworked quartzite flakes.

Artifacts

Individual artifacts have been described in the context of their placement in rooms. These and additional surface finds are tabulated in Table 11.

Food Remains

No plant products were recovered. Animal bones were common, indicating a substantial reliance on hunting. Certain lots of bone were weighed, producing the following totals.

Animal	*Room 1 Fill*	*Sub-floor Test, Rooms 1, 3, and 4*
Bison(?)		124 g
Deer and/or antelope	75 g	174 g
Intermediate-sized animals	19 g	
Small animals	6 g	54 g
Turtle shell	4 g	

Four bones identified as bison were in the size range of that animal, but only midsections of long bones were present and positive identification could not be made. Epiphyseal closure of deer bones indicated that both young and old individuals were hunted. Limb bones, ribs, and scapula were the most common body parts; one pelvic fragment and a single vertebra were found. Bone tools from this site emphasized ribs over metapodials.

Pottery

Changes in the percentages of the major types between the floor and subfloor samples were:

	Floor Room 1		*Subfloor Rooms 1, 3, and 4*	
	Count	*Weight*	*Count*	*Weight*
Chupadero Black-on-White	43%	36%	42%	39%
Corrugated	43%	55%	32%	33%
Undecorated, Jornada Brown	11%	6%	15%	13%

Corrugated increased markedly during the last occupation at the site, represented by Room 1, and undecorated Jornada Brown decreased in importance. Chupadero Black-on-White remained much the same. Glaze I and St. Johns Polychrome occurred in the sub-floor fill; Heshotauthla Polychrome was the only diagnostic trade type on the floor of Room 1.

TABLE 11
ARTIFACT TABULATION, HINER SITE 1

Artifacts	Excavated	Surface	Total
Chipped stone			
Points	4	3	7
Scrapers	2	3	5
Scraper-chopper	1		1
Worked flakes, bifacial		1	1
Worked flakes, unifacial	9	3	12
Flake gravers	2	1	3
Drill		1	1
Ground stone			
Shaft-straighteners	4		4
Metates, trough with mano rest	4		4
Metates, fragments	1		1
Manos, loaf type	5		5
Manos, undesignated	2		2
Pebble grinding stones	4		4
Grinding slabs, over 8 inches long	6		6
Grinding slabs, under 5 inches long	7		7
Polishing pebbles	5		5
Disc bead	1		1
Hammerstone	1		1
Abrading stone	1		1
Bone			
Awls	15		15
Punch	5		5
Worked deer scapula	5		5
Miscellaneous worked bones	2		2
Shell			
Glycymeris fragment	1		1

Sherd samples from Rooms 3, 4, 5, and 6 were not analyzed in detail. Superficial examination showed the sherds from these rooms to be similar to those from Room 1.

In Room 2 where the fill was only a few inches deep, 23 Jornada Brown sherds and 2 Chupadero Black-on-White were found. This suggests an earlier date for the room, but its physical location makes it appear that this was a contemporaneous outbuilding of the pueblo. See Table 12.

Ryberg Site 3

This large masonry pueblo was designated Site 3 by Wendorf (1956:89), when he described LA 2945 on the same ranch.

Location

The site is between the ranch house and the Lon-Corona Road, on the Carl Ivor Ryberg ranch.

Surface Indications

A rectangular mound ca. 100 x 200 feet had a central plaza depression. The site was well known to amateur diggers, and numerous pot holes exposed masonry walls of coursed sandstone. The Gallo Valley was quite wide at this point, and cultural debris was scattered over several acres.

Additional Remarks

It should be recorded for the sake of future archaeologists that Mr. Ryberg has been reburying Indian skeletons for some 25 years. As skeletons erode or are plowed up in his field or racetrack, Mr. Ryberg excavates them, takes them to a plot south of his house, and reinters them with a Christian ceremony.

Excavation

We tested a room already disturbed by amateurs, to expose the masonry and to acquire a ceramic sample.

Pottery

Eight Chupadero Black-on-White and one Jornada Polychrome were found in the tested room, suggesting that part of the site might be earlier than surface pottery indicates. The sample was inadequate to allow us to state the site's age with much certainty.

Surface sherds identified by Stanley Stubbs included Rio Grande Glaze I, Lincoln variant (which he dated about A.D. 1400); Chihuahua (Ramos?) incised; Mimbres Bold Face; Rio Grande Glaze III said to be almost Glaze IV (two sherds); Chaco Black-on-White II (five sherds). Additional types col-

TABLE 12
CERAMICS FROM ROOM 1 AND SUB-FLOOR TEST BY COUNT AND BY WEIGHT, HINER SITE 1

	Hiner Room 1																Rooms 1, 3, 4							
Pottery Types	Level 2				Level 3				Level 4				Level 6				Sub-floor				Total Wt.		Count	
	g	%	no.	%	g	%	no.	%	g	%	no.	%	g	%	no.	%	g	%	no.	%	g	%	no.	%
Corrugated																								
Rim	137		8		389		3						16		3		46		9					
Body	292		23		430		44		213		21		462		39		1294		160					
Total	429	80.79	31	67.39	819	64.95	47	53.41	213	22.07	21	21.65	478	56.23	42	42.86	1340	32.80	169	32.94	3279	42.63	310	36.82
Chupadero																								
Jug-body	53		7		327		24		306		36		288		38		901		130					
rim					4		1		3		1						33		1					
Bowl-body					44		8		169		15		27		5		373		66					
rim					39		5		33		3						271		23					
Total	53	9.98	7	15.22	414	32.83	38	43.18	511	52.95	55	56.70	315	37.06	43	43.88	1578	38.63	220	42.88	2871	37.32	363	43.11
Jornada Brown																								
Gallo Micaceous	45		6						119		16		51		9		461		62					
Roswell													2		2		7		2					
Other	1		1						4		1						155		15					
Total	46	8.66	7	15.22					123	12.75	17	17.52	53	6.23	11	11.22	623	15.25	79	15.40	845	10.98	114	13.54
El Paso																								
Polychrome																	7	0.17	1	0.19	7	0.09	1	0.12
Jornada Poly.																	83	2.03	5	0.97	83	1.08	5	0.59
Glaze I					8	0.63	1	1.14									76	1.86	4	0.78	84	1.09	5	0.59
Heshotauthla Poly.													4	0.47	2	2.05					4	0.05	2	0.24
St. John's Poly.									4	0.41	1	1.03					6	0.15	2	0.39	10	0.13	3	0.36
Gila Poly.	3	0.56	1	2.17																	3	0.04	1	0.12
Unident. Poly.																	2	0.04	1	0.19	2	0.03	1	0.12
Three Rivers																								
Thin-lined					16		1										20		3					
No design									110		2						13		4					
Total					16	1.27	1	1.14	110	11.40	2	2.06					33	0.81	7	1.36	159	2.07	10	1.19
Unclassified																								
Black-on-White									4	0.41	1	1.03					298	7.29	22	4.29	302	3.93	23	2.73
Other					4	0.32	1	1.14									39	0.95	3	0.58	43	0.56	4	0.47
Grand Total	531		46		1261		88		965		97		850		98		4085		513		7692		842	

lected in our survey were Rio Grande Glaze I (Middle Rio Grande in origin), Chupadero Black-on-White, El Paso Polychrome, Lincoln Black-on-Red, Jornada Polychrome, Three Rivers Red-on-Terracotta (thin-lined and red-slipped), and Corrugated with some mica in the temper. Brown sherds included several tempering agents and finishes. Stubbs examined several brown sherds and called them "unclassified general brown with paste similar to El Paso." Roswell Brown was probably imported from the east. Other sherds with the temper characteristics of the Roswell type lacked exterior polishing. Jornada Brown, Gallo Micaceous variant, was presumably manufactured locally. Decorated Jornada Brown sherds included red-slipped and red-on-brown line designs in bowls.

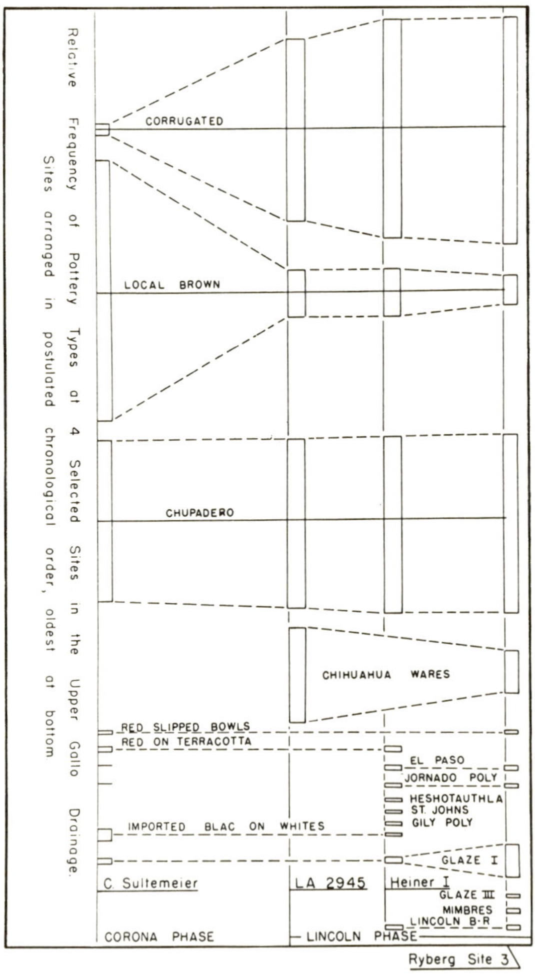

Figure 16. Relative frequency of ceramic types at four sites in the upper Gallo Drainage.

LABORATORY OF ANTHROPOLOGY SURVEY

Twelve sites from the Laboratory of Anthropology files are considered here. The sites are approximately located on Map 2, and the ceramic lists from each site are given below. Sites are roughly arranged on the list according to the latest component in the pottery complex. Many of the sites with pottery of mixed age cannot be assigned to a phase or to phases without additional information. Members of the Lino series suggest that Basketmaker III or Pueblo I sites will be found. There was probably a continuous occupation of the valley throughout the pueblo periods. Glaze III sherds are the terminal pottery type.

LA 1229: All brown sherds

LA 1273: Brown and Chupadero Black-on-White; "visited by Gila Pueblo and few sherds left." Probably Corona Phase

LA 2535: Brown, Chupadero Black-on-White, Chaco II, Alma Brown(?), a Francisco Red (?). Latter two are probably of local manufacture, probably Corona Phase

LA 1269: Brown, Chupadero Black-on-White, Lino Fugitive Red, Upper Gila Corrugated

LA 2537: Brown, Chupadero Black-on-White, coarse-tempered Pink Lino Gray, Red-on-Brown, Cibola White

LA 1565: Brown, Chupadero Black-on-White, Three Rivers Red-on-Terracotta, Chaco II,. Upper Gila Corrugated

LA 1227: Brown, Chupadero Black-on-White, Corrugated, Tularosa Black-on-White, St. Johns Polychrome, Three Rivers Red-on-Terracotta, Upper Gila Corrugated

LA 1226: Brown, Chupadero Black-on-White, Corrugated, Chaco Black-on-White, Three Rivers Red-on-Terracotta, Lincoln Black-on-Red, Glaze I (2 sherds), St. Johns Polychrome, Upper Gila Corrugated (Lincoln Phase)

LA 1228: Chupadero Black-on-White, Lincoln Black-on-Red, Glaze I (Lincoln Phase)

LA 1267: Brown, Chupadero Black-on-White, Corrugated, Socorro Black-on-White, Santa Fe Black-on-White, Three Rivers Red-on-Terracotta, Lincoln Black-on-Red, St. Johns Polychrome, Glaze I (Lincoln Phase)

LA 1225: Chupadero Black-on-White, Lincoln Black-on-Red, Red Mesa Black-on-White, Mesa Verde Black-on-White, Three Rivers Red-on-Terracotta, St. Johns Polychrome, Glaze I, San Clemente Glaze Polychrome, Arenal Glaze Polychrome, Los Lunas Smudged, Gila Polychrome, Heshotauthla Polychrome (Lincoln Phase)

LA 1268: Chupadero Black-on-White, Corrugated, Galisteo Black-on-White, Mesa Verde Black-on-White, Wingate Black-on-Red, St. Johns Polychrome, Heshotauthla Polychrome, El Paso Polychrome, Three Rivers Red-on-Terracotta, Los Padillos Polychrome, Glaze I, Klagetoli Polychrome (Lincoln Phase)

Appendix 2

SITES IN THE UPPER MACHO DRAINAGE

Carrizo and Patos creeks head in the Tucson, Carrizo, and Patos Mountains, of which Carrizo Mountain is the highest (9656 feet). Outwash fans are especially extensive and provide a favorable location for agriculture. These streams flow east along the north side of Capitan Mountain to the Pecos River. Sites are located both in the piñon-juniper belt and at the modern border of that belt where it merges with the grasslands belt of the Upper Sonoran. The steep slopes of Carrizo Mountain support oak and pine.

THE PHILLIPS SITE

Location

N ½ of S13, T7S, R13E and S ½ of S12, T7S, R13E (Map 4). This site is located along both sides of Carrizo Creek. The ranch house of what is now the Goodloe Ranch is at the west boundary of the site which extends approximately one-half mile to the east. The valley is now grassland, but piñon-juniper, oak and occasional pines grow at the valley edge.

Surface Indications

Some 49 scattered house units were partially outlined with upright stone slabs (Map 5). Sherds, chert chips, and other cultural debris were found over the entire valley floor and up onto the first flat terraces on either side of the valley.

Surface pottery collections made it clear that the house units north of the stream, tentatively assigned to the Corona Phase, were older than most of the house units south of the stream. One Corona Phase house unit was on the south terrace. Those house units having the later pottery complex were tentatively assigned to the Lincoln Phase.

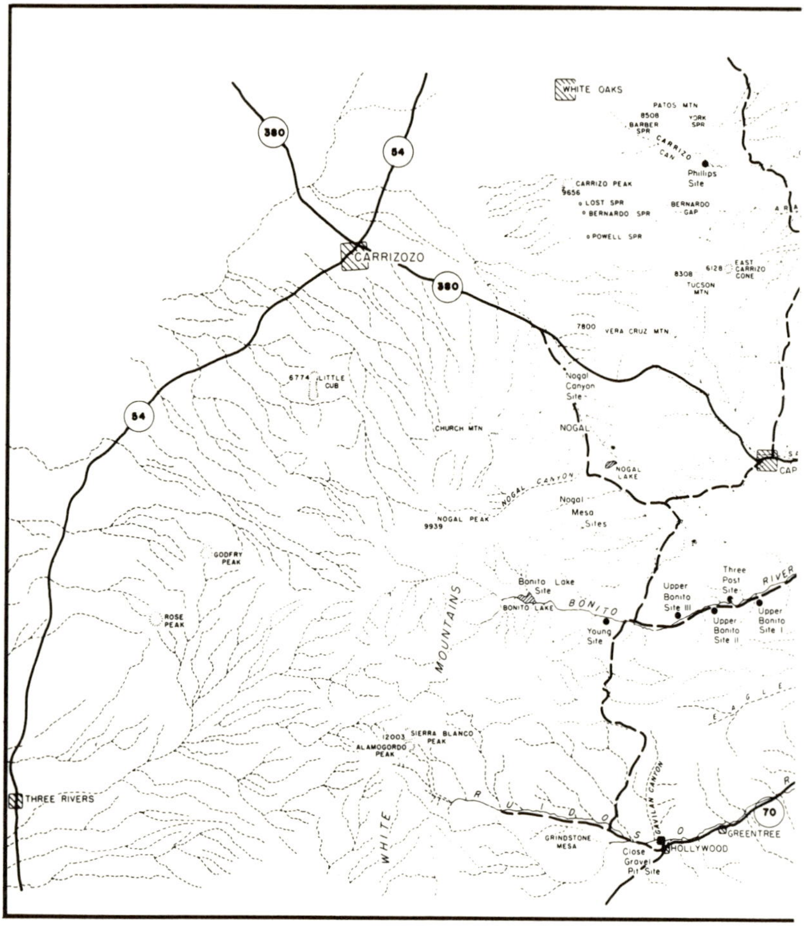

Map 4. Sites of the Macho and Hondo Drainages, New Mexico.

The Research

Work began here in 1955; we returned in 1956 with plans for extensive surveying and excavation. For reasons beyond our control, we had to discontinue work at this site before we had completed the planned research program.

Surveyed House Units

Widely scattered house units were composed of one to several rooms outlined by upright stone slabs; the surface pottery classification is given in Tables 13 and 14. A circular depression between House Units 1 and 8 was

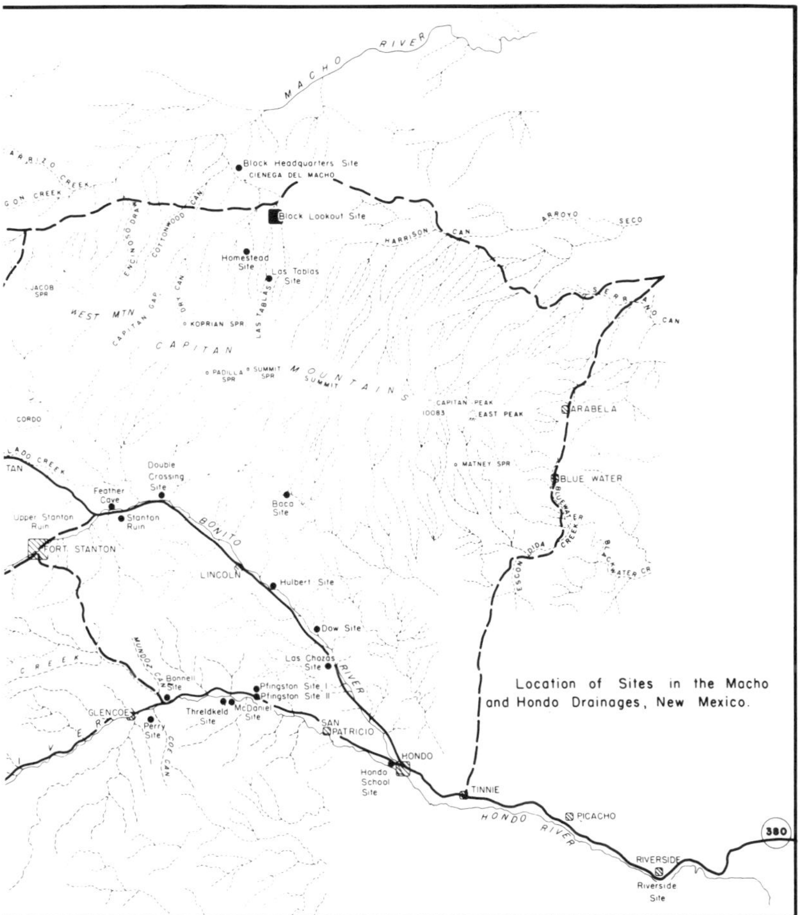

Location of Sites in the Macho and Hondo Drainages, New Mexico.

outlined with upright stone slabs. Mr. Jack Harkey of Carrizozo informed me that he dug out two small rooms just east of the circular depression, each approximately 6 x 7 feet, which were floored with flagstones but lacked the upright stone slabs.

Excavated House Units

House Unit 43, A Corona Phase House Unit

Located on a ridge south of the river, House Unit 43 was not far from the other house units, and yet the surrounding trees made it seem quite isolated

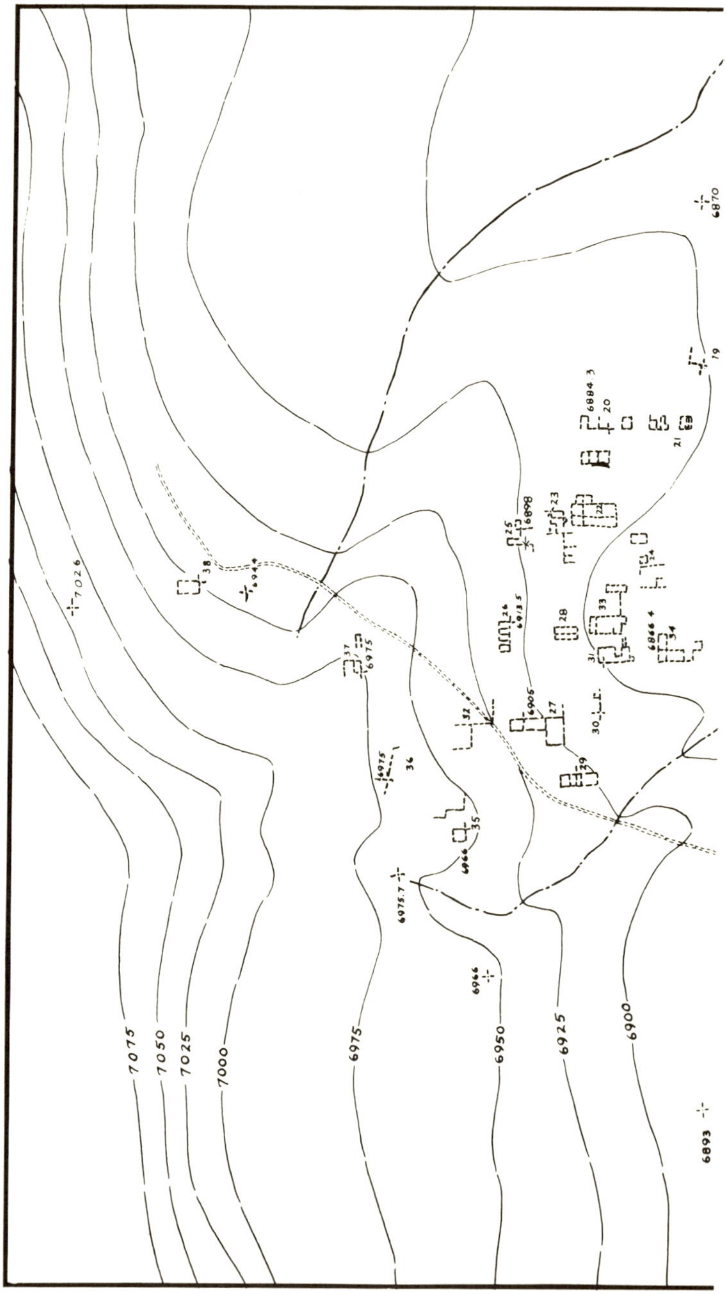
7075
7050
7025
7000
6975
6950
6925
6900
7026
6870
6893
6966

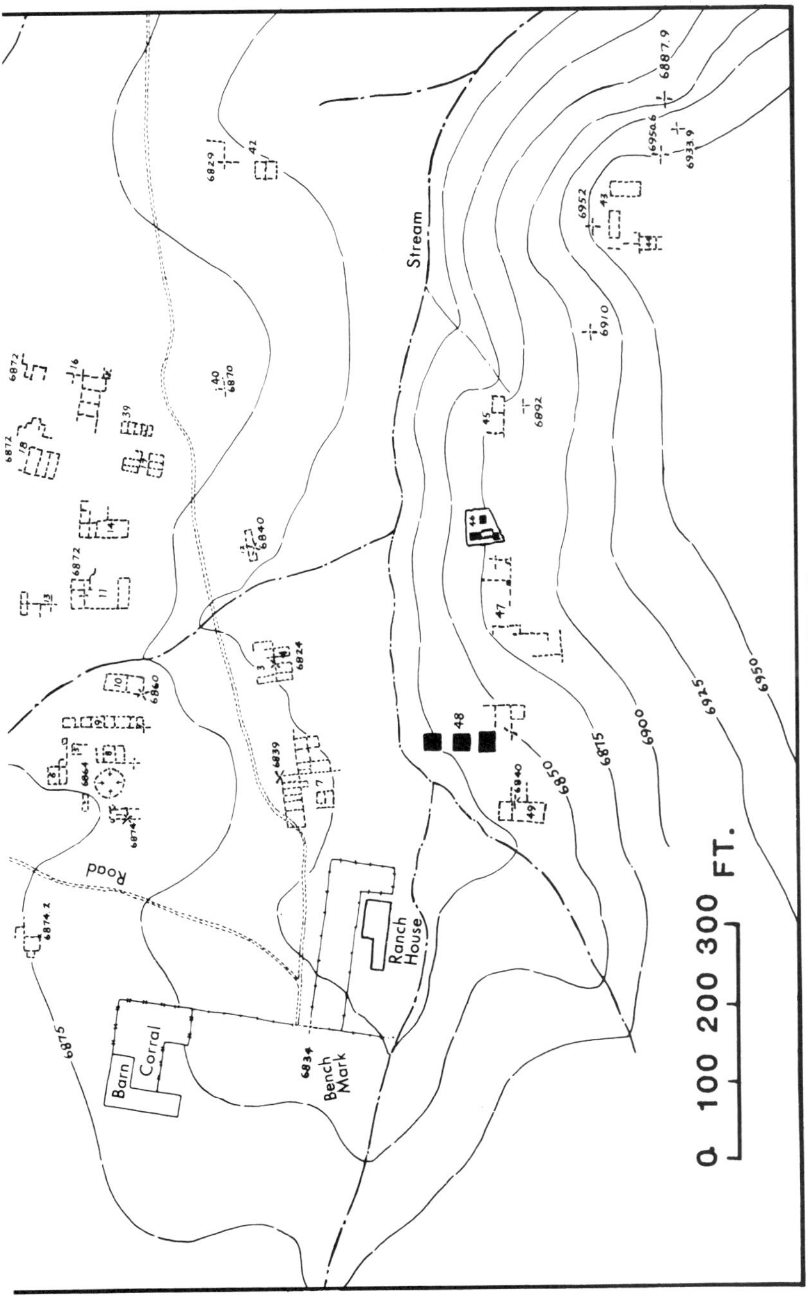

Map 5. Phillips Site.

(Map 5). At least two linear units of slab-outlined houses were visible in a clearing. We excavated one room in the west house, which had an east-west orientation. Fill was shallow. It had no internal features. Four unworked flakes of black shale were in the fill. The pottery is listed in Table 16.

Early Lincoln Phase House Excavations

House Unit 45

Both rooms of this two-room unit were cleared (Map 5; Fig. 17). The rooms, each roughly 6½ by 9 feet, had been lined with unshaped limestone slabs set on edge; three of these slabs between the rooms indicated a dividing wall. No internal features were found and trenching around the outside failed to locate any post holes. No artifacts were recovered. The pottery is listed in Table 19.

Storage Pit in House 11, House Unit 46

A circular pit remnant extended under the southwest corner of this house. Its diameter was approximately 4 feet 6 inches. The floor of the pit was well plastered. Associated sherds (Tables 17, 18) as well as stratigraphic position show that the pit was older than the house.

Late Lincoln Phase House Units

House Unit 48

Eight rooms of a linear house unit outlined with upright stone slabs were visible. (Map 5, location; Fig. 18, plan). Rooms 1, 3, and 5 were excavated in 1955. Three to six inches of fill remained; all rooms were built on sterile soil. Shallow pit rooms were ca. 10 by 12 feet in size. Construction practices are conjectural for no post holes were located inside the structures or outside the walls. No internal features, such as firepits, were present.

Room 1: The south wall of this room was not located. Other walls were clearly marked with upright slabs. The fill was 6 inches deep over most of the room.

Artifacts found in Room 1 included two Corrugated ollas which had been crushed *in situ*. One was sitting in the southeast part of the room and the second was close to the center of the room. A corner-notched obsidian projectile point with a broad straight base and a bone awl were also found. A sackful of black shale chips was collected in the room.

Room 3: No floor was recognized. It must have been a packed-earth floor within 6 inches of the surface since few cultural remains were found below this depth. Sterile soil was reached at 9 inches.

Artifacts found in Room 3 included a split deer rib which had been well smoothed on the rough interior surface. The rib's edges were deeply cut and

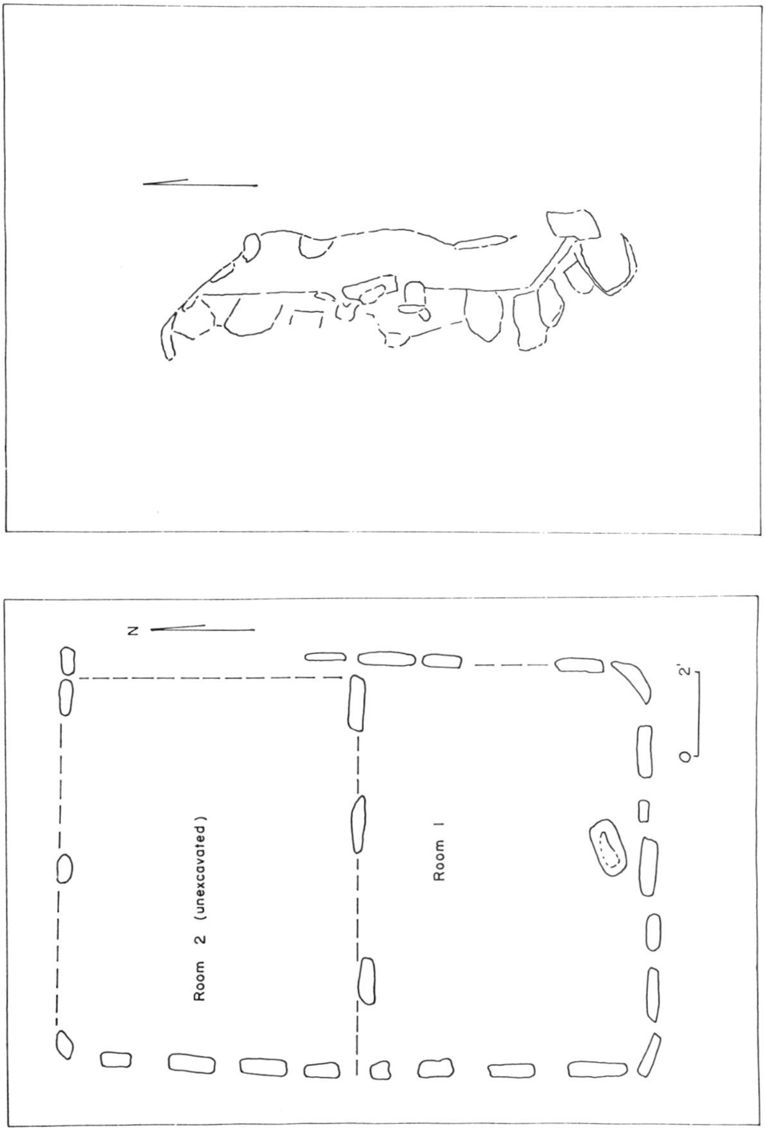

Figure 17. House Unit 45, Phillips Site: *a*, Plan; *b*, Sketch of the slab-lined pit.

nicked. Four black shale flakes from the house fill and five from the room surface showed edge retouch. A number of black shale flakes that lacked signs of use were discarded. A loaf-shaped sandstone mano was on the surface.

Room 5: A portion of floor was present across the south side of the room at a depth of 3 to 4 inches below the surface. Otherwise, erosion had proceeded below the depth of the floor.

Artifacts found in Room 5 are as follows. Sitting on the floor, about the midpoint of the south wall, was a large restorable Chupadero Black-on-White jug. A loaf-shaped mano with two parallel grinding surfaces had been well battered on one end. A large split rib had been squared off and used as a polisher or scraper. Several split deer bones were resting on the remnant of floor on the south side of the room. A large number of black shale flakes were scattered through the fill.

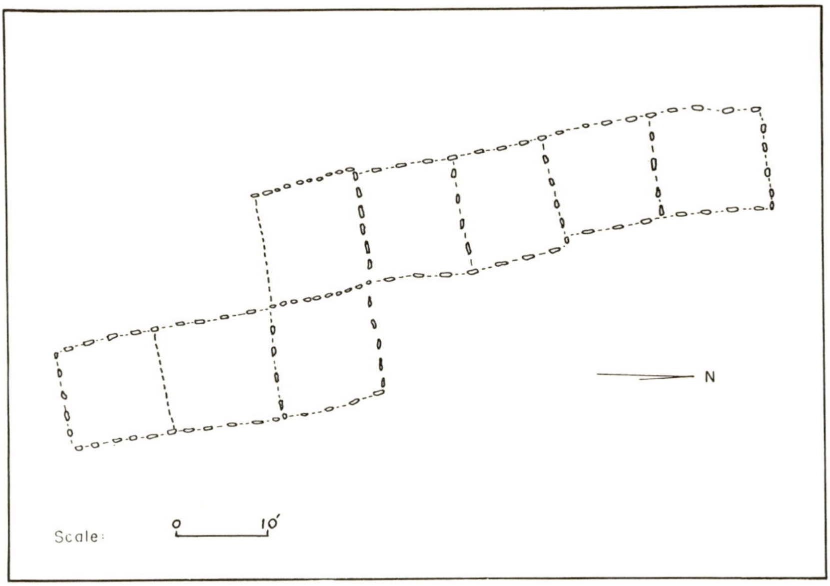

Figure 18. Plan of House Unit 48, Phillips Site.

House Unit 46

We were prompted to select this unit for excavation because several masonry walls were visible; these represent the only construction of this type to be seen at the site. Two rooms were completely excavated, three rooms were partially dug, and a sixth room, previously disturbed by pot hunters, was cleaned to make a record of masonry construction (Map 6; Pls.10–11).

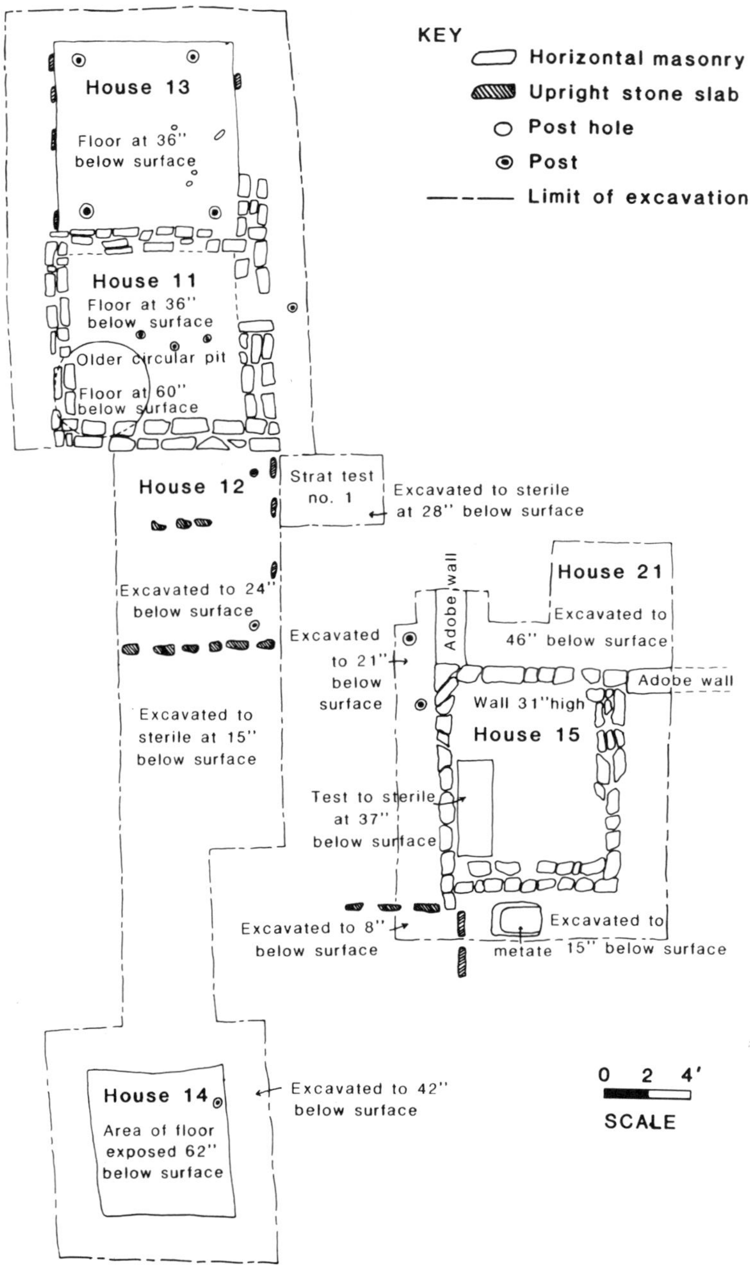

Map 6. House Unit 46, Phillips Site.

Plate 10. Room 11, House Unit 46, Phillips Site.

Houses 11, 12, and 13 form an unusual structural unit to be described below. House 15 was part of another house unit that we did not define. The relationship of the partially excavated House 14 to the others of this complex is not clear, but it was probably built earlier.

House 11: Internal dimensions were approximately 7 feet square. The massive masonry walls were of unusual construction. Large, vertical, sandstone slabs lined the house pit. A rubble-filled, double-faced, masonry wall was built above the house pit at ground level (Pl. 10). Large sandstone blocks, some of them well-squared, were laid on either side of the wall and smaller rocks and fill placed in the middle. At least one stone, in the top level of exposed masonry, was laid perpendicular to the wall to tie the two sides of the wall together.

Three small posts were charred close to the floor. They may have been roof braces or they could have had another function. Most of the weight of the roof must have been carried by the walls. No firepit was present.

A circular pit in the southwest corner of the house belonged to an older occupation, as has been described above.

Artifacts and food remains found in House 11 included four projectile

Plate 11. Room 15, House Unit 46, Phillips Site.

points (Fig. 19), three of which were on or just above the floor and one of which was in room fill. Of these, three were corner-notched, one was an unnotched triangle, and one triangular point had a notch in the concave base. A corner-notched dart (?) point was found on the dump of material previously excavated from this room. A bifacial quartzite knife had fine edge retouch. A pottery disc with a biconical hole had been made from a terracotta bowl. One bone gaming piece came from the floor. A mano fragment was present in the fill.

Black shale flakes weighing 956 grams were collected from the fill of the house. This included 2 large fragments that had well-battered surfaces, 57 apparently unworked flakes, and 1 bifacially-worked flake. Bones which could be deer or antelope were common. Two articulated lower limbs of deer,

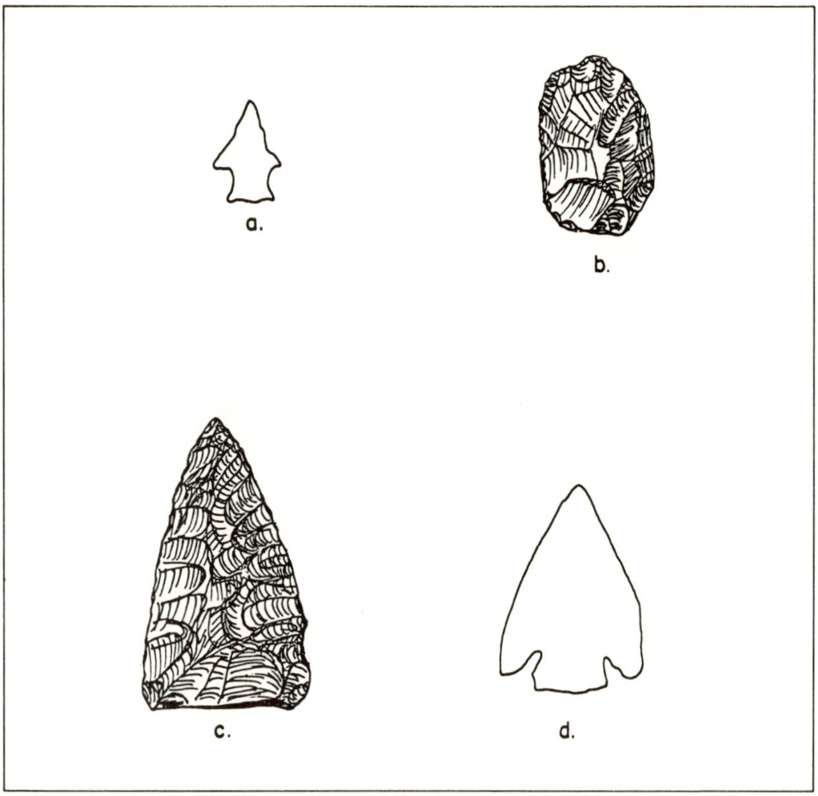

Figure 19. Artifacts from House 11, House Unit 46, Phillips Site: *a,* Projectile point, 2.0 x 1.3 cm; *b,* Scraper (unifacially worked), 4.3 x 23 cm; *c,* Knife (bifacially worked), 5.5 x 3.4 cm; *d,* Projectile point, 3.9 x 2.9 cm.

metapodial to hoof, were found against the east wall. One charred corncob was found.

House 12: This room was located immediately south of House 11 and utilized the south wall of the latter house as its north wall. East and west walls were not located. The room was exposed as a result of a test trench that was run south from House 11. A series of upright slabs across the trench were regarded as the south boundary of the room. Two posts were located on the east side of the house (Map 5). No artifacts were recorded. Approximately 500 grams of black shale flakes that showed no obvious signs of usage were found in the house fill.

House 13: This pit room adjoined House 11 on the north and shared the intervening masonry wall. Some horizontal masonry extended a few feet along the east wall of House 13, but there was no evidence that masonry walls ever extended around the entire room. A few vertical stone slabs lined the pit walls. The house was refloored once; about 15 inches separated the two floors.

Four large posts, located close to the corners, served both floors. Three additional post holes were found in the lowest floor (Map 6). The room had no firepit or fire area.

Both artifacts and animal bones were found in excavating House 13. Two projectile points were found in house fill. One was corner-notched with serrated edges and the other was a larger, asymmetrical, crudely side-notched point (Plate 12e, s). A small side-notched point of white flint was found in the backdirt from this room. A cylindrical stone, 5½ inches high and 3½ inches in diameter was on the floor by the southeast corner post; it could have served as an anvil or fire dog. About 900 grams of black shale flakes were in the fill; most appeared to be unworked. Deer bones were common. A major portion of at least two animals was present. One was full grown but the epiphyseal unions of the metapodials were not closed. The other animal was fully mature.

House 14: In excavating to sterile soil in the trench that ran south from House 11, a deeper structure was found to the south of House 12. The excavation was extended to allow testing of the deeper fill. In 1955, an area ca. 10 feet square was excavated to a depth of 42 inches below the surface, and a small test pit was sunk to the floor of this structure. The following year, a larger section of floor was exposed. We were unable to complete our work at this site, and the excavations had to be backfilled. The only structural feature present in the exposed floor area was a small post charred close to the floor. The floor was level and well plastered; it was much better made than any of the other floors examined at this site. No artifacts were found on the floor.

House 15: This surface masonry structure had been thoroughly disturbed by previous digging. It was cleaned out, and a trench was run around the walls. Internal dimensions were about 6½ x 8 feet. South and east walls were made

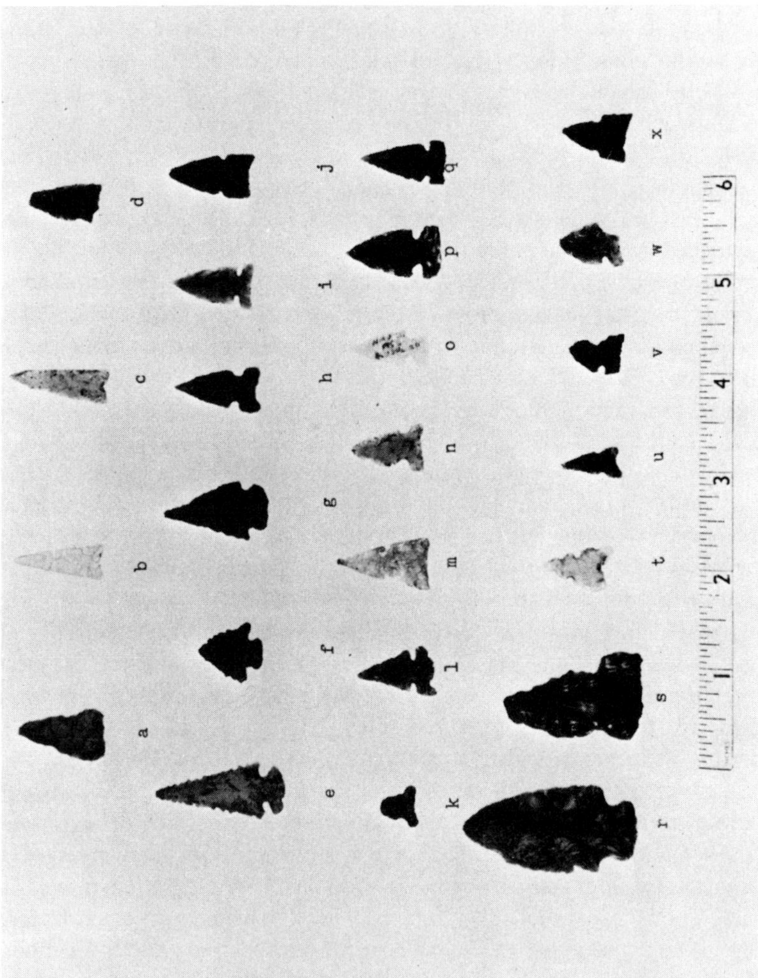

Plate 12. Projectile points, Phillips Site.

of a double row of stones with rubble fill. North and west masonry walls are now of single thickness; previous disturbance made it impossible to say if this is the original form of construction (Map 5; Pl. 11). The floor was gone. Presumably it was close to the bottom of the masonry walls, which were built on 6 to 8 inches of fill.

Trench around House 15: A trench that was merely meant to expose the outside of the masonry walls of House 15 incidentally revealed two other types of construction that apparently adjoined House 15 and were contemporary with it. Adobe walls abutted the masonry walls at the northwest and northeast corners (Map 5). On the assumption that the two adobe walls pertained to an adjacent structure, that area was tentatively designated House 21.

Upright stone slabs at the southwest corner of House 15 indicated the presence of a slab-lined house (Map 5). Two posts were found outside the northwest corner of House 15.

A number of artifacts were recovered while trenching around House 15. A trough metate and a mano were lying south of House 15. A second mano came from the northwest corner of the trench. A bone awl made from the proximal end of a deer metapodial and a rectangular tool made of a split rib came from the east portion of the trench, as did a shell ornament.

A small test of House 21 produced three small side-notched points, two drills made of triangular flakes, and an elongated black shale flake which had sufficient edge retouch to be called a side scraper. Three larger pieces of black shale had been used as hammerstones. A quartzite pebble had two polishing facets. A partially split deer rib with a blunt point had been used as a punch or gouge.

Concluding Statements on House Unit 46: It is unfortunate that our exploration of this bewildering architectural maze could not be completed. We found a hodgepodge of structures that we were unable to conclusively relate in time or order of construction. Houses 13, 11, and 12 formed a structural unit, with each of the end rooms built against a masonry wall of House 11. All three rooms were excavated below the ground surface; House 11 was the deepest and House 14 was quite shallow. No fire area was located in any of the three rooms, although House 12 was not completely cleared. The vault-like appearance of House 11 must have contrasted with the earth-covered pithouse construction of House 13 and with the postulated *jacal* construction of House 12.

House 15 was part of another house unit that was made up of still different structural components. House 15 seemed to represent a surface masonry room adjoined to an adobe surface structure on the north and a slab outlined structure on the southwest.

House 14 could have been a contemporary ceremonial chamber or pithouse.

A Private Collection

Mr. Jack Harkey of Carrizozo, New Mexico, has an extensive collection from this site that he began in 1950, and I was able to examine those items still in his possession in 1957. Mr. Harkey described specific finds for me. He reported that he excavated on the north side of the stream, as already mentioned. His largest collection was made in House Unit 49, which has been assigned to the Lincoln Phase on the basis of our surface survey and his materials.

Forty-nine Lincoln Black-on-Red bowls were said to have come from the southwest room of this house unit (six are illustrated in Pl. 14), as did an El Paso Polychrome olla containing a *Glycymeris* bracelet, three small stone bear effigies, and three peculiarly shaped rocks (Pl. 17). Another room was said to contain restorable Ramos and Gila Polychrome vessels (Pl. 16). Three Corrugated vessels are likewise reputed to be from this house unit (Pl. 15). A Chupadero Black-on-White bowl (Pl. lb) was full of walnuts.

Artifacts from Phillips Ranch Site

Large quantities of black shale flakes were found along and south of the stream, especially in and around House Units 48, 49, 46, and 45. This shale, mined at the nearby Carrizo Mines, was so abundant that flakes seem to have been used for cutting, scraping, or hammering, and then discarded. Clearly, reduction of shale from the mines occured here. Few of the flakes were shaped into recognizable artifacts. To illustrate the quantity of these flakes, a sample was counted and weighed from a 4-foot section of fill, 24 inches deep, in Room 14. Seventy-five unused flakes weighed 1940 grams, ten used flakes weighed 376 grams, and two slightly battered nodules weighed 300 grams, for a total of 2616 grams.

Small side-notched and unnotched triangular points were most frequent in our collection, which represents the Lincoln Phase. Smaller numbers of corner-notched arrow points and larger dart (?) points were found (Table 15; Pl. 12). This site had the local reputation of being one of the most prolific of arrowhead hunting locales. Jack Harkey reported that he picked up 4000 points at this site in 5 years, and he estimated that at least 20,000 were in the hands of private collectors, a statement that could not be confirmed.

Three flake and two ovate knives were each less than 2 inches in length. Three smaller flakes had bifacial edge retouch. A side-notched, chipped stone axe, 4 inches long by 2½ inches wide and 1 inch thick, had a well-blunted blade.

In the large number of used and unused flakes, purposely shaped unifacial tools were rare. Among those sorted from the mass of debitage were three flakes with one edge retouched, one flake with two edges retouched, an end

TABLE 13
SURFACE POTTERY FROM SURVEYED HOUSE UNITS, PHILLIPS SITE

	House Unit																																							
	1	2	3	4	5	6	7	8	10	11	12	13	14	15	16	17	18	20	21	22	23	24	25	26	27	28	30	31	32	33	34	35	36	37	39	40	42	43	44	47	49
	Sample Size																																							
Pottery Type	46	38	58	25	35	27	106	45	37	36	27	18	45	18	32	17	21	22	47	75	37	51	14	38	72	59	8	31	8	37	35	22	11	13	19	21	14	44	11	24	18
Chupadero Black-on-White Over 50%	X	X	X	X	X	X	X	X	X	X	X		X	X	X	X	X	X	X	X	X	X	X	X	X	X	X	X		X	X	X	X	X	X	X	X	X	X	X	
Chupadero Black-on-White 50% or less												33%																	50%												22%
Corrugated Over 30%		X																																							X
Corrugated 1-10%	X		X	X	X		X																										X	X						X	
Brown	X	X	X	X	X			X	X	X		33%	X		X	X	X		X	X	X	X	X	X	X	X		X	50%	X	X	X		X	X		X	X		X	
Three Rivers Red-on-Terracotta			X	X		X	X	X			X	33%		X	X	X	X	X	X	X		X	X	X	X	X				X		X	X	X	X	X	X		18%	X	X
Lincoln Black-on-Red			X				X						X				X				X																				
Jornada Poly.			X			X	X	X							X																		X		X	X	X			X	
El Paso Poly.			X				X	X																						X						X		X			
Mimbres Black-on-White								X																																	
Unident. Black-on-White													X																												
Carmen Red														X																											
St. Johns Poly.																																	X								
Glaze I							X	X																																	X

X = Present

TABLE 14
ARTIFACTS FROM THE PHILLIPS SITE
COLLECTED BY TEXAS TECHNOLOGICAL COLLEGE PARTY

Artifacts	House Unit 48	House Unit 46	Surface	Total
Chipped stone				
Points (See Table 15)				44
Drills		2		2
Knives and/or bifacially chipped flakes		9		9
Axe, side-notched			1	1
Retouched or used flakes	9	11		20
Unifacial choppers			4	4
Hammerstones		3		3
Anvil or pot support		1		1
Ground-stone tools				
Metate		1		1
Manos	2	3	3	8
Axe fragment, full-grooved			1	1
Pebble polisher		1	1	2
Bone artifacts				
Awls	1	4		5
Gaming piece		1		1
Bone tube		1		1
Handle (?)				
Miscellaneous	2	2		4
Worked sherds		5		5
Ceramic pipes, tubular		2		2
Shell, cut mussel fragment		1		1

scraper, two flake gravers, a core planer, and a cortex quartz flake with edge retouch. Surface finds of large, heavy, unifacial choppers or planers or blanks of black shale are shown in Figures 20 and 21 and in Plate 13. Hammerstones were also made of this shale.

Black shale was not often used to make points, scrapers, or knives. Two points were made of black shale; six were of gray chert of poor quality; two were made of obsidian and the rest of good chert. A greenish limey-chert, quartzite, and gray and other cherts were used for knives and scrapers.

The black shale mines on Carrizo Mountain seem to have been operated primarily during the Lincoln Phase. Flakes of this material, rare on earlier house units, were abundant on later parts of the site.

The single metate was of the one-end-closed trough type with a mano rest.

**TABLE 15
PROJECTILE POINTS,
PHILLIPS SITE**

Description	No.	%
Side-notched		
Asymmetrical	1	
Triangular square base	3	
Triangular, 2 side and 2 bottom notches	12	
Multiple side-notching	1	
Total	17	38.64
Unnotched triangles		
Straight base	9	
Concave base	2	
Concave base with single bottom notch	1	
Total	12	27.27
Corner-notched		
Convex base	3	
Straight base	5	
Total	8	18.18
Broken (midsections or tips)	7	
Total	7	15.91
Total Projectile Points	44	100.00

All manos were loaf forms made of sandstone. Two specimens had two parallel grinding faces and one specimen had four ground surfaces. Some were ground flat, indicating use on a flat metate. Two had convex grinding surfaces and were probably used in trough metates.

The only ground-stone axe fragment was full-grooved. Jack Harkey had a three-quarter grooved axe in his collection that he said came from between House Units 1 and 8.

Most awls were made from split deer ulnas; a split and polished awl was made from a metapodial. A bone tube, 7½ inches long, had cut and polished ends. A split bison (?) rib and a split long bone of deer had the long edges smoothed. A cut rib could have served as a handle. Another cut rib was smoothed and had an X cut on one face.

Five worked sherds—rectangular, tear-drop, and circular in shape—were made of Jornada Brown, Three Rivers Red-on-Terracotta, Chupadero Black-on-White, and Lincoln Black-on-Red. Two fragments of brown pottery tubular pipes were found.

A fragment of cut mussel shell and two other tiny pieces of mussel shell were found in our work. Jack Harkey described finding a *Glycymeris* shell bracelet in House Unit 49.

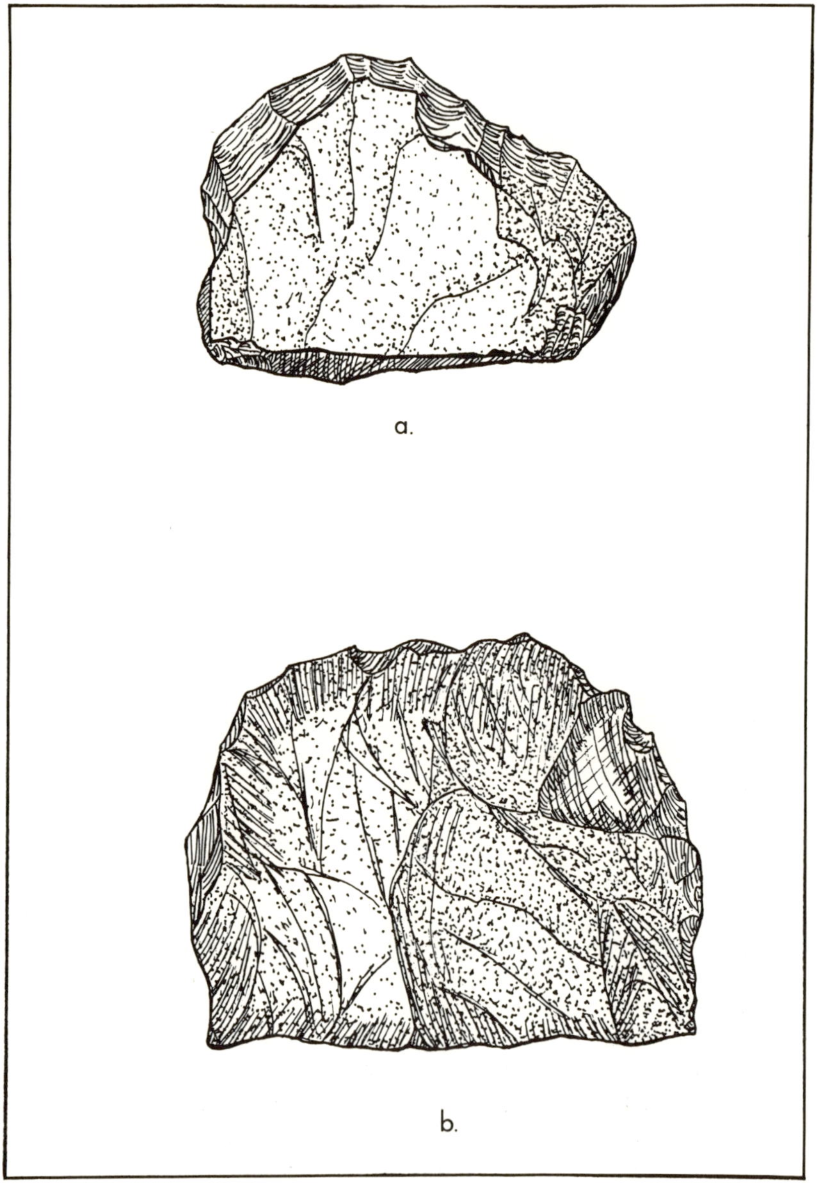

Figure 20. Unifacial silicified shale tools, Phillips Site. *a*, 5.8 x 8.0 cm; *b*, 7.3 x 9.3 cm.

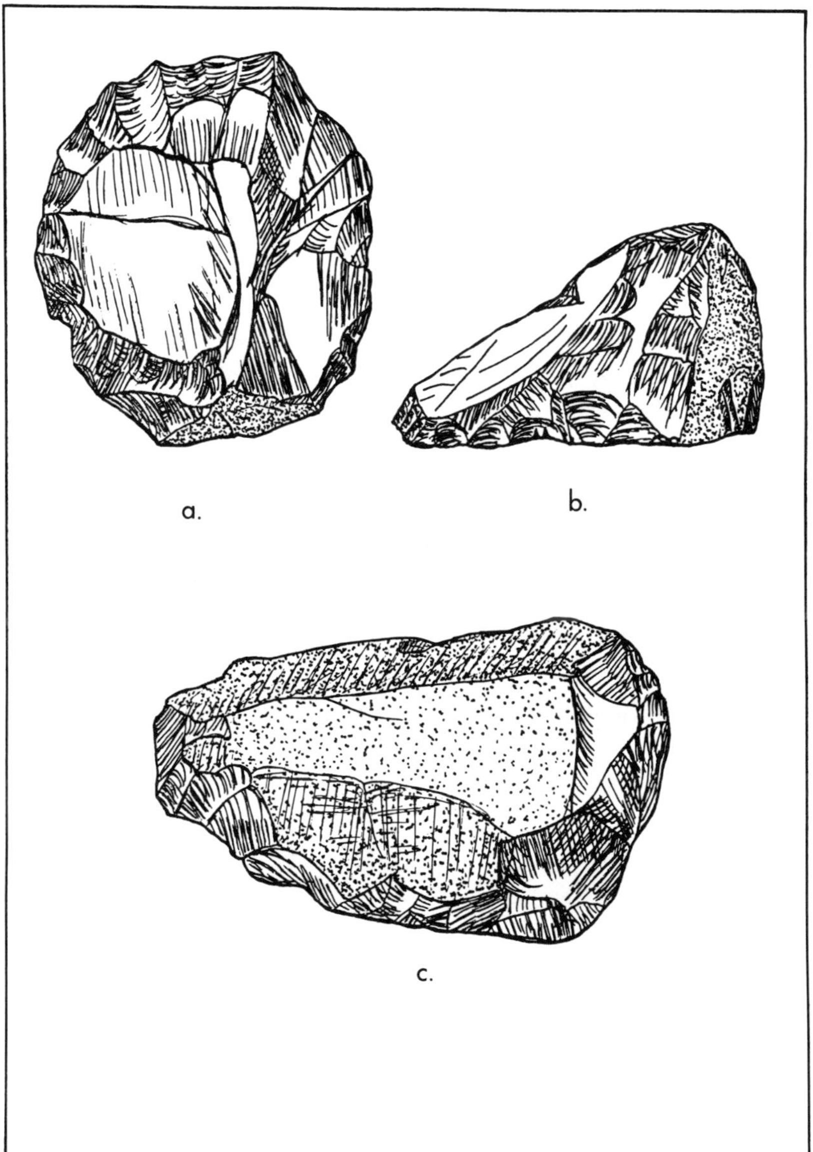

Figure 21. Black shale tools, Phillips Site: *a,* Top view of planer, 7.0 x 6.2 cm; *b,* Side view of *a,* 4.0 x 6.7 cm; *c,* Bifacial tool, 5.8 x 9.3 cm.

Plate 13. Unifacial tools, Phillips Site.

Food Remains

We obtained only one charred corncob from this site, but Mr. Harkey claimed to have found a room in House Unit 49 with corn 12 to 14 inches deep all over the floor. The abundance of animal bones implies that hunting deer or antelope contributed substantially to the diet. Three lots of bones were weighed and analyzed as to body part. Three hundred and sixty-one grams of bone came from Room 13, below Floor 1; 386 grams came from the floor and sub-floor of Room 11, and 270 grams came from a single 6-inch level of a 4 foot square strat pit. Bison bones were identified tentatively from Room 13, and a bison rib and maxilla came from the trench around Room 15. Only 45 grams of intermediate-sized bone (coyote size, for example) were weighed from these samples. Fifty-two grams of small animal bones came primarily from rabbits.

Bone fragments representing every part of deer (or antelope) were found, indicating that whole carcasses were brought into the village. Only ribs and maxillae of bison were present, suggesting that selected parts of butchered bison were transported.

Pottery

In this section, the pottery types of the local ceramic complex are described and variations in design and construction are noted. Sherd lists are given in Tables 16, 17, 18, 19, and 20.

Lincoln Black-on-Red

This site produced more of this type of pottery than any other known site. Mr. Harkey's reported find of 49 bowls in varying states of completion in addition to the frequency of this type in our collections suggests that this was a manufacturing center of this type during the Lincoln Phase. Designs typical of the type were abundantly represented (Pl. 14c). Some atypical motifs included extension of the design area into the central part of the bowl interior in two or four sections (Pl. 14a, f). Some designs seem to be copied from Glaze I bowls (Pl. 14e). Checkerboard and diamond motifs occurred, and one sherd had a circle element. Lincoln Red-on-Red variant had both typical Lincoln Black-on-Red design elements and linear motifs more reminiscent of Three Rivers Red-on-Terracotta. Both slipped and unslipped bowls were made. Some lacked painted designs but had polished red interiors. Some of the sherds contained noticeable quantities of mica, as do other locally made types. Some bowls were made of clay bands about 1 inch wide which are visible on the exterior (Pl. 14d).

Undecorated Jornada Brown

Locally made brown pottery belonged to the Gallo Micaceous variant. Roswell Brown was probably imported.

Decorated Jornada Brown Variants

This class of pottery was numerically unimportant. Two sherds had a brushed exterior, one sherd had hollow reed punctations, and a few had striated interiors. There were only four painted sherds: a red-slipped Roswell Brown olla with the red paint carried over the rim into the interior for about an inch, a Gallo Micaceous Red-on-Brown, a Roswell Red-on-Brown olla, and a Jornada Black-on-Brown.

Chupadero Black-on-White

Heavy opaque white to thin transparent slips were applied; a substantial number of sherds were unslipped. In addition to bowls and jugs, one rim sherd of a "squash" jar, two miniature vessels, and two sherds from effigy jars (?) were found. Three slipped sherds had the rim shape of the Capitan variant. One sherd was striated on both interior and exterior; one rim had a brushed exterior. Some of the paint was glazed. Atypical design elements were checkerboards and curved lines. Wide bands of clay were used to make bowls. A jug lacked the characteristic disc base; instead, a flat piece of clay had been bent up. This was successful enough to get through the firing process, but cracks reflect the structural weakness of the idea. Most of the Chupadero Black-on-White is micaceous and perhaps was made in the village.

Corrugated

Most sherds had rubbed or partially obliterated coils, but a few had distinct corrugations. Vessel shape and common degree of coil obliteration are evident in Plate 15. One sherd had a paste identical to that found in Chupadero Black-on-White. One sherd was incised at quarter-inch intervals across the coils. Another was incised with a blunt instrument about ⅛ inch wide in a diamond pattern. One sherd was called "crazy corrugated"; perhaps it should not have been called corrugated at all, for its design resembled scales on a fish. One sherd had black lines drawn over the corrugation. Much of the Corrugated had amounts of mica comparable to that present in other types of local manufacture, suggesting a common source of clay.

Three Rivers Red-on-Terracotta

Quite a number of the sherds assigned to this type from Corona Phase house units seem to have been undecorated. The type was most common in this earlier phase. In Lincoln Phase house units, there are both broad- and thin-lined designs. One sherd has two connected solid red triangles that resemble the "thunderbird" wings of modern jewelry.

El Paso Polychrome

Most sherds and vessels were typical. One rim sherd had a slightly thickened, flattened rim that contrasts with the usual rounded lip form. Some thin black sherds lacked the temper characteristic of this type and the surface was highly polished. One group of Polychrome sherds graded between this type and Jornada Polychrome in thickness.

Relative Dating of House Units and Individual Structures Using Pottery Lots

Small surface pottery collections were made from all Phillips Site house units by picking up all sherds within the limits of the visible structures (Tables 13, 14). Sherds not actually associated with a structure may be within its borders, and the samples may well be incomplete and biased, as this site has been a favorite collecting ground for amateur archaeologists and pot hunters for perhaps 40 years. In spite of these drawbacks, a chronological pattern emerges, as do some questions about relative chronological positioning of particular ceramic lots.

The Phillips Site is considerably more complex in terms of length of occupation and correlations between architectural forms and ceramic lots than any other site at which we worked. We have discrete house units and ceramic lots whose variability seems, on the basis of present knowledge, to have a strong chronological factor. Other factors, however, cannot be ruled out even though we cannot control them with the data at our disposal. In general, I have

TABLE 16
POTTERY FROM
ROOM 1, HOUSE UNIT 43,
PHILLIPS SITE

	Level 1, 2″ to 8″				Level 2, 8″ to 16″						Total	
Pottery Type	No.	%	g	%	No.	%	g	%	No.	%	g	%
Chupadero Black-on-White												
Jug	3		14		11		102		14		116	
Bowl	3		20		1		4		4		24	
Total	6	55	34	47	12	75	106	74	18	67	140	65
Jornada Brown	5	45	39	53	4	25	38	26	9	33	77	35
Total	11		73		16		144		27		217	

TABLE 17
POTTERY FROM HOUSE UNIT 46,
PHILLIPS SITE

Pottery Types	Top Floor			
	No.	%	g	%
Corrugated				
Body	53			
Rim	1		396	
Base	1			
Total	55	19.37	396	21.22
Chupadero Black-on-White				
Bowl	39		302	
Jug	47		323	
Total	86	30.28	625	33.49
Jornada, Undecorated				
Jornada				
Roswell				
Other	5		187	
Total	5	1.76	187	10.02
Jornada, Decorated				
Jornada Black-on-Brown				
Olla	1		22	
Bowl				
Textured Surface				
Jornada Red-Slipped				
Olla				
Bowl				
Total	1	.35	22	1.18
El Paso Polychrome				
Body	99			
Rim	3			
Total	102	35.91	324	17.36
Jornada Polychrome	7		74	
Rim	1		12	
Total	8	2.82	86	4.61
Lincoln Black-on-Red				
Decorated	8			
Rim	2			
Undecorated	10			
Variants				
Total	20	7.04	150	8.04
Three Rivers Red-on-Terracotta				
Body				
Rim				
Undecorated	2?		18	
Variants				
Total	2?	.70	18	.96
Glaze I	3	1.06	27	1.45
Ramos Polychrome	1	.35	10	.53
Upper Gila Corrugated				
St. Johns Polychrome				
Gila Polychrome				
Playas Red Incised				
Unidentified	1	.35	21	1.12
Unidentified Glaze				
Unidentified Black-on-White				
Undifferentiated Brown Polychrome				
Total	284		1866	

HOUSE 13							
Between Floors				Lower Floor			
No.	%	g	%	No.	%	g	%
58				93			
4		642		3		864	
62	12.75	642	18.05	96	22.33	864	26.45
78		733		73		598	
113		781		95		817	
191	39.30	1514	42.57	168	39.16	1415	43.31
62		428		32		321	
5				1			
				4			
67	13.79	428	12.03	37	8.62	321	9.82
1		5					
1	.20	5	.14				
97		428		36		144	
2							
99	20.37	428	12.03	36	8.39	144	4.41
				2			
				2			
				4	.93	30	0.92
10				13			
5				6			
16				20			
1				5			
32	6.58	249	7.00	44	10.26	277	8.48
				5			
				1			
				1			
				7	1.63	64	1.96
4	.82	38	1.07	2	.47	14	.43
22	4.53	206	5.79				
1	.20	8	.22				
4	.82	26	.73	2	.47	14	.43
3	.62	12	.34				
				33	7.69	124	3.79
486		3556		429		3267	

TABLE 17, continued
POTTERY FROM HOUSE UNIT 46,
PHILLIPS SITE

					HOUSE 11			
	Fill, Surface to 20 inches				Fill, 20 inches to Floor			
Pottery Types	No.	%	g	%	No.	%	g	%
Corrugated								
Body	163				156			
Rim	9		930		4		750	
Base								
Total	172	30.23	930	39.69	160	24.39	750	25.29
Chupadero Black-on-White								
Bowl	33		200		62		476	
Jug	108		346		148		640	
Total	141	24.78	546	23.30	210	32.01	1116	37.62
Jornada, Undecorated								
Jornada	57		240		50		262	
Roswell								
Other	1		5					
Total	58	10.19	245	10.46	50	7.62	262	8.83
Jornada, Decorated								
Jornada Black-on-Brown								
Olla					1		7	
Bowl								
Textured Surface	1		6					
Jornada Red-Slipped								
Olla					1		4	
Bowl								
Total	1	.17	6	.26	2	.30	11	.37
El Paso Polychrome								
Body	133		386		112		290	
Rim	3				3			
Total	136	23.90	386	16.47	115	17.53	290	9.78
Jornada Polychrome	2		12		13		85	
Rim					5			
Total	2	.35	12	.51	18	2.74	85	2.86
Lincoln Black-on-Red								
Decorated	10				28			
Rim	4		173		15			
Undecorated	28				46		384	
Variants					1			
Total	42	7.38	173	7.38	90	13.72	384	12.95
Three Rivers Red-on-Terracotta								
Body								
Rim					3		36	
Undecorated	4?		8		2			
Variants								
Total	4?	.70	8	.34	5	.76	36	1.21
Glaze I	2	.35	9	.38				
Ramos Polychrome	4	.70	11	.47				
Upper Gila Corrugated					2	.30	14	.47
St. Johns Polychrome					3	.46	14	.47
Gila Polychrome					1	.15	4	.13
Playas Red Incised	2	.35	4	.17				
Unidentified	1	.17	3	.13				
Unidentified Glaze								
Unidentified Black-on-White	4	.70	10	.43				
Undifferentiated Brown Polychrome								
Total	569		2343		656		2966	

Sub-floor				Older Pit, Southwest Corner				Total	
No.	%	g	%	No.	%	g	%	No.	g
35				1				549	
		165				9		21	
								1	
25	11.90	165	13.92	1	2.70	9	2.24	571	3756
17		92						302	2401
48		293		11		92		570	3292
65	30.95	385	32.49	11	29.73	92	22.88	872	5693
22		131		7		23		230	
								6	
6		47						16	
28	13.33	178	15.02	7	18.92	23	5.72	252	1644
								2	29
								1	5
								1	6
								1	4
								5	44
32		145		1		1		510	
								11	
32	15.24	145	12.25	1	2.70	1	.25	521	1718
3		29		1		29		28	
2				1				11	
5	2.38	29	2.45	2	5.40	29	7.21	39	271
12								81	
7		261		6		248		45	
33				9				162	
								7	
52	24.76	261	22.02	15	40.54	248	61.69	295	1742
								5	
								4	
								8	
								1	
								18	126
								11	88
								27	227
								2	14
1	.48	12	1.01					5	34
								1	4
								2	4
								8	64
2	.95	10	.84					5	22
								4	10
								33	124
210		1185		37		402		2671	15585

TABLE 18
POTTERY FROM HOUSE UNIT 46, PHILLIPS SITE: HOUSE 14 FILL BY 6″ LEVELS

	Level 1			
Pottery Types	No.	%	g	%
Corrugated				
Body	12			
Rim	1			
Base				
Total	13	24.07	57	34.76
Chupadero Black-on-White				
Bowl	2		5	
Jug	7		16	
Total	9	16.67	21	12.80
Jornada Brown, Undecorated				
Jornada	9		17	
Roswell				
Other				
Total	9	16.67	17	10.36
Jornada Brown, Decorated				
Jornada Black-on-Brown				
Olla				
Bowl				
Textured Surface				
Jornada Red-slipped				
Olla				
Bowl				
Total				
El Paso Polychrome				
Body	11		26	
Rim				
Total	11	20.37	26	15.85
Jornada Polychrome				
Rim				
Total				
Lincoln Black-on-Red				
Decorated				
Rim	2		31	
Undecorated	8			
Variants				
Total	10	18.52	31	18.90
Three Rivers Red-on-Terracotta				
Body				
Rim				
Undecorated				
Variants				
Total				
Glaze I	1	1.85	2	1.22
Ramos Polychrome				
Upper Gila Corrugated	1	1.85	10	6.10
St. John's Polychrome				
Gila Polychrome				
Playas Red Incised				
Unidentified				
Unidentified Glaze				
Unidentified Black-on-White				
Undiff. Brown Polychrome				
Total	54		164	

Level 2				Level 3				Level 4			
No.	%	g	%	No.	%	g	%	No.	%	g	%
9		56		38		238		13		66	
9	19.56	56	24.24	38	46.34	238	49.79	13	31.71	66	33.33
6		18		7		42		6		25	
4		46		14		45		8		38	
10	21.74	64	27.70	21	25.61	87	18.20	14	34.15	63	31.82
6		16		5		29		3		13	
6	13.04	16	6.93	5	6.10	29	6.07	3	7.32	13	6.56
13		35		1		2		6		49	
13	28.26	35	15.15	1	1.22	2	.42	6	14.63	49	24.75
3				4							
		42		2		101					
2				6				1		4	
								1			
5	10.87	42	18.18	12	14.63	101	21.13	2	4.88	4	2.02
3	6.52	18	7.79	3	3.66	8	1.67	1	2.44	1	.50
								1	2.44	1	.50
				1	1.22	3	.63				
								1	2.44	1	.50
				1	1.22	10	2.09				
46		231		82		478		41		198	

TABLE 18, continued
POTTERY FROM HOUSE UNIT 46,
PHILLIPS SITE:
HOUSE 14 FILL BY 6″ LEVELS

	Level 5			
Pottery Types	No.	%	g	%
Corrugated				
Body	31		321	
Rim	1			
Base				
Total	32	29.63	321	36.27
Chupadero Black-on-White				
Bowl	22		295	
Jug	13		104	
Total	35	32.41	399	45.08
Jornada Brown, Undecorated				
Jornada	5		21	
Roswell	1		15	
Other				
Total	6	5.55	36	4.07
Jornada Brown, Decorated				
Jornada Black-on-Brown				
Olla				
Bowl				
Textured Surface				
Jornada Red-slipped				
Olla				
Total				
El Paso Polychrome				
Body	20		56	
Rim	2			
Total	22	20.37	56	6.33
Jornada Polychrome				
Rim				
Total				
Lincoln Black-on-Red				
Decorated				
Rim				
Undecorated	2		62	
Variants	9			
Total	11	10.18	62	7.00
Three Rivers Red-on-Terracotta				
Body				
Rim				
Undecorated				
Variants				
Total				
Glaze I				
Ramos Polychrome	1	.92	1	.11
Uper Gila Corrugated	1	.92	10	1.13
St. John's Polychrome				
Gila Polychrome				
Playas Red Incised				
Unidentified				
Unidentified Glaze				
Unidentified Black-on-White				
Undiff. Brown Polychrome				
Total	108		885	

Level 6				Level 7				Total		Totals, Tables 17-18	
No.	%	g	%	No.	%	g	%	No.	g	No.	g
								103		652	
								2		23	
										1	
								105	738	676	4494
1		8						44	393	346	2794
4								50	321	620	3613
5	21.74	80	38.09					94	714	966	6407
1		9		1		5		30	110	260	
4		30						5	45	11	
										16	
5	21.74	39	18.57	1	25.00	5	35.71	35	155	287	1799
										2	29
										1	5
										1	6
										1	4
										5	44
1		3						52	171	562	
								2		13	
1	4.35	3	1.43					54	171	575	1889
										28	
										11	
										39	271
								7		88	
								4	138	49	138
2		88						21	196	183	196
10								20		27	
12	52.17	88	41.90					52	328	347	2070
										5	
										4	
										8	
				1		3		1	3	2	
				1	25.00	3	21.43	1	3	19	129
				2	50.00	6	42.86	10	35	21	123
								1	1	28	228
								2	20	4	34
										5	34
										1	4
								1	1	3	5
								1	3	9	67
								1	1	6	23
								1	10	5	20
										33	124
23		210		4		14		358	2180	3029	17765

TABLE 19
POTTERY FROM HOUSE UNIT 45, PHILLIPS SITE

Pottery Type	Count	%
Corrugated	5	16.66
Chupadero	16	53.33
Jornada Polychrome	2	6.66
Decorated Brown	2	6.66
Lincoln Black-on-Red	4	13.33
Glaze I	1	3.33
Total	30	99.97

TABLE 20
POTTERY FROM HOUSE UNIT 48, PHILLIPS SITE

Pottery Type	Room 1, 5 inches below Surface to Floor				Room 3, Surface and Fill				Room 5, 2 inches below Surface to Floor			
	No.	%	g	%	No.	%	g	%	No.	%	g	%
Corrugated												
Body	57	62.64	685	80.87	9	34.62	30	40.54	7	13.46	59	10.33
Rim												
Chupadero Black-on-White												
Jug rim	15		94		7		16		24	46.15	336	58.84
Bowl rim	1		7									
Total	16	17.58	101	11.92	7	26.92	16	21.92				
Jornada Brown												
Undifferentiated	2		13		4		9		1		12	
Roswell Brown	1		4						1	45		
Total	3	3.30	17	2.01	4	15.38	9	12.16	2	3.85	57	9.98
El Paso Polychrome	9	9.98	20	2.36	4	15.38	9	12.16	12	23.08	69	12.08
Lincoln Black-on-Red												
Decorated	1		7									
Undecorated	1		3		1		5					
Total	2	2.20	10	1.18	1	3.85	5	6.76				
Glaze I	1	1.10	5	0.59	1	3.85	5	6.76				
Gila Polychrome									5	9.61	32	5.62
St. John's Poly.									1	1.92	3	0.52
Unknown	3	3.30	9	1.06					1	1.92	15	2.63
Total	91		847		26		74		52		571	

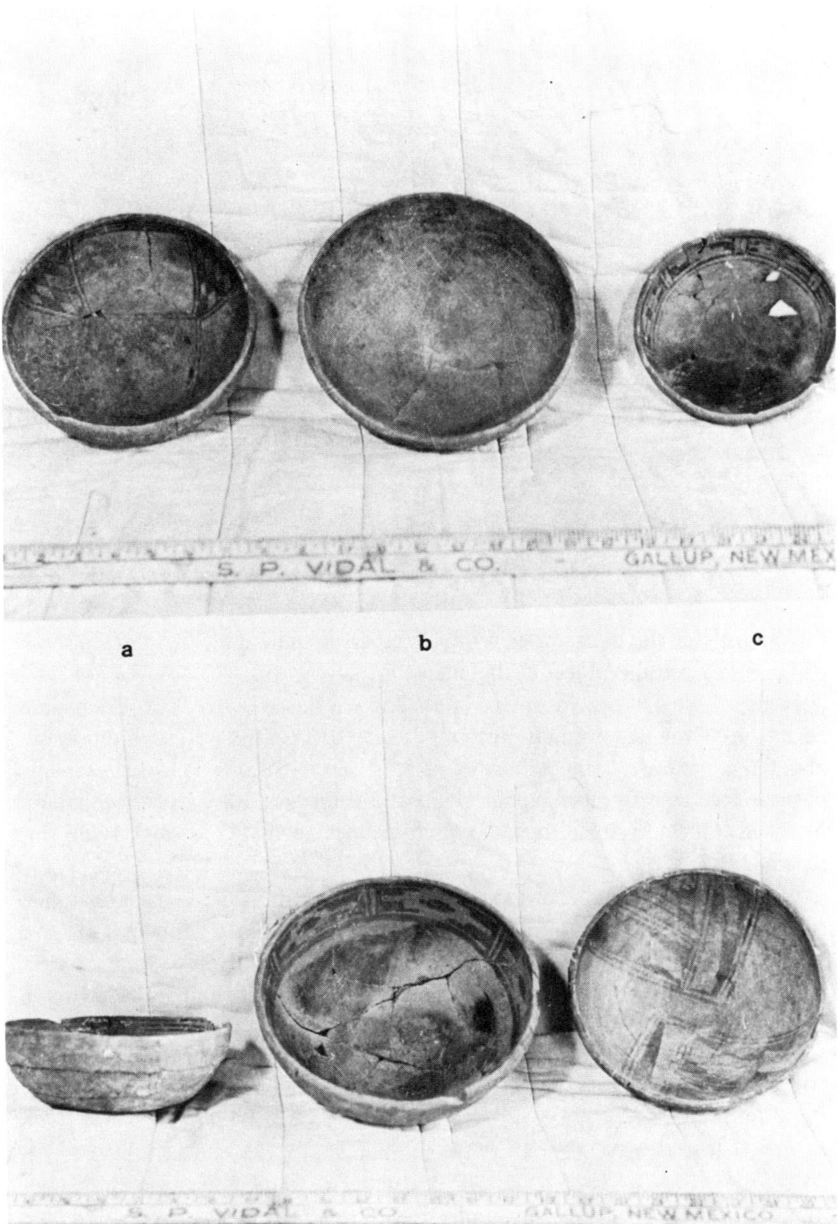

Plate 14. Lincoln Black-on-Red bowls, Phillips Site, Jack Harkey Collection.

Plate 15. Corrugated ollas, Phillips Site, Jack Harkey Collection.

the feeling that the house units north of the creek and on the first terrace south of the creek are the oldest at the site.

House Unit 43 located on the south terrace has roughly 99% Chupadero Black-on-White and Jornada Brown (Table 16). This fits well with our views about the ceramic composition of at least early Corona Phase sites using comparative date from the upper Gallo and from north of Capitan Mountain. Not only the ceramics but the architecture seems consistent with this placement.

Ceramic lots having a substantial percentage of Chupadero Black-on-White (usually over 50%) and Jornada Brown plus undecorated Three Rivers or a related terracotta-colored pottery and perhaps Jornada Polychrome may follow the chronological time when Chupadero Black-on-White and Jornada Brown were virtually the only types represented. This second group of house units, (or ceramic lots) is also characterized by the absence of Corrugated, Lincoln Black-on-Red and trade types. Twenty-seven ceramic lots from surface collections of house units meet these conditions: 6, 10, 11, 12, 13, 14 (with Mimbres Black-on-White), 15 (with Carmen Red?), 16, 17, 18, 20, 21, 22, 24, 25, 26, 27, 28, 30, 31, 32, 34, 35 (with St. Johns Polychrome), 36, 39, 42, and 44. Most of the house units are north of the creek.

Several pottery lots (and house units) seem intermediate or transitional between earlier and later pottery complexes. Corrugated pottery seems to

Plate 16. Trade pottery, Phillips Site, Jack Harkey Collection: *a*, Ramos Polychrome jar; *b*, Gila Polychrome jar.

Plate 17. El Paso Polychrome olla and its contents, Phillips Site, Jack Harkey Collection.

increase steadily in frequency after its introduction. It is not entirely clear how Lincoln Black-on-Red behaves after its introduction. The pit underlying House 11 in House Unit 46 has a low percentage of Corrugated and El Paso Polychrome but has the highest percentages of Lincoln Black-on-Red in our collections. This is hard to interpret, and of course the sample was quite small. If, as I assume, the Phillips Site was a manufacturing center for this type, its relative frequency in house units might well be correlated with its production. It might also enter the archaeological record here earlier than elsewhere.

Using 10% or less of Corrugated as a rough line of demarcation for identifying early Lincoln Phase house units, eight house units surveyed (but not excavated) can be segregated as possibly pertaining to this category: 1, 3, 4, 5, and 7 north of the creek and 36, 37, and 47 south of the creek. Of these, House Unit 7 is doubtful, since a Glaze I sherd was present. House Unit 8 lacks Corrugated but has El Paso Polychrome, Glaze I and Mimbres Bold Face, suggesting a somewhat later placement. House Unit 45 with 16% Corrugated (again a small sample) may represent an intermediate point in the increasing frequency of Corrugated between the house units with less than 10% Corrugated listed above and House Unit 46 where Corrugated is over 20% in most of the house lots (but not in the older pit of House 11). Room 13 in House Unit 46 has 14% Corrugated from the upper floor and 23% from the lower floor. This represents a reversal of expected increase in Corrugated through time, but the effects of small samples and other factors affecting the ceramic lots need to be understood before such expectations can be evaluated.

For the architectural maze encountered in House Unit 46, we assumed that the pit structure (Room 14) was the earliest except for the partial pit remnant underlying House 11. This assumption retrospectively seems to have been based on the idea that pit structures were likely to be older than other architectural components in that house unit. Also, the structural interrelationships were extremely complex; we were unable to visualize how a pit structure in such close proximity to a shallow slab-lined house could have been integrated into an architectural plan. Since we had to cease excavations before this intriguing maze could be deciphered, the temporal and spatial relationships will have to remain an unanswered question. The ceramic frequencies from Room 14 are similar to those from Rooms 11 and 13 and quite dissimilar to the older pit under Room 11, suggesting that all the structures in the maze are roughly contemporaneous.

It would appear that the last concentration of population at the Phillips Site was south of the creek at House Units 46, 48, and 49. Harkey reported Gila Polychrome and Ramos Polychrome from House Unit 49. If our assumption of progressive increases in frequencies of Corrugated through time is correct, House Unit 48, with 62% by count or 80% by weight of Corrugated in Room 1, may be the latest portion of the site to be occupied. It should be noted that the other two excavated rooms in this house unit showed considerable variation in frequencies of Corrugated (Table 20), and all ceramic lots were small samples.

The Phillips Site Petroglyphs

A ridge one-half mile east of the Phillips Site begins just south of the river, trends south-southwest, and is about one mile long. The top of this ridge is covered with large boulders that have weathered a dark gray-black. Some boulders are virtually covered with petroglyphs; others contain isolated figures (Figs. 22–26; Pls. 18–24). Most of the petroglyphs are located near the north end of the ridge. Some or all of the petroglyphs may postdate the site described above. The following analysis of subject matter and style is based on photographs and does not represent the entire group.

Subject Matter of the Petroglyphs

Human Figures: Of six semi-realistic human figures, all probably male, three have the phallus represented (Fig. 22e; Fig. 24f; Fig. 25, top). Two square human figures are covered with geometric designs (Fig. 22a; Fig. 25, bottom); these have the closest counterparts to a similar figure from Otero

County, New Mexico (Jackson 1938:47), and to a figure from the Hueco Mountains (Cosgrove 1947: Fig. 46d).

Human Masks, Heads, or Faces: Seven representations occur; three are definitely masked (Fig. 22b; Pl. 23a, b; Fig. 26). One has a bison horn headdress or mask (Fig. 24c). One probably represents a head with a *tablita* (Pl. 20).

Birds: Thirteen birds or bird-like creatures were noted (Fig. 23c, d; Pl. 18). One is a "thunderbird," one has a beak like a parrot (Fig. 22f), and one has an exaggerated long neck like a crane or heron (Fig. 22g).

Snakes (Fig. 23g; Pl. 19): Two snakes are recorded.

Fish (Fig. 24d): Three fish are depicted.

Large Quadrupeds: Two mountain sheep can be easily identified. One is a full-body profile with a small "rain" element on its back (Fig. 24c); the other is a full-face version of the horns (Fig. 23f). Two animals are probably deer (Fig. 24a).

Small Quadrupeds: There are five smaller animals; one is a rabbit, and it seems best to reserve species identification on the others (Fig. 23a).

Amphibians: There are one or two petroglyphs that could be amphibians or lizards (Pl.18b).

Turtles (?): Three possible turtles have stylized square bodies (Pl. 24a).

"Bug": One "bug" is climbing up a long line (Fig. 24b).

Crabs or Spiders (?): Two creatures with a trail or (less probably) a tail, have six legs instead of the requisite eight of crabs and spiders (Pl. 21).

Fanciful Animals: Some figures cannot be identified easily but look like real animals. Others are more fanciful, such as the two mountain sheep heads that rise from vague bodies (Pl. 23a).

Isolated Hands and Feet: Five-fingered and six-fingered hands occur (Fig. 22h; Fig. 24g).

"Rain Symbols": Six stair-stepped motifs occur (Figs. 23b); Fig. 24b). Two of them occur together as a matched pair (Fig. 22d; Pl. 19); one is the tablita headdress referred to above, under human masks.

Geometric: This category is too numerous to count effectively. Included are circles and concentric circles (Pl. 22), frets (Fig. 22c), arrows (Pl. 18b), irregular lines, and fan-shaped objects (Fig. 23e). Some elements are like the typical stepped design found on Lincoln Black-on-Red pottery.

Shield: A warrior in a buffalo horn headdress brandishing a bow and quiver of arrows in one hand and an unidentified object in the other is pictured on a shield from which feathers are suspended (Fig. 24e).

Textile (?): One geometric figure looks like an elongated textile with fringe on one end (Pl.24a).

Figure 22. Petroglyph figures, Phillips Site. Not drawn to scale.

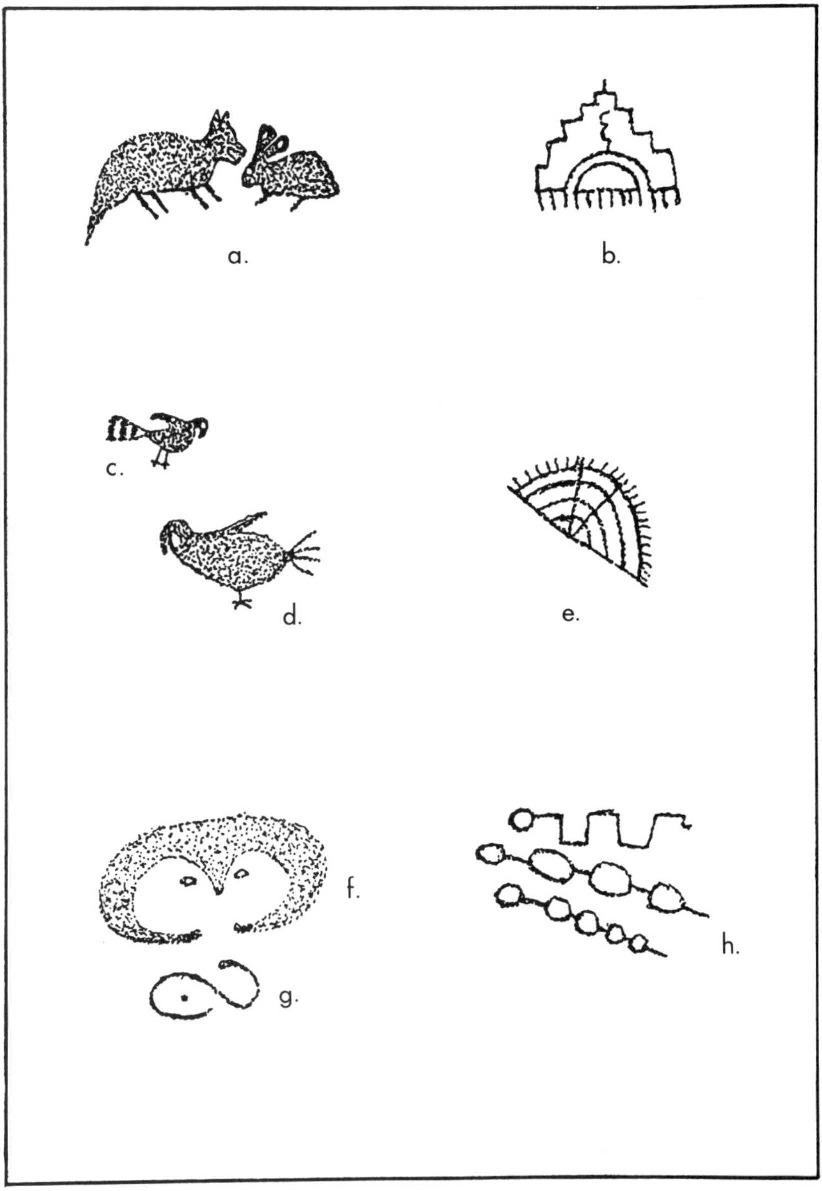

Figure 23. Petroglyphs, Phillips Site. Not drawn to scale.

Figure 24. Petroglyphs, Phillips Site. Not drawn to scale.

Figure 25. Petroglyphs, Phillips Site. Not drawn to scale. (This technique of drawing the figures better depicts the petroglyphic quality of the originals than did Figs. 22-24.)

Figure 26. Petroglyphs, Phillips Ranch. Not drawn to scale. (This technique of drawing the figures better depicts the petroglyphic quality of the originals than did Figs. 22-24.)

Plate 18. Petroglyphs, Phillips Site.

Plate 19. Petroglyphs, Phillips Site.

Plate 20. Petroglyphs, Phillips Site.

Plate 21. Petroglyphs, Phillips Site.

Plate 22. Petroglyphs, Phillips Site.

a

b

Plate 23. Petroglyphs, Phillips Site.

a

b

Plate 24. Petroglyphs, Phillips Site.

Discussion of the Petroglyphs

The only obvious element of composition occurs in a naturalistic scene of a rabbit facing a carnivore (coyote?) nose to nose (Fig. 23a).

There are at least two stylistic uses of pecking: the subject may be outlined, or it may be given an overall white or speckled effect. Subject matter includes very naturalistic animal forms such as the rabbit facing the carnivore, stylized treatment of animals or humans, and geometric forms.

There is no way to tell if all the petroglyphs are the same age. The shield showing a warrior with a buffalo headdress holding a bow and arrows probably reflects late Plains influence. If all of the petroglyphs are of this vintage, they postdate the village of the Phillips Ranch Site.

It is interesting to note, whatever their age, the blending of subject matter typical of the Southwest, such as the "tablita" on a head, a Kachina-looking mask, and the "rain" figures, with the Plains buffalo horn headdresses or masks and the shield. Quite apart from either of these traditions is the naturalistic depiction of animals and birds. As a group, the closest parallels are to be found to the south in the pictographs and petroglyphs of the Guadalupe and Hueco Mountains.

CARRIZO MOUNTAIN SILICIFIED SHALE MINES

Location

NE ¼, S11, T7S, R13E. The mines, located in the mixed oak-pine zone of Carrizo Mountain on a ridge that trends north-northeast to south-southwest, are within the Lincoln National Forest at an elevation of approximately 7100 feet.

Surface Indications

A steeply-bedded deposit of black silicified shale runs north-south. There are three quarry sites along the ridge. The easternmost is a pit some 8 feet deep and 15 feet in diameter, with flakes and slabs of shale littering the sides. This pit was once believed to be an abandoned gold mine and prospectors placed timbers inside the depression trying to find the lost shaft (Pl. 25a). The depth of quarry number 2, a depression 6 by 10 feet, could not be ascertained as it contained a great deal of washed slope debris. Number 3 quarry on the west was free of debris (Pl. 25b); it was 5 feet deep and had surface dimensions of 10 feet north-south and 6 feet east-west. The sloping sides of the pit were littered with flakes and slabs of the black shale.

The silicified shale is bedded so that slabs ½ inch to 4 or 5 inches thick could be easily broken. Many of the thinner slabs, retaining upper and lower planes of the bedded shale, were broken into manageable sizes and used. Several granite hammerstones were found in the workings. This is undoubtedly the source of the great quantities of black shale found at the Phillips Site as well as of the black shale traded south to the Hondo and Ruidoso Valleys.

ROBINSON SITE

Location

S1 and S12, T7S, R13E. The site was about 1 mile south of the Robinson ranch house on the east slope of Patos Mountain at an elevation of ca. 6850 to 6900 feet.

Surface indications

An extensive site was located in the rather sparsely wooded piñon-juniper belt. The only visible architectural remains were upright stone slabs outlining rooms and house units; a single circular depression was also outlined with upright slabs. Visible walls were mapped (Map 7). Sherds, flakes, and other cultural debris were found over several acres. No excavations were made here.

Although the use of upright stone slabs gives a superficial similarity to the Phillips Site and to Corona Phase sites in the Gallo Drainage, the settlement pattern and character of this site are different. Whereas Corona Phase sites are on a level with the modern surface and have little depth, this site has definite "mounds" 3 to 5 feet above the ground level caused by the collapse of buildings and the accumulation of cultural debris. This suggests that a more substantial architecture would be found with excavation. The function of the visible upright stone slabs cannot be determined at this time. The site has a pattern more suggestive of a pueblo, with the main group of rooms clustered around a plaza. Several linear units are located a short distance away (Map 7).

A circular depression about 30 feet in diameter located northeast of the central "pueblo" is completely ringed with upright slabs. Mr. Jack Harkey told me that this "kiva," as it is called by local amateurs, was prolific in arrow points, 175 having been collected from this single structure in one day.

Surface pottery collections from this site were unavailable for study.

SMALL SITES WEST OF THE PHILLIPS SITE

In a survey of Carrizo Creek above the Phillips Site, four sherd areas were found which had only Chupadero Black-on-White pottery, or a mixture of

a

b

Plate 25. Carrizo Mountain silicified shale mines.

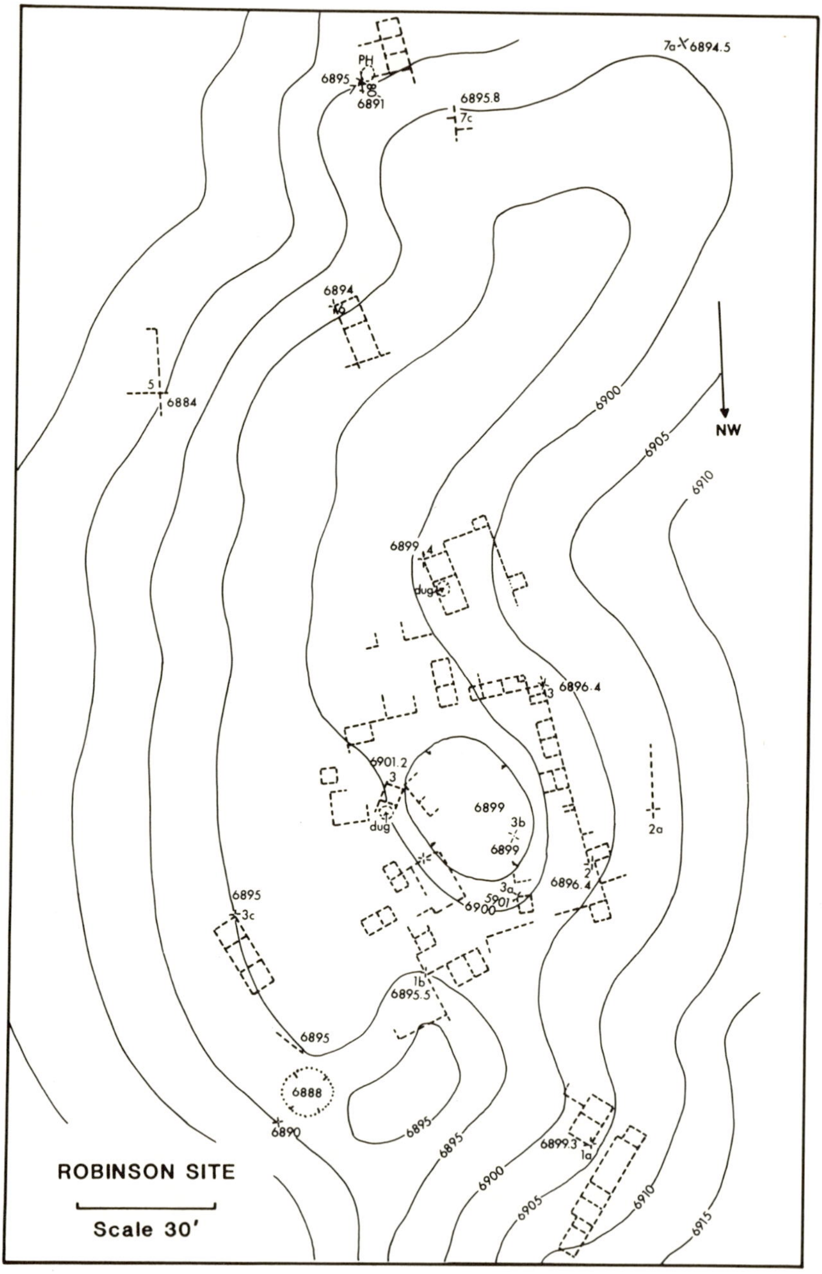

Map 7. Plan of Robinson Site, visible walls mapped with a Brunton compass.

Chupadero Black-on-White and Jornada Brown. No architectural features were reported. The survey verified our supposition that no other large sites of Corona or Lincoln Phases existed in the more mountainous terrain.

SUMMARY

The Phillips Site dominated the Carrizo Valley from the Corona Phase through the Lincoln Phase. Continuity was strong in house construction practices and in the scattered village pattern. Use of masonry and adobe in surface structures (House Unit 46) was more in keeping with architectural traits of the Lincoln Phase elsewhere, but these coexisted with the older type of slab-outlined shallow pithouses. This valley never boasted a true pueblo structure. The site was large, but only a few structures were occupied at any one time.

During the Lincoln Phase, two economic specialties of the village can be recognized. The black shale mines on Carrizo Mountain must have been worked by people from this village, and this shale was traded east along the Macho and southeast to the Hondo Drainage. Lincoln Black-on-Red pottery was probably made for trade as well as for local use.

A few miles to the north, a closely related group lived at the Robinson Site. The latter seems to have been a more substantial village, probably belonging to the Lincoln Phase.

Appendix 3

SITES NORTH OF CAPITAN MOUNTAIN

THE LOCALE

Massive Capitan Mountain dominates the landscape. Capitan Gap divides the mountain into eastern and western parts. The four sites reported here are located some 6 to 8 miles north of the crest of the eastern mountain on the edge of the rolling Pecos Plains. A number of streams that rise on the precipitous slopes of Capitan Mountain and flow north to the Macho Drainage have overlapping outwash fans which furnish extensive agricultural lands in the zone where these sites are located.

The crest of Capitan Mountain carries pine and other Canadian Zone flora. Stands of pine are visible from the sites. The precipitous slopes merge into wooded foothills forming a band 3 to 4 miles wide along the north flank of the mountains. Piñon and juniper are the main components of this zone, but oak occurs and grass is abundant. Located in this zone are the Homestead and Las Tablas Site. Block Lookout Site is located close to the border of the piñon-juniper belt with the grass belt, where the piñon is small and sparse. At Block Headquarters Site, situated beyond the piñon growth, yucca, cacti, grass, and scrub oak are the main flora.

HOMESTEAD SITE (NOT ASSIGNED TO A PHASE)

Location

Approximately NW ½, S28, T7S, R15E (Map 4 in Appendix 2). A sherd area surrounds a gate that enters 160 acres of homestead property which is surrounded by the Block Ranch.

Surface Indications

No architectural remains were visible. Sherds and flint flakes were abundant in the road close to the gate due to recent grading. Surface collections were made in 1956.

Artifacts and Pottery
A single side scraper was found. All sherds were Jornada Brown.

LAS TABLAS SITE (TENTATIVELY ASSIGNED TO THE CORONA PHASE)

Location
Approximately the NE ¼, S28, T7S, R15E; east of the Homestead Site on Block Ranch property (Map 4).

Surface Indications
This extensive site covered approximately 10 acres. Slab-outlined house units were scattered about; sherds and flakes were scarce as the site was well covered with tall grass. Surface collections were made in 1956.

Architecture
Scattered house units outlined by upright stone slabs resembled, at least superficially, the dwellings of the Corona Phase of the upper Gallo Drainage and Carrizo Stream. We did not locate a circular structure.

Pottery
Jornada Brown, Chupadero Black-on-White, and some unidentified Black-on-White sherds were collected.

BLOCK HEADQUARTERS SITE OF THE LINCOLN PHASE

Location
SW ¼, S7, T7S, R16E (see Map 4). This site is in a small pasture southeast of the barns, just east of the road that connects the ranch headquarters with the north Capitan-Roswell road.

Surface Indications
A "squared" mound with a central depression undoubtedly represents a square pueblo built around a plaza. A single row of rooms extends east from the southeast corner. To the northeast is a circular depression. Masonry walls were visible in pot hunters' holes. Metates, manos, chipped stone artifacts and

pottery were present on the surface in abundance due to rather constant digging by amateurs.

Fieldwork

A surface collection was made in 1955 and a test pit was sunk in the central depression in 1956. A disturbed room was partially cleared to expose the masonry walls.

Architecture

Visible walls were of sandstone masonry coursed without mortar. A central subterranean structure was present in the plaza. The test in the central depression reached a floor level at a depth of 6 feet below the modern surface. Two large charred posts were placed about 8 feet apart.

Artifacts and Pottery

Slab metates with a suggestion of a mano rest were observed on the surface. Excavated pottery from this site was not available for analysis. In the initial survey, Chupadero Black-on-White, Corrugated, and Glaze I were noted.

BLOCK LOOKOUT SITE OF THE LINCOLN PHASE

Introduction

Location

NE ¼, S20 and NW ½, S21, T7S, R16E (see Map 4). Some 15% of the site is on government property. The eastern section of the site is on the Block Ranch.

Terrain and Ecology

Block Lookout Station is a fire lookout post. This position was chosen because a natural hill rises out of the rather flat surrounding terrain; from this hill one can see any night light on the entire north side of Capitan Mountain. This same excellent visibility must have appealed to the Indians who built their village here, as it is a long way to water from the top of the hill.

The hill is fairly abrupt on the west side, but the east and south slopes are more gradual. The top of the hill is today devoid of any vegetation larger than a cactus, but scrub piñon and juniper grow around the foot of the hill and down the east side and large trees are found along the creek west of the hill.

Fieldwork

The site was visited in 1955 and excavations were carried out in 1956 under the direction of Herbert R. Harvey, who filed a preliminary report on the excavations with the Forest Service. Materials stored in The Museum at Lubbock, Texas, were analyzed by the author.

Surface Indications

An adobe-walled pueblo occupies the top of the hill. Walls have been exposed by the road that was graded to the Lookout Station and in countless pot holes on the Block Ranch side of the fence. Mr. Guck, Forest Ranger in Capitan, New Mexico, told us that rooms were encountered during construction of the Ranger house and the accompanying cistern.

This is one of the most devastated sites in southeastern New Mexico. Almost every square foot of surface has been disturbed or covered with back dirt from the pot holes. Fortunately for archaeologists, these holes are rarely over 2 or 3 feet deep.

A number of house units outlined with stone slabs are visible on the east slope. We cannot say at this time whether these scattered units were contemporary with the pueblo, or whether they belong to a Corona Phase occupation.

Metates were abundant down this east side of the hill. Over 60 specimens of slab metates and metates with mano rests at the closed end of the trough were counted in 1955. Other surface artifacts included manos in abundance, points (rare because they are the main object of amateur collecting), scrapers, and tubular clay pipe fragments. Animal and human bones were common. Sherds seemed to blanket the hill top and were quite abundant on the east slope. Trade wares such as Glaze I were extremely prominent in the surface collection. Charred corncobs were to be seen occasionally. Building clay fragments with twig and pole impressions were in evidence.

Excavated Structures

Four of the contiguous, adobe-walled rooms on the west of the site were completely excavated and three other rooms partially cleared (Map 8). All were on government property. A trench across the site, beginning at the Lookout road on the west and continuing east-northeast for 115 feet, exposed a large, square subterranean chamber (Structure 8) just east of the excavated surface houses, and an older subterranean structure was encountered just east of Structure 8. No pueblo rooms were encountered on the east. The amount of surface disturbance makes it difficult to estimate the original shape of the pueblo, but it may have been linear or L-shaped. In the descriptions of excavated structures, Harvey's 1956 report to the Forest Service will be followed closely; certain changes in format have been made and some statements not pertinent to this discussion have been omitted.

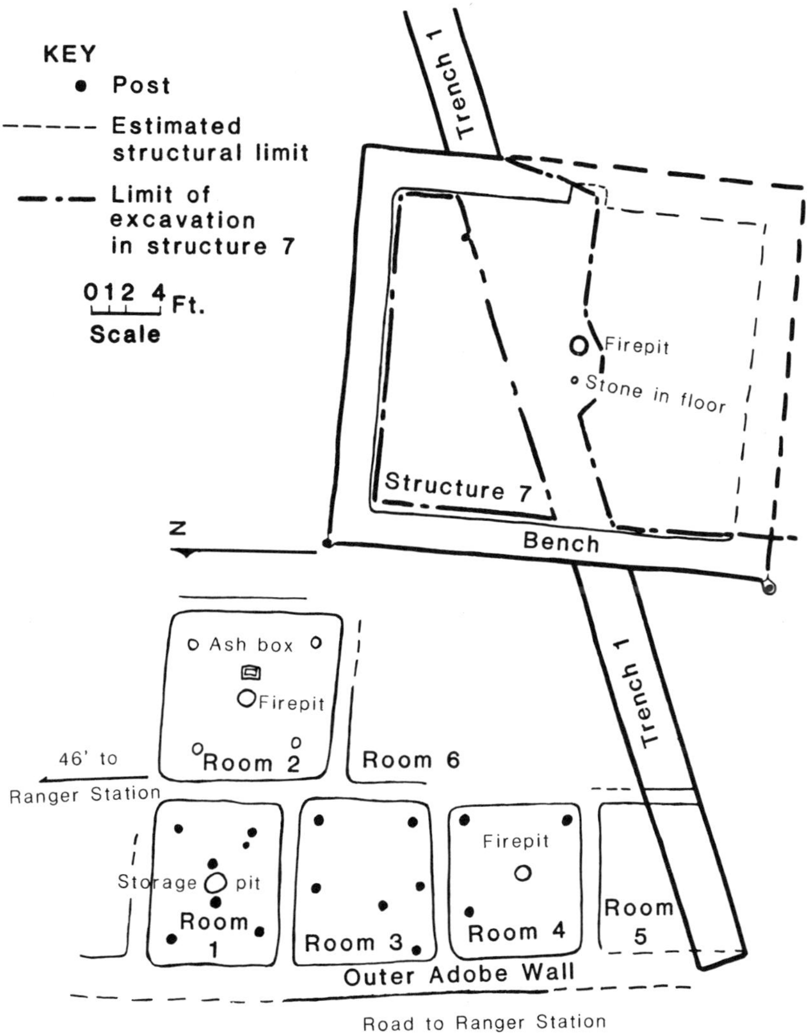

Map 8. Block Lookout Site.

Room 1

The floor area was approximately 7½ x 9½ feet with its long axis running east-west. The outside west wall of adobe two feet thick had a rock center. The other three adobe walls, shared with adjoining rooms, were 12 inches thick and also had some rock content. Both floor and walls were covered with plaster ½ inch thick. Portions of burned roof beams and baked roofing clay permeated with reeds and grasses lay 3 to 5 inches thick immediately above the floor. Cross beams were supported by eight upright posts set close to the walls. In the center of the floor was a round, crudely-shaped unplastered pit slightly over 1 foot in diameter and about 8 inches deep. It was not a firepit, and it contained no artifacts (Pl. 26).

Burials in Room 1: One adult burial without offerings was recovered from beneath the floor in the northwest corner of the room. The flexed burial lay on its right side. Remains of another adult were scattered throughout the sub-floor fill.

Along the south wall, beneath the floor, the remains of four infants were found, only one of which was fully intact. A ladle-shaped *strombus* pendant (Pl. 34) lay at the sternum of the articulated infant. Disturbance of the burials probably resulted from burying repeatedly in the same small space.

Artifacts Found in Room 1: The room contained a considerable amount of pottery, bone awls, a single-stop bone flute (Pl. 35), several projectile points and scrapers, manos, metate fragments, and an arrow shaft-straightener. Bones of deer, rabbit, and jackrabbit were abundant.

Room 2

This room, adjoining Room 1 and sharing its east wall, was the largest of the surface rooms excavated with a floor area 10 x 10 feet. The interior of the 12-inch thick adobe walls were plastered. Intact portions of the floor plaster exhibited a smooth, fine finish. In the center of the room, a small bowl-shaped firepit 10 inches in diameter had a clay lining. Ten inches to the east was a rectangular slab-stone box or ash pit, 10 x 7 inches, and 8 inches deep. The roof was supported by four upright corner posts.

Beneath the plaster of the north wall was another smooth coat of plaster which had been thoroughly burned. A heavily-charred roof beam which paralleled the north wall at floor level had been plastered over in the renovation of the room.

Artifacts in Room 2: Five manos and five metate fragments with mano rests were found. Pottery, stone, and bone was abundant. Burned walnuts and berries (thorn apples) permeated the fill.

Room 3

The roof was supported by six uprights. No interior features were located.

Room 4

A small, bowl-shaped clay-lined firepit, 8 inches in diameter, was in the center of the floor. Three upright posts were found in corners; there was none in the southwest corner.

Artifacts in Room 4: A cache of eight manos, three whole and two broken metates were on the floor.

Room 5

The south wall of this room was obliterated by the road grader; the north wall was 9 feet long.

Burial in Room 5: An infant burial in the northwest corner was accompanied by a small Lincoln Black-on-Red bowl (Pl. 27b), which covered the infant's skull, and 61 *Olivella* shell beads.

Artifacts in Room 5: Two complete miniature vessels were recovered, one a rough brownware bowl, the other a rough Corrugated jug (Pl. 27a, c).

Room 6

Trenching showed that this room was built at the same time as the first construction of Room 2. After burning, it was not rebuilt.

Room 7

The southwest corner of this room was excavated to ascertain that there was an adjoining room north of Room 1.

Summary of Surface Rooms

The surface rooms at Block Lookout are small, rectangular, adobe-walled rooms containing from 60 to 100 square feet of floor space. Inter-room walls are rockfilled adobe, ca. 1 foot thick, smoothly plastered on both sides. The exterior wall of the outside row of rooms is 2 feet thick with a center core of rock covered with adobe. Roofs of clay about 4 inches thick were supported by fairly stout cross beams. These, in turn, were supported by heavy uprights placed inside the rooms. On its western exposure, the pueblo was two rooms wide and extended more than 160 feet. This side of the pueblo probably contained in excess of 30 rooms.

Structure 8

A deep subterranean structure, in close proximity to the room block just described (see Map 8), measured 26 x 23½ feet from back wall to back wall with its long axis running approximately three degrees off true north and its short axis running six degrees off east. Depth to floor level ranged between 6 and 9 feet, depending on the surface contour. Height of the back walls on the east and west respectively was 4 feet 2 inches and 4 feet 10 inches. On all four sides, forming part of each back wall, was a bench averaging 27 inches in height and 27 inches in width. Walls, bench and floor were covered with a hard, durable plaster 2 to 4 inches thick. The entire room could not be cleared in the time available; the bench was exposed along the north and west walls and half of the east wall. The main cross trench was expanded to reveal the firepit and the ventilator.

A depression in the vertical face of the bench at the center on the east wall began 7 inches above the floor. The bench surface continued over the depression; approximately 1½ inches of plaster was supported on its underside by poles 1½ inches in diameter. A flat, rectangular, worked stone 14 inches wide was found in front of the depression at floor level. The limited excavation suggested a ventilator shaft and deflector stone.

The roof of this structure was made of baked clay with reed and grassy matter in its matrix, like the roofs of the surface structures. A considerable number of the heavily charred roof beams were found just above the floor. Corner posts were set into the bench; the southwest corner-post was intact. In the floor, 32 inches west of the east bench, an upright post 51 inches high was found. In the back wall above the bench on the west side, a series of holes probably once accommodated roof supports. Above the plaster of the back wall, a layer of heavy rocks which added a foot to wall height definitely formed an integral part of the building.

The off-center, cylindrical firepit, 14 inches in diameter, was smoothly plastered on the interior to a depth of 12 inches. Fourteen inches west of the firepit, in the center of the room, a small shallow stone "mortar" was countersunk into the floor (Pl. 29).

On its west side this structure was sunk into the natural caliche. The east side was built over older fill. The floor of an older pithouse was discovered 15½ inches beneath the floor of this structure. How far the older structure continued beneath Structure 8 is not known. At the top of the back wall on the east side, thin plaster continued for 10 inches horizontally over the fill.

No buildings were constructed above the floor area of Structure 8; the fill was continuous and contained very little pottery, bone or stone. This factor, together with the size of the structure, its physical relationship with the adobe room unit, and its probable ventilator shaft and deflector stone, all point to the probability of its being a kiva; further excavations at similar sites in the area will probably demonstrate conclusively that the square kiva is a diagnostic feature of Lincoln Phase sites.

Structure 9

The trench east of Structure 8 crossed an older, deeper house that extended under the floor of Structure 8. No structural features were found in the section of floor exposed by the trench. The house extended about 15 feet east of Structure 8. It is assigned a number for convenience of reference.

Artifacts

Provenience of artifacts is given in Table 21. Metates excavated or observed on the surface were of the slab and one-end-closed trough types. Manos were of three types: (1) Large, heavy manos, over 12 inches long and 3 to 3½ inches high, had a single convex grinding surface. (2) Manos with a single, slightly convex grinding surface which turned up at the ends, were 7 to 8 inches long. The profile of this type was low and roughly triangular or wedge shaped (Pl. 28c); one specimen had a finger depression (Pl.28f). (3) Well-shaped loaf manos are, or originally were, rectangular in cross-section with one and two flat grinding faces.

Grinding stones less than 5 inches long had one grinding face on otherwise unshaped pebbles. A well-shaped cylindrical pestle was battered on one end (Pl. 28e). One of the large, heavy manos had been grooved at the midsection and used as a maul (Pl. 28a).

Shaft-straighteners were made on pebbles ground flat on the bottom; one specimen had sides and ends shaped (Pl.28h, i). One was roughly triangular in cross-section due to the original shape of the pebble. All had single transverse grooves.

The shallow "mortar" found plastered in the middle of the kiva may have functioned as a substitute *sipapu* (Pl. 29).

A single stone ball was ½ inch in diameter. A small, cigar-shaped stone was found on the floor of Room 2 (Pl. 32, 2nd row on left). A larger stone from the floor of Room 5 had 9 horizontal lines engraved on each of two sides (Pl. 32, upper left). Polishing pebbles of less than 3 inches in diameter were found in each room and scattered through the fill.

Fifty-five points were found in our excavations, and ten more were found on the surface. Few of these were found in rooms; most came from the upper levels of fill in the long east-west trench. Two were perhaps dart points (Pl. 31, lower right); others were small arrow points. Unnotched triangular and side-notched forms outnumbered corner-notched forms (Table 22).

Four ovate knives, each less than 1¼ inches in length, could be classed as points, as could a triangular 'knife' that appeared to be a steeply retouched dart point.

Bifacial retouch occurred on a single edge of two flakes and along two long edges of six flakes. One of the drills was a long sliver of flint used with a clockwise motion (Pl. 32, upper right); the other flake drill had a slightly expanded base (Pl. 32, 2nd from right, top row).

Flakes which were unifacially retouched graded from worked flake to

TABLE 21
TABULATION OF EXCAVATED ARTIFACTS, BLOCK LOOKOUT SITE

	Rooms					Structure	Other	
Artifacts	1	2	3	4	5	8	Excavations	Total
Chipped stone								
Points (See Table 22)	5			1	2		47	55
Knives							4	4
Flakes with bifacial edge retouch							8	8
Drills	2							2
Scrapers							6	6
Core-planer							1	1
Unifacially worked flakes							16	16
Tabular object							1	1
Hammerstones							4	4
Ground stone								
Metates	1	5		5	1		1	13
Manos	2	5		8			8	23
Grinding stones							3	3
Pestle								
Maul, full-grooved							1	1
Shaft-straighteners	1				1	1	1	4
"Mortar"						1		1
"Marble"					1			1
Polishing pebbles	6	3	6		2	3	6	26
Miscellaneous		1				1		2
Shell								
Conch (*Strombus*) pendant		1						1
Olivella beads		1		1	61		1	64
Mussel shell pendants							5	5
Bone								
Awls	3	3		3		1	12	22
Gaming pieces							2	2
Whistle	1							1
Punch							4	4
Flakers, antler							2	2
Miscellaneous							5	5

scraper categories (Pls. 32-33). Among the scrapers, we found one end scraper, two side and end scrapers, two triangular scrapers with retouch on three sides, and one snub-nosed specimen. A single core-planer was found. Twelve worked flakes had one edge retouched, three had two edges retouched, and one cortex flake had the periphery retouched. Interior flakes were used for all but three of these chipped stone specimens; the latter were cortex flakes.

A rectangular piece of slate was chipped along both edges (Pl. 32, lower left). Hammerstones were numerous on the surface, but only four were found

TABLE 22
FORMS OF PROJECTILE POINTS,
BLOCK LOOKOUT SITE

Projectile Point Types	No.	%
Triangular arrow points		
Symmetrical, concave base	16	
Asymmetrical	4	
Straight base	4	
Convex base	1	
Total	25	
% of total projectile points		38.46
Side-notched arrow points		
Concave base	9	
Straight base	7	
Double side-notched	2	
Single notch on one side	3	
Total	21	
% of total projectile points		32.31
Corner-notched points		
Over 1 inch and fairly broad	2	
Less than 1 inch and slender	1	
Total	3	
% of total projectile points		4.61
Fragments		
Total	16	
% of total projectile points		24.61
Total	65	

Excavated forms = 55; forms from surface = 10.

in our excavations. Three of these were battered cores, while the fourth was a battered pebble.

Raw materials used for chipped stone artifacts are given in Table 23. Various kinds of chert were most popular. Black shale from the Carrizo Mountain mines was rare. Absence of unworked flakes and the small size of chipped stone artifacts suggested that siliceous material was a scarce and valuable commodity.

The Conch (*Strombus*) shell ornament that accompanied the infant burial in Room 1 was acquired by trade; its point of origin was the Gulf of Mexico coast. An *Olivella* shell necklace was with an infant burial in Room 5. Three *Olivella* beads were found singly. Five pendants of mussel shell are shown in Plate 34. Only seven other fragments of mussel shell were found, suggesting that shell was not worked locally.

Split bone awls were made from deer(?) ribs and long bones (Pls. 35-36). Conspicuous by their absence were ulna and metapodial awls. Many of the 22

TABLE 23
RAW MATERIALS USED FOR CHIPPED STONE TOOLS, BLOCK LOOKOUT SITE

Materials	Points	Unifacial Flakes & Scrapers	Bifacial Tools
Flint			
Red translucent	4		
Translucent	6		1
Banded	1	1	
Alibates (?)	1	3	
Gray	2		
Unspecified color		2	
Total	14	6	1
Jasper	3	3	2
Chert			
Not specified	1		1
Black	1	5	1
Gray	18	4	2
Red	2	1	2
Brown	4		
Green, limey	1	2	
Cream	4	1	2
White, chalky	3		1
Mottled	2	1	5
Total	36	14	14
Quartz	4		
Opal	2		
Unidentified	6		
Total Tools	65	23	17

awls were crude and either unpolished or slightly polished.

One of the gaming pieces came from the subterranean room that partially underlies Structure 8. The other was found in the fill of Trench 1 at a depth of 42 inches. The single whistle had one stop (Pl. 35, lower left). Four split bone punches were blunt. Two antelope antler flakers were found.

Miscellaneous bone artifacts included a thinned and rounded rib (Pl. 36, top row, 2nd from left), a handle (Pl. 36, upper left), two bison rib abraders (?) with the cancellous bone tissue exposed (Pl. 36, lower right), and part of a scapula hoe (?).

Twelve pottery "counters" or worked sherds lacked perforations or drill depressions. Ten were Chupadero Black-on-White, one was Three Rivers Red-on-Terracotta, and one was an unidentified Black-on-White. Round, oval, and rectangular forms occurred.

The complete clay pipe was unusual in that a flared "guard" separated the bowl from the mouth section (Pl. 37, left). Nine vertical incisions had been made in the body of the pipe, which had been modeled in two pieces and then joined. A pipe fragment was decorated with punched dots (Pl. 37, middle).

Food Remains

Animal Bones

Deer or antelope were the most common. The antler flakers were antelope. Rabbit and other small animals were present, and a few bison bones were found.

Wild Plants

About one gallon of charred "thorn apples" (*Crataegus*) were collected from Room 2. A charred lump of sunflower seeds (*Helianthus annuus*), a number of cholla buds (*Opuntia arborescens*?), and charred walnuts were found in the same room.

Corn

The charred cobs that we excavated from this site were taken to Harvard University by Herbert R. Harvey who, in collaboration with Walton C. Galinat of the Botanical section of Agassiz Museum, made an analysis of the most complete specimens. He has allowed me to use this data, and his unpublished manuscript is slightly edited below.

> Maize was the only cultivated plant in evidence at Block Lookout. A total of 242 whole or partial cobs were recovered. These specimens were highly carbonized and many were considered eroded. Only one kernel was recovered from the latest occupation; eleven cobs were found in the 2-3 foot level; the balance were found in the earliest occupation at a depth ranging from 5-6 feet.
>
> Seventeen cobs were completely intact. The average length of these is 4.29 cm with a range of 2.7 to 5.6 cm.
>
> There were two striking characteristics about the corn from Block Lookout, (1) the apparent homogeneity of the population, and, (2) the small size of the cob. The latter feature becomes of interest when viewed in terms of the late age of the site. Such corn might be expected from a site of considerably earlier vintage, or in a mixed population containing varieties known widely over the Southwest at the time. None of the larger more developed varieties appear at Block Lookout Site.
>
> Too little is known of the archaeological cultures, in general, in this area to attempt an empirical explanation of this conservative feature of corn agriculture. The inhabitants of Block Lookout carried on trade with areas where more highly evolved corn was being grown, so that it was not unknown or unavailable to them. It is more probable that this corn

Plate 26. Room 1, Block Lookout.

Plate 27. Three small pottery vessels, Block Lookout.

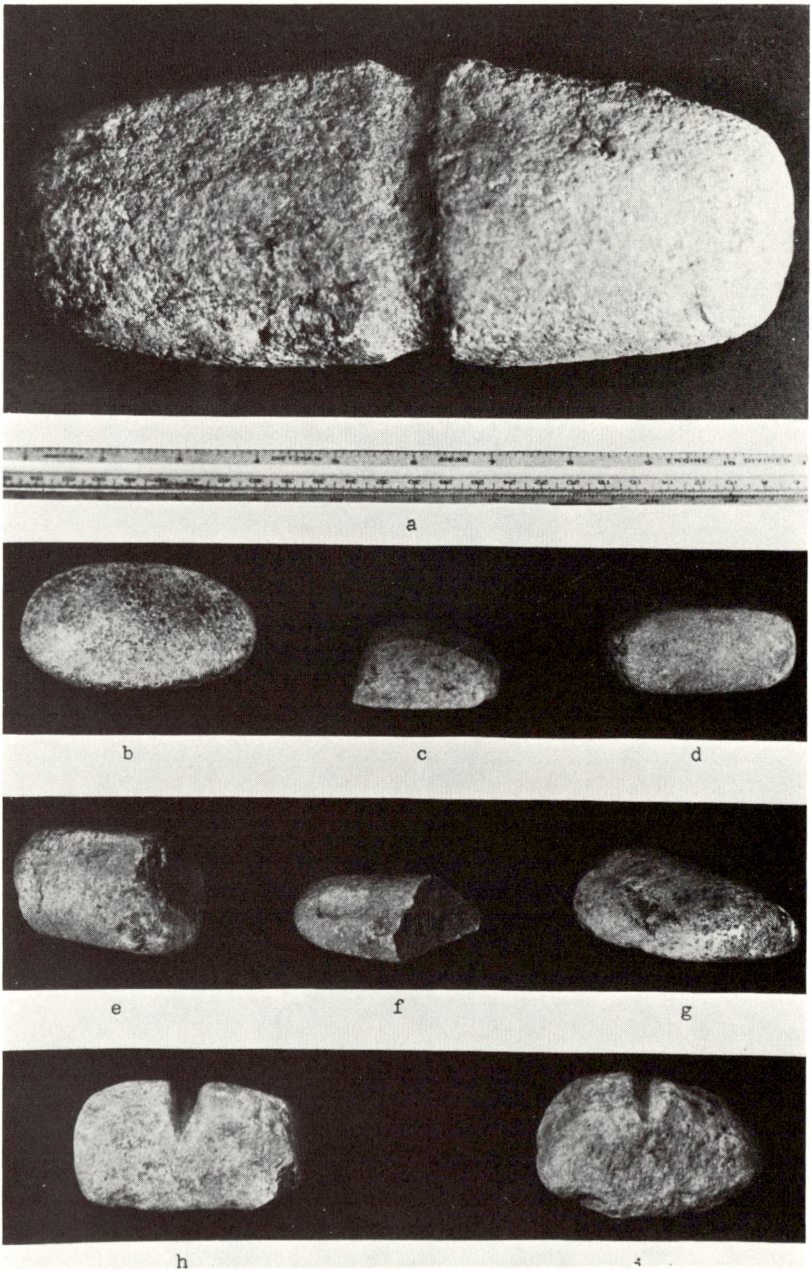

Plate 28. Maul, manos, and shaft-straightener, Block Lookout.

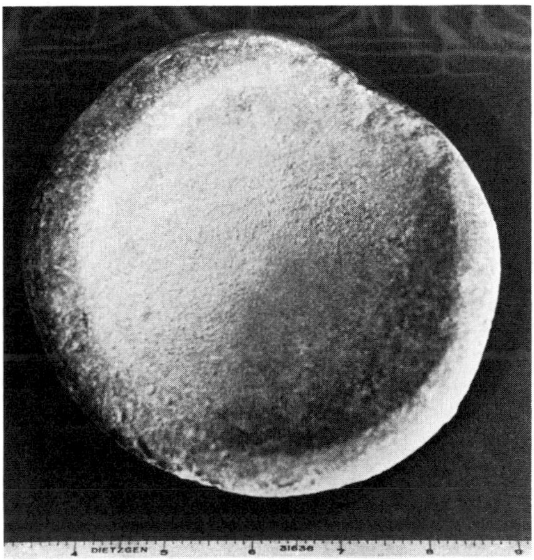

Plate 29. Stone "mortar," Block Lookout.

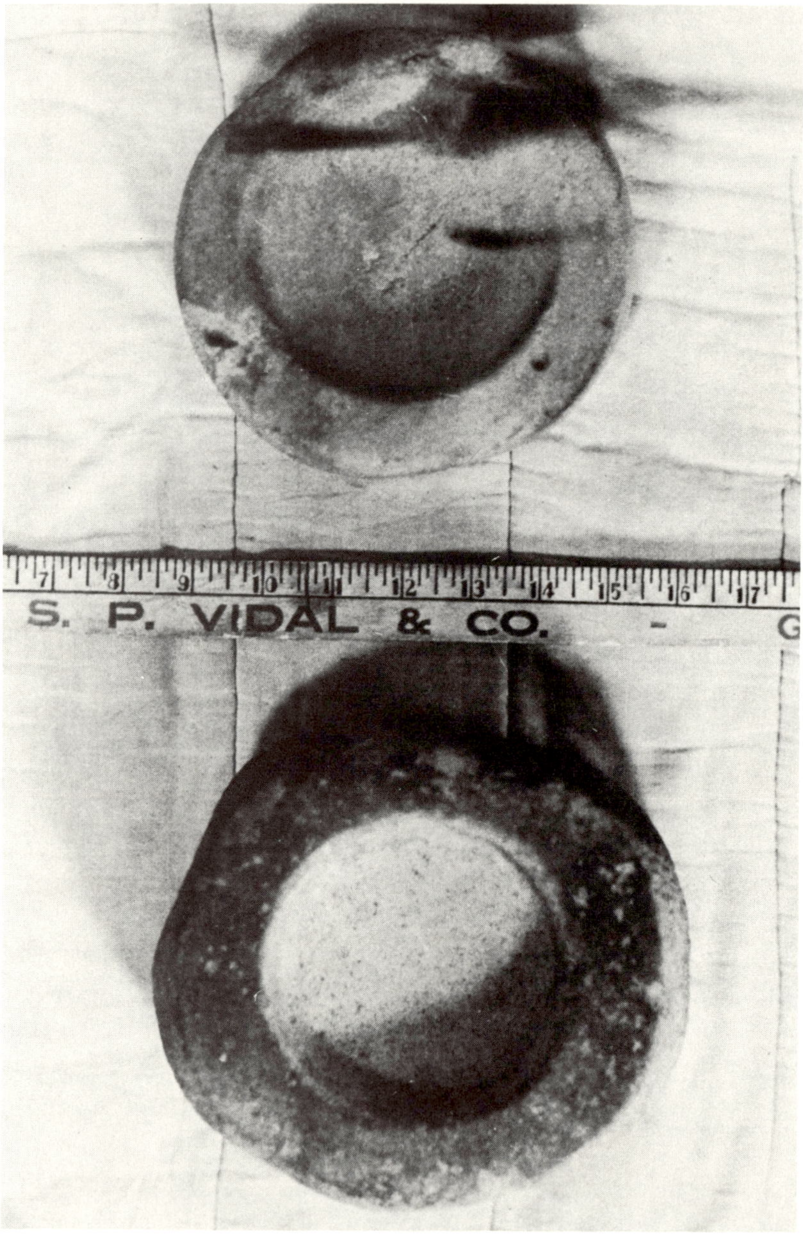

Plate 30. Two stone "mortars," Jack Harkey Collection, provenience unknown.

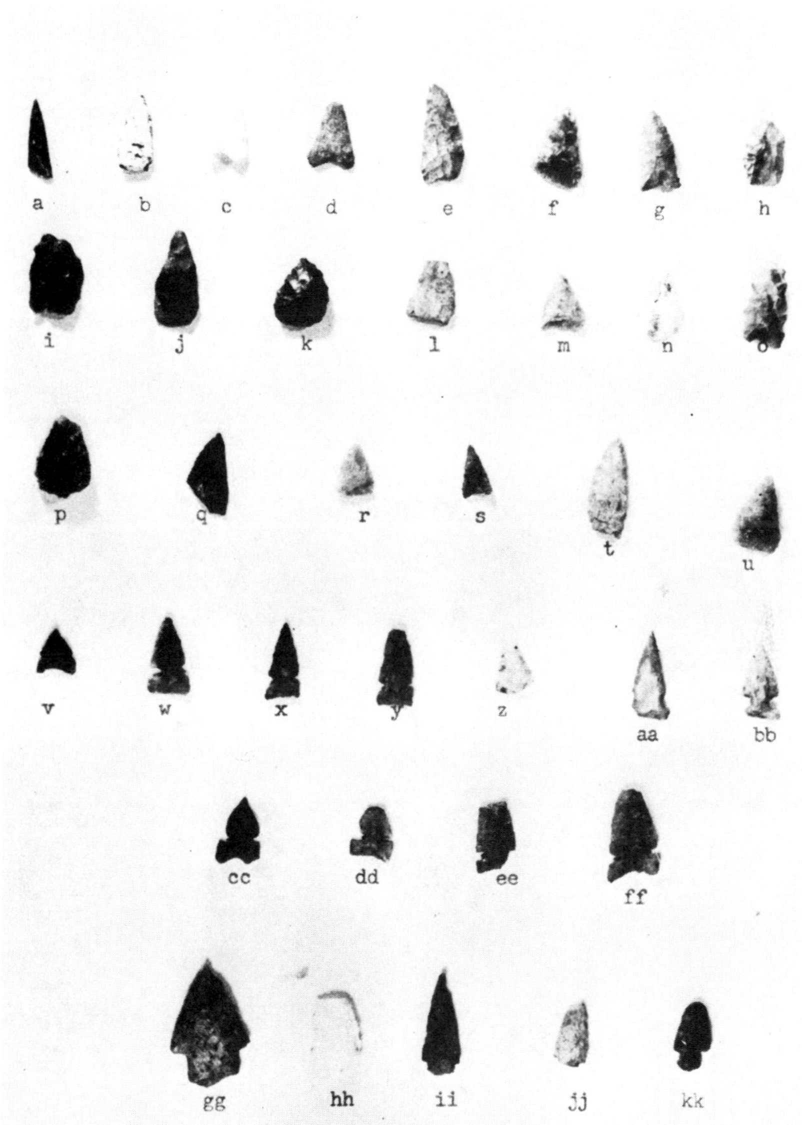

Plate 31. Projectile points, Block Lookout; *gg* measures 32 mm.

Plate 32. Stone tools, Block Lookout; *a* measures 66 mm.

Plate 33. Chipped stone tools, Block Lookout; *k* measures 26 mm.

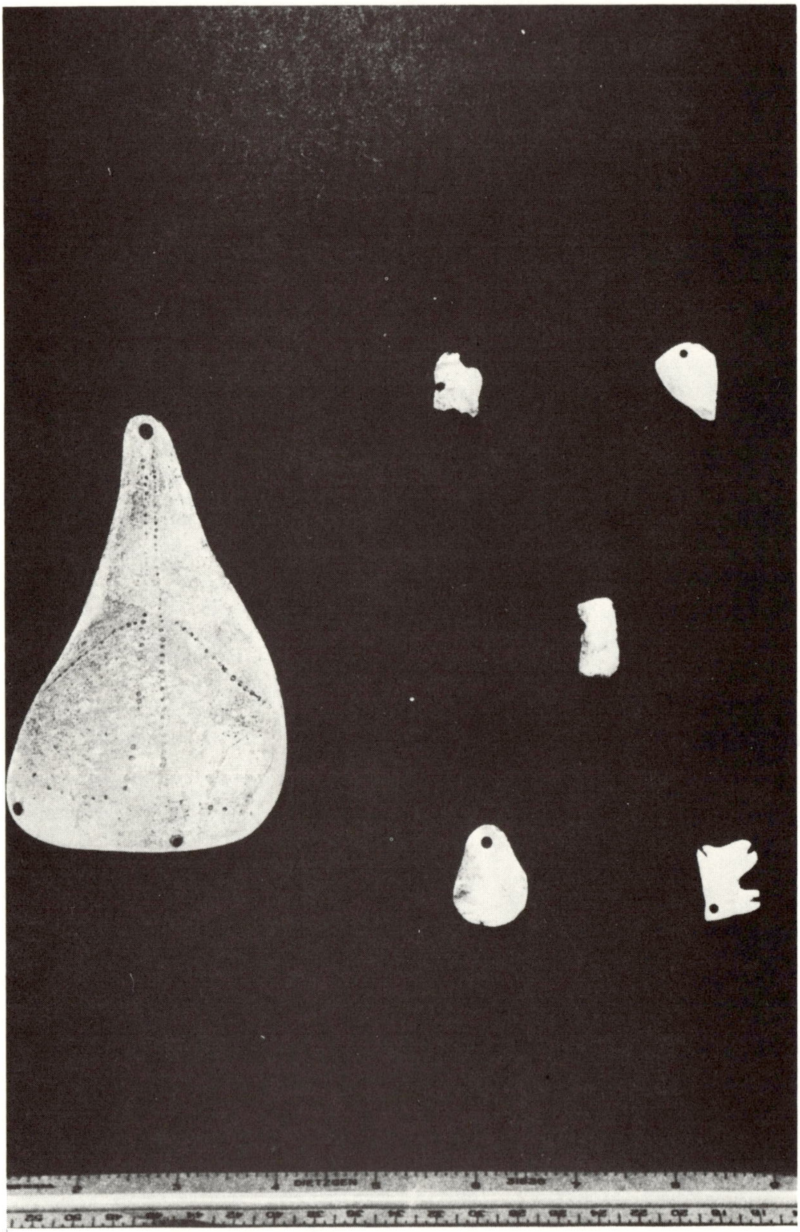

Plate 34. Shell ornaments, Block Lookout.

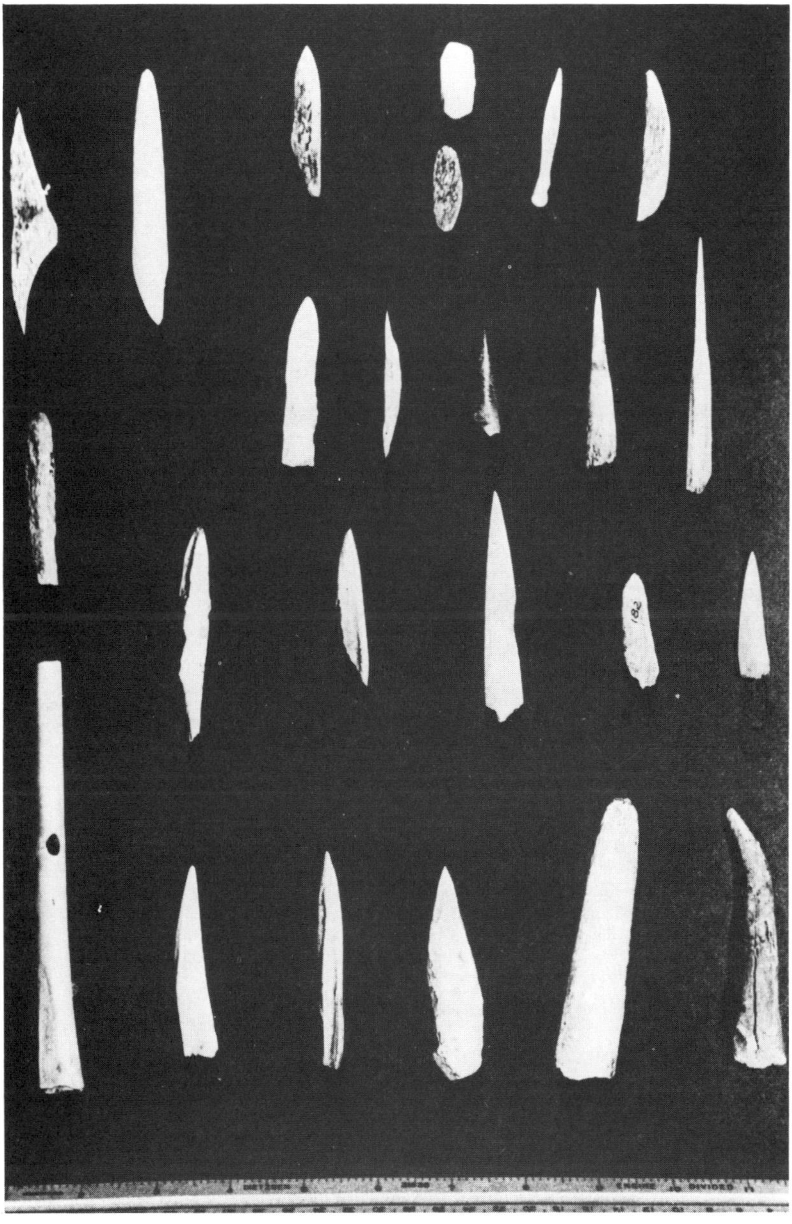

Plate 35. Bone objects, Block Lookout.

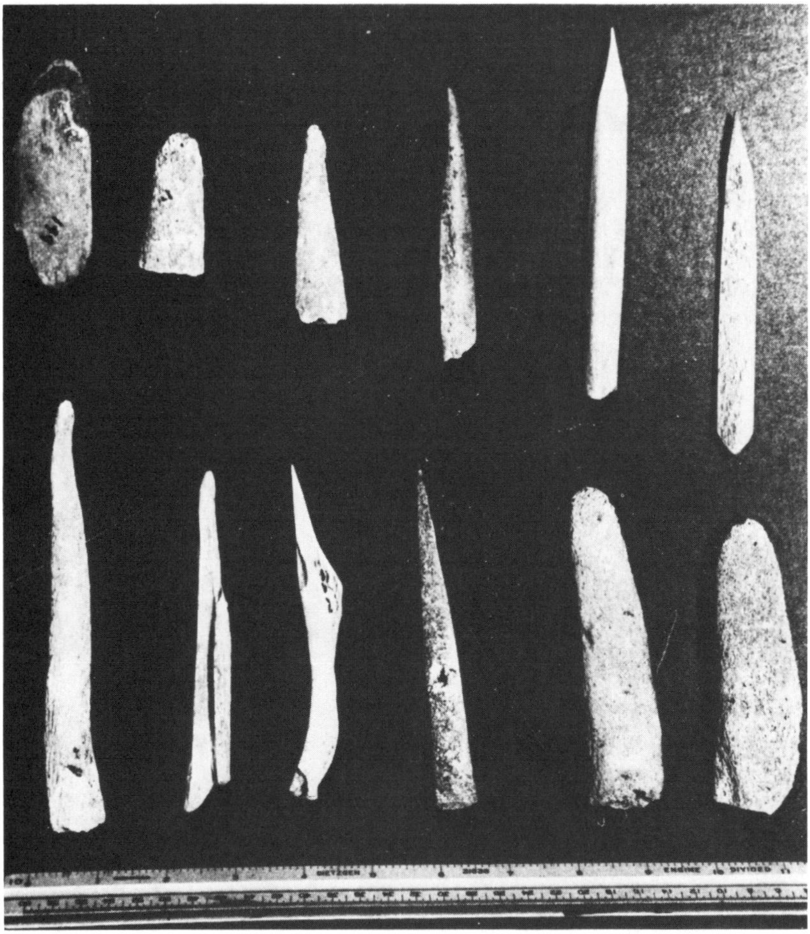

Plate 36. Bone objects, Block Lookout.

Plate 37. Tubular pipes, Block Lookout.

Plate 38. Las Lunas Smudged bowl, Block Lookout.

possessed characteristics which were better suited for growing in the rigid environment of the Lookout area, given the particular agricultural practices employed. Although agriculture was important in the subsistence pattern, hunting and gathering also played a major role.

Due to the extent of erosion, only four characters could be analysed: kernel-row number, length and diameter of the cob, and fasciation. The same procedures were used in scoring the cob characters as were employed by Galinat, Mangelsdorf, and Pierson (1956:107):

> . . .1) The number of rows of pistillate spikelets (kernel-row number) was counted in the central region of all intact and fragmentary cobs; 2) A fasciated cob was considered to be any cob which was obviously flat for at least one-quarter of its length; 3) Diameters were measured in the central region of all intact and fragmentary cobs. When cobs were fasciated, the average of maximum and minumum widths was used; 4) Length measurements were made only on obviously intact specimens. . . .

Shape: One of the most distinguishing features of the maize from Block Lookout is its cigar-shape, thickest in the central portion of the cob with tapering on both ends. It is akin to Chapalote, a distinctive race of popcorn, with a distribution centering in Northwestern Mexico.

Length: The length of the 17 intact cobs from Block Lookout averages 4.29 cm with a range from 2.7 to 6.0 cm. In terms of kernel-row number, diameter of the cob, and fasciation, this group is a fairly representative sample.

Kernel-row number: The average number of kernel-rows per cob on Block Lookout maize is 9.338. The range is from 8 to 16 rows, with 87% of the population about evenly distributed between 8 and 10 kernel-rows.

Diameter: Diameter of the cobs ranges from 10 to 22 mm, with a mean of 14.95 mm [Fig. 27]. As might be expected, kernel-row number is correlated with cob diameter. 87.5% of the 8-rowed cobs have diameters of 15 mm or less.

Fasciation: Only 52 cobs exhibit fasciation. In this population fasciation is associated with number of kernel-rows, since 88.4% occurs in cobs having more than 8 rows [see Fig. 28].

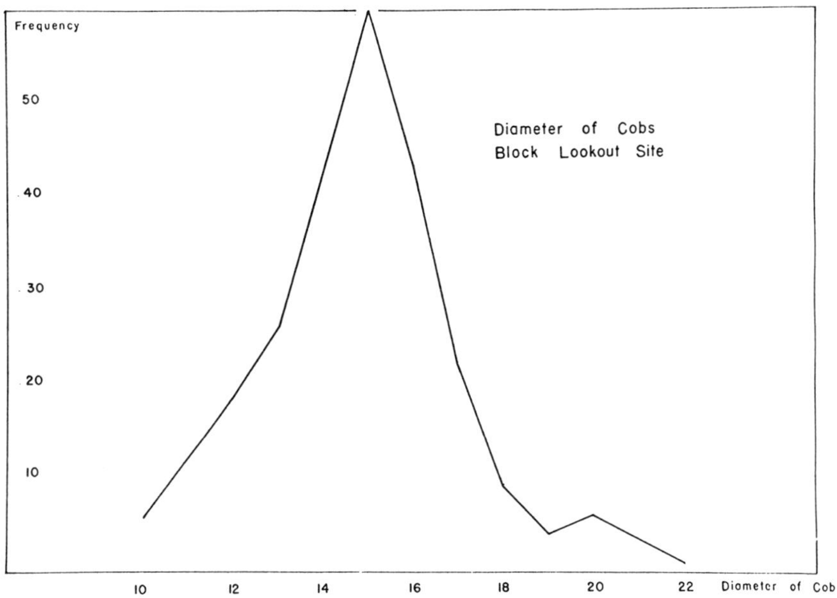

Figure 27. Diameter of corn cobs, Block Lookout.

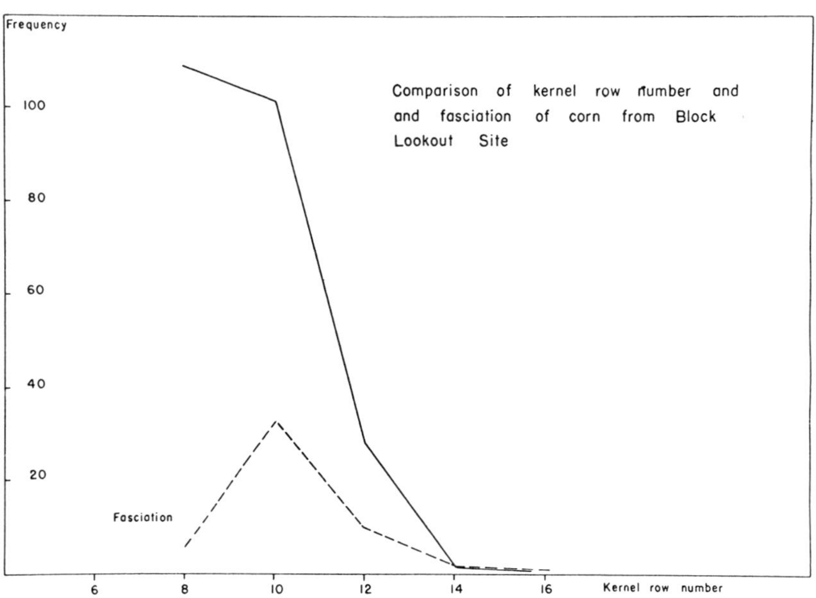

Figure 28. Comparison of row number and fasciation of corn, Block Lookout.

Burials

The one adult and four infants in Room 1 and the infant in Room 5 were the only burials that were located. Normal burial position was tightly flexed. Some individuals were buried with ornaments and pottery and others were not.

There were numerous fragments of human bones scattered around· pot holes, and the location of some of these suggests that burials also occurred outside of houses.

Skeletal Analysis of the Adult Burial in Room 1

by

Erik Reed

Small young adult male, 25-30 (all indications concur). Bones light, smooth, quite small, though definitely male. No features noted on bones of torso aside from indications of sex and age. Arms muscular though small; no perforation of olecranon. Left humerus: 302 mm long, diameter of head 46 mm. Head of right humerus missing. Radii 240 mm long (both).

Femora slender but quite muscular; slight pilastering, no third trochanter. Bicondylar length, right femur, 418 mm; diameter head 44 mm (both). Tibiae straight, flat (thin) muscular; no squatting facet, no retroversion of tibial head. Maximum length of right tibia, 347 mm — lateral length 330 mm.

Vertical occipital artificial cranial deformation, asymmetric (greater compression on the left), fairly pronounced, not quite actually vertical.

No occipital torus, no inion projection. No wormian bones; sutural complexity quite low. Parietal bosses not very prominent, even with deformation. Mastoid processes small, styloids moderate; supramastoid crests very well developed. Frontal comparatively high and well rounded. Strongly marked supraciliary ridges (over medial halves of orbits only) and glabellar prominence. No nasion depression. Maxilla small and concave in profile, but prominent, root of nose pinched up and bridge projecting. No nasal overgrowth. Large strong nasal spine. Orbits rhomboid, moderately sloping.

Malars fairly large and prominent, not notably so. Sub-orbital foramina large, fossae shallow. Very slight alveolar prognathism. Mandible small, fairly prominent, bilateral (?) chin; ascending rami broad, vertical; very, very slight gonial eversion. Dentition: no premortem losses, all third molars in, but lower left badly impacted; no caries; severe wear; shovel-shaped incisors.

Measurement	*mm*	*Measurement*	*mm*
Cranial length	160.0	R. orbit height	33.0
Cranial breadth	142.0	L. orbit height	34.0
Basion-bregma height	136.0	R. orbit breadth	38.0
Min. frontal diam.	100.0	L. orbit breadth	38.0

Max. bizygomatic diam. (est.)	140.0	Ext. pal. breadth	68.0
Total face height	112.0	Ext. pal. length	53.0
Upper face height	69.0	Basion-nasion	96.0
Nasal height	53.0	Basion-prosthion	93.0
Nasal breadth	22.0	Ht. of symphysis	29.5
		Bigonial diameter	94.0

Pottery

All excavated sherds have been analyzed; only those from surface Rooms 1, 2, 3, 4, and 5, the kiva (Structure 7), and from the deep fill of the older House 9 which underlies Structure 8 (Trench 1, Sections 9 and 10) are tabulated here (Tables 24 and 25).

Heshotauthla Polychrome, Galisteo Black-on-White, Biscuit B, Santa Fe Black-on-White, Pueblo II Black-on-White (?), Cundiyo Micaceous Corrugated(?), Tularosa Black-on-White, and most of a Los Lunas Smudged bowl (Pl. 38) were found outside of the excavations tabulated here. A brief description of some features of the local pottery types is given below.

Corrugated

A restorable olla from the floor of Room 5 is of interest to those who classify pottery. Color went from reddish brown to tan to black to gray. There was a tremendous amount of variation in the degree of prominence of coils, ranging from prominent to completely obliterated. A few other sherds had a chalk-like temper in fragments that were as large as ¼ inch in diameter. At least two partially corrugated vessels occurred, in which the upper half was corrugated and lower half was smoothed. Scalloped indented and diamond-shaped corrugations were found.

Jornada Brown

Little of this type was micaceous. Several sherds with large, rounded quartz temper also had red orthoclase feldspar inclusions typical of Roswell Brown. One handle was of this type.

Decorated Jornada Brown

Sherds of a highly polished Jornada Red-on-Black occurred in several test pits and in Trench 1. Seven Jornada Brown sherds had a textured surface. Jornada Red-slipped olla sherds were noted.

Chupadero Black-on-White

One and possibly two vessels were completely undecorated. One jug rim sherd had two vertical finger prints on the exterior. An everted bowl rim of the Capitan variant was unslipped. Glazed designs were common.

Lincoln Black-on-Red and Red-on-Red

The latter variant outnumbers the Black-on-Red. In the Red-on-Red, designs were usually thin lined. A single Lincoln Polychrome sherd had a typical Black-on-Red design with white paint added within the design area. Large checkerboards, three-quarters of an inch square, decorated one sherd.

Three Rivers Red-on-Terracotta

Undecorated bowls were rare. Thin-lined decoration dominated and broad-lined designs occurred. Two sherds were decorated with large checkerboards like that described above for Lincoln Black-on-Red.

Pottery as a Temporal Indicator

Surface Rooms

The pueblo rooms along the west side of the site represent the latest occupation. Four of the five rooms contained Glaze I, which was the terminal pottery type. The other trade wares (listed in Tables 24 and 25) were more abundant in these rooms than in other parts of the site. Corrugated formed a substantial percentage of the individual room lots (31%–72%). Chupadero Black-on-White ran from 8%–30%. Jornada Brown constituted less than 15% and Lincoln Black-on-Red and Three Rivers Red-on-Terracotta are less important.

Structure 8

Sherds collected in this structure were segregated into fill and floor lots. Very little of the floor was exposed, and so the floor sample is not complete and possibly not very representative. Percentages of the different types from the fill correspond nicely to the range of percentages of the same types from the surface houses.

Trade sherds in the fill included Mimbres Black-on-White, St. Johns Polychrome, Glaze I, and Gila Polychrome. Trade sherds off the floor, however, were of earlier types. Two sherds of Reserve Black-on-White and two sherds of an unidentified Black-on-White with carbon paint (possibly a Galisteo type) were in the firepit. These four sherds were examined by Stanley Stubbs. In view of the small sample, I do not feel that the temporal relationship of this house to the excavated surface rooms can be established at this time. The Reserve sherds argue for an earlier placement, while the structural relationship of this structure with the surface room block indicated a coexistence. Certainly no later structure was superimposed over Structure 8, and the fill contained little in the way of cultural debris, indicating the site was abandoned soon after the structure collapsed.

Trench 1, Sections 9 and 10

This was the fill in the older house (Structure 9) just east of the kiva (Structure 8). The character of the fill is shown in Plate 39, since it is quite unusual for sites in this region. Whereas most fill is hard and the proportion of dirt to cultural objects is extremely high, the fill in this older house contained much more cultural debris. The bedding was fairly horizontal. Materials from the upper two feet of fill were sacked together. Succeeding levels were 1 foot thick.

Percentages of pottery types were quite different from those in the surface rooms. Corrugated ware formed no more than 20% of the total at any level and ran as low as 2% (by weight) on the floor of Structure 9. Chupadero Black-on-White, Jornada Brown, Lincoln Black-on-Red, and Three Rivers Red-on-Terracotta were more numerous than in the surface rooms. Trade wares were more scarce, although Glaze I and St. Johns Polychrome occurred in the 5 to 6 foot level. No trade wares were found on the floor of Structure 9, but the sample was small and little of the floor was exposed.

Locality Summary

Bands of outwash fans suitable for agriculture have been created around the flanks of the Capitan Mountain by precipitous topography. Prehistoric farmers utilized this land, and as a result, their villages and fields were not limited to valley bottoms or adjacent terraces. None of the known sites were on or close to prominent streams; the many streams issuing from Capitan Mountain now are so precipitous that they only carry water during rains and are unable to retain water. The source of potable water for the prehistoric farmers is not evident.

Four sites are described in this appendix. The Homestead Site is only a sherd area. The Las Tablas Site had the house type, settlement pattern and ceramic complex typical of Corona Phase sites to the west and north. The two Lincoln Phase sites must have been contemporaneous. Block Headquarters Site was a square masonry pueblo with a subterranean structure in the center and a wing of rooms off to one side. Block Lookout Site had a double row of adobe rooms that faced east on a kiva. Exact temporal relationships of the adobe room block, the kiva, the older subterranean structure, and the slab-outlined rooms on the east slope are not clear. The location of the Lookout Site on a high, bald hill suggested a defensive position. The nearby Block Headquarters Site was not similarly protected.

We have no data on Corona Phase artifacts. The Lincoln Phase assemblage from Block Lookout was, in some respects, different from collections from

TABLE 24
SHERD LIST, BLOCK LOOKOUT SITE

	Fill, Structure 8		Floor, Structure 8		Room 1		Room 2		Room 3		Room 4		Room 5		Total
Pottery Types	No.	%	No.	%	No.	%	No.	%	No.	%	No.	%	No.	%	
Corrugated															
Rim									52		123				175
Body	92		5		121		251		52		123		242		886
Total	92	35.11	5	20.83	121	71.60	251	45.06	104	48.37	246	77.11	242	46.27	1061
Chupadero Black-on-White															
Bowl	23		1		2		23		12		6		10		77
Jug	61		4		12		100		33		11		151		372
Total	84	32.06	5	20.83	14	8.28	123	22.57	45	20.93	17	5.33	161	30.78	449
Jornada, Undecorated															
Jornada Variant	18				22		45		10		19		22		136
Roswell Variant	15		3				25		13		11		6		73
Gallo Micaceous Variant													1		1
Miniature vessels													2		2
Total	33	12.60	3	12.50	22	13.02	70	12.84	23	10.70	30	9.40	31	5.93	212
Jornada, Decorated															
Red-slipped											1		1		2
Textured	1														1
Jornada Red-on-Brown	1		3												4
Roswell Red-on-Brown	2														2
Total	4	1.53	3	12.50							1	.31	1	.19	9
Jornada Polychrome	1	.38	2	8.33			2	.37					6	1.15	11
El Paso Polychrome	10	3.82					35	6.42	9	4.19			49	9.37	103

Lincoln Black-on-Red									8						8
Decorated	8						11		4		8		1		32
Undecorated									9		5		29		43
Rim	1														1
Red-on-Red	1						1		1		3		1		7
Polychrome															0
Total	10	3.82					12	2.20	22	10.23	16	5.01	31	5.93	91
Three Rivers Red-on-Terracotta															
Thin-lined	5		1				6				2				14
Broad-lined							1								1
Red-slipped	1										2				3
Undecorated	10						22				1				33
Total	16	6.11	1	4.17			29	5.32			5	1.57			51
Biscuit A					2	1.18	1	.18							3
Socorro Black-on-White					1	.59									1
Mimbres	1	.38			1	.59									2
Reserve Black-on-White			2	8.33											2
St. Johns Polychrome	2	.76	1	4.17	7	4.14							1	.19	11
Glaze I, bowl	2	.76					17		5		1		1		26
Glaze I, olla									6						6
Glaze I, yellow									1		1				2
Total	2	.76					17	3.12	12	5.58	2	.63	1	.19	34
Gila Polychrome	1	.38					1	.18							2
Playas Red Incised							1	.18			1	.31			2
Unclassified	6	2.29					3	.55			1	.31			10
Unclassified Black-on-White					1	.59									1
Unclassified Black with carbon paint			2	8.33											2
Total	262		24		169		545		215		319		523		2057

TABLE 25
SHERD LIST, BLOCK LOOKOUT SITE

	Trench 1 Sec. 9 & 10 2′-4′ below Datum				Trench 1 Sec. 9 4′-5′ below Datum				Trench 1 Sec. 9 5′-6′ below Datum				Trench 1 Sec. 9 below 6′					
Pottery Types	g	%	No.	%	g	%	No.	%	g	%	No.	%	g	%	No.	%	Total No.	Total Wt.
Corrugated																		
Rim																		
Body	478		58		130		14		541		55		21		2		129	1170
Total	478	9.60	58	8.48	130	12.42	14	14.00	541	23.28	55	15.54	21	4.05	2	5.13	129	1170
Chupadero Black-on-White																		
Bowl	931		100		118		11		331		63		134		9		183	1514
Jug	1640		184		119		16		509		67		244		17		284	2512
Total	2571	51.65	284	41.52	237	22.64	27	27.00	840	36.14	130	36.72	378	72.97	26	66.67	467	4026
Jornada, Undecorated																		
Jornada Variant			60		6		1		206		22		21		3		86	233
Roswell Variant	1620		81		167		21		527		50						152	2314
Gallo Micaceous Variant			21						102		18						39	102
Miniature vessels																		
Total	1620	32.54	162	23.68	173	16.52	22	22.00	835	35.93	90	25.42	21	4.05	3	7.69	277	2649
Jornada, Decorated																		
Red-slipped	27		3														3	27
Textured																	0	0
Jornada Red-on-Brown	74		3		?		1		27		3		98		8		15	199
Roswell Red-on-Brown									6		2						2	6
Total	101	2.03	6	.88			1	1.00	33	1.42	5	1.41	98	18.92	8	20.51	20	232
Jornada Polychrome	64	1.29	14	2.05	87	8.31	8	8.00	19	.82	3	.85					25	170
El Paso Polychrome	115	2.31	21	3.07	16	1.53	3	3.00	44	1.89	9	2.54					33	175

Lincoln Black-on-Red																		
Decorated			2								33						35	—
Undecorated			46														46	—
Rim											15						15	—
Red-on-Red			34		404		25				1						60	404
Polychrome											1						1	—
Total			82	11.99	404	38.59	25	25.00			50	14.12					157	404
Three Rivers Red-on-Terracotta																		
Thin-lined			22								5						27	—
Broad-lined											1						1	—
Red-slipped			26								3						29	—
Undecorated																	0	—
Total			48	7.02							9	2.54					57	—
Biscuit A																	0	—
Socorro Black-on-White																	0	—
Mimbres																	0	—
Reserve Black-on-White																	0	—
St. Johns Polychrome									8	.34	2	.56					2	8
Glaze I, bowl									4		1						1	4
Glaze I, olla																	0	—
Glaze I, yellow																	0	—
Total									4	.17	1	.28					1	4
Gila Polychrome																	0	—
Playas Red Incised	25	.50	8	1.17													8	25
Unclassified	4	.08	1	.15													1	4
Unclassified Black-on-White																	0	—
Unclassified Black with carbon paint																	0	—
Total	4978		684		1047		100		2324		354		518		39		1177	8867

— = sample not weighed.

Plate 39. Trench profile across Structure 9, Block Lookout.

the Gallo Drainage and Carrizo Stream of comparable age. The sheer numbers of metates and manos was greater here than at any other site in the region. Charred corncobs were likewise more abundant. It is uncertain whether this indicates a more extensive and better developed agriculture or reflects the vagaries of preservation. The loaf-shaped mano forms typical of the Gallo Drainage Lincoln Phase were mixed with the convex, single grinding face type more characteristic of localities to the south.

Harvey's report on the corn raises some tantalizing questions. That such small, primitive corn should be the only corn grown, or that it was grown at all, is curious. The same kind of corn is the only type collected at the Bonnell Site to the south. Yet I have collected an earlier variety of corn with a large, well-developed cob from Feather Cave, which is on the south side of Capitan Mountain. Presumably the small corn was an especially drought resistant strain.

Appendix 4

SITES IN AND ADJACENT TO THE UPPER HONDO DRAINAGE

INTRODUCTION

Ruidoso and Bonito streams head high in the Sierra Blanca Mountains and join at Hondo, New Mexico, to form the Hondo River. One moves from the Lower Sonoran Zone to Transitional and Canadian Zones within 35 to 40 miles. The Lower Sonoran Zone intrudes up the Hondo Valley as far west as the town of Hondo. From Hondo to Ruidoso, Upper Sonoran vegetation includes walnuts and cottonwoods in the valleys and grass mixed with piñon and juniper along the adjacent terraces. Most of the sites are in the Upper Sonoran Zone.

Limited surveys were undertaken by our crews. Other information came from exhibits in the Lincoln County Museum, local amateur archaeologists, and published articles. The Bonnell Site of the late Glencoe Phase is fully described in Appendix 5.

The four localities recognized for the upper Hondo Drainage system present a rather complex archaeological picture, because this was the border between the Glencoe Phase to the south and the Corona-Lincoln Phases to the north. Insofar as we can determine, Ruidoso Valley sites can all be assigned to the Glencoe Phase. Certain sites in the Nogal section and in the Bonito Valley likewise seem to belong to the Glencoe Phase, while Corona Phase sites are present on the southeast fringes of Capitan Mountain. From middle or late Pueblo III times until early Pueblo IV, however, sites in the Nogal section, in the Bonito Valley, and along the southeastern slopes of Capitan Mountain belong to the Lincoln Phase. At the end of the Glaze I horizon when this drainage was abandoned, Lincoln Phase pueblos were less than 10 miles distant from the Glencoe Phase Bonnell Site, and Lincoln Phase architectural traits were beginning to be incorporated into that site. Had abandonment been deferred a few years, it is probable that Lincoln Phase culture would also have held sway in the Ruidoso Valley.

A GEOLOGICAL FEATURE: THE "AQUEDUCT"

Location

South of Hollywood, New Mexico, approximately in the N½, S31, T11S, R14E.

The "Aqueduct"

The aqueduct (Pl. 40) is firmly established in local imagination as a wonderful feat of prehistoric engineering. Periodically the *Ruidoso News* brings out a feature story that reinforces the belief. Dr. Earl Green and I examined the "aqueduct," and it is our conclusion that it is an igneous dike with a trough along the top.

Plate 40. The "Aqueduct."

PRECERAMIC SITES

Pfingsten Site 1

Location

SE ¼, S20, T10S, R16E. The site is located well back from the edge of the broad terrace north of Ruidoso River. The terrace is now grassland with isolated scrub piñon trees. It is on ranch land owned by Bert Pfingsten of Hondo, New Mexico.

Surface Indications

This is a pre-pottery site that has a number of fire-cracked rock (limestone) hearths. Occasional igneous pebbles occur. Flint flakes were percussion produced; a few show some signs of usage. Mr. Ernest McDaniel, who has periodically visited this site for several years, has found a few small dart (?) points, under 2 inches in length, which are convex-based with corner and side notches.

Feather, Chipmunk, or Smetnick Cave

Location

S16 or S17, T9S, R15E. The cave is near the top of the limestone face of the north edge of the Bonito Valley. Entrance is gained from the top side. The cave slopes rapidly down to a large chamber, 240 feet by 61 feet (Roosa 1952:133), which is far enough below the ground level that no light penetrates.

Fieldwork

This cave was partially excavated by the University of New Mexico under the direction of Dr. Paul Reiter. The sandals obtained in that dig have been described by Roosa (1952:133-46). The trench they placed across the fill of the chamber was, in places, over 5 feet deep. Amateur archaeologists are familiar with the cave, and several private collections contain materials from here. I visited the cave in November 1957, when I collected some perishable materials including a corncob ca. 6 inches long. This is a much larger variety than the corn found in Glencoe and Lincoln Phase sites.

It is to be hoped that the results of the University of New Mexico excavation will soon be fully published. Jelinek (1952:Fig. 8) showed that all of the pottery from this site was brown. It was not clear how deep pottery was found in the fill. The lower levels were preceramic.

SITES NOT ASSIGNED TO A PHASE

Threlkeld Site

Location

NW ¼, S29, T10S, R16E. This site is located on a narrow terrace remnant on the south side of the Ruidoso Valley on the property of George Threlkeld, of Roswell.

Surface Indications

The foundation or lower walls of a single masonry room is located at the widest part of the terrace remnant. Walls are nearly level with the present surface. Outside measurements of the structure are 10 feet east-west and about 12 feet north-south. The walls are about 14 inches thick, and a gap in the west wall looks like a doorway. It resembled a homestead foundation, but there is no cement in the masonry and prehistoric sherds are found on the surface.

About 6 feet to the east of this structure, there is a small depression that could represent another house. A burnt rock midden is located about 40 feet to the southwest; the ruins of an adobe homestead are 100 feet to the southeast.

Sites in the Upper Ruidoso Valley

Collections were not made at the sites listed below. They are mentioned to show site frequency in the upper 12 miles of the Ruidoso Valley.

1. At the Stetson School, there is a sherd area along both sides of U. S. Highway 70.
2. At the mouth of Gavilan Canyon is a sherd area.
3. Sherds may be found along the terrace that borders the Ruidoso Valley from Palace Motel to Biscuit Hill Cafe. Several sites were probably located in this portion of the valley.
4. The Singing Pines Cabins, for tourists, were built on a sherd area in the pine zone on the Ruidoso River, which is a rushing mountain stream at this point.
5. Grindstone Mesa is a narrow limestone outcrop with numerous bedrock mortar holes which runs along the south edge of the Ruidoso Valley within the town of Ruidoso, just south of the saloon district.

Upper Stanton Site

Location

T9S, R14E — Location cannot be precisely established.

Lincoln County Museum Collection

Two Chupadero Black-on-White bowls, 4½ and 8 inches in diameter, are from this site. A beautifully made, unused, full-grooved axe is made of a hard black stone which is referred to in the label as an "iron kidney."

Hondo Schoolyard Site

Location

NW ¼, S4, T11S, R17E. The site is in the yard of the Hondo School on a terrace above the Ruidoso River, ¼ mile from the Bonito River.

Phase

Lincoln or late Glencoe.

Surface Indications

Sherd area is roughly 100 x 100 feet. Numerous lithic remains are to be seen.

Pottery

The following types were collected: Jornada Brown, Chupadero Black-on-White, Corrugated, Lincoln Black-on-Red, El Paso Polychrome, Ramos Polychrome, and Glaze I.

Riverside Site

Location

SE ¼, S30, T11S, R19E. Just south of the Hondo River on a broad terrace.

Surface Indications

A low mound about 60 feet in diameter has fire-cracked rocks on the surface. Pottery is scarce. Three metates are of the slab type; one had an incipient mano rest.

Pottery

The following types were collected: Jornada Brown, Chupadero Black-on-White, Lincoln Black-on-Red, El Paso Polychrome, Ramos Polychrome, and Glaze I.

The Fortification

Location

Ca. NE¼, S31, T12S, R16E. This site is on the Mescalero Apache Reservation at an elevation of ca. 7000 feet. Grasses are luxurious. Oak groves and open piñon-juniper stands are present.

Description

A bare granite knoll rises some 30 feet above the valley floor. The top, which is fairly flat, is rimmed with a wall made by stacking irregular granite slabs. The wall, still 3 feet high in places, surrounds an area about 150 x 90 feet at its widest dimensions. Natural depressions within the enclosure are also rimmed with granite slabs, and a pile of these slabs stands at the southwest corner. A second wall on the north slope may be a lookout post. A permanent spring is located at the southeast edge of the knoll.

There were no artifacts within the enclosure. Arrow point tips and several sherds of an undecorated cream-colored pottery with large temper particles protruding at the surface were found around the base of the knoll.

It is assumed that this was a prehistoric fortification. The knoll top could have been defended against spears or bows and arrows on the valley floor; however, firearms placed at the higher elevations of the valley edge and nearby hills would render this location indefensible. Ernest McDaniel told me that the modern Mescalero Apache believe it to be pre-Apache.

Site on Bonito Lake

Location

NW ¼, S12, T10S, R12E. This site is located in Lincoln National Forest. It was adjacent to a small creek above the present level of Bonito Lake, created by a modern dam. The ground was rather level where the artifacts were found; the mountain rose steeply just back of this place.

Surface Indications

Jornada Brown sherds were found over an area roughly 35 feet square. At the west side of the sherd areas was a pile of rocks that might represent a burial. A finely made corner-notched arrow point of gray flint and a turquoise pendant were found within the limits of the sherd area.

A CORONA PHASE SITE

The Escondida Site

Location

N ½, S35, T9S, R17E — Doran Woods Ranch. The site lies in the valley bottom along both sides of Escondida Creek, a northern tributary of the Hondo River that heads on Capitan Mountain.

Surface Indications

A linear house unit about 50 feet long and 9 feet wide had rooms outlined by upright stone slabs. The structure paralleled the creek. One-end-closed trough metates with mano rests, manos, flint chips, and sherds were found along the creek for almost a mile. No pottery collection was made.

GLENCOE PHASE SITES

McDaniel Site

Location

On the north section line of S29, T10S, R16E, the site is located on the valley floor.

Surface Indications

The site was found when Ernest McDaniel had a loading platform cut with a bulldozer. At that time he collected exposed sherds, and he subsequently collected sherds as they eroded out of the cut bank. All of the sherds from the site were undecorated Jornada Brown.

Test Trench

Brown pottery, flint flakes, and occasional charcoal fragments were found from the surface to a depth of 12 to 14 inches.

Pfingsten Site 2

Location

Pingsten Site 2 is located along the south edge of the same terrace where Pfingsten Site 1 is found: SE ¼, S20, T10S, R16E.

Surface Indications

Close to and paralleling the terrace edge for a distance of 30 feet, occasional sherds and flint chips were found. From the surface indications, it is doubtful if any houses are present. Ernest McDaniel frequently visits this site and he reports that sherds are never numerous but are slowly eroding out. Jornada Brown and Chupadero Black-on-White were collected.

Perry Site

Location

N ½, S35, T10S, R15E. This site runs along a terrace remnant south of the Ruidoso Valley, just ½ mile southeast of the Glencoe, New Mexico, Post Office. Today part of the terrace is farmed, part is pasture, and part is in orchards, and the Perry family cemetery is located there.

Surface Indications

We could not determine the nature of a low mound 70 feet long that extended east and west along the terrace. Jornada Brown, Chupadero Black-on-White, Lincoln Black-on-Red, and Three Rivers Red-on-Terracotta were found on the mound and over much of the terrace. A large, full-grooved axe was found in digging a grave.

Close Gravel Pit Site

Location

SW ¼, S25, and NW ½, S36, T11S, R13E. A ridge about 1 mile long ran from the Close Gravel Pit in Ruidoso, New Mexico, south across the highway to the Nob Hill Restaurant.

Surface Indications

In 1954, it was possible to collect sherds, flint and chert cores, flakes, and other artifacts along the entire ridge. This site was subsequently destroyed by gravel mining operations, highway construction, and building.

We saw no evidence of structures. Mr. Close reported that a number of skeletons had been removed, some from well into the gravel. We collected a black side scraper and Jornada Brown, Three Rivers Red-on-Terracotta, Chupadero Black-on-White, Glaze I, Corrugated, El Paso Polychrome, and unclassified Black-on-White and Black-on-Red pottery.

Nogal Mesa Site

Location

South of Nogal Lake, approximately in S20, T9S, R13E.

Lincoln County Museum Collection

Two small, modeled clay animals, a tubular clay pipe, and a full-grooved axe were displayed together as having come from this site.

A stone bear effigy, 8¾ inches long and 5 inches high, was plowed up in a field on Nogal Mesa. This specimen, owned by Mr. and Mrs. Pat Murphy of White Oaks, New Mexico, may or may not be from the same site.

Nogal Canyon Site

Location

Approximately S30, T8S, R13E.

Lincoln County Museum Collection

The site was described as a pithouse village and the displayed specimens were said to have come from a pithouse 15 feet square. A large Chupadero

Black-on-White jug 12 inches high contained charred corn, wild grass seed, and cholla buds. A second jug of the same type was found, as was a shaft-straightener with a single transverse groove and a full-grooved axe 4 inches long.

Upper Bonito Site II

Location

This site is 6 miles west of Fort Stanton Hospital, south of the Bonito River (Jelinek 1952:149).

Surface Indications

Jelinek (1952:150) lists the following pottery types: Brown (42%), Chupadero Black-on-White (30%), Three Rivers Red-on-Terracotta (1%), El Paso Polychrome (2%), Corrugated (9%), and Lincoln Black-on-Red (6%).

Upper Bonito Site III

Location

Upper Bonito Site III is 2 miles west of Upper Bonito Site II (Jelinek 1952:149), north of the river.

Surface Indications

All pottery was brown.

A SITE WITH GLENCOE AND LINCOLN PHASE COMPONENTS

Fred Pfingsten Site

Location

The site is west of the Mesa Ranger Station Site (Jelinek 1952:149).

Surface Indications

"Possible remains of wall structures in the western portion and definite pithouse remains in the east, it probably includes two separate settlements, each on its own hill" (ibid.).

Pottery

Percentages and types are from Jelinek (1952:150): Brown (34%), Chupadero Black-on-White (34%),Three Rivers Red-on-Terracotta (9%), and less than 1% of El Paso Polychrome and Corrugated.

LINCOLN PHASE SITES

Mesa Ranger Station Site

Location

This site is south of Nogal Lake and west of the Mesa Ranger Station (Jelinek 1952:149).

Surface Indications

No structural remains were reported by Jelinek (ibid.), who listed the following pottery types: Brown (41%), Chupadero Black-on-White (16%), Three Rivers Red-on-Terracotta (5%), El Paso Polychrome (15%), Corrugated (19%), and Lincoln Black-on-Red (7%). Trade wares were present, but Jelinek does not specify types.

Young Site

Location

NE ¼, S16, T10S, R13E. It is on the south side of the Bonito Valley, which here is wide and flat, just 0.3 mile from the junction of the Bonito Lake Road with the Ruidoso-Capitan road. A grove of live-oak trees are on the northeast corner of the site.

Surface Indications

A large sherd area 500 feet wide parallels the creek for some 1200 feet. Piles of rock, flint, and other debris are present in the sherd area. Stewart Peckham dug a site in this vicinity on a highway salvage program, and this may be the one.

Upper Bonito Site

Location

Upper Bonito Site is 3 miles west of the Fort Stanton Hospital on the south bank of Bonito River (Jelinek 1952:147).

Surface Indications

Possible wall remains were reported by Jelinek, who gives the pottery percentages as follows: Brown (43%), Chupadero Black-on-White (30%), Three Rivers Red-on-Terracotta (5%), and El Paso Polychrome (less than 1%).

Lower Stanton or Stanton Ruin

Location

Ca. S21, T9S, R15E. This is on the south side of the valley, just south of Highway 380.

Fieldwork

This site was tested by the University of New Mexico, and local collectors have been active.

Architecture

Evidences of an adobe pueblo structure may be seen in the test trench left by the University of New Mexico and in pot holes.

Pottery

Jelinek's seriation (1952:Fig. 8) shows this to be the latest site in the Bonito Valley. Brown types comprise only 7% of the total, while Corrugated reaches 42%. Trade wares were present, but Jelinek didn't specify types.

Lincoln County Museum Collection

Two Chupadero effigy vessels (Fig. 29), a small Chupadero jug 5 inches high, and a Lincoln Black-on-Red bowl ca. 5 inches in diameter with an eroded design were said to be from this site.

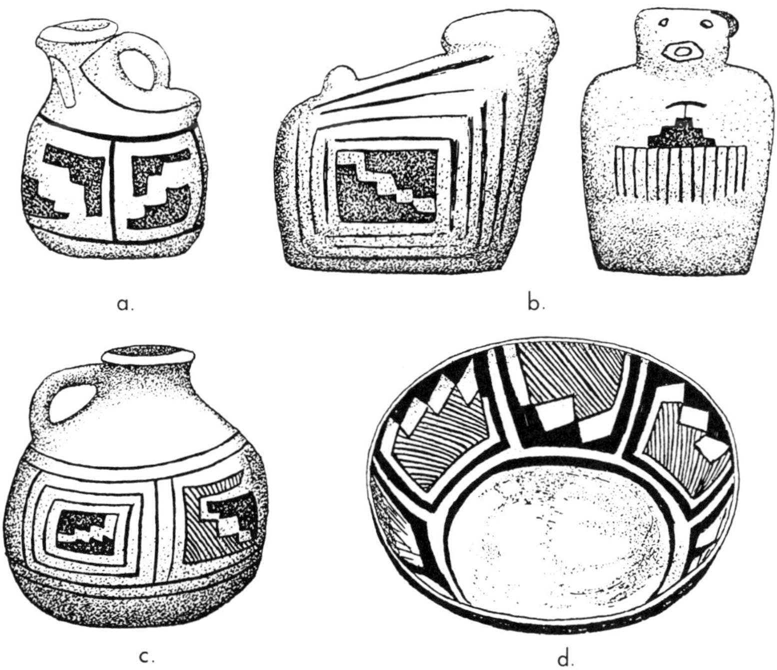

Figure 29. Chupadero Black-on-White vessels, Clark Pfingsten Collection. Not drawn to scale. *a,* Effigy pot; *b,* Side and front view of an effigy pot; *c,* Small jug, 5 inches high; *d,* Bowl, ca. 5 inches in diameter.

Double Crossing Site

Location

Approximately N½, S14, T9S, R15E. This site is located on the north bank of Bonito Stream, just below the junction of that stream with Salado Creek.

Jelinek's Survey

This is a pueblo type ruin with wall bases in evidence (Jelinek 1952:147). Eighteen percent of Brown pottery and 29% of Corrugated assign this site to the last occupational period (Jelinek 1952:150). Unspecified trade wares were present.

Lincoln County Museum Collection

A flat, full-grooved axe of limestone was only ½ inch thick. A tubular clay pipe was undecorated.

Baca Site

Location

It is in S15, 16, T9S, R16E, in Salazar Canyon, 6 miles east of Double Crossing Site.

Lincoln County Museum Collection

The placard describes the site as an "open square of houses." Five whole vessels are shown from this site: a Three Rivers Red-on-Terracotta bowl found in a burial, three Lincoln Black-on-Red bowls, and an El Paso olla with broad red-line designs. There is also a chipped stone axe with side notches that appeared to be made of compact limestone.

Hulbert Site

Location

SW ¼, S34, T9S, R16E. This site is on the valley floor just south of the Bonito River.

Surface Indications

A "square" mound with a central depression, just east of the Hulbert home, was about 150 feet across. Wall construction was not evident. Pottery, mano and metate fragments, lithic remains, roofing clay with pole impressions, and other cultural items were found. A great many one-end-closed trough metates with mano rests that leaned against the ranch house had been collected by the Hulberts.

Pottery

The following types were in our surface collection: Jornada Brown, Chupadero Black-on-White, Corrugated, Three Rivers Red-on-Terracotta, Lincoln Black-on-Red, Jornada Polychrome, El Paso Polychrome, and Glaze I.

Lincoln County Museum Collection

A Jornada Brown jug with an exterior fugitive red slip has a superficial similarity of form to Chupadero jugs.

Dow Site

Location

Approximately S24, T10S, R16E—Bert Pfingsten Ranch. It is on the valley floor, south of the Bonito River.

Surface Indications

A low, hill-like mound parallels the river for 150 feet and is 60 feet north-south. A ranch house or homestead was built on the mound. Historical rock walls, glass, nails, and other materials are mixed with prehistoric sherds.

Lincoln County Museum Collection

A small brown bowl, 3 inches in diameter and a sherd of Heshotauthla Polychrome are from this site.

Las Chosas Site

Location

SW ¼, S19, T10S, R17E, and/or SE ¼, S24, T10S, R16E.

Lincoln County Museum Collection

A Chupadero Black-on-White "squash" vessel and a large polychrome bowl from the Little Colorado came from this site.

Blue Water Sites

Location

E ½, S5 and the NE ¼, S16, T9S, R18E. A number of arroyos coalesce to form the Blackwater and Escondida tributaries of the Hondo in the piñon-juniper band of the Upper Sonoran Zone to the southeast of Capitan Mountain.

Surface Indications

A mound on the Romero Farm, ca. 330 feet long and 150 feet wide, trends northeast to southwest. An intermittent arroyo is ¼ mile east, and the permanent Blue Water spring is to the west. Masonry rooms are reported by local amateurs, but we could not confirm this. Natural dikes appeared to go through the mound, and perhaps these were utilized as a part of a building. The mound is littered with sherds, flakes, and human bones thrown out of pot holes.

In the Pryor Farm pasture, just east of the mound, sherd areas border three small north-south arroyos. Cultural debris is eroding out of the arroyo walls. A larger sherd area, ¼ mile square, lies in an adjacent plowed field on the Pryor Farm. Pottery types include Jornada Brown, Three Rivers Red-on-Terracotta with thin red lines and with thin black lines, Chupadero Black-on-White, Lincoln Black-on-Red, Corrugated, and an unclassified Glaze. A drill base, a side scraper, small shell disc beads, *Olivella* beads, mussel shell fragments, one-end-closed trough metates with mano rests, and full-grooved axes were seen.

Appendix 5

THE BONNELL SITE (LA 612) OF THE LATE GLENCOE PHASE

INTRODUCTION

The Bonnell Site (LA 612) is located in the NW ¼, S25, T10S, R15E. The site is on the edge of a broad terrace remnant on the north side of the Ruidoso Valley, bounded on the west by Eagle Creek. To the east, the terrace stretches for several miles. The site's elevation is 5760 feet. Mr. and Mrs. Bert Bonnell granted the initial permission to excavate. The property is now owned by Mr. and Mrs. Ralph Bonnell.

The Setting

The terrace, of undetermined Quaternary age, is composed of unconsolidated boulders, cobbles, gravel, sand, and clay that have been derived largely from limestone beds. Little soil has developed. It is about 40 feet above the modern valley floor where the Ruidoso River is now cutting its channel some 5 to 15 feet below the valley alluvium. The valley is fairly constricted just west of Eagle Creek, but at this point the valley is about ½ mile wide.

The U.S. Weather Bureau regards the Ruidoso River as a permanent stream as far as the Bonnell Ranch. Springs are located within a few miles both upstream and downstream.

The valley and adjacent hills are in the Upper Sonoran Zone. Within the valley confines, cottonwood and walnut trees grow large. Stream water used for modern irrigation produces double crops of alfalfa and supports numerous fruit orchards. As one approaches the valley in the summer, it has the appearance of a long, narrow, green oasis.

The terrrace remnant on which the site is located is basically grassland with a few scrub piñon trees. Where the terrace or valley edges meet the bordering hills, piñon-juniper stands are more dense. The trees become larger as you go higher, and quite large trees are visible from the site along the high ridges that border the valley.

Fieldwork at the Bonnell Site

Excavations were carried out at this site during six field seasons. Initially two trenches were run across the site. The north-south trench was laid out by the compass; the east-west trench was angled slightly in order to avoid two extensive pot holes. These two trenches became the main axis of a grid system that was applied to the whole site in 4-foot square sections. Excavation levels were 6 inches deep, until a cultural level was found. Field notes were kept of the location of structural features and important artifacts. A number of small artifacts, the sherds, and the bone materials were sacked by excavation levels in the sections.

Four low mounds are located along the terrace edge. We excavated the largest of these, Mound A, which is on a prominence that extends slightly into the valley; a small arroyo is cutting headward at the northeast edge (Fig.30; Pl. 41).

The site has long been famous locally, and the surface of the site in 1950 bore mute testimony to many Sunday afternoons of pot hunting. During the 1920s, when the Bonnells ran a guest ranch, regular excursions were arranged to dig in the ruins. In view of the devastation that the site had undergone, we were fortunate to recover as much information as we did.

In 1952, the suggestion was made that this site belonged to the San Andres Phase of the Jornada Branch of the Mogollon (Holden 1952:127). Subsequent excavation here and at other sites has demonstrated that we are dealing with a separate archaeological unit, and that a separate phase designation better reflects the realities of the situation. Accordingly, it is now regarded as a late manifestation of the Glencoe Phase.

BUILDING HISTORY OF THE VILLAGE

Four recognized building periods are presented here as an introduction or guide to the house descriptions. Alternative interpretations are possible.

Period 1

The ceramic content and stratigraphic position of Houses 5 and 6 indicated that they were the oldest excavated structures. Both were built on some 6 inches of fill. Construction details were incomplete; they were probably very shallow, rectangular pithouses some 10 to 12 feet square. These houses lacked the four central post system, and those posts which were located do not form a

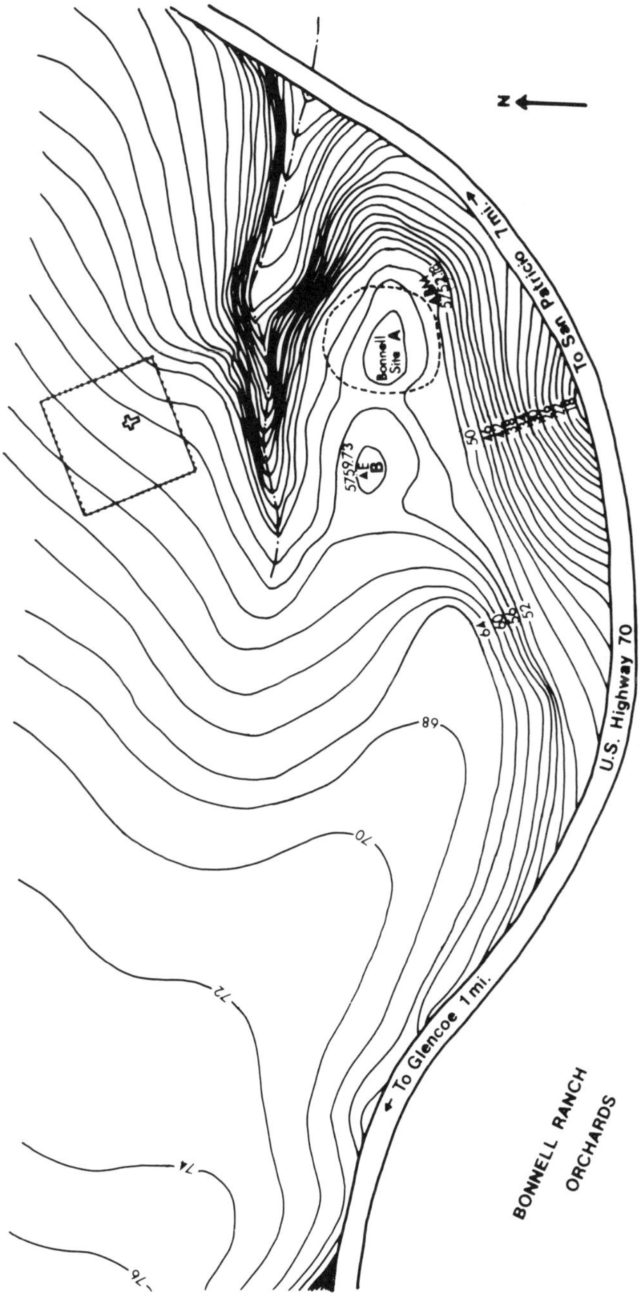

Figure 30. Contour map of the terrace on which the Bonnell Site is located.

Plate 41. The view down valley from the Bonnell Site.

definite pattern. Firepits were centrally located. The large, square pithouse, Number 1, was dug from a comparable stratigraphic level; pottery on the floor of House 1 showed that it continued in use until after the introduction of Glaze I.

Period 2

Three house units were built on the unique principle of placing shallow pithouses so closely together that they shared common walls. The west house block included Houses 2, 3, 4, and 19. The east block consisted of Houses 9, 13, 14, and 20. The south house block was formed of Houses 7 and 8. It seems probable that these house units were placed on three sides of a small plaza where Houses 5 and 6 had been leveled. At the beginning of this period, House 1 occupied the north end of the plaza. When House 1 burned, it was replaced by House 15 of comparable size and shape which was built east of House 1. Other isolated structures may have been in use during this period.

The different houses or rooms of the three house units were not all occupied at the same time. Each had a different history of abandonment, rebuilding, and remodelling, making it difficult to say which houses were occupied simultaneously. Construction practices during this period were quite varied, one might almost say eclectic.

Period 3

The experiment in multi-roomed houses was abandoned and individual houses were built once again. Since these houses were stratigraphically high in the site, they had been much disturbed by previous digging and no detailed structural data are available. Houses 10, 11, 12, 16, 22 and 23 belong to this period, and none were intact. They were probably shallow pithouses or *jacal* surface structures. All had central firepits except House 12.

Period 4

Two surface houses whose floors were only 6 inches below the modern surface were the most recent structures at the site. Both were outlined with post holes 3 or 4 inches in diameter. House 18 at the northern edge of the site was roughly oval; House 26, between Houses 1 and 15, was roughly rectangular. The former had a central hearth.

The village pattern at all periods was compact. To complete the settlement pattern of the entire site, more information is needed from the other mounds. Mound B, which joins Mound A on the west, was occupied contemporaneously. Rex Gerald's results from that mound are not detailed in this study.

DESCRIPTION OF EXCAVATED STRUCTURES

Any reconstruction of individual structures or of the village plan is made difficult by the extensive destruction that the site has undergone, and by the number of structures built in a limited space. During excavation 26 house numbers were assigned; there were actually 33 structures, as structures superimposed over older ones were given the same number. In four cases the original structure had burned before the second was built. Seven houses were refloored and remodeled. Nine houses are described in some detail; remaining structures are represented by more limited data. Multiple floors are numbered in historical rather than in excavation order. See Map 9.

House 1

Type

Large, square, individual pithouse, approximately 21 feet square.

House Pit

The pit was dug 21 to 23 inches into native clay and gravel. The top of the pit was 43 inches below modern surface in the northwest corner. Pit walls were well plastered on three walls. The south wall had large gravel cobbles exposed where the plaster had eroded away.

Floor

Part of the floor was dug into a native clay deposit and no plaster was necessary; the south side of the room was dug into gravel, and the floor was plastered with a layer of clay at least 1 inch thick. Floor plaster was smoothed continuously up to wall plaster.

Internal Posts and Post Holes

Four centrally-located posts held pine timbers 11 to 16 inches in diameter which were placed in post holes 24 to 30 inches deep. A cottonwood brace was placed on the floor adjacent to the southeast post. Smaller posts 2 to 5 inches in diameter had been placed in the interior. Two small posts about 30 inches apart in the middle of the east wall suggested an entrance that we failed to locate.

Wall Posts and Posts Holes

In the north wall close to the northwest corner, several post holes, recessed into the pit wall and set below floor level, were covered by the pit wall plaster.

Roof Construction

Beams up to 12 inches in diameter were oriented east and west. In the east section of the house a large section of collapsed, charred roofing material showed clearly the sequence of large beams, smaller poles, reeds, and grass topped with a layer of clay 4 to 6 inches thick. Three split cottonwood planks in the northwest corner measured 2 inches, 6 inches, and 11 inches in width, and were ½ inch, 1 inch, and 2 inches thick respectively.

Entrance

None was located.

Fire Area

A bowl-shaped firepit with a clay rim ½ inch high was 12 inches in diameter and 6 inches deep. Plaster was 1 inch thick at the rim.

Floor Depression

Two shallow basin-shaped depressions were found; one on the east side and a larger one on the west side.

Fill

Lower fill was largely roofing material which had collapsed toward the north. The house became a trash area after the structure burned. Smaller surface houses were built in the upper fill late in the history of the site.

Associated Artifacts

Bone awls were numerous. Projectile points were absent from the floor and the only grinding tool was a one-handed grinding stone. A Chupadero Black-on-White jar in the southeast corner contained gaming pieces; a red-slipped brown bowl contained a shell and a flake (see Fig. 31).

House 2

Type

Rectangular pithouse in the western house block of contiguous pit rooms (Fig. 32; Pl. 42A).

House Pit

Due to a large pot hole, north, east and west walls were not delineated for the upper floor although the east pit wall was found for the lower floor levels. The south wall, shared with House 3 at all floor levels, was a remnant of native soil left between the two houses that was capped with clay. Molds of the butt end of poles occurred along the length of this wall base which was about 10

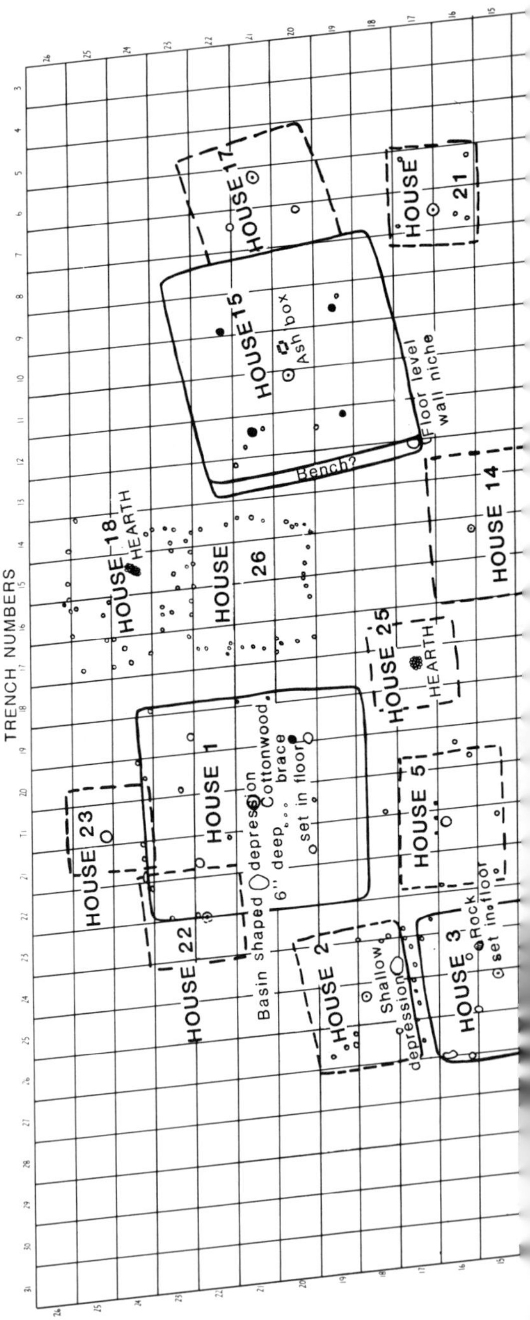
TRENCH NUMBERS
HOUSE 17
HOUSE 21
HOUSE 15
Ash box
Floor level wall niche
Bench?
HOUSE 14
HOUSE 18
HEARTH
HOUSE 26
HOUSE 25
HEARTH
HOUSE 1
Cottonwood brace set in floor
Basin shaped depression 6'' deep
HOUSE 23
HOUSE 22
HOUSE 5
HOUSE 2
Shallow depression
HOUSE 3
Rock set in floor

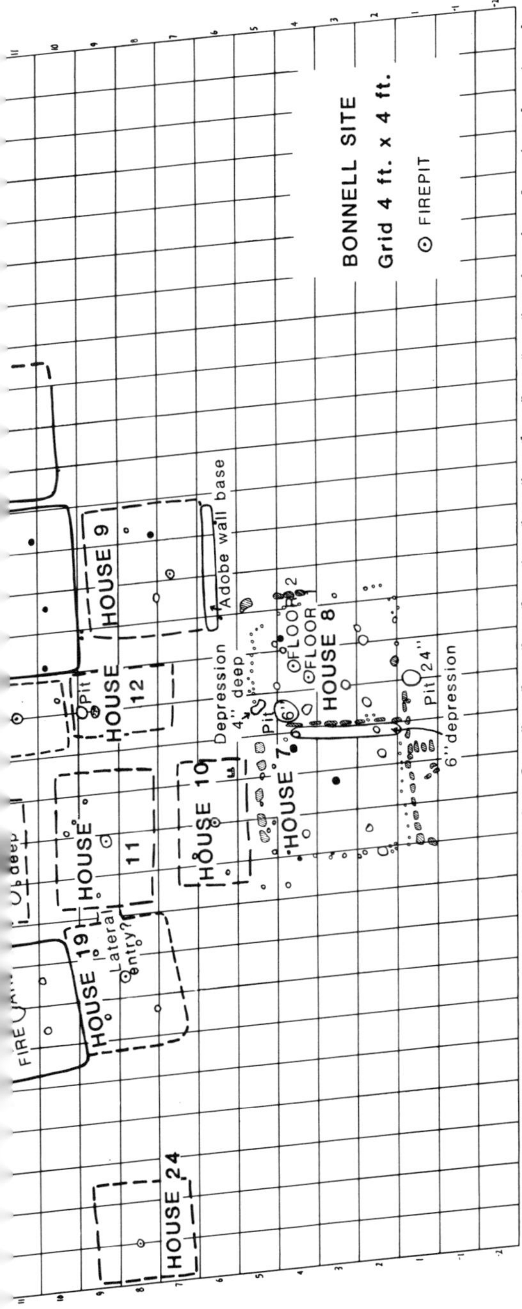

Map 9. Bonnell Site.

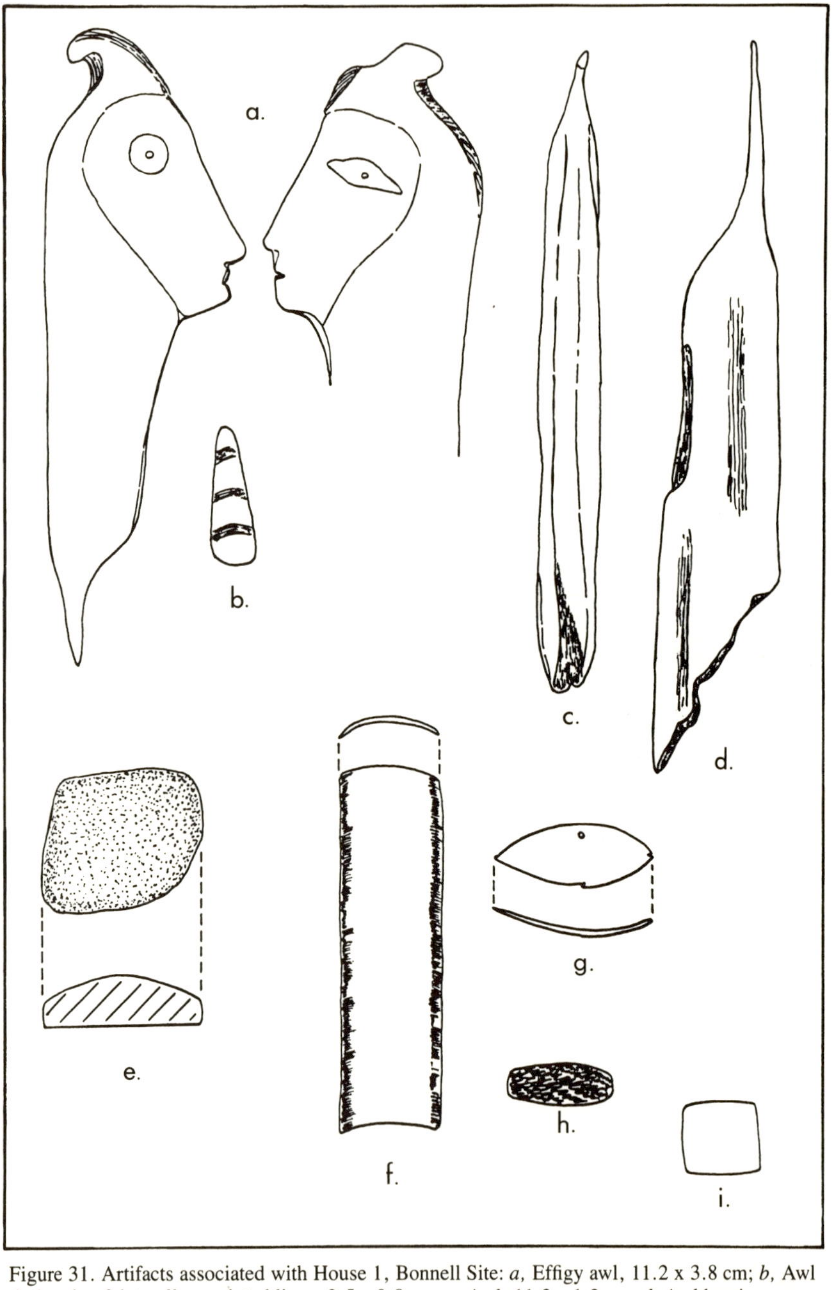

Figure 31. Artifacts associated with House 1, Bonnell Site: *a*, Effigy awl, 11.2 x 3.8 cm; *b*, Awl tip bearing faint yellow painted lines, 2.5 x 0.8 cm; *c*, Awl, 11.2 x 1.2 cm; *d*, Awl bearing green copper stains, 13.0 x 2.2 cm; *e*, Hand grinding stone, 9.6 x 11.6 x 3.6 cm; *f*, Polished bone piece, 6.2 x 1.8 x .1 cm; *g*, Perforated mussel shell pendant, 1.1 x 2.9 x .1 cm; *h*, Bone gaming piece, one of a set, 0.7 x 1.9 cm; *i*, Mussel shell, one of a pair, 1.3 x 1.4 cm.

inches high when the lower floor of House 2 was laid down; the wall stood only 3 inches above Floor 3. Pit walls were not plastered.

Floor

The lower two floors were separated by 2 to 4 inches of fill and shared the same roof support system and firepit. Both floors were plastered, the plaster being more heavily applied around the firepit. The uppermost plastered floor was equipped with some new posts and a new firepit.

Internal Posts and Post Holes

Eleven posts or post holes pertained to the earlier two floors. Disturbance of the northeast sector of the house had reached below the lowest floor in places, and no post was found there. The most recent floor incorporated the two largest posts of the lower floor and added nine new posts.

Wall Posts and Post Holes

The south wall with the imprints of small posts placed on the low dirt wall base has been described above.

Roof Construction

Charred beams above the most recent floor ran in a general northeast-southwest direction (Fig. 32).

Fire Area

In the lowest floor, a cylindrical firepit, 10 inches in diameter and 10 inches deep, with straight and well-plastered walls opened flush with the floor. For the second floor, the same firepit was used; a clay curb 22 inches in diameter was added, raising the opening about ½ inch above the new floor; it was then replastered. To construct Floor 3, the older firepit was filled, and a shallow depression 10 inches in diameter and 2 inches deep served as a firepit.

Fill

Between the floors, the fill seemed to be the result of gradual accumulation. Above the uppermost floor there was a large amount of collapsed roofing or wall material.

Associated Artifacts

Associated artifacts (Fig. 33) included a large two-handed mano which was found in the roofing debris. Projectile points, awls, a shaft-straightener, an axe, various shell ornaments, and a one-stop bone whistle were found.

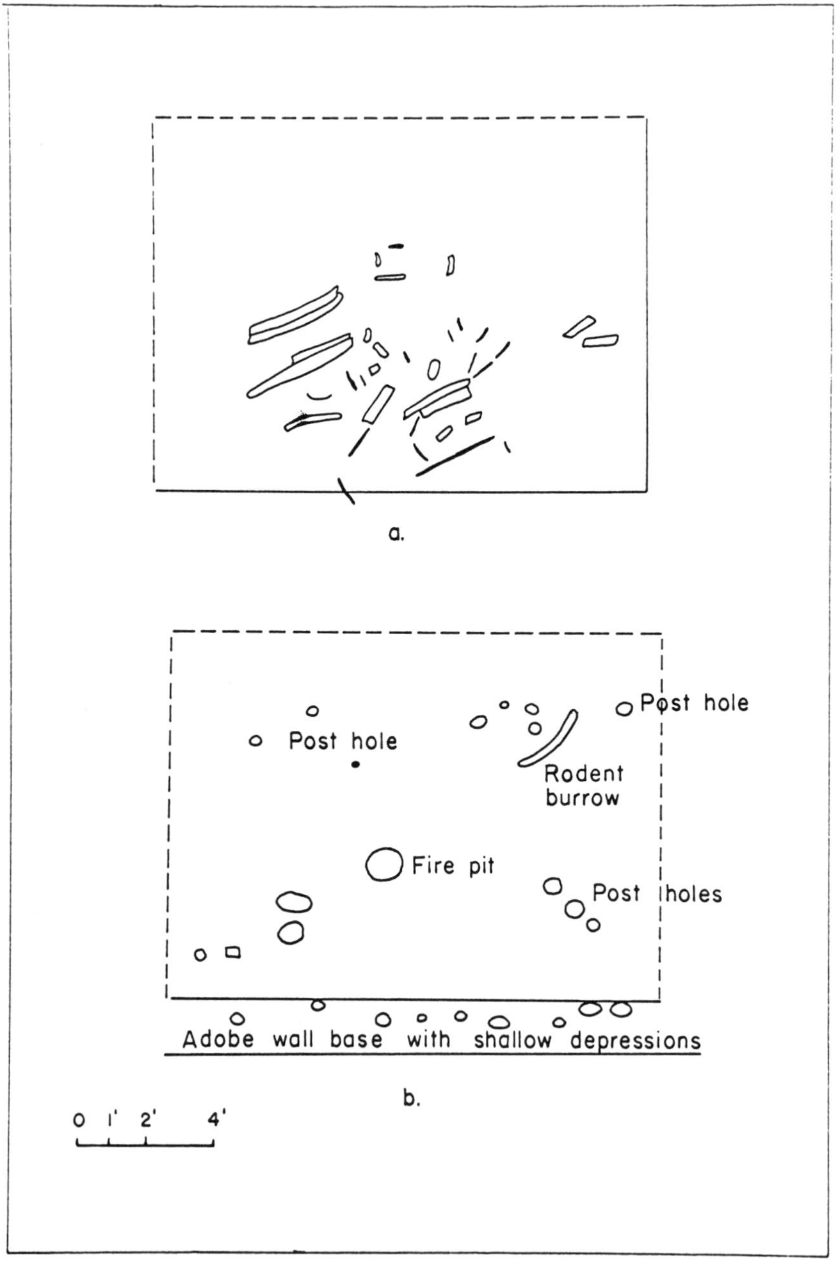

Figure 32. House 2, Bonnell Site: *a*, Pattern of charred roofing beams; *b*, Plan of floor 3.

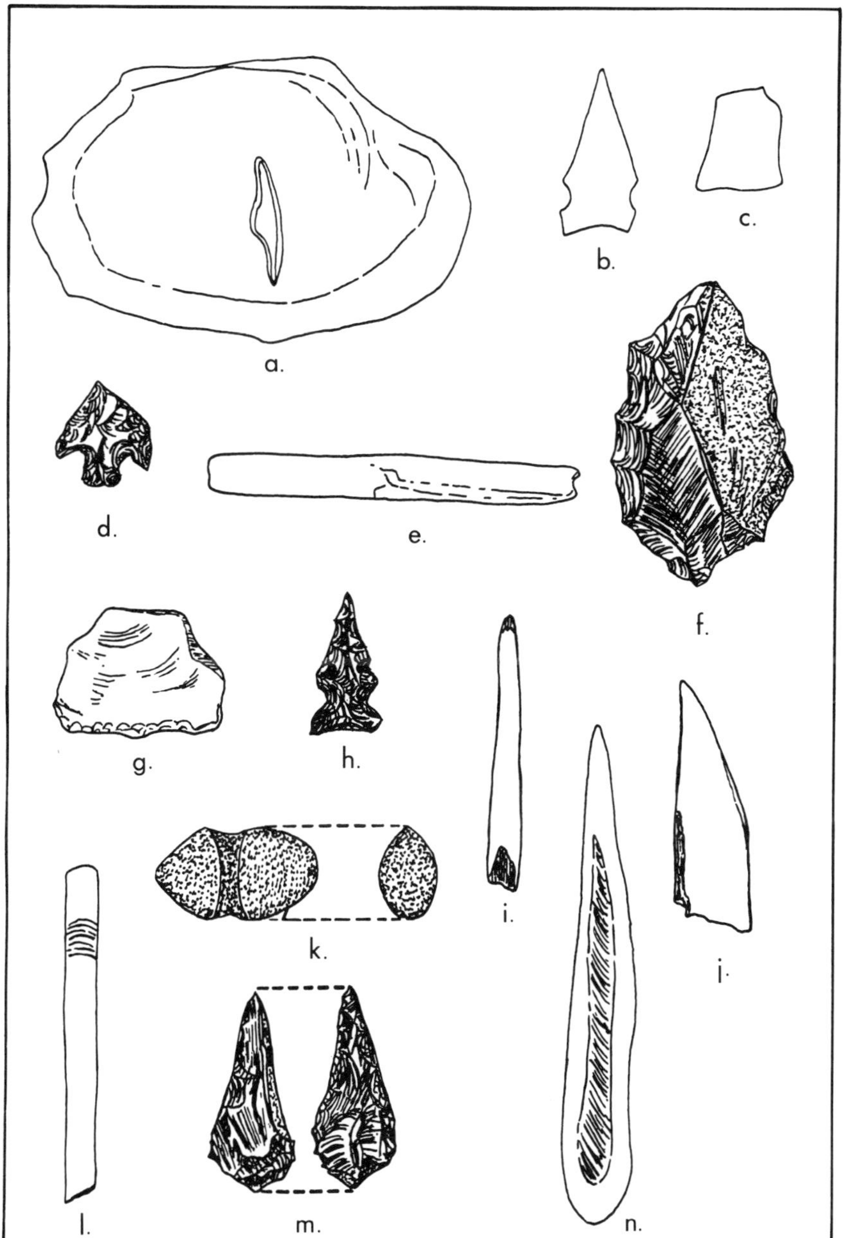

Figure 33. Artifacts associated with House 2, Bonnell Site: *a,* Half of a mussel shell showing the cut slit that was the first step in roughing out shell for the manufacture of shell ornaments, 5.2 x 8.2 cm; *b,* Projectile point, 3.2 x 1.4 cm; *c,* Projectile point base, 1.9 x 1.7 cm; *d,* Projectile point, 2.0 x 1.9 cm; *e,* One-stop bone whistle; the hole was cut, not drilled; 0.8 x 7.0 cm; *f,* Scraper, 5.7 x 3.5 cm; *g,* Scraper or unifacially worked flake, 2.5 x 3.2 cm; *h,* Projectile point, 2.7 x 1.4 cm; *i,* Polished bone with beveled tip, 5.3 x 0.6 cm; *j,* Awl fragment, 7.2 x 1.4 cm; *k,* Full-grooved axe, 7.2 x 12.4 x 4.8 cm; *l,* Bone with incised lines, 6.2 x 0.6 cm; *m,* Drill, 3.8 x 1.5 cm; *n,* Awl, 9.3 x 1.3 cm.

House 3

Type

The earlier house (Floor 1) was a rectangular pithouse in the west house block. This structure burned and was later replaced by a shallow, independent pithouse (Floor 2). See Plate 42B.

House Pit

The north wall of Floor 1, shared with House 2, was a standing remnant of native earth capped with clay; shallow post depressions were imprinted. The west pit wall was dug through sterile soil, clay, and gravel to a depth that varied from 12 inches to 18 inches. The south wall between Houses 3 and 4 was a low gravel remnant. On the east, the original pit wall stood only 4 to 6 inches as subsequent building had cut across this side of the house. The walls do not seem to have been plastered. House limits of the later structure (Floor 2) could not be accurately determined, due to enthusiastic pot-holing by amateur archaeologists.

Floor

Floor 1 was cut into the native clay and gravel. Plaster had been applied heavily around the firepit; either the periphery had never been plastered or else the plaster had worn off. Floor surface was somewhat irregular. The surviving remnants of Floor 2, 14 inches above the lower floor, were of packed earth.

Internal Posts and Post Holes

Four large posts 6 to 8 inches in diameter were centrally located in Floor 1. Large double posts of comparable diameter were placed in the northwest and southwest corners, giving a six-post support system which may indicate a gable type of roof construction. It is possible that the arrangement of several adjacent pithouses or pit rooms forming a multi-room structure would present some engineering problems and that the double posts at the corners of the middle pitroom were meant to offset some of these problems. Smaller posts were located in the eastern sector of the room. The two posts assignable to the upper structure (Floor 2) were footed on fairly flat cobbles; each post was ca. 6 inches in diameter.

Wall Posts and Post Holes

Post impressions in the north wall have been described for House 2.

Roof Construction

Collapsed roofing or wall materials were present on the northern side of the house above Floor 1. Poles 2 to 4 inches in diameter were found under a 6-inch thick layer of burned clay.

Fire Area

Walls of the Floor 1 firepit sloped in slightly toward the flat bottom; 5 inches of caked ashes remained. Plaster remnants 1 inch thick encircled the upper portion of the pit, which opened flush with the floor. The Floor 2 firepit was 12 inches in diameter, 3 inches deep, irregularly shaped, and unplastered.

Rock Feature on Floor

Northeast of the firepit on Floor 2, three unshaped cobbles had been set upright, leaving a space approximately 8 inches in diameter between the rocks where three artifacts were found.

Fill

Collapsed wall and roofing materials and charred timbers were between Floors 1 and 2.

Associated Artifacts

Manos, projectile points, and scrapers were present on both floors. A tubular bone object, a split rib tool, and a tubular clay pipe were found between the three upright cobbles on Floor 2. Associated artifacts are illustrated in Figures 34–36.

Remarks

The first house (Floor 1), which burned, formed part of a multi-roomed structural unit with Houses 2 and 4. A new, isolated, structure was built later (Floor 2). The ceramic and architectural history of House 3 closely parallels that of House 13.

House 4

Type

Rectangular, almost square, pithouse in the western house block (Pl. 43).

House Pit

Dug through heavy gravel. Depth of pit varied from 17 inches on the east to 23 inches on the north. This was the deepest pithouse in the west house block. Large cobbles protruded from unplastered pit walls.

Floor

The floor, like the walls, was irregular due to the large cobbles in the gravel.

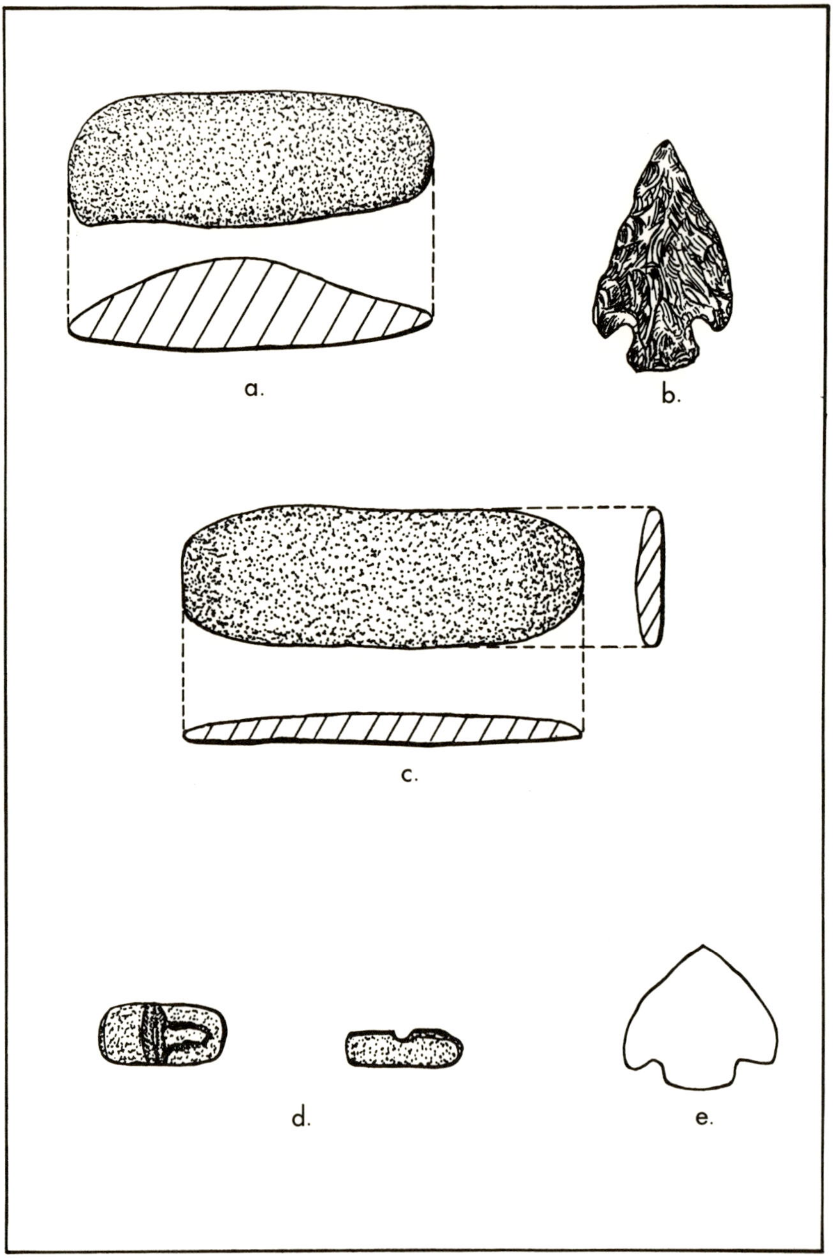

Figure 34. Artifacts associated with House 3, Bonnell Site: *a,* Mano, 10.0 x 28.0 x 6.8 cm; *b,* Projectile point, 4.3 x 2.6 cm; *c,* Flat mano, 10.0 x 30.0 x 2.5 cm; *d,* Ridged arrow shaft-straightener, 4.8 x 10.0 x 2.5 cm; *e,* Projectile point, 2.6 x 3.0 cm.

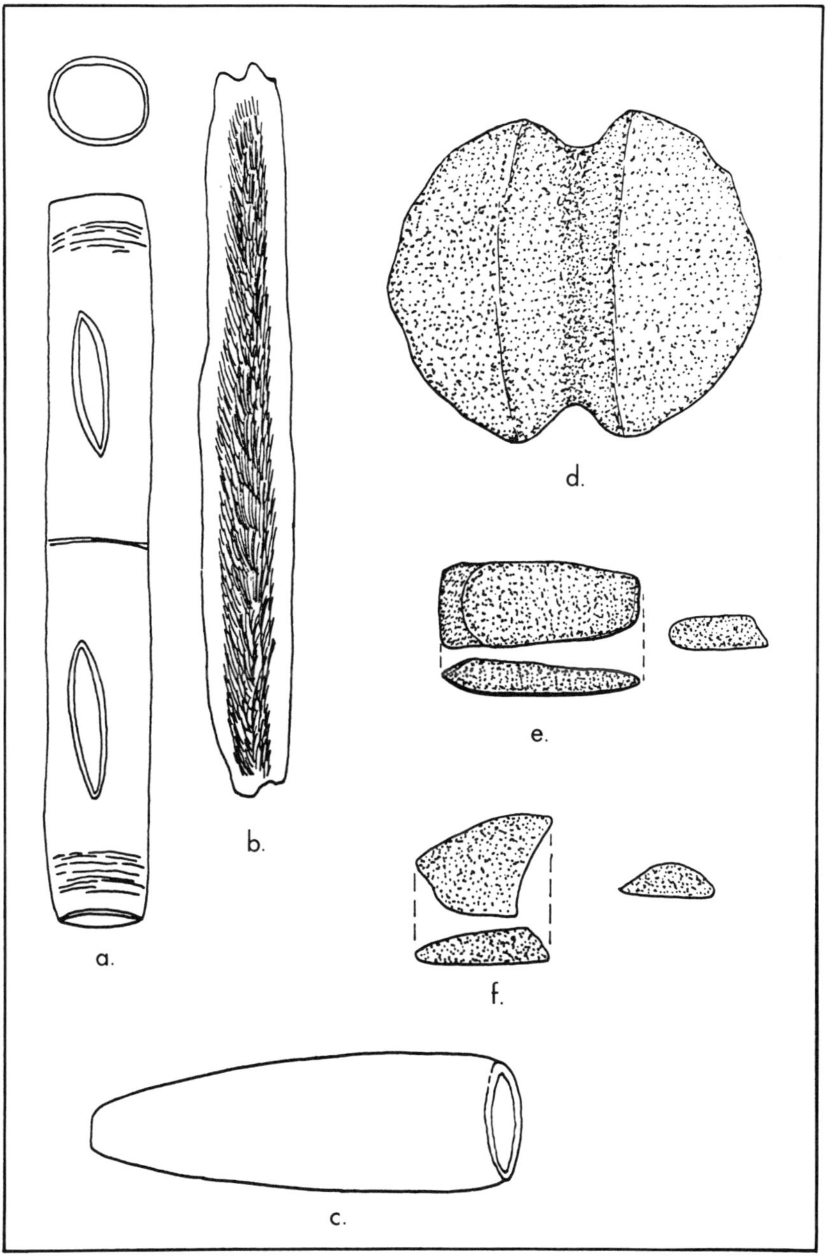

Figure 35. Artifacts associated with House 3, Bonnell Site: *a*, Tubular bone object, 13.2 x 2.0 x 1.6 cm; *b*, Bone "spatula" with thinned edges, 13.5 x 1.8 cm; *c*, Tubular clay pipe, 7.5 x 2.5 cm; *d*, Full-grooved hammerstone, 6.0 x 7.0 cm; *e*, Mano, 6.5 x 15.2 x 2.5 cm; *f*, Mano fragment, 8.0 x 10.0 x 2.5 cm.

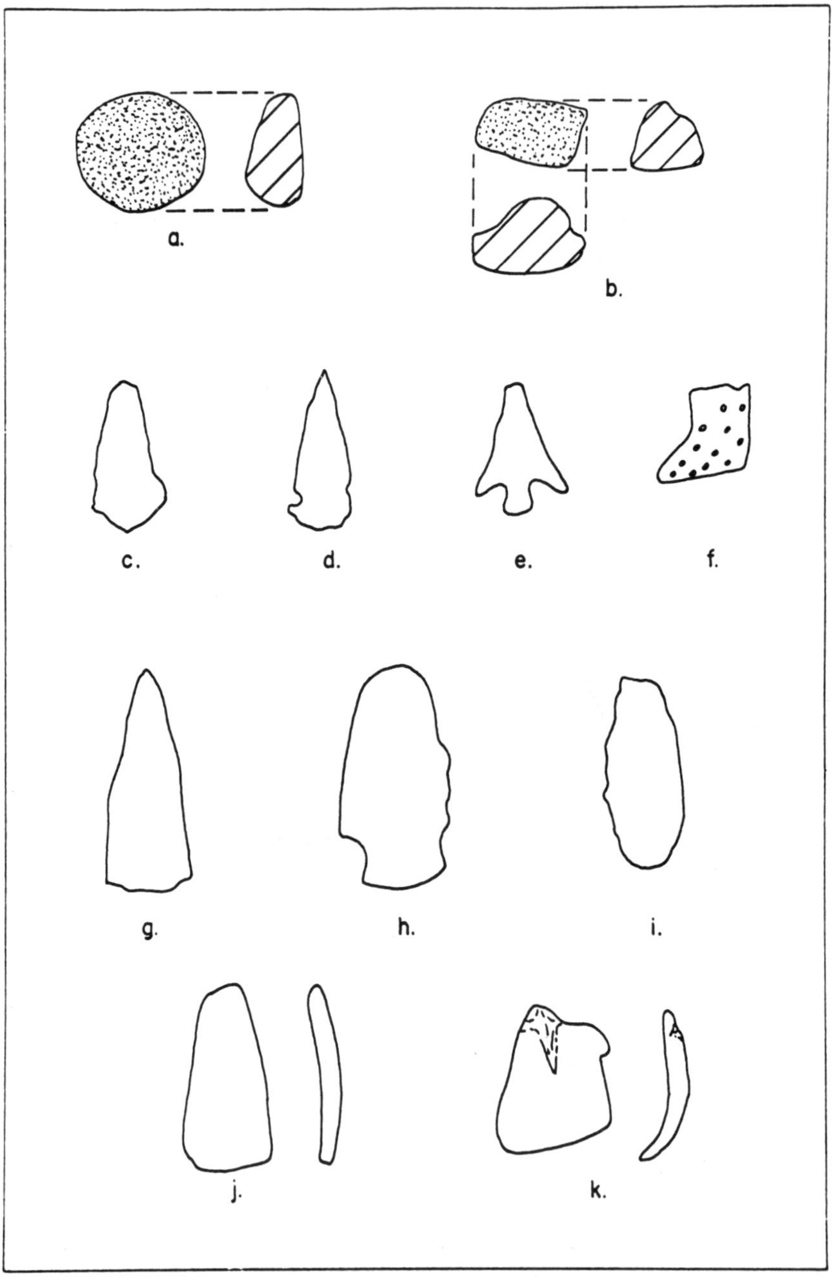

Figure 36. Artifacts associated with House 3, Bonnell Site: *a,* Hand grinding stone, 8.4 x 7.5 x 4.5 cm; *b,* Mano fragment, 5.0 x 8.5 x 6.0 cm; *c,* Projectile point, 2.8 x 1.5 cm; *d,* Projectile point, 3.0 x 1.2 cm; *e,* Projectile point, 2.5 x 1.7 cm; *f,* Mussel shell pendant (?) fragment with drill pits for surface decoration, 1.7 x 1.7 cm; *g,* Projectile point, 4.1 x 1.7 cm; *h,* Projectile point, 4.2 x 2.2 cm; *i,* Projectile point, 3.6 x 1.7 cm; *j,* Shell object, 3.5 x 1.6 x 0.4 cm; *k,* Shell object with incised decoration, 2.6 x 2.1 x 0.4 cm.

a

b

Plate 42. *a*, House 2, Bonnell Site; *b*, House 3, Bonnell Site.

A thin layer of plaster was badly worn. The floor sloped up markedly toward the walls.

Internal Posts and Post Holes

Four centrally-located posts 7 to 9 inches in diameter were sunk 18 to 24 inches below the floor. No smaller posts were inside the structure.

Wall Posts and Post Holes

None were found.

Roof Construction

No data, as the house did not burn.

Fire Area

A heavily plastered area in the center of the room was burned a bright orange and caked ashes covered an area ca. 18 x 36 inches. This room was unusual in not having a well-defined firepit.

Sub-floor Burial

A child was interred in the northwest corner (Burial 14).

Associated Artifacts

A trough metate leaned against the east wall. A pile of seven stones in the northwest corner included four black shale hammerstones, a mano fragment, a shaft-straightener fragment and a pebble with red ochre adhering to one side. Scrapers, metate fragments, a "palette," bone gaming pieces, and bone awls were present. One cut shell fragment was perforated (Figs. 37–38).

Remarks

No structure was built in this space after this house was abandoned, possibly because of the sub-floor burial.

House 5

Type

Not determined. The house was built in fill, and if pit walls were present we did not find them. This house did not burn.

Floor

Clay plaster was heavily applied to the central section of the floor around the fire area; the periphery was packed earth.

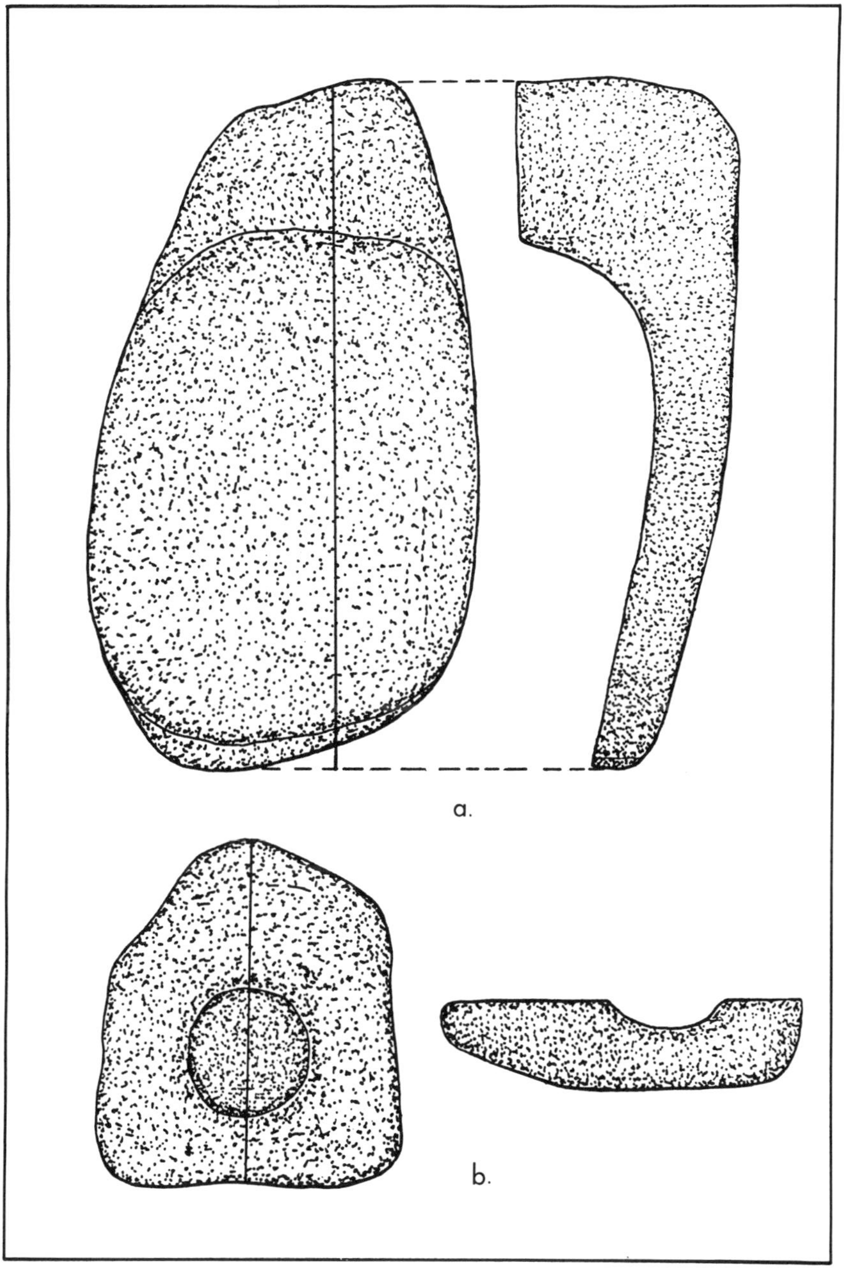

Figure 37. Artifacts associated with House 4, Bonnell Site: *a,* Metate, 50.0 x 30.0 x 16.0 cm; *b,* Stone "palette," 25.0 x 22.0 x 6.5 cm.

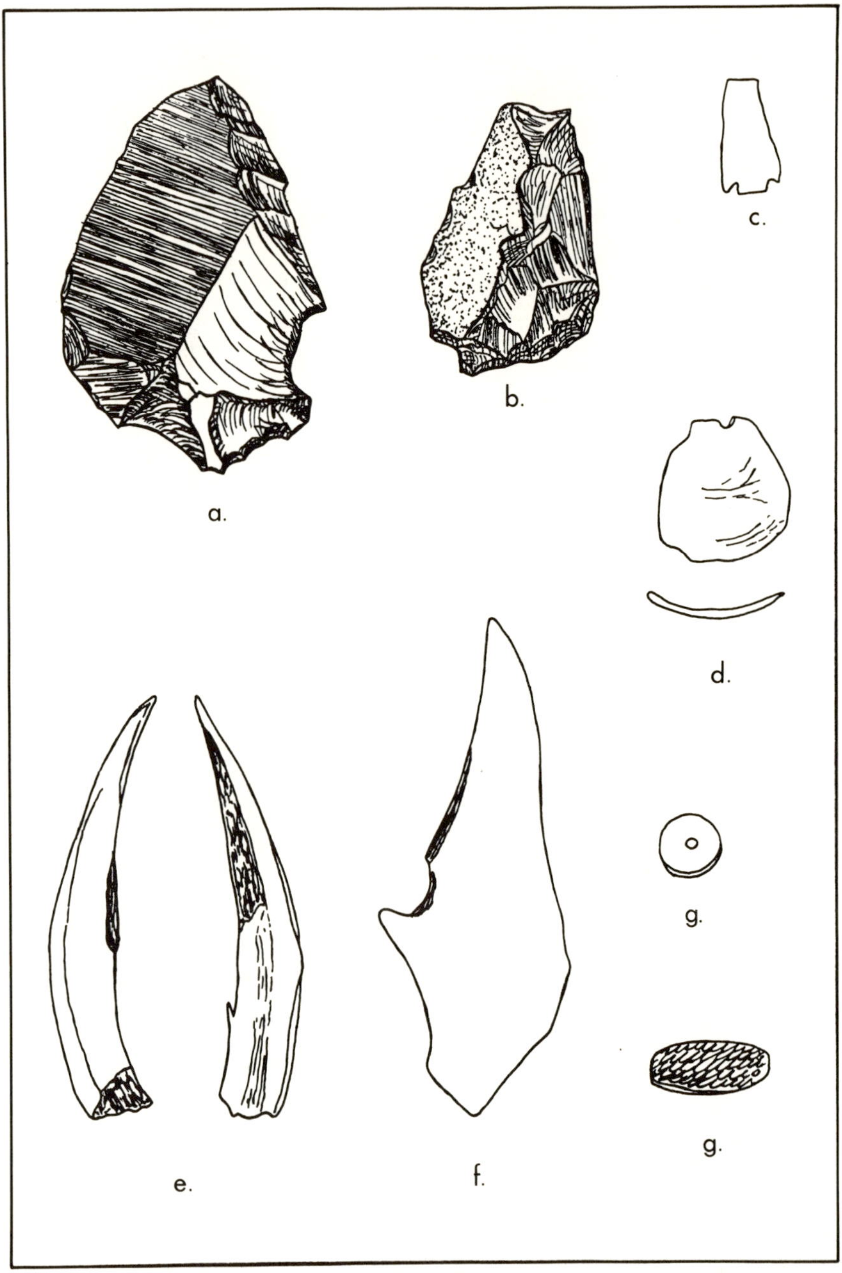

Figure 38. Artifacts associated with House 4, Bonnell Site: *a,* Unifacially worked flake, 7.2 x 5.0 cm; *b,* Unifacially worked flake, 5.0 x 3.4 cm; *c,* Projectile point, 2.1 x 1.2 cm; *d,* Shell object, 2.6 x 2.5 x 0.2 cm; *e,* Awl, 7.8 x 1.2 cm; *f,* Awl, 9.2 x 3.6 cm; *g,* Gaming Piece. One of a set, 1.1 x 1.1 cm; *h,* Gaming Piece. One of a set, 1.0 x 2.2 cm.

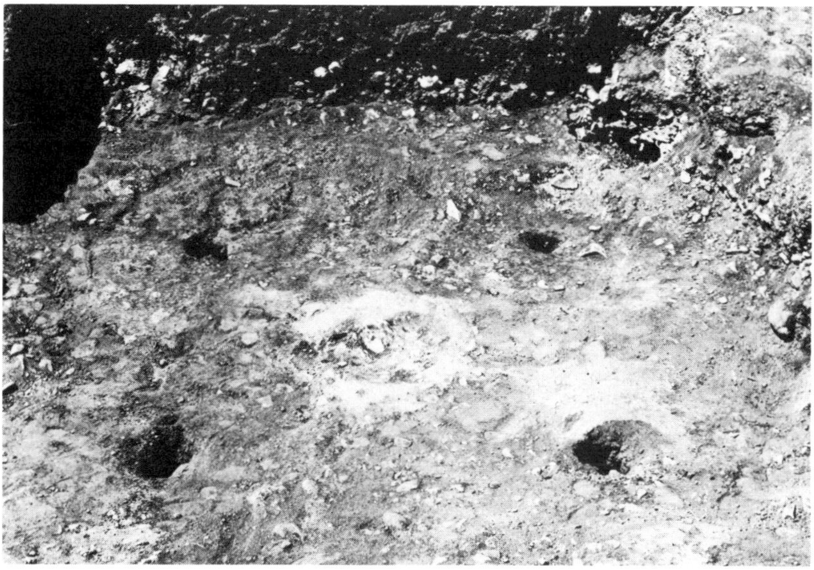

Plate 43. House 4, Bonnell Site.

Internal Posts and Post Holes

Posts that definitely belonged to this floor showed no obvious pattern.

Fire Area

Fire had been built directly on the floor, leaving a well-fired clay area and caked ashes.

Associated Artifacts

Two manos, a flat slab metate, bifacial flint tools, a scapula tool, and an awl were found in the 6-inch level above the floor (Figs. 39–40).

House 6

Type

Not determined.

Internal Posts and Post Holes

Small posts, about 3 inches in diameter, did not form a regular pattern.

Fire Area

A circular, unplastered firepit was 12 inches in diameter and 5 to 6 inches deep. Walls of the firepit sloped in slightly toward the bottom.

Floor
Packed earth.

Associated Artifacts
A metate fragment was found upside down near the firepit. A grinding pebble, paints, scrapers, awls, and gaming pieces were also present (Fig. 41).

Remarks
The house had burned.

House 7

Type
Two structures were superimposed. A rectangular shallow pithouse or partial pithouse lined with unshaped cobbles formed the west room of a two-room structure at the south edge of the site (Floor 1; see Map 9). The upper house (Floor 2) was a smaller surface structure (Fig. 42; Pl. 44).

House Pit
North and south walls of the original house (Floor 1) were cut 4 to 8 inches into gravel and lined with cobbles. The east wall was the two-course cobble wall shared with House 8. The west wall was delineated by a line of post holes at floor level. The upper house, built on the fill of the older house, utilized the existing cobblestone wall on the east.

Floor
Floor 1 was packed earth and rather uneven. There was some 8 inches of fill between this and Floor 2, which was heavily plastered.

Internal Posts and Post Holes
In the earlier house there were four centrally-located posts and a fifth in the middle of the house where the firepit usually would have been located. A long depression or shallow trench which paralleled the east wall contained three post holes.

Wall Posts and Post Holes
A line of small post holes was set between and inside of the cobbles lining the shallow pit along north and south walls and along the west side of the house. Vertical pole walls were indicated for the three outside walls. Construction of the east wall was more difficult to interpret; here, the two-course cobblestone wall shared with House 8 was made of large, flat, unshaped rocks

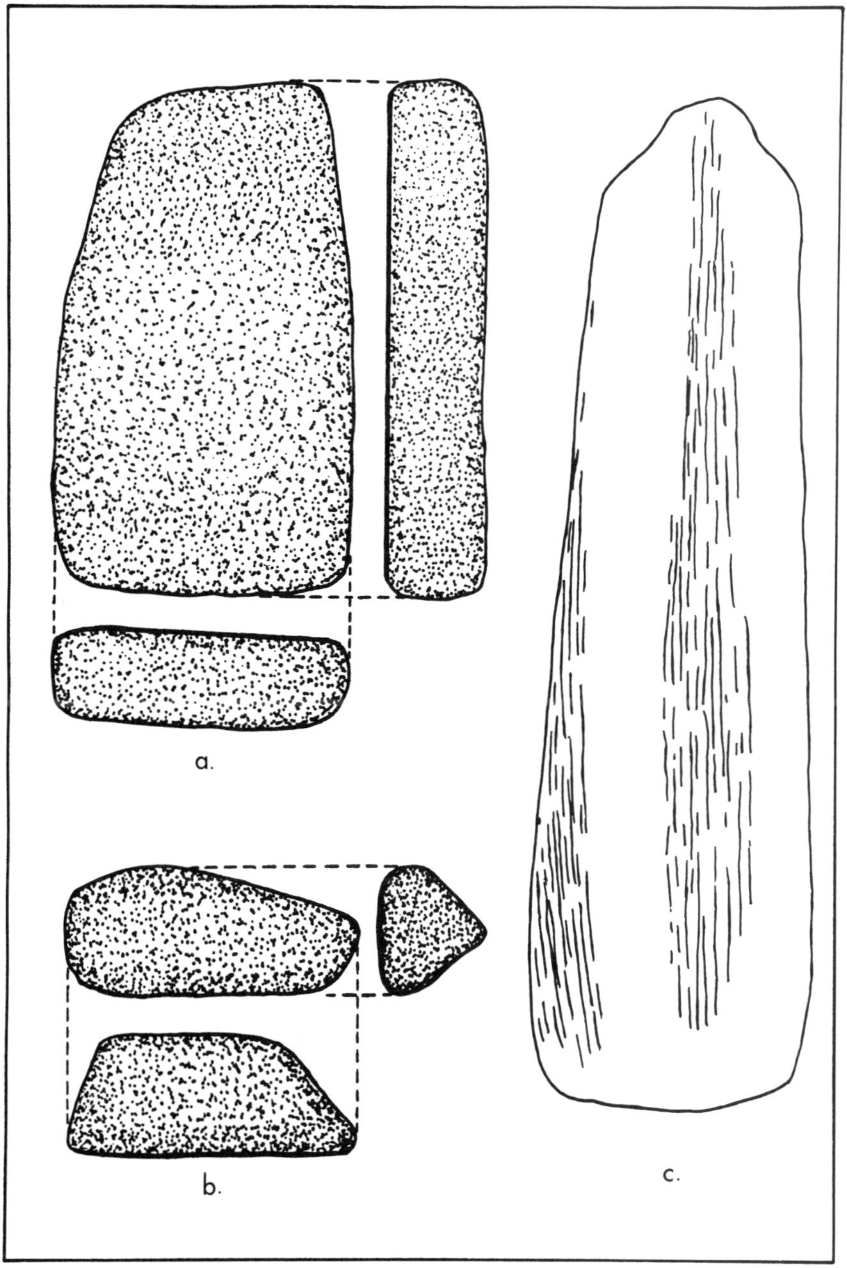

Figure 39. Artifacts associated with House 5, Bonnell Site: *a,* Slab metate, 38.0 x 22.0 x 8.0 cm; *b,* Mano, 10.0 x 22.0 x 8.0 cm; *c,* Scapula tool, 18.5 x 5.3 cm.

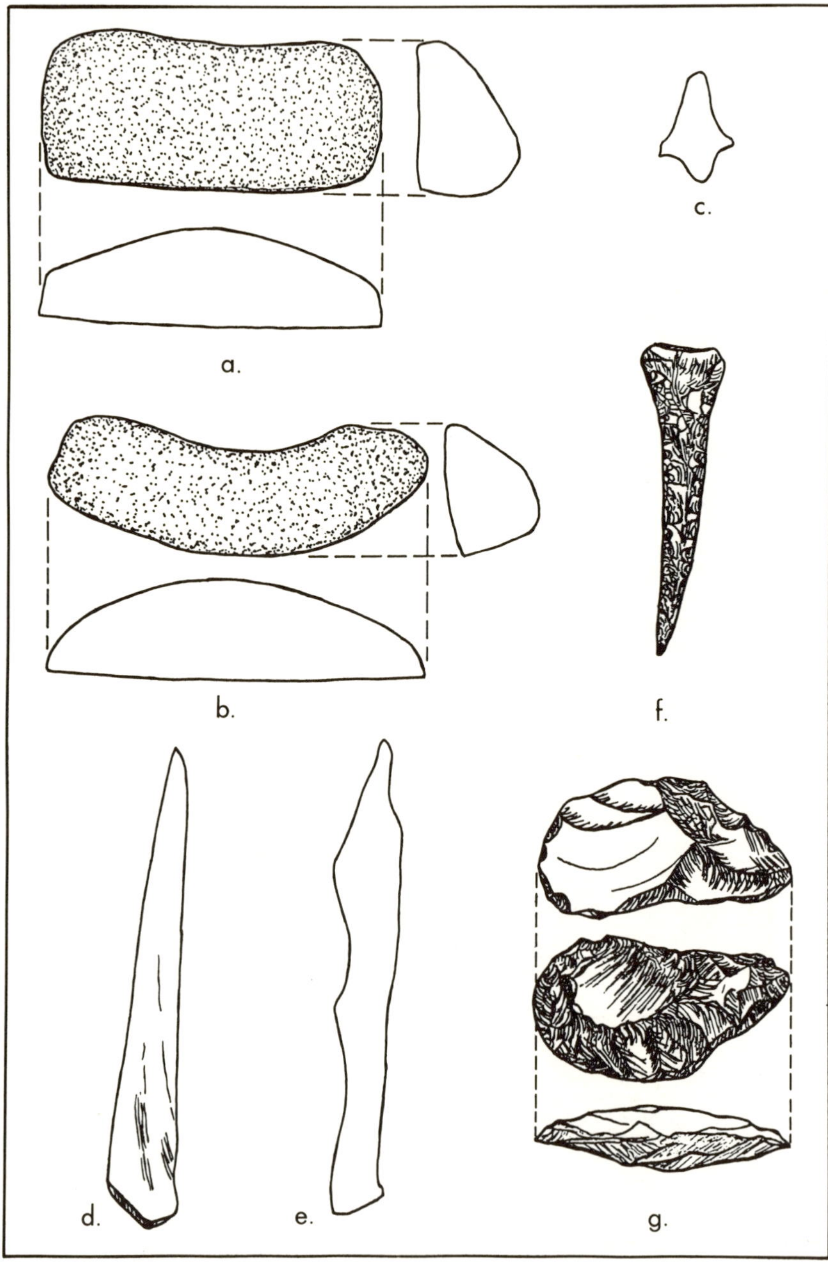

Figure 40. Artifacts associated with House 5, Bonnell Site: *a*, Mano, 11.2 x 26.0 x 8.0 cm; *b*, Mano, 10.0 x 28.0 x 8.0 cm; *c*, Projectile point, 2.0 x 1.5 cm; *d*, Awl, 8.9 x 12.0 cm; *e*, Awl or punch, 8.8 x 1.2 cm; *f*, Drill, 5.7 x 1.5 cm; *g*, Bifacially worked flake, 2.5 x 4.8 x 1.2 cm.

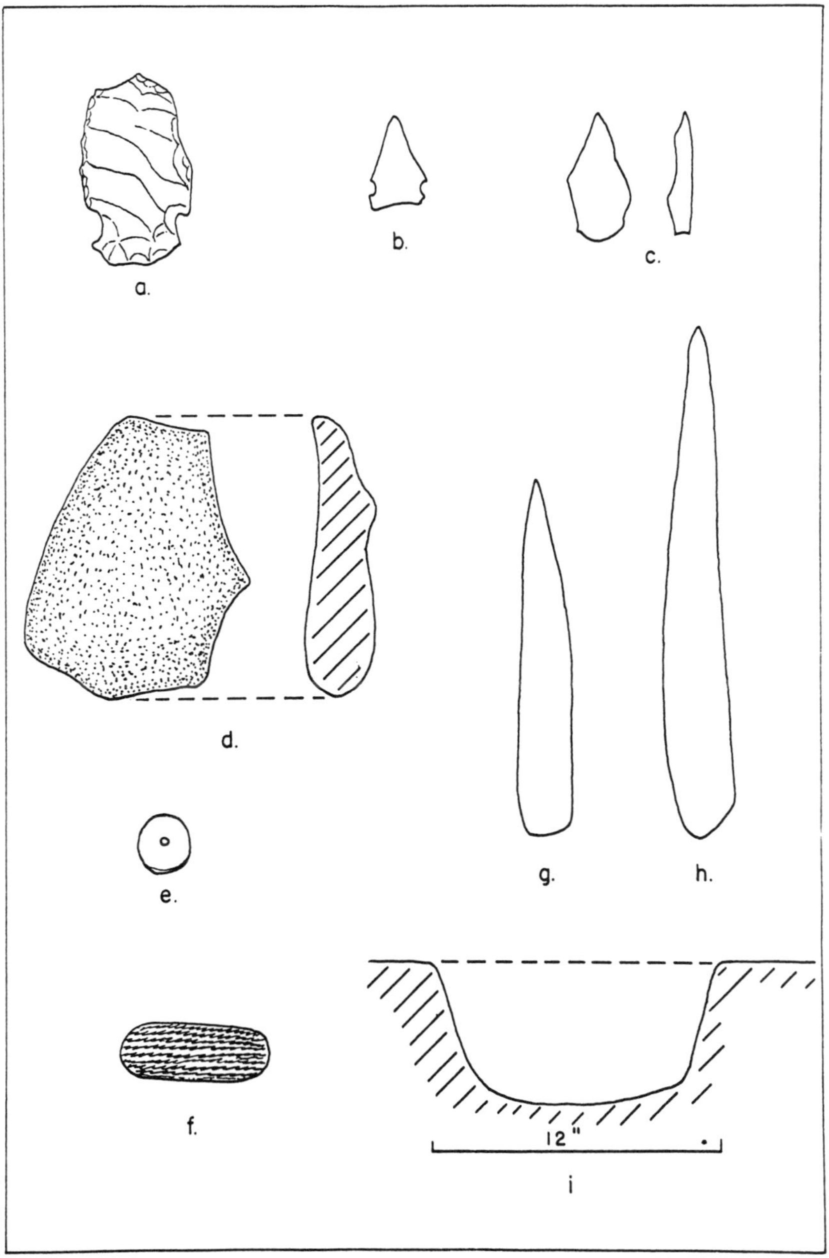

Figure 41. Artifacts associated with House 6, and firepit cross-section, House 6, Bonnell Site: *a*, Projectile point, 3.5 x 2.0 cm; *b*, Projectile point, 1.8 x 1.1 cm; *c*, Point or worked flake, 2.4 x 1.2 x 0.4 cm; *d*, Metate fragment, 21.0 x 16.0 x 4.8 cm; *e*, Round gaming piece, 1.0 x 1.1 cm; *f*, Gaming piece, 1.2 x 2.8 cm; *g*, Awl, 6.6 x 1.0 cm; *h*, Awl, 9.5 x 1.2 cm; *i*, Cross-section of firepit.

placed on edge. The precarious construction makes it unlikely that the wall was full height. It could have served as a simulated pit wall.

A post hole 2 inches in diameter was near the west edge of Floor 2. Other posts recorded from the excavation level of Floor 2 do not form a definite pattern.

Fire Area

None.

Depression in Floor

The trench or depression discussed above was 12 inches wide and about 8 inches deep. It contained three post holes which could have been part of a vertical wall between Houses 7 and 8.

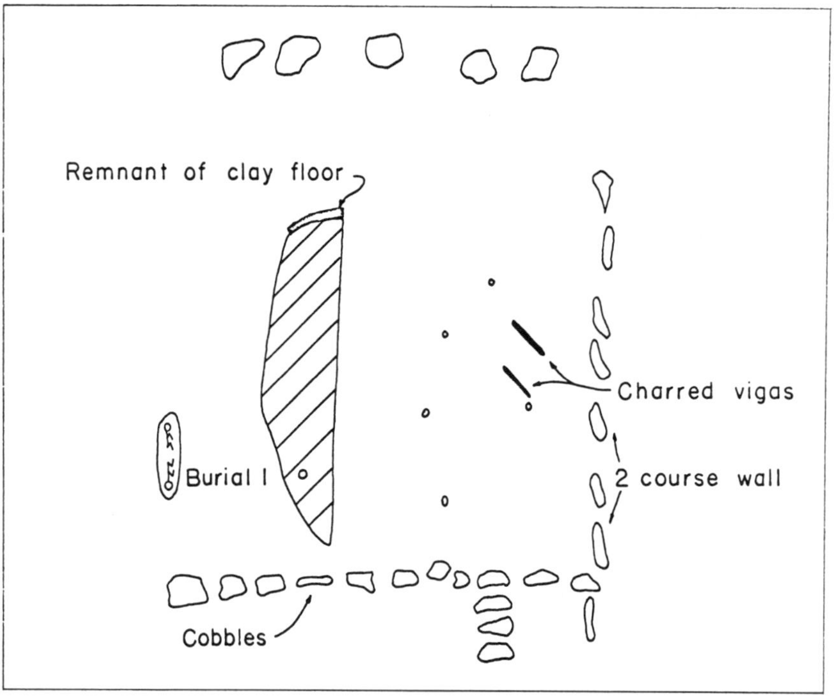

Figure 42. House 7, Bonnell Site, showing west limits of Floor 2.

Associated Artifacts

No artifacts rested on Floor 1. A double-pointed bone awl and a mano were in the fill slightly above the floor. Artifacts from the level of Floor 2 included a

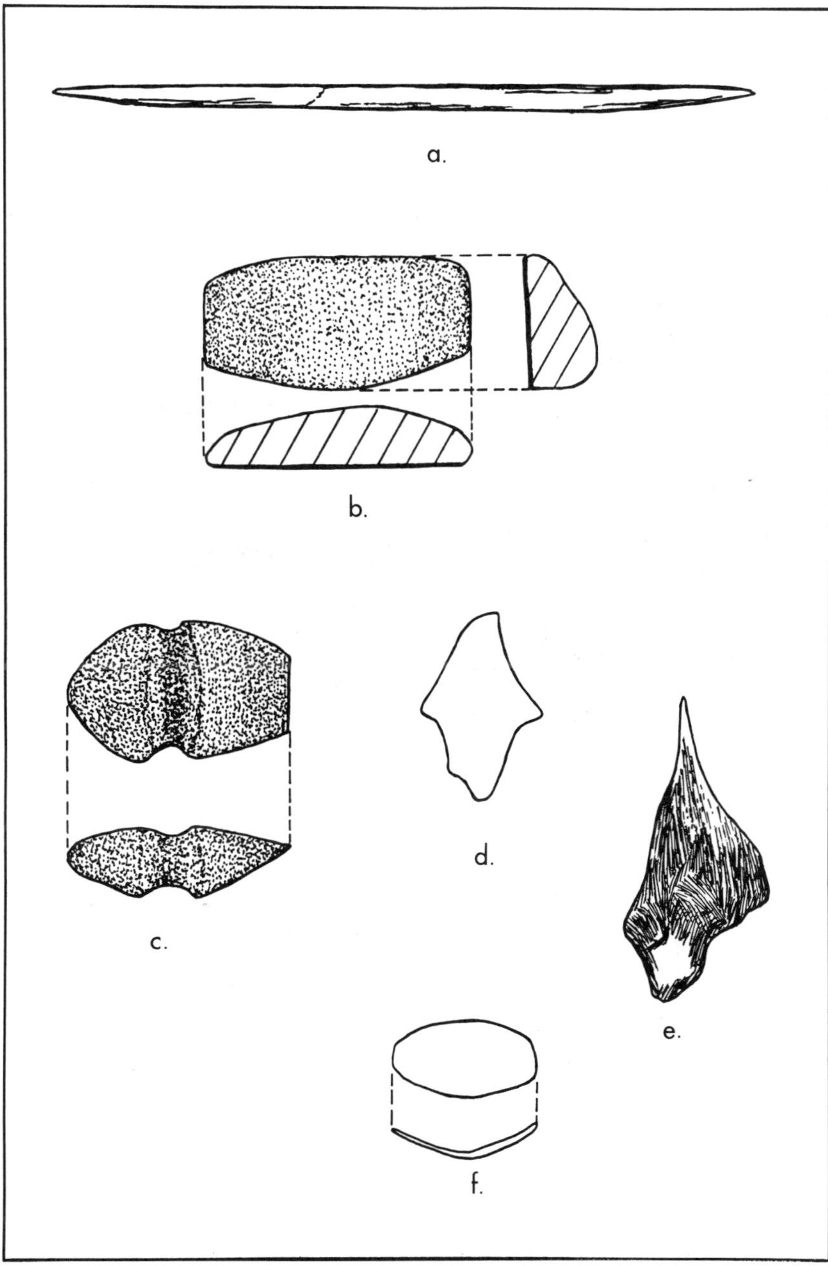

Figure 43. Artifacts associated with House 7, Bonnell Site: *a,* Double-pointed bone awl, 0.6 x 13.0 cm; *b,* Mano, 10.0 x 20.0 x 5.0 cm; *c,* Full-grooved axe, 10.0 x 16.5 x 5.0 cm; *d,* Projectile point or drill (?), 3.5 x 2.3 cm; *e,* Bone awl, 5.8 x 2.8 cm; *f,* Unperforated shell object, 2.8 x 1.4 x 0.2 cm.

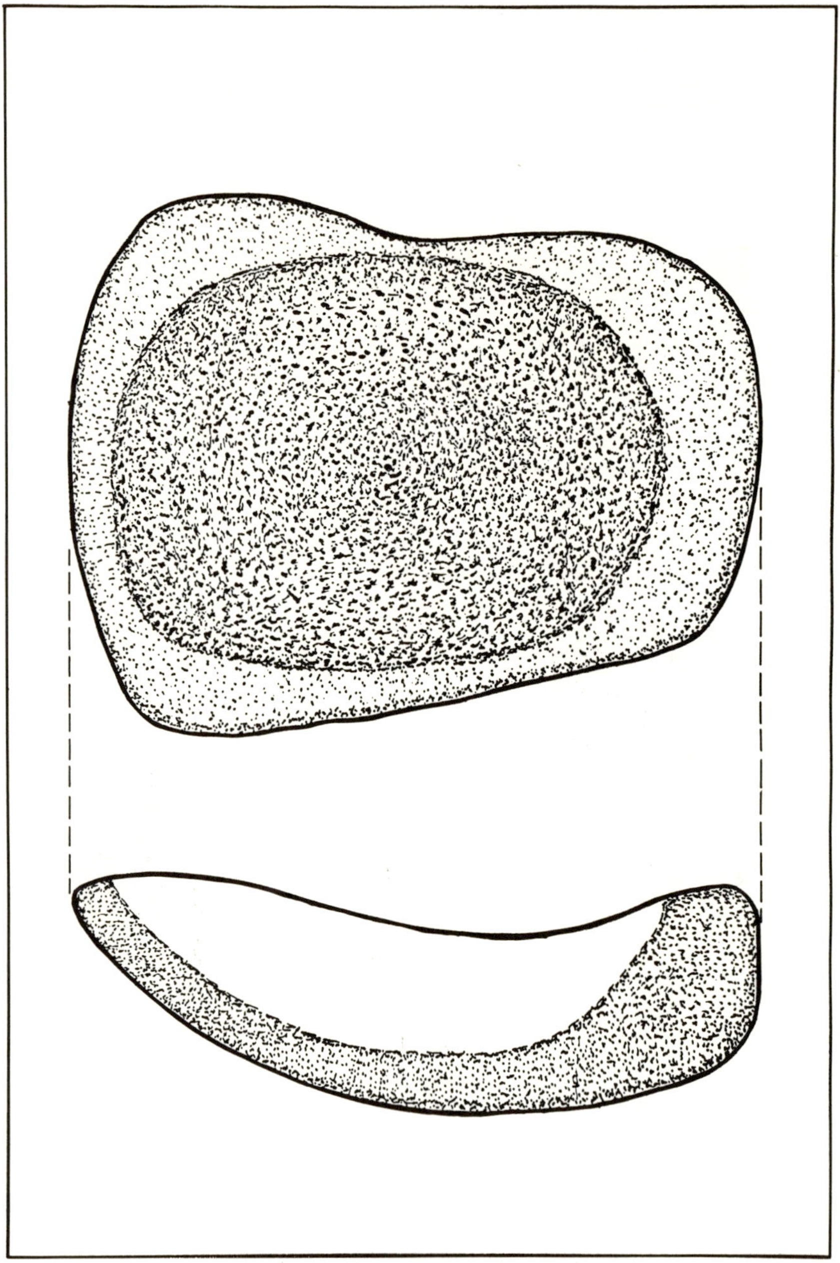

Figure 44. Basin milling stone, House 7, Bonnell Site.

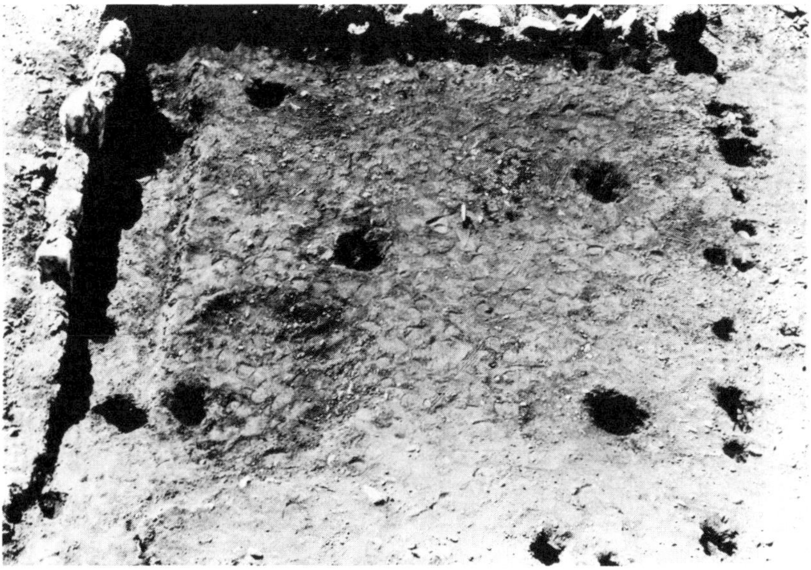

Plate 44. House 7, Bonnell Site.

metate, an axe, a bifacial knife, an awl, and an unperforated shell object (Figs. 43–44).

Remarks

Two separate structures used the east cobble stone wall. The earlier house was the west room of a two-house structure. It is not clear whether the Floor 2 structure was also associated with House 8 or was an independent structure. Neither house burned. The absence of artifacts on the lower floor suggests unusual tidiness, an orderly withdrawal, or a special function for this room.

House 8

Type

A shallow, rectangular pithouse with almost equilateral walls formed the east room of the two-room structure at the south edge of the site (Pl. 45).

House Pit

The house pit was dug into gravel; it is 14 inches deep on the north but only

3 to 6 inches deep on the south side due to surface slope at the terrace edge. Some unshaped cobbles were placed inside the pit wall and one large limestone cobble in the gravel was simply left in place in the northeast corner. Fewer cobbles were present than in adjacent House 7.

Floor

The house was refloored once; 4 to 6 inches of fill had accumulated before they made a new firepit and resurfaced the floor. Both floors were smooth packed earth.

Internal Posts and Post Holes

Eight post holes for 4- to 8-inch timbers were irregularly spaced in the interior of the room; some or all were weight-bearing columns. The northwest corner post had a stone footing, and the post butt was rounded and burned. The same post pattern and superstructure pertained to both floors.

Wall Posts and Post Holes

Some post holes at the floor level indicate that the outside walls were of vertical *jacal* construction, like House 7. The west wall of House 8 was the two-course cobblestone wall that has already been discussed in regard to House 7. If there was a vertical dividing wall between the two houses, it must have been on the House 7 side, leaving the cobbles exposed on the House 8 side.

Fire Area

The circular firepit of Floor 1 was 12 inches in diameter and 5 inches deep. That of Floor 2 was more irregular in shape, with an opening 12 by 15 inches; it was 5 to 6 inches deep. Neither firepit was plastered; both opened flush with the floor, and both had straight sides.

Floor Depressions

A shallow, basin-shaped depression, 6 inches deep, in the northwest corner contained no artifacts. A second irregular-shaped depression in the same section of the room had straight sides, a flat bottom and was 4 inches deep.

Flagstone

A flat flagstone was imbedded in the northeast corner of the upper floor.

Associated Artifacts

This structure was one of the more productive in terms of associated artifacts (Figs. 45–46); 37 were recovered. Of the 9 projectile points, the largest number found in a single structure at this site, 6 were side-notched. House 8 also produced the largest number of ornamental objects. A relative abundance of mussel shell, some cut, suggested that mussel shell objects were made here. In addition, there were bone gaming pieces, manos, an axe, a scraper, a scapula tool, and hammerstones.

Remarks

The house burned after Floor 2 remodeling.

House 9

Type

The floor plan was rectangular. Its alignment with House 13 and the similarity of the ceramic assemblages of these two houses indicated that it could have been a part of the eastern house block.

House Pit

It is not clear whether or not this was a pithouse. East and west pit walls were not recognized although the limits of the floor were found. On the south, an adobe remnant 12 to 14 inches wide standing 6 to 8 inches above the floor can be interpreted as an adobe wall base such as existed between Houses 2 and 3, or it could be a wall remnant. It was well eroded, since it was exposed on the modern surface.

Floors

The structure had been refloored once after 3 to 5 inches of fill had accumulated on Floor 1. Both floors were plastered.

Internal Posts and Post Holes

A large post hole halfway between north and south walls in the east part of the room supported a timber ca. 8 inches in diameter. Field notes showed a comparable post hole in the west side of the house, but this did not show in photographs. A two-post system is postulated. Smaller post holes occurred.

Wall Posts and Post Holes

One post was embedded in the outside of the south adobe wall and a second was placed about 5 inches south of that wall. Small posts along north and east walls may have been wall posts.

Roof Construction

No data. The postulated two-timber support system could have supported a

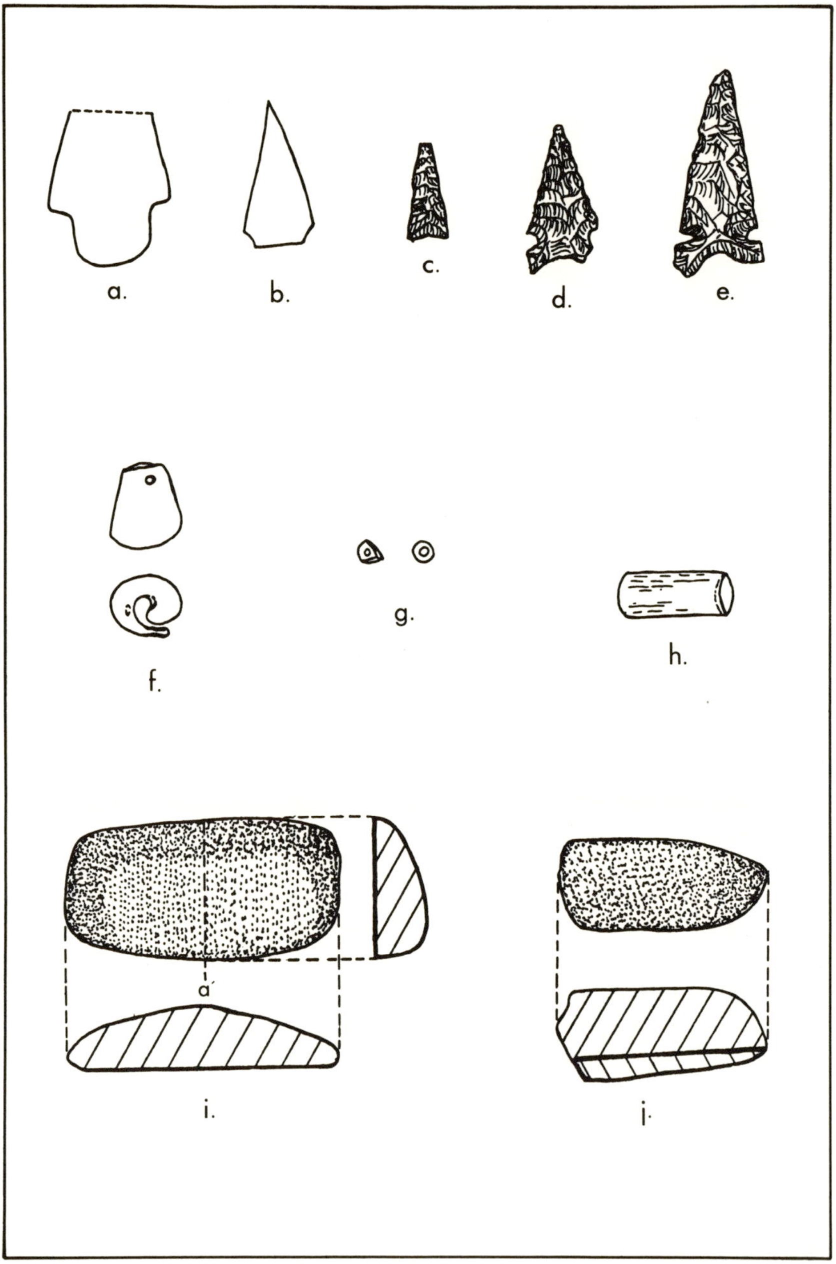

Figure 45. Artifacts associated with House 8, Bonnell Site: *a-e*, Projectile points, 2.8 x 2.5 cm; *f*, *Oliva* shell tinkler, 1.5 x 1.3 cm; *g*, Turquoise disc beads, 0.4 x 0.4 cm; *h*, Tubular bone bead, 1.3 x 1.8 cm; *i*, Mano, 10.0 x 20.0 x 4.0 cm; *j*, Mano fragment, 7.2 x 16.0 x 6.0 cm.

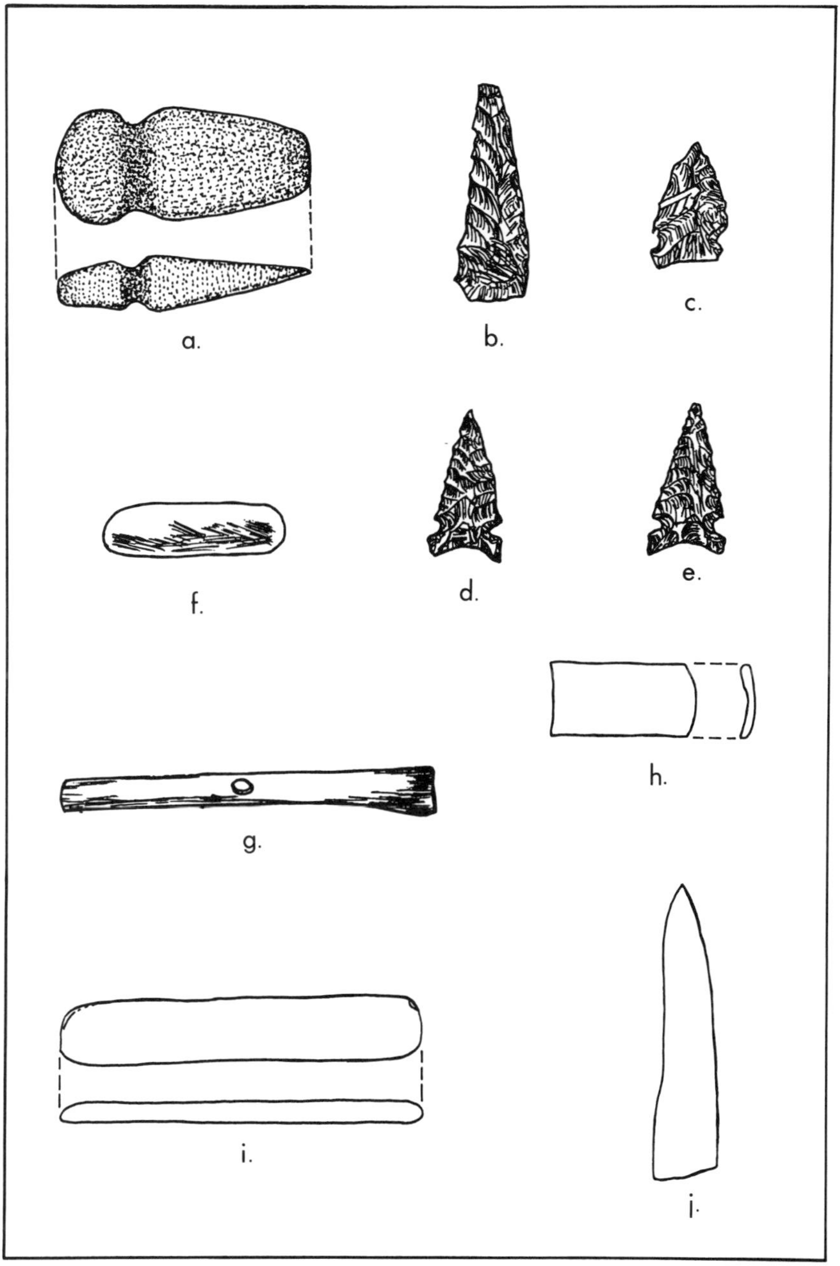

Figure 46. Artifacts associated with House 8, Bonnell Site: *a,* Full-grooved axe, 8.0 x 18.0 x 4.0 cm; *b,* Projectile point or drill, 4.0 x 1.8 cm; *c.-e,* Projectile point or drill, 2.2 x 1.3 cm; *f,* Bone gaming piece, 1.0 x 3.5 cm; *g,* One-stop bone whistle, 0.9 x 7.0 cm. The hole has been drilled. *h,* Polished bone piece, 1.3 x 2.6 x 0.2 cm; *i,* Shaped bone piece, 1.2 x 6.7 x 0.4 cm; *j,* Awl tip, 5.5 x 1.3 cm.

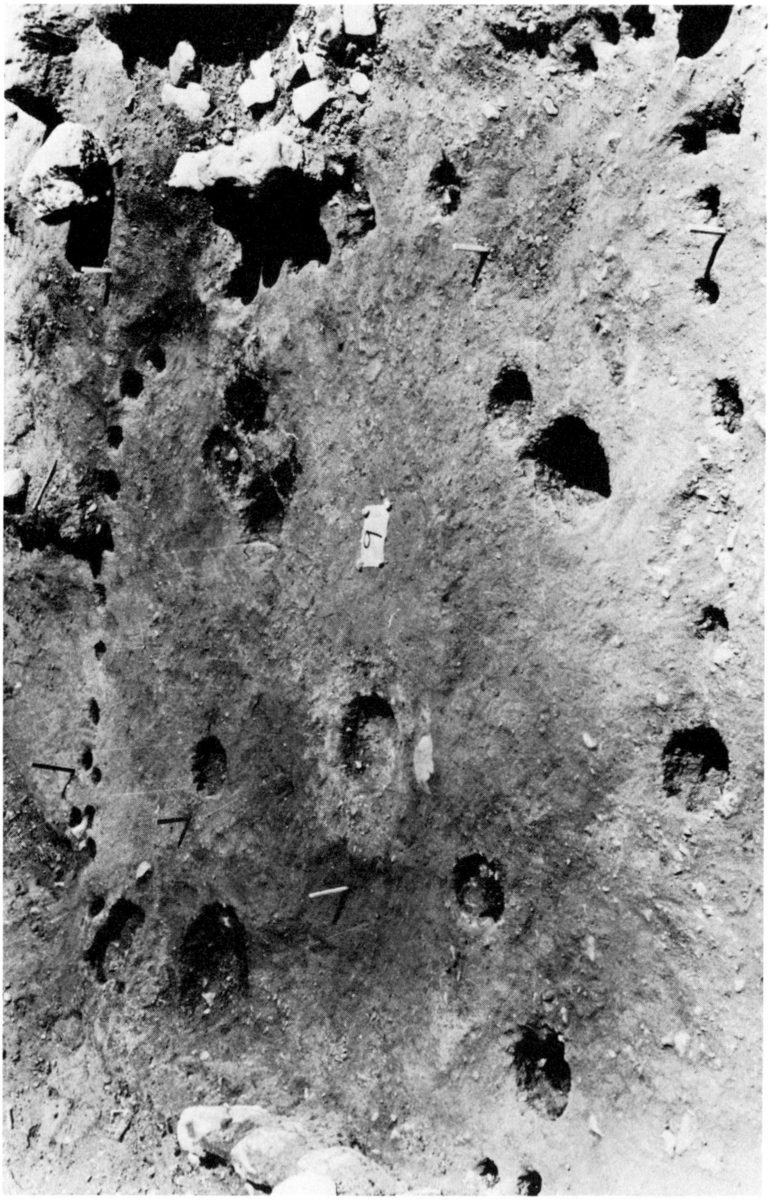

Plate 45. House 8, Bonnell Site.

gable roof. If Houses 9 and 13 were connected structurally, part of the weight of the House 9 roof could have been carried by timbers in House 13.

Fire Areas

The firepit in the lower floor, 8 inches in diameter and 9 inches deep, opened flush with the floor. Plaster had been applied to the upper 3 to 4 inches of the pit which was completely full of ashes. On the same floor just north of the firepit, in an area about 14 inches in diameter, fire had been built directly on the plaster floor, leaving the clay fired to an orange color and ashes and charcoal caked about 1 inch deep. When the house was refloored, a well-plastered firepit 12 inches in diameter and 4 inches deep was constructed above the older one.

Associated Artifacts

Artifacts from the 6 inches above the floor were sacked together. A mano, two side-notched points, an ulna awl, and a bone object that may have been a weaving batten were found (Fig. 47).

Remarks

An abundance of broken animal bones, mostly of deer or antelope, were on the floor and in the fill.

House 10

Type

Not known.

Floor

Clay had been applied to the floor around the firepit for 3 to 4 inches; the peripheral area was packed earth.

Internal Posts and Post Holes

Since the house was not excavated as a unit, data are inadequate. Six posts and one post hole occurred within the postulated house limit at the right stratigraphic position.

Fire Area

The circular firepit, 12 inches in diameter and 6 inches deep, had straight plastered sides.

Slab-lined Box

Some 5 feet southeast of the firepit, three vertical stone slabs were recessed

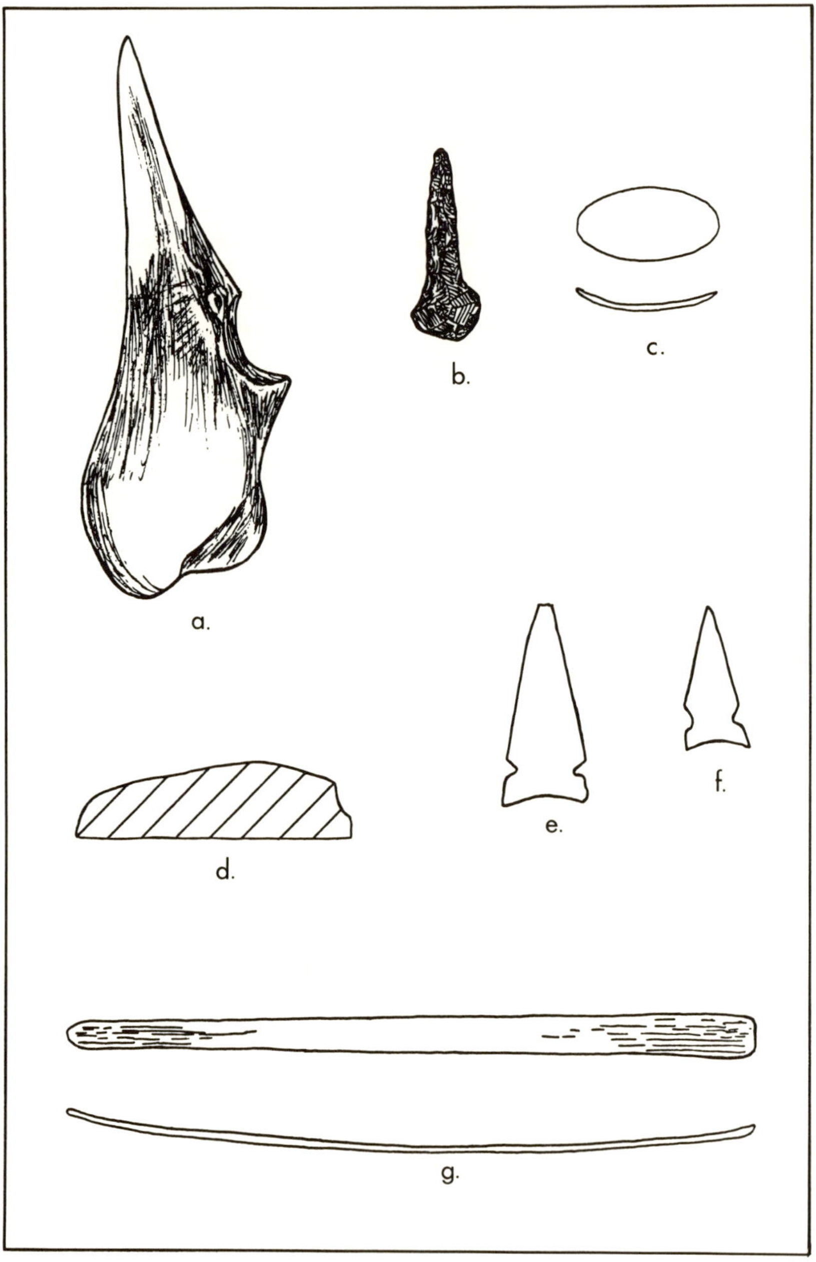

Figure 47. Artifacts associated with House 9, Bonnell Site: *a,* Awl, 10.4 x 3.4 cm; *b,* Drill, 3.5 x 1.3 cm; *c,* Mussel shell object, 1.3 x 2.6 x 0.1 cm; *d,* Mano, in cross-section, 6.5 x 20.0 cm; *e-f,* Projectile points, 3.8 x 1.6 cm; *g,* Split rib tool, 1.6 x 25.5 x 0.2 cm.

in the floor to form a rectangular pit or box. The fill between the stones was loose and dark in color.

Rock Floor Features

Two unshaped cobbles southeast of the firepit rested on the floor.

Sub-floor Burials (?)

Burials 9 and 10, made from this occupational surface, may have been under the floor or just west of the house.

Associated Artifacts

Artifacts were scarce in the excavation level containing the floor features. A shell ornament, a cut shell fragment, and a drill can be tentatively assigned to this house.

House 11

Type

No data.

Floor

Packed earth could be traced for a few feet around the firepit; outside limits were not established.

Internal Posts and Post Holes

One post was charred even with the floor.

Fire Area

A crude clay curb built on the floor, roughly 9 inches in diameter and 4 inches high, contained caked ashes.

Associated Artifacts

Three artifacts can be tentatively assigned to this house: a basalt "palette," a mano fragment, and a worked flake (see Fig. 48).

Remarks

The house burned. Large amounts of charcoal, orange clay and a post burned even with the floor were discovered in the original trenching of the site in 1950. Excavation of adjacent sections in subsequent years exposed the crude fire area and more of the floor and fallen roof.

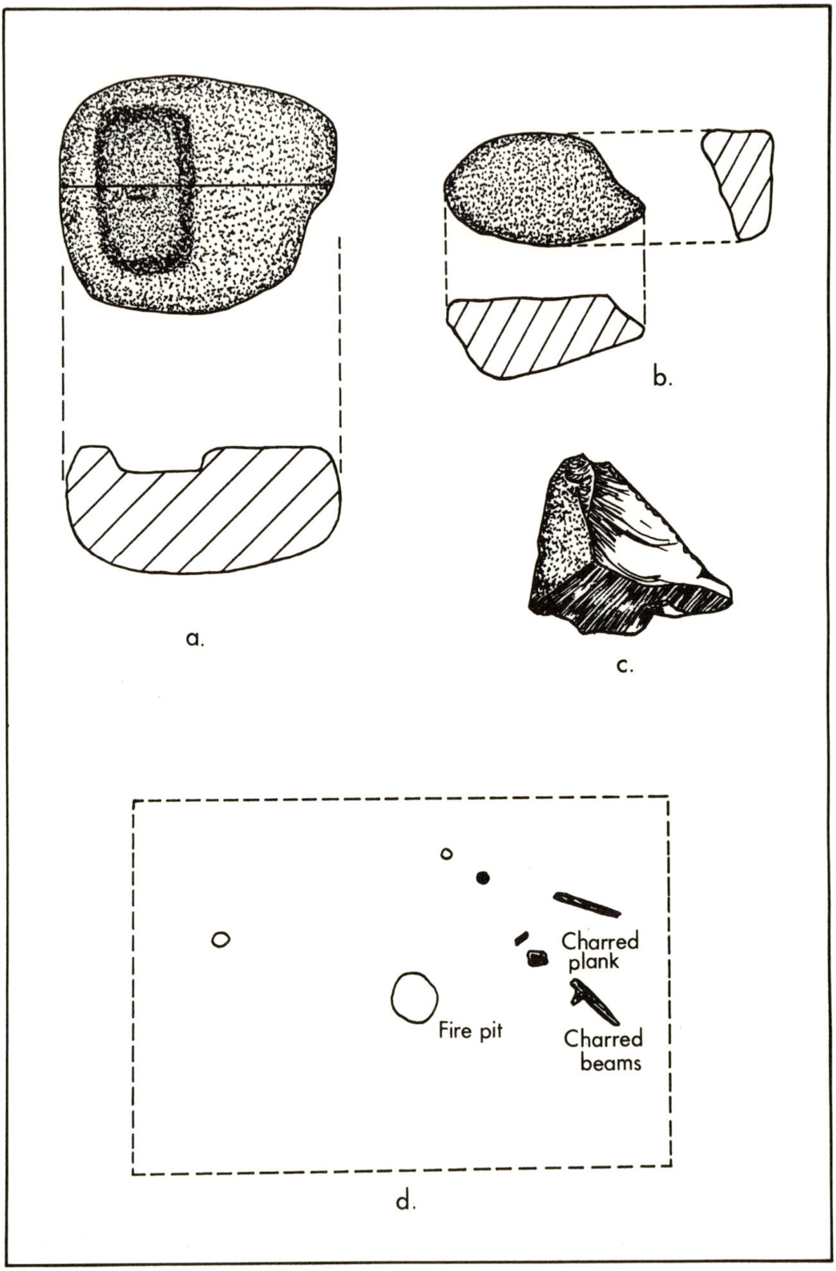

Figure 48. Artifacts associated with House 11, and location of charred roofing timbers, House 11, Bonnell Site: *a,* Stone "palette," 17.0 x 20.0 x 9.5 cm; *b,* Hand grinding stone, 8.0 x 15.0 x 5.0 cm; *c,* Unifacially worked flake, 3.3 x 3.8 cm; *d,* Plan showing location of charred plank and roofing timbers.

House 12

Type
No data.

Floor
Two floors observed in the north profile of a trench were not traced. The upper floor of packed earth was some 14 inches below the modern surface; 5 inches below this was a plastered floor (Fig. 49).

Internal Posts and Post Holes
One post was found for the lower floor.

Fire Area
None.

Sub-floor Pit
An unplastered pit, dug 18 inches into gravel from the lower floor, has an opening 18 x 14 inches.

Sub-floor Burial
The grave of a child (Burial 6) buried from the upper floor level, extended through the bottom floor (see Fig. 49).

Associated Artifacts
Half of a Black-on-Red bowl, a scapula tool, and a fire-blackened Corrugated sherd were found in the sub-floor pit. A mano 13 inches long was on the lower floor some 6 feet south of the pit. Provenience of other artifacts from the excavation level in which the two floors were located cannot be differentiated. A one-handed grinding stone, an ulna awl, shell ornaments, a stone pendant, three side-notched points, and a battered hammerstone on which hematite had been ground were found. Bison bones on the upper floor included a scapula, ribs, and broken long bones. Associated artifacts appear in Figure 50.

House 13

Type
Square pithouse in the east house block (Figs. 51–55; Pls. 46–49).

House Pit
The original pit was dug through fill into gravel to a depth of 18 to 24 inches. After this structure was refloored once, it was abandoned or filled and a new pit was dug. East and south pit walls of the latter house coincided with

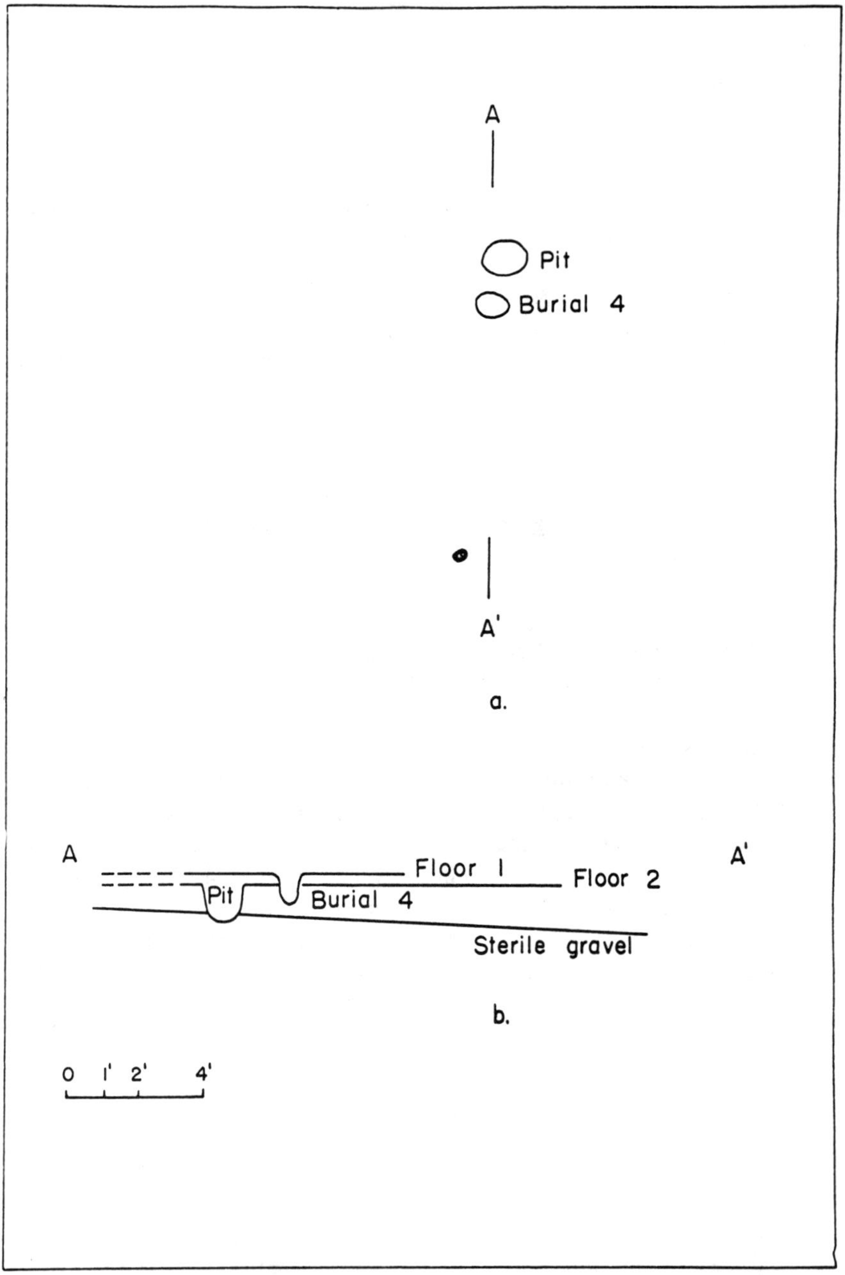

Figure 49. House 12, Bonnell Site: *a*, Plan of pit and burial; *b*, Profile of floors.

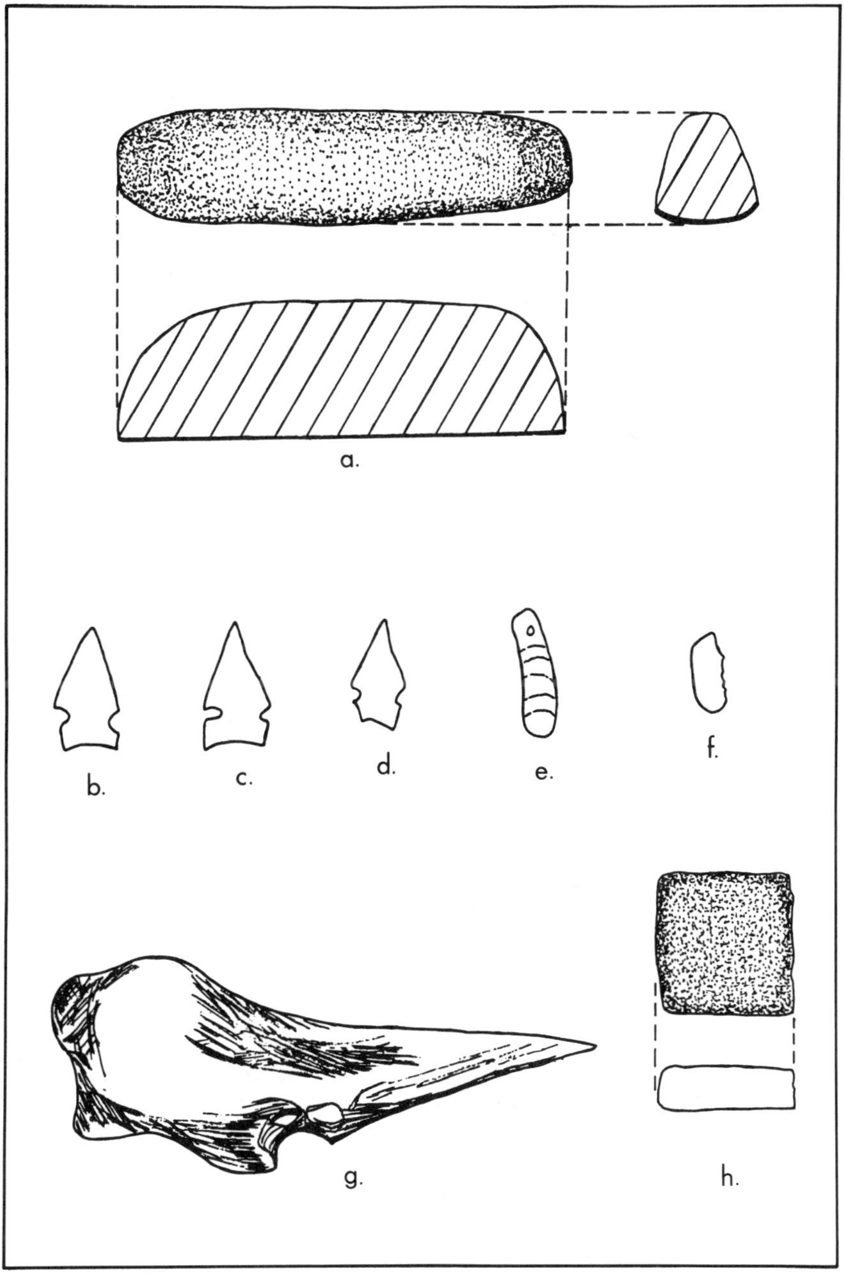

Figure 50. Artifacts associated with House 12, Bonnell Site: *a,* Large, heavy mano, 8.0 x 32.5 x 2.5 cm; *b-d,* Projectile points, 2.3 x 1.3 cm; *e,* Stone pendant, 2.5 x 0.6 cm; *f,* Worked mussel shell fragment, 1.5 x 0.6 cm; *g,* Awl, 3.2 x 10.0 cm; *h,* Mano fragment, 5.0 x 5.0 x 3.2 cm.

the older pit walls; however the new pit was cut about 6 inches beyond the old north pit wall and about 6 inches inside of the old west wall. Pit walls were never plastered in the several major remodelings. As the house was refloored, the pit became shallower, until the final floor level was in a pit only 5 to 12 inches deep.

Floors

Floors 1 and 2, only 1 inch apart, belonged to the original house pit. Both were exceptionally level and the smooth floor plaster turned up against the unplastered pit walls. These two floors shared the same four large support timbers, smaller post holes and firepit. All floors associated with the later or second house pit shared a new six-timber support system; secondary remodeling occurred as each new floor was laid down. Floors 3 through 6 were plastered, but none were as level or smoothly finished as Floors 1 and 2. Floor 3 sloped up towards the wall, a tendency that became more pronounced at each subsequent level, until the periphery of Floor 6 was 6 to 8 inches higher than the center.

Internal Posts and Post Holes

The original house pit had four large timbers, centrally located (Fig. 51). These posts were well preserved and showed no signs of having burned. Eight post holes 2 to 3 inches in diameter were clustered in the northeast corner and three other small post holes were located elsewhere in the room. After the first house pit was filled, a new pit was dug that utilized a six-timber support system (Fig. 52). Four were centrally located and two placed against the west wall with the same interval and alignment. All floor levels pertaining to the second structure, Floors 3 through 6, used these same timbers. Three of the four timbers of the first house were not used in construction of the later house, as they had been plastered over by Floor 3. Floor 4 saw the addition of smaller posts just west of three of the large central timbers and several smaller post holes were placed around the north-central support timber (Fig. 53). Floor 5 used none of the secondary posts found in Floor 4, but 25 small post holes were added in the northeast sector of the room and 8 elsewhere (Fig. 54). Floor 6 had only the six large timbers and small post holes around the firepit coping; all of the small post holes of Floor 5 were plastered over (Fig. 55).

Wall Posts and Post Holes

None were located for the older pithouse (Floors 1 and 2). A series of small post holes or post impressions were located almost one foot back from the rim of the house pit pertaining to Floors 3 through 6 (Figs. 52–55).

Roof Construction

The six timbers could have supported a flat or gabled roof. As in the case of House 3, the central location of this house in the multi-room block may have required the additional supports. The entire floor area had full head-room, as is shown by the large timbers placed in the west wall.

Fire Areas

The firepit shared by Floors 1 and 2 was unplastered and opened flush with the floor (Fig. 51). It was a cylindrical firepit with an offset ash shelf or receptacle that gave a kidney-shaped outline when viewed from the top. Cobbles imbedded in one wall were undoubtedly encountered in digging the firepit and left in place. A polished bone tube, an *Olivella* bead, and a sherd of St. Johns Polychrome were in the firepit. Floor 3 had a similar firepit with an ash shelf (Fig. 52). Floor 4 had a deep, cylindrical, well-plastered firepit that opened flush with the floor (Fig. 53). In Floor 5 was another deep, cylindrical pit that opened flush with the floor (Fig. 54). When House 13 was refloored for the last time (Floor 6), the firepit from Floor 5 was kept and a clay curb or rim was added (Fig. 55). Six post holes placed around the firepit, all slanting toward the center, suggested some arrangement of small poles to form a cooking or drying apparatus.

Rock Floor Feature

A large flat stone was plastered into Floor 4 close to the southeast support.

Bird Burial

A small bird, unidentified as to species, had been buried below Floor 4 in a small grave 6 inches deep and 3½ inches in diameter. A large Jornada Brown sherd was placed over the bird.

Sub-floor Burials

Two burials were made from Floor 3. An adult male buried against the south wall had a heavy clay cap placed over his grave. A child's skeleton in the southeast corner was badly scattered. The house was not abandoned after these burials, although remodeling may have occurred.

Associated Artifacts

Artifacts from Floors 1 and 2 are considered together (Figs. 56–57). Three manos were together in the southeast corner, and a one-handed grinding stone was in the southeast corner. Four awls and two bone tubes were found. A jasper knife, two broken projectile points, and a bifacial fragment were the major chipped stone items. A large gypsum ornament or ceremonial object was lying on the floor close to the south wall. An *Olivella* bead was in the firepit, and two mussel shell fragments were on the floor. Artifacts from Floors 3 and 4 were sacked together (Figs. 57–58). A trough metate with a mano rest at the closed end was lying upside down over two manos. Other artifacts were a triple-notched point, a side-notched concave-base point, a larger dart point with deep corner notches and a convex stem, an end scraper, a mussel shell pendant, a fragment of a worked shell object, and a small bone tube. Artifacts from Floors 5 and 6 were combined (Figs. 59–60). A basin milling stone used with an elliptical motion had a mano or grinding stone rest; it sat on the upper floor between the firepit and the west wall. Two large manos with their grinding faces together rested in the southwest corner. A fragment of a small, shallow stone mortar was found. Two full-grooved axes lay together in the northeast corner. A worked flake and a mid-section of a black chert or shale bifacial object were the only chipped stone tools. The bone inventory included three bone awls and a split rib (deer) tool. An *Olivella* bead was the only ornament. Food stuffs included six charred corncobs and half of a charred walnut shell.

House 14

Type

Two structures were represented. The earlier house (Floor 1) was a pithouse with a nearly square floor plan which formed part of the east house block. The later structure (Floor 2), only 6 to 8 inches below the modern surface, was an independent house. No walls were found.

House Pit

Pit walls pertaining to Floor 1 were not delineated on three sides. The south wall, shared with House 13, was a dirt wall base upon which a pole wall was placed. Southeast and southwest rounded corners were clear and a close approximation of these walls could be projected.

Floors

Floor 1 was 20 to 24 inches below the modern surface. It was plastered in the central part of the house around the firepit; plaster did not extend to the edges of the structure. Floor 2 had been disturbed on the south side; only the firepit and some north posts were noted.

Internal Posts and Post Holes

Of 18 internal posts and post holes in Floor 1, only 2 had a diameter of more than 5 inches. Either we failed to find large timbers, symmetrically

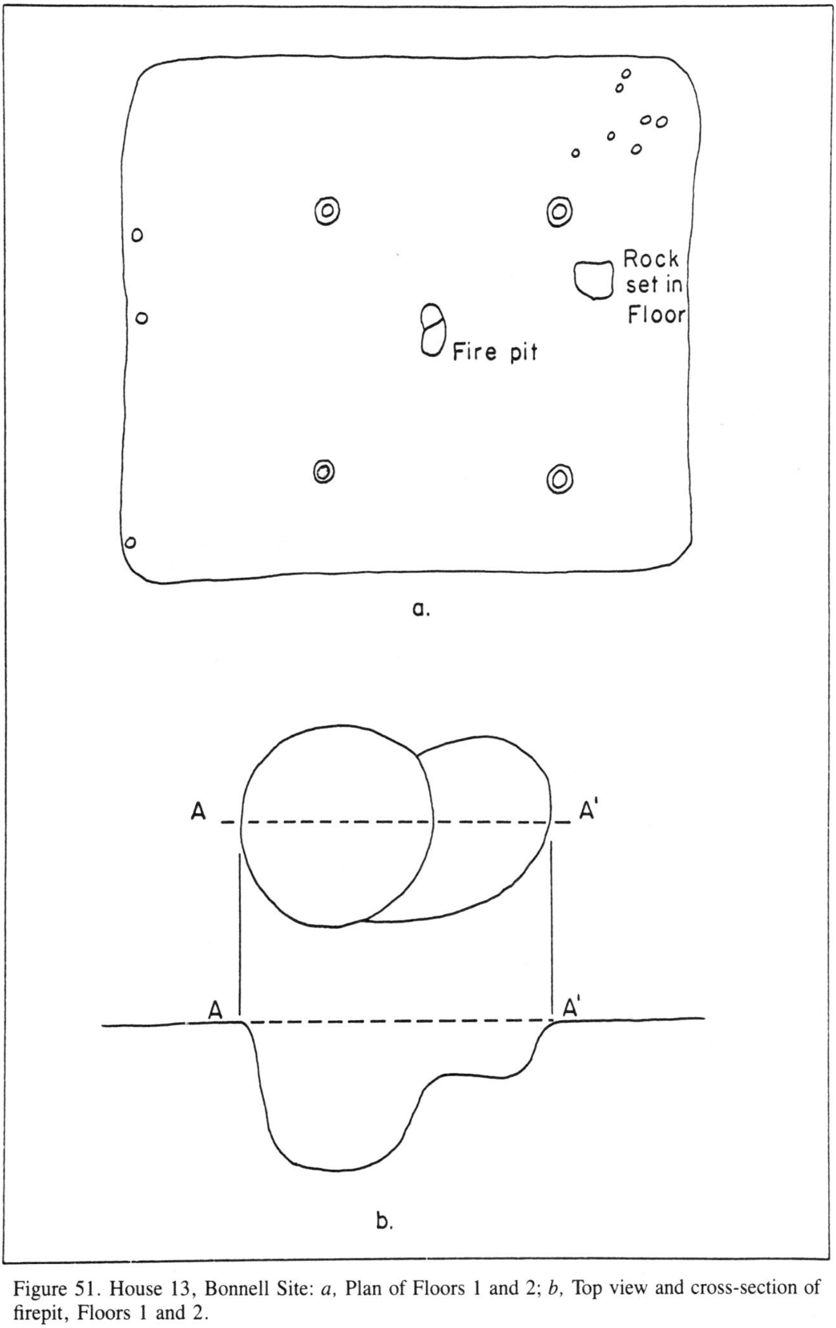

Figure 51. House 13, Bonnell Site: *a,* Plan of Floors 1 and 2; *b,* Top view and cross-section of firepit, Floors 1 and 2.

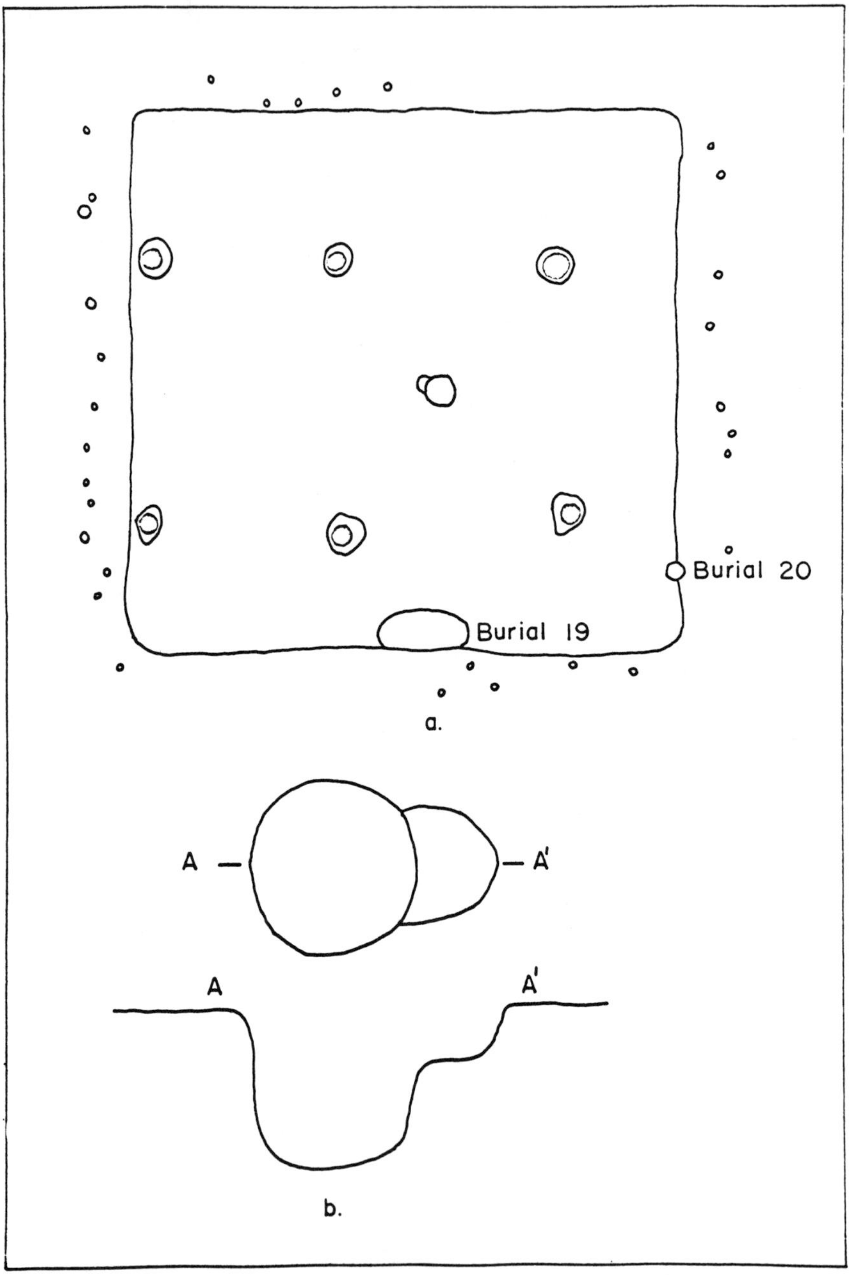

Figure 52. House 13, Bonnell Site: *a,* Plan of Floor 3; *b,* Top view and cross-section, firepit, Floor 3.

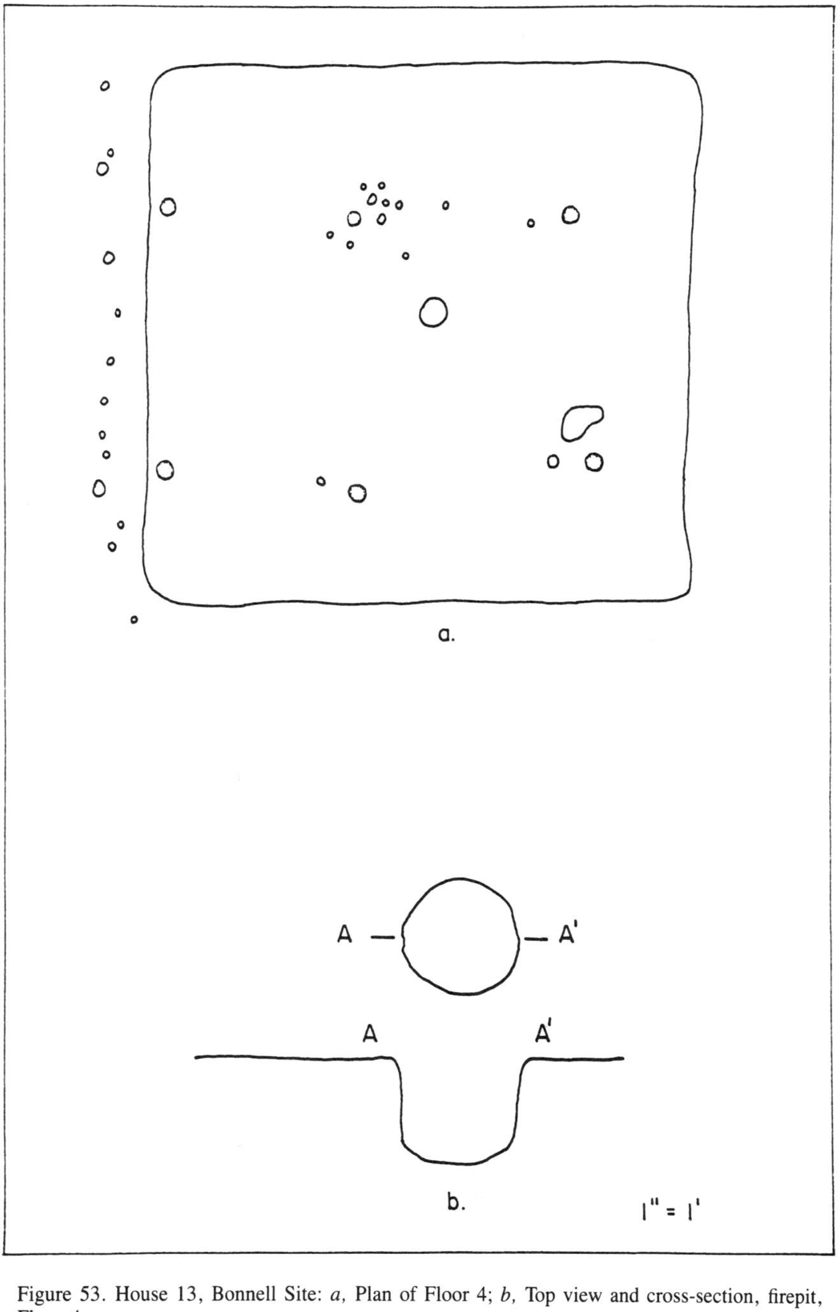

Figure 53. House 13, Bonnell Site: *a,* Plan of Floor 4; *b,* Top view and cross-section, firepit, Floor 4.

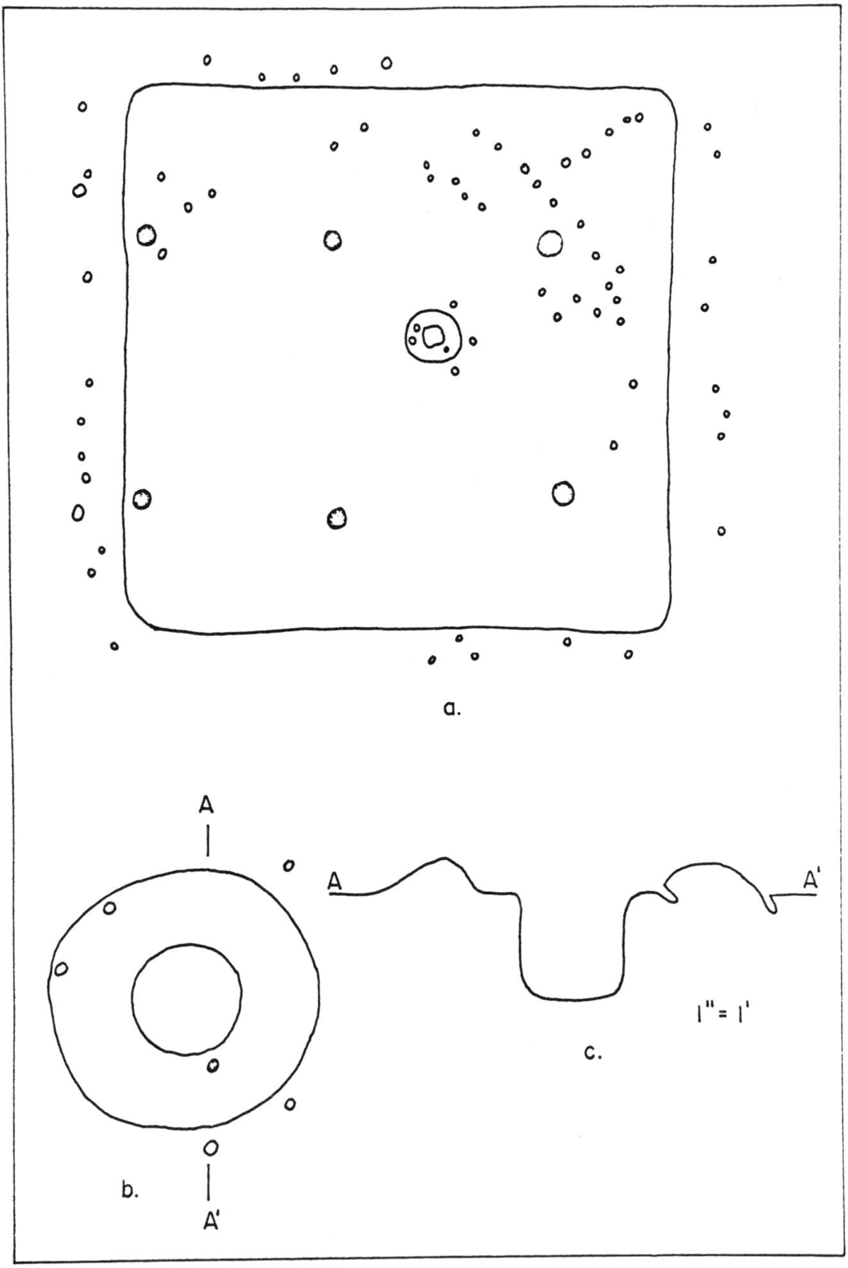

Figure 54. House 13, Bonnell Site: *a*, Plan of Floor 5; *b*, Top view and cross-section, firepit. The cylindrical firepit belongs to Floor 5. The same firepit, was used for Floor 6, with the addition of the coping.

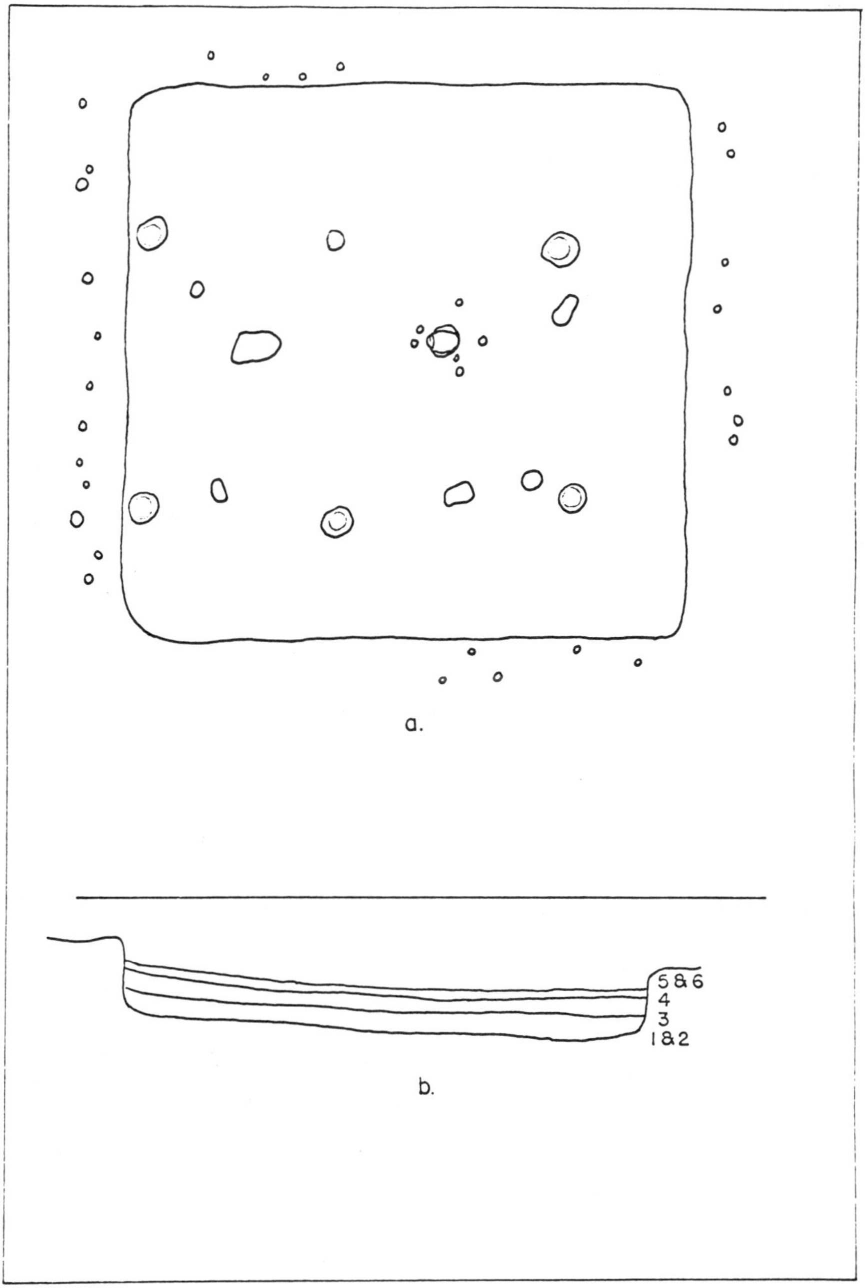

Figure 55. House 13, Bonnell Site: *a,* Plan of Floor 6; *b,* Profile of the major floor levels.

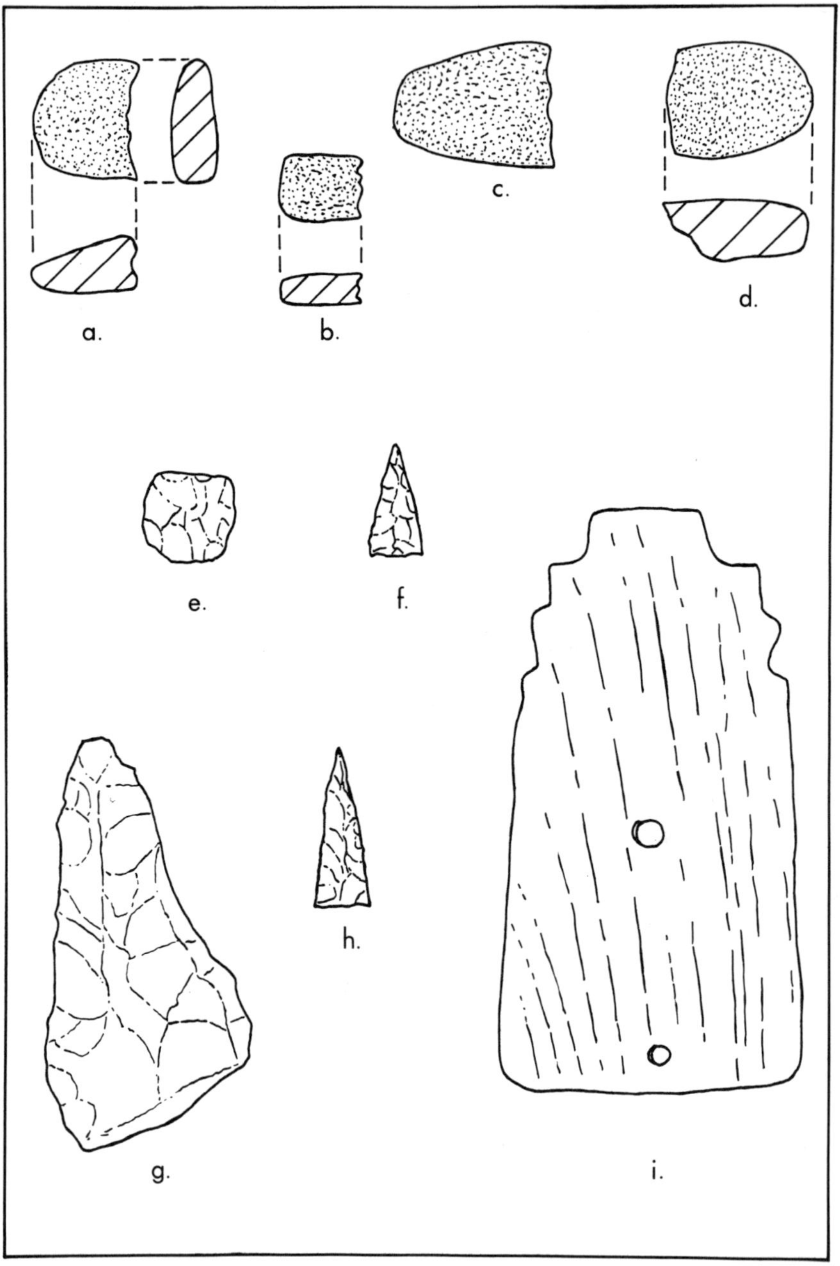

Figure 56. Artifacts associated with Floors 1 and 2, House 13, Bonnell Site: *a-d,* Mano fragments, *a,* 8.5 x 8.0 x 4.0 cm; *e,* Base of a bifacially worked artifact, actual size, 1.6 x 1.7 cm; *f* and *h,* Point tips, *f,* 1.9 x 1.0 cm; *g,* Knife, 7.5 x 3.8 cm; *i,* Gypsum ornament, 10.8 x 5.8 cm.

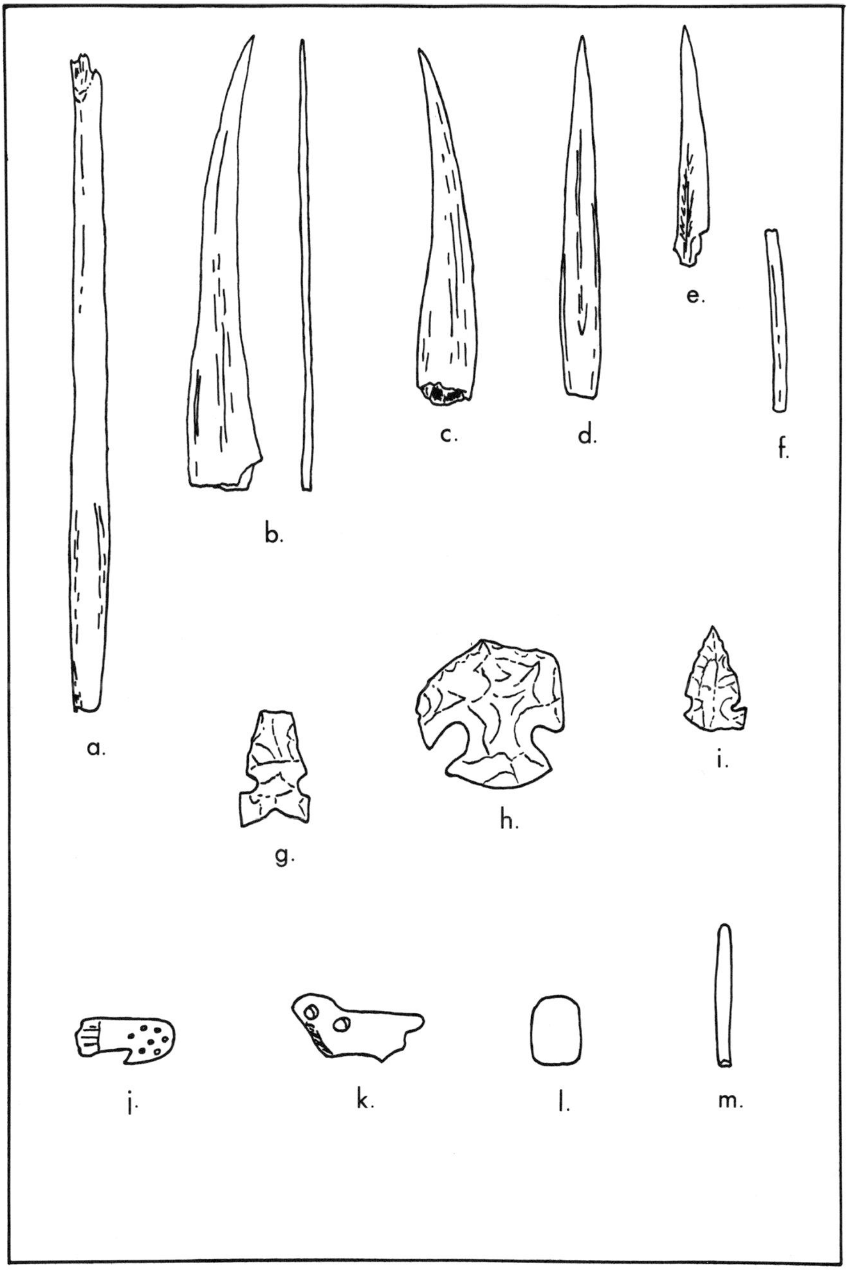

Figure 57. Artifacts associated with House 13, Bonnell Site: *a-f,* Floors 1 and 2; *g-m,* Floors 3 and 4; *a-e,* Bone awls, *a,* 12.0 x 0.7cm; *f,* Bone tube, 3.8 x 0.3 cm; *g-i,* Projectile points, *g,* 2.1 x 1.3 cm; j-k, Mussel shell ornaments, *j,* 0.8 x 1.3 cm; *l,* Unperforated turquoise object, 1.2 x 0.9 cm; *m,* Bone tube, 2.5 x 0.3 cm.

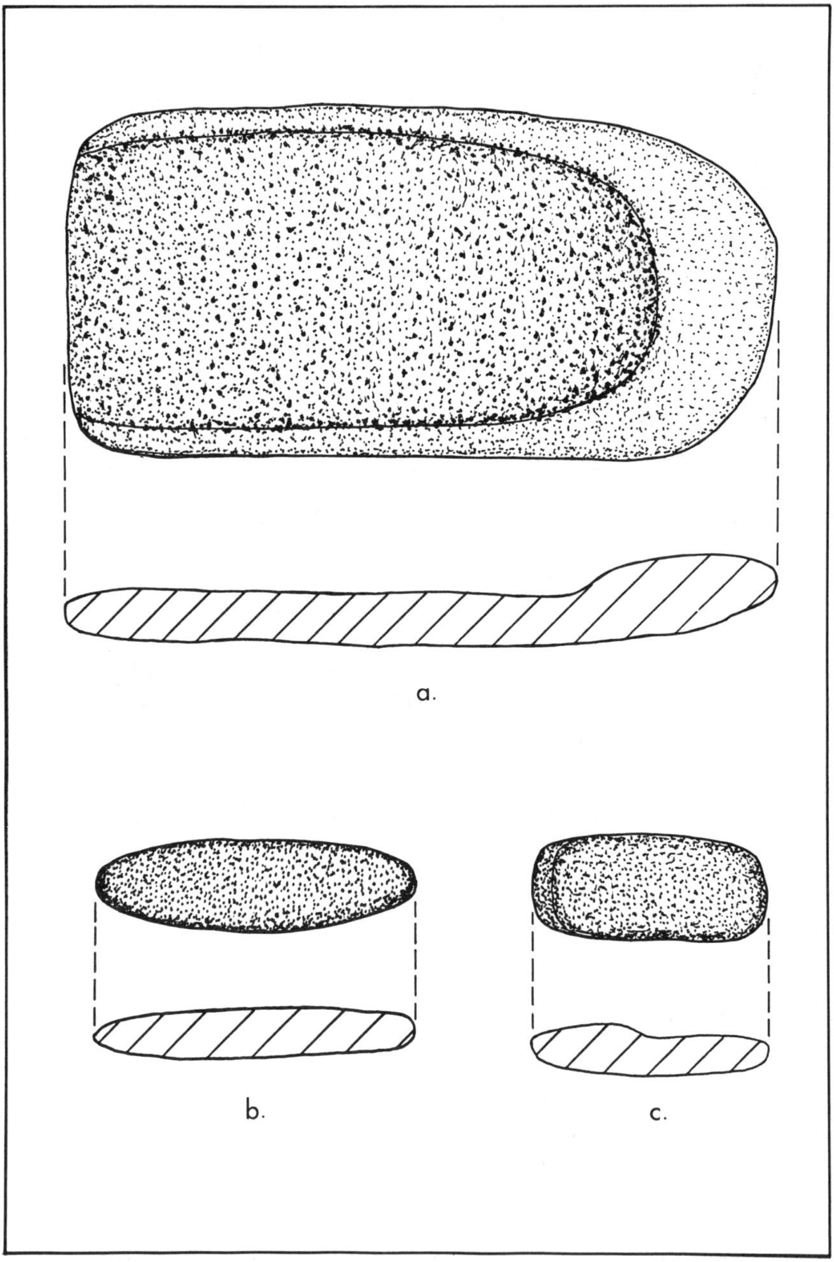

Figure 58. Artifacts associated with Floors 3 and 4, House 13, Bonnell Site. *a,* Trough metate with mano rest, 26.0 x 44.0 x 4.2 cm; *b* and *c,* Manos. *b,* 7.2 x 24.0 x 3.6 cm.

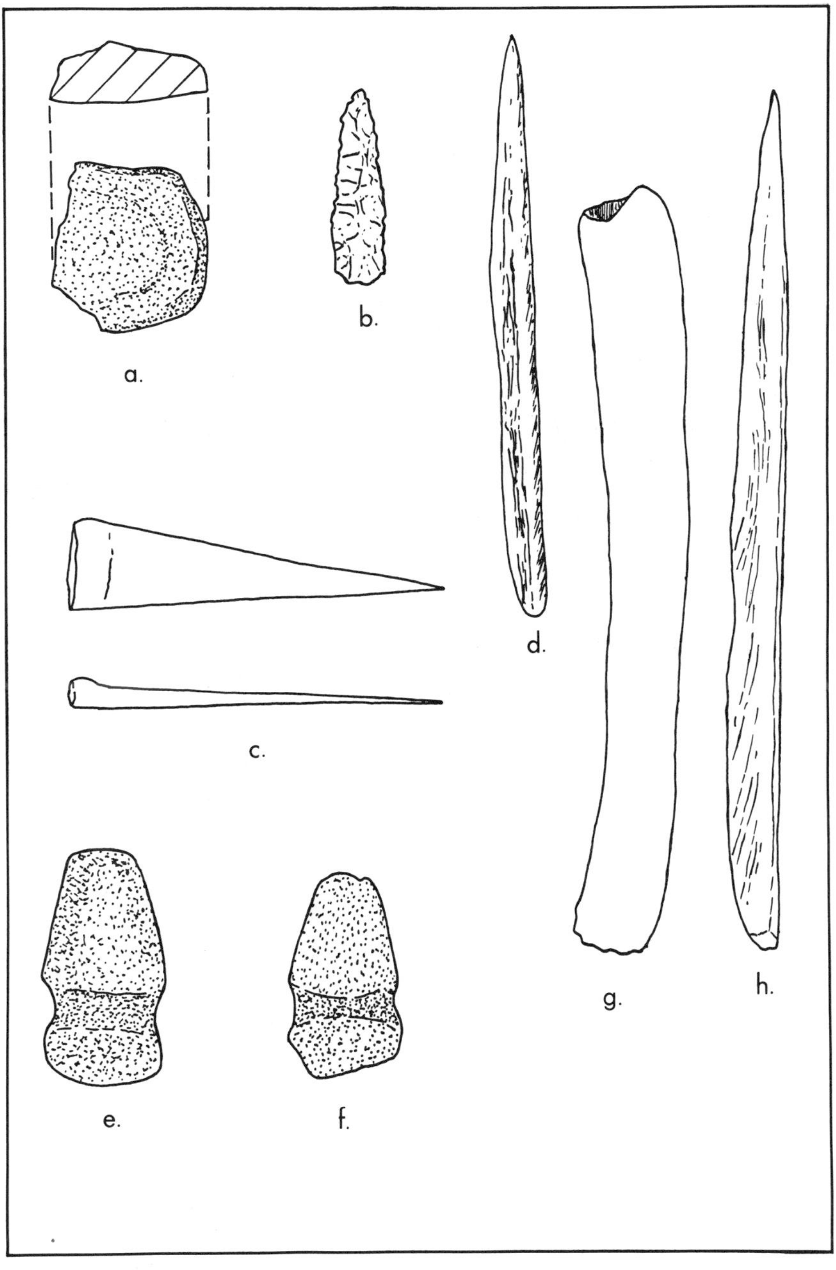

Figure 59. Artifacts associated with Floors 5 and 6, House 13, Bonnell Site: *a,* Grinding slab, 12.5 x 12.0 x 4.5 cm; *b,* Bifacial flint, 3.6 x 1.0 cm; *c,* Bone awl, 1.6 x 7.0 x 0.6 cm; *d,* Awl, 10.7 x 0.8 cm; *e* and *f,* Full-grooved axes, 17.2 x 9.2 cm; *g,* Split rib tool, 14.1 x 1.8 cm; *h,* Bone awl, 15.8 x 0.9 cm.

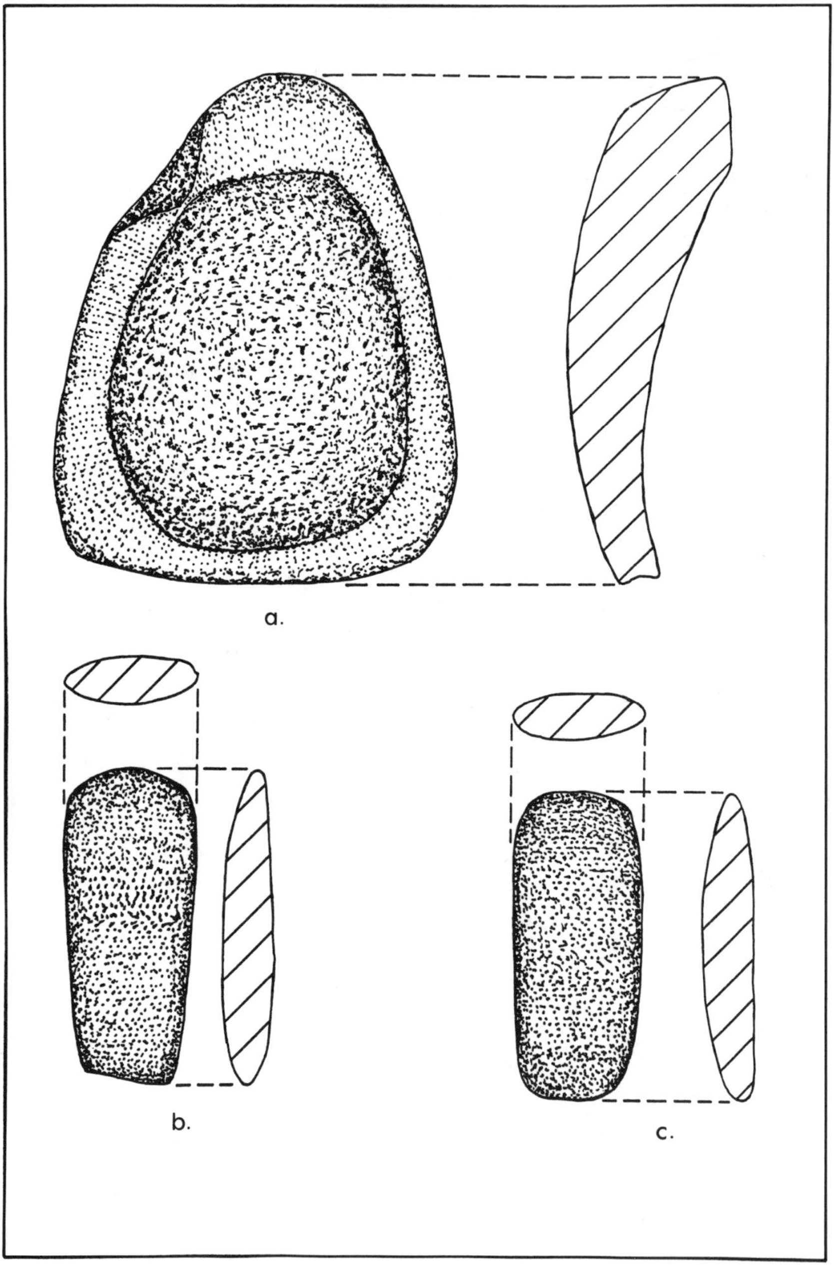

Figure 60. Artifacts associated with Floors 5 and 6, House 13, Bonnell Site: *a,* Basin milling stone, 37.2 x 30.0 x 9.6 cm; *b* and *c,* Manos, *b,* 23 x 10.0 x 4.0 cm.

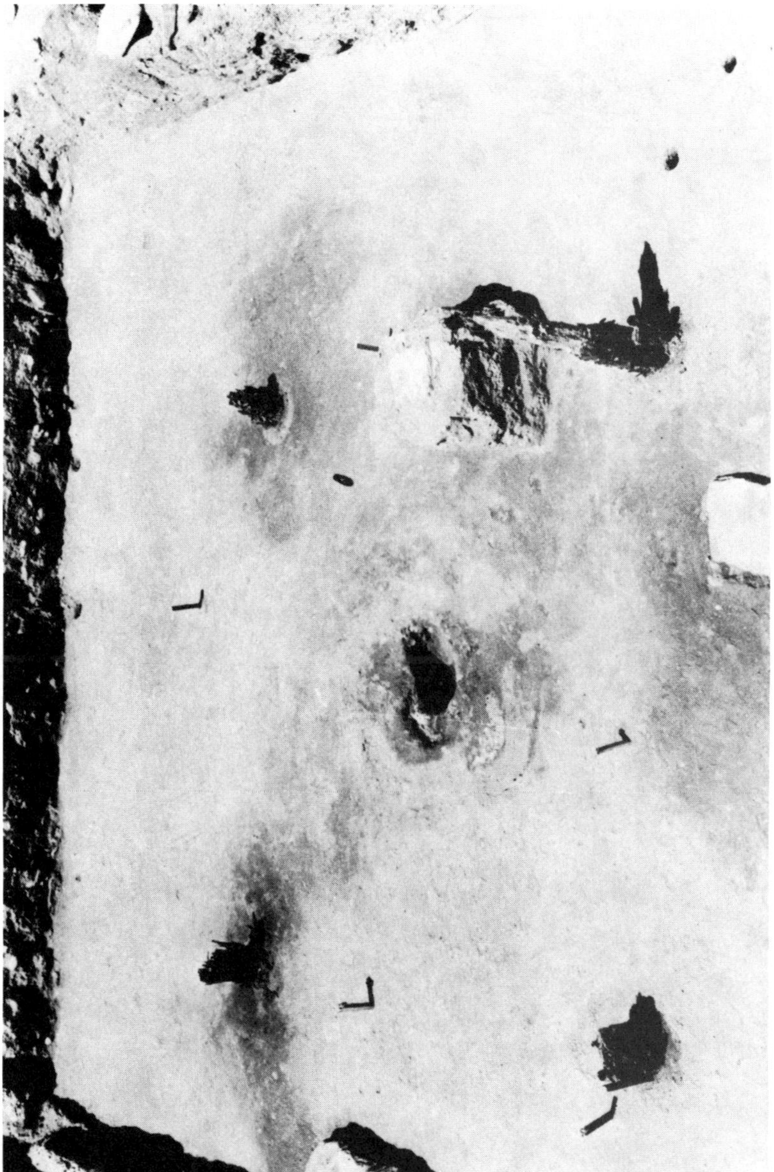

Plate 46. Floor 1, House 13, Bonnell Site.

Plate 47. Floor 4, House 13, Bonnell Site.

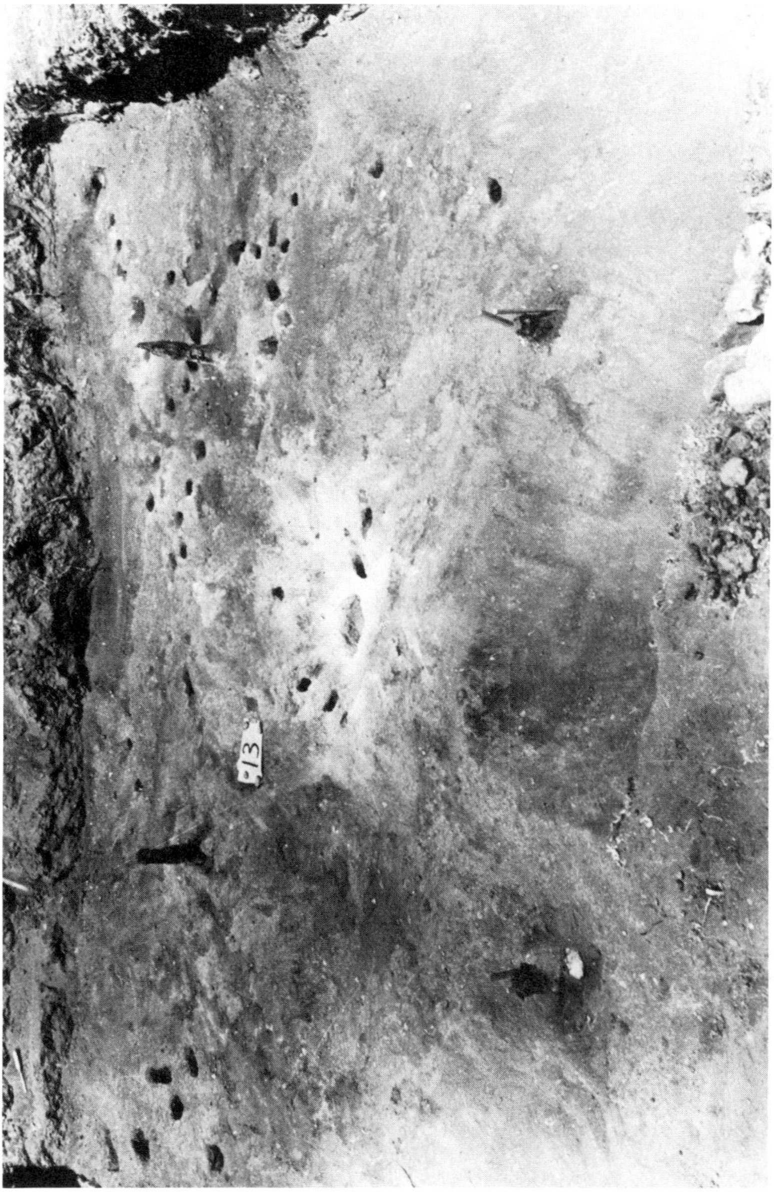

Plate 48. Floor 5, House 13, Bonnell Site.

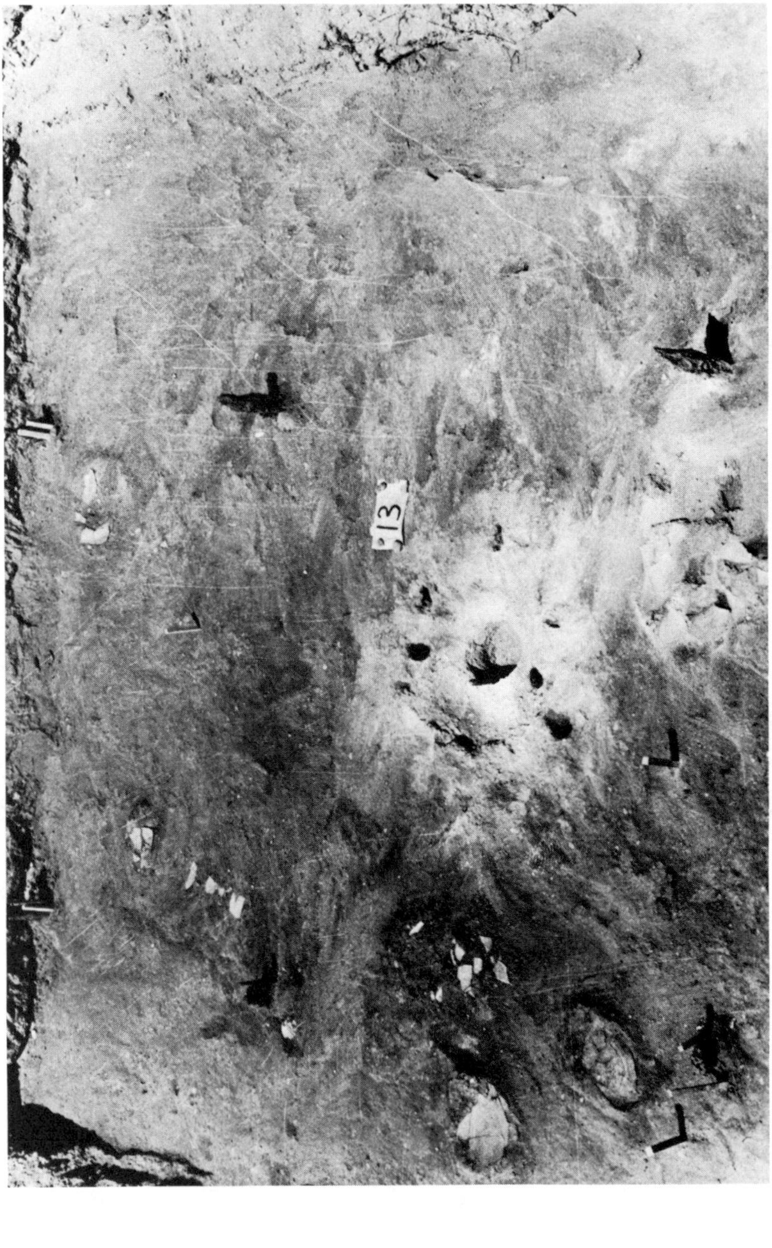

Plate 49. Floor 6, House 13, Bonnell Site.

placed, or else the roof was supported on some of these smaller, irregularly placed posts. Disturbance of the upper floor was so thorough that a pattern could only be tentatively suggested. Two posts about 5 inches in diameter, placed northeast and northwest of the fireplace, may have been part of a four-post system. Seven small posts about 2 inches in diameter and three post holes were found on the north side.

Fire Areas

That of the older house (Floor 1) was a centrally located, shallow, basin-shaped firepit, 8 inches in diameter and 2 inches deep which contained ashes. Floor plaster around the firepit was burned a bright orange. In Floor 2, a circular firepit was surrounded by a clay coping. The pit itself was 10½ inches in diameter and had in-sloping sides; the flat bottom had a diameter of 8 inches. Depth of the pit below the floor was 6 inches. The clay coping was built up 2 to 4 inches above the floor. Caked ashes were 6 inches deep.

Associated Artifacts

Three side-notched points, an elongated triangular point, awls, a scraper and a single mano could be assigned to the older floor (Floor 1). A scapula tool, an awl, a mussel shell pendant and an *Olivella* bead were assigned to the more recent occupation (Floor 2). See Figure 61.

Features under Floor 1

Fill depth was quite uneven. Several posts were sealed under Floor 1. A circular area at the bottom of the deepest fill, 3 feet deep under the southeast corner of Floor 1, may have been an earlier borrow or storage pit. Adjacent to the "borrow pit" and at the same depth, a concentration of 40 small cobbles may have been artificially placed.

House 15

Type

Large, nearly square, individual pithouse (Pl. 50).

House Pit

Depth of the unplastered pit varied from 15 to 20 inches. The old ground surface from which the pit was dug was 18 to 24 inches below the modern surface.

Floor

A sub-floor cut in the southwest corner showed 5 thin layers of clay that had been applied to the floor in this section of the room. The exposed floor was level and smoothly plastered. Sealed sub-floor features may have been present as the remaining floors were not excavated.

Internal Posts and Post Holes

Four large timbers 8 to 14 inches in diameter were centrally located. Five smaller posts were present in the interior.

Roof Construction

Charred, collapsed roofing material was 6 to 12 inches deep over most of the room. A few charred cross timbers had diameters of 5 to 8 inches. A number of small poles, 2 to 3 inches in diameter, were charred and quantities of clay baked when the house burned.

Fire Area

A shallow, cylindrical firepit was centrally located.

Ash Pit

A rectangular slab-lined pit east of the firepit was full of ashes.

Bench (?)

Along the west, a step-back in the pit wall was designated a bench; however, it is now interpreted as a by-product of archaeological procedure.

Storage Pit

In the southwest corner a "niche" or corner wall pit opened in the house wall at floor level and extended back into the gravel some 14 inches (Fig. 70c). Floor plaster extended into its mouth; the pit itself was not plastered. Two large sherds of El Paso Polychrome in the pit contained lumps of soft pinkish clay, two pieces of yellow ochre, and one of red hematite.

Associated Artifacts

Lumps of clay found in the corner storage pit, unfired clay coils found on the floor, smoothing pebbles, and a bone tool may have been employed in pottery manufacture. One projectile point was stemmed. A number of decorative objects were found. A charred wooden bead gave evidence of a normally perishable aspect of craftsmanship. See Figure 62.

House 16

Type

Not known. A small plastered area ca. 6 feet square was exposed around the firepit.

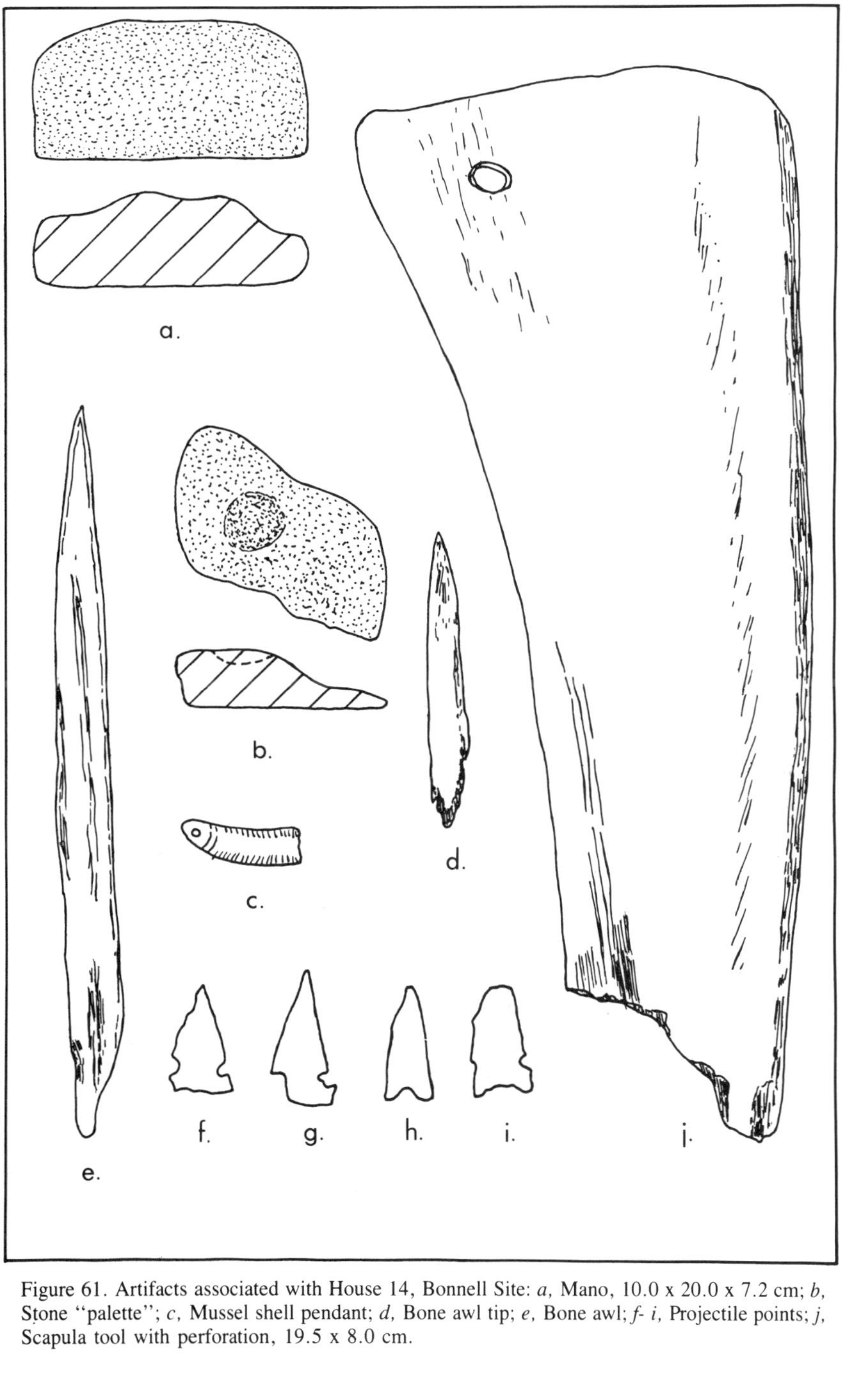

Figure 61. Artifacts associated with House 14, Bonnell Site: *a*, Mano, 10.0 x 20.0 x 7.2 cm; *b*, Stone "palette"; *c*, Mussel shell pendant; *d*, Bone awl tip; *e*, Bone awl; *f*- *i*, Projectile points; *j*, Scapula tool with perforation, 19.5 x 8.0 cm.

Fire Area

A house number was assigned on the basis of the circular firepit which was 12 inches in diameter, 6 inches deep, and which had walls that sloped inward to a flat bottom (Fig. 63c).

Associated Artifacts

A large mano, two projectile points, and a turquoise fragment with a ground edge rested on the floor. A fragment of an eggshell provides a clue to a food resource. See Figure 63.

House 17

Type

No data.

Floors

Two floors belonged to two superimposed structures. Floor 1, 22 inches below the modern surface, was lightly plastered around the firepit. Floor 2, 12 inches below the modern surface, was packed earth. A floor area approximately 12 feet square was exposed for both floor levels.

Internal Posts and Post Holes

Two large charred posts in Floor 1 were the main northwest and southwest supports; the expected eastern supports were absent. No posts or post holes were recognized for the upper floor.

Fire Areas

In Floor 1, a cylindrical firepit opened flush with the floor. A hole in the bottom of the firepit, 2 inches in diameter, contained caked ashes. The upper floor (2) had a shallow basin-shaped firepit. See Figure 71a.

Associated Artifacts

An axe, a shaft-straightener, a scraper, and a cut mussel shell fragment were found on Floor 1. A basin milling stone was sitting just southeast of the firepit on Floor 2; nearby was a one-handed grinding stone. An awl was also found on the upper floor. See Figure 64.

House 18

Type

A surface house with pole walls formed a roughly oval enclosure 12 feet by 14 feet 7 inches.

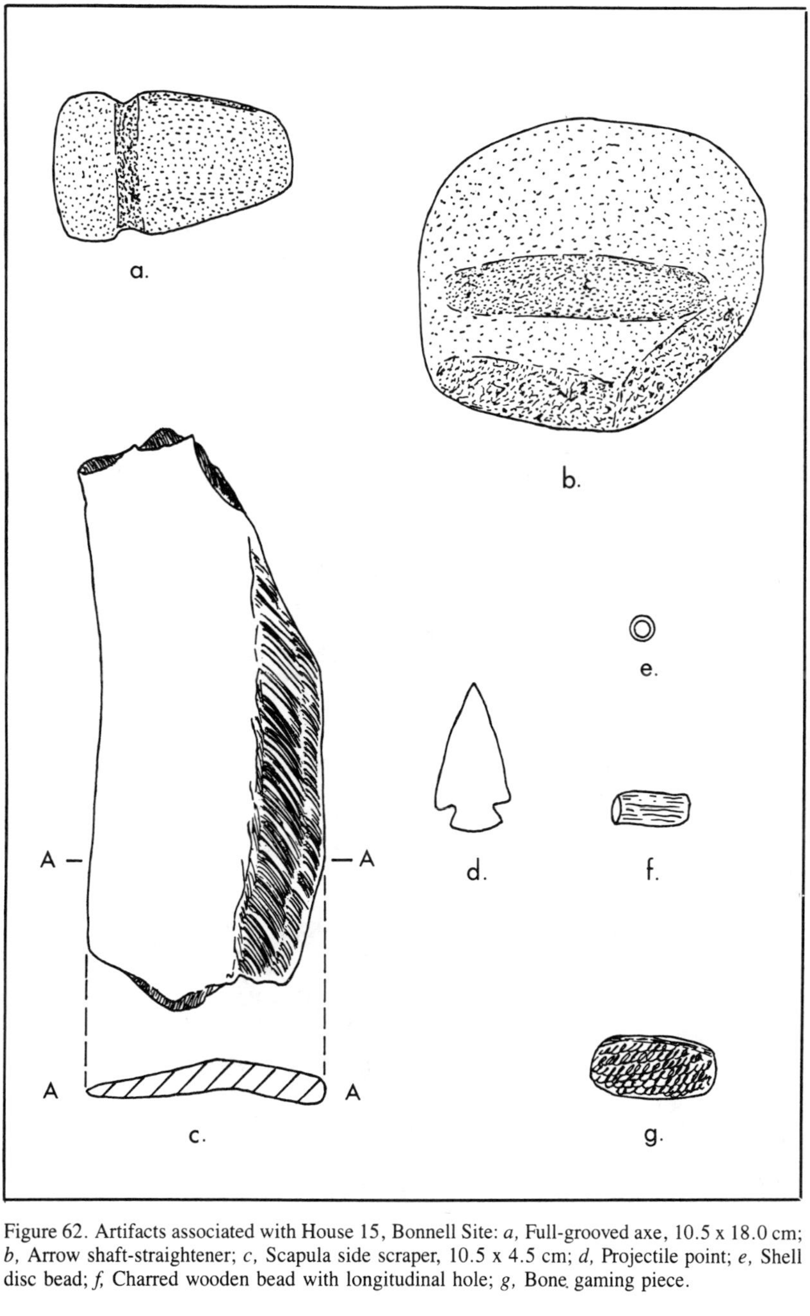

Figure 62. Artifacts associated with House 15, Bonnell Site: *a,* Full-grooved axe, 10.5 x 18.0 cm; *b,* Arrow shaft-straightener; *c,* Scapula side scraper, 10.5 x 4.5 cm; *d,* Projectile point; *e,* Shell disc bead; *f,* Charred wooden bead with longitudinal hole; *g,* Bone gaming piece.

Plate 50. House 15, Bonnell Site.

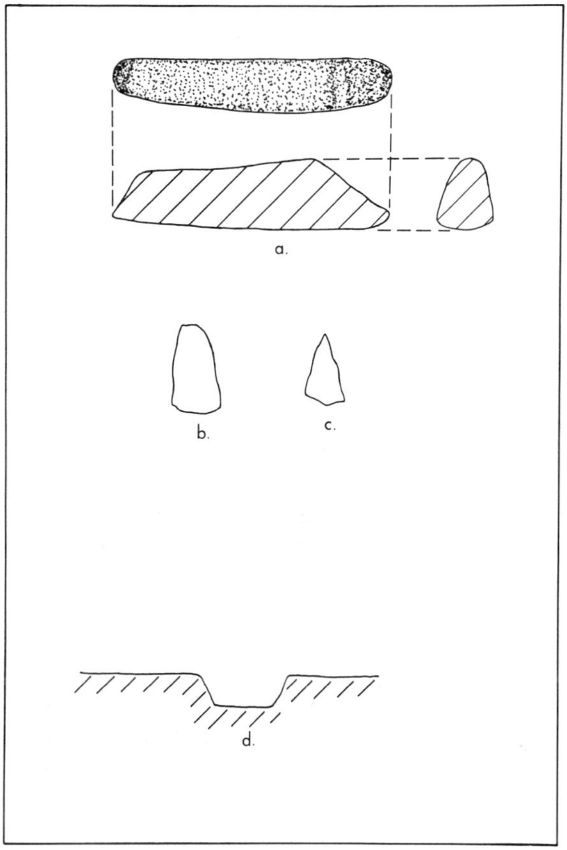

Figure 63. Artifacts and firepit associated with House 16, Bonnell Site: *a,* Large, heavy mano, 6.0 x 30.0 x 8.0 cm; *b* and *c,* Projectile point fragments. *b,* 2.5 x 1.3 cm; *d,* Cross-section of firepit, 12 inches in diameter.

Floor

The packed-earth floor was 6 inches below modern surface.

Internal Posts and Post Holes

Five post holes reaching from the east wall toward the hearth may have been part of an interior windbreak.

Wall Posts and Post Holes

Twenty-five wall post holes arranged in a roughly oval shape were each 2 to 5 inches in diameter and 3 to 6 inches deep.

Entrance

A gap in the wall posts adjacent to the line of interior posts may represent a doorway.

Fire Area

A hearth of fire-cracked rocks was slightly south of center.

Associated Artifacts

A one-handed grinding stone was the only artifact found.

Remarks

This and House 26, the last two structures built at the site, were surface *jacals*.

House 19

Type

The floor outline suggested a pithouse. Proximity and alignment of the house with adjacent House 4 suggested that this house formed part of the west house block composed of contiguous pit rooms, or it may have been an independent structure.

Floor

A large zone south of House 4 was stripped down to this floor level. While no pit walls were detected, the plastered floor of House 19 showed up clearly. The floor plan was almost square with slightly rounded corners.

Internal Posts and Post Holes

Four large centrally-located post holes carried timbers 8 to 10 inches in diameter. No secondary posts were noted.

Entrance

A lateral entry may have been present on the east.

Fire Area

A cylindrical firepit 15 inches deep contained over two gallons of fine ashes (Fig. 70b).

Rock Floor Feature

A large flat rock sat on the floor on the south side of the house.

Associated Artifacts

The only artifact resting on the floor was a splinter awl with a polished tip.

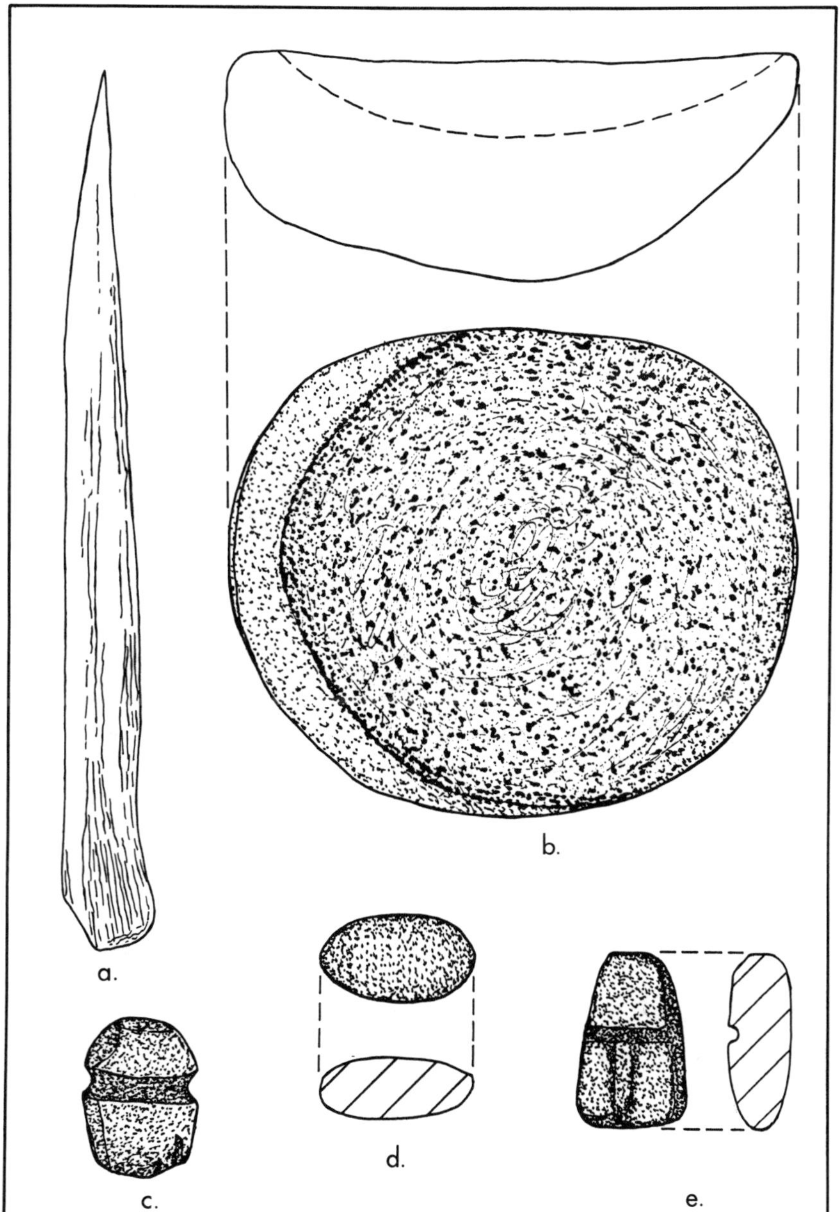

Figure 64. Artifacts associated with House 17, Bonnell Site: *a,* Bone awl, 16.2 x 1.6 cm; *b,* Basin milling stone, 36.0 x 40.5 x 12.0 cm; *c,* Full-grooved axe; *d,* Hand grinding stone; *e,* Arrow shaft-straightener.

House 20

Type

Three floors belonged to two different structures which were not directly superimposed. The lower structure (Floor 1) was a pithouse adjacent to and aligned with House 13; the two houses shared a common wall base on which pole impressions were noted. The new structure pertaining to Floors 2 and 3 was centered several feet east of the earlier structure; it was not determined whether this was a pithouse or surface structure.

House Pit

The first or earlier structure was in a pit 12 to 15 inches deep with unplastered walls. The low dirt wall base between Houses 20 and 13 was 12 to 14 inches thick and about 15 inches high.

Floors

The exposed portion of Floor 1 was level and smoothly plastered. Floors 2 and 3 of the later house were plastered around the firepit.

Internal Posts and Post Supports

None were located for Floor 1. Two small posts pertained to Floors 2 and 3.

Roof Construction

The earlier structure burned and a large section of roofing collapsed in the northwest corner (Fig. 65). Although the later structure did not burn, a number of uncharred beams with an east-west orientation were found above Floor 3.

Fire Area

The center of Floor 1 was not excavated. Floor 2 has a shallow, roughly circular cylindrical pit with a clay curb built around the opening. Floor 3 has an almost identical firepit.

Sub-floor Burial

Burial No. 17 was beneath Floor 1 against the south pit wall.

Associated Artifacts

No artifacts were associated with the part of Floor 1 that was excavated. A full-grooved axe, a side-notched concave base point, a bifacially worked flake, two radius awls, a split awl, and a perforated shell disc made of a heavy shell of an unidentified species were between Floors 2 and 3 (Fig. 66). A metate and three side-notched, straight-based points were on or above Floor 3.

Remarks

The earlier house burned and the building collapsed. A new and less well-made structure, built with its center several feet to the east, was refloored once. The latter structure did not burn.

House 21

Type

No data.

Internal Posts

Several standing posts were associated with a packed-earth floor 9 inches below the modern surface. The structure was not delineated.

Fire Area

A shallow unplastered depression 9 inches in diameter was filled with caked ashes.

Associated Artifacts

A large mano from the excavation unit containing the firepit may belong to this occupation.

Remarks

A house number was assigned on the basis of standing posts and crude fire area.

House 22

Type

Probably a surface *jacal.*

Floor

A packed earth floor, visible in the profile of House 1, was 14 inches below the modern surface.

Wall Posts or Post Holes

Four post holes, observed in the north profile of House 1 close to the northwest corner of that house, had been dug from a surface that could be followed in the profile.

Fire Area

The firepit was 12 inches in diamter, had straight unplastered sides and was

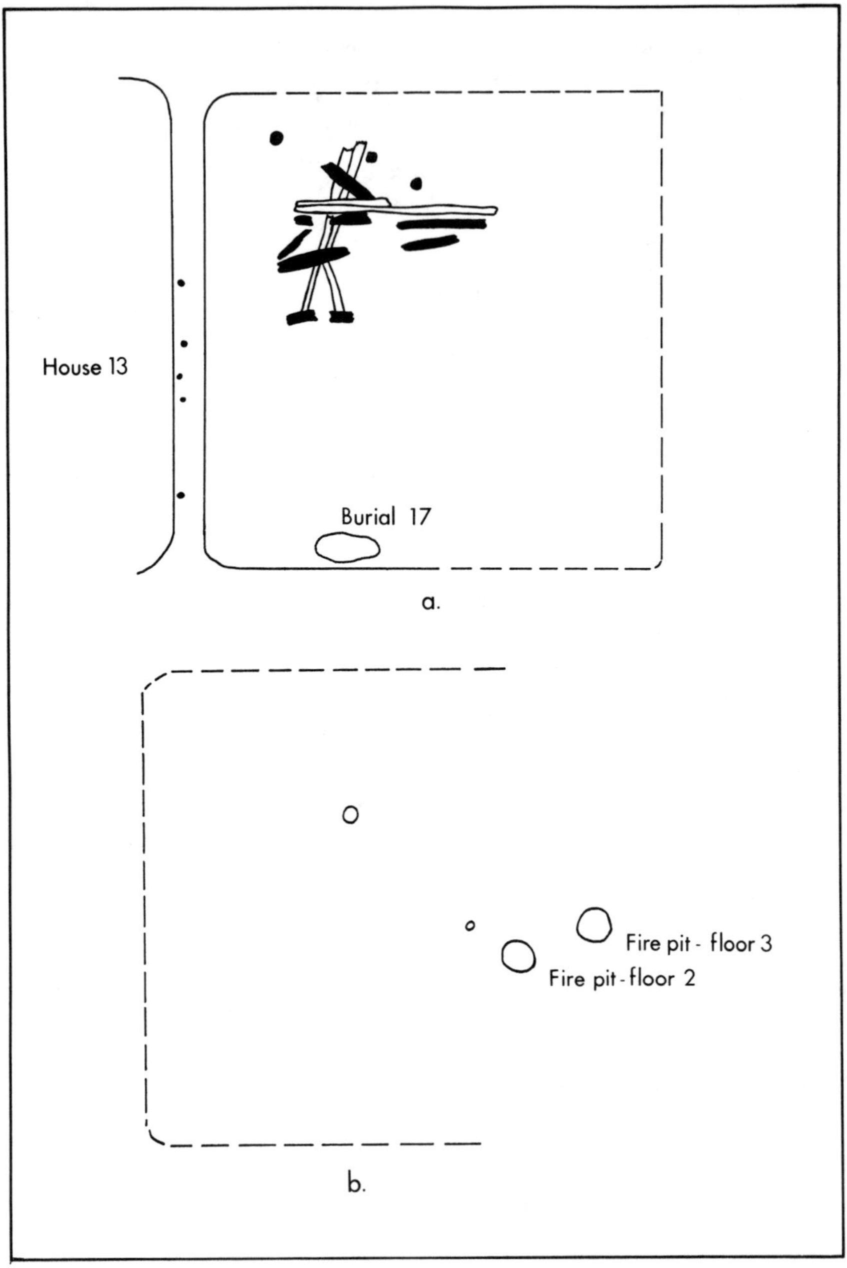

Figure 65. House 20, Bonnell Site: *a,* Plan of roofing timbers and burial associated with Floor 1; *b,* Location of firepits, Floors 2 and 3.

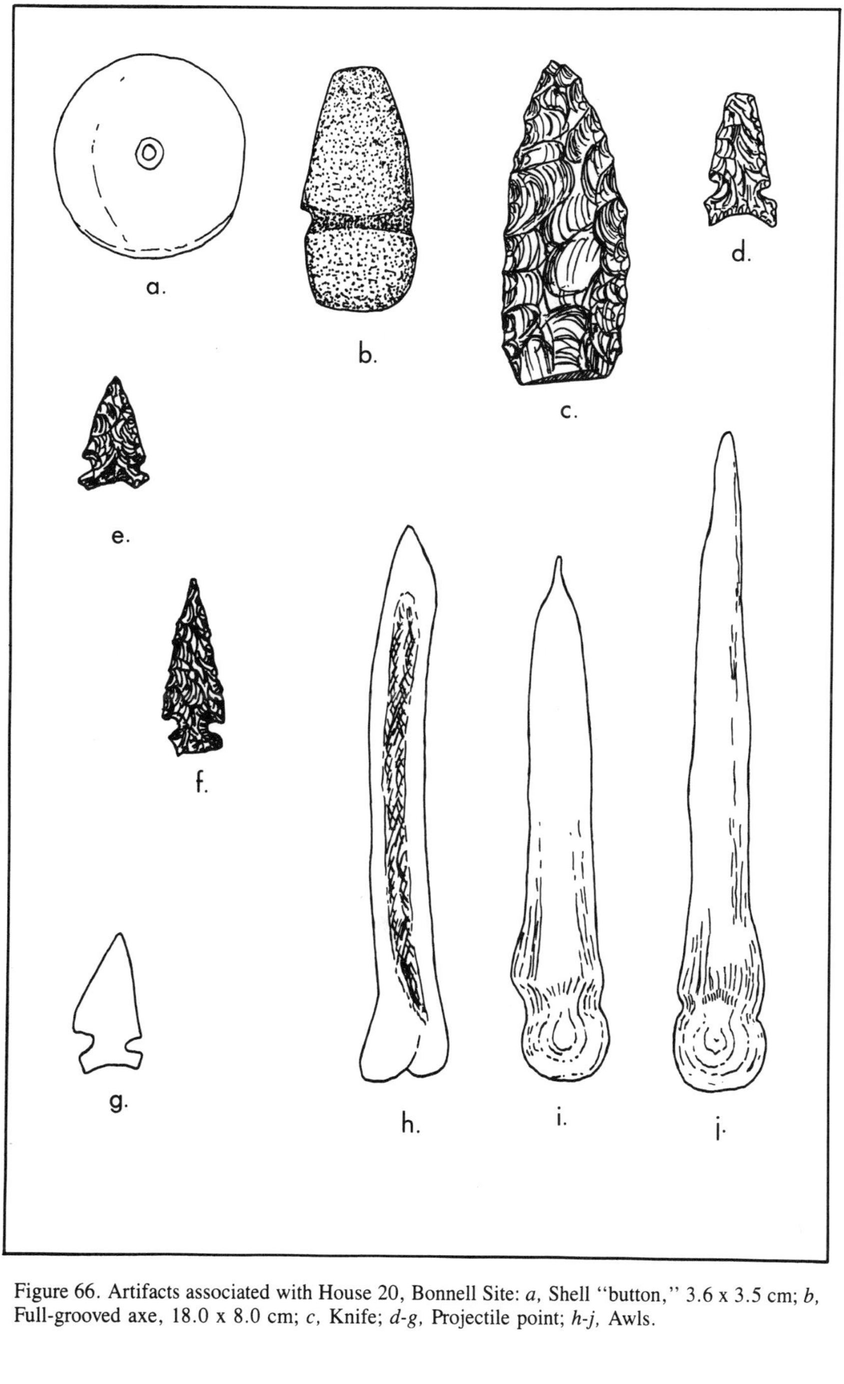

Figure 66. Artifacts associated with House 20, Bonnell Site: *a,* Shell "button," 3.6 x 3.5 cm; *b,* Full-grooved axe, 18.0 x 8.0 cm; *c,* Knife; *d-g,* Projectile point; *h-j,* Awls.

6 inches deep. Ashes were caked in the bottom.

Associated Artifacts

Objects that could have been associated with this house include a "palette" made of a broken metate, a shaft-straightener, a mano fragment, a stone pendant, and a split awl. See Figure 67.

House 23

This ill-defined structure was identified on the basis of a packed-earth floor and two small postholes visible in the upper part of the north wall of House 1 and a small firepit at the same level, located north of House 1. This was a late *jacal* structure that in part extended over House 1 fill. The artifacts associated with this structure are shown in Figure 67.

House 24

A test pit west of House 19 was made to see if structures were present this far west in Mound A. Two well-plastered floors were found. Floor 1 was ca. 36 inches below the modern surface. On top of this was an abundance of charred beams and clay. Floor 2 was 12 inches below the modern surface. A burial (No. 12) had been made from the upper floor.

House 25 (?)

A level clay area and a hearth containing 22 fire-blackened rocks were found 30 inches below the modern surface.

House 26

Type

Surface *jacal* outlined with post holes about three inches in diameter, placed in a roughly rectangular pattern 6 inches below the modern surface.

Wall Post Holes

Small post holes were placed from 8 to 18 inches apart.

Internal Posts and Post Holes

Three post holes were located along the west side of the house, a few inches in from the line of wall posts. Three other small post holes were centrally located.

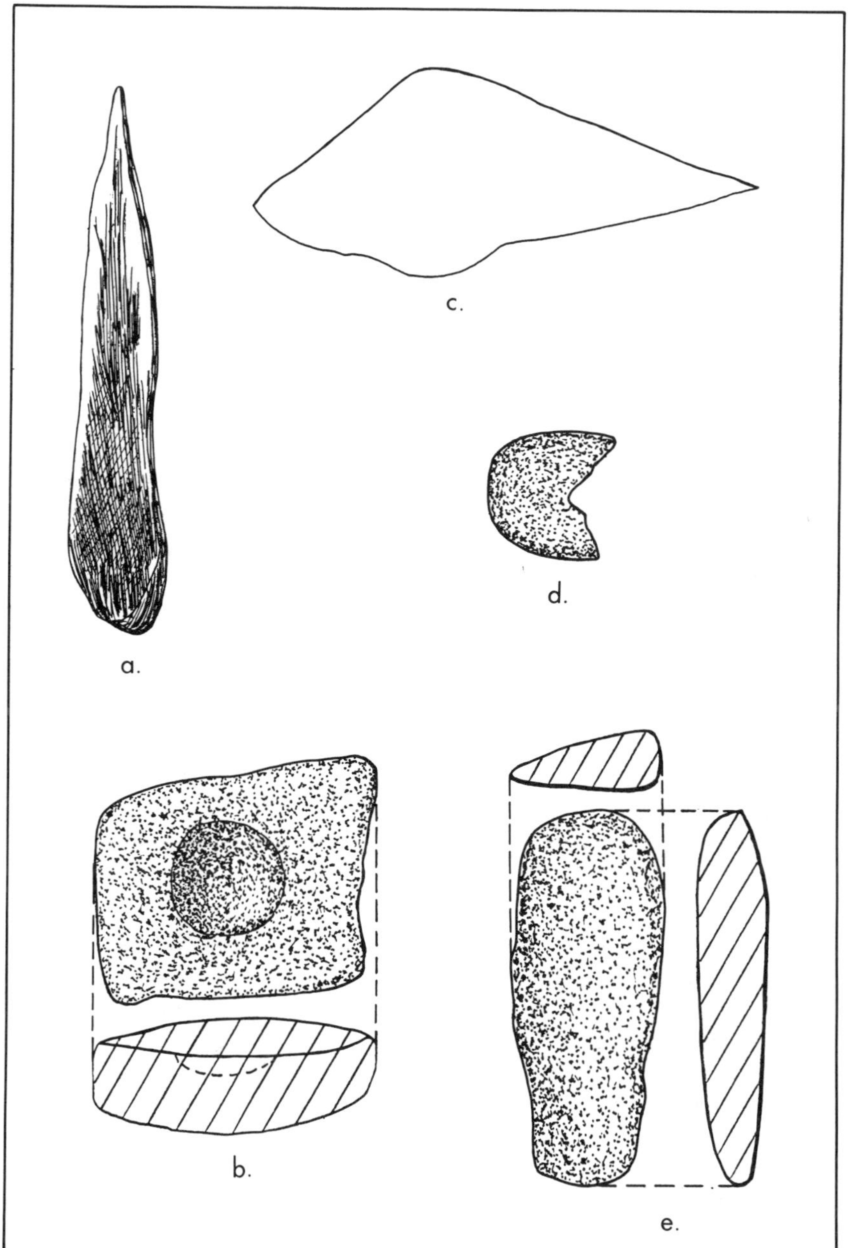

Figure 67. Artifacts associated with House 22, Bonnell Site: *a* and *c*, Bone awls, *a*, 10.0 x 1.8 cm; *b*, Paint "palette," 16.8 x 22.0 x 5.0 cm; *d*, Mano fragment; *e*, Mano.

Fire Area
None.

Entrance
A gap in the post holes in the southwest corner of the south wall may have been an entrance or a doorway.

DISCUSSION OF ARCHITECTURAL FEATURES OF HOUSES

Orientation

Structures often approached a square shape. Walls were usually placed close to the cardinal directions. House 15 departed most noticably from the cardinal placement; it was oriented 8 degrees west of magnetic north. Few entrances have been recognized, and for some houses a roof entrance was indicated. The lateral entrance of House 19 faced east. The surface level doorway of House 26, if one was correctly identified, faced south, as did the possible entrance of House 18.

House Types

Pithouses of medium to shallow depth were constructed along much the same lines as surface *jacales* and very shallow pithouses. Both had walls and roofs of poles covered with earth. The following types have been recognized.

Individual Pithouses
These can be divided on the basis of size, depth of pit, quality of workmanship, and symmetry of supports into:

1. Large pithouses, about 20 feet square, built in pits 15 to 30 inches deep. Major weight-bearing columns were four centrally-located timbers; a firepit was placed near the center of the room. Secondary posts and post holes occurred in the interior and wall posts were sometimes recessed behind the plaster of the pit wall. Houses 1 and 15 were of this type.
2. Smaller pithouses, 10 to 16 feet across, had smaller and more irregularly placed weight-bearing columns. Firepits were centrally located. Houses 5, 6, 12, and 16 were of this type.

Multi-roomed Structures
Pithouses or pit rooms were placed contiguously in pits. All had two, four, or six large internal timbers to support the superstructure. It is postulated that shared walls made of upright poles set on low earth dividing walls were sometimes clay or abode capped. The variety of roof support patterns makes it

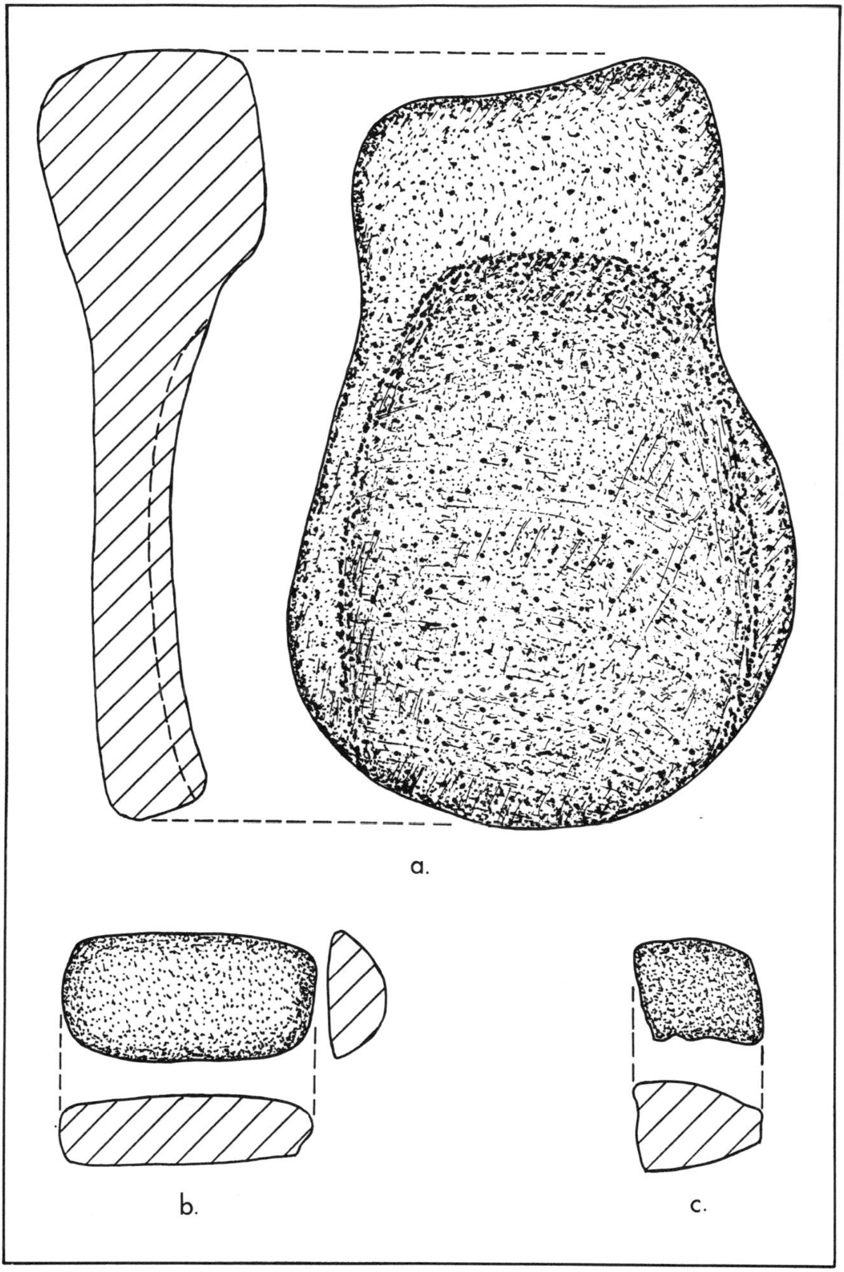

Figure 68. Artifacts associated with House 23, Bonnell Site: *a,* Metate, 56.8 x 39.2 x 16.5 cm; *b,* Mano; *c,* Mano fragment.

likely that flat, gabled, and shed roofs were in use. These structures were located so closely together and the alignment of the houses was so exact that it seems unlikely that each house could have maintained an independent structural existence from the adjacent houses. On the other hand, individual houses

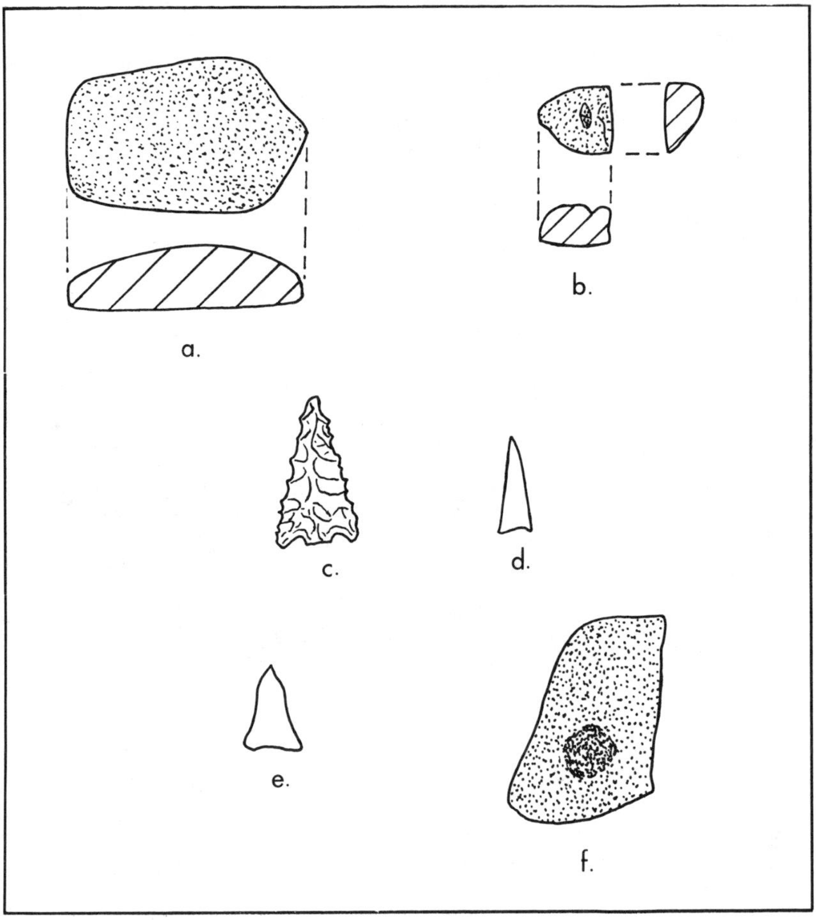

Figure 69. Artifacts associated with Houses 24 and 25, Bonnell Site: *a*, Mano, 11.5 x 18.0 x 5.0 cm; *b*, Arrow shaft straightener fragment, *c-e*, Projectile points, *c*, 2.8 x 1.5 cm; *f*, Stone "palette."

were burned or abandoned while the neighboring house continued to be inhabited. This combination of pithouse concepts in conjunction with the idea of multi-roomed structures represents a clearly defined component within the site.

Jacal Houses

Some of the individual, shallow pithouses may have had vertical pole walls. Houses 7 and 8 of the multi-roomed structures had pole walls set inside a shallow cobble-lined pit. The two surface structures of the last building period had vertical pole walls.

Function

Most or all houses must have been domiciles. There is no structure that is obviously ceremonial in nature. Houses 1 and 15 may have served in that capacity; they are set apart from the other houses by their large size, superior craftsmanship, and location. Their artifactual content was not appreciably different from other structures, and we assume that pottery was manufactured in House 15. The scarcity of storage pits suggests that storage space was allocated within the pithouses, perhaps on racks. House 7, which lacked a firepit, may have been a storage room connected to House 8.

House Pits

The amount of dirt excavated by the native builders in creating house pits varied from an estimate of more than 600 cubic feet in the case of House 1, to perhaps 70 cubic feet or less for the shallower houses. Earlier house pits were dug into native deposits which consisted of an old terrace remnant in which coarse gravel with occasional large cobbles was cross-bedded with clay and sand and the 0 to 3 inches of top soil that had developed above the terrace deposits. Some of the later houses were dug into cultural fill. Pit interiors were sometimes plastered, but more often they were left unplastered.

Floors

House 1, 13 (Floors 1 and 2), and 15 had a heavy layer of clay spread over the floor to produce a smooth, flat surface. A more sparing use of clay was seen in most of the smaller, shallower structures, some of which had clay plaster applied around the central firepit, leaving packed earth at the periphery of the floor. In at least one case, the builders partially cut their pit into a clay deposit which was used as part of the floor.

Internal Posts and Post Holes

Large houses had four, large, centrally-located posts as basic weight-bearing columns, but these were often supplemented by additional posts of various diameters. The placement of posts was more erratic in smaller houses since the weight to be supported was not so great; these posts seldom had a diameter of more than 6 inches. It can be assumed that the larger timbers, especially when symmetrically located, are roof supports. The function of the numerous smaller, internally-located posts is less certain. They could have served as roof braces or interior furnishings.

Wall Posts and Post Holes

Excavation did not reveal wall posts for all of the houses, but this reflects the amount of disturbance the site had experienced and the archaeological techniques employed. The presence of small post holes just outside the House 13 pit, just inside the shallower house pits of Houses 7 and 8, and in the clay-capped wall base between Houses 2 and 3 showed that certain structures had walls made of small upright poles, 2 to 4 inches in diameter, placed at 3 to 18 inch intervals. Posts placed on the pit edge may have slanted toward the roofing cross beams. Wall posts placed at floor level produced a vertical wall. Some of the later, more flimsy structures may have been partially open, like arbors. Large quantities of clay in the collapsed structures make it likely that pole walls were coated with clay.

Roof Construction

Flat, gabled, and shed roofs could have been built. Four centrally-located posts presumably carried flat roofs, or, if one pair of posts was slightly higher, a pitched or slanted roof would have provided better drainage. Two and six supports imply a gable construction in individual structures, but their use in multi-roomed house units introduces other engineering problems. The two cases of six-post supports occur in the middle pithouses of the multi-roomed blocks where additional weight-bearing columns could have been created, if any of the weight of adjacent structures was carried by the middle house. The two-post support system of House 9 probably supported a shed roof that headed against House 13.

Entrances

House 19 apparently had a lateral entrances on the east. The lack of entrances in other pithouses may be a reflection of archaeological technique. We made a real effort to locate entrances in Houses 1, 13, and 15, without luck. Gaps in the post pattern of Houses 18 and 26 were assumed to be entrances, and the internal poles in the former house may have created a wind break and entryway.

Fire Areas

With the exception of Houses 7, 12, and 26, all recognized structures had some centrally-located place where fire was customarily built. The presence of

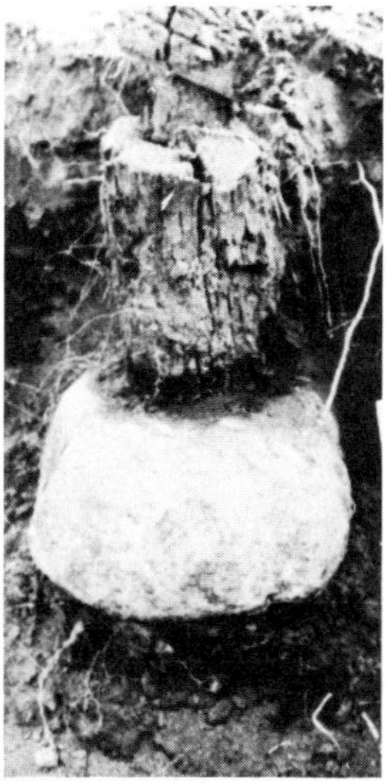

Plate 51. Posts set on a stone footing, Bonnell Site.

a firepit was, in some instances, the major stimulus to defining an incompletely excavated or partially destroyed house. There are probably no functional differences between the different kinds of internally-located firepits; a functional difference is seen between the internal firepits and outdoor hearths. Two houses that lacked firepits had an area in the center of the room where fire had been built. None had a pit diameter of more than 15 inches, and some were as small as 6 inches across. In two cases, a clay rim was built around the firepit when a new floor was laid down, thus increasing the overall floor space devoted to the fire area. Other clay copings were a part of the initial firepit design.

The following shapes occurred: (1) Basin-shaped. (2) Circular pits in which the depth was equal to or greater than the diameter. These were cylindrical pits with flat bottoms, cylindrical pits with rounded bottoms, cylindrical pits with an "ash shelf" (House 13 only); and pits with in-sloping walls. (3) Circular pits in which the diameter was greater than the depth. These were stratigraphically superimposed over older, deeper firepits in Houses 2, 3, and 9. (4) Rough clay curbs built on the floor.

Ash Pits

Two slab-lined pits were found; one contained ashes and the other did not. Two of the firepits of House 13 had an ash shelf built into the firepit.

Bench (?)

House 15 is the only structure that possibly had a bench; the questionable feature, about 12 inches high and 6 to 8 inches wide, was located at the west side of the square pithouse.

Sub-floor Pits

One sub-floor pit was recognized (House 12). It was small, unplastered, roughly shaped, and dug into native gravel.

Recess in House Pit Wall

A pit or recess opened at the floor and extended back into the southwest corner of the pit wall of House 15 (Fig. 70).

Floor Depressions

Shallow floor depressions occurred in Houses 1 and 8. All were devoid of clues as to their function.

Sub-floor Burials

These will be discussed in the section on burials.

FEATURES LOCATED OUTSIDE HOUSES

Hearths of Fire-cracked Rocks

These were usually located outside of house structures; however, Houses 18 and 25 had interior hearths. Fire-cracked limestone fragments varied in size from under 1 inch in diameter to 6 inches in length. Hearths were contained in shallow, basin-shaped depressions. Dimensions ranged in size from about 12 inches across to slightly over 3 feet. Larger hearths had up to 400 fire-cracked limestone pieces. Hearths usually lacked animal bones or artifacts.

Storage Pits

These are no more abundant outside of houses than inside. One small storage pit found just south of the south wall of House 8 was shallow and unplastered. A number of crushed, fire-blackened pots were stacked inside. The circular pit remnant underlying House 14 could have been a borrow pit for clay or a storage pit. If the latter, it was the only substantial storage pit at the site. However, since it was dug into a good clay deposit, the borrow pit interpretation is preferred.

Posts and Post Holes

Several hundred posts and post holes were found which have not been assigned to structures. Some belonged to incompletely delineated houses.

Burials

Burials occurred between houses as well as beneath floors; these are discussed in the section on burials.

SUMMARY STATEMENT ON ARCHITECTURE

Individual pithouses showed variation in size, depth of pit, and craftsmanship that probably reflected the individual ability of the builders, minor functional differences that are not clear from the archaeological record, and perhaps even minor social differences of the population. Nevertheless, these houses belong to a single building tradition which was expressed in rectangular to square pithouses with internal timbers used to support the considerable weight of the superstructure. Central firepits were typical. Equally important was the absence or scarcity of certain traits such as lateral entrances, antechambers, bell-shaped pits, ventilators, deflectors, and easily indentifiable ceremonial architecture. The peculiar combination of pithouses placed together to form multi-room houses was structurally much weaker than either individual pithouses or solid-wall multi-room structures. The pithouses used in these multi-roomed structures were so similar to the individual pithouses at the site that, apparently, an idea about multi-room housing was tried by pithouse dwellers and then discarded. Individual pithouses reappear later in the history of the site.

ARTIFACTS

The described specimens include all those transported to the laboratory, as well as adequately described artifacts not available for study. This does not represent the total of excavated specimens because certain artifact categories such as hammerstones, worked flakes, polishing pebbles, and so forth were sacked in the field without being entered in the field notebooks. Sacks from

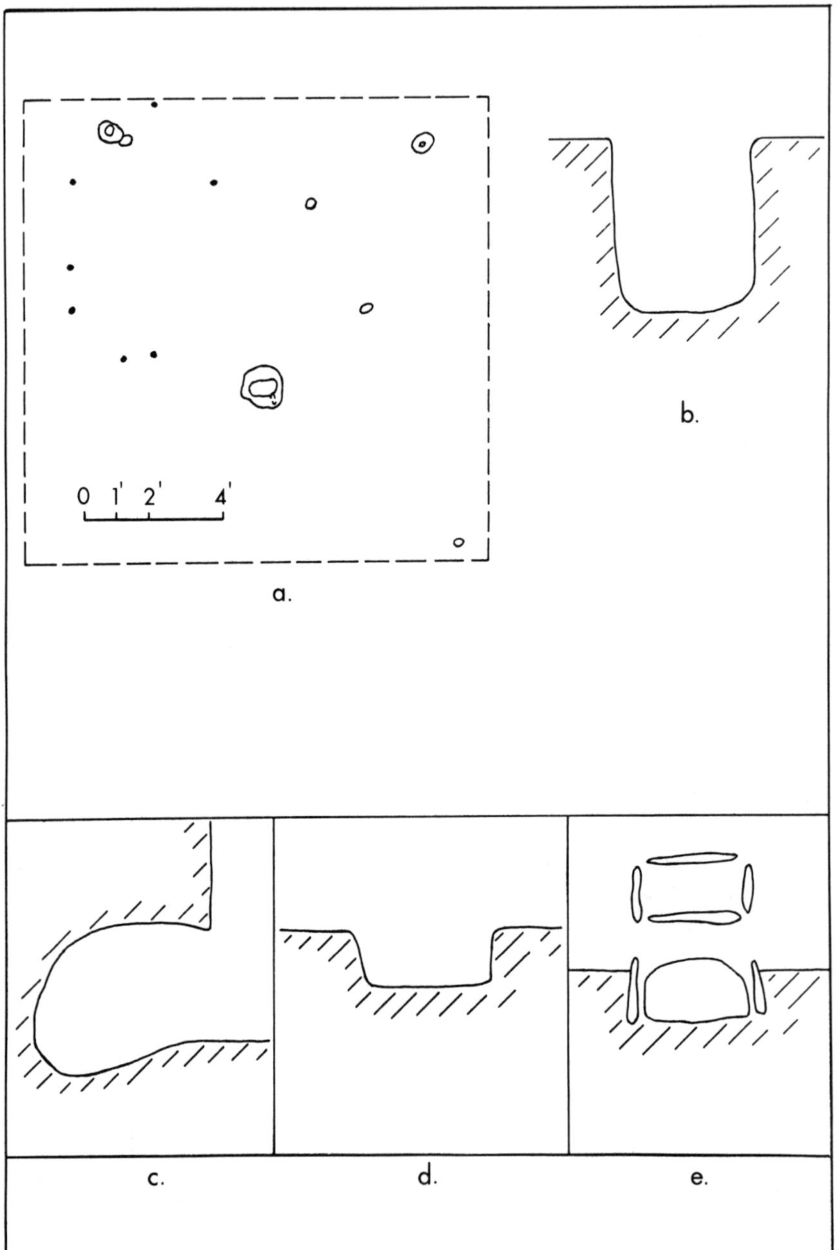

Figure 70. Architectural details of Houses 14, 19, and 15, Bonnell Site: *a,* Plan of Floor 2, House 14; *b,* Cross-section of firepit, House 19, 15 inches deep; *c,* Cross-section of niche that opens at floor level, House 15, 14 inches deep; *d,* Cross-section of firepit, House 15; *e,* Top and side views of ash pit, House 15.

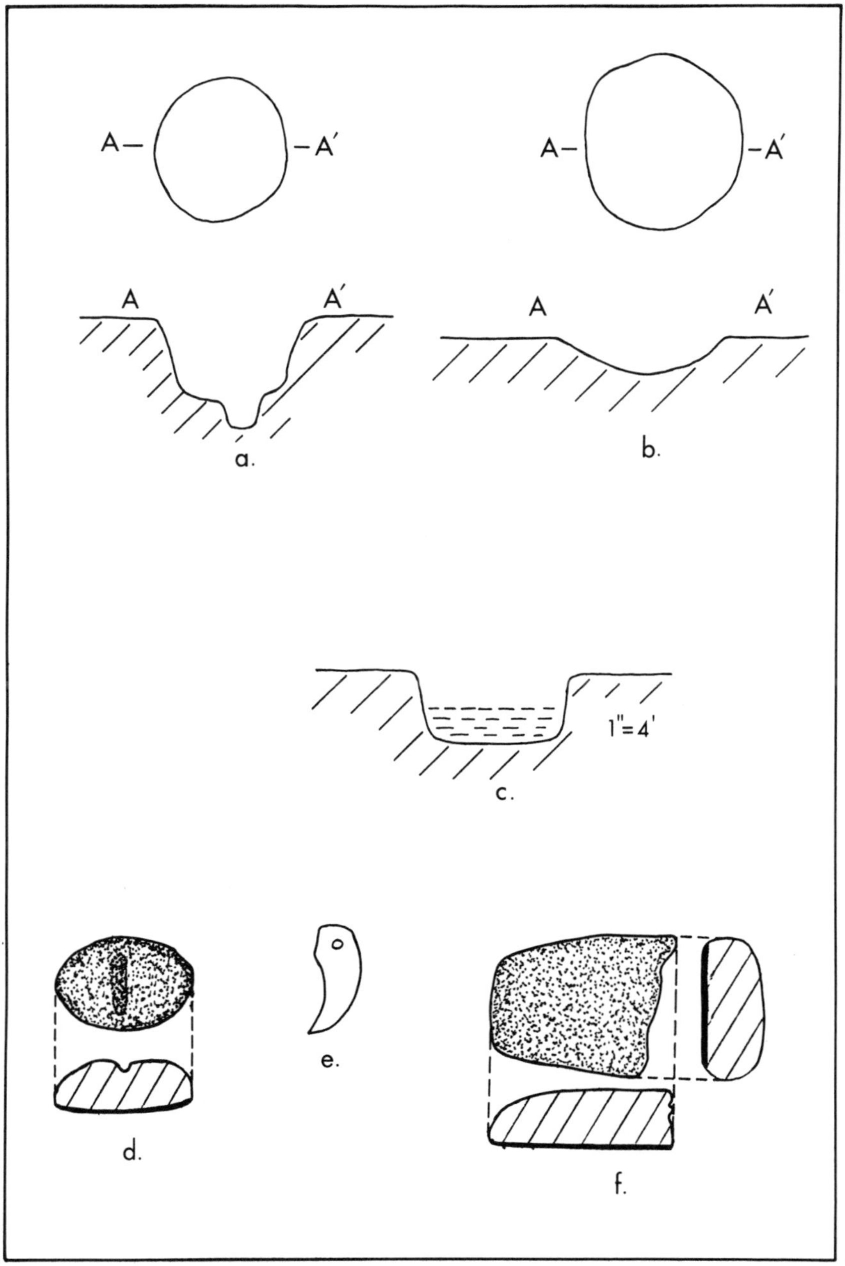

Figure 71. Associated artifacts and architectural details, Houses 17 and 22, Bonnell Site: *a,* Top view and cross-section, firepit, Floor 1, House 17; *b,* Top view and cross-section, firepit, Floor 2, House 17; *c,* Cross-section of firepit, House 22, 12 inches in diameter; *d,* Arrow shaft-straightener from House 22, 7.2 x 10.0 x 4.0 cm; *e,* Stone pendant, House 22, 1.9 x 0.9 cm; *f,* Mano fragment, House 22.

the first season's work, temporarily stored in the field, were badly damaged, and much of that material was not available for laboratory analysis.

Ground-stone Tools

Initial selection of the stone or pebble was instrumental in determining the final shape of most stone tools; few specimens were worked so completely that the original shape of the stone could not be detected. See Table 26.

Metates

Nine complete specimens of the one-end-closed trough type with "mano rests" ranged from 12 to 24 inches in length (Pl. 52). Troughs 1 to 3 inches deep had the deepest part developed close to the closed end. Three specimens had been well shaped on their sides and bottom by pecking. One of three slab metates with flat to slightly concave grinding surfaces had an incipient mano rest.

Milling Stones

Three basin-shaped milling stones were used with an elliptical motion, presumably for processing wild plant products, following the suggestion of Krieger (1945:51). The basin occupied as much of the stone as was consistent with obtaining a circular or elliptical depression. These specimens varied from 15 to 20 inches in their largest dimension. One had a "mano rest."

Manos and Hand Grinding Stones

No distinction can be made between these two categories since the specimens were left in the field and the field catalogue was inadequate on this point. Of the 121 recorded specimens, measurements are available for 75. The measured groups shows two size clusters, with a definite break at 6 inches.

Nineteen specimens, 22% of the measured sample, were less than 6 inches in length; these are tentatively called hand grinding stones. Eleven of these were unshaped except for a nearly flat grinding surface; one had a convex grinding surface, and six had been shaped toward rectangular forms. One of the latter had two grinding surfaces.

The group of larger manos was from 6 to 13½ inches in length. Fifty-two whole specimens were available, and an additional 15 fragments may be typed. The most common forms had tapered ends (Pl. 53c). The single grinding surface, nearly flat in side view, was convex in cross-section. Ends curved up to fit the trough in the metate. The largest specimens were deeper than they were wide and quite heavy. Four of this group had multiple grinding surfaces; two had two ground surfaces and two had three ground surfaces.

Ten flat, elongated manos (Pl. 54b) were much lighter in weight than the

TABLE 26
GROUND-STONE OBJECTS,
BONNELL SITE

Artifacts	No.
Metates	
Trough with mano rest	9
Slab	3
Fragments	9
Total	21
Basin milling stones	3
Manos and hand grinding stones	
Less than 6″ in length	19
Over 6″ in length	
Nearly flat grinding faces with tapered ends and convex upper surfaces	45
Thin, flat	10
Pronounced convex grinding faces	10
Fragments	37
Total	121
Pestles	3
'Palettes' with depressions	8
Shallow stone bowls or mortars	2
Axes (full-grooved)	14
Maul (full-grooved)	1
Club or full-grooved hammer	1
Shaft-straighteners	15
Polished pebbles	15
Ornaments	
Turquoise	4
Other stone	3
Gypsum	1
Stone pipes	3
Miscellaneous pebbles	8

series described above. Ten other manos had pronounced convex grinding surfaces.

Condition of Food Processing Tools

None were worn out although many were broken. None of the manos had faceted grinding surfaces.

Provenience of Food Grinding Tools

Three of the complete metates were in House 13, two definitely lying on different floors, and one in the fill above the floors. It was probable that metates or milling stones rested on the floors of Houses 4, 5, and 17. It was less certain that the metates from Houses 7 and 25 were actually on the floors.

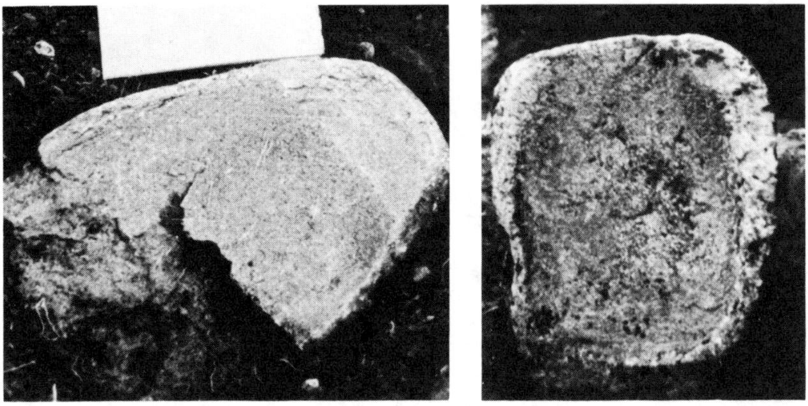

Plate 52. Metates *in situ*, Bonnell Site.

An additional four complete metates were found outside of any recognized structure. The metate above the collapsed roofing material of House 1 may been been sitting on the roof. The possibility of using the rooftops for domestic activities was further supported by the large mano lying among the charred roof timbers of House 2.

A substantial number of the whole grinding stones were inside houses. If their orientation in the house reflects the position they occupied when in use, they could be placed anywhere around the room. They were mobile and probably were leaned against the wall on occasion. We found no evidence that they were propped up to give a better grinding angle.

Pestles

Three specimens about 4 inches long were round to oval in cross-section (Pl. 53a, artifact D).

"Palettes"

Shallow depressions in a larger block of stone with a flat area around the depression are called "palettes." Eight such objects were found (Pl. 53a, artifact A). One was made on a metate fragment with the depression in the old grinding surface. The upper surface of a broken loaf-shaped mano was the setting for a small circular depression. In this case, the surface surrounding

Plate 53. Stone tools, Bonnell Site.

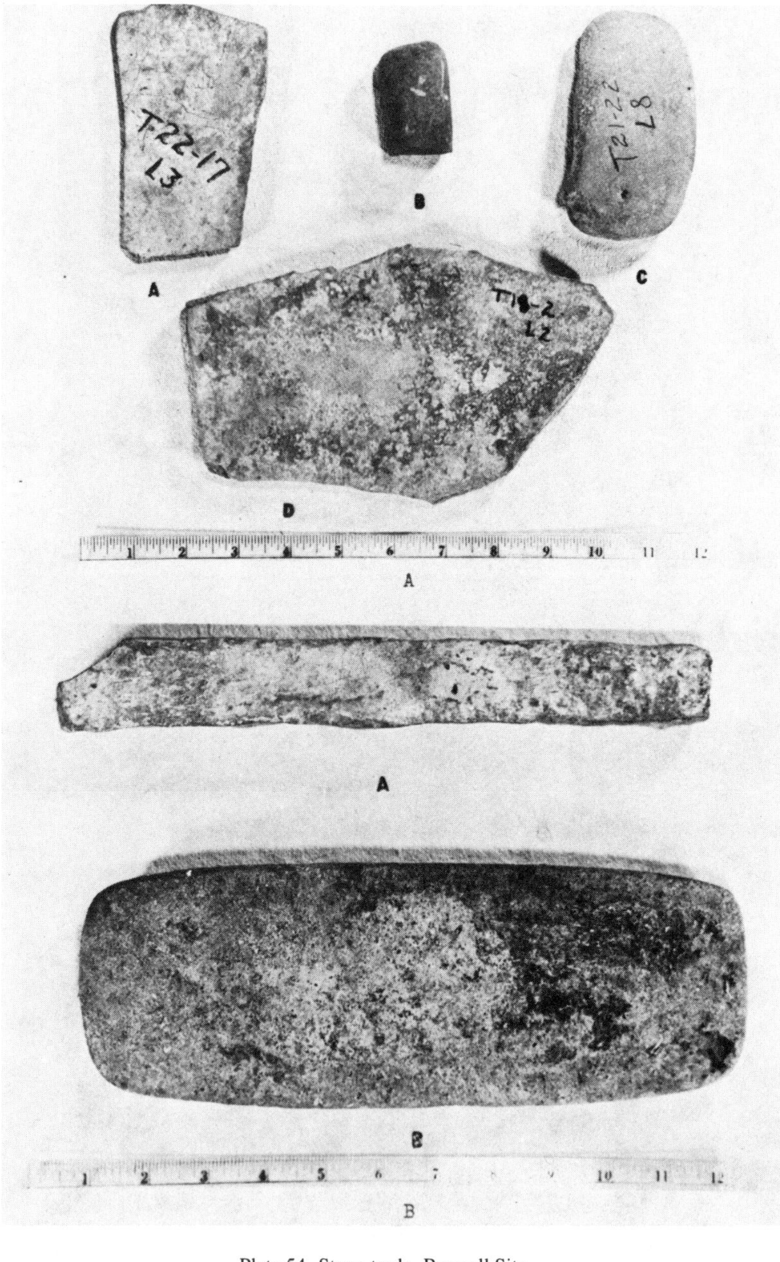

Plate 54. Stone tools, Bonnell Site.

had been ground flat. Five flat cobbles had depressions of various sizes and shapes placed into a smoothed surface. All were flat enough on the bottom to sit in a stable position. The stones varied in thickness from 1½ to 4½ inches. The depressions were from ⅜ to ⅝ inch deep. Three had round depressions from 3 to 4 inches in diameter; one had a square depression 3 inches across, and one had an elongated depression 2½ by 3½ inches. Two depressions were in a basalt cobble that was ground flat on top and bottom surfaces; a circular depression 3 inches in diameter was on one side, and a smaller depression 1⅛ inch in diameter was on the reverse side.

Paint (red ochre) adhered to only two of the specimens. In one case, there was a large red ochre stain on the flat surface of the stone, and a faint stain in the depression. In the other case, the stain was on the flat surface. Paint stains on flat surfaces may come from the dry grinding of pigment while the depressions were used to suspend the pigment in water. If they were washed out, little evidence would be left.

Shallow Stone Bowls or Mortars

The size and depth of the depression was within the range of those in "palettes," however the stones were shaped to create walls about 1 inch thick. Only two examples were found. One was 5 inches long, 4 inches wide, and 1¾ inches deep. The other was a fragment of comparable size.

Axes

Fourteen axes ranged in length from 4½ to 7 inches. The groove, from ¾ to 1⅜ inches wide, was placed from 1½ inches to 2 inches in front of the butt end. Length of the face from groove to bit varied from 1¼ to 4¼ inches. This variation in proportion of poll to face length would have affected the balance of the hafted product.

Grooves were first pecked and then ground fairly smooth. Grooves were shallow over the face of the axe, being no more than ⅛ inch deep, whereas the depression on the edges was deeper. Grooves usually have a shallow, curved profile; however, one axe had a wide, deep, squared groove.

Four of the axes showed asymmetrical or rounded polls due to the original shape of the pebble. Other specimens showed a high degree of craftsmanship and overall symmetry.

The thickest portion of the axes was located between the front of the groove and the butt of the poll. Maximum width of the axes varied from the poll to just in front of the groove. None of the axes had a shoulder.

Five axes showed signs of long and faithful service. Eight had only a few nicks removed from the bit, and one was brand new. The latter, fashioned of a compact green stone, was lying with a slightly used axe on the same surface with, and 8 feet away from, two other well-used specimens.

Provenience of Axes

Five houses had a single axe on the floor. In three cases, two axes were found together, suggesting that one man, or at least one household, frequently owned several axes.

Mauls

A maul, fully grooved at the midpoint, was nearly circular in outline and oval in cross-section. The poll, groove, and face were well polished. The blunt bit was well battered.

Club or Grooved Hammer

A well battered, roughly spherical specimen, fully grooved at the midpoint, was made of igneous rock (Pl. 53a, artifact C).

Shaft-straightener

In view of Woodbury's complaint (1954:104) that the distribution of grooved abraders is difficult to establish in the Southwest because archaeologists do not give enough information, it is well to record that none were found at Bonnell. Fifteen shaft-straighteners were found. Seven had pigment somewhere on their surfaces. Grooves, slightly convex in all specimens, ranged in width from ½ to ⅞ of an inch, in depth from 1/32 to ½ inch, and in length from 1 to 3 inches. Several descriptive categories have been set up:

A. *Transverse Groove*

1. Oval-shaped shaft-straighteners had a flat, ground bottom surface and gently rounded upper surface. Oval pebbles were selected that needed little or no shaping to give a fairly symmetrical outline. The transverse groove was placed at the middle of the stone. This type was 4 to 5 inches long, 3 to 3¾ inches wide, and 1½ to 3 inches thick. Three specimens were found.

2. Elongated shaft-straighteners that were roughly triangular in cross-section. The bottom was either naturally flat or ground flat. By selecting triangular pebbles, a natural ridge was formed down the length of the stone. The transverse groove was typically 1 to 2 inches long. This group was asymmetrical and crude looking. Complete specimens ranged in length from 3¼ to 6 inches. It is probable that the selection of elongated triangular pebbles was no accident, and that the natural ridge may have had a practical function corresponding to that of intentionally ridged shaft-straighteners. Five specimens were found.

3. Shaft-straighteners with a pentagonal cross-section. One specimen had the base and two slightly oblique sides ground flat. The other two sides converged to form the keeled upper surface containing the tranverse groove.

4. Loaf-shaped shaft-straightener. One specimen was rectangular in outline and cross-section.

5. Shaft-straightener with two transverse grooves. One squarish pebble with parallel transverse grooves was otherwise unshaped except for the customary ground bottom.

6. Ridged forms of shaft-straighteners. The flat upper surface had a single ridge perpendicular to, and at the midpoint of, the transverse groove. These were carefully shaped all over. Two specimens were found.

B. *Longitudinal Groove*

1. On pebbles. One small, oval pebble with a groove that ran the length of the pebble had a well-ground bottom (Fig. 62b). Another specimen, made of a roughly square pebble, had an unusually shallow groove (1/32 inch deep).

2. Loaf-shaped. A single well-shaped specimen was the only shaft-straightener that could possibly be used as one of a pair.

Provenience of Shaft-straighteners: Single specimens were found on Floor 1 of House 17 and the floors of House 15, House 24, and House 4. The other eleven were concentrated in the uppermost or most recent fill. Three specimens clustered in a small area on the north edge of the site.

Polished Pebbles

Small, colorful pebbles of fine-grained stone showed the effects of polishing on one or two facets. Fifteen pebbles ranging from 1 to 2½ inches in length showed moderate amounts of polishing; none were faceted. It is generally assumed that these pebbles were used to polish pottery. The battered end of two specimens and the suggestion of red pigment on another indicate that they also served other functions.

Provenience of Polishing Pebbles: Eight of these polishers were found in fill. Two were on the floor of House 15, which is the house where unfired clay coils and a lump of clay were found. Two were found on the floor of House 8, one was on the floor of House 1, and one was possibly associated with House 12.

Miscellaneous Small Pebbles

Tiny striations were visible on a fine-grained sedimentary pebble that had been ground flat on one surface; the other surface was polished and the edges had been ground perpendicular to the axis of the pebble. Six broken jasper and flint pebbles showed polishing. Three had a single break, as though a tiny pebble had been halved. Two resembled thick wedges of a Gouda cheese. Four were from the fill of House 1 and one was on the floor of that house. An angular six-faceted quartz pebble had well-smoothed edges.

Stone Pipes

An elbow pipe made of fine-grained stone, perhaps siltstone, had a stem 3 inches long; the bowl, which was 1 15/16 inches high, had an outside diameter of ⅞ inch at the mouth (Pl. 53, center photo).

Two fragments of tubular stone pipes each had a maximum diameter of ½ inch.

Stone Ornaments

A rectangular stone pendant of fine-grained limestone had a biconical hole at one end for suspension; the upper edge of the suspension hole was well worn. The pendant was 1 11/16 inches long, 1⅝ inches wide, and 9/32 inch thick. The back surface was ground flat, while the upper surface was slightly convex. The lower edge had some small chips. Surface decoration on the upper face consisted of two drilled depressions and an engraved line, so placed that if you turn the pendant upside-down, a crude face can be seen. When wet, two faint circles (⅜ inch in diameter) appear around the dots that are interpreted as eyes, suggesting that the pendant was once painted (Pl. 62a).

Turquoise is not abundant at the site. A pendant with a biconical suspension hole was found beneath the floor of House 10 (Pl. 62g). Stanley Stubbs believed that this piece of turquoise came from Oro Grande (personal communication). An unperforated, rectangular, well-polished turquoise object found amid the rib bones of Burial 20 was ⅜ inch long, ¼ inch wide, and 1/32 inch thick (Fig. 57*l*). A triangular turquoise bead, 3/32 inch across and 1/16 inch thick, had a tiny hole drilled at the center (Fig. 45g). A small, unworked chunk of turquoise was found. A small fragment of turquoise with a ground edge was only 5/16 inch long and ⅛ inch thick.

One of the most interesting objects recovered at the site was made of sheet gypsum (Fig. 56i). Two holes had been drilled, one at one end and the other at the center. The other end had a stair-stepped outline.

Two elongated stone pendants each had biconical perforations at one end. One, shaped rather like a claw in pink and white mottled stone, was ⅞ inch long and ¾ inch wide (Fig. 71b). The other, 11/16 inch long and ¼ inch wide, was very thin at the top and increased in thickness to ⅛ inch at the bottom. Five engraved lines ran across the surface (Fig. 50c).

Miscellaneous Stone Objects

Pounding and Grinding Stone

An oval, cherty limestone pebble 4 inches long had a weak grinding or polishing surface and battered ends.

Tiny Grinding Tool (?)

A midsection of a small tool 1⅛ inch long, was triangular in cross-section;

each side, about 1 inch wide, had been ground.

Skinning Tool (?)

An elongated limestone pebble 3 inches long and ½ inch in diameter at the midpoint tapered toward each end. Roughly triangular in cross-section, one end was pointed, and the other end flattened.

Comal or Griddle

A fragment of a limestone slab measuring 6½ inches x 2½ inches, was ¾ inch thick and had a heavy covering of soot on the smoother face.

Kiva Bell (?)

An elongated piece of compact limestone, rectangular in cross-section, had been chipped along the four long edges (Pl. 54B, a).

Pigments

Traces of blue-green, red, and yellow pigment were found on various grinding surfaces. The occurrence of pigment or stains on artifacts may be categorized as follows:

Artifacts	*Blue-green*	*Red*	*Yellow*
Manos	1	2	
Metate fragment		1	
Stone palettes		3	
Flat slabs		7	
Bottom of shaft-straighteners		6	1
Awls	2		
Pottery palettes		1	1
Pebble polishers		1	
Total	3	21	2

It is doubtful that the awls were used to grind pigment. It is assumed that all other cases represent pigment grinding. The two pottery "palettes," used to mix paint suspended in liquid, included about a quarter of a Broad-lined Three Rivers Red-on-Terracotta bowl with caked yellow ochre in the concavity and a large El Paso Polychrome sherd containing caked red pigment.

Otherwise, dry pigment was ground. Judging from the instances of pigment adhering to grinding surfaces, red pigment derived from hematite and limonite was the favorite. Surprisingly few pieces were found. One lump of rust-colored hematite came from the fill of House 1, and a faceted piece of brick-red limonite came from the fill of House 13. The niche of House 15 held a piece of red hematite and two small lumps of yellow ochre. Two additional pieces of yellow ochre came from the House 1 fill, and one piece came from the fill of House 5.

Blue-green stain or pigment would be a copper oxide and malachite seems the most probable source. Malachite fragments were found on the floor of House 2, and two fragments were found between the floors of House 8. Several other fragments without provenience were in the collection.

No traces of ground white pigment were found, but several well-used pieces of compact, chalky limestone were recovered.

A faceted, slate-gray piece of claystone, ⅞ inch long, came from House 13 fill.

Unaltered Stones

No count was made of unaltered pebbles. A number of broken pebbles were observed, and the modern inhabitants of the Hondo Valley referred to flat, smooth stones that were longer than they were wide as moccasin lasts (Pl. 54A). Five of these stones were excavated. All appear to be completely unworked, and they vary in length from 1¾ inches to 6 inches.

Two small, bowl-shaped concretions were excavated. One was ¾ inch in diameter, and the other was 1 inch in diameter. The latter was a coarse purple rock, and a matching purple pebble fitted the depression. A rectangular piece of mica was about 1 inch long and ¾ inch wide. A rectangular sheet of gypsum was ¾ inch long, ¼ inch wide, and 1/32 inch thick. A six-sided quartz crystal was ¾ inch long and 3/10 inch in diameter. A small chunk of amethyst, ½ inch by 3/16 inch by 5/16 inch, was among the several ornaments and shell fragments found between the two floors of House 8.

Chipped Stone Tools

The use of small, interior flakes is the outstanding characteristic of the chipped stone industry. Aside from the numerous projectile points and a few drills, flake artifacts did not receive extensive modification. Bonnell Site chipped stone tools are listed in Table 27.

Cores

No objects were found that I would regard as simple cores, in the sense of a stone remnant showing evidence of flake detachment, which was not utilized as a tool itself. There are various pieces of stone from which flakes have been removed; in every case the remaining stone was utilized. Four cores of black shale were found; one had a projection used as a graver; one was used as a hammerstone; and two were core-planers. Two specimens of black basalt with obvious flake scars had been used as hammerstones.

Unifacial Tools

This category might well be entitled "variations on a theme of random

TABLE 27
CHIPPED STONE ARTIFACTS, BONNELL SITE

Artifact Type	No.
Unifacial	
Plano-convex scraper	1
Flake scrapers	9
Worked flakes	87
Flake gravers	10
Core graver	1
Flake shavers or smoothers	2
Large flake scraping and/or chopping tools	3
Core-planers	3
Total	116
Bifacial	
Projectile points	161
Bifacial flaking over both faces (knives)	8
Bifacial retouch limited to two edges	2
Bifacial retouch limited to one edge	4
Drills	9
Large ovates, bifacially worked	2
Total	186

flakes." Over 30 scrapers were recorded in the field notes; a re-examination of available specimens caused me to shift many to the category of worked flakes (Pl. 55). The demarcation between a scraper and a worked flake rested upon a decision as to whether an edge was deliberately retouched or showed only use scars. A more exact representation would be to view the categories of flake scraper and worked flake as a continuum, with specimens showing a well-retouched edge at one end and flakes with a few use spalls at the other. Recognized types are described below.

Plano-convex Scraper: The single specimen was an oval cortex flake, plano-convex in side-section, with steep retouch around the edges (Fig. 72a, h). A projection at the end of the flake opposite the striking platform may have been used as a graver.

Flake Scrapers: Nine specimens had sufficient retouch to qualify as flake scrapers. Shape ranged from a squarish flake with the thickest part of the flake at the striking platform tapering to the opposite edge with retouch along the lower edge of the interior face, to an enlongated, triangular form with a small striking platform at the apex of the triangle. Five of the nine flakes had cortex or patina on the upper surface. Three were ¼ inch thick, while two were ⅝ inch thick.

Three had single edges worked, one had a rounded end retouched, one was an end and side scraper, three had two long edges retouched, and the final specimen had opposite edges worked on opposite faces. None of the specimens measured over 2⅛ inches in length. One had a graver projection.

Used Flakes

Ninety small, interior flakes showed some degree of usage.

Flake Gravers

Ten thin flakes had projections used as gravers (Fig. 72h). In four cases, the flake was otherwise unmodified. Two had a spall or spalls removed adjacent to the graver point to form a concavity. These and the remaining four specimens had edge retouch. The smallest was ¾ inch long, the largest 1¾ inch long.

Core-graver

A "core" of mined slab black shale with a graver projection measured 2¼ inches in length, 1¼ inch in width, and was 1½ inch thick.

Shavers

Two small flakes, each ⅝ inch long, had small, smoothed concavities. In addition, the two gravers described above as having small concavities adjacent to the graver tip may have served the same function.

Core-planers

Three plano-convex, black shale planers had numerous use marks around the periphery. Slab shale was used. The largest was 3 inches in diameter. One had been used as a hammerstone.

Large Unifacial Scraping and/or Chopping Tools

Two large chert flakes with large, crude flake scars had irregular edges showing some retouch and/or use scars. Both could have functioned as scraping or chopping tools. A third flake of black shale was extremely battered along two edges.

Bifacial Chipped Stone Tools

Projectile Points: In comparing the 86 points that are available for study with the 161 recorded specimens, field notes and drawings for points were found to be sufficiently accurate to use in describing types. Most of the forms described probably functioned as projectiles; some heavy triangular points and some thick convex base fragments may well have been small knives or drill bases. Projectile points are illustrated in Plate 56 and Figures 73-75.

"Dart" Points: Eleven points were large enough to be called darts (Fig. 73). These fall into two categories: (1) barbed-expanded stem and (2) shouldered-expanded stem. One was unique in having the edges so well ground from tip to shoulder that a flat ground edge 1/16 inch wide was attained at places (Pl. 56y).

Paleo-Indian Point: A concave-based point fragment with ground edges was made of poor quality chert (Fig. 73*l*).

Arrow Points: A total of 150 arrow points were recorded. The seven types of arrow points are described below.

1. Side-notched Points: Thirty-two of the 68 recorded points of this form were available for study (Fig. 74a–q). Most would be called Harrell points in Texas typology. Straight and concave base forms were equally common. Minor variations included triple notching and side and basal notching. One side-notched point had concave sides and a convex base (Fig. 74q).

2. Triangular Points: Two of these were so heavy that they may have served as knives (Fig. 75f–o). Most examples of this form, which were thin and had at least a 1:2 ratio of width to length, would be called Fresno points in Texas. Five beautifully-made elongated specimens with deeply concave bases (Fig. 75k–o) were like those from south-central New Mexico (Lehmer 1948:Pl. VIIa).

3. Corner-notched Points: Seventeen percent of classifiable points fall within the range of Texas Scallorn points, which Jelks (personal communication) has subdivided into Scallorn and Eddy Scallorn (Fig. 74r–cc). The former has a wider stem, and the latter is more deeply corner-notched. The Eddy Scallorn form is more numerous in this collection (Fig. 74t–x).

4. One-shouldered Points: Three crude triangular points were either naturally asymmetrical or had a slight shoulder on one side (Fig. 75p-r).

5. Shouldered-elongated Stem Point: The single specimen is a Perdiz point (Fig. 75e; Pl. 56k).

6. Shouldered-stemmed Points: Small (under 1 inch in length) almost cruciform-shaped points have shoulders that contract abruptly toward the point (Fig. 75a, b).

7. Leaf-shaped Points: Four thick, unnotched points with tapered, convex bases which had broken tips may have functioned as drills (Fig. 75s–t).

Flake-knives: Seven complete specimens and one fragment had large striking platforms 1/2 to 1 3/8 inch wide (Pl. 57A). Their original flake outline has not been substantially altered by the bifacial retouch.

One specimen of Alibates (?) flint was 2 1/2 inches long (Pl. 57A, g; Fig. 66c). The flat, symmetrical flake tapered from the striking platform (3/4 inch wide) to the tip. Even retouch along the edges produced a well-shaped knife which received most of the wear close to the tip. The edge was ground quite smooth for 5/16 inch down one edge from the tip and a second place was ground smooth about halfway down the opposite edge.

Another, made of yellow and red mottled jasper, had a striking platform 1 3/8 inches wide (Pl. 57A, h; Fig. 56g). The knife, 2 3/4 inches long, 1 1/2 inches wide, and ¼ inch thick, was asymmetrical; a shallow concavity along one side has been polished smooth.

An elongated, rectangular 'backed' flake of flint had bifacial retouch along the edge opposite the 'back' (Pl. 57A, a).

Two crude chert specimens with large and irregular flaking and wavy edges were small, measuring 1½ inches and 1⅜ inches in length (Pl. 57A, b, f).

An asymmetrical slate knife with rather obscure chipping was 1¼ inches long, ⅞ inch at the widest point, and 5⁄16 inch at the thickest point. The striking platform was ¾ inch across (Pl. 57A, c).

Grainy quartzite was used to make a crude knife that was vaguely pointed at both ends. One end had been used as a graver or punch and one edge had double beveling (Pl. 57A, e).

A chert knife fragment had a rounded tip (Pl. 57A, d).

Bifacial Retouch on Two Edges: Two specimens differed from the knives in that they were proportionally longer, thicker, and cruder, with retouch occurring only along the edge instead of across the face.

Bifacial Retouch along One Edge: Each of the four specimens assigned to this category is visually distinct. One is a true blade which was completely covered with patina before the retouching was done. Minor edge retouch was present along one edge and several flakes had been removed from the body of the blade (Fig. 72i).

A "backed" flake was struck from a flint pebble; cortex remained at the striking platform, along the "back," and at the end of the roughly rectangular flake, which had the sharpest edge retouched.

Two fairly thick chert flakes had large irregular flake scars and some irregular bifacial edge retouch.

Drills: One of the nine drills, made on a straight black flake, has bifacial retouch along one edge and unifacial retouch along the other. The remaining eight drills show some degree of basal expansion. One could be called a T-drill (Fig. 76f). The largest was 2⅞ inches long, 1⅛ inches wide, and 7⁄16 inch thick (Pl. 76b). The smaller drills have only slightly expanded bases. The four complete specimens were used with a clockwise motion.

Bifacially-worked Ovates: Both specimens were made of light-colored chert (Pl. 57B, a, e). A flat pebble with one long edge bifacially worked had an irregular edge formed by removing large spalls by percussion. The upper convex surface of an old flake was largely covered with cortex; the lower concave surface and the striking platform were largely covered with patina. Large spalls had been removed bifacially by percussion around most of the periphery, revealing fresh chert. Smaller spalls were removed along one edge. Neither specimen showed evidence of battering or chopping, and presumably they functioned as scraping or cutting tools.

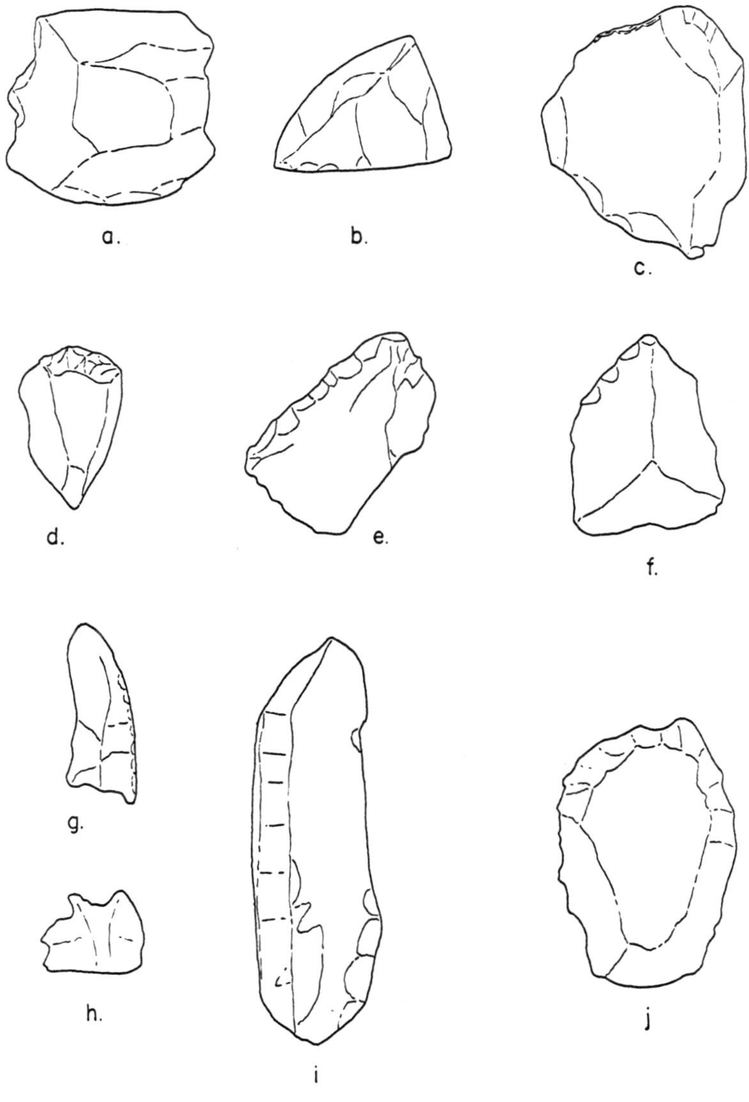

Figure 72. Chipped stone tools, Bonnell Site: *a*, Plano-convex scraper; *b*, Side view of *a*; *c-h*, and *j*, Unifacially worked flakes; *i*, Bifacially retouched flake.

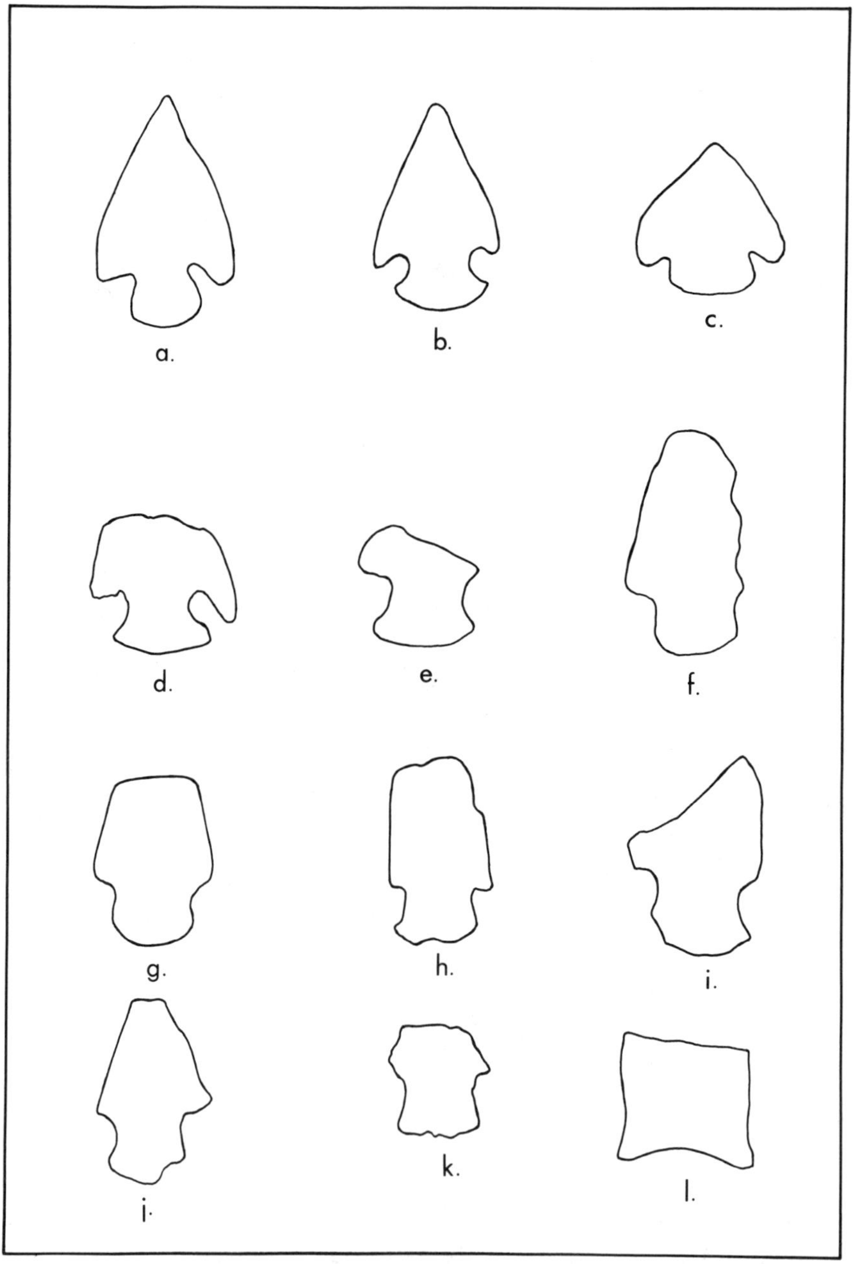

Figure 73. "Dart" Points, Bonnell Site.

Figure 74. Projectile points, Bonnell Site.

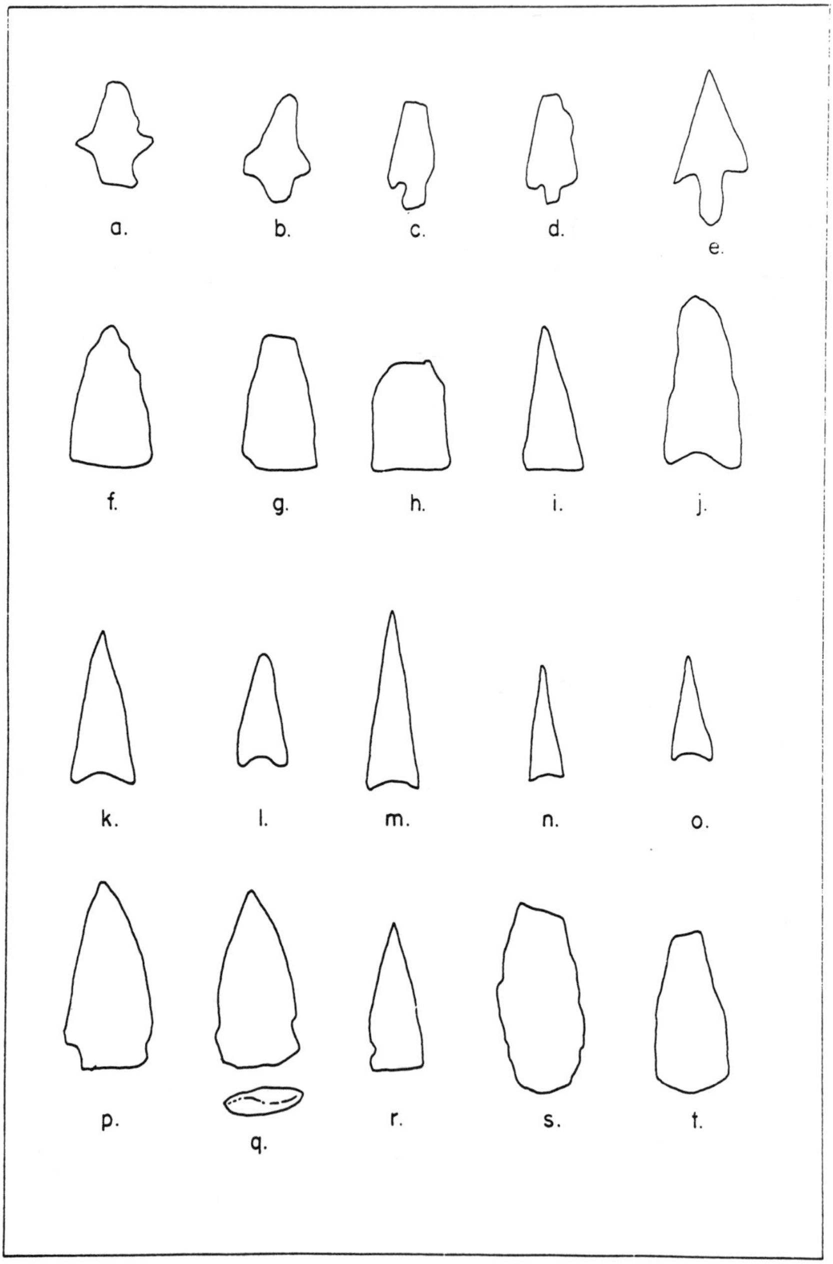

Figure 75. Projectile points, Bonnell Site.

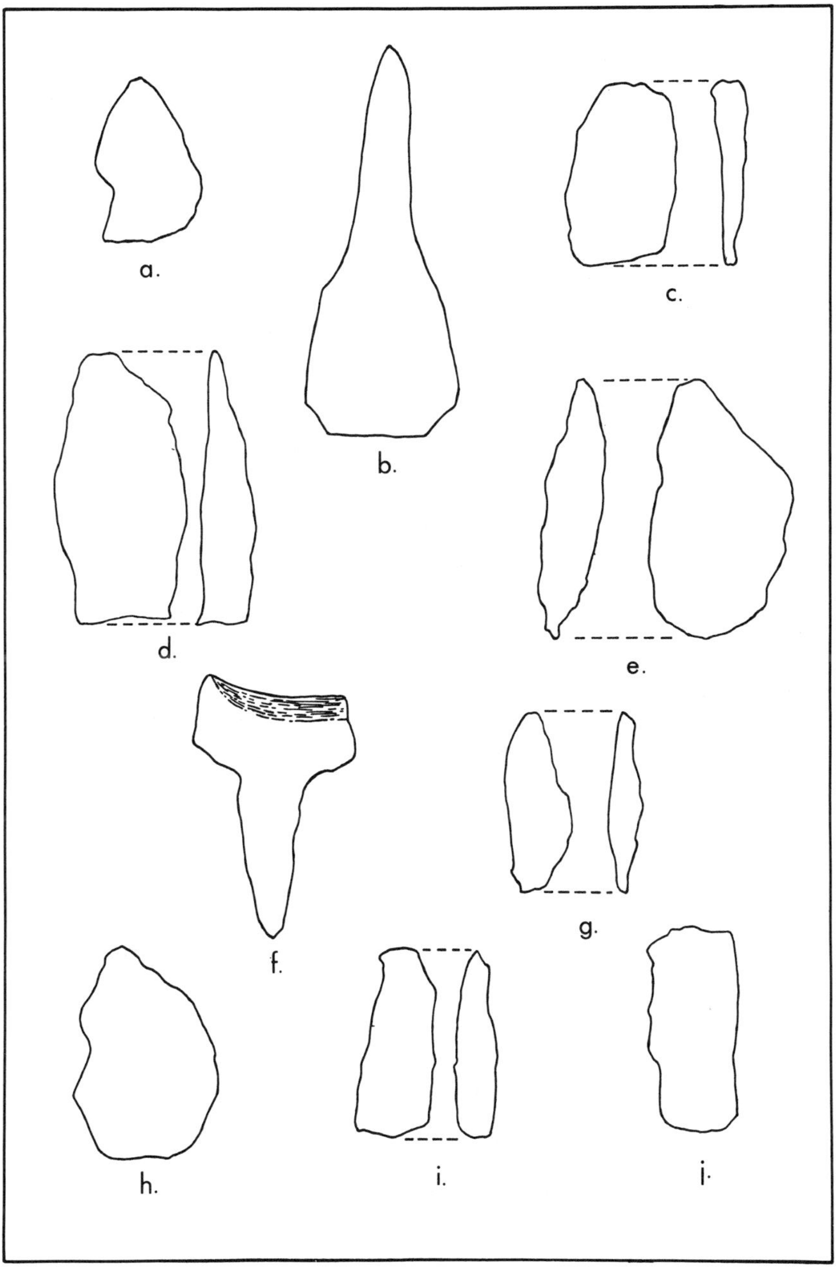

Figure 76. Bifacial chipped stone tools, Bonnell Site.

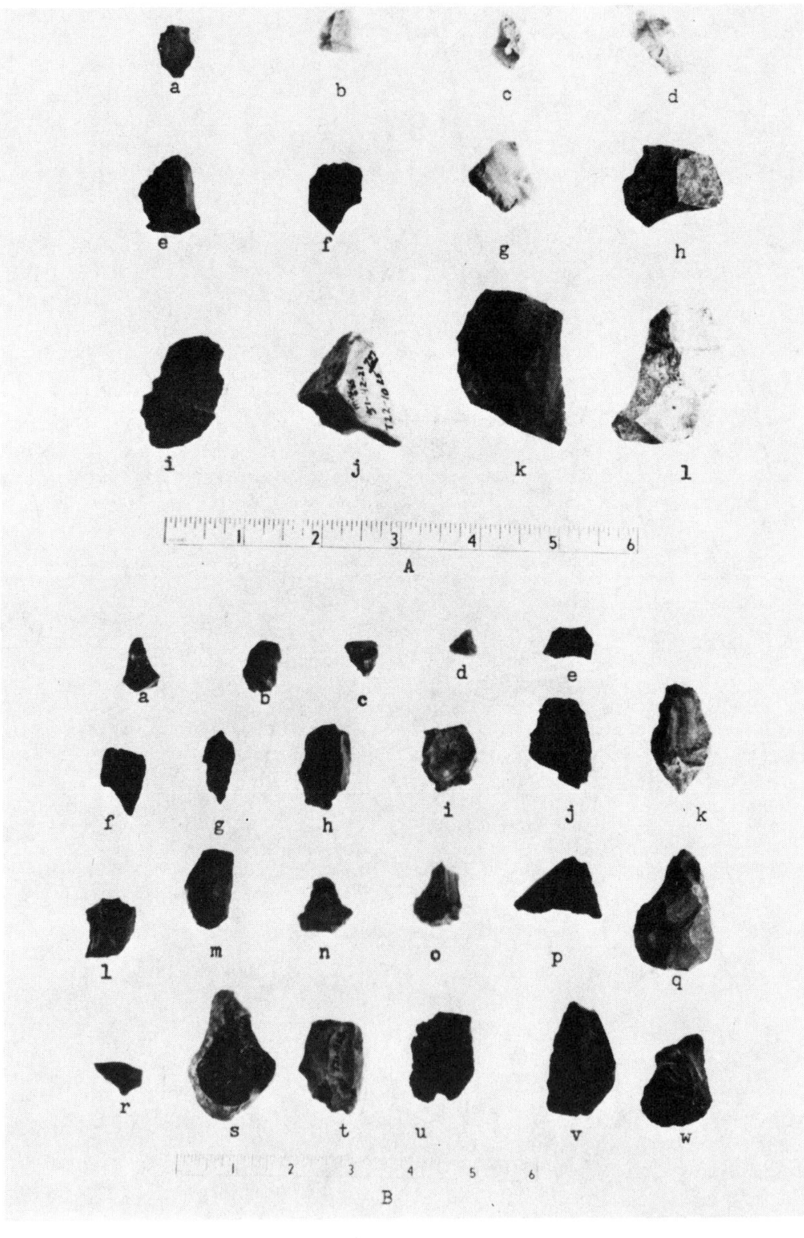

Plate 55. Unifacially flaked tools, Bonnell Site.

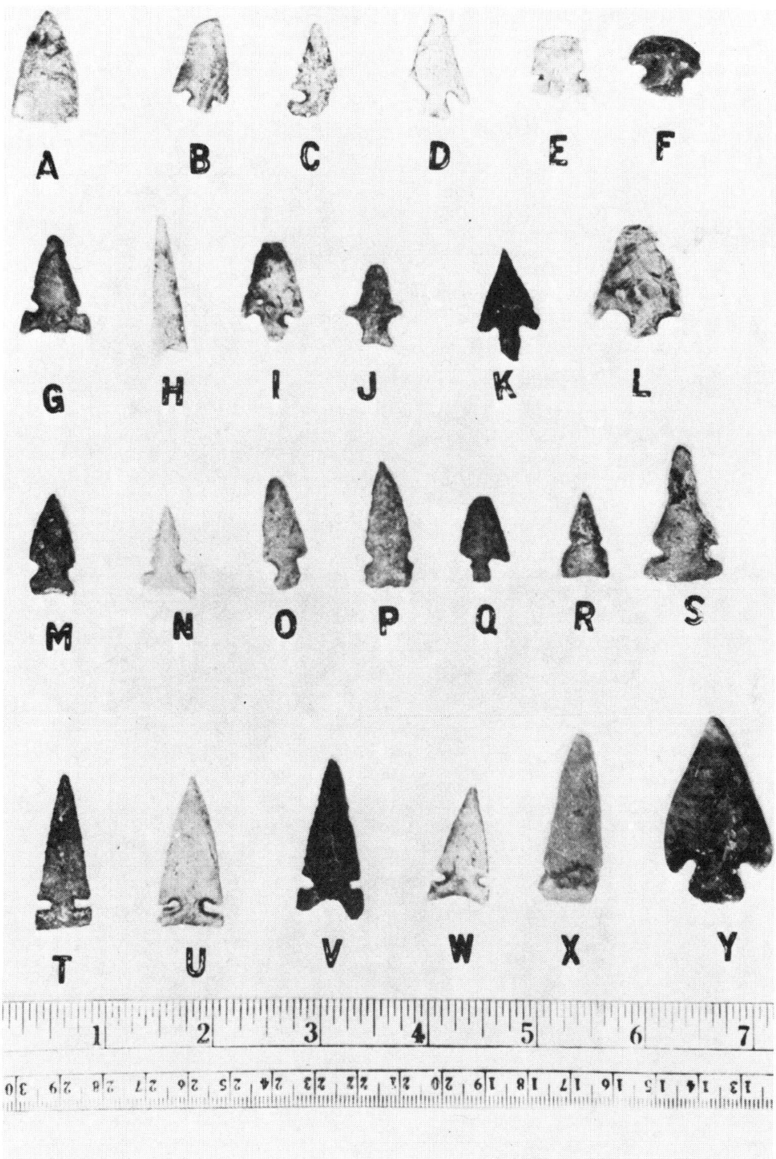

Plate 56. Projectile points, Bonnell Site.

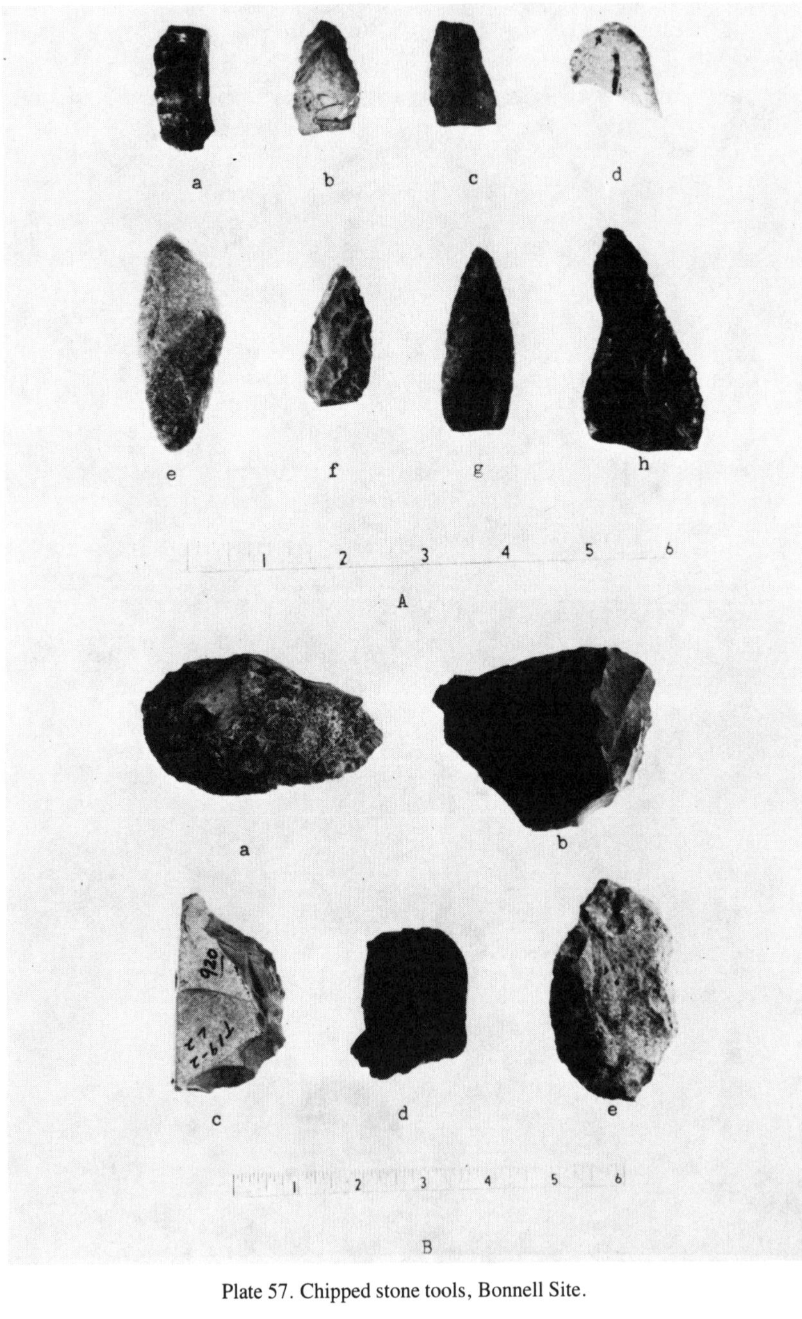

Plate 57. Chipped stone tools, Bonnell Site.

Hammerstones

The form of these 14 battered pebbles ranged from nearly spherical to oval. One nearly square specimen had a well-battered end. None of the hammerstones were over 4 inches in their maximum dimension, and a 3 inch diameter seems to have been a desirable size. Stone of high fracturability such as flint, chert, silicified shale and quartz were preferred, although igneous stone was used in two cases.

Ten of the 14 specimens came from house floors and four were in fill. Four hammerstones were found together in House 4; House 1 had two hammerstones on the floor, and individual specimens came from floors of Houses 13, 9, 12, and 8.

Bone Artifacts

Bone Awls

The general approach set forth by Kidder (1932:202–22) is followed here; emphasis is on type of bone from which the awl was made with secondary attention directed to type and degree of alteration. Awls actually available for study are separated from those for which there are only field records (Table 28). Unless otherwise specified, the following discussion deals with the former group.

Deer or antelope bones were heavily favored, and the metapodial was most often selected. Forty-three awls are clearly made from metapodials, and it is probable that the six compact-bone awls and other specimens were likewise made from this bone.

Metapodial Awls, Proximal End Present: Starting with a deer or antelope metapodial, a number of awl types were produced (Pl. 61a, o, r). Four awls were made from the proximal end, split in such a way that a long flat section of bone was obtained. They varied in length from 2¾ inches to 4¾ inches in length; basal width was ¾ to ⅝ inch. Three were polished at this stage; others were shaped more extensively. One of the awls has six small cuts along one edge close to the base.

A sturdier awl was produced by retaining an edge and part of the head of this bone; the resultant awl showed more curvature than the category above. Three awls made in this fashion were between 2⅞ inches and 6⅝ inches in length.

Metapodial Awls, Distal End Retained: In four complete specimens, the distal end of the metapodial was halved. The longest of these was 5¾ inches, the shortest, 3¾ inches. Three tapered gradually to a point; a blunt specimen could have functioned as a punch or flaker. The fourth was notched. An additional three split metapodial fragments were not tabulated.

Metapodial Awls, Head of Bone Wholly Removed: A total of 30 awls (Pl. 61p) were identified for this category. Clues to the identification of distal and proximal end have been eliminated from most specimens. Twenty-three awls were well shaped and polished. Seven of the specimens were not shaped beyond the initial splitting and polishing of the tip.

Ulna Awls, Proximal End Retained: Three of these tools were made from the bones of immature animals; one of these is a splinter awl on which the articular fossa had been split away leaving only the head of the bone as the base of an unpolished awl 3 inches long. The remaining six awls utilized the entire proximal end of the bone. On four, the end was left unaltered. One had the head of the bone cut to a square base; the articular surface was left unaltered.

The head of one awl was cleverly shaped to represent a mountain sheep and a face engraved onto each side. Cutting and polishing were carried out at the head of the ulna and below the nose of the carved face. Articular surfaces and condyles were removed and smoothed (Pl. 59e; Pl. 60A, f for reverse side; also Fig. 31a).

Ulna Awl, Distal End Retained: One specimen made from the distal end of an ulna retained less than half of the articular surface. The 2½-inch long awl tapered rapidly to a point.

Ribs: Ribs about 1 inch wide were split lengthwise to get an elongated, flat awl; the cancellous surface was smoothed. Whole specimens ranged from 3 to 6 inches in length and from 13/16 to 5/16 inch in width. Four tapered gradually to the tip; two were notched.

Compact-bone Awls: Although it is difficult to identify the parent bone of these six awls, the metapodial bone seems most suitable. The only whole specimen, 5½ inch long, is pointed at each end, resembling a knitting needle (Pl. 61*l*). The fragments are oval to rectangular in cross-section.

Splinter Awls of Unidentified Bones: Bone thickness indicated that deer or a similar sized animal supplied the raw material. Curvature of the two largest specimens (2½ inches and 2¾ inches) suggests that a long bone was used. The other three are short, narrow fragments of fairly heavy, unidentified bone.

Awls Made of Flat, Compact-bone: Eight fragments of flat, slender bones taper to a point; all specimens over 2 inches show a pronounced curvature. Six are conceivably metapodial sections, well-abraded and thinned, and two may well be scapula edges.

Awls Made of Unidentified Smaller Animal Bones: One splinter awl was made from a long bone. A highly-curved, partially-split rib had a polished tip. An ulna awl appeared to be from an intermediate-sized animal, perhaps coyote (Pl. 61j).

Awls Made of Bones of Small-sized Animals: One tiny ulna had the end cut and polished to form a delicate awl. Two tibias were cut or broken diagonally and the tips polished. The latter type was completely overlooked in the first analysis of bone materials. In a reanalysis, 83 long bones of small animals showed a diagonal break somewhere around the midsection of the bone. Of this series, only 2 showing deliberate and obvious polishing were tabulated. Any of the 83 could have been used briefly. Femurs, tibias, and ulnas of small animals which easily break diagonally in the midsection would have furnished an easily adapted point.

Awl Fragments (?): Two polished midsections of bone artifacts probably came from awls. Two shaped fragments from the proximal ends of deer or antelope metapodials probably were awl bases. Three split metapodials, distal ends, may have been awl bases.

Provenience of Awls: Of the 101 recorded awls (Table 29), 56 came from or slightly above house floors; 43 were from fill and 2 had no provenience noted. Eight were on the floor and 15 in the fill of House 1.

TABLE 28
CLASSIFICATION OF BONE AWLS, BONNELL SITE

Animal/Bone	Available Specimens	Recorded But Lost
I. Deer or antelope bone		
1. Metapodial		
(a) Proximal end present	7	1
(b) Distal end present	4	1
(c) Head of bone wholly removed		
(1) Shaped and polished	17	6
(2) Splinter	7	
2. Ulna		
(a) Proximal end present	7	2
(b) Distal end present	1	
3. Miscellaneous		
(a) Compact-bone edge	5	2
(b) Flat, compact bone		
(1) Probably metapodial	6	
(2) Probably scapula	2	
(c) Splinter, bone unidentified	5	5
II. Bones of intermediate-sized animals		
1. Long bone	1	
2. Ulna (Coyote?)		1
3. Rib, splinter	1	
III. Bones of small-sized animals		
1. Tibia	2	
2. Ulna	1	
3. Long Bone	1	
IV. Unidentifiable		6
Total	67	24
Grand total		91

TABLE 29
PROVENIENCE OF BONE AWLS, BONNELL SITE

House No.	No. On Floor	No. In Fill
1	8	15
2	5	1
3	3	
4	3	1
5	4	1
6	5	3
7	2	1
8	2	1
9	2	
10	4	4
11	1	1
13	7	5
14	1	1
15	1	1
16		1
17	1	
19	1	
20	5	
23	1	
Outside of house		7
No provenience		2
Total	56	45

Total number of awls = 101.

Other Bone Tools

Punching Tools

These tools were subdivided along the same lines as were used in the classification of awls (see Table 30).

Rib Punches: Four longitudinally split ribs were shaped and polished. The largest, 6 ⅞ inches long and ¾ inch wide, had a smoothed cancellous surface and the base was cut down or shaped on one side. Another specimen, 4½ inches long and ⅞ inch wide at the widest point, had a shaped base that formed a handle. The third, which had most of the cancellous bone removed, showed longitudinal abrasions on both faces. The fourth punch was fragmentary. The diagonally cut tip of an unsplit rib showed evidence of extensive wear.

Ulna Punch: The distal end of an ulna was split so that over half of the head of the bone remained. This splinter punch, 3⅛ inch long, had no smoothing or shaping except at the blunt working point.

Unidentified Bones: Six specimens can be called splinter punches.

Provenience of Punches: Two came from the floor of House 1 and the rest were from fill.

TABLE 30
BONE TOOLS OTHER THAN AWLS,
BONNELL SITE

Tool Type	Count
Bone punches	13
Scraping and/or polishing tools	
End scrapers	7
Deer (and/or antelope) scapula scrapers	3
Bison scapula scrapers (?)	7
Miscellaneous bones	8
Ribs	3
Weaving tools (?)	
Rib spatula	1
Miscellaneous shaped bones (flat)	
Rib handles	4
Gaming sticks	53
Rectangular, cut and polished	6
Hair ornament (?)	1
Bone bead (disc-shaped)	1
Miscellaneous cut and polished fragments	22
Tubular bone objects	
Hair ornament (?)	1
Bone whistles	2
Bone tubes	3
Bone beads	3
Broken tubular objects	3

Scraping and/or Polishing Tools

Various bones used with a pushing or pulling motion perhaps functioned as scrapers or polishers.

End Scrapers: A femur of an intermediate-sized animal with a diagonal cut across the shaft was used with a pushing motion. Four bone splinters had polished beveled ends. A deer rib, 5½ inches long, was split for 3½ inches; the split portion is smooth and the end rounded and thinned from usage. The unsplit portion forms the handle.

Scapula Scrapers: Deer scapulas were cut or broken so that a section of bone from ¼ inch to 1 inch wide remained on each side of the trimmed scapula ridge (Fig. 62c). Three specimens ranging in length from 4½ inches to 5¾ inches had longitudinal striations or abrasions on the ridged surface. The edge was nicked through usage; however, on each specimen there is a short section of the edge that has been smoothed and thinned from being used with a

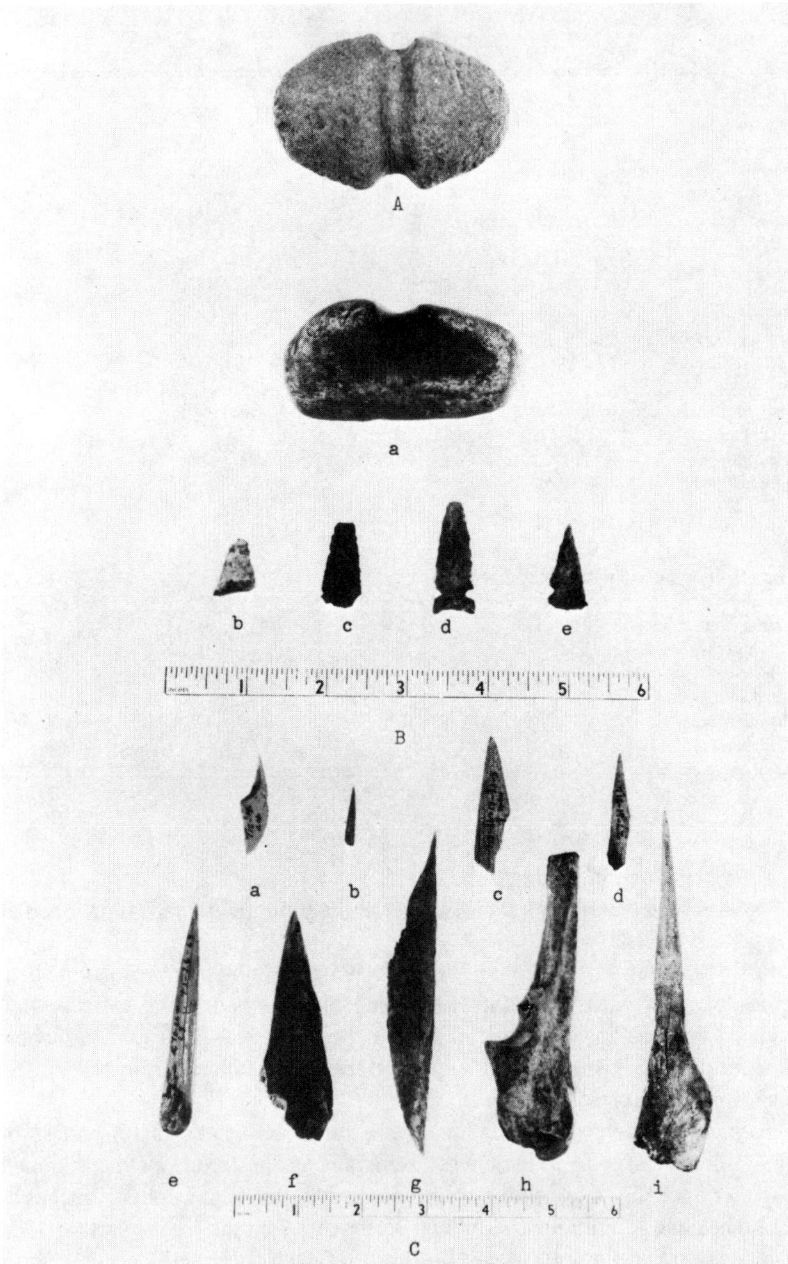

Plate 58. Artifacts from the Bonnell Site.

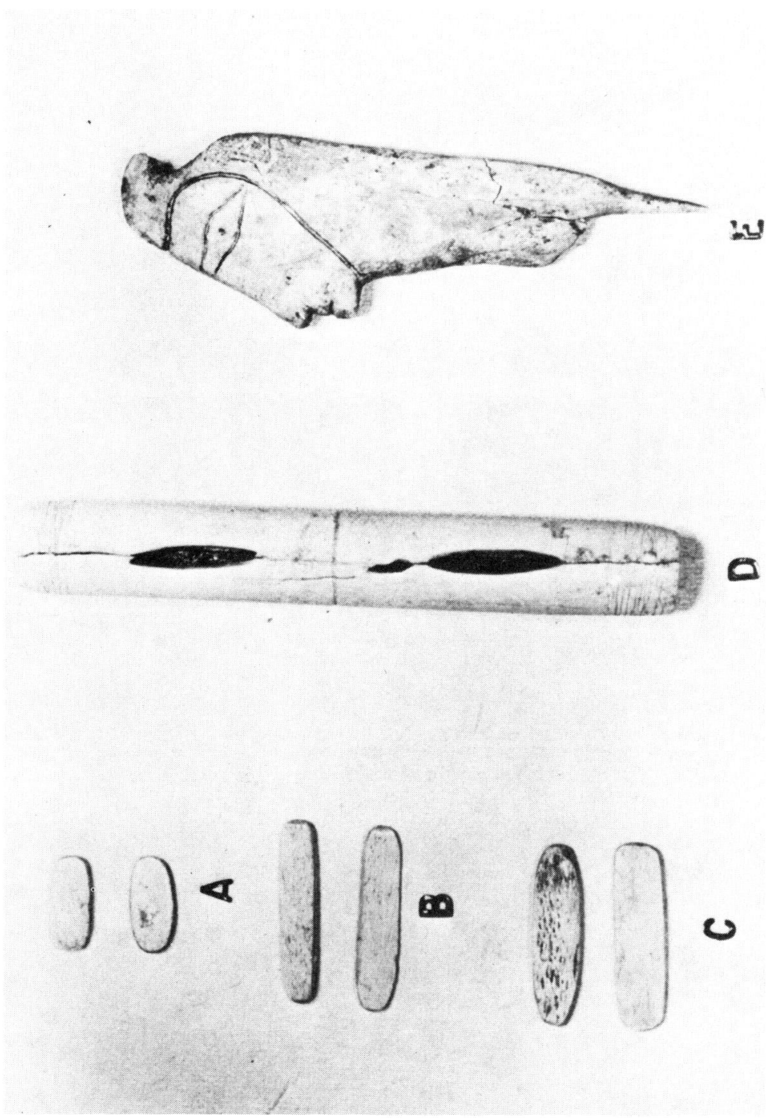

Plate 59. Bone tools, Bonnell Site.

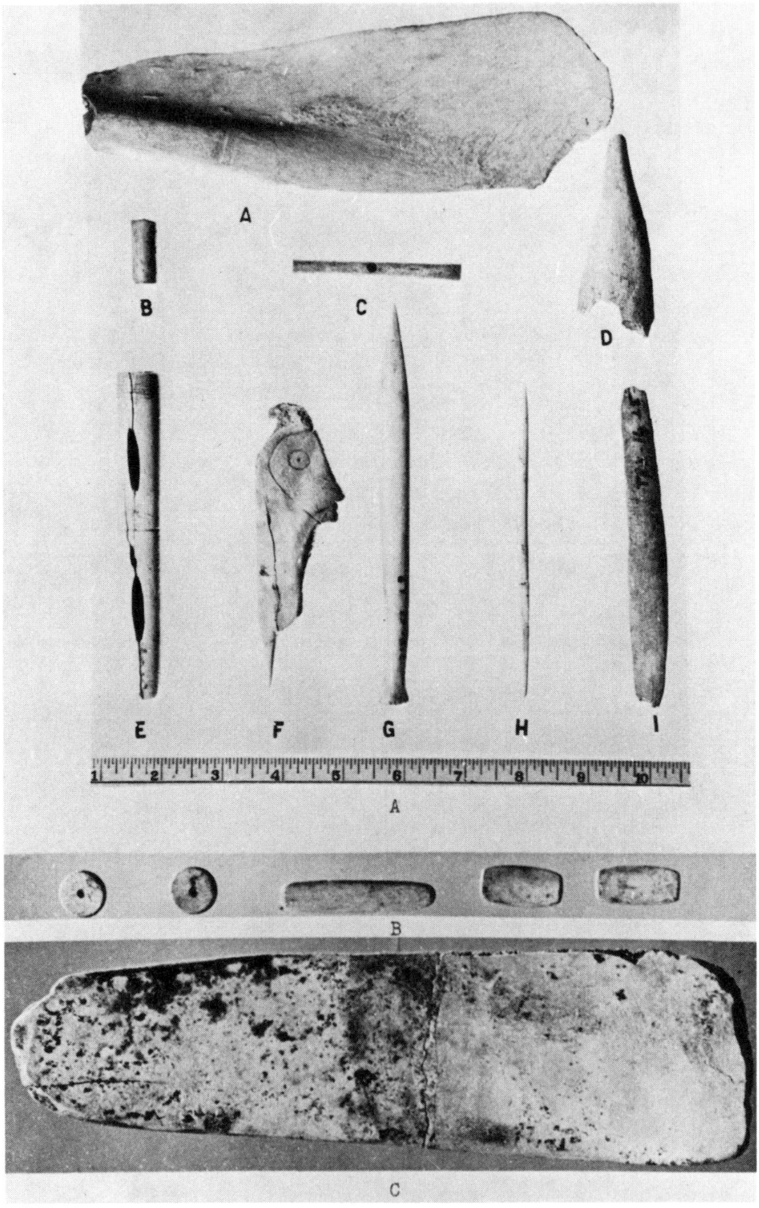

Plate 60. Bone tools, Bonnell Site.

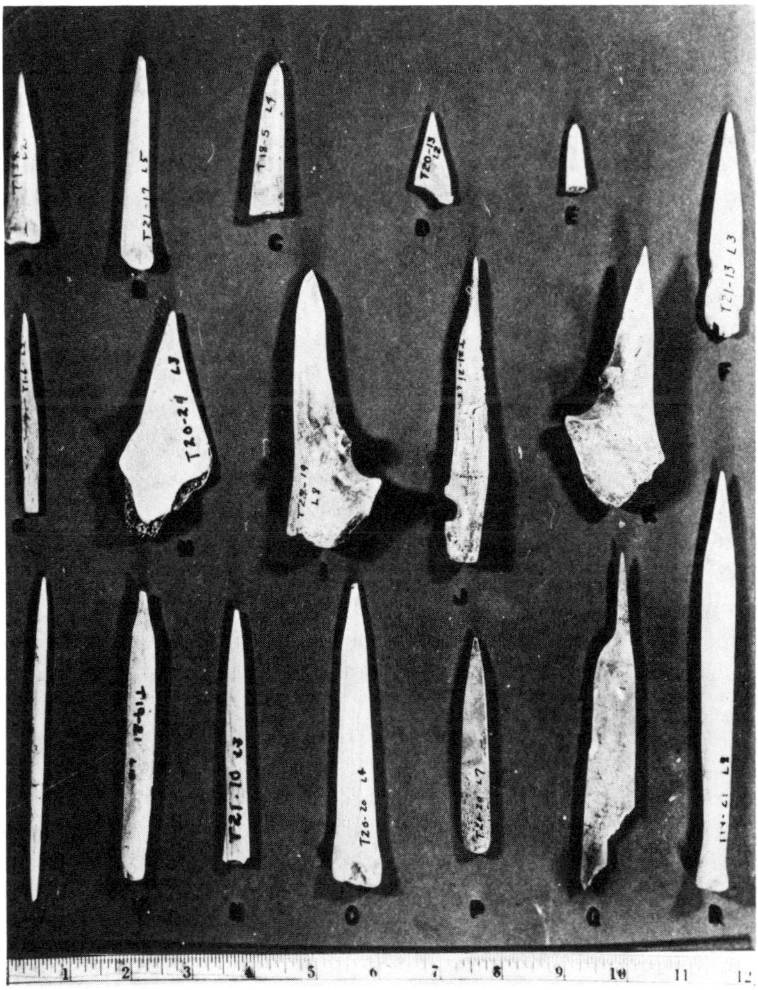

Plate 61. Bone awls, Bonnell Site.

different motion. Both edges and the ridge show signs of having been used, giving three usable edges per tool.

Proveniences of Bone Scraping (?) Tools: Scraping tools were found on the floor of Houses 9 and 13. Others came from fill.

Scapula Tools

Seven implements cut from the flat portion of the scapula were available for study and an additional specimen was adequately recorded (Pl. 60A, B, a, d). They vary in length from 3¾ inches to 8¾ inches. Two retain the ridge section, although in both cases it had been trimmed; one of these has the cut part well smoothed, but the other is rough. The dominant feature of these tools is a well-thinned, polished edge. One shows this thinning from only one surface; all others have one long edge used from two faces. One is darkened along the thinned edge. Four of the tools have longitudinal striations or abrasion marks on the face. One specimen has some indentations across the surface of the ridge that look as if they had been worn (with a cord?). A large specimen had a hole drilled through the bone close to one end (Fig. 61j).

Provenience of Scapula Tools: They were associated with floors of Houses 3, 5, 8, and 15. One was slightly above the floor of House 5 and two were in fill outside the houses. One was lying with a bison long bone splinter, 9½ inches in length, that had been used as a tool.

Worked Scapula Fragments

Eleven showed the thinned, polished edge typical of the scapula tool group. Three specimens with more than one worked edge suggested that some of these were more carefully shaped than the complete specimens. Surface abrasion was evident on five pieces; it was usually done along the long axis, but one specimen has the striations running at a 45° angle.

Provenience: Two fragments, probably of the same tool, came from the floor of House 19. Two fragments belonging to another tool were from House 21. One small fragment was from the floor of House 13. Other fragments were from fill outside of houses.

Worked Ribs

Three longitudinally split ribs, from 5¼ to 6⅞ inches long, with surface abrasions and the edge thinning were so well used as to appear fragile. In each case, the outside of the split bone was utilized so that the cancellous surface is on the inside curve of the rib. Two are from different floors of House 13 and one was from Floor 2 of House 3. They may have been used as smoothers, scrapers, polishers, or weaving battens.

Miscellaneous Bones Used for Scraping (?)

In going through the bone collection, over 20 bones were noted that had the shape of a flat *ulu,* that is, one edge was straight and the other convex. Most were split ribs, although the ilium was also used. Since many of the bones showed no polishing of the curved surface, they were eliminated from consideration. Four showed definite signs of use along the curved edge. Four other specimens, more irregular in outline, may be the same sort of "tool."

Provenience: Three of the best shaped specimens came from fill outside of houses. The fourth was from the floor of House 1. Four of the more doubtful "tools" came from the same level south and east of House 9.

Weaving Tool (?)

A single, longitudinally split rib tool is classified here, although the three ribs described above as polishing tools may have been used for the same purpose. This tool is 10⅜ inches long, 7/16 inch wide, and 3/16 inch thick. The well-shaped, smoothed edges have *not* been thinned. The cancellous surface is on the outside of the curve.

Handles (?)

Two unsplit ribs had rounded, polished ends. Both showed longitudinal striations and both were found in House 3.

Two other rib pieces could have served as hafts or handles. Both had one end cut and rounded although neither was polished. A broken specimen from House 9 was 1⅞ inches in length, while the other was 6 inches long.

Gaming Sticks

Fifty-three of these small cut and polished bone pieces were recorded. Rectangular and lenticular forms ranged from ¾ inch to 1½ inches in length. Some were wider in proportion to their length, with a ratio of less than 1:2; some were more slender, with a width-length ratio approaching 1:5. Nearly all showed longitudinal striations on the upper surface. There was variation of how much, if any, cancellous bone was retained on the lower surface. Those from House 8 were made of split ribs. All others available for study were made of heavier bones.

Round pieces had a drill pit in the center of the upper surface. A diameter of 7/16 to ½ inch was the rule.

When several gaming sticks were found together, the elongated ones tended to be consistent in size and shape, obviously forming a set. Most of the recovered sticks belonged to one of six sets.

Provenience: Six slender, elongated pieces found together on the floor of House 8 had red pigment on the lower cancellous surface.

A larger set came from the upper floor of House 3; the ten nearly identical rectangular pieces appeared to have been cut from the same heavy bone; the cancellous remnant was pitted. In addition, three round pieces had been cut from the same bone. With these, but probably not part of the same set, were two broad, rectangular sticks cut from a thinner curved bone.

In the southeast corner of House 1, seven rectangular pieces and three rounded ones (similar in shape to those in the set from House 3) were contained in a Chupadero Black-on-White jug. Three other rectangular pieces, like those in the jug, were elsewhere on the floor of House 1.

Another set from the floor of House 4 was composed of four rectangular and two round gaming sticks.

On the floor of House 6 were eight slender, elongated gaming pieces and three round ones.

A single gaming piece was on the floor of House 16 and one was in the fill east of House 6.

Other Rectangular Bone Pieces

One piece, 1⅛ inches long and ½ inch wide, was highly polished (Fig. 46h). While this falls within the size range of gaming pieces, it has a definite curvature in cross-section, and its use as a gaming stick is questionable. It came from the floor of House 8, where one of the sets of gaming sticks was found.

Two fragments of flat bone were polished along the unbroken edges. One fragment was 1¾ inches long, the other 1⅛ inches long. Both were from the fill of House 1.

Two larger rectangular pieces with rounded ends were 3 inches long, ½ inch wide, and ¼ inch thick. One came from the fill of House 5, the other from the floor of House 8.

Another specimen 1¼ inches long, 7/16 inch wide, and ¼ inch thick was within the size range of gaming pieces; however, its thickness causes it to resemble the two specimens just described. This one came from fill east of House 6.

Hair Ornament (?)

A long, flat object of compact bone had a biconical perforation near one end. The tip was broken. This object was from the fill west of House 3.

Bone Bead

A single flat, disc-shaped bone bead found in the fill of House 15 was ⅝ inch in diameter, 3/16 inch thick; a hole 1/8 inch in diameter had been drilled in the center.

Cancellous Abrader

A flat, cut, piece of heavy bone (bison?) was irregular in shape, having maximum dimensions of 2¾ inches by 1⅝ inches. The cancellous surface seems to have been used as an abrader.

Vertebral Spine with a Cut, "Beveled" End

Diagonal cuts across the spine of two deer (?) vertebrae had been use-polished.

Bone Fragments with Shaped Ends

The fragmentary nature of these two specimens precluded putting them into a functional category. A split rib that could have served as a punch or handle had diagonal cuts converging toward a broken tip; the cut portions were smoothed.

The other piece with a well-polished diagonally-cut end was broken longitudinally. It was made from a long bone and had a length of 3⅜ inches.

Cut Bones

Six long bones of small- and intermediate-sized animals were cut, showing that part of the shaft had been removed for some reason. Ten bones with cutting marks on their surfaces included five deer bone fragments, three unidentified long bone fragments, and the long bone of a small animal. One of the ribs looks as if an attempt to cut it in two had been abandoned. One of the long bone fragments (2⅛ inches long) may have served as a base for something else which was being cut.

Tubular Bone Objects

Hair Ornament (?): A "problematical" bone object 5½ inches long was found on Floor 2 of House 3 between three upright rocks accompanied by a tubular pipe and a bone "weaving tool" (Fig. 35a; Pl. 59d). Two slits were cut in one side. The ends were scratched all around the tubular bone, presumably as decoration. An indentation around the center of the tube appeared to be a more purposeful cut, perhaps for suspension by a cord.

Bone Whistles: Two of the one-stop whistles were 2⅝ inches and 2¾ inches long. The hole was drilled in one (Pl. 60A, c; also Fig. 46g), while the other hole had been cut (Fig. 33e). The latter bore green copper oxide stains.

Bone Tubes: All three bone tubes (Fig. 57f, m) came from House 13. The longest one, 4⅝ inches long, was found in the fireplace of Floor 1. The other two tubes were 1 inch or less in length and 1/8 inch in diameter.

Bone Beads: Three tubular bone beads (Pl. 60A, b; Fig. 45h) were 1 inch to 1 1/16 inches in length and 1/4 to 3/8 inch in diameter.

Broken Tubular Bone Objects: Three specimens with polished ends were broken longitudinally; they may have been tubes or beads.

Antler

Two deer antler tines had use-blunted tips. One was found in a large Gila Polychrome sherd with unworked parts of a femur and rib (deer?). A third antler punch, flat in cross-section, had a well-blunted tip; several cuts on the surface were clustered around the tip. Several other fragmented antlers and horns of deer and antelope were found.

Shell Objects

Excepting cut shell and shell fragments, all shell objects are decorative or ornamental. Mussel shell was most often used, and presumably it was obtained and worked locally. Shell objects are listed in Table 31.

TABLE 31
SHELL OBJECTS, BONNELL SITE

Type of Object	Count
I. Ornament	
1. *Olivella* beads	226
2. *Glycymeris* shell bracelet	1
3. *Oliva* shell tinklers	2
4. Mussel shell	
(1) Perforated	15
(2) Unperforated	11
5. Unidentified shell	2
II. Non-ornaments	
1. Cut shell (mussel)	24
2. Unworked shell fragments	
(1) Mussel	10
(2) Conch (?)	1

Olivella Beads

Of the 226 *Olivella* beads found at the site, 201 formed a four- or five-strand necklace in a child's burial which was also accompanied by a "killed" Chupadero Black-on-White bowl inverted over the face. The remaining 25 *Olivella* beads were found singly or in small groups (Pl. 62d).

Glycymeris Shell Bracelet

A single specimen had a maximum outside diameter of 2 3/8 inches (Pl. 62b).

Oliva Shell Tinklers

One complete specimen (Fig. 45f) and one fragment were found; the latter had a design made with a series of tiny drilled holes.

Mussel Shell

Local manufacture is assumed. A variety of forms have been recognized.

Perforated: These are subdivided into pendants with a hole for suspension at one end, buttons (?) with a hole in the center, and those specimens with other forms of perforation.

Pendants: Twelve shell pieces had circular holes drilled near an edge. It is not certain that all of the fragments served as pendants and some of the holes may have been part of a design (Fig. 57k). Zoomorphic representations of a fish and the head of a fowl were made of thinned mussel shell (Pl. 62e, f). A broken specimen shaped liked a stylized boot had 12 drilled pits in one surface (Fig. 36f). An oval specimen, $^{11}/_{16}$ inch wide and $^{5}/_{16}$ inch long, was decorated with drilled pits and engraved lines (Fig. 57j). A fragment had two holes drilled close to the upper edge.

Specimens with Other Perforations (Pl. 62k): Two specimens with slits or rectangular perforations cut at the periphery could have functioned as buttons or clothing decorations.

Unperforated Mussel Shell: Forms were zoomorphic or geometric. A zoomorphic item was a fish with two dorsal and two ventral fins. The geometric forms (Pl. 62h, l, m; Fig. 43f) included seven whole specimens that were symmetrical in outline. Three trapezoids with slightly convex ends ranged from 1$^{3}/_{8}$ inches to $^{5}/_{8}$ inches in length. One of these retained the original outer surface. A nearly rectangular shell piece with slightly convex ends was 1 inch long and $^{7}/_{16}$ inch wide. Two oval pieces were found. Two specimens, each $^{1}/_{2}$ inch square, form a pair (Fig. 31i).

Miscellaneous Unperforated Mussel Shells: One piece of shell was cut near the mussel hinge with two crossed lines deeply engraved at the apex. It was apparently broken during manufacture (Fig. 36k; Pl. 62j).

A fragment has a series of lines ($^{1}/_{4}$ inch long or less) engraved perpendicular to the edge. One specimen had been roughly cut and smoothed into a seven-sided form.

Objects of Unidentified Shell

A tiny disc bead of shell was $^{3}/_{32}$ inch in diameter (Fig. 62e). A tubular bead, probably conch shell, was 1$^{3}/_{16}$ inches long and $^{3}/_{8}$ inch in diameter. Tiny drilled pits were visible on the eroded surface. An elongated, curved pendant of heavy, unidentified shell was broken at the perforation.

"Button" (Fig. 66a): A single "button" of heavy unidentified shell about 1⅜ inches in diameter had a central perforation ⅛ inch in diameter. A deep cut had been made on the back.

Cut Shell

Twenty-four pieces of mussel shell may be by-products of shell manufacture or they may be broken fragments of intentionally shaped pieces.

Unworked Shell

Six small fragments of mussel shell showed no sign of cutting. Four bivalve shells were found; two with slits cut in the center of the shell were interpreted as showing the first step in the manufacture of shell objects (Fig. 33a). One unworked conch shell fragment was tentatively identified.

Fired Clay Objects Other Than Pottery Vessels

The types of fired clay objects other than pottery vessels are listed, and their counts are provided, in Table 32.

TABLE 32
CLASSIFICATION OF FIRED CLAY OBJECTS OTHER THAN POTTERY VESSELS, BONNELL SITE

Artifact	Count
I. Pipes	5
II. Spoon or ladle	1
III. Worked sherds	
1. Triangular, with side notches	1
2. Triangular	1
3. Circular disc with biconical hole at edge	1
4. Biconical perforation in the middle	3
5. Circular discs with drill depression	14
6. Circular discs without drill depression	9
7. Disc fragments	5
8. Pot lids (?)	2
9. Sherd with cut edge	1

Clay Pipes

Two whole tubular pipes and three fragments were located (Fig. 35c). A pipe 3⅛ inches long and about 1 inch in diameter at the bowl end had the smoke passage at the mouth end drilled or perforated with a cylindrical object while the clay was soft. The interior of the bowl has tool marks resulting from hollowing the bowl.

A stemmed tubular pipe had the mouth end cut down to form the stem after

Plate 62. Ornaments, Bonnell Site.

the clay was dry. It is 2½ inches long and about 1 inch in diameter at the bowl.

The five pipes have paste and temper that belong to local Jornada Brown.

Spoon or Ladle

A single Chupadero Black-on-White ladle fragment had the handle broken off. The interior diameter of the bowl was 1¼ inches by 1³⁄₁₆ inches; the outside diameter was 1⁹⁄₁₆ inches by 1½ inches. A V-shaped cut, ¼ inch deep, was made into the upper surface of the remaining portion of the handle. This cut was made after the ladle dried but before it was decorated and fired. Decoration on the ladle consisted of three concentric circles on the interior; on the exterior a band painted around the back served as the origin for nine lines that radiate to the forward edge.

Worked Sherds

Triangular, Notched Form: This specimen was 2³⁄₁₆ inches long and 2¹⁄₃₂ inches wide (Pl. 62c). The base of the triangle was slightly concave whereas the other two sides were slightly convex. The two sides have been beveled at a 45° angle to the interior curve of the sherd, and notched on the under side just less than ½ inch above the base. The object may have served as a pendant, worn with the apex of the triangle down. Traces of red paint or pigment on the interior surface suggested that this sherd was from a poorly red-slipped bowl.

Triangular: From the floor of House 1 came a well-shaped triangular sherd of Chupadero Black-on-White that measured 1¹⁄₁₆ inches to a side.

Sherd Disc Perforated near the Edge: A single sherd pendant or button fragment of Roswell Brown had a maximum diameter of 3⅛ inches. A biconical hole was placed close to one edge and on the opposite edge there are two biconical holes on the edge of the break. The piece may have broken during the drilling of the third hole. A straight line can be drawn through all three holes.

Sherd Discs with Biconical Holes in the Body of the Disc: Three could have functioned as pendants, buttons, spindle whorls, or drill bases. Distance from the ground hole to the edge of an irregularly shaped Chupadero Black-on-White fragment with ground edges varied from ½ inch to ¾ inch. A Roswell Brown fragment with an off-center biconical hole has a diameter of 1⅞ inches. Edges were not ground. A red-slipped Jornada bowl disc fragment was 1 inch in diameter.

Circular Discs with Drill Depressions: Fourteen sherds had a shallow depression toward the center. One was Chupadero Black-on-White; most of them were Jornada Brown. In all but one, the drill pit was on the interior curve of the sherd. Five had ground edges, the others did not. Four were complete specimens ranging from ⅞ inch to 2¼ inches in diameter.

Sherd Discs without a Drill Depression: Nine discs varied from 1 inch to 2⅝ inches in diameter. More colorful pottery was used than was the case for the discs showing drill depressions. Pottery types included a red-slipped Roswell bowl, Chupadero Black-on-White, Gila Polychrome, Glaze I, and one specimen of Jornada Brown. Some were only roughed out, others had the edges well ground.

Sherd Disc Fragments: Five of the disc fragments were too small to determine whether or not they had a drill depression. Four were brown pottery, one was Heshotauthla Polychrome.

"Pot-lids" (?): Chupadero jugs were made with a disc base that tended to break away from the rest of the vessel. Two bases had smoothed edges, resulting in a flat, circular disc that may have functioned as a pot lid. Both specimens are about 3 inches in diameter.

Sherd with a Cut Edge: A sherd of unclassified black-on-white pottery had seven cuts made transversely across one edge.

FOOD PRODUCTS

Plants

Corn was the only cultivated plant recovered. Over 50 charred cobs and a few kernels were similar, if not identical, to the variety found at Block Lookout and described in Appendix 3 of this report. Maximum cob diameter was ¾ inch; most specimens had a diameter of ⅜ to ½ inch. The longest cob was 2 inches in length. Most cobs were scattered through house fill. Corncobs and kernels were on the floors of Houses 1, 3, 13, and 15, and a single cob was found in one of the outdoor hearths.

Walnut trees grow in the Ruidoso Valley today just below the site. Walnut-shell halves were plentiful in the fill of House 1, and individual shells were associated with Houses 5 and 13.

Some small yellow seeds from House 1 were not identified. Other tiny seeds found on Floors 1 and 2 of House 2 were tentatively identified as *Opuntia*.

Animals

Animal bones were distributed throughout the fill, and deer, antelope and rabbit formed a staple element of the diet. A few bison bones were found in Houses 9 and 12. The greatest concentration of bones was in House 9, where enough broken long bones and ribs of bison and deer were found to fill two gallon containers.

Butchering of larger animals took place outside of the village, presumably at the kill site. No skulls of larger animals were found, and most antlers and tines had been used as tools. Some vertebrae were present, and so some backbone cuts were brought in. Ribs and leg bones were most numerous among the food bones; ulnas, metapodials, ribs and scapulae were important for making bone tools. Small animals were probably brought to the village whole, as all body parts of jackrabbits, cottontails, and unidentified rodents were found. The few bison bones were probably acquired from the Pecos Valley; only selected cuts were carried this greater distance.

POTTERY

Over 200,000 sherds were excavated at the Bonnell Site. Pottery lots from the 18 houses having the most complete and best labeled collection of sherd sacks were analyzed. Even though the entire sherd collection is not tabulated in this report, all available sherds have been examined. See Tables 33–35 and Plates 63–65.

Most of the pottery from the site was sacked by 6-inch levels from the 4-foot square sections. When floor sherds were not separately sacked, sherds thought to be associated with a particular structure must be inferred from the 6-inch level in which the floor was located. Tularosa Black-on-White, which is not represented in the tabulated house lots, occurred at the site.

Characteristics of the Pottery

There are certain ways in which the pottery types in this collection differ from those same types in other localities. Where types are not discussed, it may be assumed that no noteworthy local variations occurred.

Undecorated Jornada Brown

This category is most noteworthy for its prominent place in the percentage tables. A tremendous range in surface finish, color, and tempering materials was found. The vast majority of these sherds had a matte finish; occasional vessels were polished.

The most common form was a globular olla with a mouth about 4 inches in diameter. Wider-mouthed olla rims occurred as a minor form. Most of the bowl sherds may have belonged to decorated vessels.

The most common type of temper was rounded quartz particles of small to medium size. Here again there was a tremendous amount of variation from very angular feldspar temper, barely held together with clay, to temper so fine that you need a hand lens to see it.

Roswell Brown

This variant was a minor but regular member of the sherd lots. Highest percentages of Roswell Brown were found in House 1 (10% of total sherds) and House 5 (15% of total). In other house lots, it ran from a trace to 8%, with most samples having between 2% and 5%. Roswell Brown enjoyed greater popularity early in the history of the site. The ratio of bowls to ollas is higher in Roswell than in Jornada Brown. Interior striations (like Chupadero) occur. An atypical bowl had the rim everted at a 90° angle to the vessel wall.

Decorated Brown Types

Red paint decoration was much more prevalent at this site than elsewhere. Roswell bowls were more frequently decorated than Jornada Brown; similar designs were applied to both. Ollas and bowls bore broad-line decoration and red slips.

A minor form of decoration was surface alteration. Neck brushed (one vessel), exterior brushed, interior brushed, hollow reed punctation and incised decoration occurred.

Three Rivers Red-on-Terracotta

Broad-line decorations (Pl. 63b) were much more common than thin-line, and the Bonnell conservatives did little experimentation with non-linear designs. One zoomorphic (deer?) head was painted on a sherd.

Rare ollas or jugs had the vessel and paint color of the classic Three Rivers. In at least one specimen, the olla interior was striated like Chupadero; heavy handles have been found in this type.

Lincoln Black-on-Red

Design motifs tend to be typical. None of the red-on-red variant occurs, and thin black lines are rare. H. P. Mera identified a heavy handle as Lincoln Black-on-Red, suggesting the rare occurrence of a jug or pitcher form in this type.

Chupadero Black-on-White

As with the preceding type, Chupadero tends to conform to typical forms and designs (Pl. 63a; Pl. 64). The Capitan variant was not found.

Corrugated

Partially obliterated coils were most common. Little or no decoration by painting, incision, etc. occurred.

Summary

The most unusual features of this ceramic collection are (1) the high proportion of brown wares (higher than at any other site of equivalent age in the Southwest), and (2) the conservatism of the designs on locally made pottery. Design elements continue in the "classic" tradition and there is little of the exuberance and experimentation that is seen in localities to the north.

DISPOSAL OF THE DEAD

Four infant, thirteen child, and four adult burials were excavated. If each of the instances of scattered or unburied (?) finds represented an individual, perhaps one adult, one infant and two children could be added to this number.

Two cases of double burials in the same grave suggest an illness that affected several individuals simultaneously. Aside from these two double burials, there were three cases where two graves were made close together from the same surface.

Burial most typically occurred outside of structures. Graves were dug into the sheet trash deposit that covered the site. Sub-floor interment was definite for five burials, two of which were in House 13. Houses 13 and 20 were definitely occupied after burial occurred. Houses 4 and 12 were probably abandoned. Adults as well as infants and children were buried beneath floors.

No consistent orientation of the body was practiced, except that the grave orientation tended to correspond to a cardinal direction. Nine bodies had their heads to the north, two to the south, four to the west, and five to the east. One grave had an orientation that was off of a cardinal direction; Burial 15 was SSE-NNW.

Burial position was flexed in all cases where the skeleton was sufficiently intact to make this observation. Eleven skeletons were laid on their backs, three on their sides, and one in a sitting position. Children usually had their legs flexed to each side if they were on their backs. Adults were tightly flexed with their knees drawn up to the chest. Arms were usually folded across the body, under the flexed legs; one individual may have had his arms placed around his knees.

Most burials were unaccompanied by grave offerings and few individuals took their ornaments with them to the grave. Two or possibly three individuals had bowls placed over the face. The Chupadero bowl in Burial 4 had been "killed," and the Three Rivers bowl in Burial 8 had probably been "killed." The child in Burial 4 had a valuable necklace of *Olivella* shells in addition to the bowl; these signs of affluence were unique. The only other possible grave accompaniments were the turquoise object in Burial 20 and the single *Olivella* bead from the neck region of Burial 10.

The bottom of the grave in Burial 8 had been burned and burned rocks were scattered over the bottom of this grave, suggesting some variant in the burial procedures.

Burial Descriptions

Burial 1, A Double Burial

Location: Just SW of House 7.

Orientation: One individual's head was oriented to the north and one to the south.

Dimensions of Grave: 40 inches NS, 25 inches EW.

Offerings: None.

Description: Both individuals were children, one approximately 6 years old and the other approximately 12. Both bodies were apparently flexed and both faced west; bones were displaced. The bodies of the two children overlapped. For some reason, a number of bones were found in each skull. The skull on the south contained 16 vertebrae, ribs, and 1 scapula. The lower jaw was disarticulated and was found 1 foot above the skull. The skull on the north contained vertebrae, a humerus, and one pelvic bone. This latter skull has two parietal foramina, each ¼ inch in diameter, located ¼ inch above the lambdoid suture.

Burial 2, A Double Burial

Location: Between Houses 11 and 12.

Orientation: Grave was NS. Both children had their heads to the north.

Position: On their back with their legs flexed to each side.

Age: The north individual was an infant. The south individual was about 6–7 years old; some permanent teeth had erupted, but baby teeth remained.

Offerings: None.

Burial 3

Location: It was in the House 11 limits, but no evidence was found that the burial had any connection with the house.

Orientation: Head to west.

Position: The child had been placed on its back with the face up. Legs were flexed loosely over the pelvis. The disarticulated lower jaw was in the pelvic region.

Age: Child, about 4–6 years old.

Grave: Very shallow; barely deep enough to cover the skull.

Offerings: None.

TABLE 33
SHERD COUNTS FROM FLOOR LEVELS, BONNELL SITE

	House 1		House 3 Floor 1		House 5		House 6		House 7		House 8, Floor 1		
Pottery Types	No.	%	No.	%	No.	%	No.	%	No.	%	No.	%	Totals
Chupadero Black-on-White													
Bowl	25		8		19		3		1				56
Olla	56		11		61		5		12		6		151
Total	81	6.50	19	8.15	80	10.22	8	10.39	13	5.02	6	3.73	207
Corrugated	8	.64	15	6.44	12	1.53	2	2.60	4	1.54	6	3.73	47
Brown System													
Jornada Brown	2												2
Roswell Brown	40		15		126		2		12		4		199
Other	843		135		299		37		146		32		1492
Total	885	70.97	150	64.38	425	54.28	39	50.65	158	61.00	36	22.36	1693
Decorated Brown													
Undiff. Red-on-Brown	33		1										34
Jornada Red-on-Brown	5		1		1		1						8
Roswell Red-on-Brown	47								1				48
Textured Brown	3				4				3				10
Red-slipped bowl									1				1
Red-slipped olla					1								1
Total	88	7.06	2	.86	6	.77	1	1.30	5	1.93			102
Jornada Polychrome	67	5.37	5	2.15	66	8.43	2	2.60	9	3.47	5	3.11	154
El Paso Polychrome	55	4.41	27	11.59	64	8.17	14	18.18	27	10.42	90	55.90	277

Three Rivers Red-on-Terracotta													
Broad-lined	12		4		23		3		3				45
Thin-lined											1		1
Undecorated	7		2		34		4		14		10		71
Red-slipped	29		1		34		2		13		2		81
Olla	4		4		28		2		5				43
Total	52	4.17	11	4.72	119	15.20	11	14.29	35	13.51	13	8.07	241
Lincoln Black-on-Red													
Decorated	3				6						2		11
Undecorated	1		3		3				3		3		13
Red-on-Red													0
Total	4	.32	3	1.28	9	1.15			3	1.16	5	3.11	24
Glaze I	2	.16							1	.39			3
Mimbres Black-on-White	3	.24			2	.26			2	.77			7
Gila Polychrome									1	.39			1
Heshotauthla Polychrome													0
Ramos Polychrome	1	.08											1
Playas Red Incised			1	.43									1
St. Johns Polychrome													0
Unknown	1	.08							1	.39			2
Unident. Chihuahua Poly.													0
Total	1247		233		783		77		259		161		2760

TABLE 34
SHERD COUNTS FROM FLOOR LEVELS, BONNELL SITE

	House 9		House 10		House 11		House 12		House 13 Floor 1		House 14		
Pottery Types	No.	%	No.	%	No.	%	No.	%	No.	%	No.	%	Totals
Chupadero Black-on-White													
Bowl	17				4		9		17		10		57
Olla	33		3		7		14		54		18		129
Total	50	8.25	3	2.63	11	8.03	23	6.65	71	10.92	28	11.72	186
Corrugated	84	13.86	12	10.53			7	2.02	7	1.08	3	1.26	113
Brown System													
Jornada Brown													0
Roswell Brown	26		6		10		7		72		13		134
Other	256		60		90		253		267		136		1062
Total	282	46.53	66	57.89	100	72.99	260	75.14	339	52.15	149	62.34	1196
Decorated Brown													
Undiff. Red-on-Brown							2						2
Jornada Red-on-Brown	1				1		1		1				4
Roswell Red-on-Brown	1		2		1				9		1		14
Textured Brown	9		1		2		2		5		2		21
Red-slipped bowl	1				5		8						14
Red-slipped olla	3								2				5
Total	15	2.48	3	2.63	9	6.57	13	3.76	17	2.62	3	1.26	60

Jornada Polychrome			1	.88			2	.58			5	2.09	8
El Paso Polychrome	82	13.53	23	20.18	15	10.95	19	5.49	152	23.38	24	10.04	315
Three Rivers Red-on-Terracotta													
Broad-lined	3		1		1		2		3				10
Thin-lined	7						2		8		4		21
Undecorated	15		3		1		5		11		6		41
Red-slipped	16								12		5		33
Olla	10		1				4		20				35
Total	51	8.42	5	4.39	2	1.46	13	3.76	54	8.31	15	6.28	140
Lincoln Black-on-Red													
Decorated	11						2		2		3		18
Undecorated	17						3		5		5		30
Red-on-Red													0
Total	28	4.62					5	1.45	7	1.08	8	3.35	48
Glaze I	7	1.16											7
Mimbres Black-on-White	1	.17					1	.29	2	.31	1	.42	5
Gila Polychrome													0
Heshotauthla Polychrome	1	.17											1
Ramos Polychrome	1	.17							1	.15			2
Playas Red Incised													0
St. Johns Polychrome			1(?)	.88(?)							1	.42	2
Unknown	4	.66					3	.87			2	.84	9
Unident. Chihuahua Poly.													0
Total	606		114		137		346		650		239		2092

TABLE 35
SHERD COUNTS FROM FLOOR LEVELS, BONNELL SITE

	House 15		House 16		House 17 Floor 1		House 17 Floor 2		House 20 Floor 1		House 20 Floor 2		Table 35,	Totals, Tables
Pottery Types	No.	%	No.	%	No.	%	No.	%	No.	%	No.	%	Total	33, 34, & 35
Chupadero Black-on-White														
Bowl	15		22		24		8		1		5		75	188
Olla	99		72		4		36		10		17		238	518
Total	114	15.00	94	14.78	28	21.54	44	16.73	11	33.33	22	7.59	313	706
Corrugated	48	6.32	18	2.83	7	5.38	18	6.84			14	4.83	105	265
Brown System														
Jornada Brown													0	2
Roswell Brown	25		48		5		7		3		5		93	426
Other	306		275		30		95		11		156		873	3427
Total	331	43.55	323	50.79	35	26.92	102	38.78	14	42.42	161	55.52	966	3855
Decorated Brown														
Undiff. Red-on-Brown			2								3		5	41
Jornada Red-on-Brown			4		2		2				1		9	21
Roswell Red-on-Brown	3		2				1						6	68
Textured Brown	5		3				2				5		15	46
Red-slipped bowl			3										3	18
Red-slipped olla			12								17		29	35
Total	8	1.05	26	4.09	2	1.54	5	1.90			26	8.97	67	229

Jornada Polychrome	20	2.63	11	1.73	9	6.92	4	1.52	1	3.03	5	1.72	50	212
El Paso Polychrome	145	19.08	109	17.14	42	32.31	70	26.62	5	15.15	39	13.45	410	1002
Three Rivers Red-on-Terracotta														
Broad-lined	4		4		1								9	64
Thin-lined	11		11				2				7		31	53
Undecorated	24		13				3				8		48	160
Red-slipped	14												14	128
Olla	12		2		1						2		17	95
Total	65	8.55	30	4.72	2	1.54	5	1.90			17	5.86	119	500
Lincoln Black-on-Red														
Decorated	4						3						7	36
Undecorated	6				4		9		1		3		23	66
Red-on-Red	2						1				1		4	4
Total	12	1.58			4	3.08	13	4.94	1	3.03	4	1.38	34	106
Glaze I	2	.26	2	.31									4	14
Mimbres Black-on-White	4	.53			1	.77	1	.38					6	18
Gila Polychrome			1	.16					1	3.03			2	3
Heshotauthla Polychrome													0	1
Ramos Polychrome													0	3
Playas Red Incised													0	1
St. Johns Polychrome	5	.66	11	1.73									16	18
Unknown	5	.66	11	1.73			1	.38			2	.69	19	30
Unident. Chihuahua Poly.	1	.13											1	1
Total	760		636		130		263		33		290		2112	6964

a

b

c

Plate 63. *a*, Chupadero Black-on-White bowl, Bonnell Site; *b*, Three Rivers Red-on-Terracotta bowl, Bonnell Site; *c*, El Paso Polychrome olla, Bonnell Site.

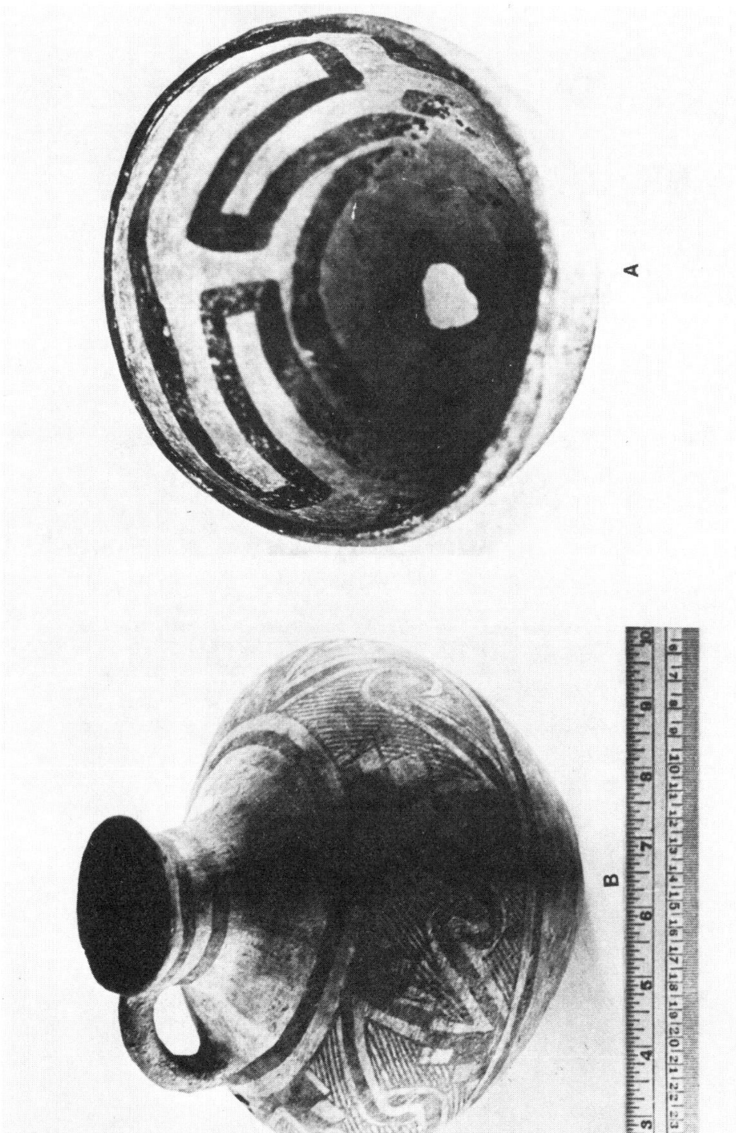

Plate 64. *a*, Chupadero Black-on-White "jug," Bonnell Site; *b*, Chupadero Black-on-White "killed" bowl, Bonnell Site.

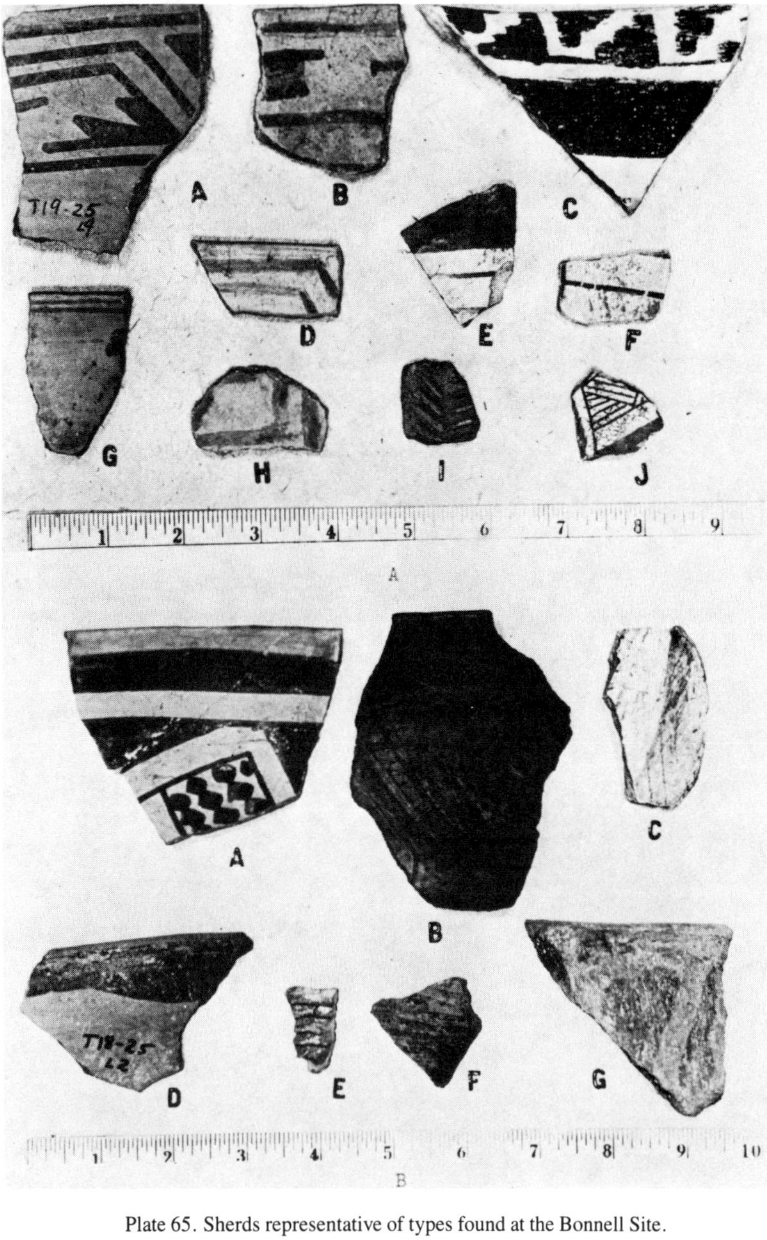

Plate 65. Sherds representative of types found at the Bonnell Site.

Burial 4

Location: Sub-floor, House 12. Burial was made from the upper floor. The grave cut through the lower floor.

Orientation: Grave EW. Head to E.

Position: On back, legs flexed to pelvic region.

Dimensions of Grave: 16 inches EW, 10 inches NS.

Age: Infant.

Offerings: A Chupadero Black-on-White bowl over the face had been "killed." A four- or five-strand necklace of 201 *Olivella* beads was around the baby's neck.

Burial 5

Location: E of House 8.

Orientation: Grave was EW. Head to E.

Position: Flexed. On right side.

Age: Child 4–6 years. All deciduous teeth.

Condition: Body was badly crushed, especially the rib cage. Several bones were in the unbroken skull; these included vertebrae, finger bones, clavicle and scapula.

Offerings: None.

Burial 6

Location: 9 inches N of Burial 5, E of House 8. This burial was made from the same surface as Burial 5.

Orientation: NS. Head to N.

Position: On left side. Legs flexed over pelvis.

Age: Child, probably under 4 years.

Offerings: None.

Burial 7

Location: Fill of House 1; 24 inches below modern surface.

Orientation: NS. Head to S.

Dimensions of Grave: 8 x 6 inches.

Position: Flexed on back.

Age: Tiny baby. Maybe premature. Certainly not over 2 months old.

Offerings: None.

Burial 8

Location: Within the limits of House 10, but no evidence that the burial was connected with the house. Depth: ca. 26 inches below surface.

Orientation: EW. Head to W.

Position: Bones were badly deteriorated, but long bones seem to indicate a flexed position, lying on its back.

Age: Child. Four erupted milk teeth in the remaining maxilla fragment.

Grave: Bottom of the grave had been burned and burned rocks more or less lined the grave. The bones had not been burned.

Offerings: A broken and possibly "killed" Three Rivers Red-on-Terracotta bowl covered the face.

Burial 10

Location: Just west of Burial 8; the two graves were dug from the same surface.

Orientation: NS. Head to N.

Position: On back. Legs flexed tightly against the chest. Arms folded across the chest under the legs.

Age and Sex: Adult male about 30 years old.

Physical Description: Asymmetrical occipital deformation is evident. The right side of the skull is larger than the left. There are two Wormian bones in the lambdoid suture. The sagittal suture is obliterated in a small area, but well marked for the rest of its length. A number of bony growths occurred on the skull but none occurred on the body bones. There is a large protuberance on the lower right parietal and a similar but smaller growth on the left parietal. Several small growths were noted in the facial region, one on the nasal bone. One third molar was extracted during the life of the individual. Rest of teeth present. No caries. Teeth well ground. Shovel-shaped incisors. The left foot was missing. Rest of the body was in excellent condition and well articulated.

Grave: Like Burial 8, this grave contained some fire-cracked rocks and charcoal.

Offering: A single *Olivella* bead lay in the neck region.

Burial 11

Location: West of House 2. Depth was 30–36 inches below the modern surface.

Description: Badly deteriorated. Skull, two femurs, one fibula and a humerus fragment were the only remaining bones. There was a hole at the back of the skull that may have been the cause of death; no scar tissue had formed.

Age: The coronoid suture was completely obliterated on the interior of the skull.

Teeth: All teeth were present in the upper jaw. Some were missing in the lower jaw. A badly decayed molar must have been painful. Teeth were badly worn.

Position: (?)

Orientation: The long bones ran in a NE-SW direction. Skull was to the

NW of the long bones.

Offerings: None.

Burial 12

Location: In fill. It was on the east edge of abandoned House 4; this burial was made so much later that it had no intentional relationship with the structure. Depth was 15 inches below the modern surface.

Orientation: The grave was oriented NS, but the exact outline could not be determined. Skull was to north, facing east.

Position: Could not be determined. Most of the bones were under the skull. The two femurs, pelvic bones, two humeri and some vertebrae were mixed in the soft fill south of the skull.

Age: Small child. The fontanelle had not closed.

Offerings: In the fill, but probably not intentionally associated with the burial, were a charred corncob, a sherd of Heshotauthla Polychrome, and a piece of worked bone.

Burial 13

Location: West of House 3.

Position: Sitting, tightly flexed arms folded over the pelvis.

Orientation: Body faced east.

Description: The skull was missing, but the scapula etc. were only 6 inches below the surface. The skull may have been collected by amateurs, as it had probably been exposed on the surface. The cervical vertebrae and sternum were displaced to the pelvic area. The rib cage was collapsed. A disarticulated femur was 18 inches from the body. A foot under the pelvis was beautifully articulated.

Age: Fully adult.

Offerings: Separated from the burial by about 18 inches, sherds of a nearly complete Chupadero Black-on-White bowl were found which could have been placed over the face.

Burial 14

Location: Room 4. Sub-floor. NW corner.

Dimensions of Grave: 2 feet NS and 2 feet EW. Dug into gravel.

Orientation: Head to N.

Age: Child, probably about 8 years. Has permanent teeth.

Offerings: None.

Burial 15

Location: Just east of Room 9. Just under the modern surface.

Orientation: Body oriented SSE-NNW. Skull to SSE.

Position: Flexed. On back. Skull was on its left side, facing east.
Age: Child.
Offerings: None.

Burial 16

Location: Just south of House 1. In sheet fill, at a depth of 28–32 inches below the surface.
Dimensions of Grave: 30 inches NS by 14 inches EW.
Orientation: Head to N.
Position: On back, legs flexed to each side. Arms across chest. Face up.
Age: Child. Had both permanent and milk teeth.
Offerings: None.

Burial 17

Location: House 20, beneath Floor 1. Against the west wall of the house.
Orientation: EW. Skull to W.
Position: (?) Bones in poor condition and scattered.
Bones Present: Skull, one femur, mandible, one rib, phalanges, one pelvic bone.
Grave: Covered with clay cap.
Age: Child 6–8 years.
Offerings: None.

Burial 18

Location: Probably just west of House 10, but burial preceded the building of that house. Top of grave was 26 inches below surface.
Grave: Very shallow. The tops of the bones were almost on a level with the surface from which the burial was made.
Orientation: EW.
Position: Body on back. Legs apparently flexed to each side. Skull was on the left side, facing north.
Age: Child. About 6 years.
Offerings: None.

Burial 19

Location: Room 13. Along the south wall. Burial had been made from Floor 3.
Grave: The grave was capped by a clay slab 9 inches thick.
Orientation: EW.
Position: Fully flexed, on right side, head to east.
Age: Adult male. No closed sutures.
Offerings: None.

Burial 20

Location: Room 13. SE corner of room. This burial was probably made from Floor 3, like Burial 19, but evidence is less clear.

Description: Some of the lower bones of the body were in the grave which was dug into the east pit wall. Remaining bones were found over the SE-¼ of the house in the soft fill between Floors 2 and 3.

Age: Child, 1¼–2 years.

Offerings: An unperforated turquoise piece was found close to the grave, amid the bones.

Burial 21

Location: West of House 19. Depth: 24 to 30 inches below modern surface.

Orientation: Body oriented NS. Top of body north.

Position: Tightly flexed on back. The right arm had been folded over the knees, and the left arm lay stretched away from the body.

Description: The skull was missing, although the mandible was present.

Age: Adult.

Offerings: None.

Other Human Bones

There were six instances of isolated human bones for which we could find no evidence of a grave. These may represent additional burials that we were unable to detect, or they may indicate less formal means of disposing of the dead.

Between Floors 1 and 2 of House 14, a rib, four human teeth and some maxillary fragments of an adult were found.

South of House 19 there were fragments of vertebrae and teeth. Scattered pieces of a baby skeleton were found in the fill of House 1. From the House 10 area, but in a level that was deposited prior to the building of that structure, there were skull fragments, one rib, one clavicle, and two femurs of a young child.

Toward the center of House 3, the group of bones described as Burial 9 (Holden 1952:125) were in an ash layer, and it was suggested that this was a cremation. Since the bones were scattered, and no grave was found, it is better to consider it here. Subsequent investigations in House 3 produced two skull fragments, two ribs and one ulna of an infant. These bones were not burned. In the fill between Floors 1 and 2, a clavicle, a petrous process and an occipital fragment were found. If all three groups of bones came from the same individual, it is doubtful that it was a cremation.

A number of bones from a small child, scattered through the fill between floors in the southeast corner of House 2, were mixed with bones of a rodent.

Two vertebrae, the sternum, two phalanges, two rib fragments, an ulna, and one of the hand or foot bones were present.

DATING

Ceramic Correlations

The initial settlement of the village cannot be dated precisely; this event may have occurred in the middle of the Pueblo III period. The presence of Corrugated in most analyzed house lots is taken as an indication of the general contemporaneity of this site with the Lincoln Phase to the north. Abandonment of the village probably occurred between A.D. 1350 and A.D. 1400, as Glaze I was common but no later Rio Grande glazes were found. The exact terminal date depends on the time lag between this region and the Middle Rio Grande.

Continuation of the popularity of Brown types on the Glaze I time horizon seems unique. Wheat (1955b:33) suggested that the high percentage of Brown pottery that was reported for this site (in Holden 1952) indicated an earlier temporal placement of the site than had been assigned. Because of his comments, the entire ceramic picture was carefully reviewed. The association of Glaze I or other late trade types with high percentages of Brown pottery seems well established by the house floor lots (Table 33). While recognizing that a great deal of mixing must have occurred as a result of the extensive pot-holing the site had endured, certain floor samples are thought to represent primary deposition.

Internal Chronology

The structural history of the site is so complex and superimpositions and rebuilding are so common that one has the impression of a long occupation. The pottery types tell a different story. The whole ceramic assemblage is relatively short lived.

The structures are divided into early, middle, and late house lots by their pottery complexes. The early lots have only a trace of Corrugated. At least one sherd of Corrugated was found on all house floors, except the lower floor of House 20, where the presence of Gila Polychrome indicated that the absence of Corrugated was not due to that house being earlier, but to other factors. A high percentage of Jornada Brown is typical of these earlier houses. Trade wares of the Glaze I horizon are lacking. The middle group of house lots likewise had little Corrugated, but Glaze I horizon trade wares are present. The latest house lots have more Corrugated (up to 21%), trade wares are present, and Gila Polychrome becomes a fad.

Early House Lots:
House 5
House 6
Middle House Lots:
House 1
House 2, Floor 1
House 3, Floor 1
House 4
House 13, Floors 1 and 2
House 14, Floor 1
House 7
House 8, Floor 1
House 15
House 20, Floor 1
Late House Lots:
House 2, Floors 2 and 3
House 3, Floor 2
House 9
House 13, Floors 3, 4, and 5
House 14, Floor 2
House 20, Floors 2 and 3
House 8, Floor 2

Houses 5 and 6 were abandoned before any trade wares of the Glaze I horizon had been acquired. The early pottery lots correspond to the first building period as defined on stratigraphic grounds.

House 1, which must have been constructed in the first building period, burned just after the introduction of Glaze I. Undecorated Jornada Brown forms 66% of the total sherd sample (of 1187 sherds), and Corrugated makes up less than .05%.

The south house block (Houses 7 and 8) and the lower floors of the east and west house blocks (Houses 2, 3, and 4 on the west, and Houses 13, 20 and 14 on the east) have low percentages of Corrugated and few trade wares. The upper floors of these house blocks (except House 4, which had been abandoned) show a marked increase in Corrugated and Gila Polychrome.

House 15 was built, or at least occupied, after House 1 had burned. We have insufficient data about the remaining houses, but they must belong to the late occupations on stratigraphic grounds.

We have no ceramic grounds for differentiating between houses assigned to Building Periods 2, 3, and 4. The increase in Corrugated and the appearance of Gila Polychrome occurred during the time when the multi-roomed structures of Building Period 2 were in use. Apparently the upper floors of the multi-roomed structures and the individual houses of Building Period 3 were occupied a very short time. Pottery from Houses 18 and 26 of Building Period 4 are not tabulated, but they contain no post-Glaze I types and are essentially like the late house lots in pottery content.

SUMMARY

Our fullest information about the late Glencoe Phase comes from the Bonnell Site. Two adjacent "mounds" represent the remains of a compact, nucleated village. The larger of these, Mound A, was excavated rather fully. Testing of Mound B established its general contemporaneity with Mound A. The village presumably was occupied from mid Pueblo III until the Glaze I horizon of Pueblo IV.

Shallow to medium depth pithouses and *jacal* structures were the basic architectural forms. At one point in the history of the site, multi-room dwellings consisting of contiguous pit rooms were built, apparently in response to the diffusion of puebloid architectural concepts from the nearby Lincoln Phase.

All excavated structures seem to have been used for domestic purposes. The size and location of Houses 1 and 15 may be indicative of a specialized function, and these structures may have been full or, more likely, part-time ceremonial chambers.

The pottery complex was somewhat similar to that of the Lincoln Phase in its general make-up. Jornada Brown formed a large percentage of the total, which is unusual in a site of this age in the Southwest. Corrugated was not of major importance, and trade types were more limited in number than they were in Lincoln Phase sites.

Close ties between the late Glencoe and Lincoln Phases were manifest in most artifact categories, including metates with "mano rests" at the closed end, slab metates, mano types, projectile point types, ornaments, and a variety of bone tools.

Subsistence depended upon corn agriculture. The variety of corn grown was small and primitive. Hunting was an important secondary food source, and wild plants were gathered.

Excavations at the Bonnell Site have revealed a rural, conservative way of life that, at the time the village was abandoned, was under considerable pressure from the more "modern" Lincoln Phase villages in the Bonito Valley. Had abandonment been postponed one or two generations, the Bonnell villagers would probably have taken over pueblo architecture and assimilated other aspects of Lincoln Phase material culture.

Appendix 6

BLOOM MOUND IN THE LOWER HONDO VALLEY

INTRODUCTION

Setting

Bloom Mound is located approximately 14 miles west-southwest of Roswell, New Mexico, on the north bank of the Hondo River some 10 miles above the junction of the Hondo with the Pecos.

The lower Hondo River meanders through valley alluvium. River flow is sporadic, and even when there is water in the upper Hondo, it often does not reach this far down-river. Elevation at the site is approximately 3775 feet. This is nominally within the Lower Sonoran Life Zone, although this section of the valley has an Upper Sonoran flora (Bailey 1913:13).

History of Research at Bloom Mound

Bloom Mound was first reported to The Roswell Archaeological Society in 1934 by Shirley Feather. Excavations began in 1936 and have continued sporadically since that date. Soon after the Society had begun excavations, Dr. H. P. Mera visited the site.

The Society has used The Roswell Museum as a repository for some excavated materials. A scrapbook written by Major M. G. Fulton, Mary K. Higgins, Colonel G. M. Sayre, Ed Raymond, and Jim Cooley gives a brief history of excavation.

This report is a reconstruction of archaeological information obtained by The Roswell Archaeological Society and Texas Technological College. The real value of the site lies not in precise details, which are elusive, but in the general corpus of information which reflects a trading center of unusual affluence for this region.

The Roswell Archaeological Society tried over the years to establish the structural limits of the site. Trenches were started from the four cardinal directions between 1938 and 1949. The west trench was carried to a depth of ten feet and sherds and other cultural materials extended to this depth. Most of the trenches were backfilled or else never proceeded very far, as only the trench on the east is now apparent. Backfilling of the western trench is specifically mentioned in the scrapbook entry for 18 September 1938. The site seems to have been honeycombed with small trenches below floors and outside of rooms. These were also backfilled.

Trenches on the east and west were adequate to show that there was no extensive building on either side, and probably the basic form of the site has been revealed.

Texas Technological College excavated one surface room (Room G) and completed the excavation of the ceremonial chamber (Room D or F) in 1954.

ARCHITECTURE

A deep, square, subterranean structure was located east of the north-south trending double tier of adobe surface rooms (Map 10). Nine of these surface rooms were cleared, and others may remain unexcavated on the northern end.

Rooms

Rooms A, B, C, E, F, and G carry letters assigned to them by the Roswell Archaeological Society. The letter C was applied to two rooms, those here called C and K. There were no designations for the remaining rooms and the letters H, I, J, and K were arbitrarily supplied by the author. The subterranean chamber was designated as Room D and Room F at different times.

Room A

This was the first room dug by the Society in fall, 1938 and fall, 1939. No architectural features were noted and artifacts were not recorded in detail, although sherds, bone, corn, a stone ring 1¼ inches in diameter, and two points were mentioned. A total of eight skeletons were said to have come from the room. Two of them were in the fill mixed with roofing charcoal; six were on the floor. Room A was backfilled and accurate measurements were not available.

Room B

This room was also dug in 1938 and 1939. A sub-floor trench produced a reed and an undescribed red jasper point.

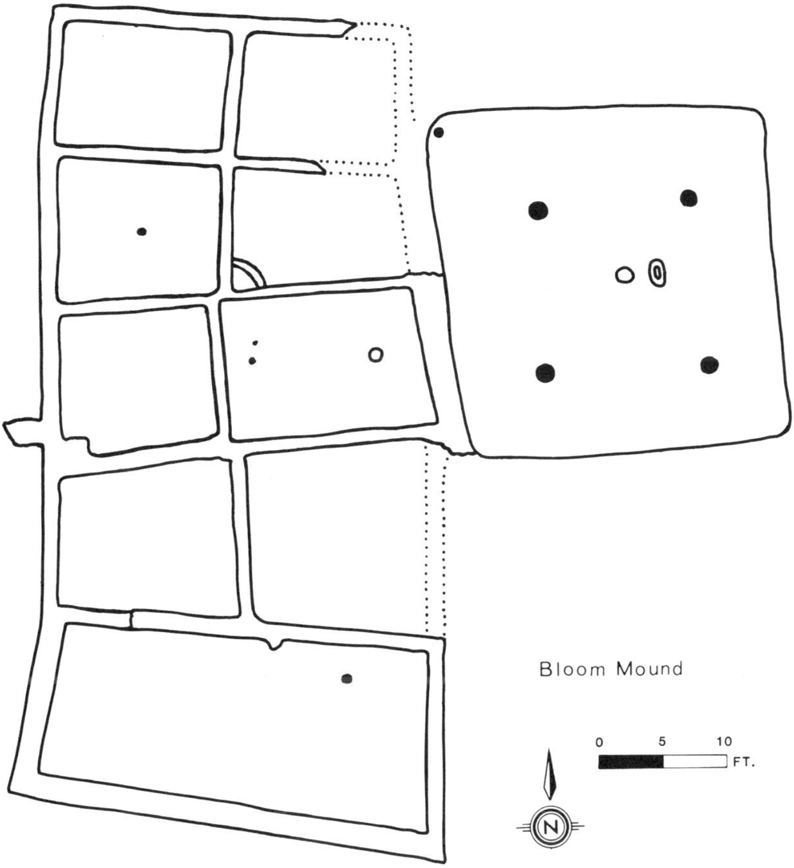

Map 10. Bloom Mound.

Room C

This room was the most productive one at the site, in spite of the fact that it had been previously looted. It was the subject of at least four days of intensive digging in 1938, and in 1939 they returned "to the old diggings" and found more artifacts. Notes in the scrapbook indicate that Room C had three floor levels.

After cleaning the middle floor, a sub-floor trench revealed a lower floor in which there was a tapering firepit 16 inches deep and 10 inches in diameter at the mouth. A strat column that had previously been left in the room was dug separately. It is likely that seven copper bells came from Room C.

A number of skeletons and parts of skeletons were recorded which are described in a later section.

Room D or F

This room (Pl. 66) received two letter designations because different groups of the Roswell Archaeological Society dug here in 1939, 1941, and 1945. The Roswell Society had exposed perhaps 4 square feet of the floor in the southwest corner.

In 1954 the Texas Technological College crew finished clearing this structure, which was nearly 20 feet square (Holden 1955b). Since the plastered wall was 7 feet high in the northwest corner, the building may have been completely subterranean. Four central posts carried the roof. A fifth post was found in the northwest corner. A cylindrical firepit was slightly east of center, and an ash pit covered with a perforated metate was 1 foot east of the firepit. The house pit had been dug several inches into a soft gypsum deposit resulting in an extremely level floor.

Points and scrapers were prominent in the artifacts recovered from the floor. No food-grinding tools were present. Ceremonial or leisure activities were represented by bone gaming pieces. Skeletal material is discussed in another section.

Room E

Excavation was carried out in 1948 and 1949 by the Roswell group. Several floors may have been present. The first was encountered at a depth of 18 to 20 inches below the surface. It seems as if another floor was found at a depth of 35 inches. A "cyst," a "burnt basin," a "Dutch oven," and a firepit were noted in the scrapbook. A Rio Grande Glaze I bowl rested on the floor, and two skulls were listed.

Room G

This was an asymmetrical, rectangular room at the west of the house block (Pl. 67; Holden 1955b). Walls 8 inches thick of coursed adobe stood 11 to 21 inches high. The only interior structural feature was a central post. Charred roofing remains were close to the modern surface.

Rooms H and I

No data.

Room J

No architectural features were mentioned in the scrapbook. A mano, a point, and the rim of a Gila Polychrome jar with a mouth opening 12 inches in diameter were noted.

Room K

The only architectural feature reported was a post, 6 inches in diameter,

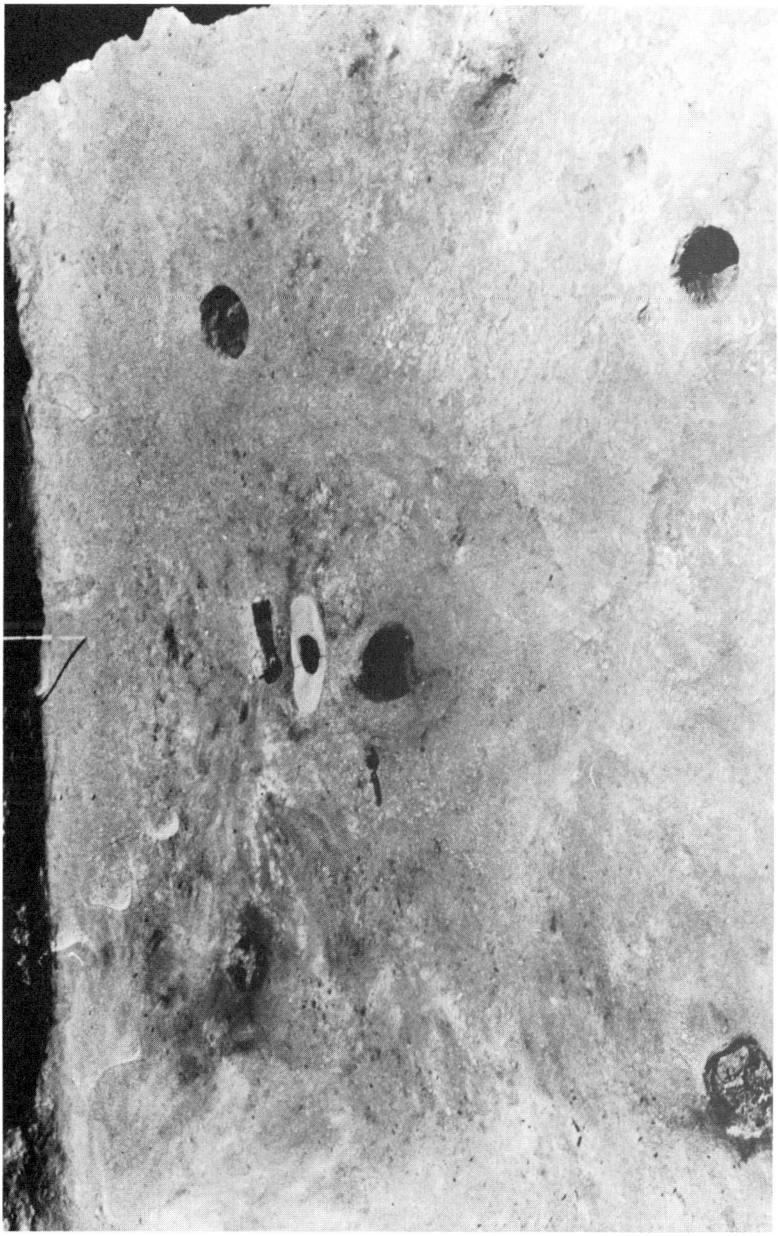

Plate 66. Room D (also designated Room F), the subterranean chamber, Bloom Mound.

Plate 67. Room G, Bloom Mound.

which rested on but did not penetrate the floor. A Glaze I bowl and a small Corrugated vessel, which was described as having the handles broken off, rested on the floor. In a photograph, two skeletons were shown close to these two vessels. A bushel of charred corncobs was removed from 1 corner; this was recorded for 5 March 1939, and it was verbally described to me by Colonel Sayre.

Function of the Rooms

Room G was a storeroom. Room C had a firepit in the lower floor, and it probably served as living quarters. The quantity of cultural materials recovered from Room C could mean that it served as a storage room later, or that it was the residence of the person who had custody of major ceremonial and decorative objects. Room E was used for domestic purposes. Information is incomplete for the other rooms. but it is clear that the surface rooms functioned as both living quarters and storage rooms. The subterranean chamber was probably a ceremonial structure.

MATERIAL CULTURE

The population of Bloom Mound could never have been large, and yet the quantity and quality of the recovered material culture is unusually rich for southeastern New Mexican sites. The fact that most of the rooms burned contributed to the apparent affluence.

The location of Bloom Mound close to the junction of the Hondo River with the Pecos River gave the residents an opportunity to engage in trade westward with other sedentary Southwesterners and eastward to the Plains. This location also placed them in a vulnerable position in regard to raiders, who finally destroyed the pueblo. It is worth trying to unravel the intricacies of 15 years of amateur archaeology to fill out the picture of this outpost. On a very small scale, it must have occupied a position much like Pecos Pueblo.

The rather lengthy lists of artifacts reported for each room indicate the relative wealth of material goods at the site (Table 37). These lists were made as complete as possible, based on notes and photographs, to stress quantitative abundance. No critical analysis was done, and if something was described as a bone implement or "a different kind of weaving" it was included because I am sure they did find a bone implement and something woven. In this discussion, on the other hand, I will deal with actual categories of artifacts that either were described well enough to furnish meaningful information, or with artifacts in our collections or in the collections of the Roswell Museum. With a few exceptions, the scrapbooks and the collections are discrete universes, unrelated to each other, as few of the collections are labeled and none were catalogued as of 1958. According to David Gebhard, The Roswell Museum was badly flooded, and the collections from Bloom Mound were mainly stored in cardboard boxes on the floor. The collections became rather badly mixed and a number of boxes were thrown out.

The list in Table 37 cannot be regarded as a complete inventory of objects from the site, as I am sure things were found that were not recorded and many objects still remain in private hands. Furthermore, the site continues to be a popular and accessible site for amateurs.

Chipped Stone Artifacts

Bifacial tools

Projectile Points: A total of 65 projectile points were recorded in the Roswell group scrapbooks or recovered from the Texas Technological College excavation. Thirty-nine points came from Room C alone. Side-notched points with straight and concave bases were the most common type in the Roswell Museum Collections (Fig. 77); one specimen of this type had a groove between the notches. At least one triple-notched point was found. My impression in 1958 was that larger points were more common than at Bonnell, but there is no detailed verification. The 10 points that we found in 1954 can be classified as follows:

1 corner-notched, convex-stemmed
1 triangular, straight base, thick and crude
1 triangular, concave base (basal fragment)
2 side-notched, concave base
1 shouldered, stemmed
3 fragments, unclassifiable
1 triangular, concave base (eccentric)

Bifacially Worked "Knives": A long, bifacially-worked blade of dark pink or red mottled flint with side notches was found in a large Chupadero Black-on-White jug sitting on the floor of House G (Pl. 68, right). Large percussion scars reached across the face, smaller spalls were removed along the edges.

A pointed ovate knife from the floor of House F, 2⅜ inches long and 1⁹⁄₁₆ inches wide, was made of chert.

A flake with a bifacial retouched end also came from the floor of House F. It was 1⅜ inches long, ⅞ inch wide, and ⅜ inch thick. The retouched end was thick and blunt.

A bifacially worked quartzite fragment was found in Level 4 fill of Room F. It was 1⁹⁄₁₆ inches wide and 1 inch long.

A flake, 1⅜ inches long, had bifacial retouch around three edges.

Chipped Axe: No provenience was given for one full-grooved chipped axe

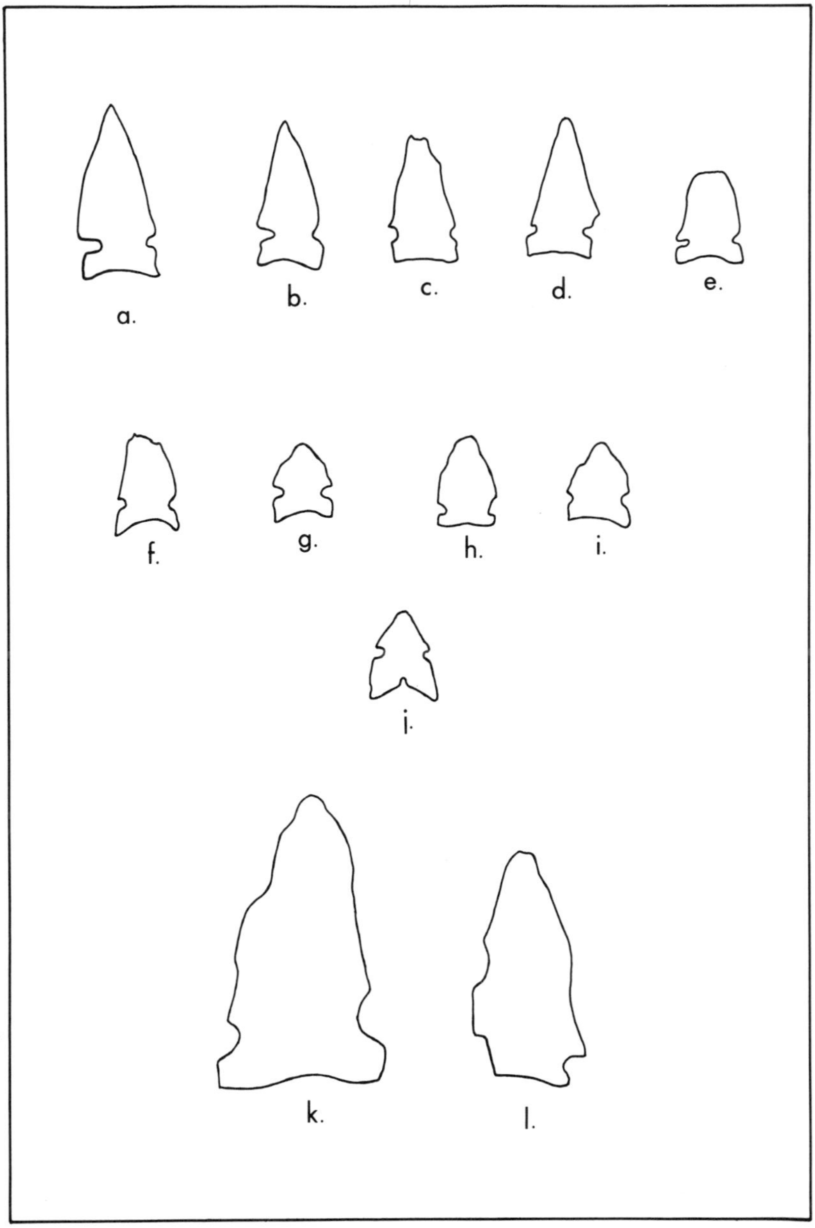

Figure 77. Projectile points, Bloom Mound. Sketches based on entries in the scrapbook of the Roswell Archaeological Society.

in the collection of the Roswell Museum (Pl. 69, left).

Drill: A flake drill base with some bifacial retouch was found on the floor of Room G (Holden 1955b; Pl. 23j; also Pl. 68m).

Unifacial Chipped Stone Tools

Scrapers or Used Flakes: Three flake tools were found in Room G. One was a flint side scraper with a graver tip (Pl. 68g). A second was a side and snub-nosed end scraper of chert (Pl. 68d). The third was flint and can be described as a "backed" flake in that a cortex "back" was perpendicular to the striking platform and ran the length of the flake. One edge was used and the opposite edge had a "shaver" concavity (Pl. 68e).

Used flakes were not recorded by the Roswell group. Nine were recovered from our excavations. Chert of various grades was most numerous. One of the flakes was black shale such as was mined in the Carrizo Shale Mines (Appendix 2).

Ground Stone

Metates

Three whole metates and four fragments were of the one-end-closed trough type with mano rests and one complete slab metate was found. One was on edge in Room K.

Manos and Hand Grinding Stones

Eleven manos were recorded; those found by the Roswell Society were not described. One mano, 7½ inches long, was in the fill of Room G. It had three grinding surfaces and both ends were battered. A small quartz grinding stone 4 inches long on the floor of Room G was ground on one surface; both ends were well battered. A granite mano fragment was also found.

Abrader

A flat sandstone abrader with longitudinal striations was found in Room C (Pl. 69c). No shaft-straighteners were recorded.

Grinding Slabs

Three metate fragments were reported in Holden (1955b:168) as having been found in a stack against the wall of Room F. They are better described as flat grinding slabs.

Axes

Four full-grooved ground-stone axes were found by the Roswell group.

Plate 68. Artifacts, Room G, Bloom Mound.

Plate 69. Stone artifacts, Roswell Museum Collection, Bloom Mound.

Stone Pipes

An unusual tubular pipe found in Room C was about 8¾ inches long (Pl. 70b). The dark reddish brown material was fine-grained, perhaps siltstone. A black stone is inlaid and a hole for a second inlay is farther down the pipe. A second stone pipe in the Roswell Museum collection with no provenience was tubular, 3¼ inches long, with a slight lip (Pl. 70c). No clay pipes have been found to my knowledge.

Pendants

Two stone pendants were recorded but not described in the scrapbook.

Objects of Micaceous Schist

Two flat ground slabs of this raw material were found in the large El Paso olla sitting on the floor of Room G (Pl. 71a, b).

Miscellaneous Stone

Hammerstones

Three hammerstones were mentioned in the scrapbook. We found a battered black core.

Polishing Pebbles

Six of these pebbles were recorded.

Unworked Stones

Various stones and fossils were kept by Bloom Mound inhabitants. Some could have been raw material, others may have been decorative in function, used by shamans, or merely regarded as curiosities. Quartz crystals, a calcite crystal, sheets of gypsum, a large obsidian chunk, unworked turquoise, mica, micaceous schist, "chalk," hematite, and small brachiopods have been found.

Objects of Bone

Awls

At least four awls were made from the distal end of a deer metapodial. One notched rib awl was on the floor of Room F. Twenty-six awls were the total recorded in the Roswell scrapbooks or found in our 1954 work. In addition, three "needles," recorded in the scrapbooks, seemed to be small awls.

Punches

The two split rib tools found in the El Paso olla on the floor of Room G are

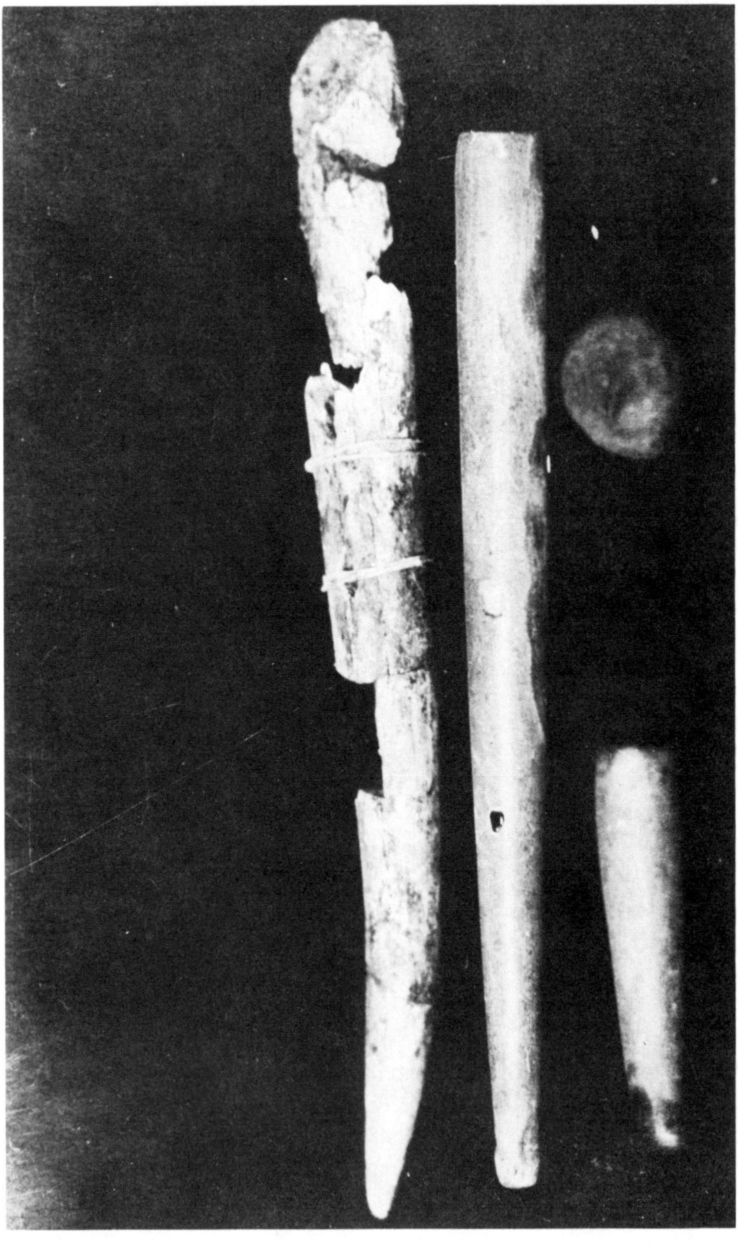

Plate 70. Artifacts, Roswell Museum Collection, Bloom Mound.

Plate 71. Three stone tools contained in an El Paso olla, Room G, which rested on charred basketry (*lower row*), Bloom Mound.

called "spatulas" in Holden (1955b:172). They are better called punches, as the functional part of the tool was the blunt tip (Pl. 72, right). An antler or horn punch about 8 inches long, also found in Room G, was in several pieces.

Batten

A bone batten was sketched in the scrapbooks.

Gaming Pieces

We recovered eight gaming pieces from the floor of Room F. Six slender, elongated pieces and a round one, all thoroughly charred, seemed to form a set. Another shorter, more rectangular piece was not burned.

Scapula Scraper

One deer (or antelope) scapula had been cut down and used as a side scraper in the same fashion as those from Bonnell Site. It was among the objects in the El Paso olla in Room G.

Bone Tube

A "cut, hollow bone" ⅝ inch in diameter and 2⅛ inches in length was reported from Room E.

Whistles

Seven whistles were listed in the scrapbooks. Two matched pieces of bone in the El Paso olla in Room G probably formed a *Bitsitsi* whistle (Pl. 72, lower center).

Miscellaneous Worked Bones

Things listed as "1 bone ornament," "bone implement," "flat bone," or "bone with square corners" cannot be elucidated further. A broken long bone in the Roswell Museum collection had a biconical hole drilled through one end. One bone was described as having a joint at one end, being pointed at the other, and having seven "saw teeth" cut along the body of the bone. A "wooden fork" may have been a companion piece to the "hair ornament" we found in Room G (Pl. 72, left). Two smoothed split ribs with rounded ends had been used as polishers or end scrapers. A flat scapula fragment with cut square corners was in a large Chupadero Black-on-White jug in Room G (Pl. 68f). An antler or horn, recovered from Room C, with two vertical holes and one longitudinal hole drilled in it (Pl. 70, top) was not well preserved.

Ornaments

Since beads were recorded when found, then totaled, and then more beads

Plate 72. Bone objects contained in an El Paso olla, Room G, Bloom Mound.

found, it is hard to give an accurate number. There were at least 1770 disc beads and maybe as many as 2182. A minimum of 473 were found close to the upper floor of Room C and perhaps 213 more on the lower floor. The first group were strung by the Roswell group to form a string 24¾ inches long. From the fill of Room F (excavated by the Roswell group), 986 disc beads were recovered and strung (54 inches; Pl. 73B), and a later entry recorded 570 more beads. A doughnut-shaped bead was found in House F during our 1954 excavations. Single entries of beads were made for Rooms C, E, and F, and we found a few beads in Room G. Disc beads were made of bone, siltstone, shell, and turquoise, as well as unidentified materials. Tubular bone beads were found. Entries about shell beads, a quartz "claw-shaped" bead, and "beads" were not specific. Mussel shell is not prominent, but it is presumed that some of the shell pendants and a "mother-of-pearl" ornament reported in the scrapbook were made of this shell. Forty-two *Oliva* shell tinklers were found in Room C (Pl. 74G), and the top of an *Oliva* shell had been cut to make a bead.

Objects of Clay other than Pottery Vessels

A fired clay incense burner 5½ inches tall was found on the upper floor of Room C (Pl. 75b). The solid cylindrical body had a depression in the upper surface; a stair-stepped back rose from the upper surface.

A sherd of Gila Polychrome, 1½ inches long and 1 inch wide, worked into a trapezoid shape, was found in the fill of House F. In addition, two pottery counters of unspecified pottery types are recorded from Room C, and one made of Black-on-Red pottery from Room E is listed.

Copper Bells

No provenience was given for seven copper bells, but they probably came from Room C (Pl. 74a). Dr. H. P. Mera, who saw the bells in 1939, told the Society that this type of copper bell probably originated at Santa Rita.

Pottery

Whole Vessels

Sherd analysis of the excavations carried on by Texas Technological College will be dealt with separately. Whole or nearly whole vessels obtained by the Roswell group will be mentioned here.

Rio Grande Glaze I

At least two vessels of this type have been reconstructed by the Society. One, from Room K, was 12 inches in diameter and 5 inches deep (Pl. 76). It was a Black-on-Red type with a panel design around the rim. Kidder

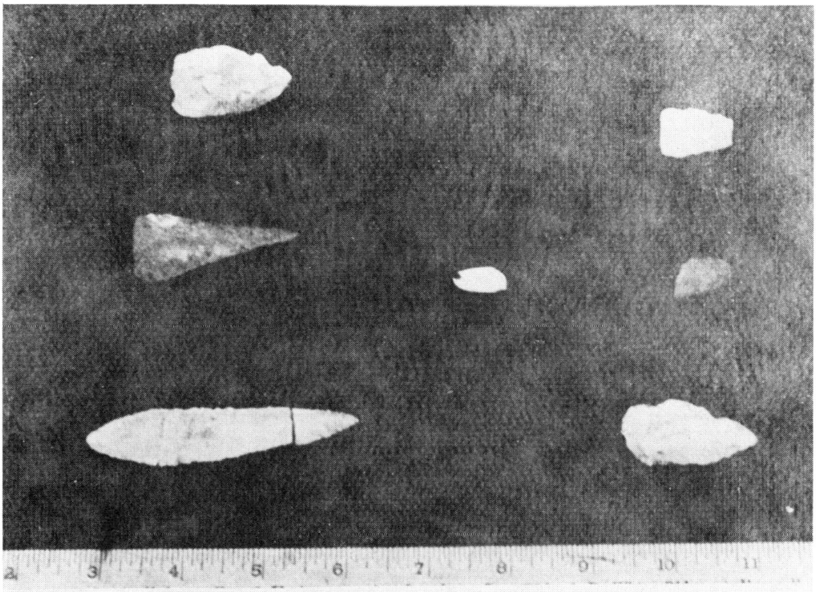

A

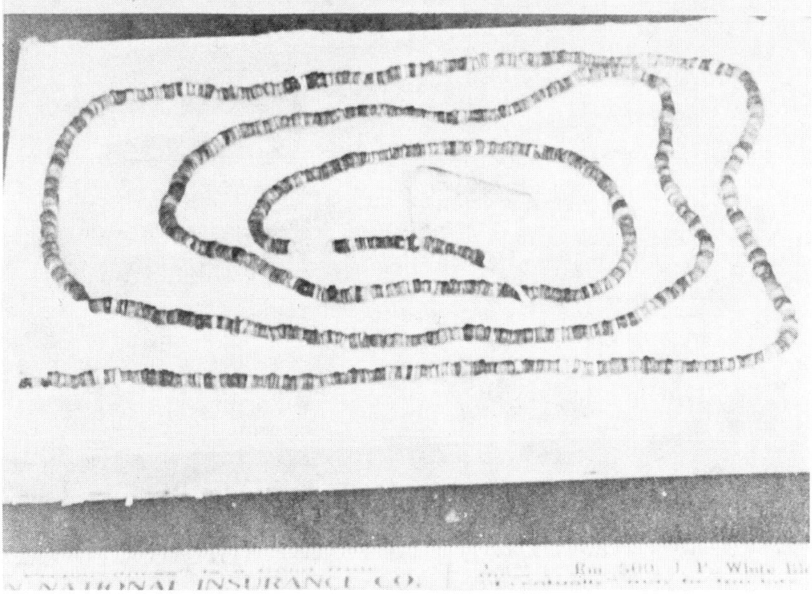

B

Plate 73. Artifacts, Roswell Museum Collection, Bloom Mound.

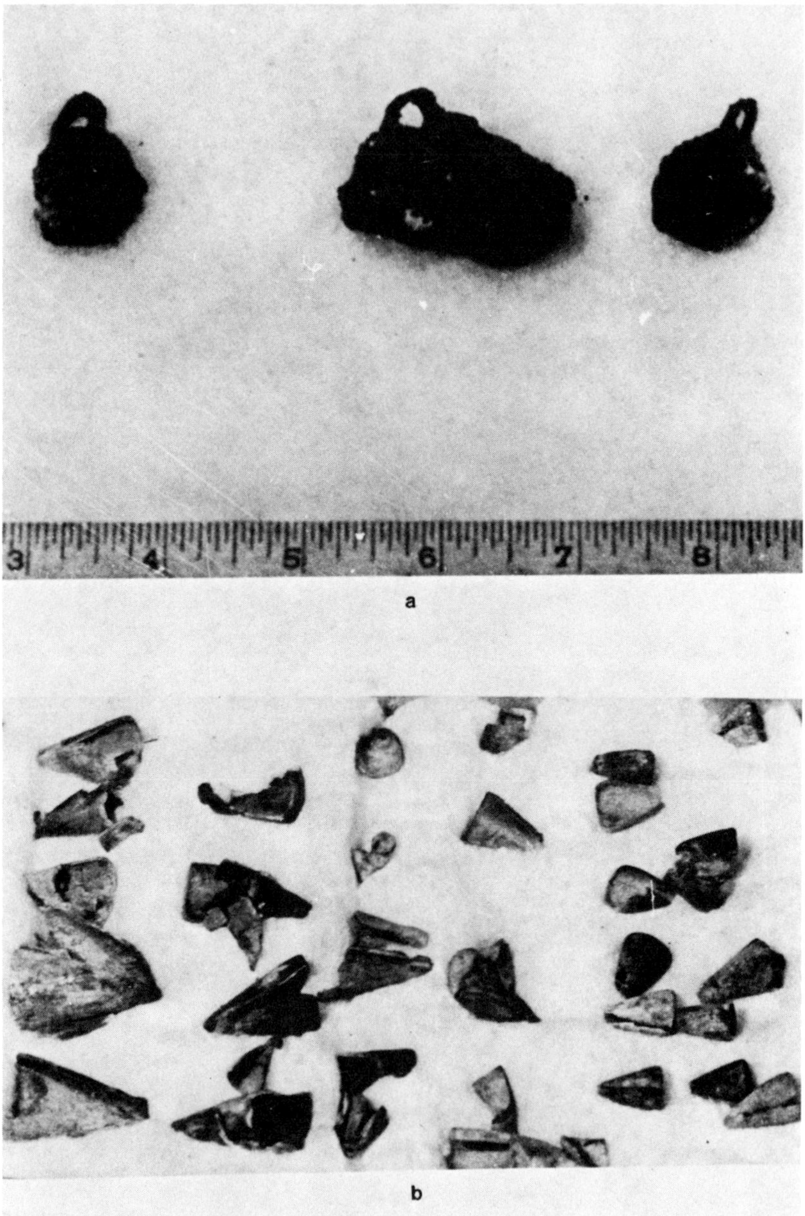

Plate 74. Copper bells and shell tinklers, Roswell Museum Collection, Room C, Bloom Mound.

(1936:49) shows a diamond panel such as this for Glaze I Yellow. A second Glaze I Red bowl came from the floor of Room E (Pl. 75a). This one was only 6½ inches in diameter. The panel design was a large Z. A third Glaze I bowl in the Roswell Museum may have come from the southwest corner of House F (Pl. 77).

Chihuahua Polychrome

A Ramos Polychrome jar was found west of House J outside the house block.

Gila Polychrome

Part of a Gila Polychrome vessel in the Roswell Museum collection was probably from House J.

Miniature Vessels

Two small Chupadero Black-on-White jugs about 2½ inches high were found on the upper floor of Room C. When cleaned, one contained 22 kernels of corn and beads of bone, turquoise, and shell. A third miniature found on Floor 2 of Room C contained unidentified seeds. A small brown vessel was in the Roswell Museum collections.

Unidentified Vessels

When the tractor was stripping off overburden in 1939, an unusual vessel was pulled up by the blade. It is a dark gray to black olla, lacking decoration, with two strap handles (Pl. 78). It has been suggested that it may have originated in Chihuahua.

Sherds from Rooms G and F

Whole and crushed vessels are not included in the sherd tabulation. Two Chupadero Black-on-White jugs (Pl. 79; Pl. 80a), an undecorated El Paso seed jar (Pl. 80b), a large El Paso Polychrome olla and a Corrugated olla were on the floor of Room G. Room G and F sherd counts appear in Table 36. (The sample from Room F did not include all excavated sherds, as some sherd sacks were poorly labeled.)

Sherds classified as Red-on-Brown, type unknown, were found throughout the lower fill of House F and on the floor. The body of the light brown sherds was thin, rather like El Paso Polychrome. Fine to medium sand temper was composed primarily of rounded quartz grains. Large ollas with a mouth about 4 to 6 inches in diameter were indicated. A red band about 1 inch wide looped around the body of the vessel. In vessel color and decoration, these sherds are much like a whole vessel found in a Malpais cave west of Carrizozo (Pl. 81B); the shape of the Bloom Mound vessel was not reconstructed.

TABLE 36
EXCAVATED SHERDS FROM ROOMS G AND F, BLOOM MOUND

	Room G		Room F												Total	
	Floor		0″-6″ Fill		6″-12″ Fill		12″-18″ Fill		18″-24″ Fill		24″-36″ Fill		36″ to Floor			
Pottery Types	No.	%	No.	%	No.	%	No.	%	No.	%	No.	%	No.	%	No.	%
Corrugated	4	11.11	4	7.14	4	6.78	7	9.46	8	8.08	3	2.63	23	5.08	53	5.95
Chupadero Black-on-White																
Bowl			6								2		12		20	
Jug	1		4		4		4		7		4		22		46	
Total	1	2.78	10	17.86	4	6.78	4	5.41	7	7.07	6	5.26	34	7.51	66	7.41
Jornada Brown	1		5	8.00	6		14		23				7		56	
Roswell Brown	1				2				3				1		7	
Micaceous Brown			1	1.00			1						3		5	
Total	2	5.56	6	10.71	8	13.56	15	20.27	26	26.26			11	2.43	68	7.63
Red-on-Brown, Type unknown							16	21.62	13	13.13	46	40.35	34	7.51	109	12.23
Jornada Poly.					6	10.17							10	2.21	16	1.80
El Paso Poly.	25	69.44	34	60.71	35	59.32	19	25.68	38	38.38	15	13.16	313	69.09	479	53.76
Three Rivers Red-on-Terracotta																
Thin-lined	1						2						2		5	
Undecorated			1								2		1		4	
Olla			1												1	
Total	1	2.78	2	3.57			2	2.70			2	1.75	3	0.66	10	1.12
Lincoln Black-on-Red																
Decorated	1						3		4		36		17		61	
Red-on-Red	2								1						3	
Undecorated					1		4								5	
Total	3	8.33			1	1.69	7	9.46	5	5.05	36	31.58	17	3.75	69	7.74
St. John's Polychrome					1	1.69									1	0.11
Glaze I							3	4.05	1	1.01	2	1.75	3	0.66	9	1.01
Gila Polychrome									1	1.01	3	2.63	3	0.66	7	0.79
Chihuahua, Incised							1	1.35			1	0.88			2	0.22
Galisteo Black-on-White													1	0.22	1	0.11
Unidentified													1	0.22	1	0.11
Total	36		56		59		74		99		114		453		891	

The percentage of El Paso Polychrome (69%) was the highest for any site described in this report, and it may well have been made locally. Corrugated ran a poor second in popularity: with 11% of the floor sherds from Room G and 5% of the floor sherds from Room D or F. Jornada Brown made up less than 3% of the sample. The low percentage of Chupadero Black-on-White (2% and 7%) may be more apparent than real because two whole vessels were found in Room G.

Woven Materials

Textiles, mats and coiled baskets have been found at the site. Three fragments of cord came from Room C. Two, examined at the Roswell Museum, were found to be three-strand cord with a left-hand twist. The longest fragment was 2½ inches long. A bound bundle of grass from Room G (Pl. 79) may have served as a broom.

Notes on Basketry and Textiles from Bloom Mound

by

Elizabeth King

Textile Museum, Washington, D.C.

Basketry, Room G

Fragments of a coiled basket. The center appears to be the usual type

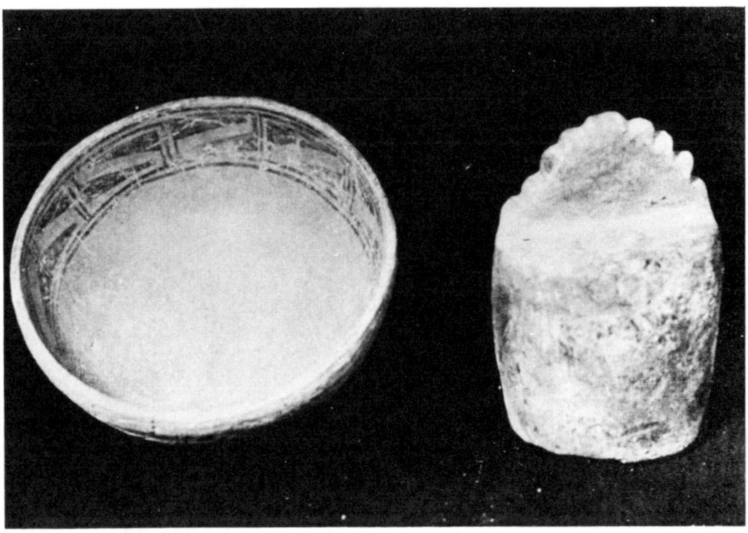

Plate 75. *a*, Glaze I bowl, Roswell Museum Collection, Room E, Bloom Mound; *b*, Stone "incense burner," Room C, Bloom Mound.

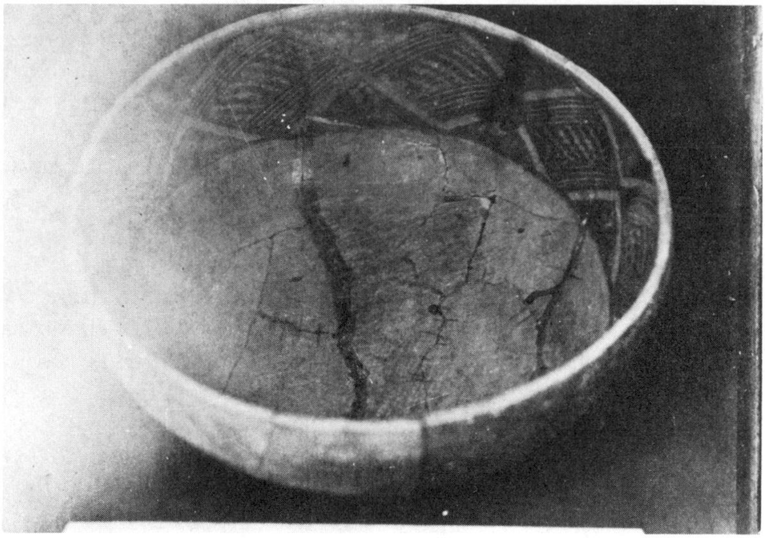

Plate 76. Glaze I bowl, Roswell Museum Collection, Bloom Mound.

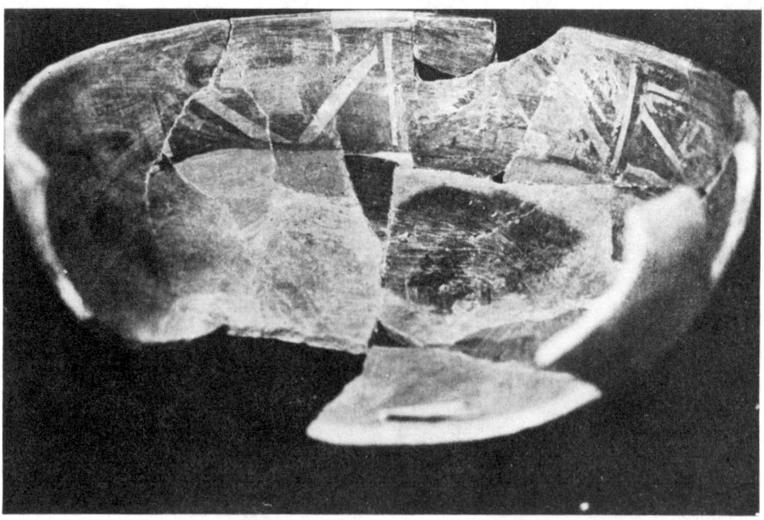

Plate 77. Glaze I bowl, Roswell Museum Collection, Bloom Mound.

Plate 78. Strap-handled vessel, Roswell Museum Collection, Bloom Mound.

Plate 79. Chupadero seed jar resting on tied grass, Room G, Bloom Mound.

Plate 80. *a*, Chupadero Black-on-White seed jar; *b*, Undecorated El Paso jar, Room G, Bloom Mound.

Plate 81. *a,* Chupadero Black-on-White "jug," Roswell Museum Collection, Bloom Mound; *b,* Olla, type unidentified, Jack Harkey Collection, found in a lava cave in the Malpais, west of Carrizozo, New Mexico.

(Morris and Burgh 1941:Fig. 7a). The straight rows of stitches indicate that the basket is probably sewn with non-interlocked stitches. The stitches do not appear to be split. Their shiny appearance may indicate that the sewing material was wood splints, rather than leaf, but this could be due to application of a preservative. The foundation contains rods, but its composition can not be determined. The basket may have been bowl shaped (see Pl. 71d, e; Pl. 82).

Charred Textiles and Basketry, Probably Room G

Items 1, 2, and 3 appear to be plain weave textiles. Items 7 and 12 are probably the same, and 9 may also be a textile fragment. Item 4 seems to be a knot. The structures of 5, 6, and 11 are not determinable from the photograph. Items 8 and 10 are coiled basketry fragments. The stitches are not interlocked, but could be split. The textile fragments could have been from a bag as suggested in the field notes, but in the Southwest, corn and other vegetable materials are sometimes just tied up in a scrap of material. The textile could be of cotton, yucca, or *Apocynum*. Since it looks quite coarse, yucca is most likely. (Notes made from photograph, Pl. 83.)

Matting Fragment, Room G

This fragment is 3 cm by 6.2 cm. It is a two-over-two interlacing. The element is probably yucca about 0.6 cm wide. There are two elements per cm in one direction, two elements per 1.5 cm in the other direction. Without an edge, it can't be determined whether the interlacing was oblique rather than at right angles, but it is likely that it was oblique.

Basketry Fragment

This fragment is about 4.5 cm by 9 cm. It is coiled basketry. The foundation appears to be a bundle with rod core but could be a rod with lateral bundle foundation. The stitches are apparently of a leaf (rather than wood-splint) element. Almost all are split on the convex surface. Those which aren't split appear to be interlocked, but this is not certain. The concave side is so worn that it is impossible to tell whether the stitches are split on that side. There are two coils and 2½ stitches per cm. This fragment seems to fall between Morris and Burgh's (1941) Figure 3g, and Cosgrove's (1947) Figure 33k and Figure 33g.

SKELETAL MATERIAL

Woodbury (1959) has recently reinstated warfare as a respectable inference for the Southwest, and the Bloom Mound material would seem to verify this idea.

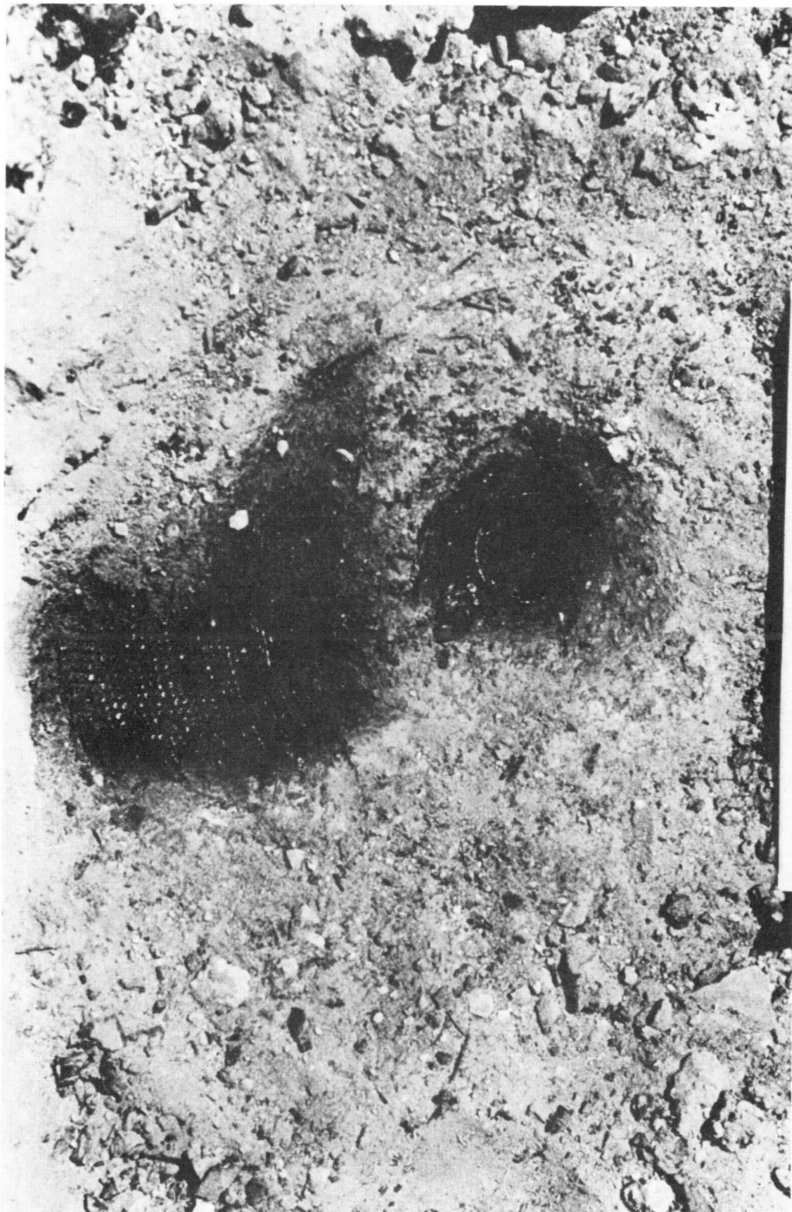

Plate 82. Charred basket, Room G, Bloom Mound.

Plate 83. Charred textiles and basketry, Roswell Museum Collection, Bloom Mound.

In our own excavation of the subterranean Room F, a badly-charred, sprawled skeleton was found beneath the charred roof (Pl. 84). A fragmentary skeleton, a skull, and part of a child's skull were scattered over the room. Notes in the scrapbooks suggested that the Roswell group found two charred skeletons in the southwest corner of the same room. One of these, removed on 9 March 1941, was described as having a crushed head, the right leg was broken twice, "the left leg went off southeast," and the left foot was broken. The other skeleton was partially charred.

In Room A, two skeletons were found in the roof debris and six skeletons were found in the room fill. Six more skeletons were discovered on the floor.

During the initial excavation of Room C, two charred skeletons were found 35 inches below the surface, close to the southwest corner of the room. A charred mat adhered to the south wall just over their heads. Another skeleton found later was not as badly charred as the first two; the left leg, left arm, and right foot were reported missing. The scrapbook notes that the epiphyseal unions of the long bones had not closed. Subsequent entries in the scrapbook about human skeletal material in Room C were much less clear. An entry for 12 March 1939 stated: "skulls in every conceivable attitude and condition. At least two in sight all the time, sometimes more." An appended sketch located seven skulls. "Broken and scattered bones," two pelvic fragments, and one sacrum were noted. A 4-foot square strat column had been reduced to 2 feet square prior to 26 March 1936, as the edges were crumbling. On this date, they removed the strat column. Ten skulls are said to have been found, two of which were directly superimposed. This seems unlikely.

It is impossible to establish how many skeletons have been removed from Bloom Mound. Fifteen skeletons at the least are indicated, plus the many skulls from Room C. The skeletons that we excavated were not intentionally buried, and presumably the people perished in a collapsing building. The charred nature of most of the skeletal material suggests that the whole village burned, trapping several of the inhabitants.

FOOD REMAINS

Corn

Entries in the scrapbook reported finding "a neat stack of corn against the wall" and "a bushel of corn." Corn was present in Rooms A, C, E, F, and K. Corn tied up in a bag or piece of material was found in Room C. Charred corncobs with kernels still on, cobs without kernels, and separate kernels were found. The corn in the Roswell Museum was a larger variety than that found at Block Lookout and at the Bonnell Site.

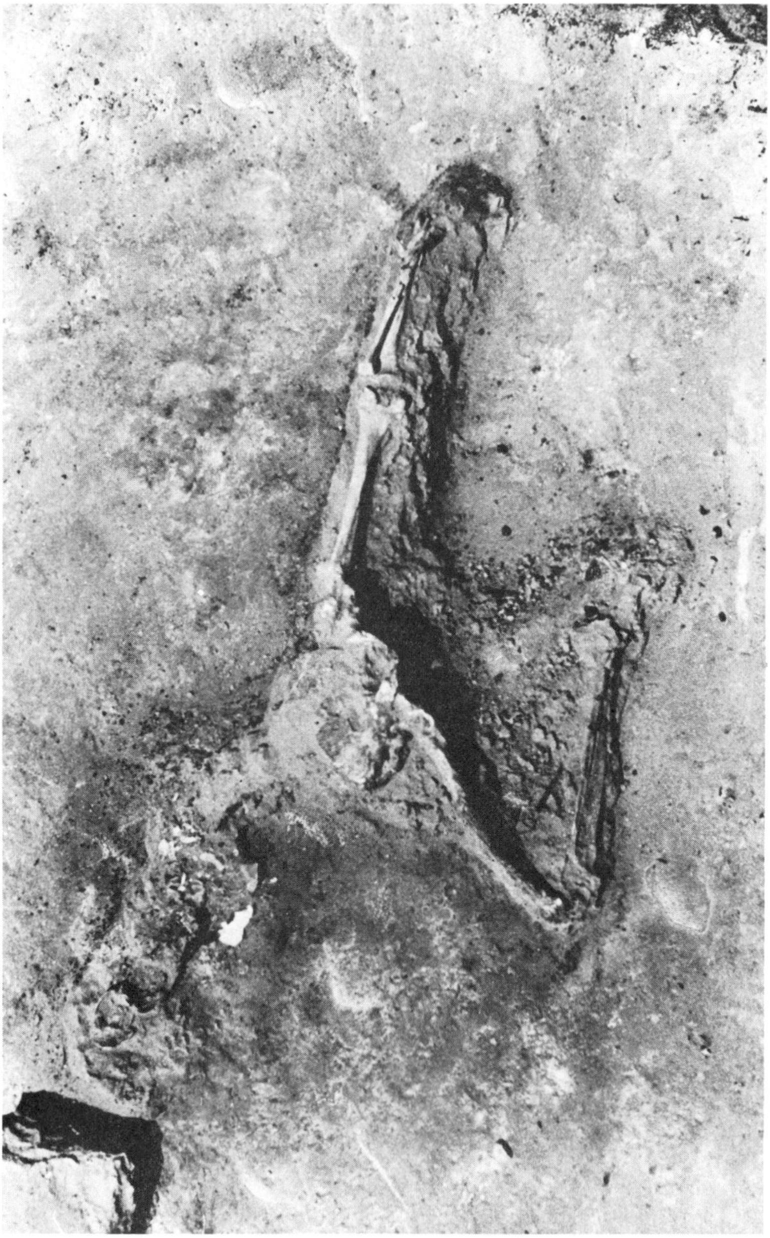

Plate 84. Skeleton, floor of Room D, Bloom Mound.

Seeds

Hackberry seeds, a bean, and "bean-shaped" seed were recorded in the scrapbooks. These identifications cannot be verified at this time.

Animal Bones

Deer and/or antelope bones were present and bison bones were more abundant here than at any other site in the region.

DATING

The adobe surface house block was built on deep cultural fill, and an earlier occupation of the site is indicated. We have no information about sherds from the deep trenches dug by the Roswell group. Our limited sherd data indicate that Room G of the surface house block and the subterranean chamber (Room D or F) were contemporaneous. The association of St. Johns Polychrome and Glaze I on the floor of the latter structure give an early Pueblo IV date. The presence of Glaze I and the absence of later Rio Grande Glazes gives the same terminal date for Bloom Mound as for other sites of the Lincoln Phase. Other trade types, such as Gila and Ramos Polychromes, have too long a life-span to be useful for precise dating. Mimbres Black-on-White, usually thought to date one or two centuries earlier, is consistently found in these later ceramic contexts east of the Sierra Blanca-Sacramento Mountains.

SUMMARY

Bloom Mound is tentatively assigned to the Lincoln Phase. The linear adobe surface structure facing east on a square subterranean chamber is similar to Lincoln Phase sites elsewhere. The high percentage of El Paso Polychrome (69%) suggests close relations with El Paso Phase sites in the lower Tularosa Basin. The rest of the ceramic complex, however, is made up of types common to the Lincoln and Glencoe Phases. The notched awl, the bone ring, the incense burner, and the emphasis on disc beads are other traits that indicate close contacts with the El Paso Phase.

The site is small; nine surface rooms and the subterranean chamber are known. It is unusually rich in material possessions, and it may have been a small trading center. The entire structure burned with material goods in place, and this has contributed to the impression of wealth.

Artifacts found in the subterranean House D (or F) were more domestic than ceremonial in nature, and there are no internal kiva structural features. Its location in front of the linear surface house block and its subterranean character suggest that it served as a communal chamber. The incense burner, which undoubtedly did have a ceremonial function, was found in one of the surface rooms.

The corn found here was a larger variety than that found at the Bonnell Site and Block Lookout. The abundance of corn and the unconfirmed bean found by the Roswell group show that farming was practiced. Bison were known historically in the Pecos Valley, and the great number of bison bones indicate that this animal was hunted regularly by the villagers. Deer and/or antelope was also acquired.

Bloom Mound is the only reported village from this section of the Hondo-Pecos Valleys. Another site exists at the edge of the valley margin, only a mile or so from Bloom Mound; it is an E-shaped, masonry pueblo with much the same pottery complex as Bloom Mound. Further investigations should delineate the settlement pattern of this part of the valley during this period, and the position of Bloom Mound may have to be reevaluated in the light of new evidence.

TABLE 37
ARTIFACTS EXCAVATED BY THE ROSWELL ARCHAEOLOGICAL SOCIETY AT BLOOM MOUND, COMPILED FROM THE SOCIETY SCRAPBOOK AND ROSWELL MUSEUM COLLECTIONS

Room C. Fill and Upper Floor

Pottery
- 2 Miniature Chupadero Black-on-White jugs
  - 1 Jug had a corncob stopper and contained
    - 22 Charred corn kernels
      - 1 Bone bead
      - 1 Shell bead
      - 1 Turquoise bead
      - 2 Pieces of turquoise
  - 1 Miniature Corrugated vessel
  - 1 Partially restorable Black-on-Red bowl (unidentified)
  - 2 Pottery counters
  - 1 Fired clay incense burner
  - 1 Fired clay ball 1¾ inches in diameter

Bone
- 2 Metapodial awls (distal end retained)
- 6 Awl fragments
- 1 Awl
- 1 Bone "batten," 8 inches long

Stone
- 4 Polishing stones
- 2 Manos (one was flat, about ½ inch thick)
- 1 Grinding slab (16 x 22 x 1½ inches thick)
- 1 Shaft-straightener

TABLE 37, continued

1 Shaft-straightener fragment
37 Projectile points
1 Chunk of obsidian (3¼ x 2½ x 1¼ inches)
1 Full-grooved axe, much battered, 5½ inches long
2 Crystals of clear quartz
1 Flat stone

Corn
"An orderly stack" on the floor
Numerous imprints of corn on the floor

Cord and Matting
Charred mat stuck to the wall
2 Fragments of twisted cord (3-strand, left hand twist 2½ inches long)

Room C. Artifacts Between Top and Middle Floors

Pottery
1 Miniature Chupadero Black-on-White jug with corncob stopper, containing unidentified seeds

Bone
2 Bone whistles
2 Bone "handles"
4 Small slender bone awls (recorded as needles)
1 "Bone with square corners"

Horn
2 "Horn ornaments" (?)

Beads
473 Beads. Made a string 24¾ inches long. Includes beads of turquoise, bone, and shell at least. Disc beads, ca. ¼ inch in diameter

Stone
1 Pipe of fine-grained red-brown stone that had one black stone inlaid and the hole for a second inlay
1 Small, flat, sandstone rock
(?) Obsidian chips
2 Point fragments
1 Turquoise fragment
2 Gypsum fragments

Cord, Matting, Etc.
1 "Different weaving"
(?) Cord
(?) Mat (?)

Corn
"Corn cobs plentiful everywhere"
"Prints on floor" of corncobs

Room C. Artifacts from Stratigraphic Column

Bone
4 Whistles
1 Small bone awl (recorded as a needle)
1 Bone ornament (?)

Stone
2 Polishing stones (recorded as marbles)
3 Projectile points (1 of obsidian)

Woven Materials

TABLE 37, continued

(?) "Woven materials"
(?) "Many basketry fragments"
1 Woven "sack" fragment containing corn
1 Knot

Shell
1 Shell bead
1 Shell fragment

Room C. Level Unknown

Shell
42 *Conus* tinklers

Room E. Fill and Floor

Pottery
1 Glaze I bowl, 6 inches in diameter
1 Black-on-Red pottery counter

Bone
1 "Bone implement"
6 Awls (2 split bone; 1 distal end of metapodial)
1 "Flat bone"
1 Bone bead
1 Bone tube (5/8 inches in diameter; 2 1/8 inches long)

Stone
2 Scrapers (one 17 inches below surface)
2 Projectile points within 2 inches of floor
6 Projectile points
1 "Spear point," 3 inches below surface
1 Broken projectile point
2 Manos (a. 9 x 4 x 2 1/2 inches; b. 6 1/4 x 3 7/8 x 2 1/4 inches)
1 Large, thick sheet of mica (?)
(?) Flints
1 Broken metate

Shell
2 Shell beads (one found 40 inches below surface)
1 Shell pendant (found 46 inches below surface)
2 "Other pendants" (shell ?)
1 "Mother-of-pearl" ornament

Perishable
"Lot of corn"
"Bean-shaped seed"

Room D (or F)
Artifacts Collected by the Roswell Archaeological Society

Stone
1 Quartz crystal
2 Turquoise fragments
1 Mano (on floor)
1 Grinding slab with paint (under roofing beam)
1 Full-grooved axe, very battered, 4 1/4 inches long
2 Pieces of "chalk"
2 Projectile points
1 Projectile point fragment

TABLE 37, continued

Bone
- 2 Bone whistles
- 1 Bone with 7 "saw-teeth" along the edge, pointed at one end, joint at the other

Beads
- 986 Disc beads of shell and bone, at least. Made a string 54 inches long. (This may not be all as several other entries of beads cannot be correlated with this entry)
- 3 *Olivella* beads
- 1 Large shell bead
- 2 Large bone beads
- 3 Large beads $\frac{5}{16}$ inches in diameter
- 1 "Button" bead of quartz

Other ornaments
- 1 Stone pendant fragment
- 1 Quartz pendant "shaped like a claw"

Wood
- 1 "Wooden fork" (?)

Room D or F. Floor
Artifacts Recovered by
Texas Technological College, 1954

Stone
- 1 Corner-notched projectile point, white chert
- 2 Triangular points (a. basal fragment with concave base; b. straight base, thick and crude)
- 1 Midsection of a projectile point
- 1 Side and end scraper
- 1 Sandstone disc, ground on both sides ($2\frac{1}{2}$ inches in diameter and $\frac{5}{8}$ inch thick)
- 1 Full-grooved maul, or very blunt axe
- 3 Grinding slabs (erroneously reported as metate fragments in Holden 1955b:168)
- 1 Stone bead ($\frac{3}{8}$ inch in diameter, doughnut-shaped)

Bone
- 7 Bone gaming sticks rectangular
- 1 Bone gaming stick, round
- 1 Split rib "spatula"
- 2 Distal end metapodial awl fragments
- 1 Split rib awl, cut at the base

Shell
- 4 Shell beads (flat beads disc, $\frac{1}{4}$ inch and $\frac{3}{16}$ inch in diameter)

Room D or F. Fill
Artifacts Recovered by
Texas Technological College, 1954

Pottery
- 1 "Counter" of Gila Polychrome

Stone
- 2 Projectile points
- 1 Bifacially worked fragment, quartzite
- 1 Battered core
- 2 Mano fragments
- 2 Polishing stones
- 5 Used flakes
- 9 Unused flakes

Shell
- 2 Unworked mussel fragments

TABLE 37, continued

Perishables
- 1 Charred corncob

Room G. Floor
Artifacts Recovered by
Texas Technological College, 1954

Pottery
- 2 Chupadero Black-on-White jugs
- 1 El Paso jar, undecorated
- 1 El Paso olla
- 1 Corrugated olla

Bone
- 2 Punches or battens
- 2 "Bitsitsi" whistle parts
- 1 "Hair ornament"
- 1 Deer (?) scapula scraper
- 4 Awl fragments
- 1 Shaped flat bone (scapula) fragment

Antler
- 1 Punch

Stone
- 3 Projectile points
- 1 Projectile point midsection
- 3 Scrapers
- 2 Ground slabs of micaceous schist
- 1 Drill base
- 1 Full-grooved axe
- 1 Slab metate (22 x 10 inches)
- 3 Metate fragments (one a trough metate)
- 1 "One-handed" mano, quartz
- 1 Round ball, ½ inch in diameter

Shell
- 1 *Oliva* bead
- 1 *Olivella* bead
- 1 Mussel shell
- 1 Shell "ornament," oval disc with drill pit

Perishables
- 1 Basketry fragment
- 2 Basketry trays
- 1 Bundle of grass tied (broom ?)
- 1 Woven mat

Room G. Fill

Stone
- 1 Mano

Room K

Pottery
- 1 Glaze I bowl (reconstructed, 12 inches in diameter, 5 inches deep)
- 1 Corrugated vessel, small

TABLE 37, continued

Bone
1 "Bone tool" fragment
213 Bone beads
2 Bone awls
1 Bone tool (bone 1 inch thick at joint end, a biconical hole)
Stone
3 Manos range from 9 x 3½ inches to 5 x 2¼ inches
1 Graver
1 Knife or scraper
1 Projectile point
1 Metate on edge (trough type with mano rest; 22 x 11-14 inches)
1 Piece of ochre
1 Stone hammer
Perishables
"Lots of corn" (2-19-39)
"Bushel of corn" (3-5-39)
"Woven material"

TABLE 38
TOTAL OF REPORTED ARTIFACTS,
BLOOM MOUND

Artifact Type	Number
Chipped stone	
Bifacial	
Projectile points (whole and fragments)	65
Knives	5
Chipped axe, full-grooved	1
Drill	1
Unifacial	
Scrapers	5
Graver	1
Ground-stone	
Axes	4
Metates (complete)	4
Metates (fragmentary)	4
Manos	11
Ground-stone axes, full-grooved	4
Abrader	1
Grinding slabs	2
Stone pipes	2
Pendants	2
Objects of micaceous schist	2
Miscellaneous worked stone	
Polishing pebbles	6
Hammerstones	3
Mauls (?)	3

TABLE 38, continued

Miscellaneous unworked stone	
Quartz crystals	3
Gypsum sheets	2
Obsidian chunk	1
Mica sheets	1
Turquoise	3
"Chalk"	2
Micaceous schist	2
Ochre	2
Bone and antler tools	
Awls	29
Punches (1 is antler)	3
Spatula or batten	1
Gaming pieces	8
Scapula scraper	1
Tube	1
Whistles	7
"Bitsitsi" whistle	1
Miscellaneous worked bones	16
Ornaments	
Beads	
Small, disc-shaped, raw material unspecified	1700
Oliva tinklers	43
Bone beads	6
Stone beads	3
Shell beads	1
Quartz "claw-shaped" bead	1
Olivella	4
Pendants	
Shell pendant	1
Pendants, raw material unspecified	2
Stone pendant	1
"Mother-of-Pearl" ornament	1
Copper bells	7
Perishables	
Cord	present
Matting	present
Basketry	present
Woven bag	present
Corn	present
Seeds (other than corn)	(2 cases reported)

Appendix 7

SITES ALONG THE UPPER AND MIDDLE PEÑASCO RIVER

The Peñasco River rises high in the Sacramento Mountains and flows east to the Pecos River. Heading in the Canadian Zone, it passes through Transitional and Upper Sonoran Zones, ending in the Lower Sonoran Life Zone.

The early Glencoe Phase was tentatively defined on the basis of three early Pueblo III sites in this locality. The late Pueblo III site 2000 was assigned to the late Glencoe Phase. This valley apparently represented the southern boundary of sedentary villages along the eastern slopes of the Sierra Blanca-Sacramento Mountains. Closest cultural ties were to Glencoe Phase sites in the Ruidoso Valley. The geographical isolation of this valley was reflected in the relative poverty of material goods found in excavated sites. A small, sparse, agriculturally-based population occupied the valley during the Pueblo III period. This was the first locality in the Sierra Blanca Region to be abandoned, probably about A. D. 1300 or slightly later.

PRECERAMIC FEATURES

Location

On the Weed-Mayhill road. SW¼, S3, T17S, R14E, Otero County.

Features

Four pits were located (Green 1956:10-16). Three were about 5 feet in diameter. The fourth was smaller and joined two of the other pits. Depth varied from 4½ to 6½ feet. Pits were slightly undercut. A complete skeleton of a dog was in the fill of one pit and a dog's skull in another. Refuse was bone scrap. No artifacts or sherds were recovered.

EARLY GLENCOE PHASE SITES

Mayhill Site 1

Location

S13, T16S, R14E. Elevation is ca. 7000 feet. This site is in the Transitional

Zone and mixed piñon-oak-pine forest alternates with grasslands. The site is on a sloping ridge on the north side of New Mexico State Highway 83 and north of the Peñasco River.

Fieldwork

Limited salvage excavations were undertaken by our crew in 1954 at the request of Fred Wendorf who was then head of Highway Salvage in New Mexico.

Results of Excavation

A house remnant was visible in a highway cut (Fig. 78a). It was 14 feet wide; the remaining section had a maximum east-west dimension of 3 feet 5 inches. Small posts were set against the pit wall, and two larger posts were found. The pit was 25 inches deep, and 40 inches of alluvium had accumulated above this. A lamellar flake was the only artifact found; there were no sherds.

Mayhill Site 2

Location

NE¼ of S26, T16S, R14E. It is at 6800 feet elevation. The house was in a road cut of New Mexico State Highway 83, on a sloping ridge on the north side of the Peñasco Valley. Life forms were those of the piñon-juniper belt of the Upper Sonoran Zone.

Fieldwork

A remnant of a house was visible in a road cut, and Fred Wendorf requested that we salvage what remained in 1954.

Results of Excavation

A rounded pithouse (Fig. 78b) had a crude bench that encircled the remaining portion of the structure. The bench continued in front of the sloping lateral entry on the east. A pit was dug through the bench on the west side. All features were unplastered. The only post located stood at the north side of the entry.

Two burials had been made in fill above the bench on the north side of the house. Both were flexed. The head of one skeleton was to the west, and the other was to the east. Neither had any grave offerings.

Three used flakes and a core tool were found. Sherds included 1 Chupadero Black-on-White and 25 Jornada Brown.

An adjacent pithouse, later excavated at this site (Steward Peckham, per-

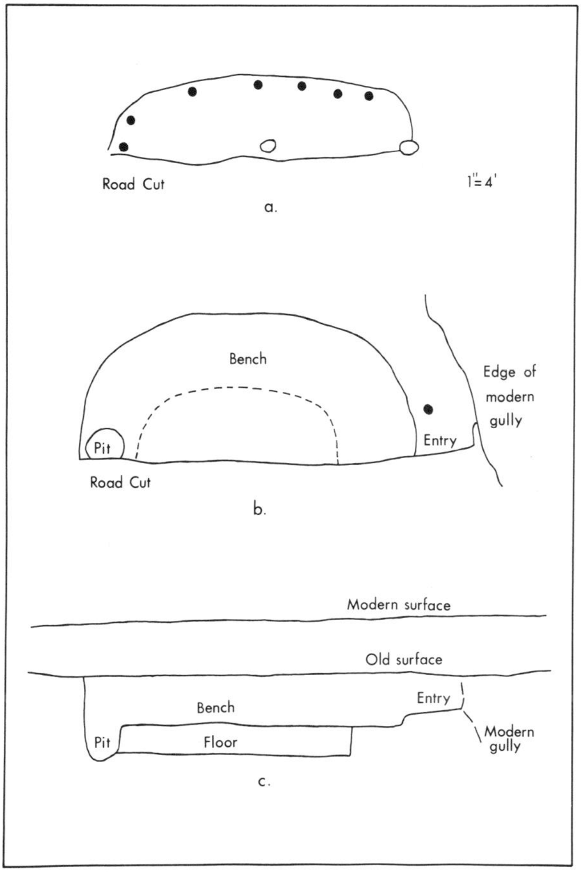

Figure 78. Pithouses, Mayhill Sites 1 and 2: *a*, Plan of pithouse remnant, Mayhill Site 1; *b*, Plan of pithouse remnant, Mayhill Site 2; *c*, Profile of pithouse remnant, Mayhill Site 2.

sonal communication), was rectangular or square, with four large supporting posts and small posts around the periphery and two deep pits on the east side.

Pithouse Excavated by Roger Green

Location

Weed-Mayhill road. SW¼, S3, T17S, R14E, Otero County.

Excavation

As part of a highway salvage operation, Roger Green excavated a pithouse remnant (Green 1956:10-16). The unplastered house was 7 feet deep. A bench extended around that section of the house that remained. A small grinding slab, a grinding stone, a hammerstone, and a bone awl were found. A locally-made Brown type of pottery predominated; a few sherds of Chupadero Black-on-White, Mimbres Black-on-White, and what Green calls San Francisco Red were found. The latter was probably a locally-made variant of Jornada Brown.

Conflicting Phase Designation

Green assigned this house remnant to the Doña Ana Phase.

LATE GLENCOE PHASE SITES

Site 2000

Location

SW¼ of S3, T16S, R16E. Broad, sloping terraces flank the Peñasco River, which has a recent history of active erosion. Elevation is between 5600 and 5800 feet. Ecologically the locality is in the lower grasslands belt of the Upper Sonoran Zone. Clump grasses and *Opuntia* cacti grow on the site. Cottonwoods, walnuts, juniper, chokecherry and scrub-oak grow in the valley. See Plates 85–86.

Previous Work

Jennings (1940:1-19) partially dug two houses at this site in 1932–33. His publication was one of the pioneer archaeological reports from this region; in it he formulated the type description of Jornada Brown pottery.

Site 2000 had four flattened circular areas, each bounded on the downhill side by an artificial embankment. These were designated 2000 A, B, C, and D; Jennings worked in 2000 A.

Jennings felt that small houses, probably brush or reed covered, were set well inside of excavated pits because floor plaster extended only as far as the main support posts (Jennings 1940:3). Our work here and at other sites demonstrated that partially plastered floors were common, and it is certain that the structures he excavated covered the entire pit. He reported that all burials were outside of houses; but three in 2000 A2 were within the pit limits and would have been in fill or sub-floor (Jennings 1940:Fig. 4).

Upper and lower levels were distinguished by a drastic shift in pottery types. In the lower level, 92% of the pottery was "common brown ware" (or Jornada Brown) with 5.7% El Paso Polychrome and a few sherds of Mimbres Black-on-White, Chupadero Black-on-White, and Three Rivers Red-on-Terracotta. The upper level had 89.2% El Paso Polychrome, and 7.8% of the

Plate 85. View of terrain and vegetation, Site 2000 C, Peñasco Valley.

"common brown ware"; the same minor types continued, and St. Johns Polychrome was added. This is the highest percentage of El Paso Polychrome reported from a single component outside of the lower Tularosa Basin. Our subsequent excavations in other parts of the site yielded only minor amounts of this type, and it is possible that this high percentage of El Paso Polychrome represented an atypical concentration.

1953 Excavations

Limited testing was carried out in 2000 B and 2000 C (Fig. 79) by Texas Technological College crews.

2000 B-1

A test pit ca. 6 x 8 feet showed remnants of two superimposed clay floors. A post ca. 6 inches in diameter was standing next to a smaller charred post. In the fill between the two floors, deer bones were numerous.

2000 B-2

Most of a shallow pithouse and a small part of an adjacent house were cleared (Fig. 80); two isolated features will be described separately.

House 1: This pithouse was probably 10 or 12 feet square, but not all of the pit walls were located. The house pit, which was ca. 10 inches deep at the time the house was constructed, was dug through topsoil. Three large posts, 7 to 11 inches in diameter, were centrally located in three corners. No large post was found in the southeast corner because an earlier, filled pit gave a poor footing. Instead the fourth large support was south of the firepit; this post hole was 22 inches deep, 9 inches in diameter and there was a rock base in the post hole. Nine smaller posts were found (Fig. 80); the five along the east were just

Plate 86. View of Site 2000 C, Peñasco Valley.

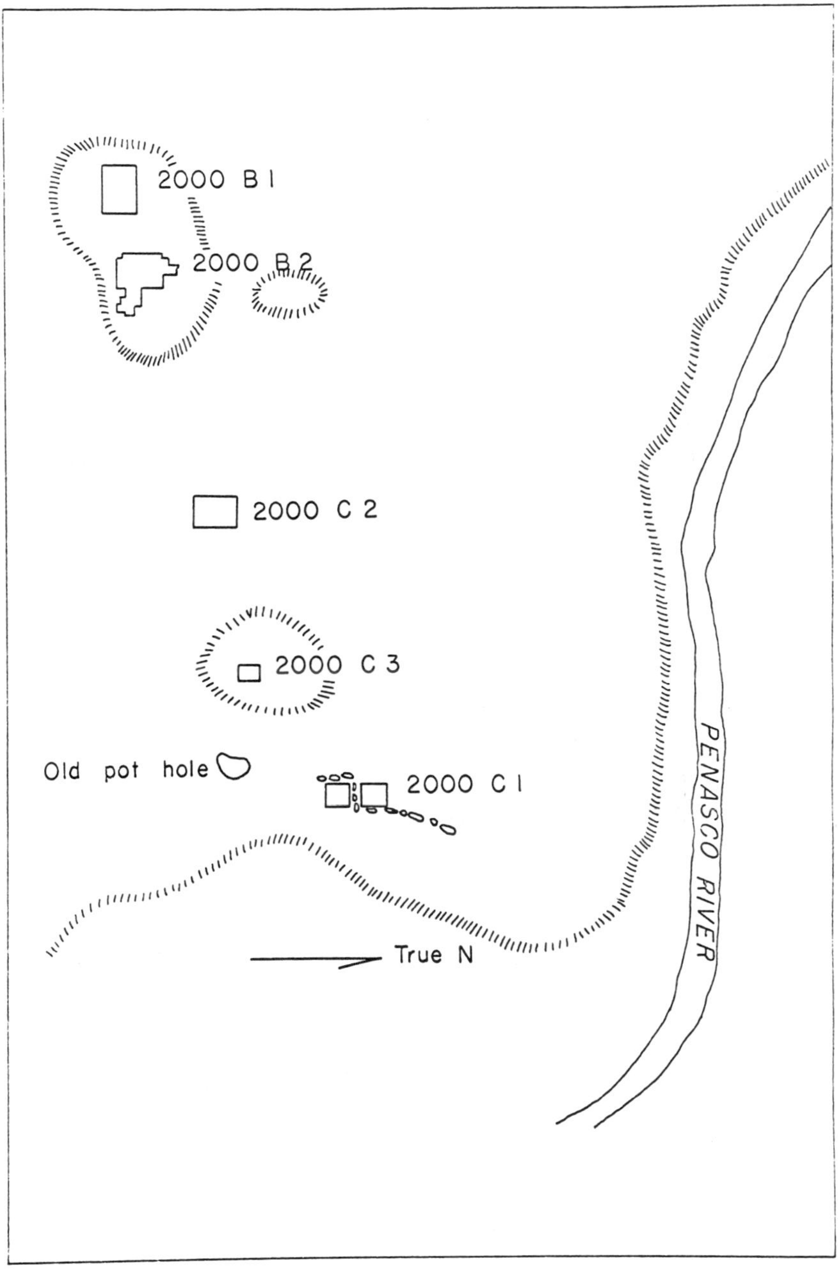

Figure 79. Sketch Map of Sites 2000 B and 2000 C in the Peñasco Valley.

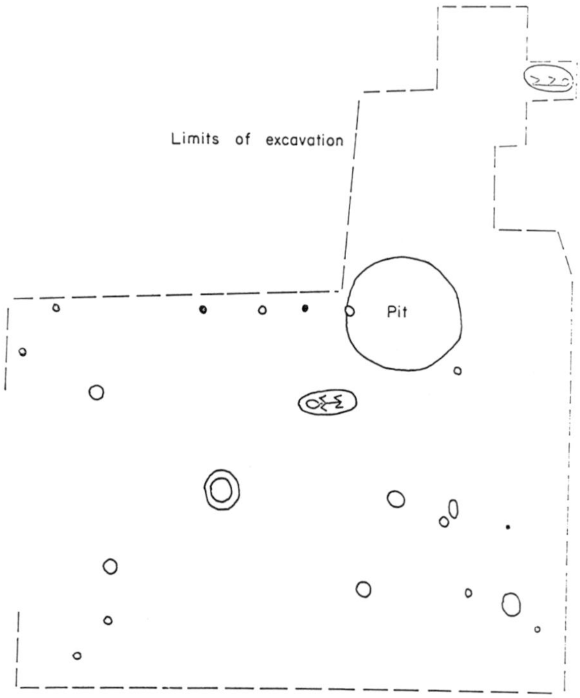

Figure 80. Excavation plan, Site 2000 B-2.

inside the pit wall. The shallow, cylindrical firepit was 12 inches in diameter, and 4 inches deep. A clay curb surrounding the firepit had a diameter of 28 inches and was built up 1 to 2 inches above the floor. An unplastered pit 26 inches deep with a mouth 16 inches in diameter in the northern half of the room contained several charred corncobs, and charcoal was scattered through its fill. A shallow grave was dug 7 inches below the floor. A child, ca. 7 to 9 years old, was flexed on its back with the head to the north. No obvious grave offering accompanied the burial. Artifacts found in the fill were two side-notched points and one corner-notched point (Fig. 83i, j, k), two fragments of trough metates with mano rests, and a grinding stone 4 inches long with a single ground surface. The house did not burn.

House 2: In extending the above excavation to the south, a second house was partially exposed. This one was built after House 1 had been abandoned and filled. The floor of House 1, which went under the House 2 floor, was not traced. The firepit must have been off-center, as it was located only 12 or 14 inches from the north edge of the floor. Three small posts pertain to this structure (Fig. 80). A basalt "palette," 8 inches long, 5 inches wide, and 1½ inches thick had a circular depression 3 inches in diameter ground into one face.

Bell-shaped Pit (Fig. 81): This feature is within House 1. It was either filled before the house was built or while the house was in use, as the house floor extended across the pit, and one of the small east posts (Fig. 80) was set inside the pit fill. This pit, 55½ inches deep, had a flat bottom 76 inches in diameter. Broken deer (?) bones were numerous in the pit fill. A bone awl was found about 24 inches below the opening. Pottery in the pit was El Paso Polychrome, Three Rivers Red-on-Terracotta, and Chupadero Black-on-White.

Burial: An adult burial, fully flexed on its back (Pl. 87), was located outside of House 1 (Fig. 80). The arms were folded across the chest. No grave offerings were in the shallow grave.

2000 C-1

Part of the floor area of two contiguous rooms partially lined with upright stone slabs was cleared (Fig. 82). The line of stone slabs continued past the room limits. This has parallels at the Bonnell Site and in Corona Phase sites to the north. No internal features were located. A corner-notched point was on the floor (Fig. 83h). Three point fragments and a stone plumb-bob were on the surface (Fig. 83b, c, d, e), and a corner-notched point was in the fill (Fig. 83g). Pottery types are listed in Table 39. These rooms were partially dug into the embankment that bounded 2000 C on the downslope side. Our testing in this embankment fully confirmed Jennings' conclusions (1940:4) that it was artificially constructed; embankment fill was a mixture of humus soil, limestone fragments and abundant cultural debris.

2000 C-2

A test pit, 8 x 8 feet, exposed a well-plastered floor 40 inches below the surface. No features and no artifacts were found.

2000 C-3

This test pit on a prominence (Fig. 79) was abandoned when sterile caliche was hit at 8 to 14 inches below the surface.

Conflicting Phase Designation

Lehmer (1948:85) assigned the lower level at Site 2000 to the Capitan Phase and the upper level to the Three Rivers Phase (Lehmer 1948:86).

Other Sites

Jennings mentioned Sites 2001 and 2002 as being near 2000 but did not describe them in detail (1940:1). Site 2001 had El Paso Polychrome and Plain

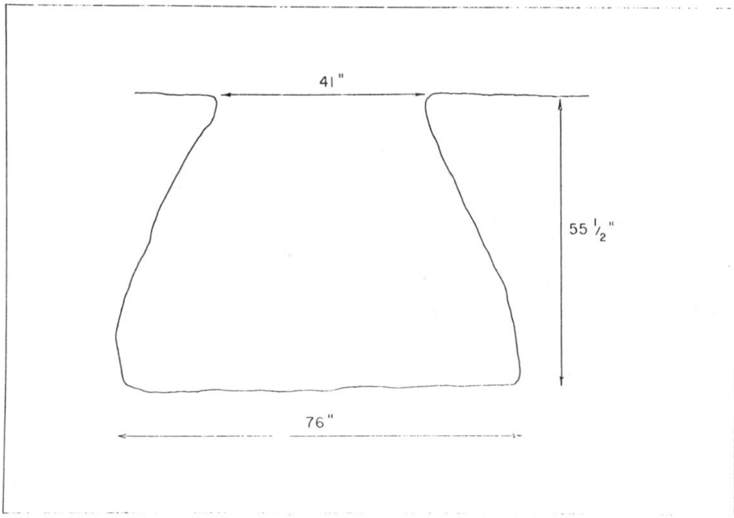

Figure 81. Cross-section of bell-shaped pit, Site 2000 B-2.

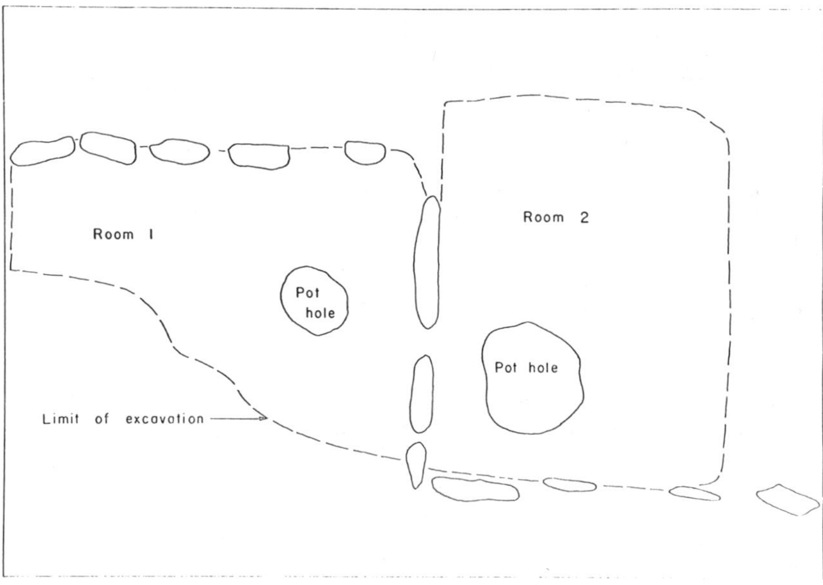

Figure 82. Excavation plan, Site 2000 C-1.

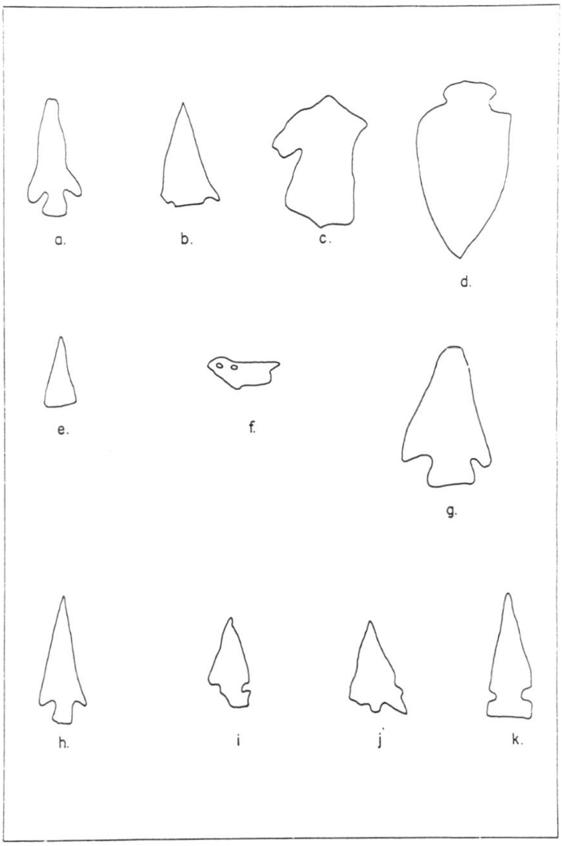

Figure 83. Artifacts from Site 2000: *a*, Projectile point from Site 2000 C-1, Level 1 (0 to 6 inches below surface); *b,c*, and *e*, Projectile points. Site 2000 C-1, surface; *d*, Stone plumb-bob, Site 2000 C-1, surface; *f*, Shell pendant fragment, Site 2000 C-1, Level 1 (0 to 6 inches below surface); *g*, Projectile point, Site 2000 C-1, Level 2 (6 to 12 inches below surface); *h*, Projectile point, Site 2000 C-1, Level 3 (12 to 18 inches below surface); *i*, Projectile point, Site 2000 B-2 (8 inches below surface); *j*, Projectile point, Site 2000 B-2 (24 inches below surface); *k*, Projectile point, Site 2000 B-2 (15 inches below surface).

Red and Brown pottery (Laboratory of Anthropology Survey). H. W. Yeo visited a site in the Mayhill schoolyard in 1930 and collected Chupadero Black-on-White, El Paso Polychrome, Three Rivers Red-on-Terracotta, Plain Red and Brown, and Springerville Polychrome (Laboratory of Anthropology Survey).

In 1953, we made a brief reconnaissance along the west side of the river adjacent to Site 2000. Three extensive sherd areas on terrace flats had the same sherd inventory as Site 2000 C-1.

SUMMARY AND DISCUSSION

This represented the southern boundary of settled life along the east slopes of the Sacramento-Guadalupe Mountains. Fewer sites existed in the Peñasco Valley than in the Hondo, Macho, and Gallo Valleys to the north, indicating a smaller farming population.

Conflicting Phase Designations

As noted, Green assigned his pithouse to the Doña Ana Phase of the southern Jornada sequence, and Lehmer assigned Site 2000 to the Capitan and Three Rivers Phases of the northern Jornada sequence. These sites are on the periphery of the Jornada Region, and each of these sites represents, insofar as I know, the only published reports of sites assigned to three Jornada phases. There are, therefore, no adequate comparative materials available from more centrally-located parts of the Jornada Region. A certain amount of confusion results from having phase members of both the northern and southern sequence present within the same valley only a few miles apart, especially when the cultural materials are so similar. On the basis of the pottery lists from the two sites, Green's pithouse is earlier than the earliest level at Site 2000 (El Paso Polychrome is absent from Green's house but present in the lowest level at Site 2000). Within the Jornada sequences, the Doña Ana Phase is equated in time with the Three Rivers Phase, resulting in a distortion of the actual temporal relationship between these two sites. The lag between cultural developments at these sites and reported cultural developments in the Tularosa Basin, and the apparent similarities to sites in the Hondo Drainage have led me to reassign these sites to the newly defined Glencoe Phase.

Early Glencoe Phase

Pithouses with and without benches were made and the pottery complex was predominantly Jornada Brown, with Chupadero Black-on-White and Mimbres Black-on-White as minor types. The lower level at Site 2000 A may be the same age (Jennings 1940:7). Green assigned his Site 1 on the Mayhill-Weed road to the Doña Ana Phase on the basis of its temporal and geographical position (1956:15), but I have placed it in the newly formulated Glencoe Phase because of its cultural content.

Late Glencoe Phase

Site 2000 was tentatively assigned to the late Glencoe Phase. The squared, medium depth pithouses, with four central supports and a center firepit, were similar to those at the Bonnell Site, and the regional pottery types were the same: Jornada Brown, El Paso Polychrome, Chupadero Black-on-White, Three Rivers Red-on-Terracotta, and Lincoln Black-on-Red. The latest pottery type collected at any site in the Peñasco Valley was Springerville Polychrome. This locality was abandoned prior to the spread of Glaze I.

Earlier sites were located in the Transitional Zone or close to its lower border where the valley was narrow. In all cases, ridges sloping into the valley were chosen. Later sites were located downstream in an arid belt of the Upper Sonoran Zone where the terraces next to the river were wide and fairly flat.

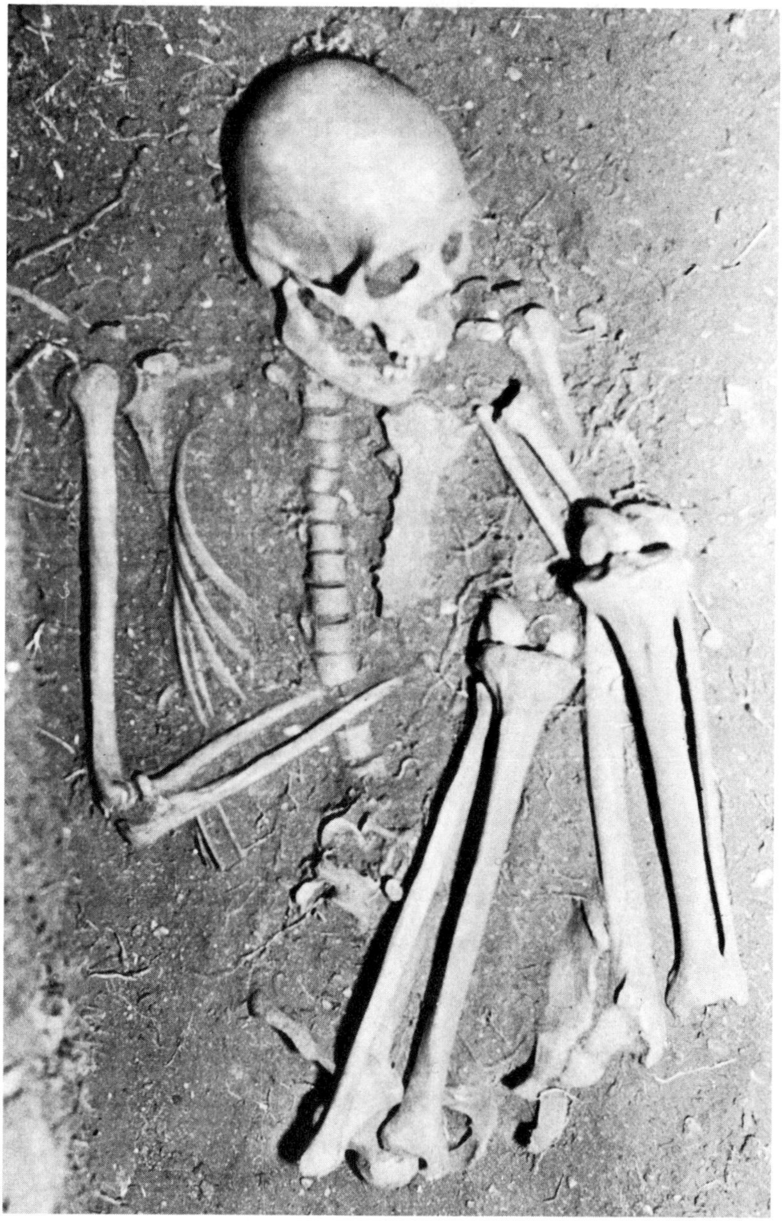

Plate 87. Extra-mural burial, Site 2000 B, Peñasco Valley.

TABLE 39
SHERDS FROM PEÑASCO 2000 C-1

Pottery Types	Fill (ca. 18″ deep)				Floor				Totals			
	Wt. (g)	%	No.	%	Wt. (g)	%	No.	%	Wt. (g)	%	No.	%
Chupadero Black-on-White												
Bowl	15		4									
Jug	153		22									
Total	168	14.43	26	11.50					168	13.66	26	10.74
Jornada Brown	558	47.94	102	45.13	58	87.88	12	75.00	616	50.08	114	47.11
Jornada Brown, Decorated												
Jornada Red-on-Brown	36		7									
Red-slipped Bowl	15		3									
Textured	22		1									
Total	73	6.27	11	4.87					73	5.93	11	4.55
Three Rivers Red-on-Terracotta												
Undecorated	91		17									
Olla	10		2									
Thin-lined	27		9									
Total	128	11.00	28	12.39					128	10.41	28	11.57
Jornada Polychrome	102	8.76	17	7.52					102	8.29	17	7.02
El Paso Polychrome	124	10.65	40	17.70	4	6.06	2	12.50	128	10.41	42	17.36
Lincoln Black-on-Red	8	0.69	1	0.44	1	1.52	1	6.25	9	0.73	2	0.83
Unidentified	3	0.26	1	0.44	3	4.55	1	6.25	6	0.49	2	0.83
Total	1164		226		66		16		1230		242	

Appendix 8

THREE SITES NORTHWEST OF ROSWELL, NEW MEXICO

SALT CREEK SITE

NE¼, S33, T5S, R19E. The site, perhaps one-half mile square, is on the north side of Salt Creek, just east of a ranch house on the Bob Marley property. Dunes alternate with small blow outs. No points were found. Flakes were numerous. Four scrapers were found, one of which was a snub-nosed thumbnail type. A hand grinding stone and a quartzite hammerstone were collected. Jornada Brown was the most common pottery type. Chupadero Black-on-White was present. Single sherds of Three Rivers Red-on-Terracotta, Thin-lined, and an unidentified white were also collected.

Directly south across Salt Creek, there is a rockshelter in limestone bluffs; it is ca. 80 feet wide and 50 feet high at the mouth. It extended some 50 feet into the bluff and diminished to 6 feet in height. Red pictographs were drawn on fallen boulders (Fig. 84). A single sherd of Chupadero Black-on-White was found in the shelter.

UPPER SALT CREEK SITE

NE¼, S16, T8S, R20E. This site is ca. ¼ to ½ mile square. Dunes and blow outs cover the locality. Pottery was mostly Jornada Brown, with rare sherds of Chupadero Black-on-White.

BLACKWATER CREEK SITE

Exact location is not certain. On the north side of Blackwater Creek, on the Clyde Marley Ranch, an overhang in the limestone bluff forms a shallow shelter that contained deposits 1 to 4 feet deep along a 50-foot front. The creek

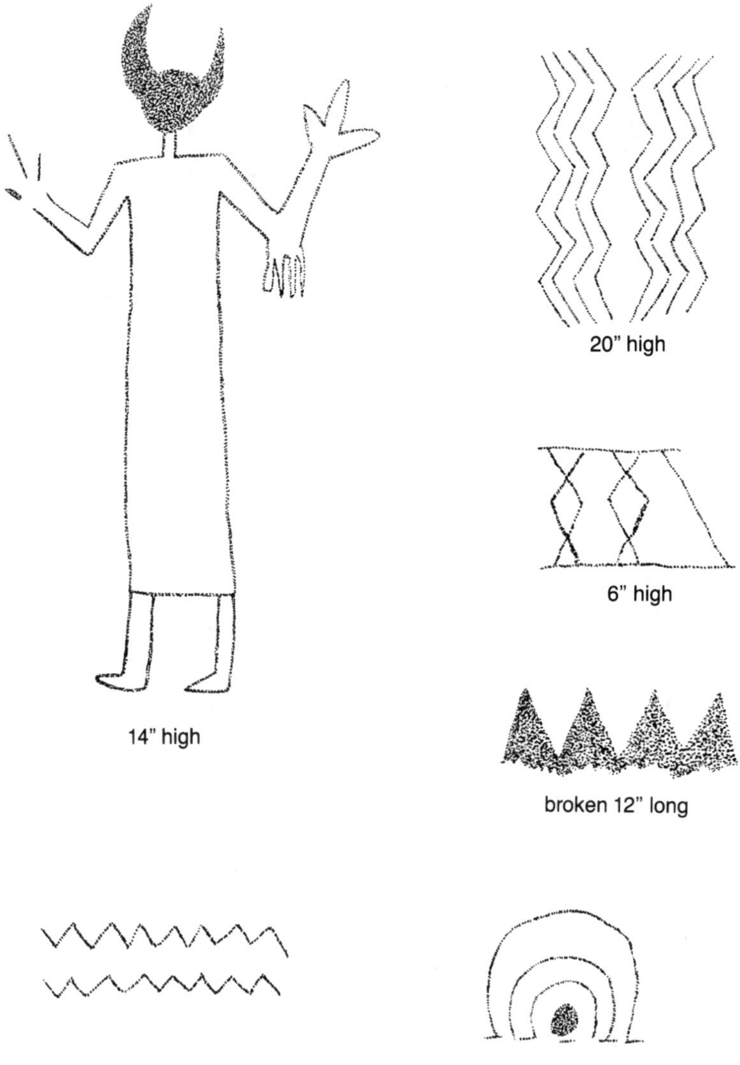

Figure 84. Red pictographs, Salt Creek Site.

was steadily eroding the site in 1955. Red and white pictographs were mainly geometric (Fig. 85). A tightly flexed burial with the skull to the west was fairly well exposed. A basin milling stone, a slab metate, and a stone palette with red paint were stacked together. There were a number of hand grinding stones. Jornada Brown was the only pottery collected.

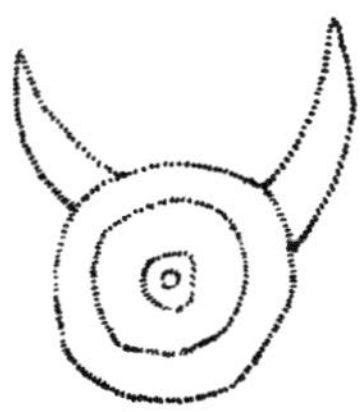

red paint

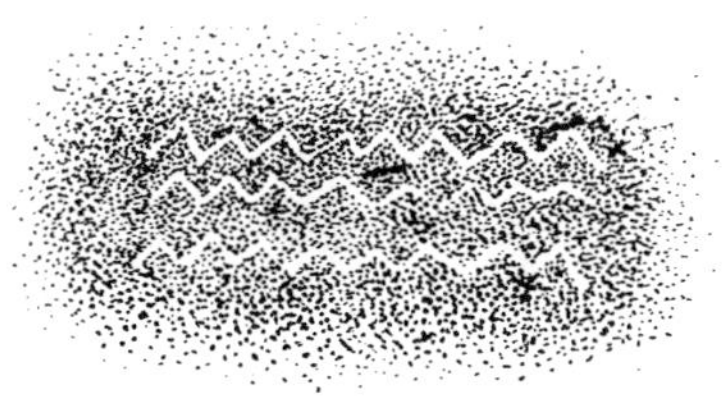

white paint

Figure 85. Pictographs at Blackwater Shelter.

BIBLIOGRAPHY

Allen, John Eliot, and Frank E. Kottlowski

1958 *Scenic Trips to the Geologic Past, No. 3, Roswell-Capitan-Ruidoso and Bottomless Lakes Park, New Mexico.* Socorro, New Mexico: State Bureau of Mines and Mineral Resources, a Division of New Mexico Institute of Mining and Technology.

Alves, Eileen E.

1932 A Small Ruin in New Mexico. *Bulletin of the Texas Archaeological and Paleontological Society* 4:40–43.

Bailey, Florence Merriam

1928 *Birds of New Mexico.* Santa Fe: New Mexico Department of Game and Fish.

Bailey, Vernon

1913 *Life Zones and Crop Zones of New Mexico. North American Fauna* 35. Washington, D. C.: U. S. Department of Agriculture, Bureau of Biological Survey.

1931 *Mammals of New Mexico. North American Fauna* 53. Washington, D.C.: United States Dept. of Agriculture, Bureau of Biological Survey.

Baker, Galen R.

1964 The Archaeology of the Park Plateau in Southeastern Colorado. Unpublished manuscript.

Bell, Willis H., and Edward F. Castetter

1937 Ethnobiological Studies in the American Southwest V. The Utilization of Mesquite and Screwbean by the Aborigines in the American Southwest. *The University of New Mexico Bulletin* 314, *Biological Series* 4(2). Albuquerque.

1941 Ethnobiological Studies in the American Southwest VII. The Utilization of Yucca, Sotol and Beargrass by the Aborigines of the American Southwest. *The University of New Mexico Bulletin* 372, *Biological Series* 5(5). Albuquerque.

Bluhm, Elaine A.

1957 The Sawmill Site. A Reserve Phase Village Pine Lawn Valley, Western New Mexico. *Fieldiana: Anthropology* 47(1).

Blumenschein, Helen

1956 Excavations in the Taos Area, 1953–1955. *El Palacio* 63(2): 53–55.

Bradfield, Wesley

1929 Excavations in the Sacramentos. *El Palacio* 82:1–7.

1931 Cameron Creek Village: A Site in the Mimbres Area in Grant County, New Mexico. *Monographs of The School of American Research* 1. Santa Fe.

Breternitz, David A.

1962 Review of the Flagstaff Area in the Light of Recent Tree-Ring Studies. Paper Delivered to the Society for American Archaeology, 27th Annual Meeting, Tucson.

Brew, John Otis
1946 Archaeology of Alkali Ridge, Southeastern Utah. *Papers of the Peabody Museum of American Archaeology and Ethnology, Harvard University* 21. Cambridge, Mass.

Bullard, William R.
1962 The Cerro Colorado Site and Pithouse Architecture in the Southwestern United States Prior to A. D. 900. *Papers of the Peabody Museum of American Archaeology and Ethnology, Harvard University* 44(2). Cambridge, Mass.

Carlson, Roy L.
1963 Basket Maker III Sites near Durango, Colorado. The Earl Morris Papers, No. 1. *University of Colorado Studies, Series in Anthropology* 8. Boulder.

Castetter, Edward F.
1935 Ethnological Studies in the American Southwest I, Uncultivated Native Plants Used as Sources of Food. *The University of New Mexico Bulletin* 266, *Biological Series* 4(1). Albuquerque.

Castetter, Edward F., and Willis H. Bell
1941 *Pima and Papago Agriculture*. Albuquerque: The University of New Mexico Press.

Castetter, Edward F., Willis H. Bell, and Alvin R. Grove
1938 Ethnobiological Studies in the American Southwest VI, The Early Utilization and the Distribution of Agave in the American Southwest. *The University of New Mexico Bulletin* 335, *Biological Series* 5(4). Albuquerque.

Castetter, Edward F., and M. E. Opler
1936 Ethnobiological Studies in the American Southwest III, The Ethnobiology of the Chiricahua and Mescalero Apache. *The University of New Mexico Bulletin* 297, *Biological Series* 4(5). Albuquerque.

Castetter, Edward F., and Ruth M. Underhill
1935 Ethnobiological Studies in the American Southwest II. The Ethnobiology of the Papago Indians. *The University of New Mexico Bulletin* 275, *Biological Series* 4(3). Albuquerque.

Chapman, Kenneth M.
1947 *A Masterpiece of Magic. Green Stone Fetish*. Silkscreen by Louie H. Ewing. Santa Fe, New Mexico: Laboratory of Anthropology.

Corley, John A., and Robert H. Leslie
n.d. Projectile Point Types of Extreme Southeastern New Mexico. *Lea County Archaeological Society Bulletin* 4.

Cosgrove, C. B.
1947 Caves of the Upper Gila and Hueco Areas in New Mexico and Texas. *Papers of the Peabody Museum of American Archaeology and Ethnology, Harvard University* 24(2). Cambridge, Mass.

Cosgrove, H. S., and C. B. Cosgrove
1932 The Swarts Ruin. A Typical Mimbres Site in Southwestern New Mexico. *Papers of the Peabody Museum of American Archaeology and Ethnology, Harvard University* 15(1). Cambridge, Mass.
1965 The Cosgrove Report. A Preliminary Survey of the El Paso Pueblo District. *El Paso Archaeological Society Special Report 3*.

Danson, Edward B.
1957 An Archaeological Survey of West Central New Mexico. *Papers of the Peabody Museum of American Archaeology and Ethnology, Harvard University* 44(1). Cambridge, Mass.

Davis, Emma Lou, and James H. Winkler
1959 A Late Mesa Verdi Site in the Rio Puerco Valley. *El Palacio* 66 (3):92–100.

Davis, Irvine
1959 Linguistic Clues to Northern Rio Grande Prehistory. *El Palacio* 66(3):73–84.

Davis, James T.
1960 An Appraisal of Certain Speculations on Prehistoric Puebloan Subsistence. *Southwest Journal of Anthropology* 16(1):15–21.

Dice, Lee R.
1943 *The Biotic Provinces of North America*. Ann Arbor: University of Michigan Press.

Dick, Herbert W.
1953 The Hodges Site, I. Two Rock Shelters Near Tucumcari, New Mexico. River Basin Survey, Paper No. 5. *Bureau of American Ethnology Bulletin* 154:267–84. Washington, D.C.

de Borhegyi, Stephan F.
1956 The Excavation of Site 9 Near Apache Creek, Catron County, New Mexico. *Highway Salvage Archaeology* (New Mexico State Highway Department and Museum of New Mexico, Santa Fe) 2(6):1–9.

Di Peso, Charles C.
1951 The Babocomari Village Site on the Babocomari River, Southeastern Arizona. *The Amerind Foundation Publication* 5. Dragoon, Arizona.
1958 The Reeve Ruin of Southeastern Arizona; A Study of A Prehistoric Western Pueblo Migration into the Middle San Pedro Valley. *The Amerind Foundation Publication* 8. Dragoon, Arizona.

Dittert, Alfred E. Jr., Jim J. Hester, and Frank W. Eddy
1961 An Archaeological Survey of the Navajo Reservoir District, Northwestern New Mexico. Navajo Project Studies II. *Monographs of the School of American Research and the Museum of New Mexico* 23. Santa Fe.

Ellis, Florence Hawley
1964 Ceramic Stratigraphy and Tribal History at Taos Pueblo. *American Antiquity* 29:316–27.

Elmore, Francis H.
1943 Ethnobotany of the Navajo. *The University of New Mexico Bulletin, Monograph Series* 1, Vol. 7. Albuquerque: University of New Mexico Press.

Fenenga, Franklin
1956 A Mogollon Village near Gran Quivira, New Mexico, Excavations at Site LA 2579. In *Pipeline Archaeology*, edited by Fred Wendorf, Nancy Fox, and Orian L. Lewis, pp. 226–32. Santa Fe and Flagstaff: Laboratory of Anthropology and Museum of Northern Arizona.

Fenenga, Franklin, and Thomas S. Cummings
1956a The Eastern Section of the Permian–San Juan Project. Archaeological Survey of the Permian–San Juan Pipeline Right-of-Way between Plains, Texas, and Correo, New Mexico. In *Pipeline Archaeology*, edited by Fred Wendorf, Nancy Fox, and Orian L. Lewis, pp. 216–26. Santa Fe and Flagstaff: The Laboratory of Anthropology and Museum of Northern Arizona.
1956b LA2569; Cerros Mojinos, A late Pueblo II - early Pueblo III Village on the Rio Puerco near Los Lunas, New Mexico. In *Pipeline Archaeology*, edited by Fred Wendorf, Nancy Fox, and Orian L. Lewis, pp. 242–55. Santa Fe and Flagstaff: The Laboratory of Anthropology and Museum of Northern Arizona.

Fenenga, Franklin, and Fred Wendorf
1956 Excavations at the Ignacio, Colorado, Field Camp: Site LA 2603. In *Pipeline Archaeology*, edited by Fred Wendorf, Nancy Fox, and Orian L. Lewis, pp. 207–14. Santa Fe and Flagstaff: Laboratory of Anthropology and Museum of Northern Arizona.

Ferdon, Edwin N., Jr.
1946 An Excavation of Hermit's Cave, New Mexico. *Monographs of the School of American Research* 10. Santa Fe.

Fiedler, A. G., and S. S. Nye
1933 Geology and Ground Water Resources of the Roswell Artisian Basin, New Mexico. *United States Geological Survey Water Supply Paper* 699.

Fontana, Bernard L., William J. Robinson, Charles W. Cormack, and Ernest E. Leavitt, Jr.
1962 *Papago Indian Pottery.* The American Ethnological Society. Monographs, Vol. 37. Seattle: University of Washington Press.

Forbes, Jack D.
1959 The Appearance of the Mounted Indian in Northern Mexico and the Southwest, to 1680. *Southwestern Journal of Anthropology* 15(2):189–212.

Fulton, W. S.
1941 A Ceremonial Cave in the Winchester Mountains. *The Amerind Foundation Publication* 1. Dragoon, Arizona.

Galinat, Walton C., Paul C. Mangelsdorf, and L. Pierson
1956 Estimates of Teosinte Introgression in Archaeological Maize. *Botanical Museum Leaflets, Harvard University* 17(4):101–24.

Green, Earl
1955 Excavations near Gran Quivira, New Mexico. *Bulletin of the Texas Archaeological and Paleontological Society* 5:182–85.

Green, Roger C.
1956 Excavations Near Mayhill, New Mexico. *Highway Salvage Archaeology* (New Mexico State Highway Department and Museum of New Mexico, Santa Fe) 2(7):1–9.

Gunnerson, Delores A.
1956 The Southern Athabascans: Their Arrival in the Southwest. *El Palacio* 63(11–12):346–65.

Gunnerson, James H.
1959 Archaeological Survey in Northeastern New Mexico. *El Palacio* 66(5):145–54.
1960 An Introduction to Plains Apache Archaeology: The Dismal River Aspect. *Bureau of American Ethnology Bulletin* 173:131–260. Washington, D. C.

Hammond, George P., and Agapito Rey
1929 *Expedition into New Mexico Made by Antonio de Espejo, 1582–1583, as Revealed in The Journal of Diego Perez de Luxan, a Member of the Party.* Vol. 1. Los Angeles: The Quivira Society.

Harvey, Herbert R.
1956 The Block Lookout Site, Capitan Area, New Mexico. Unpublished manuscript.

Haury, Emil W.
1936 The Mogollon Culture of Southwestern New Mexico. *Gila Pueblo, Medallion Papers* 20. Globe, Arizona.
1950 *The Stratigraphy and Archaeology of Ventana Cave, Arizona.* Tucson: University of Arizona Press.

Hawley, Florence M.
1936 Field Manual of Prehistoric Southwestern Pottery Types. *University of New Mexico Bulletin* 291, *Anthropological Series* 1(4). Albuquerque.

Holden, Jane
1952 The Bonnell Site. *Bulletin of the Texas Archaeological and Paleontological Society* 23:78–132.
1955a A Preliminary Report on Arrowhead Ruin. *El Palacio* 62:(4):102–19.
1955b Preliminary Report on the Bloom Mound Chaves County, New Mexico. *Bulletin of the Texas Archaeological Society* 26:166–81.
1964 Comments on The Archaeology of the Llano Estacado. *Bulletin of the Texas Archaeological Society* 35:1–17.

Holden, W. C.
1929 Some Recent Explorations and Excavations in Northwest Texas. *Bulletin of the Texas Archaeological and Paleontological Society* 1:23–35.
1930 The Canadian Valley Expedition of March, 1930. *Bulletin of the Texas Archaeological and Paleontological Society* 2:21–32.
1931 Texas Technological College Archaeological Expedition, Summer, 1930. *Bulletin of the Texas Archaeological and Paleontological Society* 3:43–52.

1933 Excavation of Saddle Back Ruin. *Bulletin of the Texas Archaeological and Paleontological Society* 5:39–52.

1938 Blue Mountain Rock Shelter. *Bulletin of the Texas Archaeological and Paleontological Society* 10:208–21.

Howard, Edgar B.

1935 Evidence of Early Man in North America. *Museum Journal* (University of Pennsylvania Museum) 24(2–3):53–171.

Howard, Richard M.

1959 Comments on The Indians' Water Supply at Gran Quivira National Monument. *El Palacio* 66(3):85–91.

1960 Tabira, Identification and Historical Sketch. *El Palacio* 67(2):68–71.

Jackson, A. T.

1938 Picture-Writing of Texas Indians. *The University of Texas Publication* 3809. Austin.

Jelinek, Arthur J.

1952 Pottery of the Rio Bonito Area of Lincoln County, New Mexico. *Bulletin of the Texas Archaeological and Paleontological Society* 23:147–67.

1960 An Archaeological Survey of the Middle Pecos River Valley and the Adjacent Llano Estacado. Ph.D. dissertation, University of Michigan, Ann Arbor.

Jennings, Jesse D.

1940 A Variation of Southwestern Culture. *New Mexico Archaeological Survey, Laboratory of Anthropology, Technical Series Bulletin* 10. Santa Fe.

Jennings, Jesse D., Erik K. Reed, James B. Griffin, J. Charles Kelley, Clement W. Meighan, Stanley Stubbs, and Joe Ben Wheat

1956 The American Southwest: A Problem in Cultural Isolation. In: Seminars in Archaeology: 1955, edited by R. Wauchope, pp. 59–27. *Society for American Archaeology Memoirs* 11. Salt Lake City.

Jennings, Noyce

1952 The Mound Lake Site. *Bulletin of the Texas Archaeological and Paleontological Society* 23:309–10, Pl. 34.

Johnson, Alfred E., and Raymond H. Thompson

1963 The Ringo Site, Southeastern Arizona. *American Antiquity* 28:465–81.

Judd, Neil M.

1954 The Material Culture of Pueblo Bonito. *Smithsonian Miscellaneous Collections* 124. Washington, D. C.

Kelley, J. Charles

1949 Archaeological Notes on Two Excavated House Structures in Western Texas. *Bulletin of the Texas Archaeological and Paleontological Society* 20:89–114.

1950 Atlatls, Bows and Arrows, Pictographs and the Pecos River Focus. *American Antiquity* 16:71–74.

1951 A Bravo River Aspect Component of the Lower Rio Conchos Valley, Chihuahua, Mexico. *American Antiquity* 17:114–19.

1952 Factors Involved in the Abandonment of Certain Peripheral Southwestern Settlements. *American Anthropologist* 54:356–87.

1954 Bravo Valley Aspect. In: An Introductory Handbook of Texas Archaeology, edited by Dee Ann Suhm and Alex D. Krieger, *Bulletin of the Texas Archaeological Society* 25:45–57.

1955 Juan Sebeata and Diffusion in Aboriginal Texas. *American Anthropologist* 57:981–95.

1957 The Livermore Focus: A Clarification. *El Palacio* 64(1–2):44–51.

Kelley, Jane H.

1979 The Sierra Blanca Restudy Project. In *Jornada Mogollon Archaeology*, edited by P. H. Beckett and R. N. Wiseman, pp.107–32. Las Cruces and Santa Fe: New Mexico State University Press and Historic Preservation Bureau, Department of

Finance and Administration, State of New Mexico.

Kidder, Alfred V.

1932 The Artifacts of Pecos. *Papers of the Phillips Academy Southwestern Expedition* 6. New Haven, Conn.: Yale University Press.

1958 Pecos, New Mexico: Archaeological Notes. *Papers of the Robert S. Peabody Foundation for Archaeology* 5. Andover, Mass.

Kidder, Alfred V., H. S. Cosgrove, and C. B. Cosgrove

1949 The Pendleton Ruin, Hidalgo County, New Mexico. *Contributions to American Anthropology and History* 10, *Carnegie Institution of Washington Publication* 585:107–52. Washington, D. C.

Kidder, Alfred V., and Samuel J. Guernsey

1919 Archaeological Explorations in Northeastern Arizona. *Bureau of American Ethnology Bulletin* 65. Washington, D. C.

Kidder, Alfred V., and Anna O. Shepard

1936 The Pottery of Pecos. Vol. 2. *Papers of the Phillips Academy Southwestern Expedition* 7. New Haven: Yale University Press.

King, P. B.

1948 Geology of the Southern Guadalupe Mountains. *United States Geological Survey, Professional Paper* 215.

Kirkland, Forrest

1942 Indian Pictographs and Petroglyphs in the Panhandle Region of Texas. *Bulletin of the Texas Archaeological and Paleontological Society* 14:9–26.

Koster, William J.

1957 *Guide to the Fishes of New Mexico*. Albuquerque: University of New Mexico Press, in cooperation with New Mexico Department of Game and Fish.

Krieger, Alex D.

1945 Some Suggestions on Archaeological Terms. *Bulletin of the Texas Archaeological and Paleontological Society* 16:41–51.

1946 Culture Complexes and Chronology in Northern Texas. *The University of Texas Publication* 4640. Austin.

Lambert, Marjorie F.

1954 Paa-ko, Archaeological Chronicle of an Indian Village in North Central New Mexico, Parts I–V; Part VI by Spencer L. Rogers: The Physical Type of the Paa-ko population. *Monographs of the School of American Research* 19. Santa Fe.

1956a A Prehistoric Stone Elbow Pipe From the Taos Area. *El Palacio* 63(2):67–68.

1956b Some Clay and Stone Figurines from the Mogollon-Mimbres Area, Luna County, New Mexico. *El Palacio* 63(9–10):259–83.

Lehmer, Donald J.

1948 The Jornada Branch of the Mogollon. *University of Arizona Social Science Bulletin* 17. Tucson.

Lister, Robert H.

1948 Notes on the Archaeology of the Watrous Valley, New Mexico. *El Palacio* 55(2):35–41.

Lutes, Eugene

1957a A Marginal Prehistoric Culture of Northeastern New Mexico. *El Palacio* 66(2):59–68.

1957b A Marginal Culture East of the Sangre de Cristo Mountains. Paper Delivered to the American Anthropological Association, Chicago.

1959MS Philmont Archaeology Report, June–September 1959. Unpublished manuscript.

1960MS Philmont Archaeological Report: June–September 1960. Unpublished manuscript.

Martin, Paul S.

1943 The SU Site: Excavations at a Mogollon Village, Western New Mexico, Second Season 1941. *Field Museum of Natural History Publication* 526, *Anthropological Series* 32(2). Chicago.

Martin, Paul S., and John B. Rinaldo
1947 The SU Site: Excavations at a Mogollon Village, Western New Mexico, Third Season, 1946. *Field Museum of Natural History Publication* 601, *Anthropological Series* 32(3). Chicago.
1950a Sites of the Reserve Phase, Pine Lawn Valley, Western New Mexico. *Fieldiana: Anthropology* 38(3).
1950b Turkey Foot Ridge Site, A Mogollon Village, Pine Lawn Valley, Western New Mexico. *Fieldiana: Anthropology* 38(2).
1960a Excavations in the Upper Little Colorado Drainage, Eastern Arizona. *Fieldiana: Anthropology* 51(1).
1960b Table Rock Pueblo, Arizona. *Fieldiana: Anthropology* 51(2).

Martin, Paul S., John B. Rinaldo, and Ernst Antevs
1949 Cochise and Mogollon Sites, Pine Lawn Valley, Western New Mexico. *Fieldiana: Anthropology* 31(1).

Martin, Paul S., John B. Rinaldo, and Elaine Bluhm
1954 Caves of the Reserve Area. *Fieldiana: Anthropology* 42.

Martin, Paul S., John B. Rinaldo, Elaine A. Bluhm, and Hugh C. Cutler
1956 Higgins Flat Pueblo Western New Mexico. *Fieldiana: Anthropology* 45.

Martin, Paul S., John B. Rinaldo, and Eloise R. Barter
1957 Late Mogollon Communities, Four Sites of the Tularosa Phase, Western New Mexico. *Fieldiana: Anthropology* 49(1).

Martin, Paul S., John B. Rinaldo, Elaine Bluhm, Hugh C. Cutler, and Roger Grange, Jr.
1952 Mogollon Cultural Continuity and Change, The Stratigraphic Analysis of Tularosa and Cordova Caves. *Fieldiana: Anthropology* 40.

Martin, Paul S., John Rinaldo, and Marjorie Kelly
1940 The SU Site. Excavations at a Mogollon Village, Western New Mexico 1939. *Field Museum of Natural History Publication* 476, *Anthropological Series* 32(1). Chicago.

Martin, Paul S., John B. Rinaldo, and William A. Longacre
1961 Mineral Creek Site and Hooper Ranch Pueblo, Eastern Arizona. *Fieldiana: Anthropology* 52.

Martin, Paul S., John B. Rinaldo, William A. Longacre, Constance Cronin, Leslie G. Freeman, Jr., and James Schoenwetter
1962 Chapters in the Prehistory of Eastern Arizona, I. *Fieldiana: Anthropology* 53.

McCluney, Eugene B.
1962 A New Name and Revised Description for a Mogollon Pottery Type from Southern New Mexico. *Southwestern Lore* 27(4):49–55.

Meinzer, O. E.
1922 Map of the Pleistocene Lakes of the Basin and Range Province and its Significance. *Bulletin of the Geologic Society of America* 33:541–52.

Meinzer, O. E., and R. F. Hare
1915 Geology and Water Resources of Tularosa Basin, New Mexico. *United States Geological Survey Water Supply Paper* 343.

Mera, Harry P.
1931 Chupadero Black on White. *New Mexico Archaeological Survey, Laboratory of Anthropology, Technical Series, Bulletin* 1. Santa Fe.
1933 A Proposed Revision of the Rio Grande Glaze Paint Sequence. *New Mexico Archaeological Survey, Laboratory of Anthropology, Technical Series Bulletin* 2. Santa Fe.
1938 Reconnaissance and Excavation in Southeastern New Mexico. *Memoirs of the American Anthropological Association* 51. Menasha.
1940a Population Changes in the Rio Grande Glaze Paint Area. *New Mexico Archaeological Survey, Laboratory of Anthropology, Technical Series Bulletin* 9. Santa Fe.

1940b An Approach to the Identity of the Jumano Puebloes in the Saline-Medano District through Archaeological Evidence. *Contributions to American Anthropology and History, Carnegie Institution of Washington* 6(34):291–99. Washington, D. C.

1943 An Outline of Ceramic Developments in Southern and Southeastern New Mexico. *New Mexico Archaeological Survey, Laboratory of Anthropology, Technical Series Bulletin* 11. Santa Fe.

Mera, Harry P., and William S. Stallings

1931 Lincoln Black-on-Red. *New Mexico Archaeological Survey, Laboratory of Anthropology, Technical Series Bulletin* 2. Santa Fe.

Montgomery, Ross Gordon, Watson Smith, and John Otis Brew

1949 Franciscan Awatovi. The Excavation and Conjectural Reconstruction of a 17th Century Spanish Mission Establishment at a Hopi Indian Town in Northeastern Arizona. *Papers of the Peabody Museum of American Archaeology and Ethnology, Harvard University* 36. Cambridge, Mass.

Moore, Mrs. Glen E.

1947 Twelve Room House Ruin. *Bulletin of the Texas Archaeological and Paleontological Society* 18:94–114.

Moore, Mrs. Glen E., and Mrs. Joe Ben Wheat

1951 An Archaeological Cache from Hueco Basin, Texas. *Bulletin of the Texas Archaeological and Paleontological Society* 22:144–63.

Morris, Earl H., and Robert F. Burgh

1941 Anasazi Basketry, Basket Maker II through Pueblo III; a Study Based on Specimens from the San Juan River Country. *Carnegie Institution of Washington Publication* 533. Washington, D. C.

1954 Basket Maker II sites near Durango, Colorado. *Carnegie Institution of Washington Publication* 604. Washington, D. C.

Munsell Color Company, Inc.

1954 *Soil Color Charts*. Baltimore, Maryland.

Mourant, Walter A.

1963 Water Resources and Geology of the Rio Hondo Drainage Basin, Chaves, Lincoln, and Otero Counties, New Mexico. *New Mexico State Engineer, Technical Report* 28. Santa Fe.

Nesbitt, Paul H.

1931 The Ancient Mimbrenos, Based on Investigations at the Mattocks Ruin, Mimbres Valley, New Mexico. *Logan Museum Publications, Bulletin* 4. Beloit, Wisconsin.

1938 Starkweather Ruin. A Mogollon Pueblo site in the Upper Gila area of New Mexico. *Logan Museum Publications in Anthropology, Bulletin* 6. Beloit, Wisconsin.

Newcomb, W. W., Jr.

1961 *The Indians of Texas From Prehistoric to Modern Times*. Austin: University of Texas Press.

Pearce, William M.

1936 A Survey of the Sand-Hill Camp Sites of Lamb and Bailey Counties. *Bulletin of the Texas Archaeological and Paleontological Society* 8:184–86.

Peckham, Stewart

1954 A Pueblo I Site Near San Felipe Pueblo, New Mexico. *Highway Salvage Archaeology* (New Mexico State Highway Department and Museum of New Mexico) 1(4):41–51.

1957a The Switchback Site. A Stratified Ruin near Reserve, New Mexico. *Highway Salvage Archaeology* (New Mexico State Highway Department and Museum of New Mexico) 3(11):10–38.

1957b Three Pithouses near Albuquerque, New Mexico. *Highway Salvage Archaeology* (New Mexico State Highway Department and Museum of New Mexico) 3(12):39–70.

1958 Hillside Pueblo: Early Masonry Architecture in the Reserve Area. New Mexico. *El Palacio* 65(3):81–94.

Peckham, Stewart, Fred Wendorf, and Edwin N. Ferdon, Jr.
1956 Excavations near Apache Creek, New Mexico. *Highway Salvage Archaeology* (New Mexico State Highway Department and Museum of New Mexico) 2(8):17–86.

Phillips, Philip
1958 Application of the Wheat-Gifford-Wasley Taxonomy to Eastern Ceramics. *American Antiquity* 24:117–125.

Reed, Erik K.
1944 The Abandonment of the San Juan Region. *El Palacio* 51(4):61–74.
1948a The Western Pueblo Archaeological Complex. *El Palacio* 55(1):9–15.
1948b The Dating of Early Mogollon Horizons. *El Palacio*
1949a The Significance of Skull Deformation in the Southwest. *El Palacio* 56(4):106–19.
1949b Sources of Upper Rio Grande Pueblo Culture and Population. *El Palacio* 56(6):163–84.
1950 Eastern-Central Arizona Archaeology in Relation to the Western Puebloes. *Southwestern Journal of Anthropology* 6:120–38.
1957 Human Skeletal Remains from Some Highway Salvage Excavations in New Mexico. *Highway Salvage Archaeology* (New Mexico State Highway Department and Museum of New Mexico) 3:85–97.

Renaud, E. B.
1937 *Northeastern New Mexico*. The Archaeological Survey of the Western High Plains. 9th Report. Denver: Department of Anthropology, University of Denver.

Reynolds, S. E.
1956 Climatological Summary, New Mexico, Temperature 1850–1954. Evaporation 1912–1954. *State Engineer Office, State of New Mexico, Technical Report* 5.

Rinaldo, John B.
1959 Foote Canyon Pueblo, Eastern Arizona. *Fieldiana: Anthropology*. 49(2).

Roberts, Frank H. H.
1929a Shabik'eshchee Village: A Late Basketmaker Site in the Chaco Canyon, New Mexico. *Bureau of American Ethnology Bulletin* 92. Washington, D. C.
1929b Recent Archaeological Developments in the Vicinity of El Paso, Texas. *Smithsonian Miscellaneous Collections* 81(7), *Smithsonian Publication* 3009:1-14. Washington, D. C.

Roosa, William B.
1952 Sandals of Feather Cave. *Bulletin of the Texas Archaeological and Palaeontological Society* 23:133–46.

Sauer, Carl
1934 The Distribution of Aboriginal Tribes and Languages in Northwestern Mexico. *Ibero-Americana* 5:65–74.

Sayles, E. B.
1936 An Archaeological Survey of Chihuahua, Mexico. *Gila Pueblo, Medallion Papers* 22. Globe, Arizona.

Scholes, France V., and H. P. Mera
1940 Some Aspects of the Jumano Problem. *Contributions to American Anthropology and History* 34, *Carnegie Institution of Washington Publication* 523:265–99. Washington, D.C.

Schroeder, Albert H., and Fred Wendorf
1954 Excavations Near Aragon, New Mexico. *Highway Salvage Archaeology* (New Mexico State Highway Department and Museum of New Mexico) 1(5):53–104.

Smiley, Terah L., Stanley A. Stubbs, and Bryant Bannister
1953 A Foundation for the Dating of Some Late Archaeological Sites in the Rio Grande Area, New Mexico: Based on Studies in Tree Ring Methods and Pottery Analysis. *University of Arizona Bulletin* 24(3), *Laboratory of Tree Ring Research Bulletin* 6. Tucson.

Smith, Watson

1952 Excavations in Big Hawk Valley, Wapatki National Monument, Arizona. *Museum of Northern Arizona Bulletin* 24. Flagstaff.

1962 Schools, Pots, and Potters. *American Anthropologist* 64:1165–78.

Stallings, W. S., Jr.

1931 El Paso Polychrome. *New Mexico Archaeological Survey, Laboratory of Anthropology, Technical Series, Bulletin* 3. Santa Fe.

Stephen, Alexander M.

1936 *Hopi Journal*, edited by Elsie Clews Parsons. *Columbia University Contributions to Anthropology* 23. New York.

Stevenson, Matilda Coxe

1915 Ethnobotany of the Zuñi Indians. *Thirtieth Annual Report of the Bureau of American Ethnology for the Years 1908–1909*, pp. 31–102. Washington, D. C.

Stubbs, Stanley A.

1930 Preliminary Report of Excavations Near La Luz and Alamogordo, New Mexico. *El Palacio* 29(1):3–14. Santa Fe.

1959 "New" Old Churches Found at Quarai and Tabira (Pueblo Blanco). *El Palacio* 66(5):162–68.

Stubbs, Stanley A., and W. S. Stallings, Jr.

1953 The Excavations of Pindi Pueblo, New Mexico. *Archaeological Institute of America and School of American Research Monographs* 18. Santa Fe.

Studer, Floyd V.

1931 Archaeological Survey of the North Panhandle of Texas. *Bulletin of the Texas Archaeological and Paleontological Society* 3:70–75.

Suhm, Dee Ann, and Edward B. Jelks

1962 Handbook of Texas Archaeology: Type Descriptions. *Texas Archaeological Society Special Publication* 1. Austin.

Taylor, Herbert C. Jr.

1949 A tentative cultural sequence for the area about the mouth of the Pecos. *Bulletin of the Texas Archaeological and Paleontological Society* 20:73–88.

Taylor, Walter W.

1948 A Study of Archaeology. *Memoirs of the American Anthropological Association* 69. Menasha, Wis.

Toulouse, Joseph H. Jr.

1949 The Mission of San Gregorio de Abó. A Report on the Excavation and Repair of a Seventeeth-Century New Mexico Mission. *Monographs of the School of American Research* 13. Santa Fe.

Toulouse, Joseph H. Jr., and Robert L. Stephenson

1960 Excavations at Pueblo Pardo: Central New Mexico. *The Museum of New Mexico Papers in Anthropology* 2. Santa Fe.

Tuthill, Carr

1947 The Tres Alamos Site on the San Pedro River. *Amerind Foundation Publication* 4. Dragoon, Arizona.

Vestal, Paul A.

1952 Ethnobotany of the Ramah Navajo, Reports of the Ramah Project. *Papers of the Peabody Museum of American Archaeology and Ethnology, Harvard University*, 40(4). Cambridge, Mass.

Vivian, Gordon

1965 The Three-C Site, an Early Pueblo II Ruin in Chaco Canyon, New Mexico. *University of New Mexico Publications in Anthropology* 13. Albuquerque.

Vytlacil, Natalie, and J. J. Brody

1958 Two Pit Houses near Zia Puebla. *El Palacio* 65(5):161–68.

Watson, Virginia

1950 The Optima Focus of the Panhandle Aspect: Description and Analysis. *Bulletin of the Texas Archaeological and Paleontological Society* 21:17–68.

Watts, W. C.

1939 Lake Sites of the South Plains of Texas. *Bulletin of the Texas Archaeological and Paleontological Society* 11:77–91.

Wedel, Waldo R.

1959 An Introduction to Kansas Archaeology. *Bureau of American Ethnology Bulletin* 174. Washington, D. C.

Wendorf, Fred

1950 A Report on the Excavation of a Small Ruin near Point of Pines, East-central Arizona. *University of Arizona Bulletin* 21(3), *Social Science Bulletin* 19. Tucson.

1953 Archaeological Studies in the Petrified Forest National Monument. *Museum of Northern Arizona Bulletin* 27. Flagstaff.

1954a The Excavation of a Small Pueblo III site near Gallup, New Mexico. *Highway Salvage Archaeology* (New Mexico State Highway Department and The Museum of New Mexico) 1(1):1–12.

1954b A Pueblo II Site near Laguna, New Mexico. *Highway Salvage Archaeology* (New Mexico State Highway Department and The Museum of New Mexico) 1(2):13–28.

1954c A Reconstruction of Northern Rio Grande Prehistory. *American Anthropologist* 56:200–27.

1956 A Fragmentary Pueblo Near Corona New Mexico, *Highway Salvage Archaeology* (New Mexico State Highway Department and The Museum of New Mexico) 2(9):87–105.

1957 A Mimbres Pueblo near Glenwood, New Mexico. *Highway Salvage Archaeology* (New Mexico State Highway Department and The Museum of New Mexico) 3(13):71–84.

1960 The Archaeology of Northeastern New Mexico. *El Palacio* 67(2):55–65.

Wheat, Joe Ben

1955a Two Archaeological Sites near Lubbock, Texas. *Panhandle-Plains Historical Review* 28:71–77.

1955b Mogollon Culture Prior to A. D. 1000. *Memoirs of the American Anthropological Association* 82. Menasha, Wis.

Wheat, Joe Ben, James C. Gifford, and William W. Wasley

1958 Ceramic Variety, Type Cluster, and Ceramic System in Southwestern Pottery Analysis. *American Antiquity* 24:34–47.

Willey, Gordon R., and Philip Phillips

1958 *Method and Theory in American Archaeology*. Chicago: University of Chicago Press.

Woodbury, Richard B.

1954 Prehistoric Stone Implements of Northeastern Arizona. *Papers of the Peabody Museum of Archaeology and Ethnology, Harvard University* 34. Cambridge, Mass.

1959 A Reconsideration of Pueblo Warfare in the Southwestern United States. *Actas del XXXIII Congreso Internacional de Americanistas* [San Jose, 1958], Vol. 2:124–33. San José, Costa Rica: Lehmann.

Wormington, H. Marie

1955 A Reappraisal of the Fremont Culture. *Denver Museum of Natural History, Proceedings* 1. Denver.